The Philosophy of Language

The Philosophy of Language

SECOND EDITION

edited by

A. P. MARTINICH

New York · Oxford

OXFORD UNIVERSITY PRESS

1990

Oxford University Press

Oxford   New York   Toronto
Delhi   Bombay   Calcutta   Madras   Karachi
Petaling   Jaya   Singapore   Hong Kong   Tokyo
Nairobi   Dar es Salaam   Cape Town
Melbourne   Auckland

and associated companies in
Berlin   Ibadan

Library of Congress Cataloging-in-Publication Data
The Philosophy of language / [edited by] A.P. Martinich.—2nd ed.
       p.   cm.
   Includes bibliographical references.
   ISBN 0-19-506254-X
   1. Languages—Philosophy.   I. Martinich, Aloysius.
P106.P455   1990
401—dc20   89-36910   CIP

10 9 8 7 6

Printed in the United States of America

Note to the Second Edition

The difficult part of preparing the second edition was the same as that of the first, namely, choosing relatively few selections from the hundreds that merit inclusion. Sometimes one selection was chosen over another because of its closeness of fit to others adjacent to it.

In this edition, there are seven rather than eight sections. Section VI of the first edition, "Possible Worlds and Situations," has been deleted, with some of its articles reassigned, and the original section VIII, "Private Languages," is now an expanded section VII, "The Nature of Language."

I want to thank the many professors who made suggestions for the contents of the second edition, especially many of the contributors to the first edition, and my editors for both editions: Cynthia Read and Susan Meigs. Also, Mark Bernstein and Deborah Nichols commented on the introduction to "The Nature of Language."

I continue to be grateful to Nicholas Asher, Dan Bonevac, and Jo Ann Carson for their help with the first edition, and I rededicate my work to my children, Carol, John, and Mary.

Contents

The Philosophy of Language

INTRODUCTION

I

Philosophers and reflective persons in general have been interested in language for a long time and for various reasons. First, since language seems to be characteristic of human beings, to know about language is to know something about being human. Although some anthropologists claim that some of the nonhuman primates can acquire language, most philosophers and linguists disagree. While conceding that these chimpanzees and gorillas have learned to communicate using a symbol system, they deny that what the primates are using counts as a human language. That is, none of the systems the primates use allows for the construction of an infinitely large number of expressions. And it is this feature that philosophers and linguists take to be characteristic of human language.

Second, since certain philosophical problems seem to arise from false beliefs about the structure of language, understanding it may help solve those problems or avoid them altogether. For example, since the sentence "Nothing came down the road" is, at least superficially, grammatically like "John came down the road" and John is something that exists, one might think that nothing is something that exists. But this absurd view would be caused by a misunderstanding of how language works. Or since "Justice is a virtue" is grammatically like "Mary is a lawyer" one might think that justice is a concrete, actual thing. Again that would be a mistake.

Third, many philosophers have held that language is a reflection of reality, so, if one could understand the structure of language, one could understand the structure of reality. It is not odd to think that the structure of language is the same or similar to the structure of reality. For language is the expression of thought, and, if human thoughts can count as knowledge about the world, thought would seem to be a reflection of reality. This view of language, thought, and reality is very old, at least as old as Plato, who has Socrates explain that this very belief is the strategy behind his own philosophizing. In Socrates' account of his turn away from the physical philosophy of Anaxagoras to his own method, he says that he feared that if he tried to figure out the structure of reality by studying reality directly, he might be intellectually blinded. Thus he resolved to use language as a kind of mirror of reality: "I decided to take refuge in language, and study the truth of things by means of it" (*Phaedo* 99E). The same idea of language as a reflection of reality continues through the middle ages, and through modern philosophy into the twentieth century. One of the most forceful statements of this view of language is Ludwig Wittgenstein's *Tractatus Logico-Philosophicus,* published in 1921. His ideas were dubbed the picture theory of language, and it has been the dominant view during the twentieth century. There is a Kantian variation on this view according to which language is not a reflection of reality, which is inaccessible to human intelligence, but a reflection of our thought about reality. Much of the philosophizing of those who do not accept any version of the picture theory of language consists of little more than criticism.

Fourth, language is, of course, interesting in itself and might be studied profitably for its own sake.

II

Philosophers distinguish three areas of the study of language: syntax, semantics, and pragmatics.

Syntax is the study of the rules that describe what a well-formed or grammatical sentence is in purely formal terms. That is, it describes what a sentence is in terms of rules that specify what sequences of words are permissible. These rules are called concatenation rules, from the metaphor of words being linked together as if in a chain. A syntactic description of language is not allowed to use the concept of meaning or any related concept in order to explain what a grammatical sentence is.

Semantics is the study of the meaning of words and sentences. A semantic theory tries to explain what meaning is, and any theory of meaning will have to describe what is and what is not a meaningful expression as well as the systematic relations between words and what they mean. The principal semantic notions are truth and reference, although pragmatics, too, has much to say about reference.

Pragmatics is the study of what speakers do with language. Speakers do not simply talk. In or by speaking, they promise, marry, swear, forgive, apologize, insult, and enrage, among many other things. Further, what is communicated is not wholly conveyed by what is said; much is implied. The treatment of these and related topics belongs to pragmatics. (Some philosophers have a different and more restrictive notion of pragmatics; they define it as the study of indexical expressions, such as "I," "here" and "now," the reference of which depends upon the context of the utterance.)

III

Several distinctions are presupposed by many of the articles in this anthology and need to be understood. First there is the use–mention distinction. For the most part, words are *used* in such a way that the word itself is not the primary object of interest. Roughly, words are signs that point beyond themselves to other things. However, it is possible for words to be used to *mention* or talk about themselves, to make the very word itself the object of interest. Consider the sentences

(1)   Cicero was a Roman senator.
(2)   Cicero is a word with six letters.

(3) "Cicero" was a Roman senator.

(4) "Cicero" is a word with six letters.

Sentences (1) and (4) are or can be used to make true statements. Sentence (1) is about the historical person Cicero; the subject expression was *used* to talk about Cicero. Sentence (4) is not about the historical person Cicero; it is about a word, about the proper name of Cicero, and it is that name that was *mentioned* in (4).

Sentences (2) and (3) are false. (2) is false because it claims that the person Cicero was a word, which is absurd; (3) is false because it claims that a word is a person.

This might seem simple and straightforward enough. But now consider this. In sentence (1), the word "Cicero" is used to talk about Cicero. In sentence (4), " 'Cicero' " is used to talk about the word "Cicero." Notice that in the preceding sentence, the subject expression contains two sets of quotation marks. The inner (single) quotation marks mention a word; the outer (double) quotation marks mention the mention of a word. These quotation marks can be stacked indefinitely, if necessary, to mention other mentioned expressions.

There are three ways to avoid the quotation mark device of mentioning a word or expression. One is to *display* the mentioned word or expression on a separate line. For example, the word

Cicero

has six letters. In the previous sentence, "Cicero" is mentioned by displaying it on a separate line. (Sometimes it is convenient to display a word or expression immediately following a colon.) The device of displaying an expression has already been used. Sentences (1) through (4) above were displayed. If I had not wanted to display them, I might have mentioned them in this way: Consider the sentences, (1) "Cicero was a Roman senator," (2) "Cicero is a word with six letters," (3) " 'Cicero' was a Roman senator," (4) " 'Cicero' is a word with six letters." Obviously, displaying expressions is often neater.

The second way to mention a word is to name it. Just as one might name an infant or pet, one can name words or expressions (or anything else). Suppose we want to talk about the word "Cicero" extensively. We might name that word "Harry." If we do, then the sentence "Harry is a word with six letters is true. Question: Is the sentence " 'Harry' has six letters" true or false?

Linguists have a third way of mentioning an expression. They italicize it. Thus, instead of (4), a linguist might write

(4') *Cicero* is a word with six letters.

IV

The use–mention distinction can be generalized in a certain way to distinguish between using a language and mentioning a language. This is the distinction between metalanguage and object language. Most areas of science and philosophy use language to talk about nonlinguistic phenomena. Linguistics and philosophy of language are unusual in that language is used to talk about language. We can distinguish then between the language used to express the science or philosophy and the language that is being studied. Since the language being studied is the *object* of study, it is called the object language. Since the language used to express the study is in a sense "outside" or "higher" than the language being studied, it is called the metalanguage. The metalanguage of a linguistic researcher will typically be his native language. English-speaking linguists typically use English as their metalanguage to talk about language. If Latin is the object of study, then Latin is the object language. When the metalanguage and the object language are different, there is relatively little risk of confusion. It is not difficult to understand what is meant by " 'Fiat lux' is a Latin sentence, consisting of a verb followed by a noun" and why it is being uttered. Yet, a linguist might take his native language as his object of study. An English-speaking linguistic researcher might take English as his object of study, in which case English is both the metalanguage and the object language. The identity of the metalanguage and object language raises philosophical problems, some of which are discussed by Alonzo Church, Alfred Tarski, and Donald Davidson in their articles in section I. There is also a kind of practical problem. When the metalanguage and the object language are the same and the discussion involves the meaning of the object language, the results can sound trivial. Philosophers have expended a lot of effort over the sentence

"Snow is white" means snow is white.

and

"Snow is white" is true just in case snow is white.

For Davidson, the truth of this latter, seemingly trivial sentence is crucial to his program for semantics. Other philosophers have called the sentence degenerate. Whatever the truth of the matter, one must keep in mind that the quoted sentence (the one mentioned) is the object of study, while the unquoted clause (the one being used) is part of the metalanguage being used to discuss the object language.

V

In the discussion of the use–mention distinction, the word "sentence" was used loosely and, one might argue, uncritically. For philosophers of language have found it necessary to distinguish between sentences, meanings, statements, and proposition, among other things; and sentences, contrary to my earlier usage, are often held *not* to be the kinds of things that can be either true or false.

To get a sense of the distinctions involved here, consider these expressions:

(5) I am a bachelor.
(6) John is a bachelor.
(7) John is an unmarried adult male.

(5) through (7) are different sentences in English. None of them has all the same words in the same order as any other. Yet, although (6) and (7) are different sentences, they are sometimes said to express the same *proposition* because they have the same meaning. Sameness of proposition is translinguistic. The English sentence "It is raining," the Italian sentence "Piove," and the German sentence "Es regnet" mean the same thing. Sentence (5), however, does not have the same meaning as (6) or (7). But suppose sentence (5) is uttered by John. Then (5) seems to be the same as (6) and (7) in some respect. They each express the same proposition: each refers to the same object and predicates the same thing of it. In order to determine whether (5) expresses the same proposition as (6) and (7), it is necessary to know something about the context. In this case, I have stipulated that John asserted the sentence. I have presupposed that the time and place of the utterance of the other sentences as well as the identities of the speakers were appropriate to make them express the same proposition. Many philosophers think this dependence

upon context is philosophically significant. Without knowing who uttered (5), it is impossible to know what proposition was expressed. More importantly, without knowing whether the sentence was asserted, or merely used as an example of a sentence of English without anyone committing himself to its truth, (5) is not used to express a proposition at all. On this view, (5) is a sentence and neither true nor false; and, in general, sentences do not have truth-values. Propositions do. Other philosophers do not think the sentence/meaning/proposition distinction is so important. They think that a proposition can be defined by relativizing a sentence to a context: a proposition is simply an ordered triple consisting of a sentence, a person, and a time of utterance.

Propositions also need to be distinguished from statements. The same proposition can be expressed with different forces. For example, consider these sentences:

> I state that John will be at the party.
> I promise that John will be at the party.
> I question whether John will be as the party.
> I order you, John, to be at the party.

All of them can be used to express the same proposition. But only the first has the potential force to make a statement directly. The other sentences, respectively, have the potential force to promise that the proposition will be made true, to question whether it is true and to order that it will be made true. Roughly, the difference between a proposition and a statement is that a proposition has a truth value without any special force attached to it, while a statement is a proposition the truth of which the speaker has committed himself to on the basis of sufficient evidence. This distinction between propositions and statements is explained by John Searle in "What Is a Speech Act?"

Related to these distinctions is a type–token distinction. Count the number of sentences displayed immediately below.

> It is raining.
> It is raining.
> It is raining.

One might count one or three. There is one sentence-type and three tokens or instances of that one sentence-type. If it seems dubious that there is only one sentence occurring three times, consider that if a teacher says, "Write the sentence 'I will not speak in class' one hundred times" she is using the word "sentence" in the sense of sentence-type. For it is the same sentence that is to be written repeatedly. She wants one sentence written: I will not speak in class. But she wants one hundred tokens of it.

VI

There was a time when philosophers were very concerned with syntax. Indeed, they thought that syntax was the sole legitimate study of language. The period lasted roughly from 1921, the date Wittgenstein's *Tractatus Logico-Philosophicus* was published, to 1935, the date that Alfred Tarski's "The Concept of Truth in Formalized Languages" was published. Wittgenstein's work was taken to show that only a syntactic description of language is possible. Tarski's work demonstrated that semantics was also possible. Most philosophers are no longer very interested in syntax. Although it still plays an important role in some philosophical discussions of language, especially those concerned with semantics, nonetheless its role is subsidiary. Most research in syntax is currently done by linguists. Many, perhaps most, philosophers of language are interested in semantics, and this volume begins with semantics. While the articles by Tarski and Church in section I sketch a syntactic theory, it is of secondary importance to the points they make about the proper shape of a semantic theory.

In addition to the meaning that words or sentences have, there is also a sense in which speakers mean things. H. P. Grice gave the first explicit, though tentative, analysis of this concept in his article "Meaning," published in 1957. He extended and revised that analysis, in response to numerous criticisms, in his "Utterer's Meaning and Intentions." On Grice's view, utterance, word, and sentence meaning are derivative concepts. That is, an analysis of utterance, word, and sentence meaning will contain the concept of utterer's meaning in the analysans. This view goes against the grain of most work in semantics. P.F. Strawson defends the Gricean project against the standard view, as represented by Tarski and Davidson. Thus, section I develops two important theories of meaning and touches on a number of related semantic issues.

Section II consists of selections about pragmatics or speech acts. It continues the line of thinking expounded in the articles by Grice and Strawson. If a person has successfully conveyed what he meant by an utterance then he has done something with those words: he has performed a speech act. The founder of speech act theory is J. L. Austin, who constructed a theory from the insights that not all cognitively significant talk is supposed to be true or false and that talking is a kind of doing. Many philosophers have extended Austin's work in various fruitful ways.

Section III concerns the single most discussed issue in the philosophy of language: reference. Reference has the importance that it does because philosophers typically think that the principal way in which language attaches to reality is through reference. This is presupposed in most of the selections in this section. The central issue of debate is whether reference is a semantic or pragmatic notion.

Section IV concerns a topic related to reference: Names and demonstratives are paradigmatic kinds of expressions that refer or are used to refer. What are names? What are demonstratives? How do they attach to reality?

In Section V a different problem is discussed. What people say is often the expression of a belief ("It is raining," or "The cat is on the mat"). Notice however that expression of belief are not in themselves expressions that someone has a belief. To say that the cat is on the mat is *not to say that anyone believes* that the cat is on the mat. Yet, one does of course often express such beliefs. In the sentences "Mary believes that it is raining" and "Mary believes that the cat is on the mat," the speaker is saying that Mary has certain beliefs. Philosophers have wondered what the objects of belief are. This question can be put in a linguistic mode: they have wondered what the object of "it is raining" and "the cat is on the mat" is when they follow the phrase "believes that." There are puzzles that seem to show that a clause occurring after the phrase "believes that" cannot refer to the same thing as it does when it occurs as the main clause of a sentence. And the same puzzles arise for a large family of words called verbs of propositional attitude, including "know," "think," "desire," and "look for."

Section VI discusses one of the most interesting uses of language: metaphor. It is also one of the most difficult to analyze because it is at once derivative from the literal use of language and extremely widespread, even in ordinary speech. The selections by John Searle and Donald Davidson are notable for developing views about metaphor that can be considered extensions of the theories of meaning introduced in section I.

Section VII deals with one of the most intriguing and elusive issues in the philosophy of language. What is the nature of language? Is it possible for one person to have his own language? Must language be a social phenomenon? Is it a formal system like logic or mathematics? Or a subsystem of the human brain? These issues overlap with the first topic discussed in this book, meaning. So, this is a good topic on which to end a philosophical reflection on language. Or to begin.

TRUTH AND MEANING

What is meaning? In what terms will meaning be analyzed, and what is the ontological status of these terms? Is it words, sentences, or persons that primarily mean or have meaning? These are the central questions raised and answered in various ways in this section.

The first two selections orient contemporary discussions of meaning by criticizing the theory of meaning espoused by logical positivism, which dominated the second quarter of this century and which was moribund shortly into the third quarter, partly because of the kinds of criticisms developed by Hempel and Quine.

Carl Hempel in "Empirical Criteria of Cognitive Significance: Problems and Changes" discusses the theory of meaning of logical positivism, according to which a sentence is meaningful just in case it is (a) analytic or contradictory or (b) verifiable or confirmable by experience. One purpose of this view was to have a criterion that would exclude certain traditional philosophical problems or solutions from scientific philosophy. As Hempel clearly and cogently shows, the criterion is both too strong and too weak. It excludes some things that the logical positivists wanted to include as philosophy and includes some that they would not want to. Hempel argues "the content of a statement with empirical import cannot, in general, be exhaustively expressed by means of any class of observation sentences." (An observation sentence is a sentence that might be verified or confirmed by some perception.) Further, "the cognitive meaning of a statement in an empirical language is reflected in the totality of its logical relationships to all other statements in that language and not to observation sentences alone." Although Hempel is critical of the standard formulations of the empiricist criterion of meaning, he is sympathetic with the project behind it.

A more unrelenting critique of empiricism is W. V. Quine's "Two Dogmas of Empiricism," which is the *locus classicus* for the attack on the alleged distinction between analytic and synthetic (or empirical) propositions. Questions of meaning seem to be different from questions of fact. Questions of meaning concern analyticity, synonymy, and entailment. Questions of fact concern the way the world is, not how we talk about the world. Quine challenges these seemingly unchallengeable views. He claims that there is no firm distinction between fact and meaning. Quine's results do not entail that there can be no theory of meaning, although they do impose restrictions on what will count as an adequate theory.

Two significantly different theories of meaning are represented in this section: a semantic and a pragmatic theory. Tarski's article, "The Semantic Conception of Truth," is an informal presentation of Tarski's technical paper "The Concept of Truth in Formalized Languages," which presented a way of rigorously treating the concept of truth. Tarski's original article was especially significant when it was first published because arguments of the then dominant school of logical positivism seemed to imply that semantics was impossible and that language could be described syntactically also. Tarski's work showed this to be mistaken.

Alonzo Church in "The Need for Abstract Entities in Semantic Analysis" presents a formal semantics for natural languages, which, though an alternative to Tarski's, still satisfies the same rigorous conditions. He modifies Frege's view that an adequate semantics for natural languages must specify both a sense and reference for almost all words.

Donald Davidson extends Tarski's work by asserting that a theory of truth for a language is at the same time a theory of meaning. H. P. Grice's theory of meaning is pragmatic in the sense that he takes as basic the notion of utterer's meaning, what it is for a person to mean something by an utterance. Utterance- or sentence-meaning is derivative in the sense that it will be analyzed in terms of utterer's meaning.

It is also important to distinguish between utterer's meaning and speaker's meaning. Utterer's meaning is the broader notion. It is whatever a person who tries to communicate something to another person means, no matter whether the utterance takes the form of a gesture, a token, or words. Speaker meaning is what a person who tries to communicate something by uttering words means. P. F. Strawson weighs the evidence between a semantic and pragmatic approach to meaning in "Meaning and Truth." He sides with Grice and against Davidson in arguing that to say something true is for a speaker to mean something, and hence the notion of a true statement must be analyzed in terms of what a speaker means.

Empiricist Criteria of Cognitive Significance: Problems and Changes   1

CARL G. HEMPEL

1. THE GENERAL EMPIRICIST CONCEPTION OF COGNITIVE AND EMPIRICAL SIGNIFICANCE

It is a basic principle of contemporary empiricism that a sentence makes a cognitively significant assertion, and thus can be said to be either true or false, if and only if either (1) it is analytic or contradictory—in which case it is said to have purely logical meaning or significance—or else (2) it is capable, at least potentially, of test by experiential evidence—in which case it is said to have empirical meaning or significance. The basic tenet of this principle, and especially of its second part, the so-called testability criterion of empirical meaning (or better: meaningfulness), is not peculiar to empiricism alone: it is characteristic also of contemporary operationism, and in a sense of pragmatism as well; for the pragmatist maxim that a difference must make a difference to be a difference may well be construed as insisting that a verbal difference between two sentences must make a difference in experiential implications if it is to reflect a difference in meaning.

How this general conception of cognitively significant discourse led to the rejection, as devoid of logical and empirical meaning, of various formulations in speculative metaphys-

ics, and even of certain hypotheses offered within empirical science, is too well known to require recounting. I think that the general intent of the empiricist criterion of meaning is basically sound, and that notwithstanding much oversimplification in its use, its critical application has been, on the whole, enlightening and salutary. I feel less confident, however, about the possibility of restating the general idea in the form of precise and general criteria which establish sharp dividing lines (a) between statements of purely logical and statements of empirical significance, and (b) between those sentences which do have cognitive significance and those which do not.

In the present paper, I propose to reconsider these distinctions as conceived in recent empiricism, and to point out some of the difficulties they present. The discussion will concern mainly the second of the two distinctions; in regard to the first, I shall limit myself to a few brief remarks.

2. THE EARLIER TESTABILITY CRITERIA OF MEANING AND THEIR SHORTCOMINGS

Let us note first that any general criterion of cognitive significance will have to meet certain

This essay combines, with certain omissions and some other changes, the contents of two articles: "Problems and Changes in the Empiricist Criterion of Meaning," *Revue Internationale de Philosophie*, no. 11, pp. 41–63 (January, 1950); and "The Concept of Cognitive Significance: A Reconsideration," *Proceedings of the American Academy of Arts and Sciences* 80, no. 1, pp. 61–77 (1951).

13

requirements if it is to be at all acceptable. Of these, we note one, which we shall consider here as expressing a necessary, though by no means sufficient, *condition of adequacy* for criteria of cognitive significance.

(A) If under a given criterion of cognitive significance, a sentence N is nonsignificant, then so must be all truth-functional compound sentences in which N occurs nonvacuously as a component. For if N cannot be significantly assigned a truth value, then it is impossible to assign truth values to the compound sentences containing N; hence, they should be qualified as nonsignificant as well.

We note two corollaries of requirement (A):

(A1) If under a given criterion of cognitive significance, a sentence S is nonsignificant, then so must be its negation, $\sim S$.

(A2) If under a given criterion of cognitive significance, a sentence N is nonsignificant, then so must be any conjunction $N \cdot S$ and any disjunction $N \vee S$, no matter whether S is significant under the given criterion or not.

We now turn to the initial attempts made in recent empiricism to establish general criteria of cognitive significance. Those attempts were governed by the consideration that a sentence, to make an empirical assertion must be capable of being borne out by, or conflicting with, phenomena which are potentially capable of being directly observed. Sentences describing such potentially observable phenomena—no matter whether the latter do actually occur or not—may be called observation sentences. More specifically, an *observation sentence* might be construed as a sentence—no matter whether true or false—which asserts or denies that a specified object, or group of objects, of macroscopic size has a particular *observable characteristic,* i.e., a characteristic whose presence or absence can, under favorable circumstances, be ascertained by direct observation.[1]

The task of setting up criteria of empirical significance is thus transformed into the problem of characterizing in a precise manner the relationship which obtains between a hypothesis and one or more observation sentences whenever the phenomena described by the latter either confirm or disconfirm the hypothesis in question. The ability of a given sentence to enter into that relationship to some set of observation sentences would then characterize its testability-in-principle, and thus its empirical significance. Let us now briefly examine the major attempts that have been made to obtain criteria of significance in this manner.

One of the earliest criteria is expressed in the so-called *verifiability requirement.* According to it, a sentence is empirically significant if and only if it is not analytic and is capable, at least in principle, of complete verification by observational evidence; i.e., if observational evidence can be described which, if actually obtained, would conclusively establish the truth of the sentence.[2] With the help of the concept of observation sentence, we can restate this requirement as follows: A sentence S has empirical meaning if and only if it is possible to indicate a finite set of observation sentences, $O_1, O_2, \ldots, O_n$, such that if these are true, then S is necessarily true, too. As stated, however, this condition is satisfied also if S is an analytic sentence or if the given observation sentences are logically incompatible with each other. By the following formulation, we rule these cases out and at the same time express the intended criterion more precisely.

2.1. Requirement of Complete Verifiability in Principle

A sentence has empirical meaning if and only if it is not analytic and follows logically from some finite and logically consistent class of observation sentences.[3] These observation sentences need not be true, for what the criterion is to explicate is testability by "potentially observable phenomena," or testability "in principle."

In accordance with the general conception of cognitive significance outlined earlier, a sentence will now be classified as cognitively significant if either it is analytic or contradictory, or it satisfies the verifiability requirement.

This criterion, however, has several serious

defects. One of them has been noted by several writers:

(a) Let us assume that the properties of being a stork and of being red-legged are both observable characteristics, and that the former does not logically entail the latter. Then the sentence

(S1)   All storks are red-legged

is neither analytic nor contradictory; and clearly, it is not deducible from a finite set of observation sentences. Hence, under the contemplated criterion, S1 is devoid of empirical significance; and so are all other sentences purporting to express universal regularities or general laws. And since sentences of this type constitute an integral part of scientific theories, the verifiability requirement must be regarded as overly restrictive in this respect.

Similarly, the criterion disqualifies all sentences such as "For any substance there exists some solvent," which contain both universal and existential quantifiers (i.e., occurrences of the terms "all" and "some" or their equivalents); for no sentences of this kind can be logically deduced from any finite set of observation sentences.

Two further defects of the verifiability requirement do not seem to have been widely noticed:

(b) As is readily seen, the negation of S1

(~S1)   There exists at least one stork that is not red-legged

is deducible from any two observation sentences of the type "a is a stork" and "a is not red-legged." Hence, ~S1 is cognitively significant under our criterion, but S1 is not, and this constitutes a violation of condition (A1).

(c) Let S be a sentence which does, and N a sentence which does not satisfy the verifiability requirement. Then S is deducible from some set of observation sentences; hence, by a familiar rule of logic, SvN is deducible from the same set, and therefore cognitively significant according to our criterion. This violates condition (A2) above.[4]

Strictly analogous considerations apply to an alternative criterion, which makes complete falsifiability in principle the defining characteristic of empirical significance. Let us formulate this criterion as follows:

2.2. Requirement of Complete Falsifiability in Principle

A sentence has empirical meaning if and only if its negation is not analytic and follows logically from some finite logically consistent class of observation sentences.

This criterion qualifies a sentence as empirically meaningful if its negation satisfies the requirement of complete verifiability; as it is to be expected, it is therefore inadequate on similar grounds as the latter:

(a) It denies cognitive significance to purely existential hypotheses, such as "There exists at least one unicorn," and all sentences whose formulation calls for mixed—i.e., universal and existential—quantification, such as "For every compound there exists some solvent," for none of these can possibly be conclusively falsified by a finite number of observation sentences.

(b) If 'P' is an observation predicate, then the assertion that all things have the property P is qualified as significant, but its negation, being equivalent to a purely existential hypothesis, is disqualified [cf. (a)]. Hence, criterion 2.2 gives rise to the same dilemma as 2.1.

(c) If a sentence S is completely falsifiable whereas N is a sentence which is not, then their conjunction S·N (i.e., the expression obtained by connecting the two sentences by the word "and") is completely falsifiable; for if the negation of S is entailed by a class of observation sentences, then the negation of S·N is, a fortiori, entailed by the same class. Thus, the criterion allows empirical significance to many sentences which an adequate empiricist criterion should rule out, such as "All swans are white and the absolute is perfect."

In sum, then, interpretations of the testability criterion in terms of complete verifiability or of complete falsifiability are inadequate because they are overly restrictive in one direction and overly inclusive in another, and because both of them violate the fundamental requirement A.

Several attempts have been made to avoid these difficulties by construing the testability criterion as demanding merely a partial and possibly indirect confirmability of empirical hypotheses by observational evidence.

A formulation suggested by Ayer[5] is characteristic of these attempts to set up a clear and sufficiently comprehensive criterion of confirmability. It states, in effect, that a sentence S has empirical import if from S in conjunction with suitable subsidiary hypotheses it is possible to derive observation sentences which are not derivable from the subsidiary hypotheses alone.

This condition is suggested by a closer consideration of the logical structure of scientific testing; but it is much too liberal as it stands. Indeed, as Ayer himself has pointed out in the second edition of his book, *Language, Truth, and Logic,*[6] his criterion allows empirical import to any sentence whatever. Thus, e.g., if S is the sentence "The absolute is perfect," it suffices to choose as a subsidiary hypothesis the sentence "If the absolute is perfect then this apple is red" in order to make possible the deduction of the observation sentence "This apple is red," which clearly does not follow from the subsidiary hypothesis alone.

To meet this objection, Ayer proposed a modified version of his testability criterion. In effect, the modification restricts the subsidiary hypothesis mentioned in the previous version to sentences which either are analytic or can independently be shown to be testable in the sense of the modified criterion.[7]

But it can readily be shown that this new criterion, like the requirement of complete falsifiability, allows empirical significance to any conjunction $S \cdot N$, where S satisfies Ayer's criterion while N is a sentence such as "The absolute is perfect," which is to be disqualified by that criterion. Indeed, whatever consequences can be deduced from S with the help of permissible subsidiary hypotheses can also be deduced from $S \cdot N$ by means of the same subsidiary hypotheses; and as Ayer's new criterion is formulated essentially in terms of

the deducibility of a certain type of consequence from the given sentence, it countenances $S \cdot N$ together with S. Another difficulty has been pointed out by Church, who has shown[8] that if there are any three observation sentences none of which alone entails any of the others, then it follows for any sentence S whatsoever that either it or its denial has empirical import according to Ayer's revised criterion.

All the criteria considered so far attempt to explicate the concept of empirical significance by specifying certain logical connections which must obtain between a significant sentence and suitable observation sentences. It seems now that this type of approach offers little hope for the attainment of precise criteria of meaningfulness: this conclusion is suggested by the preceding survey of some representative attempts, and it receives additional support from certain further considerations, some of which will be presented in the following sections.

3. CHARACTERIZATION OF SIGNIFICANT SENTENCES BY CRITERIA FOR THEIR CONSTITUENT TERMS

An alternative procedure suggests itself which again seems to reflect well the general viewpoint of empiricism: It might be possible to characterize cognitively significant sentences by certain conditions which their constituent terms have to satisfy. Specifically, it would seem reasonable to say that all extralogical terms[9] in a significant sentence must have experiential reference, and that therefore their meanings must be capable of explication by reference to observables exclusively.[10] In order to exhibit certain analogies between this approach and the previous one, we adopt the following terminological conventions.

Any term that may occur in a cognitively significant sentence will be called a *cognitively significant term.* Furthermore, we shall understand by an *observation term* any term which either (a) is an *observation predicate,* i.e., signifies some observable characteristic (as do the terms 'blue', 'warm', 'soft', 'coincident with', 'of greater apparent brightness than') or (b) names some physical object of macroscopic size (as do the terms 'the needle of this instrument', 'the Moon', 'Krakatoa Volcano', 'Greenwich, England', 'Julius Caesar').

Now while the testability criteria of meaning aimed at characterizing the cognitively significant sentences by means of certain inferential connections in which they must stand to some observation sentences, the alternative approach under consideration would instead try to specify the vocabulary that may be used in forming significant sentences. This vocabulary, the class of significant terms, would be characterized by the condition that each of its elements is either a logical term or else a term with empirical significance; in the latter case, it has to stand in certain definitional or explicative connections to some observation terms. This approach certainly avoids any violations of our earlier conditions of adequacy. Thus, e.g., if S is a significant sentence, i.e., contains cognitively significant terms only, then so is its denial, since the denial sign, and its verbal equivalents, belong to the vocabulary of logic and are thus significant. Again, if N is a sentence containing a nonsignificant term, then so is any compound sentence which contains N.

But this is not sufficient, of course. Rather, we shall now have to consider a crucial question analogous to that raised by the previous approach: Precisely how are the logical connections between empirically significant terms and observation terms to be construed if an adequate criterion of cognitive significance is to result? Let us consider some possibilities.

3.1. Requirement of Definability

The simplest criterion that suggests itself might be called the *requirement of definability*. It would demand that any term with empirical significance must be explicitly definable by means of observation terms.

This criterion would seem to accord well with the maxim of operationism that all significant terms of empirical science must be

introduced by operational definitions. However, the requirement of definability is vastly too restrictive, for many important terms of scientific and even prescientific discourse cannot be explicitly defined by means of observation terms.

In fact, as Carnap[11] has pointed out, an attempt to provide explicit definitions in terms of observables encounters serious difficulties as soon as disposition terms, such as 'soluble', 'malleable', 'electric conductor', etc., have to be accounted for; and many of these occur even on the prescientific level of discourse.

Consider, for example, the word 'fragile'. One might try to define it by saying that an object x is fragile if and only if it satisfies the following condition: If at any time t the object is sharply struck, then it breaks at that time. But if the statement connectives in this phrasing are construed truth-functionally, so that the definition can be symbolized by

(D) $Fx \equiv (t)(Sxt \supset Bxt)$

then the predicate 'F' thus defined does not have the intended meaning. For let a be any object which is not fragile (e.g., a raindrop or a rubber band), but which happens not to be sharply struck at any time throughout its existence. Then 'Sat' is false and hence '$Sat \supset Bat$' is true for all values of 't'; consequently, 'Fa' is true though a is not fragile.

To remedy this defect, one might construe the phrase 'if . . . then . . .' in the original definiens as having a more restrictive meaning than the truth-functional conditional. This meaning might be suggested by the subjunctive phrasing 'If x were to be sharply struck at any time t, then x would break at t.' But a satisfactory elaboration of this construal would require a clarification of the meaning and the logic of counterfactual and subjunctive conditionals, which is a thorny problem.[12]

An alternative procedure was suggested by Carnap in his theory of reduction sentences.[13] These are sentences which, unlike definitions, specify the meaning of a term only conditionally or partially. The term 'fragile', for example, might be introduced by the following reduction sentence:

(R) $(x)(t)[Sxt \supset (Fx \equiv Bxt)]$

which specifies that if x is sharply struck at any time t, then x is fragile if and only if x breaks at t.

Our earlier difficulty is now avoided, for if a is a nonfragile object that is never sharply struck, then that expression in R which follows the quantifiers is true of a; but this does not imply that 'Fa' is true. But the reduction sentence R specifies the meaning of 'F' only for application to those objects which meet the "test condition" of being sharply struck at some time; for these it states that fragility then amounts to breaking. For objects that fail to meet the test condition, the meaning of 'F' is left undetermined. In this sense, reduction sentences have the character of partial or conditional definitions.

Reduction sentences provide a satisfactory interpretation of the experiential import of a large class of disposition terms and permit a more adequate formulation of so-called operational definitions, which, in general, are not complete definitions at all. These considerations suggest a greatly liberalized alternative to the requirement of definability.

3.2. Requirement of Reducibility

Every term with empirical significance must be capable of introduction, on the basis of observation terms, through chains of reduction sentences.

This requirement is characteristic of the liberalized versions of positivism and physicalism which, since about 1936, have superseded the older, overly narrow conception of a full definability of all terms of empirical science by means of observables,[14] and it avoids many of the shortcomings of the latter. Yet, reduction sentences do not seem to offer an adequate means for the introduction of the central terms of advanced scientific theories, often referred to as theoretical constructs. This is indicated by the following considerations: A chain of reduction sentences provides a necessary and a sufficient condition for the applicability of the term it introduces. (When the two conditions coincide, the chain is tantamount

to an explicit definition.) But now take, for example, the concept of length as used in classical physical theory. Here, the length in centimeters of the distance between two points may assume any positive real number as its value; yet it is clearly impossible to formulate, by means of observation terms, a sufficient condition for the applicability of such expressions as 'having a length of $\sqrt{2}$ cm' and 'having a length of $\sqrt{2} + 10^{-100}$ cm'; for such conditions would provide a possibility for discrimination, in observational terms, between two lengths which differ by only 10^{-100} cm.[15]

It would be ill-advised to argue that for this reason, we ought to permit only such values of the magnitude, length, as permit the statement of sufficient conditions in terms of observables. For this would rule out, among others, all irrational numbers and would prevent us from assigning, to the diagonal of a square with sides of length 1, the length $\sqrt{2}$, which is required by Euclidean geometry. Hence, the principles of Euclidean geometry would not be universally applicable in physics. Similarly, the principles of the calculus would become inapplicable, and the system of scientific theory as we know it today would be reduced to a clumsy, unmanageable torso. This, then, is no way of meeting the difficulty. Rather, we shall have to analyze more closely the function of constructs in scientific theories, with a view to obtaining through such an analysis a more adequate characterization of cognitively significant terms.

Theoretical constructs occur in the formulation of scientific theories. These may be conceived of, in their advanced stages; as being stated in the form of deductively developed axiomatized systems. Classical mechanics, or Euclidean or some non-Euclidean form of geometry in physical interpretation, present examples of such systems. The extralogical terms used in a theory of this kind may be divided, in familiar manner, into primitive or basic terms, which are not defined within the theory, and defined terms, which are explicitly defined by means of the primitives. Thus, e.g., in Hilbert's axiomatization of Euclidean geometry, the terms 'point', 'straight line', 'between' are among the primitives, while 'line segment', 'angle', 'triangle', 'length' are among the defined terms. The basic and the defined terms together with the terms of logic constitute the vocabulary out of which all the sentences of the theory are constructed. The latter are divided, in an axiomatic presentation, into primitive statements (also called postulates or basic statements) which, in the theory, are not derived from any other statements, and derived ones, which are obtained by logical deduction from the primitive statements.

From its primitive terms and sentences, an axiomatized theory can be developed by means of purely formal principles of definition and deduction, without any consideration of the empirical significance of its extralogical terms. Indeed, this is the standard procedure employed in the axiomatic development of uninterpreted mathematical theories such as those of abstract groups or rings or lattices, or any form of pure (i.e., noninterpreted) geometry.

However, a deductively developed system of this sort can constitute a scientific theory only if it has received an empirical interpretation[16] which renders it relevant to the phenomena of our experience. Such interpretation is given by assigning a meaning, in terms of observables, to certain terms or sentences of the formalized theory. Frequently, an interpretation is given not for the primitive terms or statements but rather for some of the terms definable by means of the primitives, or for some of the sentences deducible from the postulates.[17] Furthermore, interpretation may amount to only a partial assignment of meaning. Thus, e.g., the rules for the measurement of length by means of a standard rod may be considered as providing a *partial* empirical interpretation for the term 'the length, in centimeters, of interval *i*', or alternatively, for some sentences of the form 'the length of interval *i* is *r* centimeters'. For the method is applicable only to intervals of a certain medium size, and even for the latter it does not constitute a full interpretation since the use of a standard rod does not constitute the only way of determining length: various

alternative procedures are available involving the measurement of other magnitudes which are connected, by general laws, with the length that is to be determined.

This last observation, concerning the possibility of an indirect measurement of length by virtue of certain laws, suggests an important reminder. It is not correct to speak, as is often done, of "the experiential meaning" of a term or a sentence in isolation. In the language of science, and for similar reasons even in prescientific discourse, a single statement usually has no experiential implications. A single sentence in a scientific theory does not, as a rule, entail any observation sentences; consequences asserting the occurrence of certain observable phenomena can be derived from it only by conjoining it with a set of other, subsidiary, hypotheses. Of the latter, some will usually be observation sentences, others will be previously accepted theoretical statements. Thus, e.g., the relativistic theory of the deflection of light rays in the gravitational field of the sun entails assertions about observable phenomena only if it is conjoined with a considerable body of astronomical and optical theory as well as a large number of specific statements about the instruments used in those observations of solar eclipses which serve to test the hypothesis in question.

Hence, the phrase, 'the experiential meaning of expression *E*' is elliptical: What a given expression "means" in regard to potential empirical data is relative to two factors, namely:

(1) *The linguistic framework L* to which the expression belongs. Its rules determine, in particular, what sentences—observational or otherwise—may be inferred from a given statement or class of statements.

(2) The theoretical context in which the expression occurs, i.e., the class of those statements in *L* which are available as subsidiary hypotheses.

Thus, the sentence formulating Newton's law of gravitation has no experiential meaning by itself; but when used in a language whose logical apparatus permits the development of the calculus, and when combined with a suitable system of other hypotheses—including sentences which connect some of the theoretical terms with observation terms and thus establish a partial interpretation—then it has a bearing on observable phenomena in a large variety of fields. Analogous considerations are applicable to the term 'gravitational field', for example. It can be considered as having experiential meaning only within the context of a theory, which must be at least partially interpreted; and the experiential meaning of the term—as expressed, say, in the form of operational criteria for its application—will depend again on the theoretical system at hand, and on the logical characteristics of the language within which it is formulated.

4. COGNITIVE SIGNIFICANCE AS A CHARACTERISTIC OF INTERPRETED SYSTEMS

The preceding considerations point to the conclusion that a satisfactory criterion of cognitive significance cannot be reached through the second avenue of approach here considered, namely by means of specific requirements for the terms which make up significant sentences. This result accords with a general characteristic of scientific (and, in principle, even prescientific) theorizing: Theory formation and concept formation go hand in hand; neither can be carried on successfully in isolation from the other.

If, therefore, cognitive significance can be attributed to anything, then only to entire theoretical systems formulated in a language with a well-determined structure. And the decisive mark of cognitive significance in such a system appears to be the existence of an interpretation for it in terms of observables. Such an interpretation might be formulated, for example, by means of conditional or biconditional sentences connecting nonobservational terms of the system with observation terms in the given language; the latter as well as the connecting sentences may or may not belong to the theoretical system.

But the requirement of partial interpretation is extremely liberal; it is satisfied, for example, by the system consisting of contemporary physical theory combined with some set of principles of speculative metaphysics, even if the latter have no empirical interpretation at all. Within the total system, these metaphysical principles play the role of what K. Reach and also O. Neurath liked to call *isolated sentences:* They are neither purely formal truths or falsehoods, demonstrable or refutable by means of the logical rules of the given language system; nor do they have any experiential bearing; i.e., their omission from the theoretical system would have no effect on its explanatory and predictive power in regard to potentially observable phenomena (i.e., the kind of phenomena described by observation sentences). Should we not, therefore, require that a cognitively significant system contain no isolated sentences? The following criterion suggests itself.

4.1.

A theoretical system is cognitively significant if and only if it is partially interpreted to at least such an extent that none of its primitive sentences is isolated.

But this requirement may bar from a theoretical system certain sentences which might well be viewed as permissible and indeed desirable. By way of a simple illustration, let us assume that our theoretical system *T* contains the primitive sentence

(S1) $(x)[P_1x \supset (Qx \equiv P_2x)]$

where 'P_1' and 'P_2' are observation predicates in the given language *L*, while 'Q' functions in *T* somewhat in the manner of a theoretical construct and occurs in only one primitive sentence of *T*, namely S1. Now S1 is not a truth or falsehood of formal logic; and furthermore, if S1 is omitted from the set of primitive sentences of *T,* then the resulting system, *T'*, possesses exactly the same systematic, i.e., explanatory and predictive, power as *T.* Our contemplated criterion would therefore qualify S1 as an isolated sentence which has to be eliminated—excised by means of Occam's razor, as it were—if the theoretical system at hand is to be cognitively significant.

But it is possible to take a much more liberal view of $S1$ by treating it as a partial definition for the theoretical term 'Q'. Thus conceived, $S1$ specifies that in all cases where the observable characteristic P_1 is present, 'Q' is applicable if and only if the observable characteristic P_2 is present as well. In fact, $S1$ is an instance of those partial, or conditional, definitions which Carnap calls bilateral reduction sentences. These sentences are explicitly qualified by Carnap as analytic (though not, of course, as truths of formal logic), essentially on the ground that all their consequences which are expressible by means of observation predicates (and logical terms) alone are truths of formal logic.[18]

Let us pursue this line of thought a little further. This will lead us to some observations on analytic sentences and then back to the question of the adequacy of 4.1.

Suppose we add to our system T the further sentence

($S2$) $(x)[P_3x \supset (Qx \equiv P_4x)]$

where 'P_3', 'P_4' are additional observation predicates. Then, on the view that "every bilateral reduction sentence is analytic,"[19] $S2$ would be analytic as well as $S1$. Yet, the two sentences jointly entail nonanalytic consequences which are expressible in terms of observation predicates alone, such as[20]

(O) $(x)[\sim(P_1x \cdot P_2x \cdot Px_3 \cdot \sim P_4x) \cdot$
$\sim(P_1x \cdot \sim P_2x \cdot P_3x \cdot P_4x)]$

But one would hardly want to admit the consequence that the conjunction of two analytic sentences may be synthetic. Hence if the concept of analyticity can be applied at all to the sentences of interpreted deductive systems, then it will have to be relativized with respect to the theoretical context at hand. Thus, e.g., $S1$ might be qualified as analytic relative to the system T, whose remaining postulates do not contain the term 'Q', but as synthetic relative to the system T enriched by $S2$. Strictly speaking, the concept of analyticity has to be relativized also in regard to the rules of the language at hand, for the latter determine what observational or other consequences are entailed by a given sentence. This need for at least a twofold relativization of the concept of analyticity was almost to be expected in view of those considerations which required the same twofold relativization for the concept of experiential meaning of a sentence.

If, on the other hand, we decide not to permit $S1$ in the role of a partial definition and instead reject it as an isolated sentence, then we are led to an analogous conclusion. Whether a sentence is isolated or not will depend on the linguistic frame and on the theoretical context at hand: While $S1$ is isolated relative to T (and the language in which both are formulated), it acquires definite experiential implications when T is enlarged by $S2$.

Thus we find, on the level of interpreted theoretical systems, a peculiar rapprochement, and partial fusion, of some of the problems pertaining to the concepts of cognitive significance and of analyticity: Both concepts need to be relativized; and a large class of sentences may be viewed, apparently with equal right, as analytic in a given context, or as isolated, or nonsignificant, in respect to it.

In addition to barring, as isolated in a given context, certain sentences which could just as well be construed as partial definitions, the criterion 4.1 has another serious defect. Of two logically equivalent formulations of a theoretical system it may qualify one as significant while barring the other as containing an isolated sentence among its primitives. For assume that a certain theoretical system $T1$ contains among its primitive sentences S', S'', . . . exactly one, S', which is isolated. Then $T1$ is not significant under 4.1. But now consider the theoretical system $T2$ obtained from $T1$ by replacing the two first primitive sentences, S', S'', by one, namely their conjunction. Then, under our assumptions, none of the primitive sentences of $T2$ is isolated, and $T2$, though equivalent to $T1$, is qualified as significant by 4.1. In order to do justice to the intent of 4.1, we would therefore have to lay down the following stricter requirement.

4.2.

A theoretical system is cognitively significant if and only if it is partially interpreted to such an extent that in no system equivalent to it at least one primitive sentence is isolated.

Let us apply this requirement to some theoretical system whose postulates include the two sentences $S1$ and $S2$ considered before, and whose other postulates do not contain 'Q' at all. Since the sentences $S1$ and $S2$ together entail the sentence O, the set consisting of $S1$ and $S2$ is logically equivalent to the set consisting of $S1$, $S2$, and O. Hence, if we replace the former set by the latter, we obtain a theoretical system equivalent to the given one. In this new system, both $S1$ and $S2$ are isolated since, as can be shown, their removal does not affect the explanatory and predictive power of the system in reference to observable phenomena. To put it intuitively, the systematic power of $S1$ and $S2$ is the same as that of O. Hence, the original system is disqualified by 4.2. From the viewpoint of a strictly sensationalist positivism as perhaps envisaged by Mach, this result might be hailed as a sound repudiation of theories making reference to fictitious entities, and as a strict insistence on theories couched exclusively in terms of observables. But from a contemporary vantage point, we shall have to say that such a procedure overlooks or misjudges the important function of constructs in scientific theory: The history of scientific endeavor shows that if we wish to arrive at precise, comprehensive, and well-confirmed general laws, we have to rise above the level of direct observation. The phenomena directly accessible to our experience are not connected by general laws of great scope and rigor. Theoretical constructs are needed for the formulation of such higher-level laws. One of the most important functions of a well-chosen construct is its potential ability to serve as a constituent in ever new general connections that may be discovered; and to such connections we would blind ourselves if we insisted on banning from scientific theories all those terms and sentences which could be "dispensed with" in the sense indicated in 4.2. In following such a narrowly phenomenalistic or positivistic course, we would deprive ourselves of the tremendous fertility of theoretical constructs, and we would often render the formal structure of the expurgated theory clumsy and inefficient.

Criterion 4.2, then, must be abandoned, and considerations such as those outlined in this paper seem to lend strong support to the conjecture that no adequate alternative to it can be found; i.e., that it is not possible to formulate general and precise criteria which would separate those partially interpreted systems whose isolated sentences might be said to have a significant function from those in which the isolated sentences are, so to speak, mere useless appendages.

We concluded earlier that cognitive significance in the sense intended by recent empiricism and operationism can at best be attributed to sentences forming a theoretical system, and perhaps rather to such systems as wholes. Now, rather than try to replace 4.2 by some alternative, we will have to recognize further that cognitive significance in a system is a matter of degree: Significant systems range from those whose entire extralogical vocabulary consists of observation terms, through theories whose formulation relies heavily on theoretical constructs, on to systems with hardly any bearing on potential empirical findings. Instead of dichotomizing this array into significant and nonsignificant systems it would seem less arbitrary and more promising to appraise or compare different theoretical systems in regard to such characteristics as these:

(a) the clarity and precision with which the theories are formulated, and with which the logical relationships of their elements to each other and to expressions couched in observational terms have been made explicit;

(b) the systematic, i.e., explanatory and predictive, power of the systems in regard to observable phenomena;

(c) the formal simplicity of the theoretical system with which a certain systematic power is attained;

(d) the extent to which the theories have been confirmed by experiential evidence.

Many of the speculative philosophical approaches to cosmology, biology, or history, for example, would make a poor showing on practically all of these counts and would thus prove no matches to available rival theories, or would be recognized as so unpromising as not to warrant further study or development.

If the procedure here suggested is to be carried out in detail, so as to become applicable also in less obvious cases, then it will be necessary, of course, to develop general standards, and theories pertaining to them, for the appraisal and comparison of theoretical systems in the various respects just mentioned. To what extent this can be done with rigor and precision cannot well be judged in advance. In recent years, a considerable amount of work has been done towards a definition and theory of the concept of degree of confirmation, or logical probability, of a theoretical system;[21] and several contributions have been made towards the clarification of some of the other ideas referred to above.[22] The continuation of this research represents a challenge for further constructive work in the logical and methodological analysis of scientific knowledge.

NOTES

1. Observation sentences of this kind belong to what Carnap has called the thing-language, cf., e.g. (1938), pp. 52–53. That they are adequate to formulate the data which serve as the basis for empirical tests is clear in particular for the intersubjective testing procedures used in science as well as in large areas of empirical inquiry on the common-sense level. In epistemological discussions, it is frequently assumed that the ultimate evidence for beliefs about empirical matters consists in perceptions and sensations whose description calls for a phenomenalistic type of language. The specific problems connected with the phenomenalistic approach cannot be discussed here; but it should be mentioned that at any rate all the critical considerations presented in this article in regard to the testability criterion are applicable, *mutatis mutandis*, to the case of a phenomenalistic basis as well.

2. Originally, the permissible evidence was meant to be restricted to what is observable by the speaker and perhaps his fellow beings during their lifetimes. Thus construed, the criterion rules out, as cognitively meaningless, all statements about the distant future or the remote past, as has been pointed out, among others, by Ayer (1946), chapter 1; by Pap (1949), chapter 13, esp. pp. 333ff.; and by Russell (1948), pp. 445–47. This difficulty is avoided, however, if we permit the evidence to consist of any finite set of "logically possible observation data", each of them formulated in an observation sentence. Thus, e.g., the sentence S_1, "The tongue of the largest dinosaur in New York's Museum of Natural History was blue or black" is completely verifiable in our sense; for it is a logical consequence of the sentence S_2, "The tongue of the largest dinosaur in New York's Museum of Natural History was blue"; and this is an observation sentence, in the sense just indicated.

   And if the concept of *verifiability in principle* and the more general concept of *confirmability in principle,* which will be considered later, are construed as referring to *logically possible evidence* as expressed by observation sentences, then it follows similarly that the class of statements which are verifiable, or at least confirmable, in principle include such assertions as that the planet Neptune and the Antarctic Continent existed before they were discovered, and that atomic warfare, if not checked, will lead to the extermination of this planet. The objections which Russell (1948), pp. 445 and 447, raises against the verifiability criterion by reference to those examples do not apply therefore if the criterion is understood in the manner here suggested. Incidentally, statements of the kind mentioned by Russell, which are not actually verifiable by any human being, were explicitly recognized as cognitively significant already by Schlick (1936), part V, who argued that the impossibility of verifying them was "merely empirical." The characterization of verifiability with the help of the concept of observation sentence as suggested here might serve as a more explicit and rigorous statement of that conception.

3. As has frequently been emphasized in the empiricist literature, the term "verifiability" is to indicate, of course, the conceivability, or better, the logical possibility, of evidence of an observational kind which, if actually encountered, would constitute conclusive evidence for the given sentence; it is not intended to mean the technical possibility of performing the tests needed to obtain such evidence, and even less the possibility of actually finding directly observable phenomena which constitute conclusive evidence for that sentence— which would be tantamount to the actual existence of such evidence and would thus imply the truth of the given sentence. Analogous remarks apply to the terms "falsifiability" and "confirmability". This point has clearly

been disregarded in some critical discussions of the verifiability criterion. Thus, e.g., Russell (1948), p. 448 construes verifiability as the actual existence of a set of conclusively verifying occurrences. This conception, which has never been advocated by any logical empiricist, must naturally turn out to be inadequate since according to it the empirical meaningfulness of a sentence could not be established without gathering empirical evidence, and moreover enough of it to permit a conclusive proof of the sentence in question! It is not surprising, therefore, that his extraordinary interpretation of verifiability leads Russell to the conclusion: "In fact, that a proposition is verifiable is itself not verifiable" (*l.c.*). Actually, under the empiricist interpretation of complete verifiability, any statement asserting the verifiability of some sentence S whose text is quoted, is either analytic or contradictory; for the decision whether there exists a class of observation sentences which entail S, i.e., whether such observation sentences can be formulated, no matter whether they are true or false—that decision is a purely logical matter.

4. The arguments here adduced against the verifiability criterion also prove the inadequacy of a view closely related to it, namely that two sentences have the same cognitive significance if any set of observation sentences which would verify one of them would also verify the other, and conversely. Thus, e.g., under this criterion, any two general laws would have to be assigned the same cognitive significance, for no general law is verified by any set of observation sentences. The view just referred to must be clearly distinguished from a position which Russell examines in his critical discussion of the positivistic meaning criterion. It is "the theory that two propositions whose verified consequences are identical have the same significance" (1948), p. 448. This view is untenable indeed, for what consequences of a statement have actually been verified at a given time is obviously a matter of historical accident which cannot possibly serve to establish identity of cognitive significance. But I am not aware that any logical empiricist ever subscribed to that "theory."

5. Ayer (1936, 1946), chapter I. The case against the requirements of verifiability and of falsifiability, and in favor of a requirement of partial confirmability and disconfirmability, is very clearly presented also by Pap (1949), chapter 13.

6. Ayer (1946), 2d ed., pp. 11–12.

7. This restriction is expressed in recursive form and involves no vicious circle. For the full statement of Ayer's criterion, see Ayer (1946), p. 13.

8. Church (1949). An alternative criterion recently suggested by O'Connor (1950) as a revision of Ayer's formulation is subject to a slight variant of Church's stricture: It can be shown that if there are three observation sentences none of which entails any of the others, and if S is any noncompound sentence, then either S or $\sim S$ is significant under O'Connor's criterion.

9. An extralogical term is one that does not belong to the specific vocabulary of logic. The following phrases, and those definable by means of them, are typical examples of logical terms: 'not', 'or', 'if . . . then', 'all', 'some', '. . . is an element of class. . . .' Whether it is possible to make a sharp theoretical distinction between logical and extralogical terms is a controversial issue related to the problem of discriminating between analytic and synthetic sentences. For the purpose at hand, we may simply assume that the logical vocabulary is given by enumeration.

10. For a detailed exposition and critical discussion of this idea, see H. Feigl's stimulating and enlightening article (1950).

11. Cf. Carnap (1936–37), especially section 7.

12. On this subject, see for example Langford (1941); Lewis (1946), pp. 210–30; Chisholm (1946); Goodman (1947); Reichenbach (1947), chapter VIII; Hempel and Oppenheim (1948), part III; Popper (1949); and especially Goodman's further analysis (1955).

13. Cf. Carnap, *loc. cit.* note 11. For a brief elementary presentation of the main idea, see Carnap (1938), part III. The sentence R here formulated for the predicate 'F' illustrates only the simplest type of reduction sentence, the so-called bilateral reduction sentence.

14. Cf. the analysis in Carnap (1936–37), especially section 15; also see the briefer presentation of the liberalized point of view in Carnap (1938).

15. (Added in 1964.) This is not strictly correct. For a more circumspect statement, see note 12 in "A Logical Appraisal of Operationism" and the fuller discussion in section 7 of the essay "The Theoretician's Dilemma."

16. The interpretation of formal theories has been studied extensively by Reichenbach, especially in his pioneer analyses of space and time in classical and in relativistic physics. He describes such interpretation as the establishment of *coordinating definitions* (Zuordnungsdefinitionen) for certain terms of the formal theory. See, for example, Reichenbach (1928). More recently, Northrop [cf. (1947), chapter VII, and also the detailed study of the use of deductively formulated theories in science, ibid., chapters IV, V, VI] and H. Margenau [cf., for example, (1935)] have discussed certain aspects of this process under the title of *epistemic correlation*.

17. A somewhat fuller account of this type of interpretation may be found in Carnap (1939), §24. The articles by Spence (1944) and by MacCorquodale and Meehl (1948) provide en-

lightening illustrations of the use of theoretical constructs in a field outside that of the physical sciences, and of the difficulties encountered in an attempt to analyze in detail their function and interpretation.
18. Cf. Carnap (1936–37), especially sections 8 and 10.
19. Carnap (1936–37), p. 452.
20. The sentence *O* is what Carnap calls the *representative sentence* of the couple consisting of the sentences *S*1 and *S*2; see (1936–37), pp. 450–53.
21. Cf., for example, Carnap (1945)1 and (1945)2, and especially (1950). Also see Helmer and Oppenheim (1945).
22. On simplicity, cf. especially Popper (1935), chapter V; Reichenbach (1938), §42; Goodman (1949)1, (1949)2, (1950); on explanatory and predictive power, cf. Hempel and Oppenheim (1948), part IV.

REFERENCES

Ayer, A. J., *Language, Truth and Logic* (London: 1936) 2d ed. 1946.

Carnap, R., "Testability and Meaning," *Philosophy of Science,* 3 (1936) and 4 (1937).

Carnap, R., "Logical Foundations of the Unity of Science," in *International Encyclopedia of Unified Science,* I, 1 (Chicago: 1938).

Carnap, R., *Foundations of Logic and Mathematics* (Chicago: 1939).

Carnap, R., "On Inductive Logic," *Philosophy of Science,* 12 (1945). Referred to as (1945)1 in this article.

Carnap, R., "The Two Concepts of Probability," *Philosophy and Phenomenological Research,* 5 (1945). Referred to as (1945)2 in this article.

Carnap, R., *Logical Foundations of Probability* (Chicago: 1950).

Chisholm, R. M., "The Contrary-to-Fact Conditional," *Mind,* 55 (1946).

Church, A., Review of Ayer (1946), *The Journal of Symbolic Logic,* 14 (1949), 52–53.

Feigl, H., "Existential Hypotheses: Realistic vs. Phenomenalistic Interpretations," *Philosophy of Science,* 17 (1950).

Goodman, N., "The Problem of Counterfactual Conditionals," *The Journal of Philosophy,* 44 (1947).

Goodman, N., "The Logical Simplicity of Predicates," *The Journal of Symbolic Logic,* 14 (1949). Referred to as (1949)1 in this article.

Goodman, N., "Some Reflections on the Theory of Systems," *Philosophy and Phenomenological Research,* 9 (1949). Referred to as (1949)2 in this article.

Goodman, N., "An Improvement in the Theory of Simplicity," *The Journal of Symbolic Logic,* 15 (1950).

Goodman, N., *Fact, Fiction, and Forecast* (Cambridge, Mass.: 1955).

Helmer, O. and P. Oppenheim, "A Syntactical Definition of Probability and of Degree of Confirmation." *The Journal of Symbolic Logic,* 10 (1945).

Hempel, C. G, "A Logical Appraisal of Operationalism," in *Aspects of Scientific Explanation* (New York: 1965).

Hempel, C. G., "A Theoretician's Dilemma: A Study in the Logic of Theory Construction," in *Aspects of Scientific Explanation* (New York: 1965).

Hempel, C. G. and P. Oppenheim, "Studies in the Logic of Explanation," *Philosophy of Science,* 15 (1948).

Langford, C. H., Review in *The Journal of Symbolic Logic,* 6 (1941), 67–68.

Lewis, C. I., *An Analysis of Knowledge and Valuation* (La Salle, Ill.: 1946).

MacCorquodale, K. and P. E. Meehl, "On a Distinction Between Hypothetical Constructs and Intervening Variables," *Psychological Review,* 55 (1948).

Margenau, H., "Methodology of Modern Physics," *Philosophy of Science,* 2 (1935).

Northrop, F. S. C., *The Logic of the Sciences and the Humanities* (New York: 1947).

O'Connor, D. J., "Some Consequences of Professor A. J. Ayer's Verification Principle," *Analysis,* 10 (1950).

Pap, A., *Elements of Analytic Philosophy* (New York: 1949).

Popper, K., *Logik der Forschung* (Vienna: 1935).

Popper, K., "A Note on Natural Laws and So-Called 'Contrary-to-Fact Conditionals'," *Mind,* 58 (1949).

Reichenbach, H., *Philosophie der Raum-Zeit-Lehre* (Berlin: 1928).

Reichenbach, H., *Elements of Symbolic Logic* (New York: 1947).

Russell, B., *Human Knowledge* (New York: 1948).

Schlick, M., "Meaning and Verification," *Philosophical Review,* 45 (1936). Also reprinted in Feigl, H. and W. Sellars, eds. *Readings in Philosophical Analysis* (New York: 1949).

Spence, Kenneth W., "The Nature of Theory Construction in Contemporary Psychology," *Psychological Review,* 51 (1944).

Two Dogmas of Empiricism 2

W. V. QUINE

Modern empiricism has been conditioned in large part by two dogmas. One is a belief in some fundamental cleavage between truths which are *analytic,* or grounded in meanings independently of matters of fact, and truths which are *synthetic,* or grounded in fact. The other dogma is *reductionism:* the belief that each meaningful statement is equivalent to some logical construct upon terms which refer to immediate experience. Both dogmas, I shall argue, are ill-founded. One effect of abandoning them is, as we shall see, a blurring of the supposed boundary between speculative metaphysics and natural science. Another effect is a shift toward pragmatism.

1. BACKGROUND FOR ANALYTICITY

Kant's cleavage between analytic and synthetic truths was foreshadowed in Hume's distinction between relations of ideas and matters of fact, and in Leibniz's distinction between truths of reason and truths of fact. Leibniz spoke of the truths of reason as true in all possible worlds. Picturesqueness aside, this is to say that the truths of reason are those which could not possibly be false. In the same vein we hear analytic statements defined as statements whose denials are self-contradictory. But this definition has small explanatory value; for the notion of self-contradictoriness,

in the quite broad sense needed for this definition of analyticity, stands in exactly the same need of clarification as does the notion of analyticity itself. The two notions are the two sides of a single dubious coin.

Kant conceived of an analytic statement as one that attributes to its subject no more than is already conceptually contained in the subject. This formulation has two shortcomings: it limits itself to statements of subject-predicate form, and it appeals to a notion of containment which is left at a metaphorical level. But Kant's intent, evident more from the use he makes of the notion of analyticity than from his definition of it, can be restated thus: a statement is analytic when it is true by virtue of meanings and independently of fact. Pursuing this line, let us examine the concept of *meaning* which is presupposed.

Meaning, let us remember, is not to be identified with naming. Frege's example of "Evening Star" and "Morning Star," and Russell's of "Scott" and "the author of *Waverley,*" illustrate that terms can name the same thing but differ in meaning. The distinction between meaning and naming is no less important at the level of abstract terms. The terms "9" and "the number of the planets" name one and the same abstract entity but presumably must be regarded as unlike in meaning; for astronomical observation was needed, and not mere reflection on meanings,

From *From A Logical Point of View,* 2d ed. (Cambridge: Harvard University Press, 1961).

to determine the sameness of the entity in question.

The above examples consist of singular terms, concrete and abstract. With general terms, or predicates, the situation is somewhat different but parallel. Whereas a singular term purports to name an entity, abstract or concrete, a general term does not; but a general term is *true of* an entity, or of each of many, or of none. The class of all entities of which a general term is true is called the *extension* of the term. Now paralleling the contrast between the meaning of a singular term and the entity named, we must distinguish equally between the meaning of a general term and its extension. The general terms "creature with a heart" and "creature with kidneys," for example, are perhaps alike in extension but unlike in meaning.

Confusion of meaning with extension, in the case of general terms, is less common than confusion of meaning with naming in the case of singular terms. It is indeed a commonplace in philosophy to oppose intension (or meaning) to extension, or, in a variant vocabulary, connotation to denotation.

The Aristotelian notion of essence was the forerunner, no doubt, of the modern notion of intension or meaning. For Aristotle it was essential in men to be rational, accidental to be two-legged. But there is an important difference between this attitude and the doctrine of meaning. From the latter point of view it may indeed be conceded (if only for the sake of argument) that rationality is involved in the meaning of the word "man" while two-leggedness is not; but two-leggedness may at the same time be viewed as involved in the meaning of "biped" while rationality is not. Thus from the point of view of the doctrine of meaning it makes no sense to say of the actual individual, who is at once a man and a biped, that his rationality is essential and his two-leggedness accidental or vice versa. Things had essences, for Aristotle, but only linguistic forms have meanings. Meaning is what essence becomes when it is divorced from the object of reference and wedded to the word.

For the theory of meaning a conspicuous question is the nature of its objects: what sort of things are meanings? A felt need for meant entities may derive from an earlier failure to appreciate that meaning and reference are distinct. Once the theory of meaning is sharply separated from the theory of reference, it is a short step to recognizing as the primary business of the theory of meaning simply the synonymy of linguistic forms and the analyticity of statements; meanings themselves, as obscure intermediary entities, may well be abandoned.

The problem of analyticity then confronts us anew. Statements which are analytic by general philosophical acclaim are not, indeed, far to seek. They fall into two classes. Those of the first class, which may be called *logically true*, are typified by:

(1) No unmarried man is married.

The relevant feature of this example is that it not merely is true as it stands, but remains true under any and all reinterpretations of "man" and "married." If we suppose a prior inventory of *logical* particles, comprising "no," "un-," "not," "if," "then," "and," etc., then in general a logical truth is a statement which is true and remains true under all reinterpretations of its components other than the logical particles.

But there is also a second class of analytic statements, typified by:

(2) No bachelor is married.

The characteristic of such a statement is that it can be turned into a logical truth by putting synonyms for synonyms; thus (2) can be turned into (1) by putting "unmarried man" for its synonym "bachelor." We still lack a proper characterization of this second class of analytic statements, and therewith of analyticity generally, inasmuch as we have had in the above description to lean on a notion of 'synonymy' which is no less in need of clarification than analyticity itself.

In recent years Carnap has tended to explain analyticity by appeal to what he calls state-descriptions.[1] A state-description is any exhaustive assignment of truth values to the atomic, or noncompound, statements of the language. All other statements of the language are, Carnap assumes, built up of their component clauses by means of the familiar logical devices, in such a way that the truth value of any complex statement is fixed for each state-description by specifiable logical laws. A statement is then explained as analytic when it comes out true under every state description. This account is an adaptation of Leibniz's "true in all possible worlds." But note that this version of analyticity serves its purpose only if the atomic statements of the language are, unlike "John is a bachelor" and "John is married," mutually independent. Otherwise there would be a state-description which assigned truth to "John is a bachelor" and to "John is married," and consequently "No bachelors are married" would turn out synthetic rather than analytic under the proposed criterion. Thus the criterion of analyticity in terms of state-descriptions serves only for languages devoid of extralogical synonym-pairs, such as "bachelor" and "unmarried man"—synonym-pairs of the type which give rise to the 'second class' of analytic statements. The criterion in terms of state-descriptions is a reconstruction at best of logical truth, not of analyticity.

I do not mean to suggest that Carnap is under any illusions on this point. His simplified model language with its state-descriptions is aimed primarily not at the general problem of analyticity but at another purpose, the clarification of probability and induction. Our problem, however, is analyticity; and here the major difficulty lies not in the first class of analytic statements, the logical truths, but rather in the second class, which depends on the notion of synonymy.

2. DEFINITION

There are those who find it soothing to say that the analytic statements of the second class reduce to those of the first class, the logical truths, by *definition;* "bachelor," for example, is *defined* as "unmarried man." But how do we find that "bachelor" is defined as "unmarried man"? Who defined it thus, and when? Are we to appeal to the nearest dictionary,

and accept the lexicographer's formulation as law? Clearly this would be to put the cart before the horse. The lexicographer is an empirical scientist, whose business is the recording of antecedent facts; and if he glosses "bachelor" as "unmarried man" it is because of his belief that there is a relation of synonymy between those forms, implicit in general or preferred usage prior to his own work. The notion of synonymy presupposed here has still to be clarified, presumably in terms relating to linguistic behavior. Certainly the 'definition' which is the lexicographer's report of an observed synonymy cannot be taken as the ground of the synonymy.

Definition is not, indeed, an activity exclusively of philologists. Philosophers and scientists frequently have occasion to 'define' a recondite term by paraphrasing it into terms of a more familiar vocabulary. But ordinarily such a definition, like the philologist's, is pure lexicography, affirming a relation of synonymy antecedent to the exposition in hand.

Just what it means to affirm synonymy, just what the interconnections may be which are necessary and sufficient in order that two linguistic forms be properly describable as synonymous, is far from clear; but, whatever these interconnections may be, ordinarily they are grounded in usage. Definitions reporting selected instances of synonymy come then as reports upon usage.

There is also, however, a variant type of definitional activity which does not limit itself to the reporting of pre-existing synonymies. I have in mind what Carnap calls *explication*— an activity to which philosophers are given, and scientists also in their more philosophical moments. In explication the purpose is not merely to paraphrase the definiendum into an outright synonym, but actually to improve upon the definiendum by refining or supplementing its meaning. But even explication, though not merely reporting a pre-existing synonymy between definiendum and definiens, does rest nevertheless on *other* pre-existing synonymies. The matter may be viewed as follows. Any word worth explicating has some contexts which, as wholes, are clear and precise enough to be useful; and the purpose of explication is to preserve the usage of these favored contexts while sharpening the usage of other contexts. In order that a given definition be suitable for purposes of explication, therefore, what is required is not that the definiendum in its antecedent usage be synonymous with the definiens, but just that each of these favored contexts of the definiendum, taken as a whole in its antecedent usage, be synonymous with the corresponding context of the definiens.

Two alternative definientia may be equally appropriate for the purposes of a given task of explication and yet not be synonymous with each other; for they may serve interchangeably within the favored contexts but diverge elsewhere. By cleaving to one of these definientia rather than the other, a definition of explicative kind generates, by fiat, a relation of synonymy between definiendum and definiens which did not hold before. But such a definition still owes its explicative function, as seen, to pre-existing synonymies.

There does, however, remain stil! an extreme sort of definition which does not hark back to prior synonymies at all: namely, the explicitly conventional introduction of novel notations for purposes of sheer abbreviation. Here the definiendum becomes synonymous with the definiens simply because it has been created expressly for the purpose of being synonymous with the definiens. Here we have a really transparent case of synonymy created by definition; would that all species of synonymy were as intelligible. For the rest, definition rests on synonymy rather than explaining it.

The word "definition" has come to have a dangerously reassuring sound, owing no doubt to its frequent occurrence in logical and mathematical writings. We shall do well to digress now into a brief appraisal of the role of definition in formal work.

In logical and mathematical systems either of two mutually antagonistic types of economy may be striven for, and each has its peculiar practical utility. On the one hand we may seek economy of practical expression—ease and brevity in the statement of multifarious relations. This sort of economy calls usually for distinctive concise notations for a wealth of concepts. Second, however, and oppositely, we may seek economy in grammar and vocabulary; we may try to find a minimum of basic concepts such that, once a distinctive notation has been appropriated to each of them, it becomes possible to express any desired further concept by mere combination and iteration of our basic notations. This second sort of economy is impractical in one way, since a poverty in basic idioms tends to a necessary lengthening of discourse. But it is practical in another way: it greatly simplifies theoretical discourse *about* the language, through minimizing the terms and the forms of construction wherein the language consists.

Both sorts of economy, though prima facie incompatible, are valuable in their separate ways. The custom has consequently arisen of combining both sorts of economy by forging in effect two languages, the one a part of the other. The inclusive language, though redundant in grammar and vocabulary, is economical in message lengths, while the part, called primitive notation, is economical in grammar and vocabulary. Whole and part are correlated by rules of translation whereby each idiom not in primitive notation is equated to some complex built up of primitive notation. These rules of translation are the so-called *definitions* which appear in formalized systems. They are best viewed not as adjuncts to one language but as correlations between two languages, the one a part of the other.

But these correlations are not arbitrary. They are supposed to show how the primitive notations can accomplish all purposes, save brevity and convenience, of the redundant language. Hence the definiendum and its definiens may be expected, in each case, to be related in one or another of the three ways lately noted. The definiens may be a faithful paraphrase of the definiendum into the narrower notation, preserving a direct synonymy[2] as of antecedent usage; or the definiens may, in the spirit of explication, improve upon the antecedent usage of the definiendum; or finally, the definiendum may be a newly created notation, newly endowed with meaning here and now.

In formal and informal work alike, thus, we find that definition—except in the extreme case of the explicitly conventional introduction of new notations—hinges on prior relations of synonymy. Recognizing then that the notion of definition does not hold the key to synonymy and analyticity, let us look further into synonymy and say no more of definition.

3. INTERCHANGEABILITY

A natural suggestion, deserving close examination, is that the synonymy of two linguistic forms consists simply in their interchangeability in all contexts without change of truth value—interchangeability, in Leibniz's phrase, *salva veritate*.[3] Note that synonyms so conceived need not even be free from vagueness, as long as the vaguenesses match.

But it is not quite true that the synonyms "bachelor" and "unmarried man" are everywhere interchangeable *salva veritate*. Truths which become false under substitution of "unmarried man" for "bachelor" are easily constructed with the help of "bachelor of arts" or "bachelor's buttons"; also with the help of quotation, thus:

"Bachelor" has less than ten letters.

Such counterinstances can, however, perhaps be set aside by treating the phrases "bachelor of arts" and "bachelor's buttons" and the quotation "bachelor" each as a single indivisible word and then stipulating that the interchangeability *salva veritate* which is to be the touchstone of synonymy is not supposed to apply to fragmentary occurrences inside of a word. This account of synonymy, supposing it acceptable on other counts, has indeed the drawback of appealing to a prior conception of 'word' which can be counted on to present difficulties of formulation in its turn. Nevertheless some progress might be claimed in having reduced the problem of synonymy to a problem of wordhood. Let us pursue this line a bit, taking 'word' for granted.

The question remains whether interchangeability *salva veritate* (apart from occurrences within words) is a strong enough condition for synonymy, or whether, on the contrary, some

heteronymous expressions might be thus interchangeable. Now let us be clear that we are not concerned here with synonymy in the sense of complete identity in psychological associations or poetic quality; indeed no two expressions are synonymous in such a sense. We are concerned only with what may be called *cognitive* synonymy. Just what this is cannot be said without successfully finishing the present study; but we know something about it from the need which arose for it in connection with analyticity in §1. The sort of synonymy needed there was merely such that any analytic statement could be turned into a logical truth by putting synonyms for synonyms. Turning the tables and assuming analyticity, indeed, we could explain cognitive synonymy of terms as follows (keeping to the familiar example): to say that "bachelor" and "unmarried man" are cognitively synonymous is to say no more nor less than that the statement:

(3)   All and only bachelors are unmarried men

is analytic.[4]

What we need is an account of cognitive synonymy not presupposing analyticity—if we are to explain analyticity conversely with help of cognitive synonymy as undertaken in §1. And indeed such an independent account of cognitive synonymy is at present up for consideration, namely, interchangeability *salva veritate* everywhere except within words. The question before us, to resume the thread at last, is whether such interchangeability is a sufficient condition for cognitive synonymy. We can quickly assure ourselves that it is, by examples of the following sort. The statement:

(4)   Necessarily all and only bachelors are
      bachelors

is evidently true, even supposing "necessarily" so narrowly construed as to be truly applicable only to analytic statements. Then, if "bachelor" and "unmarried man" are interchangeable *salva veritate*, the result:

(5)   Necessarily all and only bachelors are unmarried men

of putting "unmarried man" for an occurrence of "bachelor" in (4) must, like (4), be true. But to say that (5) is true is to say that (3) is analytic, and hence that "bachelor" and "unmarried man" are cognitively synonymous.

Let us see what there is about the above argument that gives it its air of hocus-pocus. The condition of interchangeability *salva veritate* varies in its force with variations in the richness of the language at hand. The above argument supposes we are working with a language rich enough to contain the adverb "necessarily," this adverb being so construed as to yield truth when and only when applied to an analytic statement. But can we condone a language which contains such an adverb? Does the adverb really make sense? To suppose that it does is to suppose that we have already made satisfactory sense of "analytic." Then what are we so hard at work on right now?

Our argument is not flatly circular, but something like it. It has the form, figuratively speaking, of a closed curve in space.

Interchangeability *salva veritate* is meaningless until relativized to a language whose extent is specified in relevant respects. Suppose now we consider a language containing just the following materials. There is an indefinitely large stock of one-place predicates (for example, "F" where "Fx" means that x is a man) and many-place predicates (for example, "G" where "Gxy" means that x loves y), mostly having to do with extralogical subject matter. The rest of the language is logical. The atomic sentences consist each of a predicate followed by one or more variables "x," "y," etc.; and the complex sentences are built up of the atomic ones by truth functions ("not," "and," "or," etc.) and quantification. In effect such a language enjoys the benefits also of descriptions and indeed singular terms generally, these being contextually definable in known ways. Even abstract singular terms naming classes, classes of classes, etc., are contextually definable in case the assumed stock of predicates includes the two-place predicate of class membership. Such a language can be adequate to classical mathematics and indeed to scientific discourse generally, except in so far as the latter involves debatable devices such as contrary-to-fact conditionals or modal adverbs like "necessarily".[5] Now a language of this type is extensional, in this sense: any two predicates which agree extensionally (that is, are true of the same objects) are interchangeable *salva veritate*.[6]

In an extensional language, therefore, interchangeability *salva veritate* is no assurance of cognitive synonymy of the desired type. That "bachelor" and "unmarried man" are interchangeable *salva veritate* in an extensional language assures us of no more than that (3) is true. There is no assurance here that the extensional agreement of "bachelor" and "unmarried man" rests on meaning rather than merely on accidental matters of fact, as does the extensional agreement of "creature with a heart" and "creature with kidneys."

For most purposes extensional agreement is the nearest approximation to synonymy we need care about. But the fact remains that extensional agreement falls far short of cognitive synonymy of the type required for explaining analyticity in the manner of §1. The type of cognitive synonymy required there is such as to equate the synonymy of "bachelor" and "unmarried man" with the analyticity of (3), not merely with the truth of (3).

So we must recognize that interchangeability *salva veritate,* if construed in relation to an extensional language, is not a sufficient condition of cognitive synonymy in the sense needed for deriving analyticity in the manner of §1. If a language contains an intensional adverb "necessarily" in the sense lately noted, or other particles to the same effect, then interchangeability *salva veritate* in such a language does afford a sufficient condition of cognitive synonymy; but such a language is intelligible only in so far as the notion of analyticity is already understood in advance.

The effort to explain cognitive synonymy first, for the sake of deriving analyticity from it afterward as in §1, is perhaps the wrong approach. Instead we might try explaining analyticity somehow without appeal to cognitive synonymy. Afterward we could doubtless derive cognitive synonymy from analyticity satisfactorily enough if desired. We have seen that cognitive synonymy of "bachelor" and "unmarried man" can be explained as analyticity of (3). The same explanation works for any pair of one-place predicates, of course, and it can be extended in obvious fashion to many-place predicates. Other syntactical categories can also be accommodated in fairly parallel fashion. Singular terms may be said to be cognitively synonymous when the statement of identity formed by putting "=" between them is analytic. Statements may be said simply to be cognitively synonymous when their biconditional (the result of joining them by "if and only if") is analytic.[7] If we care to lump all categories into a single formulation, at the expense of assuming again the notion of 'word' which was appealed to early in this section, we can describe any two linguistic forms as cognitively synonymous when the two forms are interchangeable (apart from occurrences within 'words') *salva* (no longer *veritate* but) *analyticitate*. Certain technical questions arise, indeed, over cases of ambiguity or homonymy; let us not pause for them, however, for we are already digressing. Let us rather turn our backs on the problem of synonymy and address ourselves anew to that of analyticity.

4. SEMANTICAL RULES

Analyticity at first seemed most naturally definable by appeal to a realm of meanings. On refinement, the appeal to meanings gave way to an appeal to synonymy or definition. But definition turned out to be a will-o'-the-wisp, and synonymy turned out to be best understood only by dint of a prior appeal to analyticity itself. So we are back at the problem of analyticity.

I do not know whether the statement "Everything green is extended" is analytic. Now does my indecision over this example really betray an incomplete understanding, an incomplete grasp of the 'meanings', of "green" and "extended"? I think not. The trouble is not with "green" or "extended," but with "analytic."

It is often hinted that the difficulty in separating analytic statements from synthetic ones in ordinary language is due to the vagueness of ordinary language and that the distinction is clear when we have a precise artificial language with explicit 'semantical rules'. This, however, as I shall now attempt to show, is a confusion.

The notion of analyticity about which we are worrying is a purported relation between statements and languages: a statement S is said to be *analytic for* a language L, and the problem is to make sense of this relation generally, that is, for variable "S" and "L." The gravity of this problem is not perceptibly less for artificial languages than for natural ones. The problem of making sense of the idiom "S is analytic for L," with variable "S" and "L," retains its stubbornness even if we limit the range of the variable "L" to artificial languages. Let me now try to make this point evident.

For artificial languages and semantical rules we look naturally to the writings of Carnap. His semantical rules take various forms, and to make my point I shall have to distinguish certain of the forms. Let us suppose, to begin with, an artificial language L_0 whose semantical rules have the form explicitly of a specification, by recursion or otherwise, of all the analytic statements of L_0. The rules tell us that such and such statements, and only those, are the analytic statements of L_0. Now here the difficulty is simply that the rules contain the word "analytic," which we do not understand! We understand what expressions the rules attribute analyticity to, but we do not understand what the rules attribute to those expressions. In short, before we can understand a rule which begins "A statement S is analytic for language L_0 if and only if . . . ," we must understand the general relative term "analytic for"; we must understand "S is analytic for L" where "S" and "L" are variables.

Alternatively we may, indeed, view the so-called rule as a conventional definition of a new simple symbol "analytic-for-L_0," which might better be written untendentiously as "K" so as not to seem to throw light on the interesting word "analytic." Obviously any number of classes K, M, N, etc. of statements of L_0 can be specified for various purposes or for no purpose; what does it mean to say that K, as against M, N, etc., is the class of the 'analytic' statements of L_0?

By saying what statements are analytic for L_0 we explain "analytic-for-L_0" but not "analytic," not "analytic for." We do not begin to explain the idiom "S is analytic for L" with variable "S" and "L," even if we are content to limit the range of "L" to the realm of artificial languages.

Actually we do know enough about the intended significance of "analytic" to know that analytic statements are supposed to be true. Let us then turn to a second form of semantical rule, which says not that such and such statements are analytic but simply that such and such statements are included among the truths. Such a rule is not subject to the criticism of containing the un-understood word "analytic"; and we may grant for the sake of argument that there is no difficulty over the broader term "true." A semantical rule of this second type, a rule of truth, is not supposed to specify all the truths of the language; it merely stipulates, recursively or otherwise, a certain multitude of statements which, along with others unspecified, are to count as true. Such a rule may be conceded to be quite clear. Derivatively, afterward, analyticity can be demarcated thus: a statement is analytic if it is (not merely true but) true according to the semantical rule.

Still there is really no progress. Instead of appealing to an unexplained word "analytic," we are now appealing to an unexplained phrase "semantical rule." Not every true statement which says that the statements of some class are true can count as a semantical rule—otherwise *all* truths would be 'analytic' in the sense of being true according to semantical rules. Semantical rules are distinguishable, apparently, only by the fact of appearing on a page under the heading "Semantical Rules"; and this heading is itself then meaningless.

We can say indeed that a statement is *analytic-for-L_0* if and only if it is true according to such and such specifically appended 'semantical rules', but then we find ourselves back at essentially the same case which was originally discussed: "S is analytic-for-L_0 if and only if. . . ." Once we seek to explain "S is analytic for L" generally for variable "L" (even allowing limitation of "L" to artificial languages), the explanation "true according to the semantical rules of L" is unavailing; for the relative term "semantical rule of" is as much in need of clarification, at least, as "analytic for."

It may be instructive to compare the notion of semantical rule with that of postulate. Relative to a given set of postulates, it is easy to say what a postulate is: it is a member of the set. Relative to a given set of semantical rules, it is equally easy to say what a semantical rule is. But given simply a notation, mathematical or otherwise, and indeed as thoroughly understood a notation as you please in point of the translations or truth conditions of its statements, who can say which of its true statements rank as postulates? Obviously the question is meaningless—as meaningless as asking which points in Ohio are starting points. Any finite (or effectively specifiable infinite) selection of statements (preferably true ones, perhaps) is as much *a* set of postulates as any other. The word "postulate" is significant only relative to an act of inquiry; we apply the word to a set of statements just in so far as we happen, for the year or the moment, to be thinking of those statements in relation to the statements which can be reached from them by some set of transformations to which we have seen fit to direct our attention. Now the notion of semantical rule is as sensible and meaningful as that of postulate, if conceived in a similarly relative spirit—relative, this time, to one or another particular enterprise of schooling unconversant persons in sufficient conditions for truth of statements of some natural or artificial language L. But from this point of view no one signalization of a subclass of the truths of L is intrinsically more a semantical rule than another; and, if "analytic" means "true by semantical rules," no one truth of L is analytic to the exclusion of another.[8]

It might conceivably be protested that an artificial language L (unlike a natural one) is a language in the ordinary sense *plus* a set of explicit semantical rules—the whole constituting, let us say, an ordered pair; and that the semantical rules of L then are specifiable simply as the second component of the pair L. But, by the same token and more simply, we might construe an artificial language L outright as an ordered pair whose second component is the class of its analytic statements; and then the analytic statements of L become specifiable simply as the statements in the second component of L. Or better still, we might just stop tugging at our bootstraps altogether.

Not all the explanations of analyticity known to Carnap and his readers have been covered explicitly in the above considerations, but the extension to other forms is not hard to see. Just one additional factor should be mentioned which sometimes enters: sometimes the semantical rules are in effect rules of translation into ordinary language, in which case the analytic statements of the artificial language are in effect recognized as such from the analyticity of their specified translations in ordinary language. Here certainly there can be no thought of an illumination of the problem of analyticity from the side of the artificial language.

From the point of view of the problem of analyticity the notion of an artificial language with semantical rules is a *feu follet par excellence*. Semantical rules determining the analytic statements of an artificial language are of interest only in so far as we already understand the notion of analyticity; they are of no help in gaining this understanding.

Appeal to hypothetical languages of an artificially simple kind could conceivably be useful in clarifying analyticity, if the mental or behavioral or cultural factors relevant to analyticity—whatever they may be—were somehow sketched into the simplified model. But a model which takes analyticity merely as an irreducible character is unlikely to throw light on the problem of explicating analyticity.

It is obvious that truth in general depends on both language and extralinguistic fact. The statement "Brutus killed Caesar" would be false if the world had been different in certain ways, but it would also be false if the word "killed" happened rather to have the sense of "begat." Thus one is tempted to suppose in general that the truth of a statement is somehow analyzable into a linguistic component and a factual component. Given this supposition, it next seems reasonable that in some statements the factual component should be null; and these are the analytic statements. But, for all its a priori reasonableness, a boundary between analytic and synthetic statements simply has not been drawn. That there is such a distinction to be drawn at all is an unempirical dogma of empiricists, a metaphysical article of faith.

5. THE VERIFICATION THEORY AND REDUCTIONISM

In the course of these somber reflections we have taken a dim view first of the notion of meaning, then of the notion of cognitive synonymy, and finally of the notion of analyticity. But what, it may be asked, of the verification theory of meaning? This phrase has established itself so firmly as a catchword of empiricism that we should be very unscientific indeed not to look beneath it for a possible key to the problem of meaning and the associated problems.

The verification theory of meaning, which has been conspicuous in the literature from Peirce onward, is that the meaning of a statement is the method of empirically confirming or infirming it. An analytic statement is that limiting case which is confirmed no matter what.

As urged in §1, we can as well pass over the question of meanings as entities and move straight to sameness of meaning, or synonymy. Then what the verification theory says is that statements are synonymous if and only if they are alike in point of method of empirical confirmation or infirmation.

This is an account of cognitive synonymy not of linguistic forms generally, but of statements.[9] However, from the concept of synonymy of statements we could derive the concept of synonymy for other linguistic forms, by considerations somewhat similar to those at the end of §3. Assuming the notion of 'word,' indeed, we could explain any two forms as synonymous when the putting of the one form for an occurrence of the other in any statement (apart from occurrences within 'words') yields a synonymous statement. Finally, given the concept of synonymy thus for linguistic forms generally, we could define analyticity in terms of synonymy and logical truth as in §1. For that matter, we could define analyticity more simply in terms of just synonymy of statements together with logical truth; it is not necessary to appeal to synonymy of linguistic forms other than statements. For a statement may be described as analytic simply when it is synonymous with a logically true statement.

So, if the verification theory can be accepted as an adequate account of statement synonymy, the notion of analyticity is saved after all. However, let us reflect. Statement synonymy is said to be likeness of method of empirical confirmation or infirmation. Just what are these methods which are to be compared for likeness? What, in other words, is the nature of the relation between a statement and the experiences which contribute to or detract from its confirmation?

The most naïve view of the relation is that it is one of direct report. This is *radical reductionism*. Every meaningful statement is held to be translatable into a statement (true or false) about immediate experience. Radical reductionism, in one form or another, well antedates the verification theory of meaning explicitly so called. Thus Locke and Hume held that every idea must either originate directly in sense experience or else be compounded of ideas thus originating; and taking a hint from Tooke we might rephrase this doctrine in semantical jargon by saying that a term, to be significant at all, must be either a name of a sense datum or a compound of such names or an abbreviation of such a compound. So stated, the doctrine remains ambiguous as between sense data as sensory events and sense data as sensory qualities; and it remains vague as to the admissible ways of compounding. Moreover, the doctrine is unnecessarily and intolerably restrictive in the

term-by-term critique which it imposes. More reasonably, and without yet exceeding the limits of what I have called radical reductionism, we may take full statements as our significant units—thus demanding that our statements as wholes be translatable into sense-datum language, but not that they be translatable term by term.

This emendation would unquestionably have been welcome to Locke and Hume and Tooke, but historically it had to await an important reorientation in semantics—the reorientation whereby the primary vehicle of meaning came to be seen no longer in the term but in the statement. This reorientation, explicit in Frege ([1], §60), underlies Russell's concept of incomplete symbols defined in use; also it is implicit in the verification theory of meaning, since the objects of verification are statements.

Radical reductionism, conceived now with statements as units, set itself the task of specifying a sense-datum language and showing how to translate the rest of significant discourse, statement by statement, into it. Carnap embarked on this project in the *Aufbau*.

The language which Carnap adopted as his starting point was not a sense-datum language in the narrowest conceivable sense, for it included also the notations of logic, up through higher set theory. In effect it included the whole language of pure mathematics. The ontology implicit in it (that is, the range of values of its variables) embraced not only sensory events but classes, classes of classes, and so on. Empiricists there are who would boggle at such prodigality. Carnap's starting point is very parsimonious, however, in its extralogical or sensory part. In a series of constructions in which he exploits the resources of modern logic with much ingenuity, Carnap succeeds in defining a wide array of important additional sensory concepts which, but for his constructions, one would not have dreamed were definable on so slender a basis. He was the first empiricist who, not content with asserting the reducibility of science to terms of immediate experience, took serious steps toward carrying out the reduction.

If Carnap's starting point is satisfactory, still his constructions were, as he himself stressed, only a fragment of the full program. The construction of even the simplest statements about the physical world was left in a sketchy state. Carnap's suggestions on this subject were, despite their sketchiness, very suggestive. He explained spatio-temporal point-instants as quadruples of real numbers and envisaged assignment of sense qualities to point-instants according to certain canons. Roughly summarized, the plan was that qualities should be assigned to point-instants in such a way as to achieve the laziest world compatible with our experience. The principle of least action was to be our guide in constructing a world from experience.

Carnap did not seem to recognize, however, that his treatment of physical objects fell short of reduction not merely through sketchiness, but in principle. Statements of the form "Quality q is at point-instant $x;y;z;t$" were, according to his canons, to be apportioned truth values in such a way as to maximize and minimize certain overall features, and with growth of experience the truth values were to be progressively revised in the same spirit. I think this is a good schematization (deliberately oversimplified, to be sure) of what science really does; but it provides no indication, not even the sketchiest, of how a statement of the form "Quality q is at $x;y;z;t$" could ever be translated into Carnap's initial language of sense data and logic. The connective "is at" remains an added undefined connective; the canons counsel us in its use but not in its elimination.

Carnap seems to have appreciated this point afterward; for in his later writings he abandoned all notion of the translatability of statements about the physical world into statements about immediate experience. Reductionism in its radical form has long since ceased to figure in Carnap's philosophy.

But the dogma of reductionism has, in a subtler and more tenuous form, continued to influence the thought of empiricists. The notion lingers that to each statement, or each synthetic statement, there is associated a unique range of possible sensory events such that the occurrence of any of them would add to the likelihood of truth of the statement, and that there is associated also another unique range of possible sensory events whose occurrence would detract from that likelihood. This notion is of course implicit in the verification theory of meaning.

The dogma of reductionism survives in the supposition that each statement, taken in isolation from its fellows, can admit of confirmation or infirmation at all. My countersuggestion, issuing essentially from Carnap's doctrine of the physical world in the *Aufbau*, is that our statements about the external world face the tribunal of sense experience not individually but only as a corporate body.[10]

The dogma of reductionism, even in its attenuated form, is intimately connected with the other dogma—that there is a cleavage between the analytic and the synthetic. We have found ourselves led, indeed, from the latter problem to the former through the verification theory of meaning. More directly, the one dogma clearly supports the other in this way: as long as it is taken to be significant in general to speak of the confirmation and infirmation of a statement, it seems significant to speak also of a limiting kind of statement which is vacuously confirmed, *ipso facto*, come what may; and such a statement is analytic.

The two dogmas are, indeed, at root identical. We lately reflected that in general the truth of statements does obviously depend both upon language and upon extralinguistic fact; and we noted that this obvious circumstance carries in its train, not logically but all too naturally, a feeling that the truth of a statement is somehow analyzable into a linguistic component and a factual component. The factual component must, if we are empiricists, boil down to a range of confirmatory experiences. In the extreme case where the linguistic component is all that matters, a true statement is analytic. But I hope we are now impressed with how stubbornly the distinction between analytic and synthetic has resisted any straightforward drawing. I am impressed also, apart from prefabricated examples of black and white balls in an urn, with how baffling the problem has always been of arriving at any explicit theory of the empirical confirmation of a synthetic statement. My present suggestion is that it is nonsense, and the root of much nonsense, to speak of a linguistic component and a factual component in the truth of any individual statement. Taken collectively, science has its double dependence upon language and experience; but this duality is not significantly traceable into the statements of science taken one by one.

The idea of defining a symbol in use was, as remarked, an advance over the impossible term-by-term empiricism of Locke and Hume. The statement, rather than the term, came with Frege to be recognized as the unit accountable to an empiricist critique. But what I am now urging is that even in taking the statement as unit we have drawn our grid too finely. The unit of empirical significance is the whole of science.

6. EMPIRICISM WITHOUT THE DOGMAS

The totality of our so-called knowledge or beliefs, from the most casual matters of geography and history to the profoundest laws of atomic physics or even of pure mathematics and logic, is a man-made fabric which impinges on experience only along the edges. Or, to change the figure, total science is like a field of force whose boundary conditions are experience. A conflict with experience at the periphery occasions readjustments in the interior of the field. Truth values have to be redistributed over some of our statements. Reevaluation of some statements entails reevaluation of others, because of their logical interconnections—the logical laws being in turn simply certain further statements of the system, certain further elements of the field. Having reevaluated one statement we must reevaluate some others, which may be statements logically connected with the first or may be the statements of logical connections themselves. But the total field is so underdetermined by its boundary conditions, experience, that there is much latitude of choice as to what

statements to reevaluate in the light of any single contrary experience. No particular experiences are linked with any particular statements in the interior of the field, except indirectly through considerations of equilibrium affecting the field as a whole.

If this view is right, it is misleading to speak of the empirical content of an individual statement—especially if it is a statement at all remote from the experiential periphery of the field. Furthermore it becomes folly to seek a boundary between synthetic statements, which hold contingently on experience, and analytic statements, which hold come what may. Any statement can be held true come what may, if we make drastic enough adjustments elsewhere in the system. Even a statement very close to the periphery can be held true in the face of recalcitrant experience by pleading hallucination or by amending certain statements of the kind called logical laws. Conversely, by the same token, no statement is immune to revision. Revision even of the logical law of the excluded middle has been proposed as a means of simplifying quantum mechanics; and what difference is there in principle between such a shift and the shift whereby Kepler superseded Ptolemy, or Einstein Newton, or Darwin Aristotle?

For vividness I have been speaking in terms of varying distances from a sensory periphery. Let me try now to clarify this notion without metaphor. Certain statements, though *about* physical objects and not sense experience, seem peculiarly germane to sense experience—and in a selective way: some statements to some experiences, others to others. Such statements, especially germane to particular experiences, I picture as near the periphery. But in this relation of 'germaneness' I envisage nothing more than a loose association reflecting the relative likelihood, in practice, of our choosing one statement rather than another for revision in the event of recalcitrant experience. For example, we can imagine recalcitrant experiences to which we would surely be inclined to accommodate our system by reevaluating just the statement that there are brick houses on Elm Street, together with related statements on the same topic. We can imagine other recalcitrant experiences to which we would be inclined to accommodate our system by reevaluating just the statement that there are no centaurs, along with kindred statements. A recalcitrant experience can, I have urged, be accommodated by any of various alternative reevaluations in various alternative quarters of the total system; but, in the cases which we are now imagining, our natural tendency to disturb the total system as little as possible would lead us to focus our revisions upon these specific statements concerning brick houses or centaurs. These statements are felt, therefore, to have a sharper empirical reference than highly theoretical statements of physics or logic or ontology. The latter statements may be thought of as relatively centrally located within the total network, meaning merely that little preferential connection with any particular sense data obtrudes itself.

As an empiricist I continue to think of the conceptual scheme of science as a tool, ultimately, for predicting future experience in the light of past experience. Physical objects are conceptually imported into the situation as convenient intermediaries—not by definition in terms of experience, but simply as irreducible posits comparable, epistemologically, to the gods of Homer. For my part I do, qua lay physicist, believe in physical objects and not in Homer's gods; and I consider it a scientific error to believe otherwise. But in point of epistemological footing the physical objects and the gods differ only in degree and not in kind. Both sorts of entities enter our conception only as cultural posits. The myth of physical objects is epistemologically superior to most in that it has proved more efficacious than other myths as a device for working a manageable structure into the flux of experience.

Positing does not stop with macroscopic physical objects. Objects at the atomic level are posited to make the laws of macroscopic objects, and ultimately the laws of experience, simpler and more manageable; and we need not expect or demand full definition of atomic and subatomic entities in terms of macroscopic ones, any more than definition of

macroscopic things in terms of sense data. Science is a continuation of common sense, and it continues the common-sense expedient of swelling ontology to simplify theory.

Physical objects, small and large, are not the only posits. Forces are another example; and indeed we are told nowadays that the boundary between energy and matter is obsolete. Moreover, the abstract entities which are the substance of mathematics—ultimately classes and classes of classes and so on up—are another posit in the same spirit. Epistemologically these are myths on the same footing with physical objects and gods, neither better nor worse except for differences in the degree to which they expedite our dealings with sense experiences.

The overall algebra of rational and irrational numbers is underdetermined by the algebra of rational numbers, but is smoother and more convenient; and it includes the algebra of rational numbers as a jagged or gerrymandered part. Total science, mathematical and natural and human, is similarly but more extremely underdetermined by experience. The edge of the system must be kept squared with experience; the rest, with all its elaborate myths or fictions, has as its objective the simplicity of laws.

Ontological questions, under this view, are on a par with questions of natural science.[11] Consider the question whether to countenance classes as entities. This, as I have argued elsewhere, is the question whether to quantify with respect to variables which take classes as values. Now Carnap [3] has maintained that this is a question not of matters of fact but of choosing a convenient language form, a convenient conceptual scheme or framework for science. With this I agree, but only on the proviso that the same be conceded regarding scientific hypotheses generally. Carnap ([3], p. 32n) has recognized that he is able to preserve a double standard for ontological questions and scientific hypotheses only by assuming an absolute distinction between the analytic and the synthetic; and I need not say again that this is a distinction which I reject.[12]

The issue over there being classes seems more a question of convenient conceptual scheme; the issue over there being centaurs, or brick houses on Elm Street, seems more a question of fact. But I have been urging that this difference is only one of degree, and that it turns upon our vaguely pragmatic inclination to adjust one strand of the fabric of science rather than another in accommodating some particular recalcitrant experience. Conservatism figures in such choices, and so does the quest for simplicity.

Carnap, Lewis, and others take a pragmatic stand on the question of choosing between language forms, scientific frameworks; but their pragmatism leaves off at the imagined boundary between the analytic and the synthetic. In repudiating such a boundary I espouse a more thorough pragmatism. Each man is given a scientific heritage plus a continuing barrage of sensory stimulation; and the considerations which guide him in warping his scientific heritage to fit his continuing sensory promptings are, where rational, pragmatic.

NOTES

1. Carnap [1], pp. 9ff; [2], pp. 70ff.
2. According to an important variant sense of "definition," the relation preserved may be the weaker relation of mere agreement in reference. But definition in this sense is better ignored in the present connection, being irrelevant to the question of synonymy.
3. Cf. Lewis [1], p. 373.
4. This is cognitive synonymy in a primary, broad sense. Carnap ([1], pp. 56ff) and Lewis ([2], pp. 83ff) have suggested how, once this notion is at hand, a narrower sense of cognitive synonymy which is preferable for some purposes can in turn be derived. But this special ramification of concept-building lies aside from the present purposes and must not be confused with the broad sort of cognitive synonymy here concerned.
5. On such devices see also Quine [1].
6. This is the substance of Quine [2], *121.
7. The 'if and only if' itself is intended in the truth functional sense. See Carnap [1], p. 14.
8. The foregoing paragraph was not part of the present essay as originally published. It was prompted by Martin.
9. The doctrine can indeed be formulated with

terms rather than statements as the units. Thus Lewis describes the meaning of a term as "*a criterion in mind*, by reference to which one is able to apply or refuse to apply the expression in question in the case of presented, or imagined, things or situations" ([2], p. 133).—For an instructive account of the vicissitudes of the verification theory of meaning, centered however on the question of meaning*fulness* rather than synonymy and analyticity, see Hempel.
10. This doctrine was well argued by Duhem, pp. 303–328. Or see Lowinger, pp. 132–140.
11. "L'ontologie fait corps avec la science elle-même et ne peut en être separée." Meyerson, p. 439.
12. For an effective expression of further misgivings over this distinction, see White.

BIBLIOGRAPHY

Carnap, R. [1]. *Meaning and Necessity*. (Chicago: University of Chicago Press, 1947.)
——[2]. *Logical Foundations of Probability*. (Chicago: University of Chicago Press, 1950.)
——[3]. "Empiricism, semantics, and ontology," *Revue Internationale de Philosophie*, vol. IV (1950), pp. 20–40.
Duhem, P. *La Théorie physique: son objet et sa structure*. (Paris: 1906.)
Frege, Gottlob. *Foundations of Arithmetic*. (New York: Philosophical Library, 1950.)
Hempel, C. G. "Problems and Changes in the Empiricist Criterion of Meaning." *Revue Internationale de Philosophie*, vol. IV (1950), pp. 41–63.
Lewis, C. I. [1]. *A Survey of Symbolic Logic*. (Berkeley: 1918.)
——[2]. *An Analysis of Knowledge and Valuation*. (La Salle, Ill.: Open Court Publishing Co., 1946.)
Lowinger, A. *The Methodology of Pierre Duhem*. (New York: Columbia University Press, 1941.)
Martin, R. M., "On 'Analytic'." *Philosophical Studies*, vol. III (1952), pp. 42–47.
Meyerson, Émile. *Identité et realité*. (Paris: 1908; 4th ed., 1932.)
Quine, W. V. [1]. *From A Logical Point of View*. (New York: Harper & Row, 1961.)
——[2]. *Mathematical Logic*. (New York: W. W. Norton & Company, Inc., 1940; Cambridge: Harvard University Press, 1947; rev. ed., 1951.)
White, Morton. "The Analytic and the Synthetic: An Untenable Dualism." In Sidney Hook, ed., *John Dewey: Philosopher of Science and Freedom*. (New York: The Dial Press, Inc., 1950), pp. 316–30.

Intensional Semantics 3

ALONZO CHURCH

We distinguish between a *logistic system* and a *formalized language* on the basis that the former is an abstractly formulated calculus for which no interpretation is fixed, and thus has a syntax but no semantics; but the latter is a logistic system together with an assignment of meanings to its expressions.

As primitive basis of a logistic system it suffices to give, in familiar fashion: (1) The list of primitive symbols or *vocabulary* of the system (together usually with a classification of the primitive symbols into categories, which will be used in stating the formation rules and rules of inference). (2) The *formation rules,* determining which finite sequences of primitive symbols are to be *well-formed* expressions, determining certain categories of well-formed expressions, among which we shall assume that at least the category of *sentence* is included, and determining (in case *variables* are included among the primitive symbols) which occurrences of variables in a well-formed expression are *free* occurrences and which are *bound* occurrences.[1] (3) The transformation rules or *rules of inference,* by which from the *assertion* of certain sentences (the *premisses,* finite in number) a certain sentence (the *conclusion*) may be *inferred.* (4) Certain asserted sentences, the *axioms.*

In order to obtain a formalized language it is necessary to add to these *syntactical rules* of

the logistic system, *semantical rules* assigning meanings (in some sense) to the well-formed expressions of the system.[2] The character of the semantical rules will depend on the theory of meaning adopted, and this in turn must be justified by the purpose which it is to serve.

Let us take it as our purpose to provide an abstract theory of the actual use of language for human communication—not a factual or historical report of what has been observed to take place, but a norm to which we may regard everyday linguistic behavior as an imprecise approximation, in the same way that e.g. elementary (applied) geometry is a norm to which we may regard as imprecise approximations the practical activity of the land-surveyor in laying out a plot of ground, or of the construction foreman in seeing that building plans are followed. We must demand of such a theory that it have a place for all observably informative kinds of communication—including such notoriously troublesome cases as belief statements, modal statements, conditions contrary to fact—or at least that it provide a (theoretically) workable substitute for them. And solutions must be available for puzzles about meaning which may arise, such as the so-called "paradox of analysis."

There exist more than one theory of meaning showing some promise of fulfilling these requirements, at least so far as the formula-

Originally published under the title "The Need for Abstract Entities," in the *American Academy of Arts and Sciences Proceedings*, 80 (1951), pp. 100–113.

40

tion and development have presently been carried. But the theory of Frege seems to recommend itself above others for its relative simplicity, naturalness, and explanatory power—or, as I would advocate, Frege's theory as modified by elimination of his somewhat problematical notion of a function (and in particular of a *Begriff*) as *ungesättigt*, and by some other changes which bring it closer to present logistic practice without loss of such essentials as the distinction of sense and denotation.

This modified Fregean theory may be roughly characterized by the tendency to minimize the category of *syncategorematic* notations—i.e., notations to which no meaning at all is ascribed in isolation but which may combine with one or more meaningful expressions to form a meaningful expression[3]—and to reduce the categories of meaningful expressions to two, (proper) *names* and *forms,* for each of which two kinds of meaning are distinguished in a parallel way.

A name, or a *constant* (as we shall also say, imitating mathematical terminology), has first its *denotation,* or that of which it is a name.[4] And each name has also a *sense*—which is perhaps more properly to be called its meaning, since it is held that complete understanding of a language involves the ability to recognize the sense of any name in the language, but does not demand any knowledge beyond this of the denotations of names. (Declarative) *sentences,* in particular, are taken as a kind of names, the denotation being the *truth-value* of the sentence, *truth* or *falsehood,* and the sense being the *proposition* which the sentence expresses.

A name is said to *denote* its denotation and to *express* its sense, and the sense is said to be *a concept of* the denotation. The abstract entities which serve as senses of names let us call *concepts*—although this use of the word 'concept' has no analogue in the writings of Frege, and must be carefully distinguished from Frege's use of 'Begriff'. Thus anything which is or is capable of being the sense of some name in some language, actual or possible, is a concept.[5] The terms *individual concept, function concept,* and the like are

then to mean a concept which is a concept of an individual, of a function, etc. A *class concept* may be identified with a *property*, and a *truth-value concept* (as already indicated) with a proposition.

Names are to be meaningful expressions without free variables, and expressions which are analogous to names except that they contain free variables, we call forms (a rather wide extension of the ordinary mathematical usage, here adopted for lack of a better term).[6] Each variable has a *range*, which is the class of admissible *values* of the variable.[7] And analogous to the denotation of a name, a form has a *value* for every system of admissible values of its free variables.[8]

The assignment of a value to a variable, though it is not a syntactical operation, corresponds in a certain way to the syntactical operation of substituting a constant for the variable. The denotation of the substituted constant represents the value of the variable.[9] And the sense of the substituted constant may be taken as representing a *sense-value* of the variable. Thus every variable has, besides its range, also a *sense-range*, which is the class of admissible sense-values of the variable. And analogous to the sense of a name, a form has a *sense-value* for every system of admissible sense-values of its free variables.[10]

The following principles are assumed[11]: (i) Every concept is a concept of at most one thing. (ii) Every constant has a unique concept as its sense. (iii) Every variable has a non-empty class of concepts as its sense-range. (iv) For any assignment of sense-values, one to each of the free variables of a given form, if each sense-value is admissible in the sense that it belongs to the sense-range of the corresponding variable, the form has a unique concept as its sense-value. (v) The denotation of a constant is that of which its sense is a concept. (vi) The range of a variable is the class of those things of which the members of the sense-range are concepts. (vii) If S, $s_1, s_2, \ldots, s_m$ are concepts of A, a_1, $a_2, \ldots, a_m$ respectively, and if S is the sense-value of a form F for the system of sense-values $s_1, s_2, \ldots, s_m$ of its free variables $x_1, x_2, \ldots, x_m$, then the value of F for the system of values a_1, a_2, . . . a_m of x_1, x_2, . . . , x_m is A. (viii) If C' is obtained from a constant C by replacing a particular occurrence of a constant c by a constant c' that has the same sense as c, then C' is a constant having the same sense as C.[12] (ix) If C' is obtained from a constant C by replacing a particular occurrence of a constant c by a constant c' that has the same denotation as c, then C' is a constant having the same denotation as C.[13] (x) If C' is obtained from a constant C by replacing a particular occurrence of a form f by a form f' that has the same free variables as f, and if, for every admissible system of sense-values of their free variables, f and f' have the same sense-value, then C' is a constant having the same sense as C.[12] (xi) If C' is obtained from a constant C by replacing a particular occurrence of a form f by a form f' that has the same free variables as f, and if, for every system of values of their free variables which are admissible in the sense that each value belongs to the range of the corresponding variable, f and f' have the same value, then C' is a constant having the same denotation as C.[13] (xii) If x_1, x_2, . . . , x_m are all the distinct variables occurring (necessarily as bound variables) in a constant C, if y_1, y_2, . . . , y_m are distinct variables having the same sense-ranges as x_1, x_2, . . . , x_m respectively, and if C' is obtained from C by substituting y_1, y_2, . . . , y_m throughout for x_1, x_2, . . . , x_m respectively, then C' is a constant having the same sense as C. (xiii) If x_1, x_2, . . . , x_m are the distinct variables occurring in a constant C, if y_1, y_2, . . . , y_m are distinct variables having the same ranges as x_1, x_2, . . . , x_m respectively, and if C' is obtained from C by substituting y_1, y_2, . . . , y_m throughout for x_1, x_2, . . . , x_m respectively, then C' is a constant having the same denotation as C. (xiv) The result of substituting constants for all the free variables of a form is a constant, if the sense of each substituted constant belongs to the sense-range of the corresponding variable.[12] (xv) The sense of a constant C thus obtained by substituting constants c_1, c_2, . . . , c_m for the free variables x_1, x_2, . . . , x_m of a form F is the same as the sense-value of F when the senses of c_1,

c_2, . . . , c_m are assigned as the sense-values of x_1, x_2, . . . , x_m.

To these must still be added principles which are similar to (viii)–(xv), except that substitution is made in forms instead of constants, or that forms and variables as well as constants are substituted for the free variables of a form. Instead of stating these here, it may be sufficient to remark that they follow if arbitrary extensions of the language are allowed by adjoining (as primitive symbols) constants which have as their senses any concepts that belong to sense-ranges of variables in the language, if the foregoing principles are assumed to hold also for such extensions of the language, and if there is assumed further: (xvi) Let an expression F contain the variables x_1, x_2, . . . , x_m; and suppose that in every extension of the language of the kind just described and for every substitution of constants c_1, c_2, . . . , c_m for the variables x_1, x_2, . . . , x_m respectively, if the sense of each constant belongs to the sense-range of the corresponding variable, F becomes a constant; then F is a form having x_1, x_2, . . . , x_m as its free variables.

To those who find forbidding the array of abstract entities and principles concerning them which is here proposed, I would say that the problems which give rise to the proposal are difficult and a simpler theory is not known to be possible.[14]

To those who object to the introduction of abstract entities at all I would say that I believe that there are more important criteria by which a theory should be judged. The extreme demand for a simple prohibition of abstract entities under all circumstances perhaps arises from a desire to maintain the connection between theory and observation. But the preference of (say) *seeing* over *understanding* as a method of observation seems to me capricious. For just as an opaque body may be seen, so a concept may be understood or grasped. And the parallel between the two cases is indeed rather close. In both cases the observation is not direct but through intermediaries—light, lens of eye or optical instrument, and retina in the case of the visible body, linguistic expressions in the case of the concept. And in both cases there are or may be tenable theories according to which the entity in question, opaque body or concept, is not assumed, but only those things which would otherwise be called its effects.

The variety of entities (whether abstract or concrete) which a theory assumes is indeed one among other criteria by which it may be judged. If multiplication of entities is found beyond the needs of the workability, simplicity, and generality of the theory, then the razor shall be applied.[15] The theory of meaning here outlined I hold exempt from such treatment no more than any other, but I do advocate its study.

Let us return now to our initial question, as to the character of the semantical rules which are to be added to the syntactical rules of a logistic system in order to define a particular formalized language.

On the foregoing theory of meaning the semantical rules must include at least the following: (5) *Rules of sense,* by which a sense is determined for each well-formed expression without free variables (all such expressions thus becoming names). (6) *Rules of sense-range,* assigning to each variable a sense-range. (7) *Rules of sense-value,* by which a sense-value is determined for every well-formed expression containing free variables and every admissible system of sense-values of its free variables (all such expressions thus becoming forms).

In the case of both syntactical and semantical rules there is a distinction to be drawn between *primitive* and *derived* rules, the primitive rules being those which are stated in giving the primitive basis of the formalized language, and the derived rules being rules of similar kind which follow as consequences of the primitive rules. Thus besides primitive rules of inference there are also derived rules of inference, besides primitive rules of sense also derived rules of sense, and so on. (But instead of "derived axioms" it is usual to say *theorems.*)

A statement of the denotation of a name, the range of a variable, or the value of a form does not necessarily belong to the semantics of a language. For example, that 'the number of planets' denotes the number nine is a fact as much of astronomy as it is of the semantics of the English language, and can be described only as belonging to a discipline broad enough to include both semantics and astronomy. On the other hand, a statement that 'the number of planets' denotes the number of planets is a purely semantical statement about the English language. And indeed it would seem that a statement of this kind may be considered as purely semantical only if it is a consequence of the rules of sense, sense-range, and sense-value, together with the syntactical rules and the general principles of meaning (i)–(xvi).

Thus as derived semantical rules rather than primitive, there will be also: (8) *Rules of denotation,* by which a denotation is determined for each name. (9) *Rules of range,* assigning to each variable a range. (10) *Rules of value,* by which a value is determined for every form and for every admissible system of values of its free variables.

By stating (8), (9), and (10) as primitive rules, without (5), (6), and (7) there results what may be called the *extensional part* of the semantics of a language. The remaining *intensional part* of the semantics does not follow from the extensional part. For the sense of a name is not uniquely determined by its denotation, and thus a particular rule of denotation does not of itself have as a consequence the corresponding rule of sense.

On the other hand, because the metalinguistic phrase which is used in the rule of denotation must itself have a sense, there is a certain sense (though not that of logical consequence) in which the rule of denotation, by being given as a primitive rule of denotation, uniquely indicates the corresponding rule of sense. Since the like is true of the rules of range and rules of value, it is permissible to say that we have fixed an *interpretation* of a given logistic system, and thus a formalized language, if we have stated only the extensional part of the semantics.[16]

Although all the foregoing account has been concerned with the case of a formalized language, I would go on to say that in my opinion there is no difference in principle between this case and that of one of the natural languages. In particular, it must not be thought that a formalized language depends for its meaning or its justification (in any sense in which a natural language does not) upon some prior natural language, say English, through some system of translation of its sentences into English—or, more plausibly, through the statement of its syntactical and semantical rules in English. For speaking in principle, and leaving all questions of practicality aside, the logician must declare it a mere historical accident that you and I learned from birth to speak English rather than a language with less irregular, and logically simpler, syntactical rules, similar to those of one of the familiar logistic systems in use today—or that we learned in school the content of conventional English grammars and dictionaries rather than a more precise statement of a system of syntactical and semantical rules of the kind which has been described in this present sketch. The difference of a formalized language from a natural language lies not in any matter of principle, but in the degree of completeness that has been attained in the laying down of explicit syntactical and semantical rules and the extent to which vaguenesses and uncertainties have been removed from them.

For this reason the English language itself may be used as a convenient though makeshift illustration of a language for which syntactical and semantical rules are to be given. Of course only a few illustrative examples of such rules can be given in brief space. And even for this it is necessary to avoid carefully the use of examples involving English constructions that raise special difficulties or show too great logical irregularities, and to evade the manifold equivocacy of English words by selecting and giving attention to just one meaning of each word mentioned. It must also not be asked whether the rules given as examples are among the "true" rules of the English language or are "really" a part of what is implied in an understanding of English; for the laying down of rules for a natural language, because of the need to fill gaps and to decide doubtful

points, is as much a process of legislation as of reporting.

With these understandings, and with no attempt made to distinguish between primitive and derived rules, following are some examples of syntactical and semantical rules of English according to the program which has been outlined.[17]

(1) Vocabulary: 'equals' 'five' 'four' 'if' 'is' 'nine' 'number' 'of' 'planet' 'planets' 'plus' 'round' 'the' 'then' 'the world'—besides the bare list of primitive symbols (words) there must be statements regarding their classification into categories and systematic relations among them, e.g., that 'planet' is a common noun,[18] that 'planets' is the plural of 'planet,'[19] that 'the world' is a proper noun, that 'round' is an adjective.

(2) Formation Rules: If A is the plural of a common noun, then 'the' ⌐ 'number' ⌐ 'of' ⌐ A is a singular term. A proper noun standing alone is a singular term. If A and B are singular terms, then A ⌐ 'equals' ⌐ B is a sentence. If A is a singular term and B is an adjective, then A ⌐ 'is' ⌐ B is a sentence.[20] If A and B are sentences, then 'if' ⌐ A ⌐ 'then' ⌐ B is a sentence.—Here singular terms and sentences are to be understood as categories of well-formed expressions; a more complete list of formation rules would no doubt introduce many more such.

(3) Rules of Inference: Where A and B are sentences, from 'if' ⌐ A ⌐ 'then' ⌐ B and A to infer B. Where A and B are singular terms and C is an adjective, from A ⌐ 'equals' ⌐ B and B ⌐ 'is' ⌐ C to infer A ⌐ 'is' ⌐ C.

(4) Axioms-Theorems: 'if the world is round, then the world is round'; 'four plus five equals nine.'

(5) Rules of Sense: 'round' expresses the property of roundness. 'the world' expresses the (individual) concept of the world. 'the world is round' expresses the proposition that the world is round.

(8) Rules of Denotation: 'round' denotes the class of round things. 'the world' denotes the world. 'the world is round' denotes the truth-value thereof that the world is round.[21]

On a Fregean theory of meaning, rules of truth in Tarski's form—e.g., " 'the world is round' is true if and only if the world is round"—follow from the rules of denotation for sentences. For that a sentence is true is taken to be the same as that it denotes truth.

NOTES

1. For convenience of the present brief exposition we make the simplifying assumption that sentences are without free variables, and that only sentences are asserted.

2. The possibility that the meaningful expressions may be a proper subclass of the well-formed expressions must not ultimately be excluded, But again for the present sketch it will be convenient to treat the two classes as identical—the simplest and most usual case. Compare, however, note 13.

3. Such notations can be reduced to at most two, namely the notation (consisting, say, of juxtaposition between parentheses) which is used in application of a singulary function to its argument, and the abstraction operator λ. By the methods of the Schönfinkel-Curry combinatory logic it may even be possible further to eliminate the abstraction operator, and along with it the use of variables altogether. But this final reduction is not contemplated here—nor even necessarily the simpler reduction to two syncategorematic notations.

4. The complicating possibility is here ignored of *denotationless names*, or names which have a sense but no denotation. For though it may be held that these do occur in the natural languages, it is possible, as Frege showed, to construct a formalized language in such a way as to avoid them.

5. This is meant only as a preliminary rough description. In logical order, the notion of a concept must be postulated and that of a possible language defined by means of it.

6. Frege's term in German is *Marke*.—The form or *Marke* must of course not be confused with its associated abstract entity, the *function*. The function differs from the form in that it is not a linguistic entity, and belongs to no particular language. Indeed the same function may be associated with different forms; and if there is more than one free variable the same form may have several associated functions. But in some languages it is possible from the form to construct a name (or names) of the associated function (or functions) by means of an abstraction operator.

7. The idea of allowing variables of different ranges is not Fregean, except in the case of functions in Frege's sense (i.e., as *ungesättigt*),

the different categories of which appear as ranges for different variables. The introduction of *Gegenstandsbuchstaben* with restricted ranges is one of the modifications here advocated in Frege's theory.

8. Exceptions to this are familiar in common mathematical notation. E.g. the form x/y has no value for the system of values $0,0$ of x, y. However, the semantics of a language is much simplified if a value is assigned to a form for every system of values of the free variables which are admissible in the sense that each value belongs to the range of the corresponding variable. And for purposes of the present exposition we assume that this has been done. (Compare note 4.)

9. Even if the language contains no constant denoting the value in question, it is possible to consider an extension of the language obtained by adjoining such a constant.

10. The notion of a sense-value of a form is not introduced by Frege, at least not explicitly, but it can be argued that it is necessarily implicit in his theory. For Frege's question, "How can $a=b$ if true ever differ in meaning from $a=a$?" can be asked as well for forms a and b as for constants, and leads to the distinction of value and sense-value of a form just as it does to the distinction of denotation and sense of a constant. Even in a language like that of *Principia Mathematica*, having no forms other than propositional forms, a parallel argument can be used to show that from the equivalence of two propositional forms A and B the identity in meaning of A and B in all respects is not to be inferred. For otherwise how could A ≡ B if true (i.e., true for all values of the variables) ever differ in meaning from A ≡ A?

11. For purposes of the preliminary sketch, the metalanguage is left unformalized, and such questions are ignored as whether the metalanguage shall conform to the theory of types or to some alternative such as transfinite type theory or axiomatic set theory. Because of the extreme generality which is attempted in laying down these principles, it is clear that there may be some difficulty in rendering them precise (in their full attempted generality) by restatement in a formalized metalanguage. But it should be possible to state the semantical rules of a particular object language so as to conform, so that the principles are clarified to this extent by illustration.

It is not meant that the list of principles is necessarily complete or in final form, but rather a tentative list is here proposed for study and possible amendment. Moreover it is not meant that it may not be possible to formulate a language not conforming to the principles, but only that a satisfactory general theory may result by making conformity to these principles a part of the definition of a formalized language (compare note 12).

12. In the case of some logistic systems which have been proposed (e.g., by Hilbert and Bernays), if semantical rules are to be added, in conformity with the theory here described and with the informally intended interpretation of the system, it is found to be impossible to satisfy (viii), (x), and (xiv), because of restriction imposed on the bound variables which may appear in a constant or form used in a particular context. But it would seem that modifications in the logistic system necessary to remove the restriction may reasonably be considered nonessential, and that in this sense (viii), (x), (xiv) may still be maintained.

In regard to all of the principles it should be understood that nonessential modifications in existing logistic systems may be required to make them conform. In particular the principles have been formulated in a way which does not contemplate the distinction in typographical style between free and bound variables that appears in systems of Frege and of Hilbert-Bernays.

In (x) and (xi), the condition that f' have the same free variables as f can in many cases be weakened to the condition that every free variable of f' occur also as a free variable of f.

13. Possibly (ix) and (xi) should be weakened to require only that if C' is well-formed then it is a constant having the same denotation as C. Since there is in general no syntactical criterion by which to ascertain whether two constants c and c' have the same denotation, or whether two forms have always the same values, there is the possibility that the stronger forms of (ix) and (xi) might lead to difficulty in some cases. However, (ix) as here stated has the effect of preserving fully the rule of substitutivity of equality—where the equality sign is so interpreted that $[c_1 = c_2]$ is a sentence denoting truth if and only if c_1 and c_2 are constants having the same denotation—and if in some formalized languages, (ix) and (xi) should prove to be inconsistent with the requirement that every well-formed expression be meaningful (note 2), it may be preferable to abandon the latter. Indeed the preservation of the rule of substitutivity of equality may be regarded as an important advantage of a Fregean theory of meaning over some of the alternatives that suggest themselves.

14. At the present stage it cannot be said with assurance that a modification of Frege's theory will ultimately prove to be the best or the simplest. Alternative theories demanding study are: the theory of Russell, which relies on the elimination of names by contextual definition to an extent sufficient to render the distinction of sense and denotation unnecessary; the modifi-

cation of Russell's theory, briefly suggested by Smullyan [*The Journal of Symbolic Logic*, 13 (1948), pp. 31–37], according to which descriptive phrases are to be considered as actually contained in the logistic system rather than being (in the phrase of Whitehead and Russell) "mere typographical conveniences," but are to differ from names in that they retain their need for scope indicators; and finally, the theory of Carnap's *Meaning and Necessity*.

Though the Russell theory has an element of simplicity in avoiding the distinction of two kinds of meaning, it leads to complications of its own of a different sort, in connection with the matter of scope of descriptions. The same should be said of Smullyan's proposed modification of the theory. And the distinctions of scope become especially important in modal statements, where they cannot be eliminated by the convention of always taking the minimum scope, as Smullyan has shown (loc. cit.).

Moreover, in its present form it would seem that the Russell theory requires some supplementation. For example, "I am thinking of Pegasus," "Ponce de Leon searched for the fountain of youth," "Barbara Villiers was less chaste than Diana" cannot be analyzed as "$(Ec)[x$ is a Pegasus $\equiv_x x=c]$ [I am thinking of c]," "$(Ec)[x$ is a fountain of youth $\equiv_x x=c]$ [Ponce de Leon searched for c]," "$(Ec)[x$ is a Diana $\equiv_x x=c]$ [Barbara Villiers was less chaste than c]" respectively—if only because of the (probable or possible) difference of truth-value between the given statements and their proposed analyses. On a Fregean theory of meaning the given statements might be analyzed as being about the individual concepts of Pegasus, of the fountain of youth, and of Diana rather than about some certain winged horse, some certain fountain, and some certain goddess. For the Russell theory it might be suggested to analyze them as being about the property of being a Pegasus, the property of being a fountain of youth, and the property of being a Diana. This analysis in terms of properties would also be possible on a Fregean theory, though perhaps slightly less natural. On a theory of the Russell type the difficulty arises that names of properties seem to be required, and on pain of readmitting Frege's puzzle about equality (which leads to the distinction of sense and denotation in connection with names of any kind), such names of properties either must be analyzed away by contextual definition—it is not clear how—or must be so severely restricted that two names of the same property cannot occur unless trivially synonymous.

15. Here a warning is necessary against spurious economies, since not every subtraction from the entities which a theory assumes is a reduction in the variety of entities.

For example, in the simple theory of types it is well known that the individuals may be dispensed with if classes and relations of all types are retained; or one may abandon also classes and relations of the lowest type, retaining only those of higher type. In fact any finite number of levels at the bottom of the hierarchy of types may be deleted. But this is no reduction in the variety of entities, because the truncated hierarchy of types, by appropriate deletions of entities in each type, can be made isomorphic to the original hierarchy—and indeed the continued adequacy of the truncated hierarchy to the original purposes depends on this isomorphism.

Similarly the idea may suggest itself to admit the distinction of sense and denotation at the nth level and above in the hierarchy of types, but below the nth level to deny this distinction and to adopt instead Russell's device of contextual elimination of names. The entities assumed would thus include only the usual extensional entities below the nth level, but at the nth level and above they would include also concepts, concepts of concepts, and so on. However, this is no reduction in the variety of entities assumed, as compared to the theory which assumes at all levels in the hierarchy of types not only the extensional entities but also concepts of them, concepts of concepts of them, and so on. For the entities assumed by the former theory are reduced again to isomorphism with those assumed by the latter, if all entities below the nth level are deleted and appropriate deletions are made in every type at the nth level and above.

Some one may object that the notion of isomorphism is irrelevant which is here introduced, and insist that any subtraction from the entities assumed by a theory must be considered a simplification. But to such objector I would reply that his proposal leads (in the cases just named, and others) to perpetual oscillation

between two theories T_1 and T_2, T_1 being reduced to T_2 and T_2 to T_1 by successive "simplifications" *ad infinitum.*

16. As is done in the revised edition of my *Introduction to Mathematical Logic, Part I.*

17. For convenience, English is used also as the metalanguage, although this gives a false appearance of triviality or obviousness to some of the semantical rules. Since the purpose is only illustrative, the danger of semantical antinomies is ignored.

18. For present illustrative purposes the question may be avoided whether common nouns in English, in the singular, shall be considered to be variables (e.g., 'planet' or 'a planet' as a variable having planets as its range), or to be class names (e.g., 'planet' as a proper name of the class of planets), or to have "no status at all in a logical grammar" (see Quine's *Methods of Logic*, p. 207), or perhaps to vary from one of these uses to another according to context.

19. Or possibly 'planet' and 's' could be regarded as two primitive symbols, by making a minor change in existing English so that all common nouns form the plural by adding 's.'

20. If any of you finds unacceptable the conclusion that therefore 'the number of planets is round' is a sentence, he may try to alter the rules to suit, perhaps by distinguishing different types of terms. This is an example of a doubtful point, on the decision of which they may well be differences of opinion. The advocate of a set-theoretic language may decide one way and the advocate of type theory another, but it is hard to say that either decision is the "true" decision for the English language as it is.

21. But of course it would be wrong to include as a rule of denotation: 'the world is round' denotes truth. For this depends on a fact of geography extraneous to semantics (namely that the world is round).

The Semantic Conception of Truth and the Foundations of Semantics

ALFRED TARSKI

This paper consists of two parts; the first has an expository character, and the second is rather polemical.

In the first part I want to summarize in an informal way the main results of my investigations concerning the definition of truth and the more general problem of the foundations of semantics. These results have been embodied in a work which appeared in print several years ago.[1] Although my investigations concern concepts dealt with in classical philosophy, they happen to be comparatively little known in philosophical circles, perhaps because of their strictly technical character. For this reason I hope I shall be excused for taking up the matter once again.[2]

Since my work was published, various objections, of unequal value, have been raised to my investigations; some of these appeared in print, and others were made in public and private discussions in which I took part.[3] In the second part of the paper I should like to express my views regarding these objections. I hope that the remarks which will be made in this context will not be considered as purely polemical in character, but will be found to contain some constructive contributions to the subject.

In the second part of the paper I have made extensive use of material graciously put at my disposal by Dr. Marja Kokoszyńska (University of Lwów). I am especially indebted and grateful to Professors Ernest Nagel (Colum-

bia University) and David Rynin (University of California, Berkeley) for their help in preparing the final text and for various critical remarks.

I. EXPOSITION

1. The Main Problem—A Satisfactory Definition of Truth

Our discussion will be centered around the notion[4] of *truth*. The main problem is that of giving a *satisfactory definition* of this notion, i.e., a definition which is *materially adequate* and *formally correct*. But such a formulation of the problem, because of its generality, cannot be considered unequivocal, and requires some further comments.

In order to avoid any ambiguity, we must first specify the conditions under which the definition of truth will be considered adequate from the material point of view. The desired definition does not aim to specify the meaning of a familiar word used to denote a novel notion; on the contrary, it aims to catch hold of the actual meaning of an old notion. We must then characterize this notion precisely enough to enable anyone to determine whether the definition actually fulfills its task.

Secondly, we must determine on what the formal correctness of the definition depends. Thus, we must specify the words or concepts which we wish to use in defining the notion of

From *Philosophy and Phenomenological Research,* volume 4 (1944), pp. 341–375.

truth; and we must also give the formal rules to which the definition should conform. Speaking more generally, we must describe the formal structure of the language in which the definition will be given.

The discussion of these points will occupy a considerable portion of the first part of the paper.

2. The Extension of the Term "True"

We begin with some remarks regarding the extension of the concept of truth which we have in mind here.

The predicate "true" is sometimes used to refer to psychological phenomena such as judgments or beliefs, sometimes to certain physical objects, namely, linguistic expressions and specifically sentences, and sometimes to certain ideal entities called "propositions." By "sentence" we understand here what is usually meant in grammar by "declarative sentence"; as regards the term "proposition," its meaning is notoriously a subject of lengthy disputations by various philosophers and logicians, and it seems never to have been made quite clear and unambiguous. For several reasons it appears most convenient to *apply the term "true" to sentences,* and we shall follow this course.[5]

Consequently, we must always relate the notion of truth, like that of a sentence, to a specific language; for it is obvious that the same expression which is a true sentence in one language can be false or meaningless in another.

Of course, the fact that we are interested here primarily in the notion of truth for sentences does not exclude the possibility of a subsequent extension of this notion to other kinds of objects.

3. The Meaning of the Term "True"

Much more serious difficulties are connected with the problem of the meaning (or the intension) of the concept of truth.

The word "true," like other words from our everyday language, is certainly not unambiguous. And it does not seem to me that the philosophers who have discussed this concept have helped to diminish its ambiguity. In works and discussions of philosophers we meet many different conceptions of truth and falsity, and we must indicate which conception will be the basis of our discussion.

We should like our definition to do justice to the intuitions which adhere to the *classical Aristotelian conception of truth*—intuitions which find their expression in the well-known words of Aristotle's *Metaphysics:*

> To say of what is that it is not, or of what is not that it is, is false, while to say of what is that it is, or of what is not that it is not, is true.

If we wished to adapt ourselves to modern philosophical terminology, we could perhaps express this conception by means of the familiar formula:

> The truth of a sentence consists in its agreement with (or correspondence to) reality.

(For a theory of truth which is to be based upon the latter formulation the term "correspondence theory" has been suggested.)

If, on the other hand, we should decide to extend the popular usage of the term "designate" by applying it not only to names, but also to sentences, and if we agreed to speak of the designata of sentences as "states of affairs," we could possibly use for the same purpose the following phrase:

> A sentence is true if it designates an existing state of affairs.[6]

However, all these formulations can lead to various misunderstandings, for none of them is sufficiently precise and clear (though this applies much less to the original Aristotelian formulation than to either of the others); at any rate, none of them can be considered a satisfactory definition of truth. It is up to us to look for a more precise expression of our intuitions.

4. A Criterion for the Material Adequacy of the Definition[7]

Let us start with a concrete example. Consider the sentence "snow is white." We ask the question under what conditions this sentence is true or false. It seems clear that if we base ourselves on the classical conception of truth, we shall say that the sentence is true if snow is white, and that it is false if snow is not white. Thus, if the definition of truth is to conform to our conception, it must imply the following equivalence:

> The sentence "snow is white" is true if, and only if, snow is white.

Let me point out that the phrase "snow is white" occurs on the left side of this equivalence in quotation marks, and on the right without quotation marks. On the right side we have the sentence itself, and on the left the name of the sentence. Employing the medieval logical terminology we could say that on the right side the words "snow is white" occur in *suppositio formalis,* and on the left in *suppositio materialis.* It is hardly necessary to explain why we must have the name of the sentence, and not the sentence itself, on the left side of the equivalence. For, in the first place, from the point of view of the grammar of our language, an expression of the form "*X* is true" will not become a meaningful sentence if we replace in it '*X*' by a sentence or by anything other than a name—since the subject of a sentence may be only a noun or an expression functioning like a noun. And, in the second place, the fundamental conventions regarding the use of any language require that in any utterance we make about an object it is the name of the object which must be employed, and not the object itself. In consequence, if we wish to say something about a sentence, for example that it is true, we must use the name of this sentence, and not the sentence itself.[8]

It may be added that enclosing a sentence in quotation marks is by no means the only way of forming its name. For instance, by assuming the usual order of letters in our alphabet, we can use the following expression as the name (the description) of the sentence "snow is white":

> the sentence constituted by three words, the first of which consists of the 19th, 14th, 15th, and 23rd

letters, the second of the 9th and 19th letters, and the third of the 23rd, 8th, 9th, 20th, and 5th letters of the English alphabet.

We shall now generalize the procedure which we have applied above. Let us consider an arbitrary sentence; we shall replace it by the letter '*p.*' We form the name of this sentence and we replace it by another letter, say '*X.*' We ask now what is the logical relation between the two sentences "*X* is true" and '*p.*' It is clear that from the point of view of our basic conception of truth these sentences are equivalent. In other words, the following equivalence holds:

(T)   X is true if, and only if, p.

We shall call any such equivalence (with '*p*' replaced by any sentence of the language to which the word "true" refers, and '*X*' replaced by a name of this sentence) an "*equivalence of the form* (T)."

Now at last we are able to put into a precise form the conditions under which we will consider the usage and the definition of the term "true" as adequate from the material point of view: we wish to use the term "true" in such a way that all equivalences of the form (T) can be asserted, and *we shall call a definition of truth "adequate" if all these equivalences follow from it.*

It should be emphasized that neither the expression (T) itself (which is not a sentence, but only a schema of a sentence) nor any particular instance of the form (T) can be regarded as a definition of truth. We can only say that every equivalence of the form (T) obtained by replacing '*p*' by a particular sentence, and '*X*' by a name of this sentence, may be considered a partial definition of truth, which explains wherein the truth of this one individual sentence consists. The general definition has to be, in a certain sense, a logical conjunction of all these partial definitions.

(The last remark calls for some comments. A language may admit the construction of infinitely many sentences; and thus the number of partial definitions of truth referring to sentences of such a language will also be infinite. Hence to give our remark a precise sense we should have to explain what is meant by a "logical conjunction of infinitely many sentences"; but this would lead us too far into technical problems of modern logic.)

5. Truth as a Semantic Concept

I should like to propose the name "*the semantic conception of truth*" for the conception of truth which has just been discussed.

Semantics is a discipline which, speaking loosely, *deals with certain relations between expressions of a language and the objects* (or "states of affairs") "*referred to*" *by those expressions*. As typical examples of semantic concepts we may mention the concepts of *designation, satisfaction,* and *definition* as these occur in the following examples:

> the expression "the father of his country" designates (denotes) George Washington;
>
> snow satisfies the sentential function (the condition) "x is white";
>
> the equation "$2 \cdot x = 1$" defines (uniquely determines) the number 1/2.

While the words "designates," "satisfies," and "defines" express relations (between certain expressions and the objects "referred to" by these expressions), the word "true" is of a different logical nature: it expresses a property (or denotes a class) of certain expressions, viz., of sentences. However, it is easily seen that all the formulations which were given earlier and which aimed to explain the meaning of this word (cf. sections 3 and 4) referred not only to sentences themselves, but also to objects "talked about" by these sentences, or possibly to "states of affairs" described by them. And, moreover, it turns out that the simplest and the most natural way of obtaining an exact definition of truth is one which involves the use of other semantic notions, e.g., the notion of satisfaction. It is for these reasons that we count the concept of truth which is discussed here among the concepts of semantics, and the problem of defining truth proves to be closely related to the more general problem of setting up the foundations of theoretical semantics.

It is perhaps worthwhile saying that semantics as it is conceived in this paper (and in former papers of the author) is a sober and modest discipline which has no pretensions of being a universal patent-medicine for all the ills and diseases of mankind, whether imaginary or real. You will not find in semantics any remedy for decayed teeth or illusions of grandeur or class conflicts. Nor is semantics a device for establishing that everyone except the speaker and his friends is speaking nonsense.

From antiquity to the present day the concepts of semantics have played an important role in the discussions of philosophers, logicians, and philologists. Nevertheless, these concepts have been treated for a long time with a certain amount of suspicion. From a historical standpoint, this suspicion is to be regarded as completely justified. For although the meaning of semantic concepts as they are used in everyday language seems to be rather clear and understandable, still all attempts to characterize this meaning in a general and exact way miscarried. And what is worse, various arguments in which these concepts were involved, and which seemed otherwise quite correct and based upon apparently obvious premises, led frequently to paradoxes and antinomies. It is sufficient to mention here the *antinomy of the liar,* Richard's *antinomy of definability* (by means of a finite number of words), and Grelling-Nelson's *antinomy of heterological terms.*[9]

I believe that the method which is outlined in this paper helps to overcome these difficulties and assures the possibility of a consistent use of semantic concepts.

6. Languages with a Specified Structure

Because of the possible occurrence of antinomies, the problem of specifying the formal structure and the vocabulary of a language in which definitions of semantic concepts are to be given becomes especially acute; and we turn now to this problem.

There are certain general conditions under which the structure of a language is regarded as *exactly specified.* Thus, to specify the structure of a language, we must characterize unambiguously the class of those words and expressions which are to be considered *meaningful*. In particular, we must indicate all words which we decide to use without defining them, and which are called "*undefined* (or *primitive*) *terms*"; and we must give the so-called *rules of definition* for introducing new or *defined terms*. Furthermore, we must set up criteria for distinguishing within the class of expressions those which we call "*sentences*." Finally, we must formulate the conditions under which a sentence of the language can be *asserted*. In particular, we must indicate all *axioms* (or *primitive sentences*), i.e., those sentences which we decide to assert without proof; and we must give the so-called *rules of inference* (or *rules of proof*) by means of which we can deduce new asserted sentences from other sentences which have been previously asserted. Axioms, as well as sentences deduced from them by means of rules of inference, are referred to as "*theorems*" or "*provable sentences*."

If in specifying the structure of a language we refer exclusively to the form of the expressions involved, the language is said to be *formalized*. In such a language theorems are the only sentences which can be asserted.

At the present time the only languages with a specified structure are the formalized languages of various systems of deductive logic, possibly enriched by the introduction of certain nonlogical terms. However, the field of application of these languages is rather comprehensive; we are able, theoretically, to develop in them various branches of science, for instance, mathematics and theoretical physics.

(On the other hand, we can imagine the construction of languages which have an exactly specified structure without being formalized. In such a language the assertability of sentences, for instance, may depend not always on their form, but sometimes on other, nonlinguistic factors. It would be interesting and important actually to construct a language of this type, and specifically one which would prove to be sufficient for the development of a comprehensive branch of empirial science; for this would justify the hope that languages with specified structure could finally replace everyday language in scientific discourse.)

The problem of the definition of truth obtains a precise meaning and can be solved in a rigorous way only for those languages whose structure has been exactly specified. For other languages—thus, for all natural, "spoken" languages—the meaning of the problem is more or less vague, and its solution can have only an approximate character. Roughly speaking, the approximation consists in replacing a natural language (or a portion of it in which we are interested) by one whose structure is exactly specified, and which diverges from the given language "as little as possible."

7. The Antinomy of the Liar

In order to discover some of the more specific conditions which must be satisfied by languages in which (or for which) the definition of truth is to be given, it will be advisable to begin with a discussion of that antinomy which directly involves the notion of truth, namely, the antinomy of the liar.

To obtain this antinomy in a perspicuous form,[10] consider the following sentence:

> The sentence printed in this paper on p. 52, column B, ll. 28–29, is not true.

For brevity we shall replace the sentence just stated by the letter 's.'

According to our convention concerning the adequate usage of the term 'true', we assert the following equivalence of the form (T):

(1) 's' is true if, and only if, the sentence printed in this paper on p. 52, column B, ll. 28–29 is not true.

On the other hand, keeping in mind the meaning of the symbol 's,' we establish empirically the following fact:

(2) 's' is identical with the sentence printed in this paper on p. 52, column B, ll. 28–29.

Now, by a familiar law from the theory of identity (Leibniz's law), it follows from (2) that we may replace in (1) the expression "the sentence printed in this paper on p. 52, column B, ll. 28–29" by the symbol " 's.' " We thus obtain what follows:

(3) 's' is true if, and only if, 's' is not true.

In this way we have arrived at an obvious contradiction.

In my judgment, it would be quite wrong and dangerous from the standpoint of scientific progress to depreciate the importance of this and other antinomies, and to treat them as jokes or sophistries. It is a fact that we are here in the presence of an absurdity, that we have been compelled to assert a false sentence [since (3), as an equivalence between two contradictory sentences, is necessarily false]. If we take our work seriously, we cannot be reconciled with this fact. We must discover its cause, that is to say, we must analyze premises upon which the antinomy is based; we must then reject at least one of these premises, and we must investigate the consequences which this has for the whole domain of our research.

It should be emphasized that antinomies have played a preeminent role in establishing the foundations of modern deductive sciences. And just as class-theoretical antinomies, and in particular Russell's antinomy (of the class of all classes that are not members of themselves), were the starting point for the successful attempts at a consistent formalization of logic and mathematics, so the antinomy of the liar and other semantic antinomies give rise to the construction of theoretical semantics.

8. The Inconsistency of Semantically Closed Languages[7]

If we now analyze the assumptions which lead to the antinomy of the liar, we notice the following:

(I) We have implicitly assumed that the language in which the antinomy is constructed contains, in addition to its expressions, also the names of these expressions, as well as semantic terms such as the term "*true*" referring to sentences of this language; we have also assumed that all sentences which determine the adequate usage of this term can be

asserted in the language. A language with these properties will be called "*semantically closed.*"

(II) We have assumed that in this language the ordinary laws of logic hold.

(III) We have assumed that we can formulate and assert in our language an empirical premise such as the statement (2) which has occurred in our argument.

It turns out that the assumption (III) is not essential, for it is possible to reconstruct the antinomy of the liar without its help.[11] But the assumptions (I) and (II) prove essential. Since every language which satisfies both of these assumptions is inconsistent, we must reject at least one of them.

It would be superfluous to stress here the consequences of rejecting the assumption (II), that is, of changing our logic (supposing this were possible) even in its more elementary and fundamental parts. We thus consider only the possibility of rejecting the assumption (I). Accordingly, we decide *not to use any language which is semantically closed* in the sense given.

This restriction would of course be unacceptable for those who, for reasons which are not clear to me, believe that there is only one "genuine" language (or, at least, that all "genuine" languages are mutually translatable). However, this restriction does not affect the needs or interests of science in any essential way. The languages (either the formalized languages or—what is more frequently the case—the portions of everyday language) which are used in scientific discourse do not have to be semantically closed. This is obvious in case linguistic phenomena and, in particular, semantic notions do not enter in any way into the subject matter of a science; for in such a case the language of this science does not have to be provided with any semantic terms at all. However, we shall see in the next section how semantically closed languages can be dispensed with even in those scientific discussions in which semantic notions are essentially involved.

The problem arises as to the position of everyday language with regard to this point. At first blush it would seem that this language satisfies both assumptions (I) and (II), and that therefore it must be inconsistent. But actually the case is not so simple. Our everyday language is certainly not one with an exactly specified structure. We do not know precisely which expressions are sentences, and we know even to a smaller degree which sentences are to be taken as assertible. Thus the problem of consistency has no exact meaning with respect to this language. We may at best only risk the guess that a language whose structure has been exactly specified and which resembles our everyday language as closely as possible would be inconsistent.

9. Object Language and Metalanguage

Since we have agreed not to employ semantically closed languages, we have to use two different languages in discussing the problem of the definition of truth and, more generally, any problems in the field of semantics. The first of these languages is the language which is "talked about" and which is the subject matter of the whole discussion; the definition of truth which we are seeking applies to the sentences of this language. The second is the language in which we "talk about" the first language, and in terms of which we wish, in particular, to construct the definition of truth for the first language. We shall refer to the first language as "the object language," and to the second as "the metalanguage."

It should be noticed that these terms "object language" and "metalanguage" have only a relative sense. If, for instance, we become interested in the notion of truth applying to sentences, not of our original object language, but of its metalanguage, the latter becomes automatically the object language of our discussion; and in order to define truth for this language, we have to go to a new metalanguage—so to speak, to a metalanguage of a higher level. In this way we arrive at a whole hierarchy of languages.

The vocabulary of the metalanguage is to a large extent determined by previously stated conditions under which a definition of truth will be considered materially adequate. This definition, as we recall, has to imply all equivalences of the form (T):

(T)   X is true if, and only if, p.

The definition itself and all the equivalences implied by it are to be formulated in the metalanguage. On the other hand, the symbol 'p' in (T) stands for an arbitrary sentence of our object language. Hence it follows that every sentence which occurs in the object language must also occur in the metalanguage; in other words, the metalanguage must contain the object language as a part. This is at any rate necessary for the proof of the adequacy of the definition—even though the definition itself can sometimes be formulated in a less comprehensive metalanguage which does not satisfy this requirement.

[The requirement in question can be somewhat modified, for it suffices to assume that the object-language can be translated into the metalanguage; this necessitates a certain change in the interpretation of the symbol 'p' in (T). In all that follows we shall ignore the possibility of this modification.]

Furthermore, the symbol 'X' in (T) represents the name of the sentence which 'p' stands for. We see therefore that the metalanguage must be rich enough to provide possibilities of constructing a name for every sentence of the object language.

In addition, the metalanguage must obviously contain terms of a general logical character, such as the expression "if, and only if."[12]

It is desirable for the metalanguage not to contain any undefined terms except such as are involved explicitly or implicitly in the remarks above, i.e.: terms of the object language; terms referring to the form of the expressions of the object language, and used in building names for these expressions; and terms of logic. In particular, we desire *semantic terms* (referring to the object language) *to be introduced into the metalanguage only by definition*. For, if this postulate is satisfied, the definition of truth, or of any other semantic concept, will fulfill what we intuitively expect from every definition; that is, it will explain the meaning of the term being defined in terms whose meaning appears to be completely clear and unequivocal. And, moreover, we have then a kind of guarantee that the use of semantic concepts will not involve us in any contradictions.

We have no further requirements as to the formal structure of the object language and the metalanguage; we assume that it is similar to that of other formalized languages known at the present time. In particular, we assume that the usual formal rules of definition are observed in the metalanguage.

10. Conditions for a Positive Solution of the Main Problem

Now, we have already a clear idea both of the conditions of material adequacy to which the definition of truth is subjected, and of the formal structure of the language in which this definition is to be constructed. Under these circumstances the problem of the definition of truth acquires the character of a definite problem of a purely deductive nature.

The solution of the problem, however, is by no means obvious, and I would not attempt to give it in detail without using the whole machinery of contemporary logic. Here I shall confine myself to a rough outline of the solution and to the discussion of certain points of a more general interest which are involved in it.

The solution turns out to be sometimes positive, sometimes negative. This depends upon some formal relations between the object language and its metalanguage; or, more specifically, upon the fact whether the metalanguage in its logical part is "essentially richer" than the object language or not. It is not easy to give a general and precise definition of this notion of "essential richness." If we restrict ourselves to languages based on the logical theory of types, the condition for the metalanguage to be "essentially richer" than the object language is that it contain variables of a higher logical type than those of the object language.

If the condition of "essential richness" is not satisfied, it can usually be shown that an interpretation of the metalanguage in the object language is possible; that is to say, with any given term of the metalanguage a well-determined term of the object language can be correlated in such a way that the assertible sentences of the one language turn out to be correlated with assertible sentences of the other. As a result of this interpretation, the hypothesis that a satisfactory definition of truth has been formulated in the metalanguage turns out to imply the possibility of reconstructing in that language the antinomy of the liar; and this in turn forces us to reject the hypothesis in question.

(The fact that the metalanguage, in its nonlogical part, is ordinarily more comprehensive than the object language does not affect the possibility of interpreting the former in the latter. For example, the names of expressions of the object language occur in the metalanguage, though for the most part they do not occur in the object language itself; but, nevertheless, it may be possible to interpret these names in terms of the object language.)

Thus we see that the condition of "essential richness" is necessary for the possibility of a satisfactory definition of truth in the metalanguage. If we want to develop the theory of truth in a metalanguage which does not satisfy this condition, we must give up the idea of defining truth with the exclusive help of those terms which were indicated above (in section 8). We have then to include the term "true," or some other semantic term, in the list of undefined terms of the metalanguage, and to express fundamental properties of the notion of truth in a series of axioms. There is nothing essentially wrong in such an axiomatic procedure, and it may prove useful for various purposes.[13]

It turns out, however, that this procedure can be avoided. For *the condition of the "essential richness" of the metalanguage proves to be, not only necessary, but also sufficient for the construction of a satisfactory definition of truth;* i.e., if the metalanguage satisfies this condition, the notion of truth can be defined in it. We shall now indicate in general terms how this construction can be carried through.

11. The Construction (in Outline) of the Definition[14]

A definition of truth can be obtained in a very simple way from that of another semantic notion, namely, of the notion of *satisfaction.*

Satisfaction is a relation between arbitrary objects and certain expressions called "*sentential functions.*" These are expressions like "*x* is white," "*x* is greater than *y*," etc. Their formal structure is analogous to that of sentences; however, they *may* contain the so-called free variables (like '*x*' and '*y*' in "*x* is greater than *y*"), which cannot occur in sentences.

In defining the notion of a sentential function in formalized languages, we usually apply what is called a "recursive procedure"; i.e., we first describe sentential functions of the simplest structure (which ordinarily presents no difficulty), and then we indicate the operations by means of which compound functions can be constructed from simpler ones. Such an operation may consist, for instance, in forming the logical disjunction or conjunction of two given functions, i.e., by combining them by the word "or" or "and." A sentence can now be defined simply as a sentential function which contains no free variables.

As regards the notion of satisfaction, we might try to define it by saying that given objects satisfy a given function if the latter becomes a true sentence when we replace in it free variables by names of given objects. In this sense, for example, snow satisfies the sentential function "*x* is white" since the sentence "snow is white" is true. However, apart from other difficulties, this method is not available to us, for we want to use the notion of satisfaction in defining truth.

To obtain a definition of satisfaction we have rather to apply again a recursive procedure. We indicate which objects satisfy the simplest sentential functions; and then we state the conditions under which given objects satisfy a compound function—assuming that we know which objects satisfy the simpler functions from which the compound one has been constructed. Thus, for instance, we say

that given numbers satisfy the logical disjunction "*x* is greater than *y* or *x* is equal to *y*" if they satisfy at least one of the functions "*x* is greater than *y*" or "*x* is equal to *y*."

Once the general definition of satisfaction is obtained, we notice that it applies automatically also to those special sentential functions which contain no free variables, i.e., to sentences. It turns out that for a sentence only two cases are possible: a sentence is either satisfied by all objects, or by no objects. Hence we arrive at a definition of truth and falsehood simply by saying that *a sentence is true if it is satisfied by all objects, and false otherwise.*[15]

(It may seem strange that we have chosen a roundabout way of defining the truth of a sentence, instead of trying to apply, for instance, a direct recursive procedure. The reason is that compound sentences are constructed from simpler sentential functions, but not always from simpler sentences; hence no general recursive method is known which applies specifically to sentences.)

From this rough outline it is not clear where and how the assumption of the "essential richness" of the metalanguage is involved in the discussion; this becomes clear only when the construction is carried through in a detailed and formal way.[16]

12. Consequences of the Definition

The definition of truth which was outlined above has many interesting consequences.

In the first place, the definition proves to be not only formally correct, but also materially adequate (in the sense established in section 4); in other words, it implies all equivalences of the form (T). In this connection it is important to notice that the conditions for the material adequacy of the definition determine uniquely the extension of the term "true." Therefore, every definition of truth which is materially adequate would necessarily be equivalent to that actually constructed. The semantic conception of truth gives us, so to speak, no possibility of choice between various nonequivalent definitions of this notion.

Moreover, we can deduce from our definition various laws of a general nature. In particular, we can prove with its help the *laws of contradiction and of excluded middle,* which are so characteristic of the Aristotelian conception of truth; i.e., we can show that one and only one of any two contradictory sentences is true. These semantic laws should not be identified with the related logical laws of contradiction and excluded middle; the latter belong to the sentential calculus, i.e., to the most elementary part of logic, and do not involve the term "true" at all.

Further important results can be obtained by applying the theory of truth to formalized languages of a certain very comprehensive class of mathematical disciplines; only disciplines of an elementary character and a very elementary logical structure are excluded from this class. It turns out that for a discipline of this class *the notion of truth never coincides with that of provability;* for all provable sentences are true, but there are true sentences which are not provable.[17] Hence it follows further that every such discipline is consistent, but incomplete; that is to say, of any two contradictory sentences at most one is provable, and—what is more—there exists a pair of contradictory sentences neither of which is provable.[18]

13. Extension of the Results to Other Semantic Notions

Most of the results at which we arrived in the preceding sections in discussing the notion of truth can be extended with appropriate changes to other semantic notions, for instance, to the notion of satisfaction (involved in our previous discussion), and to those of *designation* and *definition.*

Each of these notions can be analyzed along the lines followed in the analysis of truth. Thus, criteria for an adequate usage of these notions can be established; it can be shown that each of these notions, when used in a semantically closed language according to those criteria, leads necessarily to a contradiction;[19] a distinction between the object language and the metalanguage becomes again indispensable; and the "essential rich-

ness" of the metalanguage proves in each case to be a necessary and sufficient condition for a satisfactory definition of the notion involved. Hence the results obtained in discussing one particular semantic notion apply to the general problem of the foundations of theoretical semantics.

Within theoretical semantics we can define and study some further notions, whose intuitive content is more involved and whose semantic origin is less obvious; we have in mind, for instance, the important notions of *consequence, synonymity,* and *meaning.*[20]

We have concerned ourselves here with the theory of semantic notions related to an individual object language (although no specific properties of this language have been involved in our arguments). However, we could also consider the problem of developing *general semantics* which applies to a comprehensive class of object languages. A considerable part of our previous remarks can be extended to this general problem; however, certain new difficulties arise in this connection, which will not be discussed here. I shall merely observe that the axiomatic method (mentioned in section 10) may prove the most appropriate for the treatment of the problem.[21]

II. POLEMICAL REMARKS

14. Is the Semantic Conception of Truth the "Right" One?

I should like to begin the polemical part of the paper with some general remarks.

I hope nothing which is said here will be interpreted as a claim that the semantic conception of truth is the "right" or indeed the "only possible" one. I do not have the slightest intention to contribute in any way to those endless, often violent discussions on the subject: "What is the right conception of truth?"[22] I must confess I do not understand what is at stake in such disputes; for the problem itself is so vague that no definite solution is possible. In fact, it seems to me that the sense in which the phrase "the right conception" is used has never been made clear. In most cases one gets the impression that the phrase is used in an almost mystical sense based upon the belief that every word has only one "real" meaning (a kind of Platonic or Aristotelian idea), and that all the competing conceptions really attempt to catch hold of this one meaning; since, however, they contradict each other, only one attempt can be successful, and hence only one conception is the "right" one.

Disputes of this type are by no means restricted to the notion of truth. They occur in all domains where—instead of an exact, scientific terminology—common language with its vagueness and ambiguity is used; and they are always meaningless, and therefore in vain.

It seems to me obvious that the only rational approach to such problems would be the following: We should reconcile ourselves with the fact that we are confronted, not with one concept, but with several different concepts which are denoted by one word; we should try to make these concepts as clear as possible (by means of definition, or of an axiomatic procedure, or in some other way); to avoid further confusions, we should agree to use different terms for different concepts; and then we may proceed to a quiet and systematic study of all concepts involved, which will exhibit their main properties and mutual relations.

Referring specifically to the notion of truth, it is undoubtedly the case that in philosophical discussions—and perhaps also in everyday usage—some incipient conceptions of this notion can be found that differ essentially from the classical one (of which the semantic conception is but a modernized form). In fact, various conceptions of this sort have been discussed in the literature, for instance, the pragmatic conception, the coherence theory, etc.[6]

It seems to me that none of these conceptions have been put so far in an intelligible and unequivocal form. This may change, however; a time may come when we find ourselves confronted with several incompatible, but equally clear and precise, conceptions of truth. It will then become necessary to abandon the ambiguous usage of the word "true,"

and to introduce several terms instead, each to denote a different notion. Personally, I should not feel hurt if a future world congress of the "theoreticians of truth" should decide—by a majority of votes—to reserve the word "true" for one of the nonclassical conceptions, and should suggest another word, say, "frue," for the conception considered here. But I cannot imagine that anybody could present cogent arguments to the effect that the semantic conception is "wrong" and should be entirely abandoned.

15. Formal Correctness of the Suggested Definition of Truth

The specific objections which have been raised to my investigations can be divided into several groups; each of these will be discussed separately.

I think that practically all these objections apply, not to the special definition I have given, but to the semantic conception of truth in general. Even those which were leveled against the definition actually constructed could be related to any other definition which conforms to this conception.

This holds, in particular, for those objections which concern the formal correctness of the definition. I have heard a few objections of this kind; however, I doubt very much whether anyone of them can be treated seriously.

As a typical example let me quote in substance such an objection.[23] In formulating the definition we use necessarily sentential connectives, i.e., expressions like "if . . . , then," "or," etc. They occur in the definiens; and one of them, namely, the phrase "if, and only if" is usually employed to combine the definiendum with the definiens. However, it is well known that the meaning of sentential connectives is explained in logic with the help of the words "true" and "false"; for instance, we say that an equivalence, i.e., a sentence of the form "p if, and only if, q," is true if either both of its members, i.e., the sentences represented by 'p' and 'q,' are true or both are false. Hence the definition of truth involves a vicious circle.

If this objection were valid, no formally correct definition of truth would be possible; for we are unable to formulate any compound sentence without using sentential connectives, or other logical terms defined with their help. Fortunately, the situation is not so bad.

It is undoubtedly the case that a strictly deductive development of logic is often preceded by certain statements explaining the conditions under which sentences of the form "if p, then q," etc., are considered true or false. (Such explanations are often given schematically, by means of the so-called truth-tables.) However, these statements are outside of the system of logic, and should not be regarded as definitions of the terms involved. They are not formulated in the language of the system, but constitute rather special consequences of the definition of truth given in the metalanguage. Moreover, these statements do not influence the deductive development of logic in any way. For in such a development we do not discuss the question whether a given sentence is true, we are only interested in the problem whether it is provable.[24]

On the other hand, the moment we find ourselves within the deductive system of logic—or of any discipline based upon logic, e.g., of semantics—we either treat sentential connectives as undefined terms, or else we define them by means of other sentential connectives, but never by means of semantic terms like "true" or "false." For instance, if we agree to regard the expressions "not" and "if . . . , then" (and possibly also "if, and only if") as undefined terms, we can define the term "or" by stating that a sentence of the form "p or q" is equivalent to the corresponding sentence of the form "if not p, then q." The definition can be formulated, e.g., in the following way:

(p or q) if, and only if, (if not p, then q).

This definition obviously contains no semantic terms.

However, a vicious circle in definition arises only when the definiens contains either the term to be defined itself, or other terms defined with its help. Thus we clearly see that the use of sentential connectives in defining the semantic term "$true$" does not involve any circle.

I should like to mention a further objection which I have found in the literature and which seems also to concern the formal correctness, if not of the definition of truth itself, then at least of the arguments which lead to this definition.[25]

The author of this objection mistakenly regards scheme (T) (from section 4) as a definition of truth. He charges this alleged definition with "inadmissible brevity, i.e., incompleteness," which "does not give us the means of deciding whether by 'equivalence' is meant a logical-formal, or a nonlogical and also structurally nondescribable relation." To remove this "defect" he suggests supplementing (T) in one of the two following ways:

(T′) X is true if, and only if, p is true,

or

(T″) X is true if, and only if, p is the case (i.e., if what p states is the case).

Then he discusses these two new "definitions," which are supposedly free from the old, formal "defect," but which turn out to be unsatisfactory for other, nonformal reasons.

This new objection seems to arise from a misunderstanding concerning the nature of sentential connectives (and thus to be somehow related to that previously discussed). The author of the objection does not seem to realize that the phrase "if, and only if" (in opposition to such phrases as "are equivalent" or "is equivalent to") expresses no relation between sentences at all since it does not combine names of sentences.

In general, the whole argument is based upon an obvious confusion between sentences and their names. It suffices to point out that—in contradistinction to (T)—schemata (T′) and (T″) do not give any meaningful expressions if we replace in them 'p' by a sentence; for the phrases "p is true" and "p is the case" (i.e., "what p states is the case") become meaningless if 'p' is replaced by a sentence, and not by the name of a sentence (cf. section 4).[26]

While the author of the objection considers schema (T) "inadmissibly brief," I am inclined, on my part, to regard schemata (T') and (T'') as "inadmissibly long." And I think even that I can rigorously prove this statement on the basis of the following definition: An expression is said to be "inadmissibly long" if (i) it is meaningless, and (ii) it has been obtained from a meaningful expression by inserting superfluous words.

16. Redundancy of Semantic Terms— Their Possible Elimination

The objection I am going to discuss now no longer concerns the formal correctness of the definition, but is still concerned with certain formal features of the semantic conception of truth.

We have seen that this conception essentially consists in regarding the sentence "X is true" as equivalent to the sentence denoted by 'X' (where 'X' stands for a name of a sentence of the object language). Consequently, the term "true" when occurring in a simple sentence of the form "X is true" can easily be eliminated, and the sentence itself, which belongs to the metalanguage, can be replaced by an equivalent sentence of the object language; and the same applies to compound sentences provided the term "*true*" occurs in them exclusively as a part of the expressions of the form "X is true."

Some people have therefore urged that the term "true" in the semantic sense can always be eliminated, and that for this reason the semantic conception of truth is altogether sterile and useless. And since the same considerations apply to other semantic notions, the conclusion has been drawn that semantics as a whole is a purely verbal game and at best only a harmless hobby.

But the matter is not quite so simple.[27] The sort of elimination here discussed cannot always be made. It cannot be done in the case of universal statements which express the fact that all sentences of a certain type are true, or that all true sentences have a certain property. For instance, we can prove in the theory of truth the following statement:

All consequences of true sentences are true.

However, we cannot get rid here of the word "true" in the simple manner contemplated.

Again, even in the case of particular sentences having the form "X is true" such a simple elimination cannot always be made. In fact, the elimination is possible only in those cases in which the name of the sentence which is said to be true occurs in a form that enables us to reconstruct the sentence itself. For example, our present historical knowledge does not give us any possibility of eliminating the word "true" from the following sentence:

The first sentence written by Plato is true.

Of course, since we have a definition for truth and since every definition enables us to replace the definiendum by its definiens, an elimination of the term "true" in its semantic sense is always theoretically possible. But this would not be the kind of simple elimination discussed above, and it would not result in the replacement of a sentence in the metalanguage by a sentence in the object language.

If, however, anyone continues to urge that—because of the theoretical possibility of eliminating the word "true" on the basis of its definition—the concept of truth is sterile, he must accept the further conclusion that all defined notions are sterile. But this outcome is so absurd and so unsound historically that any comment on it is unnecessary. In fact, I am rather inclined to agree with those who maintain that the moments of greatest creative advancement in science frequently coincide with the introduction of new notions by means of definition.

17. Conformity of the Semantic Conception of Truth with Philosophical and Common-sense Usage

The question has been raised whether the semantic conception of truth can indeed be regarded as a precise form of the old, classical conception of this notion.

Various formulations of the classical conception were quoted in the early part of this paper (section 3). I must repeat that in my judgment none of them is quite precise and clear. Accordingly, the only sure way of settling the question would be to confront the authors of those statements with our new formulation, and to ask them whether it agrees with their intentions. Unfortunately, this method is impractical since they died quite some time ago.

As far as my own opinion is concerned, I do not have any doubts that our formulation does conform to the intuitive content of that of Aristotle. I am less certain regarding the later formulations of the classical conception, for they are very vague indeed.[28]

Furthermore, some doubts have been expressed whether the semantic conception does reflect the notion of truth in its common-sense and everyday usage. I clearly realize (as I already indicated) that the common meaning of the word "true"—as that of any other word of everyday language—is to some extent vague, and that its usage more or less fluctuates. Hence the problem of assigning to this word a fixed and exact meaning is relatively unspecified, and every solution of this problem implies necessarily a certain deviation from the practice of everyday language.

In spite of all this, I happen to believe that the semantic conception does conform to a very considerable extent with the common-sense usage—although I readily admit I may be mistaken. What is more to the point, however, I believe that the issue raised can be settled scientifically, though of course not by a deductive procedure, but with the help of the statistical questionnaire method. As a matter of fact, such research has been carried on, and some of the results have been reported at congresses and in part published.[29]

I should like to emphasize that in my opinion such investigations must be conducted with the utmost care. Thus, if we ask a high-school boy, or even an adult intelligent man having no special philosophical training, whether he regards a sentence to be true if it agrees with reality, or if it designates an existing state of affairs, it may simply turn out that he does not understand the question; in consequence his response, whatever it may be, will be of no value for us. But his answer to the question whether he would admit that the sentence "it is snowing" could be true although it is not snowing, or could be false although it is snowing, would naturally be very significant for our problem.

Therefore, I was by no means surprised to learn (in a discussion devoted to these problems) that in a group of people who were questioned only 15% agreed that "true" means for them "agreeing with reality," while 90% agreed that a sentence such as "it is snowing" is true if, and only if, it is snowing. Thus, a great majority of these people seemed to reject the classical conception of truth in its "philosophical" formulation, while accepting the same conception when formulated in plain words (waiving the question whether the use of the phrase "the same conception" is here justified).

18. The Definition in Its Relation to "The Philosophical Problem of Truth" and to Various Epistemological Trends

I have heard it remarked that the formal definition of truth has nothing to do with "the philosophical problem of truth."[30] However, nobody has ever pointed out to me in an intelligible way just what this problem is. I have been informed in this connection that my definition, though it states necessary and sufficient conditions for a sentence to be true, does not really grasp the "essence" of this concept. Since I have never been able to understand what the "essence" of a concept is, I must be excused from discussing this point any longer.

In general, I do not believe that there is such a thing as "the philosophical problem of truth." I do believe that there are various intelligible and interesting (but not necessarily philosophical) problems concerning the notion of truth, but I also believe that they can be exactly formulated and possibly solved only on the basis of a precise conception of this notion.

While on the one hand the definition of truth has been blamed for not being philosophical enough, on the other a series of objections have been raised charging this definition with serious philosophical implications, always of a very undesirable nature. I shall discuss now one special objection of this type; another group of such objections will be dealt with in the next section.

It has been claimed that—due to the fact that a sentence like "snow is white" is taken to be semantically true if snow is *in fact* white (italics by the critic)—logic finds itself involved in a most uncritical realism.[31]

If there were an opportunity to discuss the objection with its author, I should raise two points. First, I should ask him to drop the words "in fact," which do not occur in the original formulation and which are misleading, even if they do not affect the content. For these words convey the impression that the semantic conception of truth is intended to establish the conditions under which we are warranted in asserting any given sentence, and in particular any empirical sentence. However, a moment's reflection shows that this impression is merely an illusion; and I think that the author of the objection falls victim to the illusion which he himself created.

In fact, the semantic definition of truth implies nothing regarding the conditions under which a sentence like (1):

(1)   snow is white

can be asserted. It implies only that, whenever we assert or reject this sentence, we must be ready to assert or reject the correlated sentence (2):

(2)   the sentence "snow is white" is true.

Thus, we may accept the semantic conception of truth without giving up any epistemological attitude we may have had; we may remain naive realists, critical realists or idealists, empiricists or metaphysicians—whatever we were before. The semantic conception is completely neutral toward all these issues.

In the second place, I should try to get some information regarding the conception of truth which (in the opinion of the author of the objection) does not involve logic in a most naive realism. I would gather that this conception must be incompatible with the semantic one. Thus, there must be sentences which are true in one of these conceptions without being true in the other. Assume, e.g., the sentence (1) to be of this kind. The truth of this sentence in the semantic conception is determined by an equivalence of the form (T):

> The sentence "snow is white" is true if, and only if, snow is white.

Hence in the new conception we must reject this equivalence, and consequently we must assume its denial:

> The sentence "snow is white" is true if, and only if, snow is not white (*or perhaps:* snow, in fact, is not white).

This sounds somewhat paradoxical. I do not regard such a consequence of the new conception as absurd; but I am a little fearful that someone in the future may charge this conception with involving logic in a "most sophisticated kind of irrealism." At any rate, it seems to me important to realize that every conception of truth which is incompatible with the semantic one carries with it consequences of this type.

I have dwelt a little on this whole question, not because the objection discussed seems to me very significant, but because certain points which have arisen in the discussion should be taken into account by all those who for various epistemological reasons are inclined to reject the semantic conception of truth.

19. Alleged Metaphysical Elements in Semantics

The semantic conception of truth has been charged several times with involving certain metaphysical elements. Objections of this sort have been made to apply not only to the theory of truth, but to the whole domain of theoretical semantics.[32]

I do not intend to discuss the general problem whether the introduction of a metaphysical element into a science is at all objectionable. The only point which will interest me here is whether and in what sense metaphysics is involved in the subject of our present discussion.

The whole question obviously depends

upon what one understands by "metaphysics." Unfortunately, this notion is extremely vague and equivocal. When listening to discussions in this subject, sometimes one gets the impression that the term "metaphysical" has lost any objective meaning, and is merely used as a kind of professional philosophical invective.

For some people metaphysics is a general theory of objects (ontology)—a discipline which is to be developed in a purely empirical way, and which differs from other empirical sciences only by its generality. I do not know whether such a discipline actually exists (some cynics claim that it is customary in philosophy to baptize unborn children); but I think that in any case metaphysics in this conception is not objectionable to anybody, and has hardly any connections with semantics.

For the most part, however, the term "metaphysical" is used as directly opposed—in one sense or another—to the term "empirical"; at any rate, it is used in this way by those people who are distressed by the thought that any metaphysical elements might have managed to creep into science. This general conception of metaphysics assumes several more specific forms.

Thus, some people take it to be symptomatic of a metaphysical element in a science when methods of inquiry are employed which are neither deductive nor empirical. However, no trace of this symptom can be found in the development of semantics (unless some metaphysical elements are involved in the object language to which the semantic notions refer). In particular, the semantics of formalized languages is constructed in a purely deductive way.

Others maintain that the metaphysical character of a science depends mainly on its vocabulary and, more specifically, on its primitive terms. Thus, a term is said to be metaphysical if it is neither logical nor mathematical, and if it is not associated with an empirical procedure which enables us to decide whether a thing is denoted by this term or not. With respect to such a view of metaphysics it is sufficient to recall that a metalanguage includes only three kinds of undefined terms: (i) terms taken from logic, (ii) terms of the corresponding object language, and (iii) names of expressions in the object language. It is thus obvious that no metaphysical undefined terms occur in the metalanguage (again, unless such terms appear in the object language itself).

There are, however, some who believe that, even if no metaphysical terms occur among the primitive terms of a language, they may be introduced by definitions; namely, by those definitions which fail to provide us with general criteria for deciding whether an object falls under the defined concept. It is argued that the term "true" is of this kind, since no universal criterion of truth follows immediately from the definition of this term, and since it is generally believed (and in a certain sense can even be proved) that such a criterion will never be found. This comment on the actual character of the notion of truth seems to be perfectly just. However, it should be noticed that the notion of truth does not differ in this respect from many notions in logic, mathematics, and theoretical parts of various empirical sciences, e.g., in theoretical physics.

In general, it must be said that if the term "metaphysical" is employed in so wide a sense as to embrace certain notions (or methods) of logic, mathematics, or empirical sciences, it will apply a fortiori to those of semantics. In fact, as we know from part I of the paper, in developing the semantics of a language we use all the notions of this language, and we apply even a stronger logical apparatus than that which is used in the language itself. On the other hand, however, I can summarize the arguments given above by stating that in no interpretation of the term "metaphysical" which is familiar and more or less intelligible to me does semantics involve any metaphysical elements peculiar to itself.

I should like to make one final remark in connection with this group of objections. The history of science shows many instances of concepts which were judged metaphysical (in a loose, but in any case derogatory sense of this term) before their meaning was made precise; however, once they received a rigorous, formal definition, the distrust in them evaporated. As typical examples we may mention the concepts of negative and imaginary numbers in mathematics. I hope a similar fate awaits the concept of truth and other semantic concepts; and it seems to me, therefore, that those who have distrusted them because of their alleged metaphysical implications should welcome the fact that precise definitions of these concepts are now available. If in consequence semantic concepts lose philosophical interest, they will only share the fate of many other concepts of science, and this need give rise to no regret.

20. Applicability of Semantics to Special Empirical Sciences

We come to the last and perhaps the most important group of objections. Some strong doubts have been expressed whether semantic notions find or can find applications in various domains of intellectual activity. For the most part such doubts have concerned the applicability of semantics to the field of empirical science—either to special sciences or to the general methodology of this field; although similar skepticism has been expressed regarding possible applications of semantics to mathematical sciences and their methodology.

I believe that it is possible to allay these doubts to a certain extent, and that some optimism with respect to the potential value of semantics for various domains of thought is not without ground.

To justify this optimism, it suffices I think to stress two rather obvious points. First, the development of a theory which formulates a precise definition of a notion and establishes its general properties provides *eo ipso* a firmer basis for all discussions in which this notion is involved; and, therefore, it cannot be irrelevant for anyone who uses this notion, and desires to do so in a conscious and consistent way. Secondly, semantic notions are actually involved in various branches of science, and in particular of empirical science.

The fact that in empirical research we are concerned only with natural languages and that theoretical semantics applies to these languages only with certain approximation,

does not affect the problem essentially. However, it has undoubtedly this effect that progress in semantics will have but a delayed and somewhat limited influence in this field. The situation with which we are confronted here does not differ essentially from that which arises when we apply laws of logic to arguments in everyday life—or, generally, when we attempt to apply a theoretical science to empirical problems.

Semantic notions are undoubtedly involved, to a larger or smaller degree, in psychology, sociology, and in practically all the humanities. Thus, a psychologist defines the so-called intelligence quotient in terms of the numbers of *true* (right) and *false* (wrong) answers given by a person to certain questions; for a historian of culture the range of objects for which a human race in successive stages of its development possesses adequate *designations* may be a topic of great significance; a student of literature may be strongly interested in the problem whether a given author always uses two given words with the same *meaning*. Examples of this kind can be multiplied indefinitely.

The most natural and promising domain for the applications of theoretical semantics is clearly linguistics—the empirical study of natural languages. Certain parts of this science are even referred to as "semantics," sometimes with an additional qualification. Thus, this name is occasionally given to that portion of grammar which attempts to classify all words of a language into parts of speech, according to what the words mean or designate. The study of the evolution of meanings in the historical development of a language is sometimes called "historical semantics." In general, the totality of investigations on semantic relations which occur in a natural language is referred to as "descriptive semantics." The relation between theoretical and descriptive semantics is analogous to that between pure and applied mathematics, or perhaps to that between theoretical and empirical physics; the role of formalized languages in semantics can be roughly compared to that of isolated systems in physics.

It is perhaps unnecessary to say that

semantics cannot find any direct applications in natural sciences such as physics, biology, etc.; for in none of these sciences are we concerned with linguistic phenomena, and even less with semantic relations between linguistic expressions and objects to which these expressions refer. We shall see, however, in the next section that semantics may have a kind of indirect influence even on those sciences in which semantic notions are not directly involved.

21. Applicability of Semantics to the Methodology of Empirical Science

Besides linguistics, another important domain for possible applications of semantics is the methodology of science; this term is used here in a broad sense so as to embrace the theory of science in general. Independent of whether a science is conceived merely as a system of statements or as a totality of certain statements and human activities, the study of scientific language constitutes an essential part of the methodological discussion of a science. And it seems to me clear that any tendency to eliminate semantic notions (like those of truth and designation) from this discussion would make it fragmentary and inadequate.[33] Moreover, there is no reason for such a tendency today, once the main difficulties in using semantic terms have been overcome. The semantics of scientific language should be simply included as a part in the methodology of science.

I am by no means inclined to charge methodology and, in particular, semantics— whether theoretical or descriptive—with the task of clarifying the meanings of all scientific terms. This task is left to those sciences in which the terms are used, and is actually fulfilled by them (in the same way in which, e.g., the task of clarifying the meaning of the term "*true*" is left to, and fulfilled by, semantics). There may be, however, certain special problems of this sort in which a methodological approach is desirable or indeed necessary (perhaps, the problem of the notion of causality is a good example here); and in a methodological discussion of such problems semantic

notions may play an essential role. Thus, semantics may have some bearing on any science whatsoever.

The question arises whether semantics can be helpful in solving general and, so to speak, classical problems of methodology. I should like to discuss here with some detail a special, though very important, aspect of this question.

One of the main problems of the methodology of empirical science consists in establishing conditions under which an empirical theory or hypothesis should be regarded as acceptable. This notion of acceptability must be relativized to a given stage of the development of a science (or to a given amount of presupposed knowledge). In other words, we may consider it as provided with a time coefficient; for a theory which is acceptable today may become untenable tomorrow as a result of new scientific discoveries.

It seems a priori very plausible that the acceptability of a theory somehow depends on the truth of its sentences, and that consequently a methodologist in his (so far rather unsuccessful) attempts at making the notion of acceptability precise, can expect some help from the semantic theory of truth. Hence we ask the question: Are there any postulates which can be reasonably imposed on acceptable theories and which involve the notion of truth? And, in particular, we ask whether the following postulate is a reasonable one:

> An acceptable theory cannot contain (or imply) any false sentences.

The answer to the last question is clearly negative. For, first of all, we are practically sure, on the basis of our historical experience, that every empirical theory which is accepted today will sooner or later be rejected and replaced by another theory. It is also very probable that the new theory will be incompatible with the old one; i.e., will imply a sentence which is contradictory to one of the sentences contained in the old theory. Hence, at least one of the two theories must include false sentences, in spite of the fact that each of them is accepted at a certain time. Secondly, the postulate in question could hardly ever be satisfied in practice; for we do not know, and are very unlikely to find, any criteria of truth which enable us to show that no sentence of an empirical theory is false.

The postulate in question could be at most regarded as the expression of an ideal limit for successively more adequate theories in a given field of research; but this hardly can be given any precise meaning.

Nevertheless, it seems to me that there is an important postulate which can be reasonably imposed on acceptable empirical theories and which involves the notion of truth. It is closely related to the one just discussed, but is essentially weaker. Remembering that the notion of acceptability is provided with a time coefficient, we can give this postulate the following form:

> As soon as we succeed in showing that an empirical theory contains (or implies) false sentences, it cannot be any longer considered acceptable.

In support of this postulate, I should like to make the following remarks.

I believe everybody agrees that one of the reasons which may compel us to reject an empirical theory is the proof of its inconsistency: a theory becomes untenable if we succeed in deriving from it two contradictory sentences. Now we can ask what are the usual motives for rejecting a theory on such grounds. Persons who are acquainted with modern logic are inclined to answer this question in the following way: A well-known logical law shows that a theory which enables us to derive two contradictory sentences enables us also to derive every sentence; therefore, such a theory is trivial and deprived of any scientific interest.

I have some doubts whether this answer contains an adequate analysis of the situation. I think that people who do not know modern logic are as little inclined to accept an inconsistent theory as those who are thoroughly familiar with it; and probably this applies even to those who regard (as some still do) the logical law on which the argument is based as a highly controversial issue, and almost as a paradox. I do not think that our attitude toward an incon-

sistent theory would change even if we decided for some reasons to weaken our system of logic so as to deprive ourselves of the possibility of deriving every sentence from any two contradictory sentences.

It seems to me that the real reason of our attitude is a different one: We know (if only intuitively) that an inconsistent theory must contain false sentences; and we are not inclined to regard as acceptable any theory which has been shown to contain such sentences.

There are various methods of showing that a given theory includes false sentences. Some of them are based upon purely logical properties of the theory involved; the method just discussed (i.e., the proof of inconsistency) is not the sole method of this type, but is the simplest one, and the one which is most frequently applied in practice. With the help of certain assumptions regarding the truth of empirical sentences, we can obtain methods to the same effect which are no longer of a purely logical nature. If we decide to accept the general postulate suggested above, then a successful application of any such method will make the theory untenable.

22. Applications of Semantics to Deductive Science

As regards the applicability of semantics to mathematical sciences and their methodology, i.e., to metamathematics, we are in a much more favorable position than in the case of empirical sciences. For, instead of advancing reasons which justify some hopes for the future (and thus making a kind of pro-semantics propaganda), we are able to point out concrete results already achieved.

Doubts continue to be expressed whether the notion of a true sentence—as distinct from that of a provable sentence—can have any significance for mathematical disciplines and play any part in a methodological discussion of mathematics. It seems to me, however, that just this notion of a true sentence constitutes a most valuable contribution to metamathematics by semantics. We already possess a series of interesting metamathematical results gained with the help of the theory of truth. These results concern the mutual relations between the notion of truth and that of provability; establish new properties of the latter notion (which, as well known, is one of the basic notions of metamathematics); and throw some light on the fundamental problems of consistency and completeness. The most significant among these results have been briefly discussed in section 12.[34]

Furthermore, by applying the method of semantics we can adequately define several important metamathematical notions which have been used so far only in an intuitive way—such as, e.g., the notion of definability or that of a model of an axiom system; and thus we can undertake a systematic study of these notions. In particular, the investigations on definability have already brought some interesting results, and promise even more in the future.[35]

We have discussed the applications of semantics only to metamathematics, and not to mathematics proper. However, this distinction between mathematics and metamathematics is rather unimportant. For metamathematics is itself a deductive discipline and hence, from a certain point of view, a part of mathematics; and it is well known that—due to the formal character of deductive method—the results obtained in one deductive discipline can be automatically extended to any other discipline in which the given one finds an interpretation. Thus, for example, all metamathematical results can be interpreted as results of number theory. Also from a practical point of view there is no clearcut line between metamathematics and mathematics proper; for instance, the investigations on definability could be included in either of these domains.

23. Final Remarks

I should like to conclude this discussion with some general and rather loose remarks concerning the whole question of the evaluation of scientific achievements in terms of their applicability. I must confess I have various doubts in this connection.

Being a mathematician (as well as a logician, and perhaps a philosopher of a sort), I have had the opportunity to attend many discussions between specialists in mathematics, where the problem of applications is especially acute, and I have noticed on several occasions the following phenomenon: If a mathematician wishes to disparage the work of one of his colleagues, say, A, the most effective method he finds for doing this is to ask where the results can be applied. The hard-pressed man, with his back against the wall, finally unearths the researches of another mathematician B as the locus of the application of his own results. If next B is plagued with a similar question, he will refer to another mathematician C. After a few steps of this kind we find ourselves referred back to the researches of A, and in this way the chain closes.

Speaking more seriously, I do not wish to deny that the value of a man's work may be increased by its implications for the research of others and for practice. But I believe, nevertheless, that it is inimical to the progress of science to measure the importance of any research exclusively or chiefly in terms of its usefulness and applicability. We know from the history of science that many important results and discoveries have had to wait centuries before they were applied in any field. And, in my opinion, there are also other important factors which cannot be disregarded in determining the value of a scientific work. It seems to me that there is a special domain of very profound and strong human needs related to scientific research, which are similar in many ways to aesthetic and perhaps religious needs. And it also seems to me that the satisfaction of these needs should be considered an important task of research. Hence, I believe, the question of the value of any research cannot be adequately answered without taking into account the intellectual satisfaction which the results of that research bring to those who understand it and care for it. It may be unpopular and out-of-date to say—but I do not think that a scientific result which gives us a better understanding of the world and makes it more harmonious in our eyes should be held in lower esteem than, say, an invention which reduces the cost of paving roads, or improves household plumbing.

It is clear that the remarks just made become pointless if the word "application" is used in a very wide and liberal sense. It is perhaps not less obvious that nothing follows from these general remarks concerning the specific topics which have been discussed in this paper; and I really do not know whether research in semantics stands to gain or lose by introducing the standard of value I have suggested.

NOTES

1. Compare Tarski [2] (see Bibliography following Notes). This work may be consulted for a more detailed and formal presentation of the subject of the paper, especially of the material included in sections 6 and 9–13. It contains also references to my earlier publications on the problems of semantics (a communication in Polish, 1930; the article Tarski [1] in French, 1931; a communication in German, 1932; and a book in Polish, 1933). The expository part of the present paper is related in its character to Tarski [3]. My investigations on the notion of truth and on theoretical semantics have been reviewed or discussed in Hofstadter [1], Juhos [1], Kokoszyńska [1] and [2], Kotarbiński [2], Scholz [1], Weinberg [1], et al.

2. It may be hoped that the interest in theoretical semantics will now increase, as a result of the recent publication of the important work Carnap [2].

3. This applies, in particular, to public discussions during the I. International Congress for the Unity of Science (Paris, 1935) and the Conference of International Congresses for the Unity of Science (Paris, 1937); cf., e.g., Neurath [1] and Gonseth [1].

4. The words "notion" and "concept" are used in this paper with all of the vagueness and ambiguity with which they occur in philosophical literature. Thus, sometimes they refer simply to a term, sometimes to what is meant by a term, and in other cases to what is denoted by a term. Sometimes it is irrelevant which of these interpretations is meant; and in certain cases perhaps none of them applies adequately. While on principle I share the tendency to avoid these words in any exact discussion, I did not consider it necessary to do so in this informal presentation.

5. For our present purposes it is somewhat more convenient to understand by "expressions,"

"sentences," etc., not individual inscriptions, but classes of inscriptions of similar form (thus, not individual physical things, but classes of such things).

6. For the Aristotelian formulation see Aristotle [1], γ, 7, 27. The other two formulations are very common in the literature, but I do not know with whom they originate. A critical discussion of various conceptions of truth can be found, e.g., in Kotarbiński [1] (so far available only in Polish), pp. 123ff., and Russell [1], pp. 362ff.

7. For most of the remarks contained in sections 4 and 8, I am indebted to the late S. Leśniewski who developed them in his unpublished lectures in the University of Warsaw (in 1919 and later). However, Leśniewski did not anticipate the possibility of a rigorous development of the theory of truth, and still less of a definition of this notion; hence, while indicating equivalences of the form (T) as premises in the antinomy of the liar, he did not conceive them as any sufficient conditions for an adequate usage (or definition) of the notion of truth. Also the remarks in section 8 regarding the occurrence of an empirical premiss in the antinomy of the liar, and the possibility of eliminating this premiss, do not originate with him.

8. In connection with various logical and methodological problems involved in this paper the reader may consult Tarski [6].

9. The antinomy of the liar (ascribed to Eubulides or Epimenides) is discussed here in sections 7 and 8. For the antinomy of definability (due to J. Richard) see, e.g., Hilbert-Bernays [1], vol. 2, pp. 263ff.; for the antinomy of heterological terms see Grelling-Nelson [1], p. 307.

10. Due to Professor J. Łukasiewicz (University of Warsaw).

11. This can roughly be done in the following way. Let S be any sentence beginning with the words "Every sentence." We correlate with S a new sentence S^* by subjecting S to the following two modifications: we replace in S the first word, "Every," by "The"; and we insert after the second word, "sentence," the whole sentence S enclosed in quotation marks. Let us agree to call the sentence S "(self-)applicable" or "non-(self-)applicable" dependent on whether the correlated sentence S^* is true or false. Now consider the following sentence:

Every sentence is nonapplicable.

It can easily be shown that the sentence just stated must be both applicable and nonapplicable; hence a contradiction. It may not be quite clear in what sense this formulation of the antinomy does not involve an empirical premiss; however, I shall not elaborate on this point.

12. The terms "logic" and "logical" are used in this paper in a broad sense, which has become

almost traditional in the last decades; logic is assumed here to comprehend the whole theory of classes and relations (i.e., the mathematical theory of sets). For many different reasons I am personally inclined to use the term "logic" in a much narrower sense, so as to apply it only to what is sometimes called "elementary logic," i.e., to the sentential calculus and the (restricted) predicate calculus.

13. Cf. here, however, Tarski [3], pp. 5f.

14. The method of construction we are going to outline can be applied—with appropriate changes—to all formalized languages that are known at the present time; although it does not follow that a language could not be constructed to which this method would not apply.

15. In carrying through this idea a certain technical difficulty arises. A sentential function may contain an arbitrary number of free variables; and the logical nature of the notion of satisfaction varies with this number. Thus, the notion in question when applied to functions with one variable is a binary relation between these functions and single objects; when applied to functions with two variables it becomes a ternary relation between functions and couples of objects; and so on. Hence, strictly speaking, we are confronted, not with one notion of satisfaction, but with infinitely many notions; and it turns out that these notions cannot be defined independently of each other, but must all be introduced simultaneously.

To overcome this difficulty, we employ the mathematical notion of an infinite sequence (or, possibly, of a finite sequence with an arbitrary number of terms). We agree to regard satisfaction, not as a many-termed relation between sentential functions and an indefinite number of objects, but as a binary relation between functions and sequences of objects. Under this assumption the formulation of a general and precise definition of satisfaction no longer presents any difficulty; and a true sentence can now be defined as one which is satisfied by every sequence.

16. To define recursively the notion of satisfaction, we have to apply a certain form of recursive definition which is not admitted in the object-language. Hence the "essential richness" of the metalanguage may simply consist in admitting this type of definition. On the other hand, a general method is known which makes it possible to eliminate all recursive definitions and to replace them by normal, explicit ones. If we try to apply this method to the definition of satisfaction, we see that we have either to introduce into the metalanguage variables of a higher logical type than those which occur in the object language; or else to assume axiomatically in the metalanguage the existence of classes that are more comprehensive than all those whose existence can be established in the object-language. See here Tarski [2], pp. 393ff., and Tarski [5], p. 110.

17. Due to the development of modern logic, the notion of mathematical proof has undergone a far-reaching simplification. A sentence of a given formalized discipline is provable if it can be obtained from the axioms of this discipline by applying certain simple and purely formal rules of inference, such as those of detachment and substitution. Hence to show that all provable sentences are true, it suffices to prove that all the sentences accepted as axioms are true, and that the rules of inference when applied to true sentences yield new true sentences; and this usually presents no difficulty.

On the other hand, in view of the elementary nature of the notion of provability, a precise definition of this notion requires only rather simple logical devices. In most cases, those logical devices which are available in the formalized discipline itself (to which the notion of provability is related) are more than sufficient for this purpose. We know, however, that as regards the definition of truth just the opposite holds. Hence, as a rule, the notions of truth and provability cannot coincide; and since every provable sentence is true, there must be true sentences which are not provable.

18. Thus the theory of truth provides us with a general method for consistency proofs for formalized mathematical disciplines. It can be easily realized, however, that a consistency proof obtained by this method may possess some intuitive value—i.e., may convince us, or strengthen our belief, that the discipline under consideration is actually consistent—only in case we succeed in defining truth in terms of a metalanguage which does not contain the object language as a part (cf. here a remark in section 9). For only in this case the deductive assumptions of the metalanguage may be intuitively simpler and more obvious than those of the object-language—even though the condition of "essential richness" will be formally satisfied. Cf. here also Tarski [3], p. 7.

The incompleteness of a comprehensive class of formalized disciplines constitutes the essential content of a fundamental theorem of K. Gödel; cf. Gödel [1], pp. 187ff. The explanation of the fact that the theory of truth leads so directly to Gödel's theorem is rather simple. In deriving Gödel's result from the theory of truth we make an essential use of the fact that the definition of truth cannot be given in a meta-language which is only as "rich" as the object language (cf. note 17); however, in establishing this fact, a method of reasoning has been applied which is very closely related to that used (for the first time) by Gödel. It may be added that Gödel was clearly guided in his proof by certain intuitive considerations regarding the notion of truth, although this notion does not occur in the proof explicitly; cf. Gödel [1], pp. 174f.

19. The notions of designation and definition lead respectively to the antinomies of Grelling-Nelson and Richard (cf. note 9). To obtain an antinomy for the notion of satisfaction, we construct the following expression:

    The sentential function X does not satisfy X.

    A contradiction arises when we consider the question whether this expression, which is clearly a sentential function, satisfies itself or not.

20. All notions mentioned in this section can be defined in terms of satisfaction. We can say, e.g., that a given term designates a given object if this object satisfies the sentential function "x is identical with T" where 'T' stands for the given term. Similarly, a sentential function is said to define a given object if the latter is the only object which satisfies this function. For a definition of consequence see Tarski [4], and for that of synonymity, Carnap [2].

21. General semantics is the subject of Carnap [2]. Cf. here also remarks in Tarski [2], pp. 388f.

22. Cf. various quotations in Ness [1], pp. 13f.

23. The names of persons who have raised objections will not be quoted here, unless their objections have appeared in print.

24. It should be emphasized, however, that as regards the question of an alleged vicious circle the situation would not change even if we took a different point of view, represented, e.g., in Carnap [2]; i.e., if we regarded the specification of conditions under which sentences of a language are true as an essential part of the description of this language. On the other hand, it may be noticed that the point of view represented in the text does not exclude the possibility of using truth-tables in a deductive development of logic. However, these tables are to be regarded then merely as a formal instrument for checking the provability of certain sentences; and the symbols 'T' and 'F' which occur in them and which are usually considered abbreviations of "true" and "false" should not be interpreted in any intuitive way.

25. Cf. Juhos [1]. I must admit that I do not clearly understand von Juhos' objections and do not know how to classify them; therefore, I confine myself here to certain points of a formal character. Von Juhos does not seem to know my definition of truth; he refers only to an informal presentation in Tarski [3] where the definition has not been given at all. If he knew the actual definition, he would have to change his argument. However, I have no doubt that he would discover in this definition some "defects" as well. For he believes he has proved that "on ground of principle it is impossible to give such a definition at all."

26. The phrases "p is true" and "p is the case" (or better "it is true that p" and "it is the case that p") are sometimes used in informal discussions, mainly for stylistic reasons; but they are considered then as synonymous with the sentence represented by 'p'. On the other hand, as far as I understand the situation, the phrases in question cannot be used by von Juhos synonymously with 'p'; for otherwise the replacement of (T) by (T') or (T'') would not constitute any "improvement."

27. Cf. the discussion of this problem in Kokoszyńska [1], pp. 161ff.

28. Most authors who have discussed my work on the notion of truth are of the opinion that my definition does conform with the classical conception of this notion; see, e.g., Kotarbiński [2] and Scholz [1].

29. Cf. Ness [1]. Unfortunately, the results of that part of Ness' research which is especially relevant for our problem are not discussed in his book; compare p. 148, footnote 1.

30. Though I have heard this opinion several times, I have seen it in print only once and, curiously enough, in a work which does not have a philosophical character—in fact, in Hilbert-Bernays [1], vol. II, p. 269 (where, by the way, it is not expressed as any kind of objection). On the other hand, I have not found any remark to this effect in discussions of my work by professional philosophers (cf. note 1).

31. Cf. Gonseth [1], pp. 187f.

32. See Nagel [1], and Nagel [2], pp. 471f. A remark which goes, perhaps, in the same direction is also to be found in Weinberg [1], p. 77; cf., however, his earlier remarks, pp. 75f.

33. Such a tendency was evident in earlier works of Carnap (see, e.g., Carnap [1], especially part V) and in writings of other members of Vienna Circle. Cf. Kokoszyńska [1] and Weinberg [1].

34. For other results obtained with the help of the theory of truth see Gödel [2]; Tarski [2], pp. 401ff.; and Tarski [5], pp. 111f.

35. An object—e.g., a number or a set of numbers—is said to be definable (in a given formalism) if there is a sentential function which defines it; cf. note 20. Thus, the term "definable," though of a metamathematical (semantic) origin, is purely mathematical as to its extension, for it expresses a property (denotes a class) of mathematical objects. In consequence, the notion of definability can be redefined in purely mathematical terms, though not within the formalized discipline to which this notion refers; however, the fundamental idea of the definition remains unchanged. Cf. here—also for further bibliographic references—Tarski [1]; various other results concerning definability can also be found in the literature, e.g., in Hilbert-Bernays [1], vol. I, pp. 354ff., 369ff., 456ff., etc., and in Linden-

baum-Tarski [1]. It may be noticed that the term "definable" is sometimes used in another, metamathematical (but not semantic), sense; this occurs, for instance, when we say that a term is definable in other terms (on the basis of a given axiom system). For a definition of a model of an axiom system see Tarski [4].

BIBLIOGRAPHY

Only the books and articles actually referred to in the paper will be listed here.

Aristotle [1]. *Metaphysica.* (*Works,* vol. VIII.) English translation by W. D. Ross. (Oxford: 1908).

Carnap, R. [1]. *Logical Syntax of Language.* (London and New York: 1937).

—— [2]. *Introduction to Semantics.* (Cambridge: 1942).

Gödel, K. [1]. "Über formal unentscheidbare Sätze der *Principia Mathematica* und verwandter Systeme, I." *Monatshefte für Mathematik und Physik,* XXXVIII (1931), pp. 173–198.

—— [2]. "Über die Länge von Beweisen." *Ergebnisse eines mathematischen Kolloquiums,* vol. VII (1936), pp. 23–24.

Gonseth, F. [1]. "Le Congrès Descartes. Questions de Philosophie scientifique." *Revue thomiste,* vol. XLIV (1938), pp. 183–193.

Grelling, K., and Nelson, L. [1]. "Bemerkungen zu den Paradoxien von Russell und Burali-Forti." *Abhandlungen der Fries'schen Schule,* vol. II (new series), (1908), pp. 301–334.

Hofstadter, A. [1]. "On Semantic Problems." *The Journal of Philosophy,* vol. XXXV (1938), pp. 225–232.

Hilbert, D., and Bernays, P. [1]. *Grundlagen der Mathematik.* 2 vols. (Berlin: 1934–1939).

Juhos, B. von. [1]. "The Truth of Empirical Statements." *Analysis,* vol. IV (1937), pp. 65–70.

Kokoszyńska, M. [1]. "Über den absoluten Wahrheitsbegriff und einige andere semantische Begriffe." *Erkenntnis,* vol. VI (1936), pp. 143–165.

—— [2]. "Syntax, Semantik und Wissenschaftslogik." *Actes du Congrès International de Philosophie Scientifique,* vol. III (Paris: 1936), pp. 9–14.

Kotarbiński, T. [1]. *Elementy teorji poznania, logiki formalnej i metodologji nauk.* (*Elements of Epistemology, Formal Logic, and the Methodology of Sciences,* in Polish.) (Lwów: 1929).

—— [2]. "W sprawie pojęcia prawdy." ("*Concerning the Concept of Truth,*" in Polish.) *Przeglgd filozoficzny,* vol. XXXVII, pp. 85–91.

Lindenbaum, A., and Tarski, A. [1]. "Über die Beschränktheit der Ausdrucksmittel deduktiver Theorien." *Ergebnisse eines mathematischen Kolloquiums,* vol. VII, (1936), pp. 15–23.

Nagel, E. [1]. Review of Hofstadter [1]. *The Journal of Symbolic Logic,* vol. III, (1938), p. 90.

—— [2]. Review of Carnap [2]. *The Journal of Philosophy,* vol. XXXIX, (1942), pp. 468–473.

Ness, A. [1]. " 'Truth' As Conceived by Those Who Are Not Professional Philosophers." *Skrifter utgitt av Det Norske Videnskaps-Akademi i Oslo, II. Hist.-Filos. Klasse,* vol. IV (Oslo: 1938).

Neurath, O. [1]. "Erster Internationaler Kongress für Einheit der Wissenschaft in Paris 1935." *Erkenntnis,* vol. V (1935), pp. 377–406.

Russell, B. [1]. *An Inquiry Into Meaning and Truth.* (New York: 1940).

Scholz, H. [1]. Review of *Studia philosophica,* vol. I. *Deutsche Literaturzeitung,* vol. LVIII (1937), pp. 1914–1917.

Tarski, A. [1]. "Sur les ensembles définissables de nombres réels. I." *Fundamenta mathematicae,* vol. XVII (1931), pp. 210–239.

—— [2]. "Der Wahrheitsbegriff in den formalisierten Sprachen." (German translation of a book in Polish, 1933.) *Studia philosophica,* vol. I (1935), pp. 261–405.

——. [3]. "Grundlegung der wissenschaftlichen Semantik." *Actes du Congrès International de Philosophie Scientifique,* vol. III (Paris: 1936), pp. 1–8.

—— [4]. "Über den Begriff der logischen Folgerung." *Actes du Congrès International de Philosophie Scientifique,* vol. VII (Paris: 1937), pp. 1–11.

—— [5]. "On Undecidable Statements in Enlarged Systems of Logic and the Concept of Truth." *The Journal of Symbolic Logic,* vol. IV, 1939, pp. 105–112.

—— [6]. *Introduction to Logic.* (New York: 1941).

Weinberg, J. [1]. Review of *Studia philosophica,* vol. I. *The Philosophical Review,* vol. XLVII, pp. 70–77.

Meaning   5

H. P. GRICE

Consider the following sentences:

"Those spots mean (meant) measles."

"Those spots didn't mean anything to me, but to the doctor they meant measles."

"The recent budget means that we shall have a hard year."

(1) I cannot say, "Those spots meant measles, but he hadn't got measles," and I cannot say, "The recent budget means that we shall have a hard year, but we shan't have." That is to say, in cases like the above, *x meant that p* and *x means that p* entail *p*.

(2) I cannot argue from "Those spots mean (meant) measles" to any conclusion about "what is (was) meant by those spots"; for example, I am not entitled to say, "What was meant by those spots was that he had measles." Equally I cannot draw from the statement about the recent budget the conclusion "What is meant by the recent budget is that we shall have a hard year."

(3) I cannot argue from "Those spots meant measles" to any conclusion to the effect that somebody or other meant by those spots so-and-so. *Mutatis mutandis,* the same is true of the sentence about the recent budget.

(4) For none of the above examples can a restatement be found in which the verb "mean" is followed by a sentence or phrase in inverted commas. Thus "Those spots meant measles" cannot be reformulated as "Those spots meant 'measles' " or "Those spots meant 'he has measles.' "

(5) On the other hand, for all these examples an approximate restatement can be found beginning with the phrase "The fact that . . ."; for example, "The fact that he had those spots meant that he had measles" and "The fact that the recent budget was as it was means that we shall have a hard year."

Now contrast the above sentences with the following:

"Those three rings on the bell (of the bus) mean that the 'bus is full.' "

"That remark, 'Smith couldn't get on without his trouble and strife,' meant that Smith found his wife indispensable."

(1) I can use the first of these and go on to say, "But it isn't in fact full—the conductor has made a mistake"; and I can use the second and go on, "But in fact Smith deserted her seven years ago." That is to say, here *x means that p* and *x meant that p* do not entail *p*.

(2) I can argue from the first to some statement about "what is (was) meant" by the rings on the bell and from the second to some statement about "what is (was) meant" by the quoted remark.

(3) I can argue from the first sentence to the conclusion that somebody (viz., the con-

From *Philosophical Review*, volume 66 (1957), pp. 377–388.

ductor) meant, or at any rate should have meant, by the rings that the bus is full, and I can argue analogously for the second sentence.

(4) The first sentence can be restated in a form in which the verb "mean" is followed by a phrase in inverted commas, that is, "Those three rings on the bell mean 'the bus is full.' " So also can the second sentence.

(5) Such a sentence as "The fact that the bell has been rung three times means that the bus is full" is not a restatement of the meaning of the first sentence. Both may be true, but they do not have, even approximately, the same meaning.

When the expressions "means," "means something," "means that" are used in the kind of way in which they are used in the first set of sentences, I shall speak of the sense, or senses, in which they are used, as the *natural* sense, or senses, of the expressions in question. When the expressions are used in the kind of way in which they are used in the second set of sentences, I shall speak of the sense, or senses, in which they are used, as the *nonnatural* sense, or senses, of the expressions in question. I shall use the abbreviation "means$_{NN}$" to distinguish the nonnatural sense or senses.

I propose, for convenience, also to include under the head of natural senses of "mean" such senses of "mean" as may be exemplified in sentences of the pattern "A means (meant) *to do* so-and-so (by x)," where A is a human agent. By contrast, as the previous examples show, I include under the head of nonnatural senses of "mean" any senses of "mean" found in sentences of the patterns "A means (meant) something by x" or "A means (meant) by x that. . . ." (This is overrigid; but it will serve as an indication.)

I do not want to maintain that *all* our uses of "mean" fall easily, obviously, and tidily into one of the two groups I have distinguished; but I think that in most cases we should be at least fairly strongly inclined to assimilate a use of "mean" to one group rather than to the other. The question which now arises is this: "What more can be said about the distinction between the cases where we should say that the word is applied in a natural sense and the cases where we should say that the word is applied in a nonnatural sense?" Asking this

question will not of course prohibit us from trying to give an explanation of "meaning$_{NN}$" in terms of one or another natural sense of "mean."

This question about the distinction between natural and nonnatural meaning is, I think, what people are getting at when they display an interest in a distinction between "natural" and "conventional" signs. But I think my formulation is better. For some things which can mean$_{NN}$ something are not signs (e.g., words are not), and some are not conventional in any ordinary sense (e.g., certain gestures); while some things which mean naturally are not signs of what they mean (cf. the recent budget example).

I want first to consider briefly, and reject, what I might term a causal type of answer to the question, "What is meaning$_{NN}$?" We might try to say, for instance, more or less with C. L. Stevenson,[1] that for x to mean$_{NN}$ something, x must have (roughly) a tendency to produce in an audience some attitude (cognitive or otherwise) and a tendency, in the case of a speaker, to *be* produced *by* that attitude, these tendencies being dependent on "an elaborate process of conditioning attending the use of the sign in communication"[2] This clearly will not do.

(1) Let us consider a case where an utterance, if it qualifies at all as meaning$_{NN}$ something, will be of a descriptive or informative kind and the relevant attitude, therefore, will be a cognitive one, for example, a belief. (I use "utterance" as a neutral word to apply to any candidate for meaning$_{NN}$; it has a convenient act-object ambiguity.) It is no doubt the case that many people have a tendency to put on a tail coat when they think they are about to go to a dance, and it is also no doubt the case that many people, on seeing someone put on a tail coat, would conclude that the person in question was about to go to a dance. Does this satisfy us that putting on a tail coat means$_{NN}$ that one is about to go to a dance (or indeed means$_{NN}$ anything at all)? Obviously not. It is no help to refer to the qualifying phrase "dependent on an elaborate process of conditioning. . . ." For if all this means is that the response to the sight of a tail coat being put on is in some way learned or acquired, it will not exclude the present case

from being one of meaning$_{NN}$. But if we have to take seriously the second part of the qualifying phrase ("attending the use of the sign in communication"), then the account of meaning$_{NN}$ is obviously circular. We might just as well say, "X has meaning$_{NN}$ if it is used in communication," which, though true, is not helpful.

(2) If this is not enough, there is a difficulty—really the same difficulty, I think—which Stevenson recognizes: how we are to avoid saying, for example, that "Jones is tall" is part of what is meant by "Jones is an athlete," since to tell someone that Jones is an athlete would tend to make him believe that Jones is tall. Stevenson here resorts to invoking linguistic rules, namely, a permissive rule of language that "athletes may be nontall." This amounts to saying that we are not prohibited by rule from speaking of "nontall athletes." But why are we not prohibited? Not because it is not bad grammar, or is not impolite, and so on, but presumably because it is not meaningless (or, if this is too strong, does not in any way violate the rules of meaning for the expressions concerned). But this seems to involve us in another circle. Moreover, one wants to ask why, if it is legitimate to appeal here to rules to distinguish what is meant from what is suggested, this appeal was not made earlier, in the case of groans, for example, to deal with which Stevenson originally introduced the qualifying phrase about dependence on conditioning.

A further deficiency in a causal theory of the type just expounded seems to be that, even if we accept it as it stands, we are furnished with an analysis only of statements about the *standard* meaning, or the meaning in general, of a "sign." No provision is made for dealing with statements about what a particular speaker or writer means by a sign on a particular occasion (which may well diverge from the standard meaning of the sign); nor is it obvious how the theory could be adapted to make such provision. One might even go further in criticism and maintain that the causal theory ignores the fact that the meaning (in general) of a sign needs to be explained in terms of what users of the sign do

(or should) mean by it on particular occasions; and so the latter notion, which is unexplained by the causal theory, is in fact the fundamental one. I am sympathetic to this more radical criticism, though I am aware that the point is controversial.

I do not propose to consider any further theories of the "causal-tendency" type. I suspect no such theory could avoid difficulties analogous to those I have outlined without utterly losing its claim to rank as a theory of this type.

I will now try a different and, I hope, more promising line. If we can elucidate the meaning of

"x meant$_{NN}$ something (on a particular occasion)" and

"x meant$_{NN}$ that so-and-so (on a particular occasion)"

and of

"A meant$_{NN}$ something by x (on a particular occasion)" and

"A meant$_{NN}$ by x that so-and-so (on a particular occasion),"

this might reasonably be expected to help us with

"x means$_{NN}$ (timeless) something (that so-and-so),"

"A means$_{NN}$ (timeless) by x something (that so-and-so),"

and with the explication of "means the same as," "understands," "entails," and so on. Let us for the moment pretend that we have to deal only with utterances which might be informative or descriptive.

A first shot would be to suggest that "x meant$_{NN}$ something" would be true if x was intended by its utterer to induce a belief in some "audience" and that to say what the belief was would be to say what x meant$_{NN}$. This will not do. I might leave B's handkerchief near the scene of a murder in order to induce the detective to believe that B was the murderer; but we should not want to say that the handkerchief (or my leaving it there) meant$_{NN}$ anything or that I had meant$_{NN}$ by leaving it that B was the murderer. Clearly we must at least add that, for x to have meant$_{NN}$

anything, not merely must it have been "uttered" with the intention of inducing a certain belief but also the utterer must have intended an "audience" to recognize the intention behind the utterance.

This, though perhaps better, is not good enough. Consider the following cases:

(1) Herod presents Salome with the head of St. John the Baptist on a charger.
(2) Feeling faint, a child lets its mother see how pale it is (hoping that she may draw her own conclusion and help).
(3) I leave the china my daughter has broken lying around for my wife to see.

Here we seem to have cases which satisfy the conditions so far given for meaning$_{NN}$. For example, Herod intended to make Salome believe that John the Baptist was dead and no doubt also intended Salome to recognize that he intended her to believe that St. John the Baptist was dead. Similarly for the other cases. Yet I certainly do not think that we should want to say that we have here cases of meaning$_{NN}$.

What we want to find is the difference between, for example, "deliberately and openly letting someone know" and "telling" and between "getting someone to think" and "telling."

The way out is perhaps as follows. Compare the following two cases:

(1) I show Mr. X a photograph of Mr. Y displaying undue familiarity to Mrs. X.
(2) I draw a picture of Mr. Y behaving in this manner and show it to Mr. X.

I find that I want to deny that in (1) the photograph (or my showing it to Mr. X) meant$_{NN}$ anything at all; while I want to assert that in (2) the picture (or my drawing and showing it) meant$_{NN}$ something (that Mr. Y had been unduly unfamiliar), or at least that I had meant$_{NN}$ by it that Mr. Y had been unduly familiar. What is the difference between the two cases? Surely that in case (1) Mr. X's recognition of my intention to make him believe that there is something between Mr. Y and Mrs. X is (more or less) irrelevant to the production of this effect by the photograph. Mr. X would be led by the photograph at least

to suspect Mrs. X even if instead of showing it to him I had left it in his room by accident; and I (the photograph shower) would not be unaware of this. But it will make a difference to the effect of my picture on Mr. X whether or not he takes me to be intending to inform him (make him believe something) about Mrs. X, and not to be just doodling or trying to produce a work of art.

But now we seem to be landed in a further difficulty if we accept this account. For consider now, say, frowning. If I frown spontaneously, in the ordinary course of events, someone looking at me may well treat the frown as a natural sign of displeasure. But if I frown deliberately (to convey my displeasure), an onlooker may be expected, provided he recognizes my intention, *still* to conclude that I am displeased. Ought we not then to say, since it could not be expected to make any difference to the onlooker's reaction whether he regards my frown as spontaneous or as intended to be informative, that my frown (deliberate) does *not* mean$_{NN}$ anything? I think this difficulty can be met; for though in general a deliberate frown may have the same effect (as regards inducing belief in my displeasure) as a spontaneous frown, it can be expected to have the same effect only *provided* the audience takes it as intended to convey displeasure. That is, if we take away the recognition of intention, leaving the other circumstances (including the recognition of the frown as deliberate), the belief-producing tendency of the frown must be regarded as being impaired or destroyed.

Perhaps we may sum up what is necessary for A to mean something by x as follows. A must intend to induce by x a belief in an audience, and he must also intend his utterance to be recognized as so intended. But these intentions are not independent; the recognition is intended by A to play its part in inducing the belief, and if it does not do so something will have gone wrong with the fulfillment of A's intentions. Moreover, A's intending that the recognition should play this part implies, I think, that he assumes that there is some chance that it will in fact play this part, that he does not regard it as a foregone conclusion that the belief will be induced in the audience whether or not the intention behind the utterance is recognized. Shortly, perhaps, we may say that "A meant$_{NN}$ something by x" is roughly equivalent to "A uttered x with the intention of inducing a belief by means of the recognition of this intention." (This seems to involve a reflexive paradox, but it does not really do so.)

Now perhaps it is time to drop the pretense that we have to deal only with "informative" cases. Let us start with some examples of imperatives or quasi-imperatives. I have a very avaricious man in my room, and I want him to go; so I throw a pound note out of the window. Is there here any utterance with a meaning$_{NN}$? No, because in behaving as I did, I did not intend his recognition of my purpose to be in any way effective in getting him to go. This is parallel to the photograph case. If on the other hand I had pointed to the door or given him a little push, then my behavior might well be held to constitute a meaningful$_{NN}$ utterance, just because the recognition of my intention would be intended by me to be effective in speeding his departure. Another pair of cases would be (1) a policeman who stops a car by standing in its way and (2) a policeman who stops a car by waving.

Or, to turn briefly to another type of case, if as an examiner I fail a man, I may well cause him distress or indignation or humiliation; and if I am vindictive, I may intend this effect and even intend him to recognize my intention. But I should not be inclined to say that my failing him meant$_{NN}$ anything. On the other hand, if I cut someone in the street I do feel inclined to assimilate this to the cases of meaning$_{NN}$, and this inclination seems to me dependent on the fact that I could not reasonably expect him to be distressed (indignant, humiliated) unless he recognized my intention to affect him in this way. (Cf., if my college stopped my salary altogether I should accuse them of ruining me; if they cut it by 2/6^d I might accuse them of insulting me; with some intermediate amounts I might not know quite what to say.)

Perhaps then we may make the following generalizations:

(1) "A meant$_{NN}$ something by x" is (roughly) equivalent to "A intended the utterance of x to produce some effect in an audience by means of the recognition of this intention"; and we may add to that to ask what A meant is to ask for a specification of the intended effect (though, of course, it may not always be possible to get a straight answer involving a "that" clause, for example, "a belief that . . .").

(2) "x meant something" is (roughly) equivalent to "Somebody meant$_{NN}$ something by x." Here again there will be cases where this will not quite work. I feel inclined to say that (as regards traffic lights) the change to red meant$_{NN}$ that the traffic was to stop; but it would be very unnatural to say, "Somebody (e.g., the Corporation) meant$_{NN}$ by the red-light change that the traffic was to stop." Nevertheless, there seems to be *some* sort of reference to somebody's intentions.

(3) "x means$_{NN}$ (timeless) that so-and-so" might as a first shot be equated with some statement of disjunction of statements about what "people" (vague) intend (with qualifications about "recognition") to effect by x. I shall have a word to say about this.

Will any kind of intended effect do, or may there be cases where any effect is intended (with the required qualifications) and yet we should not want to talk of meaning$_{NN}$? Suppose I discovered some person so constituted that, when I told him that whenever I grunted in a special way I wanted him to blush or to incur some physical malady, thereafter whenever he recognized the grunt (and with it my intention), he did blush or incur the malady. Should we then want to say that the grunt meant$_{NN}$ something? I do not think so. This points to the fact that for x to have meaning$_{NN}$, the intended effect must be something which in some sense is within the control of the audience, or that in some sense of "reason" the recognition of the intention behind x is for the audience a reason and not merely a cause. It might look as if there is a sort of pun here ("reason for believing" and "reason for doing"), but I do not think this is serious. For though no doubt from one point of view questions about reasons for believing are questions about evidence and so quite different from questions about reasons for doing, nevertheless to recognize an utterer's intention in uttering x (descriptive utterance), to have a reason for believing that so-and-so, is at least quite like "having a motive for" accepting so-and-so. Decisions "that" seem to involve decisions "to" (and this is why we can "refuse to believe" and also be "compelled to believe"). (The "cutting" case needs slightly different treatment, for one cannot in any straightforward sense "decide" to be offended; but one can refuse to be offended.) It looks then as if the intended effect must be something with the control of the audience, or at least the *sort* of thing which is within its control.

One point before passing to an objection or two. I think it follows that from what I have said about the connection between meaning$_{NN}$ and recognition of intention that (insofar as I am right) only what I may call the primary intention of an utterer is relevant to the meaning$_{NN}$ of an utterance. For if I utter x, intending (with the aid of the recognition of this intention) to induce an effect E, and intend this effect E to lead to a further effect F, then insofar as the occurrence of F is thought to be dependent solely on E, I cannot regard F as in the least dependent on recognition of my intention to induce E. That is, if (say) I intend to get a man to do something by giving him some information, it cannot be regarded as relevant to the meaning$_{NN}$ of my utterance to describe what I intend him to do.

Now some question may be raised about my use, fairly free, of such words as "intention" and "recognition." I must disclaim any intention of peopling all our talking life with armies of complicated psychological occurrences. I do not hope to solve any philosophical puzzles about intending, but I do want briefly to argue that no special difficulties are raised by my use of the word "intention" in connection with meaning. First, there will be cases where an utterance is accompanied or preceded by a conscious "plan" or explicit formulation of intention (e.g., I declare how I am going to use x, or ask myself how to "get something across"). The presence of such an explicit "plan" obviously counts fairly heavily in favor of the utterer's intention (meaning) being as "planned"; though it is not, I think, conclusive; for example, a speaker who has declared

an intention to use a familiar expression in an unfamiliar way may slip into the familiar use. Similarly in nonlinguistic cases: if we are asking about an agent's intention, a previous expression counts heavily; nevertheless, a man might plan to throw a letter in the dustbin and yet take it to the post; when lifting his hand he might "come to" and say *either* "I didn't intend to do this at all" *or* "I suppose I must have been intending to put it in."

Explicitly formulated linguistic (or quasi-linguistic) intentions are no doubt comparatively rare. In their absence we would seem to rely on very much the same kinds of criteria as we do in the case of nonlinguistic intentions where there is a general usage. An utterer is held to intend to convey what is normally conveyed (or normally intended to be conveyed), and we require a good reason for accepting that a particular use diverges from the general usage (e.g., he never knew or had forgotten the general usage). Similarly in nonlinguistic cases: we are presumed to intend the normal consequences of our actions.

Again, in cases where there is doubt, say, about which of two or more things an utterer intends to convey, we tend to refer to the context (linguistic or otherwise) of the utterance and ask which of the alternatives would be relevant to other things he is saying or doing, or which intention in a particular situation would fit in with some purpose he obviously has (e.g., a man who calls for a "pump" at a fire would not want a bicycle pump). Nonlinguistic parallels are obvious: context is a criterion in settling the question of why a man who has just put a cigarette in his mouth has put his hand in his pocket; relevance to an obvious end is a criterion in settling why a man is running away from a bull.

In certain linguistic cases we ask the utterer afterward about his intention, and in a few of these cases (the very difficult ones, like a philosopher asked to explain the meaning of an unclear passage in one of his works), the answer is not based on what he remembers but is more like a decision, a decision about how what he said is to be taken. I cannot find a nonlinguistic parallel here; but the case is so special as not to seem to contribute a vital difference.

All this is very obvious; but surely to show that the criteria for judging linguistic intentions are very like the criteria for judging nonlinguistic intentions is to show that linguistic intentions are very like nonlinguistic intentions.

NOTES

1. *Ethics and Language* (New Haven: 1944), ch. 3.
2. *Ibid.*, p. 57.

Truth and Meaning   6

DONALD DAVIDSON

It is conceded by most philosophers of language, and recently even by some linguists, that a satisfactory theory of meaning must give an account of how the meanings of sentences depend upon the meanings of words. Unless such an account could be supplied for a particular language, it is argued, there would be no explaining the fact that we can learn the language: no explaining the fact that, on mastering a finite vocabulary and a finitely stated set of rules, we are prepared to produce and to understand any of a potential infinitude of sentences. I do not dispute these vague claims, in which I sense more than a kernel of truth.[1] Instead I want to ask what it is for a theory to give an account of the kind adumbrated.

One proposal is to begin by assigning some entity as meaning to each word (or other significant syntactical feature) of the sentence; thus we might assign Theaetetus to "Theaetetus" and the property of flying to "flies" in the sentence "Theaetetus flies." The problem then arises how the meaning of the sentence is generated from these meanings. Viewing concatenation as a significant piece of syntax, we may assign to it the relation of participating in or instantiating; however, it is obvious that we have here the start of an infinite regress. Frege sought to avoid the regress by saying that the entities corresponding to predicates (for example) are 'unsaturated' or 'incom-plete' in contrast to the entities that correspond to names, but this doctrine seems to label a difficulty rather than solve it.

The point will emerge if we think for a moment of complex singular terms, to which Frege's theory applies along with sentences. Consider the expression "the father of Annette"; how does the meaning of the whole depend on the meaning of the parts? The answer would seem to be that the meaning of "the father of" is such that when this expression is prefixed to a singular term the result refers to the father of the person to whom the singular term refers. What part is played, in this account, by the unsaturated or incomplete entity for which "the father of" stands? All we can think to say is that this entity 'yields' or 'gives' the father of x as value when the argument is x, or perhaps that this entity maps people onto their fathers. It may not be clear whether the entity for which "the father of" is said to stand performs any genuine explanatory function as long as we stick to individual expressions; so think instead of the infinite class of expressions formed by writing "the father of" zero or more times in front of "Annette." It is easy to supply a theory that tells, for an arbitrary one of these singular terms, what it refers to: if the term is "Annette" it refers to Annette, while if the term is complex, consisting of "the father of" prefixed to a singular term t, then it refers to

From *Synthese*, 17 (1967), pp. 304–323. © D. Reidel Publishing Co., Dordrecht, Holland.

the father of the person to whom t refers. It is obvious that no entity corresponding to "the father of" is, or needs to be, mentioned in stating this theory.

It would be inappropriate to complain that this little theory *uses* the words "the father of" in giving the reference of expressions containing those words. For the task was to give the meaning of all expressions in a certain infinite set on the basis of the meaning of the parts; it was not in the bargain also to give the meanings of the atomic parts. On the other hand, it is now evident that a satisfactory theory of the meanings of complex expressions may not require entities as meanings of all the parts. It behooves us then to rephrase our demand on a satisfactory theory of meaning so as not to suggest that individual words must have meanings at all, in any sense that transcends the fact that they have a systematic effect on the meanings of the sentences in which they occur. Actually, for the case at hand we can do better still in stating the criterion of success: what we wanted, and what we got, is a theory that entails every sentence of the form "t refers to x" where 't' is replaced by a structural description[2] of a singular term, and 'x' is replaced by that term itself. Further, our theory accomplishes this without appeal to any semantical concepts beyond the basic "refers to." Finally, the theory clearly suggests an effective procedure for determining, for any singular term in its universe, what that term refers to.

A theory with such evident merits deserves wider application. The device proposed by Frege to this end has a brilliant simplicity: count predicates as a special case of functional expressions, and sentences as a special case of complex singular terms. Now, however, a difficulty looms if we want to continue in our present (implicit) course of identifying the meaning of a singular term with its reference. The difficulty follows upon making two reasonable assumptions: that logically equivalent singular terms have the same reference; and that a singular term does not change its reference if a contained singular term is replaced by another with the same reference. But now suppose that 'R' and 'S' abbreviate

any two sentences alike in truth value. Then the following four sentences have the same reference:

(1) R
(2) $\hat{x}(x=x.R)=\hat{x}(x=x)$
(3) $\hat{x}(x=x.S)=\hat{x}(x=x)$
(4) S

For (1) and (2) are logically equivalent, as are (3) and (4), while (3) differs from (2) only in containing the singular term '$\hat{x}(x=x.S)$' where (2) contains '$\hat{x}(x=x.R)$' and these refer to the same thing if S and R are alike in truth value. Hence any two sentences have the same reference if they have the same truth value.[3] And if the meaning of a sentence is what it refers to, all sentences alike in truth value must be synonymous—an intolerable result.

Apparently we must abandon the present approach as leading to a theory of meaning. This is the natural point at which to turn for help to the distinction between meaning and reference. The trouble, we are told, is that questions of reference are, in general, settled by extralinguistic facts, questions of meaning not, and the facts can conflate the references of expressions that are not synonymous. If we want a theory that gives the meaning (as distinct from reference) of each sentence, we must start with the meaning (as distinct from reference) of the parts.

Up to here we have been following in Frege's footsteps; thanks to him, the path is well known and even well worn. But now, I would like to suggest, we have reached an impasse: the switch from reference to meaning leads to no useful account of how the meanings of sentences depend upon the meanings of the words (or other structural features) that compose them. Ask, for example, for the meaning of "Theaetetus flies." A Fregean answer might go something like this: given the meaning of "Theaetetus" as argument, the meaning of "flies" yields the meaning of "Theaetetus flies" as value. The vacuity of this answer is obvious. We wanted to know what the meaning of "Theaetetus flies" is; it is no progress to be told that it is the meaning of "Theaetetus flies." This much we knew before any theory was in sight. In the bogus account just given, talk of the structure of the sentence and of the meanings of words was idle, for it played no role in producing the given description of the meaning of the sentence.

The contrast here between a real and pretended account will be plainer still if we ask for a theory, analogous to the miniature theory of reference of singular terms just sketched, but different in dealing with meanings in place of references. What analogy demands is a theory that has as consequences all sentences of the form "*s* means *m*" where '*s*' is replaced by a structural description of a sentence and '*m*' is replaced by a singular term that refers to the meaning of that sentence; a theory, moreover, that provides an effective method for arriving at the meaning of an arbitrary sentence structurally described. Clearly some more articulate way of referring to meanings than any we have seen is essential if these criteria are to be met.[4] Meanings as entities, or the related concept of synonymy, allow us to formulate the following rule relating sentences and their parts: sentences are synonymous whose corresponding parts are synonymous ("corresponding" here needs spelling out of course). And meanings as entities may, in theories such as Frege's, do duty, on occasion as references, thus losing their status as entities distinct from references. Paradoxically, the one thing meanings do not seem to do is oil the wheels of a theory of meaning—at least as long as we require of such a theory that it nontrivially give the meaning of every sentence in the language. My objection to meanings in the theory of meaning is not that they are abstract or that their identity conditions are obscure, but that they have no demonstrated use.

This is the place to scotch another hopeful thought. Suppose we have a satisfactory theory of syntax for our language, consisting of an effective method of telling, for an arbitrary expression, whether or not it is independently meaningful (i.e., a sentence), and assume as usual that this involves viewing each sentence as composed, in allowable ways, out of elements drawn from a fixed finite stock of atomic syntactical elements (roughly, words). The hopeful thought is that syntax, so conceived, will yield semantics when a dictionary giving the meaning of each syntactic atom is added. Hopes will be dashed, however, if semantics is to comprise a theory of meaning in our sense, for knowledge of the structural characteristics that make for meaningfulness in a sentence, plus knowledge of the meanings of the ultimate parts, does not add up to knowledge of what a sentence means. The point is easily illustrated by belief sentences. Their syntax is relatively unproblematic. Yet, adding a dictionary does not touch the standard semantic problem, which is that we cannot account for even as much as the truth conditions of such sentences on the basis of what we know of the meanings of the words in them. The situation is not radically altered by refining the dictionary to indicate which meaning or meanings an ambiguous expression bears in each of its possible contexts; the problem of belief sentences persists after ambiguities are resolved.

The fact that recursive syntax with dictionary added is not necessarily recursive semantics has been obscured in some recent writing on linguistics by the intrusion of semantic criteria into the discussion of purportedly syntactic theories. The matter would boil down to a harmless difference over terminology if the semantic criteria were clear; but they are not. While there is agreement that it is the central task of semantics to give the semantic interpretation (the meaning) of every sentence in the language, nowhere in the linguistic literature will one find, so far as I know, a straightforward account of how a theory performs this task, or how to tell when it has been accomplished. The contrast with syntax is striking. The main job of a modest syntax is to characterize *meaningfulness* (or sentencehood). We may have as much confidence in the correctness of such a characterization as we have in the representativeness of our sample and our ability to say when particular expressions are meaningful (sentences). What clear and analogous task and test exist for semantics?[5]

We decided a while back not to assume that parts of sentences have meanings except in the ontologically neutral sense of making a systematic contribution to the meaning of the sentences in which they occur. Since postulating meanings has netted nothing, let us return to that insight. One direction in which it points is a certain holistic view of meaning. If sentences depend for their meaning on their structure, and we understand the meaning of each item in the structure only as an abstraction from the totality of sentences in which it features, then we can give the meaning of any sentence (or word) only by giving the meaning of every sentence (and word) in the language. Frege said that only in the context of a sentence does a word have meaning; in the same vein he might have added that only in the context of the language does a sentence (and therefore a word) have meaning.

This degree of holism was already implicit in the suggestion that an adequate theory of meaning must entail *all* sentences of the form "*s* means *m*." But now, having found no more help in meanings of sentences than in meanings of words, let us ask whether we can get rid of the troublesome singular terms supposed to replace '*m*' and to refer to meanings. In a way, nothing could be easier: just write "*s* means that *p*," and imagine '*p*' replaced by a sentence. Sentences, as we have seen, cannot name meanings, and sentences with "that" prefixed are not names at all, unless we decide so. It looks as though we are in trouble on another count, however, for it is reasonable to expect that in wrestling with the logic of the apparently nonextensional "means that" we will encounter problems as hard as, or perhaps identical with, the problems our theory is out to solve.

The only way I know to deal with this difficulty is simple, and radical. Anxiety that we are enmeshed in the intensional springs from using the words "means that" as filling between description of sentence and sentence, but it may be that the success of our venture depends not on the filling but on what it fills. The theory will have done its work if it provides, for every sentence *s* in the language under study, a matching sentence (to replace

'*p*') that, in some way yet to be made clear, 'gives the meaning' of *s*. One obvious candidate for matching sentence is just *s* itself, if the object language is contained in the metalanguage; otherwise a translation of *s* in the metalanguage. As a final bold step, let us try treating the position occupied by '*p*' extensionally: to implement this, sweep away the obscure "means that," provide the sentence that replaces '*p*' with a proper sentential connective, and supply the description that replaces '*s*' with its own predicate. The plausible result is

(*T*)   *s* is *T* if and only if *p*.

What we require of a theory of meaning for a language *L* is that without appeal to any (further) semantical notions it place enough restrictions on the predicate "is *T*" to entail all sentences got from schema *T* when '*s*' is replaced by a structural description of a sentence of *L* and '*p*' by that sentence.

Any two predicates satisfying this condition have the same extension,[6] so if the metalanguage is rich enough, nothing stands in the way of putting what I am calling a theory of meaning into the form of an explicit definition of a predicate "is *T*." But whether explicitly defined or recursively characterized, it is clear that the sentences to which the predicate "is *T*" applies will be just the true sentences of *L*, for the condition we have placed on satisfactory theories of meaning is in essence Tarski's Convention *T* that tests the adequacy of a formal semantical definition of truth.[7]

The path to this point has been tortuous, but the conclusion may be stated simply: a theory of meaning for a language *L* shows "how the meanings of sentences depend upon the meanings of words" if it contains a (recursive) definition of truth-in-L. And, so far at least, we have no other idea how to turn the trick. It is worth emphasizing that the concept of truth played no ostensible role in stating our original problem. That problem, upon refinement, led to the view that an adequate theory of meaning must characterize a predicate meeting certain conditions. It was in the nature of a discovery that such a predicate would apply exactly to the true sentences. I hope that what I am doing may be described in part as defending the philosophical importance of Tarski's semantical concept of truth. But my defense is only distantly related, if at all, to the question whether the concept Tarski has shown how to define is the (or a) philosophically interesting conception of truth, or the question whether Tarski has cast any light on the ordinary use of such words as "true" and "truth." It is a misfortune that dust from futile and confused battles over these questions has prevented those with a theoretical interest in language—philosophers, logicians, psychologists, and linguists alike—from recognizing in the semantical concept of truth (under whatever name) the sophisticated and powerful foundation of a competent theory of meaning.

There is no need to suppress, of course, the obvious connection between a definition of truth of the kind Tarski has shown how to construct, and the concept of meaning. It is this: the definition works by giving necessary and sufficient conditions for the truth of every sentence, and to give truth conditions is a way of giving the meaning of a sentence. To know the semantic concept of truth for a language is to know what it is for a sentence—any sentence—to be true, and this amounts, in one good sense we can give to the phrase, to understanding the language. This at any rate is my excuse for a feature of the present discussion that is apt to shock old hands: my freewheeling use of the word "meaning," for what I call a theory of meaning has after all turned out to make no use of meanings, whether of sentences or of words. Indeed since a Tarski-type truth definition supplies all we have asked so far of a theory of meaning, it is clear that such a theory falls comfortably within what Quine terms the "theory of reference" as distinguished from what he terms the "theory of meaning." So much to the good for what I call a theory of meaning, and so much, perhaps, against my so calling it.[8]

A theory of meaning (in my mildly perverse sense) is an empirical theory, and its ambition it to account for the workings of a natural language. Like any theory, it may be tested by comparing some of its consequences with the facts. In the present case this is easy, for the theory has been characterized as issuing in an infinite flood of sentences each giving the truth conditions of a sentence; we only need to ask, in selected cases, whether what the theory avers to be the truth conditions for a sentence really are. A typical test case might involve deciding whether the sentence "Snow is white" *is* true if and only if snow is white. Not all cases will be so simple (for reasons to be sketched), but it is evident that this sort of test does not invite counting noses. A sharp conception of what constitutes a theory in this domain furnishes an exciting context for raising deep questions about when a theory of language is correct and how it is to be tried. But the difficulties are theoretical, not practical. In application, the trouble is to get a theory that comes close to working; anyone can tell whether it is right.[9] One can see why this is so. The theory reveals nothing new about the conditions under which an individual sentence is true; it does not make those conditions any clearer than the sentence itself does. The work of the theory is in relating the known truth conditions of each sentence to those aspects ('words') of the sentence that recur in other sentences, and can be assigned identical roles in other sentences. Empirical power in such a theory depends on success in recovering the structure of a very complicated ability—the ability to speak and understand a language. We can tell easily enough when particular pronouncements of the theory comport with our understanding of the language; this is consistent with a feeble insight into the design of the machinery of our linguistic accomplishments.

The remarks of the last paragraph apply directly only to the special case where it is assumed that the language for which truth is being characterized is part of the language used and understood by the characterizer. Under these circumstances, the framer of a theory will as a matter of course avail himself when he can of the built-in convenience of a metalanguage with a sentence guaranteed equivalent to each sentence in the object language. Still, this fact ought not to con us into thinking a theory any more correct that entails " 'Snow is white' is true if and only if snow is white" than one that entails instead:

(S)   "Snow is white" is true if and only if grass is green,

provided, of course, we are as sure of the truth of (S) as we are of that of its more celebrated predecessor. Yet (S) may not encourage the same confidence that a theory that entails it deserves to be called a theory of meaning.

The threatened failure of nerve may be counteracted as follows. The grotesqueness of (S) is in itself nothing against a theory of which it is a consequence, provided the theory gives the correct results for every sentence (on the basis of its structure, there being no other way). It is not easy to see how (S) could be party to such an enterprise, but if it were—if, that is, (S) followed from a characterization of the predicate "is true" that led to the invariable pairing of truths with truths and falsehoods with falsehoods—then there would not, I think, be anything essential to the idea of meaning that remained to be captured.

What appears to the right of the biconditional in sentences of the form "s is true if and only if p," when such sentences are consequences of a theory of truth, plays its role in determining the meaning of s not by pretending synonymy but by adding one more brushstroke to the picture which, taken as a whole, tells what there is to know of the meaning of s; this stroke is added by virtue of the fact that the sentence that replaces 'p' is true if and only if s is.

It may help to reflect that (S) is acceptable, if it is, because we are independently sure of the truth of "snow is white" and "grass is green"; but in cases where we are unsure of the truth of a sentence, we can have confidence in a characterization of the truth predicate only if it pairs that sentence with one we have good reason to believe equivalent. It would be ill advised for someone who had any doubts about the color of snow or grass to accept a theory that yielded (S), even if his doubts were of equal degree, unless he thought the color of the one was tied to the color of the other. Omniscience can obviously afford more bizarre theories of meaning than ignorance; but then, omniscience has less need of communication.

It must be possible, of course, for the speaker of one language to construct a theory of meaning for the speaker of another, though in this case the empirical test of the correctness of the theory will no longer be trivial. As before, the aim of theory will be an infinite correlation of sentences alike in truth. But this time the theory-builder must not be assumed to have direct insight into likely equivalences between his own tongue and the alien. What he must do is find out, however he can, what sentences the alien holds true in his own tongue (or better, to what degree he holds them true). The linguist then will attempt to construct a characterization of truth-for-the-alien which yields, so far as possible, a mapping of sentences held true (or false) by the alien onto sentences held true (or false) by the linguist. Supposing no perfect fit is found, the residue of sentences held true translated by sentences held false (and vice versa) is the margin for error (foreign or domestic). Charity in interpreting the words and thoughts of others is unavoidable in another direction as well: just as we must maximize agreement, or risk not making sense of what the alien is talking about, so we must maximize the self-consistency we attribute to him, on pain of not understanding *him*. No single principle of optimum charity emerges; the constraints therefore determine no single theory. In a theory of radical translation (as Quine calls it) there is no completely disentangling questions of what the alien means from questions of what he believes. We do not know what someone means unless we know what he believes; we do not know what someone believes unless we know what he means. In radical translation we are able to break into this circle, if only incompletely, because we can sometimes tell that a person accedes to a sentence we do not understand.[10]

In the past few pages I have been asking how a theory of meaning that takes the form of a truth definition can be empirically tested, and have blithely ignored the prior question whether there is any serious chance such a theory can be given for a natural language. What are the prospects for a formal semantical theory of a natural language? Very poor, according to Tarski; and I believe most logicians, philosophers of language, and linguists agree.[11] Let me do what I can to dispel the pessimism. What I can in a general and programmatic way, of course; for here the proof of the pudding will certainly be in the proof of the right theorems.

Tarski concludes the first section of his classic essay on the concept of truth in formalized languages with the following remarks, which he italicizes:

The very possibility of a consistent use of the expression 'true sentence' which is in harmony with the laws of logic and the spirit of everyday language seems to be very questionable, and consequently the same doubt attaches to the possibility of constructing a correct definition of this expression.[12]

Late in the same essay, he returns to the subject:

the concept of truth (as well as other semantical concepts) when applied to colloquial language in conjunction with the normal laws of logic leads inevitably to confusions and contradictions. Whoever wishes, in spite of all difficulties, to pursue the semantics of colloquial language with the help of exact methods will be driven first to undertake the thankless task of a reform of this language. He will find it necessary to define its structure, to overcome the ambiguity of the terms which occur in it, and finally to split the language into a series of languages of greater and greater extent, each of which stands in the same relation to the next in which a formalized language stands to its metalanguage. It may, however be doubted whether the language of everyday life, after being 'rationalized' in this way, would still preserve its naturalness and whether it would not rather take on the characteristic features of the formalized languages.[13]

Two themes emerge: that the universal character of natural languages leads to contradiction (the semantic paradoxes), and that natural languages are too confused and amorphous to permit the direct application of formal methods. The first point deserves a serious answer, and I wish I had one. As it is, I will say only why I think we are justified in carrying on without having disinfected this particular source of conceptual anxiety. The semantic paradoxes arise when the range of the quantifiers in the object language is too generous in certain ways. But it is not really clear how unfair to Urdu or to Hindi it would be to view the range of their quantifiers as insufficient to yield an explicit definition of 'true-in-Urdu' or 'true-in-Hindi'. Or, to put the matter in another, if not more serious way, there may in the nature of the case always be something we grasp in understanding the language of another (the concept of truth) that we cannot communicate to him. In any case, most of the problems of general philosophical interest arise within a fragment of the relevant natural language that may be conceived as containing very little set theory. Of course these comments do not meet the claim that natural languages are universal. But it seems to me this claim, now that we know such universality leads to paradox, is suspect.

Tarski's second point is that we would have to reform a natural language out of all recognition before we could apply formal semantical methods. If this is true, it is fatal to my project, for the task of a theory of meaning as I conceive it is not to change, improve or reform a language, but to describe and understand it. Let us look at the positive side. Tarski has shown the way to giving a theory for interpreted formal languages of various kinds; pick one as much like English as possible. Since this new language has been explained in English and contains much English we not only may, but I think must, view it as part of English for those who understand it. For this fragment of English we have, *ex hypothesi*, a theory of the required sort. Not only that, but in interpreting this adjunct of English in old English we necessarily gave hints connecting old and new. Wherever there are sentences of old English with the same truth conditions as sentences in the adjunct we may extend the theory to cover them. Much of what is called for is just to mechanize as far as possible what we now do by art when we put ordinary English into one or another canonical notation. The point is not that canonical notation is better than the rough original idiom, but rather that if we know what idiom the canonical notation is canonical *for,* we have as good a theory for the idiom as for its kept companion.

Philosophers have long been at the hard work of applying theory to ordinary language by the device of matching sentences in the vernacular with sentences for which they have a theory. Frege's massive contribution was to show how "all," "some," "every," "each," "none," and associated pronouns, in some of their uses, could be tamed; for the first time, it was possible to dream of a formal semantics for a significant part of a natural language. This dream came true in a sharp way with the work of Tarski. It would be a shame to miss the fact that as a result of these two magnificent achievements, Frege's and Tarski's, we have gained a deep insight into the structure of our mother tongues. Philosophers of a logical bent have tended to start where the theory was and work out towards the complications of natural language. Contemporary linguists, with an aim that cannot easily be seen to be different, start with the ordinary and work toward a general theory. If either party is successful, there must be a meeting. Recent work by Chomsky and others is doing much to bring the complexities of natural languages within the scope of serious semantic theory. To give an example: suppose success in giving the truth conditions for some significant range of sentences in the active voice. Then with a formal procedure for transforming each such sentence into a corresponding sentence in the passive voice, the theory of truth could be extended in an obvious way to this new set of sentences.[14]

One problem touched on in passing by Tarski does not, at least in all its manifestations, have to be solved to get ahead with theory: the existence in natural languages of "ambiguous terms." As long as ambiguity does not affect grammatical form, and can be translated, ambiguity for ambiguity, into the metalanguage, a truth definition will not tell us any lies. The trouble, for systematic semantics, with the phrase "believes that" in English is not its vagueness, ambiguity, or unsuitabil-

ity for incorporation in a serious science: let our metalanguage be English, and all *these* problems will be translated without loss or gain into the metalanguage. But the central problem of the logical grammar of "believes that" will remain to haunt us.

The example is suited to illustrating another, and related, point, for the discussion of belief sentences has been plagued by failure to observe a fundamental distinction between tasks: uncovering the logical grammar or form of sentences (which is in the province of a theory of meaning as I construe it), and the analysis of individual words or expressions (which are treated as primitive by the theory). Thus Carnap, in the first edition of *Meaning and Necessity,* suggested we render "John believes that the earth is round" as "John responds affirmatively to 'the earth is round' as an English sentence." He gave this up when Mates pointed out that John might respond affirmatively to one sentence and not to another no matter how close in meaning. But there is a confusion here from the start. The semantic structure of a belief sentence, according to this idea of Carnap's, is given by a three-place predicate with places reserved for expressions referring to a person, a sentence, and a language. It is a different sort of problem entirely to attempt an analysis of this predicate, perhaps along behavioristic lines. Not least among the merits of Tarski's conception of a theory of truth is that the purity of method it demands of us follows from the formulation of the problem itself, not from the self-imposed restraint of some adventitious philosophical puritanism.

I think it is hard to exaggerate the advantages to philosophy of language of bearing in mind this distinction between questions of logical form or grammar, and the analysis of individual concepts. Another example may help advertise the point.

If we suppose questions of logical grammar settled, sentences like "Bardot is good" raise no special problems for a truth definition. The deep differences between descriptive and evaluative (emotive, expressive, etc.) terms do not show here. Even if we hold there is some important sense in which moral or evaluative sentences do not have a truth value (for example, because they cannot be 'verified'), we ought not to boggle at " 'Bardot is good' is true if and only if Bardot is good"; in a theory of truth, this consequence should follow with the rest, keeping track, as must be done, of the semantic location of such sentences in the language as a whole—of their relation to generalizations, their role in such compound sentences as "Bardot is good and Bardot is foolish," and so on. What is special to evaluative words is simply not touched: the mystery is transferred from the word "good" in the object language to its translation in the metalanguage.

But "good" as it features in "Bardot is a good actress" is another matter. The problem is not that the translation of this sentence is not in the metalanguage—let us suppose it is. The problem is to frame a truth definition such that " 'Bardot is a good actress' is true if and only if Bardot is a good actress"—and all other sentences like it—are consequences. Obviously "good actress" does not mean "good and an actress." We might think of taking "is a good actress" as an unanalyzed predicate. This would obliterate all connection between "is a good actress" and "is a good mother," and it would give us no excuse to think of "good," in these uses, as a word or semantic element. But worse, it would bar us from framing a truth definition at all, for there is no end to the predicates we would have to treat as logically simple (and hence accomodate in separate clauses in the definition of satisfaction): "is a good companion to dogs," "is a good 28-years-old conversationalist," and so forth. The problem is not peculiar to the case: it is the problem of attributive adjectives generally.

It is consistent with the attitude taken here to deem it usually a strategic error to undertake philosophical analysis of words or expressions which is not preceded by or at any rate accompanied by the attempt to get the logical grammar straight. For how can we have any confidence in our analyses of words like "right," "ought," "can," and "obliged," or the phrases we use to talk of actions, events, and causes, when we do not know what (logical, semantical) parts of speech we have to deal with? I would say much the same about studies of the 'logic' of these and other words, and the sentences containing them. Whether the effort and ingenuity that has gone into the study of deontic logics, modal logics, imperative and erotetic logics has been largely futile or not cannot be known until we have acceptable semantic analyses of the sentences such systems purport to treat. Philosophers and logicians sometimes talk or work as if they were free to choose between, say, the truth-functional conditional and others, or free to introduce non-truth-functional sentential operators like "Let it be the case that" or "It ought to be the case that." But in fact the decision is crucial. When we depart from idioms we can accomodate in a truth definition, we lapse into (or create) language for which we have no coherent semantical account—that is, no account at all of how such talk can be integrated into the language as a whole.

To return to our main theme: we have recognized that a theory of the kind proposed leaves the whole matter of what individual words mean exactly where it was. Even when the metalanguage is different from the object language, the theory exerts no pressure for improvement, clarification or analysis of individual words, except when, by accident of vocabulary, straightforward translation fails. Just as synonomy, as between expressions, goes generally untreated, so also synonomy of sentences, and analyticity. Even such sentences as "A vixen is a female fox" bear no special tag unless it is our pleasure to provide it. A truth definition does not distinguish between analytic sentences and others, except for sentences that owe their truth to the presence alone of the constants that give the theory its grip on structure: the theory entails not only that these sentences are true but that they will remain true under all significant rewritings of their nonlogical parts. A notion of logical truth thus given limited application, related notions of logical equivalence and entailment will tag along. It is hard to imagine how a theory of meaning could fail to read a logic into its object language to this degree;

and to the extent that it does, our intuitions of logical truth, equivalence, and entailment may be called upon in constructing and testing the theory.

I turn now to one more, and very large, fly in the ointment: the fact that the same sentence may at one time or in one mouth be true and at another time or in another mouth be false. Both logicians and those critical of formal methods here seem largely (though by no means universally) agreed that formal semantics and logic are incompetent to deal with the disturbances caused by demonstratives. Logicians have often reacted by downgrading natural language and trying to show how to get along without demonstratives; their critics react by downgrading logic and formal semantics. None of this can make me happy: clearly, demonstratives cannot be eliminated from a natural language without loss or radical change, so there is no choice but to accommodate theory to them.

No logical errors result if we simply treat demonstratives as constants[15]; neither do any problems arise for giving a semantic truth definition. " 'I am wise' is true if and only if I am wise," with its bland ignoring of the demonstrative element in "I" comes off the assembly line along with " 'Socrates is wise' is true if and only if Socrates is wise" with *its* bland indifference to the demonstrative element in "is wise" (the tense).

What suffers in this treatment of demonstratives is not the definition of a truth predicate, but the plausibility of the claim that what has been defined is truth. For this claim is acceptable only if the speaker and circumstances of utterance of each sentence mentioned in the definition is matched by the speaker and circumstances of utterance of the truth definition itself. It could also be fairly pointed out that part of understanding demonstratives is knowing the rules by which they adjust their reference to circumstance; assimilating demonstratives to constant terms obliterates this feature. These complaints can be met, I think, though only by a fairly far-reaching revision in the theory of truth. I shall barely suggest how this could be done, but bare suggestion is all that is needed: the

idea is technically trivial, and quite in line with work being done on the logic of the tenses.[16]

We could take truth to be a property, not of sentences, but of utterances, or speech acts, or ordered triples of sentences, times, and persons; but it is simplest just to view truth as a relation between a sentence, a person, and a time. Under such treatment, ordinary logic as now read applies as usual, but only to sets of sentences relativized to the same speaker and time; further logical relations between sentences spoken at different times and by different speakers may be articulated by new axioms. Such is not my concern. The theory of meaning undergoes a systematic but not puzzling change: corresponding to each expression with a demonstrative element there must in the theory be a phrase that relates the truth conditions of sentences in which the expression occurs to changing times and speakers. Thus the theory will entail sentences like the following:

> "I am tired" is true as (potentially) spoken by p at t if and only if p is tired at t.

> "That book was stolen" is true as (potentially) spoken by p at t if and only if the book demonstrated by p at t is stolen prior to t.[17]

Plainly, this course does not show how to eliminate demonstratives; for example, there is no suggestion that "the book demonstrated by the speaker" can be substituted ubiquitously for "that book" *salva veritate*. The fact that demonstratives are amenable to formal treatment ought greatly to improve hopes for a serious semantics of natural language, for it is likely that many outstanding puzzles, such as the analysis of quotations or sentences about propositional attitudes, can be solved if we recognize a concealed demonstrative construction.

Now that we have relativized truth to times and speakers, it is appropriate to glance back at the problem of empirically testing a theory of meaning for an alien tongue. The essence of the method was, it will be remembered, to correlate held-true sentences with held-true sentences by way of a truth definition, and within the bounds of intelligible error. Now the picture must be elaborated to allow for the fact that sentences are true, and held true, only relative to a speaker and a time. The real task is therefore to translate each sentence by another that is true for the same speakers at the same times. Sentences with demonstratives obviously yield a very sensitive test of the correctness of a theory of meaning, and constitute the most direct link between language and the recurrent macroscopic objects of human interest and attention.[18]

In this paper I have assumed that the speakers of a language can effectively determine the meaning or meanings of an arbitrary expression (if it has a meaning), and that it is the central task of a theory of meaning to show how this is possible. I have argued that a characterization of a truth predicate describes the required kind of structure, and provides a clear and testable criterion of an adequate semantics for a natural language. No doubt there are other reasonable demands that may be put on a theory of meaning. But a theory that does no more than define truth for a language comes far closer to constituting a complete theory of meaning than superficial analysis might suggest; so, at least, I have urged.

Since I think there is no alternative, I have taken an optimistic and programmatic view of the possibilities for a formal characterization of a truth predicate for a natural language. But it must be allowed that a staggering list of difficulties and conundrums remains. To name a few: we do not know the logical form of counterfactual or subjunctive sentences, nor of sentences about probabilities and about causal relations; we have no good idea what the logical role of adverbs is, nor the role of attributive adjectives; we have no theory for mass terms like "fire," "water," and "snow," nor for sentences about belief, perception, and intention, nor for verbs of action that imply purpose. And finally, there are all the sentences that seem not to have truth values at all: the imperatives, optatives, interrogatives, and a host more. A comprehensive theory of meaning for a natural language must cope successfully with each of these problems.

ACKNOWLEDGMENTS

An earlier version of this paper was read at the Eastern Division meeting of the American Philosophical Association in December, 1966; the main theme traces back to an unpublished paper delivered to the Pacific Division of the American Philosophical Association in 1953. Present formulations owe much to John Wallace, with whom I have discussed these matters since 1962. My research was supported by the National Science Foundation.

NOTES

1. Elsewhere I have urged that it is a necessary condition, if a language is to be learnable, that it have only a finite number of semantical primitives: see "Theories of Meaning and Learnable Languages," in *Proceedings of the 1964 International Congress for Logic, Methodology and Philosophy of Science* (North-Holland Publishing Company, Amsterdam: 1965), pp. 383–394.
2. A 'structural description' of an expression describes the expression as a concatenation of elements drawn from a fixed finite list (for example of words or letters).
3. The argument is essentially Frege's. See A. Church, *Introduction to Mathematical Logic*, vol. I (Princeton: 1956), pp. 24–25. It is perhaps worth mentioning that the argument does not depend on any particular identification of the entities to which sentences are supposed to refer.
4. It may be thought that Church, in "A Formulation of the Logic of Sense and Denotation," in *Structure, Method and Meaning: Essays in Honor of H. M. Sheffer*, Henle, Kallen and Langer, eds. (Liberal Arts Press, New York: 1951), pp. 3–24, has given a theory of meaning that makes essential use of meanings as entities. But this is not the case: Church's logics of sense and denotation are interpreted as being about meanings, but they do not mention expressions and so cannot of course be theories of meaning in the sense now under discussion.
5. For a recent and instructive statement of the role of semantics in linguistics, see Noam Chomsky, "Topics in the Theory of Generative Grammar," in *Current Trends in Linguistics*, Thomas A. Sebeok, ed., vol. III (The Hague: 1966). In this article, Chomsky (1) emphasizes the central importance of semantics in linguistic theory, (2) argues for the superiority of transformational grammars over phrase structure grammars largely on the grounds that, although phrase structure grammars may be adequate to define sentencehood for (at least) some natural languages, they are inadequate as a foundation

for semantics, and (3) comments repeatedly on the 'rather primitive state' of the concepts of semantics and remarks that the notion of semantic interpretation "still resists any deep analysis".

6. Assuming, of course, that the extension of these predicates is limited to the sentences of L.

7. Alfred Tarski, "The Concept of Truth in Formalized Languages," in *Logic, Semantics, Metamathematics* (Oxford: 1956), pp. 152–278.

8. But Quine may be quoted in support of my usage: ". . . in point of *meaning* . . . a word may be said to be determined to whatever extent the truth or falsehood of its contexts is determined." "Truth by Convention," first published in 1936; now in *The Ways of Paradox* (New York: 1966), p. 82. Since a truth definition determines the truth value of every sentence in the object language (relative to a sentence in the metalanguage), it determines the meaning of every word and sentence. This would seem to justify the title Theory of Meaning.

9. To give a single example: it is clearly a count in favor of a theory that it entails " 'Snow is white' is true if and only if snow is white." But to contrive a theory that entails this (and works for all related sentences) is not trivial. I do not know a theory that succeeds with this very case (the problem of 'mass terms').

10. This sketch of how a theory of meaning for an alien tongue can be tested obviously owes its inspiration to Quine's account of radical translation in chapter II of *Word and Object* (New York: 1960). In suggesting that an acceptable theory of radical translation take the form of a recursive characterization of truth, I go beyond anything explicit in Quine. Toward the end of this paper, in the discussion of demonstratives, another strong point of agreement will turn up.

11. So far as I am aware, there has been very little discussion of whether a formal truth definition can be given for a natural language. But in a more general vein, several people have urged that the concepts of formal semantics be applied to natural language. See, for example, the contributions of Yehoshua Bar-Hillel and Evert Beth to *The Philosophy of Rudolph Carnap*, Paul A. Schilpp, ed., (La Salle, Ill.: 1963), and Bar-Hillel's "Logical Syntax and Semantics," *Language* 30, 230–237.

12. Tarski, *ibid.*, p. 165.

13. *Ibid.*, p. 267.

14. The rapprochement I prospectively imagine between transformational grammar and a sound theory of meaning has been much advanced by a recent change in the conception of transformational grammar described by Chomsky in the article referred to above (note 5). The structures generated by the phrase-structure part of the grammar, it has been realized for some time, are those suited to semantic interpretation; but this view is inconsistent with the idea, held by Chomsky until recently, that recursive operations are introduced only by the transformation rules. Chomsky now believes the phrase-structure rules are recursive. Since languages to which formal semantic methods directly and naturally apply are ones for which a (recursive) phrase-structure grammar is appropriate, it is clear that Chomsky's present picture of the relation between the structures generated by the phrase-structure part of the grammar, and the sentences of the language, is very much like the picture many logicians and philosophers have had of the relation between the richer formalized languages and ordinary language. (In these remarks I am indebted to Bruce Vermazen.)

15. Quine has good things to say about this in *Methods of Logic* (New York: 1950). See §8.

16. For an up-to-date bibliography, and discussion, see A. N. Prior, *Past, Present, and Future* (Oxford: 1967).

17. There is more than an intimation of this approach to demonstratives and truth in Austin's 1950 article 'Truth', reprinted in *Philosophical Papers* (Oxford: 1961). See pp. 89–90.

18. These remarks clearly derive from Quine's idea that 'occasion sentences' (those with a demonstrative element) must play a central role in constructing a translation manual.

Meaning and Truth   7

P. F. STRAWSON

What is it for anything to have a *meaning* at all, in the way, or in the sense, in which words or sentences or signals have meaning? What is it for a particular sentence to have the meaning or meanings it does have? What is it for a particular phrase, or a particular word, to have the meaning or meanings it does have? These are obviously connected questions. Any account we give of meaning in general (in the relevant sense) must square with the account we give of what it is for particular expressions to have particular meanings; and we must acknowledge, as two complementary truths, first, that the meaning of a sentence in general depends, in some systematic way, on the meanings of the words that make it up and, second, that for a word to have a particular meaning is a matter of its making a particular systematic contribution to the meanings of the sentences in which it occurs.

I am not going to undertake to try to answer these so obviously connected questions. That is not a task for one lecture; or for one man. I want rather to discuss a certain conflict, or apparent conflict, more or less dimly discernible in current approaches to these questions. For the sake of a label, we might call it the conflict between the theorists of communication-intention and the theorists of formal semantics. According to the former, it is impossible to give an adequate account of the concept of meaning without reference to the possession by speakers of audience-directed intentions of a certain complex kind. The particular meanings of words and sentences are, no doubt, largely a matter of rule and convention; but the general nature of such rules and conventions can be ultimately understood only by reference to the concept of communication-intention. The opposed view, at least in its negative aspect, is that this doctrine simply gets things the wrong way round or the wrong way up, or mistakes the contingent for the essential. Of course we may expect a certain regularity of relationship between what people intend to communicate by uttering certain sentences and what those sentences conventionally mean. But the system of semantic and syntactical rules, in the mastery of which knowledge of a language consists—the rules which determine the meanings of sentences—is not a system of rules *for* communicating at all. The rules can be exploited for this purpose; but this is incidental to their essential character. It would be perfectly possible for someone to understand a language completely—to have a perfect linguistic competence—without having even the implicit thought of the function of communication; provided, of course, that the language in question did not contain words explicitly referring to this function.

A struggle on what seems to be such a

From *Meaning and Truth* (Oxford: Oxford University Press, 1970).

central issue in philosophy should have something of a Homeric quality; and a Homeric
struggle calls for gods and heroes. I can at
least, though tentatively, name some living
captains and benevolent shades: on the one
side, say, Grice, Austin, and the later Wittgenstein; on the other, Chomsky, Frege, and
the earlier Wittgenstein.

First, then, as to the theorists of communication-intention. The simplest, and most
readily intelligible, though not the only way of
joining their ranks is to present your general
theory of meaning in two stages: first, present
and elucidate a primitive concept of *communication* (or communication-intention) in terms
which do not presuppose the concept of
linguistic meaning; then show that the latter
concept can be, and is to be, explained in
terms of the former.[1] For any theorist who
follows this path, the fundamental concept in
the theory of meaning is that of a speaker's,
or, generally, an utterer's, *meaning something
by* an audience-directed utterance on a particular occasion. An utterance is something
produced or executed by an utterer; it need
not be vocal; it could be a gesture or a drawing
or the moving or disposing of objects in a
certain way. What an utterer means by his
utterance is incidentally specified in specifying
the complex intention with which he produces
the utterance. The analysis of the kind of
intention in question is too complex to be
given in detail here, so I shall confine myself
to incomplete description. An utterer might
have, as one of his intentions in executing his
utterance, that of bringing his audience to
think that he, the utterer, believes some
proposition, say the proposition that *p;* and he
might intend this intention to be wholly overt,
to be clearly recognized by the audience. Or
again he might have the intention of bringing
his audience to think that he, the utterer,
wants his audience to perform some action,
say *a;* and he might intend this intention of his
to be wholly overt, to be clearly recognized by
the audience. Then, provided certain other
conditions on utterer's intention are fulfilled,
the utterer may be said, in the relevant sense,
to mean something by his utterance: specifically, to mean that *p,* in the declarative mode,

in the first case and to mean, in the imperative
mode, that the audience is to perform action *a*
in the second case. Grice, for one, has given
us reason to think that, with sufficient care,
and far greater refinement than I have indicated, it is possible to expound such a concept
of communication-intention or, as he calls it,
utterer's meaning, which is proof against
objection and which does not presuppose the
notion of linguistic meaning.

Now a word about how the analyis of
linguistic meaning in terms of utterer's meaning is supposed to proceed. Here again I shall
not go into details. The details would be very
complex. But the fundamental idea is comparatively simple. We are accustomed, and reasonably, to think of linguistic meaning in
terms of rules and conventions, semantic and
syntactic. And when we consider the enormous elaboration of these rules and conventions—their capacity, as the modern linguists
stress, to generate an infinite number of
sentences in a given language—we may feel
infinitely removed from the sort of primitive
communication situation which we naturally
think of when trying to understand the notion
of utterer's meaning in terms which clearly do
not presuppose linguistic meaning. But rules
or conventions govern human practices and
purposive human activities. So we should ask
what purposive activities are governed by
these conventions. What are *these* rules rules
for doing? And the very simple thought I
spoke of which underlies the suggested type of
analysis is that these rules are, precisely, rules
for communicating, rules by the observance of
which the utterer may achieve his purpose,
fulfil his communication-intention; and that
this is their *essential* character. That is, it is not
just a fortunate fact that these rules allow of
use for this purpose; rather, the very nature of
the rules concerned can be understood only if
they are seen as rules whereby this purpose
can be achieved.

This simple thought may seem too simple,
and in several ways. For it is clear that we can,
and do, communicate very complicated things
by the use of language; and if we are to think
of language as, fundamentally, a system of
rules for facilitating the achievement of our

communication-intentions, and if the analysis is not to be circular, must we not credit ourselves with extremely complicated communication-intentions (or at least desires) independently of having at our disposal the linguistic means of fulfilling those desires? And is not this absurd? I think this is absurd. But the program of analysis does not require it. All that the analysis requires is that we can explain the notion of conventions of communication in terms of the notion of preconventional communication at a rather basic level. Given that we can do this, then there is more than one way in which we can start pulling ourselves up by our own linguistic boot-straps. And it looks as if we can explain the notion of conventions of communication in terms of the notion of pre-conventional communication at a rather basic level.

We can, for example, tell ourselves a story of the analytic-genetic variety. Suppose an utterer achieves a pre-conventional communication success with a given audience by means of an utterance, say x. He has a complex intention, vis-à-vis the audience of the sort which counts as a communication-intention and succeeds in fulfilling that intention by uttering x. Let us suppose that the primary intention was such that the utterer *meant* that p by uttering x; and, since, by hypothesis, he achieved a communication-success, he was so *understood* by his audience. Now if the same communication-problem presents itself later to the same utterer in relation to the same audience, the fact, known to both of them, that the utterer meant that p by uttering x before, gives the utterer a reason for uttering x again and the audience a reason for interpreting the utterance in the same way as before. (The reason which each has is the knowledge that the other has the knowledge which he has.) So it is easy to see how the utterance of x could become established as between this utterer and this audience as a means of meaning that p. Because it has worked, it becomes established; and then it works *because* it is established. And it is easy to see how this story could be told so as to involve not just a group of two, but a wider group. So we can have a movement from an

utterer pre-conventionally meaning that p by an utterance of x to the utterance-type x conventionally meaning that p within a group and thence back to utterer-members of the group meaning that p by a token of the type, but now *in accordance with the conventions*.

Now of course this explanation of conventional meaning in terms of utterer's meaning is not enough by itself. For it only covers the case, or only obviously covers the case, of utterance-types without structure—i.e. of utterance-types of which the meaning is not systematically derived from the meanings of their parts. But it is characteristic of linguistic utterance-types to have structure. The meaning of a sentence is a syntactic function of the meanings of its parts and their arrangement. But there is no reason in principle why a pre-conventional utterance should not have a certain complexity—a kind of complexity which allowed an utterer, having achieved one communication-success, to achieve another by repeating one part of the utterance while varying the other part, what he means on the second occasion having something in common with, and something which differentiates it from, what he meant on the first occasion. And if he does thus achieve a second success, the way is open for a rudimentary *system* of utterance-types to become established, i.e., to become conventional within a group.

A system of conventions can be modified to meet needs which we can scarcely imagine existing before the system existed. And its modification and enrichment may in turn create the possibility of thoughts such as we cannot understand what it would be for one to have, without supposing such modification and enrichment to have taken place. In this way we can picture a kind of alternating development. Primitive communication-intentions and successes give rise to the emergence of a limited conventional meaning-system, which makes possible its own enrichment and development which in turn makes possible the enlargement of thought and of communication-needs to a point at which there is once more pressure on the existing resources of language which is in turn responsive to such pressure. . . . And of course there is an element of mystery in this;

but so there is in human intellectual and social creativity anyway.

All the foregoing is by way of the roughest possible sketch of some salient features of a communication-intention theory of meaning and of a hint as to how it might meet the obvious objection that certain communication-intentions presuppose the existence of language. It has all been said before, and with far greater refinement. But it will serve, I hope, as a sufficient basis for the confrontation of views that I wish to arrange.

Now, then, for the at least apparently opposed view, which I have so far characterized only in its negative aspect. Of course the holders of this view share some ground with their opponents. Both agree that the meanings of the sentences of a language are largely determined by the semantic and syntactic rules or conventions of that language. Both agree that the members of any group or community of people who share knowledge of a language—who have a common linguistic competence—have at their disposal a more or less powerful instrument or means of communicating, and thereby of modifying each other's beliefs or attitudes or influencing each other's actions. Both agree that these means are regularly used in a quite conventional way, that what people intend to communicate by what they say is regularly related to the conventional meanings of the sentences they utter. Where they differ is as to the relations between the meaning-determining rules of the language, on the one hand, and the function of communication, on the other: one party insists, and the other (apparently) refuses to allow, that the general nature of those rules can be understood only by reference to this function.

The refusal naturally prompts a question, viz. What *is* the general character of those rules which must in some sense have been mastered by anyone who speaks and understands a given language? The rejected answer grounds their general character in the social function of communicating, for example, beliefs or wishes or instructions. If this answer is rejected, another must be offered. So we ask again: What is the general character of these meaning-determining rules?

It seems to me that there is only one type of answer that has ever been seriously advanced or developed, or needs to be seriously considered, as providing a possible alternative to the thesis of the communication theorist. This is an answer which rests on the motion of truth-conditions. The thought that the sense of a sentence is determined by its truth-conditions is to be found in Frege and in the early Wittgenstein, and we find it again in many subsequent writers. I take, as an example, a recent article by Professor Davidson. Davidson is rightly concerned with the point that an adequate account of the meaning rules for a language L will show how the meanings of sentences depend on the meanings of words in L; and a theory of meaning for L will do this, he says, if it contains a recursive definition of truth-in-L. The "obvious connection," he says, between such a definition of truth and the concept of meaning is this: "the definition works by giving the necessary and sufficient conditions for the truth of every sentence, and *to give truth-conditions is a way of giving the meaning of a sentence.* To know the semantic concept of truth for a language is to know what it is for a sentence—any sentence—to be true, and *this amounts, in one good sense we can give to the phrase, to understanding the language.*"[2]

Davidson, in the article I quote from, has a limited concern. But the concern finds its place inside a more general idea; and the general idea, plainly enough, is that the syntactic and semantic rules together determine the meanings of all the sentences of a language and do this by means, precisely, of determining their truth-conditions.

Now if we are to get at the root of the matter, to isolate the crucial issue, it seems to me important to set aside, at least initially, one class of objections to the adequacy of such a conception of meaning. I say one class of objections; but it is a class which admits of subdivisions. Thus it may be pointed out that there are some kinds of sentences—e.g., imperatives, optatives, and interrogatives—to which the notion of truth-conditions seems inappropriate, in that the conventional utterance of such sentences does not result in the saying of anything true or false. Or again it may be pointed out that even sentences to which the notion of truth-conditions does seem appropriate may contain expressions which certainly make a difference to their conventional meaning, but not the sort of difference which can be explained in terms of their truth-conditions. Compare the sentence "Fortunately, Socrates is dead" with the sentence "Unfortunately, Socrates is dead." Compare a sentence of the form "p and q" with the corresponding sentence of the form "p but q." It is clear that the meanings of the members of each pair of sentences differ; it is far from clear that their truth-conditions differ. And there are not just one or two expressions which give rise to this problem, but many such expressions.

Obviously both a comprehensive general theory of meaning and a comprehensive semantic theory for a particular language must be equipped to deal with these points. Yet they may reasonably be regarded as peripheral points. For it is a truth implicitly acknowledged by communication theorists themselves[3] that in almost all the things we should count as sentences there is a substantial central core of meaning which is explicable either in terms of truth-conditions or in terms of some related notion quite simply derivable from that of a truth-condition, for example the notion, as we might call it, of a compliance-condition in the case of an imperative sentence or a fulfillment-condition in the case of an optative. If we suppose, therefore, that an account can be given of the notion of a truth-condition itself, an account which is indeed independent of reference to communication-intention, then we may reasonably think that the greater part of the task of a general theory of meaning has been accomplished without such reference. And by the same token, on the same supposition, we may think that the greater part of the particular theory of meaning of a particular language L can also be given, free of any such, even implicit, reference; for it can be given by systematically setting out the syntactic and semantical rules which determine truth-conditions for sentences of L.

Of course, as already admitted, something will have to be added to complete our general theory and to complete our particular theories. Thus for a particular theory an account will have to be added of the transformations that yield sentences with compliance-conditions or fulfillment-conditions out of sentences with truth-conditions; and the general theory will have to say what sort of thing, semantically speaking, such a derived sentence in general is. But this, though yielding a large harvest in sentences, is in itself a relatively small addition to either particular or general theory. Again, other additions will be necessary in connection with the other objections I mentioned. But, heartened by his hypothesized success into confidence, the theorist may reckon on dealing with some of these additions without essential reference to communication-intention; and, heartened by his hypothesized success into generosity, he may be happy to concede rights in some small outlying portion of the *de facto* territory of theoretical semantics to the theorist of communication-intention, instead of confining the latter entirely to some less appetizing territory called theoretical pragmatics.

I hope it is now clear what the central issue is. It consists in nothing other than the simple-seeming question whether the notion of truth-conditions can itself be explained or understood without reference to the function of communication. One minor clarification is called for before I turn to examine the question directly. I have freely used the phrase "the truth-conditions of sentences" and I have spoken of these truth-conditions as determined by the semantical and syntactical rules of the language to which the sentences belong. In such a context we naturally understand the word "sentence" in the sense of a 'type-sentence'. (By a sentence in the sense of a type I mean the sense in which there is just one English sentence, say, "I am feeling shivery," or just one English sentence, say, "She had her sixteenth birthday yesterday," which one and the same sentence may be uttered on countless different occasions by different people and with different references or applications.) But for many type-sentences, such as those just mentioned, the question whether they, the *sentences,* are true or false is one that has no natural application: it is not the invariant type-sentences themselves that are naturally said to be true or false, but rather the systematically varying things that people say, the propositions they express, when they utter those sentences on different particular occasions. But if the notion of truth-*values* is in general inappropriate to type-sentences, how can the notion of truth-*conditions* be appropriate? For presumably the truth-conditions of something are the conditions under which it is true.

The difficulty, however, is quite easily resolved. All that needs to be said is that the statement of truth-conditions for many type-sentences—perhaps most that are actually uttered in ordinary conversation—has to be, and can be, relativized in a systematic way to contextual conditions of utterance. A general statement of truth-conditions for such a sentence will then be, not a statement of conditions under which that sentence is a truth, but a general statement of a type of conditions under which different particular utterances of it will issue in different particular truths. And there are other more or less equivalent, though rather less natural, ways of resolving the difficulty.

So now, at last, to the central issue. For the theorists of formal semantics, as I have called them, the whole weight, or most of the weight, both of a general theory of meaning and of particular semantic theories, falls on the notion of truth-conditions and hence on the notion of truth. We agree to let it rest there. But we still cannot be satisfied that we have an adequate general understanding of the notion of meaning unless we are satisfied that we have an adequate general understanding of the notion of truth.

There is one maneuver here that would completely block all hope of achieving adequate understanding; and, if I am not mistaken, it is a maneuver which has a certain appeal for some theorists of formal semantics. This is to react to a demand for a general explication of the notion of truth by referring us back to a Tarski-like conception of truth-in-

a-given-language, *L,* a conception which is elucidated precisely by a recursive statement of the rules which determine the truth-conditions for sentences of *L.* This amounts to a refusal to face the general philosophical question altogether. Having agreed to the general point that the meanings of the sentences of a language are determined, or largely determined, by rules which determine truth-conditions, we then raise the general question what sort of thing truth-conditions are, or what truth-conditions are conditions *of;* and we are told that the concept of truth for a given language is defined by the rules which determine the truth-conditions for sentences of that language.

Evidently we cannot be satisfied with this. So we return to our general question about truth. And immediately we feel some embarrassment. For we have come to think there is very little to say about truth *in general.* But let us see what we can do with this very little. Here is one way of saying something uncontroversial and fairly general about truth. One who makes a statement or assertion makes a true statement if and only if things are as, in making that statement, he states them to be. Or again: one who expresses a supposition expresses a true supposition if and only if things are as, in expressing that supposition, he expressly supposes them to be. Now let us interweave with such innocuous remarks as these the agreed thoughts about meaning and truth-conditions. Then we have, first: the meaning of a sentence is determined by those rules which determine how things are stated to be by one who, in uttering the sentence, makes a statement; or, how things are expressly supposed to be by one who, in uttering the sentence, expresses a supposition. And then, remembering that the rules are relativized to contextual conditions, we can paraphrase as follows: the meaning of a sentence is determined by the rules which determine *what* statement is made by one who, in uttering the sentence in given conditions, makes a statement; or, which determine *what* supposition is expressed by one who, in uttering the sentence in given conditions, expresses a supposition; and so on.

Thus we are led, by way of the notion of truth, back to the notion of the *content* of such speech acts as stating, expressly supposing, and so on. And here the theorist of communication-intention sees his chance. There is no hope, he says, of elucidating the notion of the content of such speech acts without paying some attention to the notions of those speech acts themselves. Now of all the speech acts in which something true or false may, in one mode or another, be put forward, it is reasonable to regard that of statement or assertion as having an especially central position. (Hot for certainties, we value speculation primarily because we value information.) And we cannot, the theorist maintains, elucidate the notion of stating or asserting except in terms of audience-directed intention. For the fundamental case of stating or asserting, in terms of which all variants must be understood, is that of uttering a sentence with a certain intention—an intention wholly, overt in the sense required by the analysis of utterer's meaning—which can be incompletely described as that of letting an audience know, or getting it to think, that the speaker has a certain belief; as a result of which there may, or may not, be activated or produced in the audience that same belief. The rules determining the conventional meaning of the sentence join with the contextual conditions of its utterance to determine what the belief in question *is* in such a primary and fundamental case. And in determining what the belief in question is in such a case, the rules determine what statement is made in such a case. To determine the former *is* to determine the latter. But this is precisely what we wanted. For when we set out from the agreed point that the rules which determine truth-conditions thereby determine meaning, the conclusion to which we were led was precisely that those rules determined what statement was made by one who, in uttering the sentence, made a statement. So the agreed point, so far from being an alternative to a communication theory of meaning, leads us straight in to such a theory of meaning.

The conclusion may seem a little too swift. So let us see if there is any way of avoiding it.

The general condition of avoiding it is clear. It is that we should be able to give an account of the notion of truth-conditions which involves no essential reference to communicative speech acts. The alternative of refusing to give any account at all—of just resting on the notion of truth-conditions—is, as I have already indicated, simply not open to us if we are concerned with the philosophical elucidation of the notion of meaning: it would simply leave us with the concepts of meaning and truth each pointing blankly and unhelpfully at the other. Neither would it be helpful, though it might at this point be tempting, to retreat from the notion of truth-conditions to the less specific notion of correlation in general; to say, simply, that the rules which determine the meanings of sentences do so by correlating the sentences, envisaged as uttered in certain contextual conditions, with certain possible states of affairs. One reason why this will not do is that the notion of correlation in general is simply too unspecific. There are many kinds of behavior (including verbal behavior)—and many more kinds could be imagined—which are correlated by rule with possible states of affairs without its being the case that such correlation confers upon them the kind of relation to those possible states of affairs that we are concerned with.

Another reason why it will not do is the following. Consider the sentence "I am tired." The rules which determine its meaning are indeed such as to correlate the sentence, envisaged as uttered by a particular speaker at a particular time, with the possible state of affairs of the speaker's being tired at that time. But this feature is not peculiar to that sentence or to the members of the class of sentences which have the same meaning as it. For consider the sentence "I am not tired." The rules which determine its meaning are also such as to correlate the sentence, envisaged as uttered by a certain speaker at a certain time, with the possible state of affairs of that speaker's being tired at that time. Of course the kinds of correlation are different. They are respectively such that one who uttered the first sentence would normally be understood as affirming, and one who uttered the second sentence would normally be understood as denying, that the state of affairs in question obtained; or again they are such that one who utters the first sentence when the state of affairs in question obtains has made a true statement and one who utters the second sentence in these circumstances has made a false statement. But to invoke these differences would be precisely to give up the idea of employing only the unspecific notion of correlation in general. It is not worth labouring the point further. But it will readily be seen not only that sentences different, and even opposed, in meaning are correlated, in one way or another, with the same possible state of affairs, but also that one and the same unambiguous sentence is correlated, in one way or another, with very many different and in some cases mutually incompatible states of affairs. The sentence "I am tired" is correlated with the possible state of affairs of the speaker's being at the point of total exhaustion and also with the state of affairs of his being as fresh as a daisy. The sentence "I am over 40" is correlated with any possible state of affairs whatever regarding the speaker's age; the sentence "Swans are white" with any state of affairs whatever regarding the color of swans.

The quite unspecific notion of correlation, then, is useless for the purpose in hand. It is necessary to find some way of specifying a particular correlation in each case, viz. the correlation of the sentence with the possible state of affairs the obtaining of which would be necessary and sufficient for something *true* to have been said in the uttering of the sentence under whatever contextual conditions are envisaged. So we are back once more with the notion of truth-conditions and with the question, whether we can give an account of this notion which involves no essential reference to communicative speech acts, i.e. to communication-intention.

I can at this point see only one resource open, or apparently open, to the theorist of meaning who still holds that the notion of communication-intention has no essential place in the analysis of the concept of meaning. If he is not to swallow his opponent's hook, he must take some leaves out of his

book. He sees now that he cannot stop with the idea of truth. That idea leads straight to the idea of *what is said,* the content of what is said, when utterances are made; and that in turn to the question of what is being *done* when utterances are made. But may not the theorist go some way along this path without going as far along it as his opponent? Might it not be possible to *delete* the reference to communication-intention while *preserving* a reference to, say, belief-expression? And will not this, incidentally, be more realistic in so far as we often voice our thoughts to ourselves, with no communicative intention?

The maneuver proposed merits a fuller description. It goes as follows. First, follow the communication-theorist in responding to the challenge for an elucidation of the notion of truth-conditions by invoking the notion of, e.g. and centrally, statement or assertion (accepting the uncontroversial point that one makes a true statement or assertion when things are as, in making that assertion, one asserts them to be). Second, follow the communication-theorist again in responding to the challenge for an elucidation of the notion of asserting by making a connection with the notion of belief (conceding that to make an assertion is, in the primary case, to give expression to a belief; to make a true assertion is to give expression to a correct belief; and a belief is correct when things are as one who holds that belief, in so far as he holds that belief, believes them to be). But third, part company with the communication-theorist over the nature of this connection between assertion and belief; deny, that is, that the analysis of the notion of asserting involves essential reference to an intention, for example, to get an audience to think that the maker of the assertion holds the belief; deny that the analysis of the notion of asserting involves *any* kind of reference to audience-directed intention; maintain, on the contrary, that it is perfectly satisfactory to accept as fundamental here the notion of simply voicing or expressing a belief. Then conclude that the meaning-determining rules for a sentence of the language are the rules which determine *what* belief is conventionally articulated by one who, in given contextual conditions, utters the sentence. As before, determining what this belief is, is the same thing as determining what assertion is made. So all the merits of the opponent's theory are preserved while the reference to communication is extruded.

Of course, more must be said by this theorist, as by his opponent. For sentences which can be used to express beliefs need not always be so used. But the point is one to be made on both sides. So we may neglect it for the present.

Now will this do? I do not think it will. But in order to see that it will not, we may have to struggle hard against a certain illusion. For the notion of expressing a belief may seem to us perfectly straightforward; and hence the notion of expressing a belief in accordance with certain conventions may seem equally straightforward. Yet, in so far as the notion of expressing a belief is the notion we need, it may borrow all its force and apparent straightforwardness from precisely the communication situation which it was supposed to free the analysis of meaning from depending on. We may be tempted to argue as follows. Often we express beliefs with an audience-directed intention; we intend that our audience should take us to have the belief we express and perhaps that that belief should be activated or produced in the audience as well. But then what could be plainer than this: that what we can do with an audience-directed intention we can also do without any such intention? That is to say, the audience-directed intention, when it is present, is something added on to the activity of expressing a belief and in no way essential to it—or to the concept of it.

Now what a mixture of truth and falsity, of platitude and illusion, we have here! Suppose we reconsider for a moment that analysis of utterer's meaning which was roughly sketched at the beginning. The utterer produces something—his utterance x—with a complex audience-directed intention, involving, say, getting the audience to think that he has a certain belief. We cannot detach or extract from the analysis an element which corresponds to his expressing a belief with no such intention—

though we could indeed produce the following description and imagine a case for it: he acts *as if* he had such an intention though as a matter of fact he has not. But here the description depends on the description of the case in which he has such an intention.

What I am suggesting is that we may be tempted, here as elsewhere, by a kind of bogus arithmetic of concepts. Given the concept of Audience Directed Belief Expression (ADBE), we can indeed think of Belief Expression (BE) without Audience Direction (AD), and find cases of this. But it does not follow that the concept of ADBE is a kind of logical compound of the two simpler concepts of AD and BE and hence that BE is conceptually independent of ADBE.

Of course these remarks do not show that there is no such thing as an independent concept of belief-expression which will meet the needs of the anti-communication theorist. They are only remarks directed against a too simple argument to the effect that there is such a concept.

This much is clear. If there is such an essentially independent concept of belief-expression which is to meet the needs of the analysis of the notion of meaning, we cannot just stop with the phrase 'expressing a belief'. We must be able to give some *account* of this concept, to tell ourselves some intelligible story about it. We can sometimes reasonably talk of a man's actions or his behavior as expressing a belief when, for example, we see those actions as directed towards an end or goal which it is plausible to ascribe to him in so far as it is also plausible to ascribe to him that belief. But this reflection by itself does not get us very far. For one thing, on the present program, we are debarred from making reference to the end or goal of communication an essential part of our story. For another, the sort of behavior we are to be concerned with must be, or be capable of being, formalized or conventionalized in such a way that it can be regarded as subjected to, or performed in observance of, rules; and of rules, moreover, which regulate the behavior precisely in its aspect as expression of belief. It will not do to say simply: we might suppose a man to find *some* satisfaction (unspecified) or *some* point (unspecified) in performing certain formalized (perhaps vocal) actions on some occasions, these actions being systematically related to his having certain beliefs. For suppose a man had a practice of vocalizing in a certain way whenever he saw the sun rise and in another, partly similar, partly different, way whenever he saw it set. Then this practice would be regularly related to certain beliefs, i.e. that the sun was rising or that it was setting. But this description gives us no reason at all for saying that when the man indulged in this practice he was *expressing the belief* that the sun was rising or setting, in accordance with a rule for doing so. We really have not enough of a description to know *what* to say. As far as we could tell, we might say, he just seems to have this ritual of *saluting* the rising or the setting sun in this way. What need of his it satisfies we don't know.

Let us suppose, however—for the sake of the argument—that we can elaborate some relevant conception of expressing a belief which presupposes nothing which, on the present program, we are debarred from presupposing; and that we draw on this concept of expressing a belief in order to give an account, or analysis, on the lines indicated, of the notion of linguistic meaning. Then an interesting consequence ensues. That is, it will appear as a quite contingent truth about language that the rules or conventions which determine the meanings of the sentences of a language are public or social rules or conventions. This will be, as it were, a natural fact, a fact of nature, in no way essential to the concept of a language, and calling for a natural explanation which must not be allowed to touch or modify that concept. There must be nothing in the *concept* to rule out the idea that every individual might have his own language which only he understands. But then one might ask: Why should each individual observe his own rules? or any rules? Why shouldn't he express any belief he likes in any way he happens to fancy when he happens to have the urge to express it? There is one answer at least which the theorist is debarred from giving to this question, if only in the

interests of his own programme. He cannot say: Well, a man might wish to *record* his beliefs so that he could refer to the records later, and then he would find it convenient to have rules to interpret his own records. The theorist is debarred from giving this answer because it introduces, though in an attenuated form, the concept of communication-intention: the earlier man communicates with his later self.

There might be one way of stilling the doubts which arise so rapidly along this path. That would be to offer possible natural explanations of the supposed natural fact that language is public, that linguistic rules are more or less socially common rules; explanations which successfully avoided any suggestion that the connection of public rules with communication was anything but incidental and contingent. How might such an explanation go? We might say that it was an agreed point that the possession of a language enlarges the mind, that there are beliefs one could not express without a language to express them in, thoughts one could not entertain without a rule-governed system of expressions for articulating them. And it is a fact about human beings that they simply would not acquire mastery of such a system unless they were exposed, as children, to conditioning or training by adult members of a community. Without concerning ourselves about the remote origins of language, then, we may suppose the adult members of a community to wish their successors to have this mind-enlarging instrument at their disposal—and evidently the whole procedure of training will be simplified if they all teach the same, the common language. We may reasonably suppose that the learners, to begin with, do not quite appreciate what they will ultimately be doing with language; that it is for them, to begin with, a matter of learning to do the right thing rather than learning to say the true thing, i.e. a matter of responding vocally to situations in a way which will earn them reward or avoid punishment rather than a matter of *expressing their beliefs*. But later they come to realize that they have mastered a system which enables them to perform this (still unexplained) activity whenever they wish to; and *then* they are speaking a language.

Of course it must be admitted that in the process they are liable also to acquire the *secondary* skill of communicating their beliefs. But this is simply something added on, an extra and conceptually uncovenanted benefit, quite incidental to the description of what it is to have mastered the meaning-rules of the language. If, indeed, you pointedly direct utterances, of which the essential function is belief-expression, to another member of the community, he will be apt to take it that you hold whatever beliefs are in question and indeed that you intend him to take this to be so; and this fact may give rise, indeed, it must be admitted, does give rise, to a whole cluster of social consequences; and opens up all sorts of possibilities of kinds of linguistic communication other than that which is based on belief-expression. This is why, as already acknowledged, we may have ultimately to allow some essential reference to communication-intention into outlying portions of our semantic theory. But this risk is incurred only when we go beyond the central core of meaning, determined by the rules which determine truth-conditions. As far as the central core is concerned, the function of communication remains secondary, derivative, conceptually inessential.

I hope it is clear that any such story is going to be too perverse and arbitrary to satisfy the requirements of an acceptable theory. If this is the way the game has to be played, then the communication theorist must be allowed to have won it.

But must the game, finally, be played in this way? I think, finally, it must. It is indeed a generally harmless and salutary thing to say that to know the meaning of a sentence is to know under what conditions one who utters it says something true. But if we wish for a philosophical elucidation of the concept of meaning, then the dictum represents, not the end, but the beginning, of our task. It simply narrows, and relocates, our problem, forcing us to inquire what is contained in the little phrase ". . . says something true." Of course there are many ways in which one can say

something which is in fact true, give expression, if you like, to a true proposition, without thereby expressing belief in it, without asserting that proposition: for example when the words in question form certain sorts of subordinate or coordinate clauses, and when one is quoting or playacting and so on. But when we come to try to explain in general what it is to say something true, to express a true proposition, reference to belief or to assertion (and thereby to belief) is inescapable. Thus we may harmlessly venture: Someone says something true if things are as he says they are. But this "says" already has the force of "asserts." Or, to eschew the "says" which equals "asserts," we may harmlessly venture: Someone propounds, in some mode or other, a true proposition if things are as anyone who believed what he propounds would thereby believe them to be. And here the reference to belief is explicit.

Reference, direct or indirect, to belief-expression is inseparable from the analysis of saying something true (or false). And, as I have tried to show, it is unrealistic to the point of unintelligibility—or, at least, of extreme perversity—to try to free the notion of the linguistic expression of belief from all essential connection with the concept of communication-intention.

Earlier I hinted that the habit of some philosophers of speaking as if "true" were a predicate of type-sentences was only a minor aberration, which could readily enough be accommodated to the facts. And so it can. But it is not a simple matter of pedantry to insist on correcting the aberration. For if we are not careful, it is liable to lead us totally wrong. It is liable, when we inquire into the nature of meaning, to make us forget what sentences are *for*. We connect meaning with truth and truth, too simply, with sentences; and sentences belong to language. But, as theorists, we know nothing of human *language* unless we understand human *speech*.

NOTES

1. Not the *only* way; for to say that a concept φ cannot be adequately elucidated without refer-

ence to a concept ψ is not the same thing as to say that it is possible to give a classical analysis of ϕ in terms of ψ. But the *simplest* way; for the classical method of analysis is that in terms of which, in our tradition, we most naturally think.

2. "Truth and Meaning," *Synthese*, 1967, p. 310. My italics. [Reprinted in this volume.]

3. This acknowledgement is probably implicit, though not very clearly so, in Austin's concept of *locutionary meaning* (see *How to do things with Words*, Oxford: 1962); it is certainly implicit in Grice's distinction between what speakers *actually say*, in a favored sense of 'say', and what they imply (see "Utterer's Meaning, Sentence-Meaning and Word-Meaning," in *Foundations of Language*, 1968); and again in Searle's distinction between the *proposition* put forward and the illocutionary mode in which it is put forward (see *Speech Acts*, Cambridge: 1969).

SUGGESTED FURTHER READING

Alston, William, Semantic Rules, in *Semantics and Philosophy,* ed. Milton Munitz and Peter Unger (New York: New York University Press, 1974), pp. 17–48.

Bennett, Jonathan, *Linguistic Behavior* (Cambridge: Cambridge University Press, 1976).

Biro, John, Intentionalism in the Theory of Meaning, *The Monist* 62 (1979), 238–58.

Black, Max, Meaning and Intention: An Examination of Grice's Views, *New Literary History* 4 (1973), 257–79.

Davidson, Donald, A Nice Derangement of Epitaphs, in *Truth and Interpretation,* ed. Ernest LePore (Oxford: Basil Blackwell, 1986), pp. 433–46.

Dummett, Michael, What Is a Theory of Meaning? in *Mind & Language,* ed. Samuel Guttenplan (Oxford: Clarendon Press, 1975), pp. 97–138.

Dummett, Michael, What Is a Theory of Meaning? (II) in *Truth & Meaning,* ed. Gareth Evans and John McDowell (Oxford: Clarendon Press, 1976), pp. 67–137.

Field, Hartry, Tarski's Theory of Truth, *Journal of Philosophy* 79 (1972), 347–75.

Grandy, Richard E. and Richard Warner, eds., *Philosophical Grounds of Rationality* (Oxford: Clarendon Press, 1986).

Grice, H. P. and P. F. Strawson, In Defense of a Dogma, *Philosophical Review* 55 (1956), 141–15.

Grice, H. P., Utterer's Meaning and Intentions, *Philosophical Review* 78 (1969), 147–77.

Grice, H. P., Utterer's Meaning, Sentence-Meaning and Word-Meaning, *Foundations of Language* 4 (1968), 1–18.

Grice, H. P., Meaning Revisited, in *Mutual Knowledge,* ed. N. V. Smith (New York: Academic Press, 1982), pp. 223–43.

Kempson, Ruth, *Semantic Theory* (Cambridge: Cambridge University Press, 1977).

Linsky, Leonard, *Semantics and the Philosophy of Language* (Urbana, Ill.: University of Illinois Press, 1952).

McDowell, John, Meaning, Communication, and Knowledge, in *Philosophical Subjects,* ed. Zak Van Straaten (Oxford: Clarendon Press, 1980), pp. 117–39.

Platts, Mark, *Ways of Meaning* (London: Routledge & Kegan Paul, 1979).

Quine, W. V., Cognitive Meaning, *Monist* 62 (1979), 129–42.

Searle, John, The Background of Meaning, in *Speech Act Theory and Pragmatics,* ed. John R. Searle and Ferenc Kiefer (Dordrecht, Holland: D. Reidel, 1980), pp. 221–32.

Searle, John, Indeterminacy and the First Person, *Journal of Philosophy* 84 (1987), 123–46.

Shiffer, Stephen, *Meaning* (Oxford: Clarendon Press, 1972).

Strawson, P. F., Truth, *Analysis* 9 (1949), 83–97.

Tarski, Alfred, The Concept of Truth in Formalized Languages, in *Logic, Semantics and Metamathematics* (Oxford: Clarendon Press, 1956), pp. 152–278.

Ziff, Paul, On H. P. Grice's Account of Meaning, *Analysis* 28 (1967), 1–8.

II

SPEECH ACTS

According to Grice, to mean something is first of all for a person to mean something; and, if the person successfully communicates what he means, he has performed a speech act. Although there are hints of speech act theory in earlier philosophers as different as Avicenna and Hobbes, the first to study the issue explicitly and at length was J. L. Austin. In "Performative Utterances," Austin introduces the idea that to say something is to do something. He argues dialectically against the logical positiivists who held that a sentence is meaningful only if it has a truth-value. Austin shows that there are perfectly ordinary and meaningful sentences that are neither true nor false.

Austin presented a tentative though relatively comprehensive theory of speech acts in *How to Do Things with Words*. John Searle substantially revised that theory and presented what has become the standard theory in *Speech Acts*. His article, "What is a Speech Act?" sketches the central portions of that theory.

Zeno Vendler does not follow Searle but revises and extends in his own way Austin's views about what it is to say something. Vendler's work is highly influenced by Noam Chomsky's transformational grammar. He lauds Austin for intuitively discovering conceptual patterns that are verified by empirically based linguistic theory. Vendler then relates the structure of what is said to the structure of our thought.

What is said is just one part of what a speaker communicates. Much, perhaps most, of what is communicated is implied in one way or another. Although this is a kind of commonplace, it had not been incorporated into a theory of meaning until Grice sketched the main types of implication and roughly characterized them in his William James Lectures for 1967, titled "Logic and Conversation." His theory also has substantial applications to traditional philosophical problems.

The central kind of implication is conversational implication. One kind of conversational implication involves indirect speech acts, which are speech acts that result from the performance of some other speech acts. For example, the explicit speech act performed by saying "Can you pass the salt?" is a question ("Are you able to . . . ?"); yet, at a dinner table it is typically used to make a request. The explicit speech act performed by saying "You are standing on my feet" is a statement, yet it too is sometimes used to request that a person get off the speaker's feet. Searle's analysis of these indirect speech acts is an extension of his theory of speech acts and has a place within Grice's theory of conversation.

Because of its unprecedented character, Grice's statement of his theory in "Logic and Conversation" contains some easily identifiable and easily correctible errors. For example, he distinguishes between four ways in which a conversational maxim can go unfulfilled: (1) by violating a maxim; (2) by opting out of a maxim; (3) by flouting a maxim; and (4) by being faced with a clash of maxims. The first, violating a maxim, is a specific way of not fulfilling a maxim in a broad sense. It is to quietly and unonstentatiously not fulfill a maxim. But Grice sometimes mistakenly uses "violate" where he should have used the broader term, "not fulfill." Watch for this.

Also, it is clear that (4) does not belong with (1)–(3). (4) is not a way in which a maxim can go unfulfilled. Rather, it is a reason why a maxim might go unfulfilled. If a speaker is faced with a clash of two maxims, that is, a situation in which he can fulfill one or the other but not both, then he will have to sacrifice one in order to fulfill the other. (Suppose someone is asked to give a brief and complete explanation of Hegel's theory of Absolute Idealism.) Thus, in being faced with a clash, the speaker may violate, opt out of, or flout one of the maxims.

It is plausible that these remaining three maxims need to be supplemented with a fourth. Just as violating a maxim is complemented by flouting a maxim, that is, openly and ostentatiously not fulfilling one, opting out of a maxim seems to have a complement. Opting out of a maxim is temporarily not accepting the force of a maxim. A person might opt out of the maxim of saying as much as is required by an interlocutor when that person must keep a secret. Thus, to the remaining three, we might add *suspending* a maxim, that is, permanently not accepting the force of a maxim in certain situations. For example, because the United States Senate allows filibustering, it suspends the maxim of relevance; and because it also does not allow a senator to be prosecuted for anything he says on the Senate floor, it suspends the maxim of quality: "Say what is true."

Robert Stalnaker provides a different sort of approach to pragmatics in his essay with that name. He is interested in handling pragmatic phenomena within a model theoretic system. An important element of that system is the notion of a possible world. The intuitive idea behind a possible world is that the way the world actually is could have been different; it is possible that the world might have been different. This idea of a different world is the foundation for the notion of possible worlds.

Performative Utterances   8

J. L. AUSTIN

I

You are more than entitled not to know what the word "performative" means. It is a new word and an ugly word, and perhaps it does not mean anything very much. But at any rate there is one thing in its favor, it is not a profound word. I remember once when I had been talking on this subject that somebody afterwards said: "You know, I haven't the least idea what he means, unless it could be that he simply means what he says." Well, that is what I should like to mean.

Let us consider first how this affair arises. We have not got to go very far back in the history of philosophy to find philosophers assuming more or less as a matter of course that the sole business, the sole interesting business, of any utterance—that is, of anything we say—is to be true or at least false. Of course they had always known that there are other kinds of things which we say—things like imperatives, the expressions of wishes, and exclamations—some of which had even been classified by grammarians, though it wasn't perhaps too easy to tell always which was which. But still philosophers have assumed that the only things that they are interested in are utterances which report facts or which describe situations truly or falsely. In recent times this kind of approach has been

questioned—in two stages, I think. First of all people began to say: "Well, if these things are true or false it ought to be possible to decide which they are, and if we can't decide which they are they aren't any good but are, in short, nonsense." And this new approach did a great deal of good; a great many things which probably are nonsense were found to be such. It is not the case, I think, that all kinds of nonsense have been adequately classified yet, and perhaps some things have been dismissed as nonsense which really are not; but still this movement, the verification movement, was, in its way, excellent.

However, we then come to the second stage. After all, we set some limits to the amount of nonsense that we talk, or at least the amount of nonsense that we are prepared to admit we talk; and so people began to ask whether after all some of those things which, treated as statements, were in danger of being dismissed as nonsense did after all really set out to be statements at all. Mightn't they perhaps be intended not to report facts but to influence people in this way or that, or to let off steam in this way or that? Or perhaps at any rate some elements in these utterances performed such functions, or, for example, drew attention in some way (without actually reporting it) to some important feature of the circumstances in which the utterance was

From *Philosophical Papers*, 2d ed., J. O. Urmson and G. J. Warnock, eds. (Oxford: Oxford University Press 1970), pp. 233–252.

105

being made. On these lines people have now adopted a new slogan, the slogan of the "different uses of language." The old approach, the old statemental approach, is sometimes called even a fallacy, the descriptive fallacy.

Certainly there are a great many uses of language. It's rather a pity that people are apt to invoke a new use of language whenever they feel so inclined, to help them out of this, that, or the other well-known philosophical tangle; we need more of a framework in which to discuss these uses of language; and also I think we should not despair too easily and talk, as people are apt to do, about the *infinite* uses of language. Philosophers will do this when they have listed as many, let us say, as seventeen; but even if there were something like ten thousand uses of language, surely we could list them all in time. This, after all, is no larger than the number of species of beetle that entomologists have taken the pains to list. But whatever the defects of either of these movements—the 'verification' movement or the 'use of language' movement—at any rate they have effected, nobody could deny, a great revolution in philosophy and, many would say, the most salutary in its history. (Not, if you come to think of it, a very immodest claim.)

Now it is one such sort of use of language that I want to examine here. I want to discuss a kind of utterance which looks like a statement and grammatically, I suppose, would be classed as a statement, which is not nonsensical, and yet is not true or false. These are not going to be utterances which contain curious verbs like "could" or "might," or curious words like "good," which many philosophers regard nowadays simply as danger signals. They will be perfectly straightforward utterances, with ordinary verbs in the first person singular present indicative active, and yet we shall see at once that they couldn't possibly be true or false. Furthermore, if a person makes an utterance of this sort we should say that he is *doing* something rather than merely *saying* something. This may sound a little odd, but the examples I shall give will in fact not be odd at all, and may even seem decidedly dull.

Here are three or four. Suppose, for example, that in the course of a marriage ceremony I say, as people will, "I do"—(sc. take this woman to be my lawful wedded wife). Or again, suppose that I tread on your toe and say "I apologize." Or again, suppose that I have the bottle of champagne in my hand and say "I name this ship the *Queen Elizabeth*." Or suppose I say "I bet you sixpence it will rain tomorrow." In all these cases it would be absurd to regard the thing that I say as a report of the performance of the action which is undoubtedly done—the action of betting, or christening, or apologizing. We should say rather that, in saying what I do, I actually perform that action. When I say "I name this ship the *Queen Elizabeth*" I do not describe the christening ceremony, I actually perform the christening; and when I say "I do" (sc. take this woman to be my lawful wedded wife), I am not reporting on a marriage, I am indulging in it.

Now these kinds of utterance are the ones that we call *performative* utterances. This is rather an ugly word, and a new word, but there seems to be no word already in existence to do the job. The nearest approach that I can think of is the word "operative," as used by lawyers. Lawyers when talking about legal instruments will distinguish between the preamble, which recites the circumstances in which a transaction is effected, and on the other hand the operative part—the part of it which actually performs the legal act which it is the purpose of the instrument to perform. So the word "operative" is very near to what we want. "I give and bequeath my watch to my brother" would be an operative clause and is a performative utterance. However, the word 'operative' has other uses, and it seems preferable to have a word specially designed for the use we want.

Now at this point one might protest, perhaps even with some alarm, that I seem to be suggesting that marrying is simply saying a few words, that just saying a few words *is* marrying. Well, that certainly is not the case. The words have to be said in the appropriate circumstances, and this is a matter that will come up again later. But the one thing we must not suppose is that what is needed in addition to the saying of the words in such cases is the performance of some internal spiritual act, of which the words then are to be the report. It's very easy to slip into this view at least in difficult, portentous cases, though perhaps not so easy in simple cases like apologizing. In the case of promising—for example, "I promise to be there tomorrow"— it's very easy to think that the utterance is simply the outward and visible (that is, verbal) sign of the performance of some inward spiritual act of promising, and this view has certainly been expressed in many classic places. There is the case of Euripides' Hippolytus, who said "My tongue swore to, but my heart did not"—perhaps it should be "mind" or "spirit" rather than "heart," but at any rate some kind of backstage artiste. Now it is clear from this sort of example that, if we slip into thinking that such utterances are reports, true or false, of the performance of inward and spiritual acts, we open a loophole to perjurers and welshers and bigamists and so on, so that there are disadvantages in being excessively solemn in this way. It is better, perhaps, to stick to the old saying that our word is our bond.

However, although these utterances do not themselves report facts and are not themselves true or false, saying these things does very often *imply* that certain things are true and not false, in some sense at least of that rather woolly word "imply." For example, when I say "I do take this woman to be my lawful wedded wife," or some other formula in the marriage ceremony, I do imply that I'm not already married, with wife living, sane, undivorced, and the rest of it. But still it is very important to realize that to imply that something or other is true, is not at all the same as saying something which is true itself.

These performative utterances are not true or false, then. But they do suffer from certain disabilities of their own. They can fail to come off in special ways, and that is what I want to consider next. The various ways in which a performative utterance may be unsatisfactory we call, for the sake of a name, the infelicities; and an infelicity arises—that is to say, the utterance is unhappy—if certain rules, transparently simple rules, are broken. I will mention some of these rules and then give examples of some infringements.

First of all, it is obvious that the conventional procedure which by our utterance we are purporting to use must actually exist. In the examples given here this procedure will be a verbal one, a verbal procedure for marrying or giving or whatever it may be; but it should be borne in mind that there are many nonverbal procedures by which we can perform exactly the same acts as we perform by these verbal means. It's worth remembering too that a great many of the things we do are at least in part of this conventional kind. Philosophers at least are too apt to assume that an action is always in the last resort the making of a physical movement, whereas it's usually, at least in part, a matter of convention.

The first rule is, then, that the convention invoked must exist and be accepted. And the second rule, also a very obvious one, is that the circumstances in which we purport to invoke this procedure must be appropriate for its invocation. If this is not observed, then the act that we purport to perform would not come off—it will be, one might say, a misfire. This will also be the case if, for example, we do not carry through the procedure—whatever it may be—correctly and completely, without a flaw and without a hitch. If any of these rules are not observed, we say that the act which we purported to perform is void, without effect. If, for example, the purported act was an act of marrying, then we should say that we "went through a form" of marriage, but we did not actually succeed in marrying.

Here are some examples of this kind of misfire. Suppose that, living in a country like our own, we wish to divorce our wife. We may try standing her in front of us squarely in the room and saying, in a voice loud enough for all to hear, "I divorce you." Now this procedure is not accepted. We shall not thereby have succeeded in divorcing our wife, at least in this country and others like it. This is a case where the convention, we should say, does not exist or is not accepted. Again, suppose that, picking sides at a children's party, I say "I pick

George." But George turns red in the face and says "Not playing." In that case I plainly, for some reason or another, have not picked George—whether because there is no convention that you can pick people who aren't playing, or because George in the circumstances is an inappropriate object for the procedure of picking. Or consider the case in which I say "I appoint you Consul," and it turns out that you have been appointed already—or perhaps it may even transpire that you are a horse; here again we have the infelicity of inappropriate circumstances, inappropriate objects, or what not. Examples of flaws and hitches are perhaps scarcely necessary—one party in the marriage ceremony says "I will," the other says "I won't"; I say "I bet sixpence," but nobody says "Done," nobody takes up the offer. In all these and other such cases, the act which we purport to perform, or set out to perform, is not achieved.

But there is another and a rather different way in which this kind of utterance may go wrong. A good many of these verbal procedures are designed for use by people who hold certain beliefs or have certain feelings or intentions. And if you use one of these formulae when you do not have the requisite thoughts or feelings or intentions then there is an abuse of the procedure, there is insincerity. Take, for example, the expression, "I congratulate you." This is designed for use by people who are glad that the person addressed has achieved a certain feat, believe that he was personally responsible for the success, and so on. If I say "I congratulate you" when I'm not pleased or when I don't believe that the credit was yours, then there is insincerity. Likewise if I say I promise to do something, without having the least intention of doing it or without believing it feasible. In these cases there is something wrong certainly, but it is not like a misfire. We should not say that I didn't in fact promise, but rather that I did promise but promised insincerely; I did congratulate you but the congratulations were hollow. And there may be an infelicity of a somewhat similar kind when the performative utterance commits the speaker to future conduct of a certain description and then in the future he does not in fact behave in the expected way. This is very obvious, of course, if I promise to do something and then break my promise, but there are many kinds of commitment of a rather less tangible form than that in the case of promising. For instance, I may say "I welcome you," bidding you welcome to my home or wherever it may be, but then I proceed to treat you as though you were exceedingly unwelcome. In this case the procedure of saying "I welcome you" has been abused in a way rather different from that of simple insincerity.

Now we might ask whether this list of infelicities is complete, whether the kinds of infelicity are mutually exclusive, and so forth. Well, it is not complete, and they are not mutually exclusive; they never are. Suppose that you are just about to name the ship, you have been appointed to name it, and you are just about to bang the bottle against the stem; but at that very moment some low type comes up, snatches the bottle out of your hand, breaks it on the stem, shouts out "I name this ship the *Generalissimo Stalin*," and then for good measure kicks away the chocks. Well, we agree of course on several things. We agree that the ship certainly isn't now named the *Generalissimo Stalin,* and we agree that it's an infernal shame and so on and so forth. But we may not agree as to how we should classify the particular infelicity in this case. We might say that here is a case of a perfectly legitimate and agreed procedure which, however, has been invoked in the wrong circumstances, namely by the wrong person, this low type instead of the person appointed to do it. But on the other hand we might look at it differently and say that this is a case where the procedure has not as a whole been gone through correctly, because part of the procedure for naming a ship is that you should first of all get yourself appointed as the person to do the naming and that's what this fellow did not do. Thus the way we should classify infelicities in different cases will be perhaps rather a difficult matter, and may even in the last resort be a bit arbitrary. But of course lawyers, who have to deal very much with this kind of thing, have invented all kinds of technical terms and have made numerous rules about different kinds of cases, which enable them to classify fairly rapidly what in particular is wrong in any given case.

As for whether this list is complete, it certainly is not. One further way in which things may go wrong is, for example, through what in general may be called misunderstanding. You may not hear what I say, or you may understand me to refer to something different from what I intended to refer to, and so on. And apart from further additions which we might make to the list, there is the general overriding consideration that, as we are performing an act when we issue these performative utterances, we may of course be doing so under duress or in some other circumstances which make us not entirely responsible for doing what we are doing. That would certainly be an unhappiness of a kind—any kind of nonresponsibility might be called an unhappiness; but of course it is a quite different kind of thing from what we have been talking about. And I might mention that, quite differently again, we could be issuing any of these utterances, as we can issue an utterance of any kind whatsoever, in the course, for example, of acting a play or making a joke or writing a poem—in which case of course it would not be seriously meant and we shall not be able to say that we seriously performed the act concerned. If the poet says "Go and catch a falling star" or whatever it may be, he doesn't seriously issue an order. Considerations of this kind apply to any utterance at all, not merely to performatives.

That, then, is perhaps enough to be going on with. We have discussed the performative utterance and its infelicities. That equips us, we may suppose, with two shining new tools to crack the crib of reality maybe. It also equips us—it always does—with two shining new skids under our metaphysical feet. The question is how we use them.

II

So far we have been going firmly ahead, feeling the firm ground of prejudice glide away beneath our feet which is always rather

exhilarating, but what next? You will be waiting for the bit when we bog down, the bit where we take it all back, and sure enough that's going to come but it will take time. First of all let us ask a rather simple question. How can we be sure, how can we tell, whether any utterance is to be classed as a performative or not? Surely, we feel, we ought to be able to do that. And we should obviously very much like to be able to say that there is a grammatical criterion for this, some grammatical means of deciding whether an utterance is performative. All the examples I have given hitherto do in fact have the same grammatical form; they all of them begin with the verb in the first person singular present indicative active—not just any kind of verb of course, but still they all are in fact of that form. Furthermore, with these verbs that I have used there is a typical asymmetry between the use of this person and tense of the verb and the use of the same verb in other persons and other tenses, and this asymmetry is rather an important clue.

For example, when we say "I promise that . . . ," the case is very different from when we say "He promises that . . . ," or in the past tense "I promised that . . . ." For when we say "I promise that . . ." we do perform an act of promising—we give a promise. What we do *not* do is to report on somebody's performing an act of promising—in particular, we do not report on somebody's use of the expression "I promise." We actually do use it and do the promising. But if I say "He promises," or in the past tense "I promised," I precisely do report on an act of promising, that is to say an act of using this formula "I promise"—I report on a present act of promising by him, or on a past act of my own. There is thus a clear difference between our first person singular present indicative active, and other persons and tenses. This is brought out by the typical incident of little Willie whose uncle says he'll give him half-a-crown if he promises never to smoke till he's 55. Little Willie's anxious parent will say "Of course he promises, don't you, Willie?" giving him a nudge, and little Willie just doesn't vouchsafe. The point here is that he must do the promising himself by saying "I promise," and his parent is going too fast in saying he promises.

That, then, is a bit of a test for whether an utterance is performative or not, but it would not do to suppose that every performative utterance has to take this standard form. There is at least one other standard form, every bit as common as this one, where the verb is in the passive voice and in the second or third person, not in the first. The sort of case I mean is that of a notice inscribed "Passengers are warned to cross the line by the bridge only," or of a document reading "You are hereby authorized" to do so-and-so. These are undoubtedly performative, and in fact a signature is often required in order to show who it is that is doing the act of warning, or authorizing, or whatever it may be. Very typical of this kind of performative—especially liable to occur in written documents of course—is that the little word 'hereby' either actually occurs or might naturally be inserted.

Unfortunately, however, we still can't possibly suggest that every utterance which is to be classed as a performative has to take one or another of these two, as we might call them, standard forms. After all it would be a very typical performative utterance to say "I order you to shut the door." This satisfies all the criteria. It is performing the act of ordering you to shut the door, and it is not true or false. But in the appropriate circumstances surely we could perform exactly the same act by simply saying "Shut the door," in the imperative. Or again, suppose that somebody sticks up a notice "This bull is dangerous," or simply "Dangerous bull," or simply "Bull." Does this necessarily differ from sticking up a notice, appropriately signed, saying "You are hereby warned that this bull is dangerous"? It seems that the simple notice "Bull" can do just the same job as the more elaborate formula. Of course the difference is that if we just stick up "Bull" it would not be quite clear that it is a warning; it might be there just for interest or information, like "Wallaby" on the cage at the zoo, or "Ancient Monument." No doubt we should know from the nature of the case that it was a warning, but it would not be explicit.

Well, in view of this breakdown of grammatical criteria, what we should like to suppose—and there is a good deal in this—is that any utterance which is performative could be reduced or expanded or analysed into one of these two standard forms beginning "I . . . " so and so or beginning "You (or he) hereby . . . " so and so. If there was any justification for this hope, as to some extent there is, then we might hope to make a list of all the verbs which can appear in these standard forms, and then we might classify the kinds of acts that can be performed by performative utterances. We might do this with the aid of a dictionary, using such a test as that already mentioned—whether there is the characteristic asymmetry between the first person singular present indicative active and the other persons and tenses—in order to decide whether a verb is to go into our list or not. Now if we make such a list of verbs we do in fact find that they fall into certain fairly well-marked classes. There is the class of cases where we deliver verdicts and make estimates and appraisals of various kinds. There is the class where we give undertakings, commit ourselves in various ways by saying something. There is the class where by saying something we exercise various rights and powers, such as appointing and voting and so on. And there are one or two other fairly well-marked classes.

Suppose this task accomplished. Then we could call these verbs in our list explicit performative verbs, and any utterance that was reduced to one or the other of our standard forms we could call an explicit performative utterance. "I order you to shut the door" would be an explicit performative utterance, whereas "Shut the door" would not—that is simply a 'primary' performative utterance or whatever we like to call it. In using the imperative we may be ordering you to shut the door, but it just isn't made clear whether we are ordering you or entreating you or imploring you or beseeching you or inciting you or tempting you, or one or another of many other subtly different acts which, in an unsophisticated primitive language, are very likely not yet discriminated.

But we need not overestimate the unsophistication of primitive languages. There are a great many devices that can be used for making clear, even at the primitive level, what act it is we are performing when we say something—the tone of voice, cadence, gesture—and above all we can rely upon the nature of the circumstances, the context in which the utterance is issued. This very often makes it quite unmistakable whether it is an order that is being given or whether, say, I am simply urging you or entreating you. We may, for instance, say something like this: "Coming from him I was bound to take it as an order." Still, in spite of all these devices, there is an unfortunate amount of ambiguity and lack of discrimination in default of our explicit performative verbs. If I say something like "I shall be there," it may not be certain whether it is a promise, or an expression of intention, or perhaps even a forecast of my future behavior, of what is going to happen to me; and it may matter a good deal, at least in developed societies, precisely which of these things it is. And that is why the explicit performative verb is evolved—to make clear exactly which it is, how far it commits me and in what way, and so forth.

This is just one way in which language develops in tune with the society of which it is the language. The social habits of the society may considerably affect the question of which performative verbs are evolved and which, sometimes for rather irrelevant reasons, are not. For example, if I say "You are a poltroon," it might be that I am censuring you or it might be that I am insulting you. Now since apparently society approves of censuring or reprimanding, we have here evolved a formula "I reprimand you," or "I censure you," which enables us expeditiously to get this desirable business over. But on the other hand, since apparently we don't approve of insulting, we have not evolved a simple formula "I insult you," which might have done just as well.

By means of these explicit performative verbs and some other devices, then, we make explicit what precise act it is that we are performing when we issue our utterance. But

here I would like to put in a word of warning. We must distinguish between the function of making explicit what act it is we are performing, and the quite different matter of *stating* what act it is we are performing. In issuing an explicit performative utterance we are not stating what act it is, we are showing or making explicit what act it is. We can draw a helpful parallel here with another case in which the act, the conventional act that we perform, is not a speech act but a physical performance. Suppose I appear before you one day and bow deeply from the waist. Well, this is ambiguous. I may be simply observing the local flora, tying my shoelace, something of that kind; on the other hand, conceivably I might be doing obeisance to you. Well, to clear up this ambiguity we have some device such as raising the hat, saying "Salaam," or something of that kind, to make it quite plain that the act being performed is the conventional one of doing obeisance rather than some other act. Now nobody would want to say that lifting your hat was stating that you were performing an act of obeisance; it certainly is not, but it does make it quite plain that you are. And so in the same way to say "I warn you that . . ." or "I order you to . . ." or "I promise that . . ." is not to state that you are doing something, but makes it plain that you are—it does constitute your verbal performance, a performance of a particular kind.

So far we have been going along as though there was a quite clear difference between our performative utterances and what we have contrasted them with, statements or reports or descriptions. But now we begin to find that this distinction is not as clear as it might be. It's now that we begin to sink in a little. In the first place, of course, we may feel doubts as to how widely our performatives extend. If we think up some odd kinds of expression we use in odd cases, we might very well wonder whether or not they satisfy our rather vague criteria for being performative utterances. Suppose, for example, somebody says "Hurrah." Well, not true or false; he is performing the act of cheering. Does that make it a performative utterance in our sense or not? Or suppose he says "Damn"; he is performing the act of swearing, and it is not true or false. Does that make it performative? We feel that in a way it does and yet it's rather different. Again, consider cases of 'suiting the action to the words'; these too may make us wonder whether perhaps the utterance should be classed as performative. Or sometimes, if somebody says "I am sorry," we wonder whether this is just the same as "I apologize"— in which case of course we have said it's a performative utterance—or whether perhaps it's to be taken as a description, true or false, of the state of his feelings. If he had said "I feel perfectly awful about it," then we should think it must be meant to be a description of the state of his feelings. If he had said "I apologize," we should feel this was clearly a performative utterance, going through the ritual of apologizing. But if he says "I am sorry" there is an unfortunate hovering between the two. This phenomenon is quite common. We often find cases in which there is an obvious pure performative utterance and obvious other utterances connected with it which are not performative but descriptive, but on the other hand a good many in between where we're not quite sure which they are. On some occasions of course they are obviously used the one way, on some occasions the other way, but on some occasions they seem positively to revel in ambiguity.

Again, consider the case of the umpire when he says "Out" or "Over," or the jury's utterance when they say that they find the prisoner guilty. Of course, we say, these are cases of giving verdicts, performing the act of appraising and so forth, but still in a way they have some connection with the facts. They seem to have something like the duty to be true or false, and seem not to be so very remote from statements. If the umpire says "Over," this surely has at least something to do with six balls in fact having been delivered rather than seven, and so on. In fact in general we may remind ourselves that "I state that . . ." does not look so very different from "I warn you that . . ." or "I promise to . . . ." It makes clear surely that the act that we are performing is an act of stating, and

so functions just like 'I warn' or 'I order'. So isn't "I state that . . ." a performative utterance? But then one may feel that utterances beginning "I state that . . ." do have to be true or false, that they *are* statements.

Considerations of this sort, then, may well make us feel pretty unhappy. If we look back for a moment at our contrast between statements and performative utterances, we realize that we were taking statements very much on trust from, as we said, the traditional treatment. Statements, we had it, were to be true or false; performative utterances on the other hand were to be felicitous or infelicitous. They were the doing of something, whereas for all we said making statements was not doing something. Now this contrast surely, if we look back at it, is unsatisfactory. Of course statements are liable to be assessed in this matter of their correspondence or failure to correspond with the facts, that is, being true or false. But they are also liable to infelicity every bit as much as are performative utterances. In fact some troubles that have arisen in the study of statements recently can be shown to be simply troubles of infelicity. For example, it has been pointed out that there is something very odd about saying something like this: "The cat is on the mat but I don't believe it is." Now this is an outrageous thing to say, but it is not self-contradictory. There is no reason why the cat shouldn't be on the mat without my believing that it is. So how are we to classify what's wrong with this peculiar statement? If we remember now the doctrine of infelicity we shall see that the person who makes this remark about the cat is in much the same position as somebody who says something like this: "I promise that I shall be there, but I haven't the least intention of being there." Once again you can of course perfectly well promise to be there without having the least intention of being there, but there is something outrageous about saying it, about actually avowing the insincerity of the promise you give. In the same way there is insincerity in the case of the person who says "The cat is on the mat but I don't believe it is," and he is actually avowing that insincerity—which makes a peculiar kind of nonsense.

A second case that has come to light is the one about John's children—the case where somebody is supposed to say "All John's children are bald but John hasn't got any children." Or perhaps somebody says "All John's children are bald," when as a matter of fact—he doesn't say so—John has no children. Now those who study statements have worried about this; ought they to say that the statement "All John's children are bald" is meaningless in this case? Well, if it is, it is not a bit like a great many other more standard kinds of meaninglessness; and we see, if we look back at our list of infelicities, that what is going wrong here is much the same as what goes wrong in, say, the case of a contract for the sale of a piece of land when the piece of land referred to does not exist. Now what we say in the case of this sale of land, which of course would be effected by a performative utterance, is that the sale is void—void for lack of reference or ambiguity of reference; and so we can see that the statement about all John's children is likewise void for lack of reference. And if the man actually says that John has no children in the same breath as saying they're all bald, he is making the same kind of outrageous utterance as the man who says "The cat is on the mat and I don't believe it is," or the man who says "I promise to but I don't intend to."

In this way, then, ills that have been found to afflict statements can be precisely paralleled with ills that are characteristic of performative utterances. And after all when we state something or describe something or report something, we do perform an act which is every bit as much an act as an act of ordering or warning. There seems no good reason why stating should be given a specially unique position. Of course philosophers have been wont to talk as though you or I or anybody could just go round stating anything about anything and that would be perfectly in order, only there's just a little question: is it true or false? But besides the little question, is it true or false, there is surely the question: *is* it in order? Can you go round just making statements about anything? Suppose for example you say to me "I'm feeling pretty moldy this

morning." Well, I say to you "You're not"; and you say "What the devil do you mean, I'm not?" I say "Oh nothing—I'm just stating you're not, is it true or false?" And you say "Wait a bit about whether it's true or false, the question is what did you mean by making statements about somebody else's feelings? I told you I'm feeling pretty moldy. You're just not in a position to say, to state that I'm not." This brings out that you can't just make statements about other people's feelings (though you can make guesses if you like); and there are very many things which, having no knowledge of, not being in a position to pronounce about, you just can't state. What we need to do for the case of stating, and by the same token describing and reporting, is to take them a bit off their pedestal, to realize that they are speech acts no less than all these other speech acts that we have been mentioning and talking about as performative.

Then let us look for a moment at our original contrast between the performative and the statement from the other side. In handling performatives we have been putting it all the time as though the only thing that a performative utterance had to do was to be felicitous, to come off, not to be a misfire, not to be an abuse. Yes, but that's not the end of the matter. At least in the case of many utterances which, on what we have said, we should have to class as performative—cases where we say "I warn you to . . . ," "I advise you to . . ." and so on—there will be other questions besides simply: was it in order, was it all right, as a piece of advice or a warning, did it come off? After that surely there will be the question: was it good or sound advice? Was it a justified warning? Or in the case, let us say, of a verdict or an estimate: was it a good estimate, or a sound verdict? And these are questions that can only be decided by considering how the content of the verdict or estimate is related in some way to fact, or to evidence available about the facts. This is to say that we do require to assess at least a great many performative utterances in a general dimension of correspondence with fact. It may still be said, of course, that this does not make them *very* like statements because still they are not true or false, and that's a little black and white speciality that distinguishes statements as a class apart. But actually—though it would take too long to go on about this—the more you think about truth and falsity the more you find that very few statements that we ever utter are just true or just false. Usually there is the question are they fair or are they not fair, are they adequate or not adequate, are they exaggerated or not exaggerated? Are they too rough, or are they perfectly precise, accurate, and so on? 'True' and 'false' are just general labels for a whole dimension of different appraisals which have something or other to do with the relation between what we say and the facts. If, then, we loosen up our ideas of truth and falsity we shall see that statements, when assessed in relation to the facts, are not so very different after all from pieces of advice, warnings, verdicts, and so on.

We see then that stating something is performing an act just as much as is giving an order or giving a warning; and we see, on the other hand, that, when we give an order or a warning or a piece of advice, there is a question about how this is related to fact which is not perhaps so very different from the kind of question that arises when we discuss how a statement is related to fact. Well, this seems to mean that in its original form our distinction between the performative and the statement is considerably weakened, and indeed breaks down. I will just make a suggestion as to how to handle this matter. We need to go very much farther back, to consider all the ways and senses in which saying anything at all is doing this or that—because of course it is always doing a good many different things. And one thing that emerges when we do do this is that, besides the question that has been

very much studied in the past as to what a certain utterance *means,* there is a further question distinct from this as to what was the *force,* as we may call it, of the utterance. We may be quite clear what "Shut the door" means, but not yet at all clear on the further point as to whether as uttered at a certain time it was an order, an entreaty, or whatnot. What we need besides the old doctrine about meanings is a new doctrine about all the possible forces of utterances, towards the discovery of which our proposed list of explicit performative verbs would be a very great help; and then, going on from there, an investigation of the various terms of appraisal that we use in discussing speech-acts of this, that, or the other precise kind—orders, warnings, and the like.

The notions that we have considered then, are the performative, the infelicity, the explicit performative, and lastly, rather hurriedly, the notion of the forces of utterances. I dare say that all this seems a little unremunerative, a little complicated. Well, I suppose in some ways it is unremunerative, and I suppose it ought to be remunerative. At least, though, I think that if we pay attention to these matters we can clear up some mistakes in philosophy; and after all philosophy is used as a scapegoat, it parades mistakes which are really the mistakes of everybody. We might even clear up some mistakes in grammar, which perhaps is a little more respectable.

And is it complicated? Well, it is complicated a bit; but life and truth and things do tend to be complicated. It's not things, it's philosophers that are simple. You will have heard it said, I expect, that oversimplification is the occupational disease of philosophers, and in a way one might agree with that. But for a sneaking suspicion that it's their occupation.

What Is a Speech Act?   9

JOHN R. SEARLE

I. INTRODUCTION

In a typical speech situation involving a speaker, a hearer, and an utterance by the speaker, there are many kinds of acts associated with the speaker's utterance. The speaker will characteristically have moved his jaw and tongue and made noises. In addition, he will characteristically have performed some acts within the class which includes informing or irritating or boring his hearers; he will further characteristically have performed acts within the class which includes referring to Kennedy or Khrushchev or the North Pole; and he will also have performed acts within the class which includes making statements, asking questions, issuing commands, giving reports, greeting, and warning. The members of this last class are what Austin[1] called illocutionary acts and it is with this class that I shall be concerned in this paper, so the paper might have been called "What is an Illocutionary Act?" I do not attempt to define the expression 'illocutionary act', although if my analysis of a particular illocutionary act succeeds it may provide the basis for a definition. Some of the English verbs and verb phrases associated with illocutionary acts are: state, assert, describe, warn, remark, comment, command, order, request, criticize, apologize, censure, approve, welcome, promise, express approval, and express regret. Austin claimed that there were over a thousand such expressions in English.

By way of introduction, perhaps I can say why I think it is of interest and importance in the philosophy of language to study speech acts, or, as they are sometimes called, language acts or linguistic acts. I think it is essential to any specimen of linguistic communication that it involve a linguistic act. It is not, as has generally been supposed, the symbol or word or sentence, or even the token of the symbol or word or sentence, which is the unit of linguistic communication, but rather it is the *production* of the token in the performance of the speech act that constitutes the basic unit of linguistic communication. To put this point more precisely, the production of the sentence token under certain conditions is the illocutionary act, and the illocutionary act is the minimal unit of linguistic communication.

I do not know how to *prove* that linguistic communication essentially involves acts but I can think of arguments with which one might attempt to convince someone who was sceptical. One argument would be to call the sceptic's attention to the fact that when he takes a noise or a mark on paper to be an instance of linguistic communication, as a message, one of the things that is involved in his so taking that noise or mark is that he should regard it as having been produced by a

From *Philosophy in America*, Max Black, ed. (Ithaca: Cornell University Press, 1965), pp. 221–239.

being with certain intentions. He cannot just regard it as a natural phenomenon, like a stone, a waterfall, or a tree. In order to regard it as an instance of linguistic communication one must suppose that its production is what I am calling a speech act. It is a logical presupposition, for example, of current attempts to decipher the Mayan hieroglyphs that we at least hypothesize that the marks we see on the stones were produced by beings more or less like ourselves and produced with certain kinds of intentions. If we were certain the marks were a consequence of, say, water erosion, then the question of deciphering them or even calling them hieroglyphs could not arise. To construe them under the category of linguistic communication necessarily involves construing their production as speech acts.

To perform illocutionary acts is to engage in a rule-governed form of behavior. I shall argue that such things as asking questions or making statements are rule-governed in ways quite similar to those in which getting a base hit in baseball or moving a knight in chess are rule-governed forms of acts. I intend therefore to explicate the notion of an illocutionary act by stating a set of necessary and sufficient conditions for the performance of a particular kind of illocutionary act, and extracting from it a set of semantic rules for the use of the expression (or syntactic device) which marks the utterance as an illocutionary act of that kind. If I am successful in stating the conditions and the corresponding rules for even one kind of illocutionary act, that will provide us with a pattern for analyzing other kinds of acts and consequently for explicating the notion in general. But in order to set the stage for actually stating conditions and extracting rules for performing an illocutionary act I have to discuss three other preliminary notions: *rules, propositions,* and *meaning.* I shall confine my discussion of these notions to those aspects which are essential to my main purposes in this paper, but, even so, what I wish to say concerning each of these notions, if it were to be at all complete, would require a paper for each; however, sometimes it may be worth sacrificing thoroughness for the sake of scope and I shall therefore be very brief.

II. RULES

In recent years there has been in the philosophy of language considerable discussion involving the notion of rules for the use of expressions. Some philosophers have even said that knowing the meaning of a word is simply a matter of knowing the rules for its use or employment. One disquieting feature of such discussions is that no philosopher, to my knowledge at least, has ever given anything like an adequate formulation of the rules for the use of even one expression. If meaning is a matter of rules of use, surely we ought to be able to state the rules for the use of expressions in a way which would explicate the meaning of those expressions. Certain other philosophers, dismayed perhaps by the failure of their colleagues to produce any rules, have denied the fashionable view that meaning is a matter of rules and have asserted that there are no semantic rules of the proposed kind at all. I am inclined to think that this scepticism is premature and stems from a failure to distinguish different sorts of rules, in a way which I shall now attempt to explain.

I distinguish between two sorts of rules: Some regulate antecedently existing forms of behavior; for example, the rules of etiquette regulate interpersonal relationships, but these relationships exist independently of the rules of etiquette. Some rules on the other hand do not merely regulate but create or define new forms of behavior. The rules of football, for example, do not merely regulate the game of football but as it were create the possibility of or define that activity. The activity of playing football is constituted by acting in accordance with these rules; football has no existence apart from these rules. I call the latter kind of rules constitutive rules and the former kind regulative rules. Regulative rules regulate a pre-existing activity, an activity whose existence is logically independent of the existence of the rules. Constitutive rules constitute (and also regulate) an activity the existence of which is logically dependent on the rules.[2]

Regulative rules characteristically take the form of or can be paraphrased as imperatives, e.g. "When cutting food hold the knife in the right hand," or "Officers are to wear ties at dinner." Some constitutive rules take quite a different form, e.g. a checkmate is made if the king is attacked in such a way that no move will leave it unattacked; a touchdown is scored when a player crosses the opponents' goal line in possession of the ball while a play is in progress. If our paradigms of rules are imperative regulative rules, such nonimperative constitutive rules are likely to strike us as extremely curious and hardly even as rules at all. Notice that they are almost tautological in character, for what the 'rule' seems to offer is a partial definition of 'checkmate' or 'touchdown'. But, of course, this quasi-tautological character is a necessary consequence of their being constitutive rules: the rules concerning touchdowns must define the notion of 'touchdown' in the same way that the rules concerning football define 'football'. That, for example, a touchdown can be scored in such and such ways and counts six points can appear sometimes as a rule, sometimes as an analytic truth; and that it can be construed as a tautology is a clue to the fact that the rule in question is a constitutive one. Regulative rules generally have the form "Do X" or "If Y do X." Some members of the set of constitutive rules have this form but some also have the form "X counts as Y."[3]

The failure to perceive this is of some importance in philosophy. Thus, e.g., some philosophers ask "How can a promise create an obligation?" A similar question would be "How can a touchdown create six points?" And as they stand both questions can only be answered by stating a rule of the form "X counts as Y."

I am inclined to think that both the failure of some philosophers to state rules for the use of expressions and the scepticism of other philosophers concerning the existence of any such rules stem at least in part from a failure to recognize the distinctions between constitutive and regulative rules. The model or paradigm of a rule which most philosophers have is that of a regulative rule, and if one looks in semantics for purely regulative rules one is not likely to find anything interesting

from the point of view of logical analysis. There are no doubt social rules of the form "One ought not to utter obscenities at formal gatherings," but that hardly seems a rule of the sort that is crucial in explicating the semantics of a language. The hypothesis that lies behind the present paper is that the semantics of a language can be regarded as a series of systems of constitutive rules and that illocutionary acts are acts performed in accordance with these sets of constitutive rules. One of the aims of this paper is to formulate a set of constitutive rules for a certain kind of speech act. And if what I have said concerning constitutive rules is correct, we should not be surprised if not all these rules take the form of imperative rules. Indeed we shall see that the rules fall into several different categories, none of which is quite like the rules of etiquette. The effort to state the rules for an illocutionary act can also be regarded as a kind of test of the hypothesis that there are constitutive rules underlying speech acts. If we are unable to give any satisfactory rule formulations, our failure could be construed as partially disconfirming evidence against the hypothesis.

III. PROPOSITIONS

Different illocutionary acts often have features in common with each other. Consider utterances of the following sentences:

(1)   Will John leave the room?
(2)   John will leave the room.
(3)   John, leave the room!
(4)   Would that John left the room.
(5)   If John will leave the room, I will leave also.

Utterances of each of these on a given occasion would characteristically be performances of different illocutionary acts. The first would, characteristically, be a question, the second an assertion about the future, that is, a prediction, the third a request or order, the fourth an expression of a wish, and the fifth a hypothetical expression of intention. Yet in the performance of each the speaker would characteristically perform some subsidiary acts which are common to all five illocutionary acts. In the utterance of each the speaker *refers* to a particular person John and *predicates* the act of leaving the room of that person. In no case is that all he does, but in every case it is a part of what he does. I shall say, therefore, that in each of these cases, although the illocutionary acts are different, at least some of the nonillocutionary acts of reference and predication are the same.

The reference to some person John and predication of the same thing of him in each of these illocutionary acts inclines me to say that there is a common *content* in each of them. Something expressible by the clause "that John will leave the room" seems to be a common feature of all. We could, with not too much distortion, write each of these sentences in a way which would isolate this common feature: "I assert that John will leave the room," "I ask whether John will leave the room," etc.

For lack of a better word I propose to call this common content a proposition, and I shall describe this feature of these illocutionary acts by saying that in the utterance of each of (1)–(5) the speaker expresses the proposition that John will leave the room. Notice that I do not say that the sentence expresses the proposition; I do not know how sentences could perform acts of that kind. But I shall say that in the utterance of the sentence the speaker expresses a proposition. Notice also that I am distinguishing between a proposition and an assertion or statement of that proposition. The proposition that John will leave the room is expressed in the utterance of all of (1)–(5) but only in (2) is that proposition asserted. An assertion is an illocutionary act, but a proposition is not an act at all, although the act of expressing a proposition is a part of performing certain illocutionary acts.

I might summarize this by saying that I am distinguishing between the illocutionary act and the propositional content of an illocutionary act. Of course, not all illocutionary acts have a propositional content, for example, an utterance of "Hurrah!" or "Ouch!" does not. In one version or another this distinction is an old one and has been marked in different ways by authors as diverse as Frege, Sheffer, Lewis, Reichenbach and Hare, to mention only a few.

From a semantical point of view we can distinguish between the propositional indicator in the sentence and the indicator of illocutionary force. That is, for a large class of sentences used to perform illocutionary acts, we can say for the purpose of our analysis that the sentence has two (not necessarily separate) parts, the proposition indicating element and the function indicating device.[4] The function indicating device shows how the proposition is to be taken, or, to put it in another way, what illocutionary force the utterance is to have, that is, what illocutionary act the speaker is performing in the utterance of the sentence. Function indicating devices in English include word order, stress, intonation contour, punctuation, the mood of the verb, and finally a set of so-called performative verbs: I may indicate the kind of illocutionary act I am performing by beginning the sentence with "I apologize," "I warn," "I state," etc. Often in actual speech situations the context will make it clear what the illocutionary force of the utterance is, without its being necessary to invoke the appropriate function indicating device.

If this semantical distinction is of any real importance, it seems likely that it should have some syntactical analogue, and certain recent developments in transformational grammar tend to support the view that it does. In the underlying phrase marker of a sentence there is a distinction between those elements which correspond to the function indicating device and those which correspond to the propositional content.

The distinction between the function indicating device and the proposition indicating device will prove very useful to us in giving an analysis of an illocutionary act. Since the same proposition can be common to all sorts of illocutionary acts, we can separate our analysis of the proposition from our analysis of kinds of illocutionary acts. I think there are rules for expressing propositions, rules for such things as reference and predication, but those rules can be discussed independently of the rules for function indicating. In this paper

I shall not attempt to discuss propositional rules but shall concentrate on rules for using certain kinds of function indicating devices.

IV. MEANING

Speech acts are characteristically performed in the utterance of sounds or the making or marks. What is the difference between *just* uttering sounds or making marks and performing a speech act? One difference is that the sounds or marks one makes in the performance of a speech act are characteristically said to *have meaning,* and a second related difference is that one is characteristically said to *mean something* by those sounds or marks. Characteristically when one speaks one means something by what one says, and what one says, the string of morphemes that one emits, is characteristically said to have a meaning. Here, incidentally, is another point at which our analogy between performing speech acts and playing games breaks down. The pieces in a game like chess are not characteristically said to have a meaning, and furthermore when one makes a move one is not characteristically said to mean anything by that move.

But what is it for one to mean something by what one says, and what is it for something to have a meaning? To answer the first of these questions I propose to borrow and revise some ideas of Paul Grice. In an article entitled "Meaning,"[5] Grice gives the following analysis of one sense of the notion of 'meaning'. To say that *A* meant something by *x* is to say that "*A* intended the utterance of *x* to produce some effect in an audience by means of the recognition of this intention." This seems to me a useful start on an analysis of meaning, first because it shows the close relationship between the notion of meaning and the notion of intention, and secondly because it captures something which is, I think, essential to speaking a language: In speaking a language I attempt to communicate things to my hearer by means of getting him to recognize my intention to communicate just those things. For example, characteristically, when I make an assertion, I attempt to communicate to and

convince my hearer of the truth of a certain proposition; and the means I employ to do this are to utter certain sounds, which utterance I intend to produce in him the desired effect by means of his recognition of my intention to produce just that effect. I shall illustrate this with an example. I might on the one hand attempt to get you to believe that I am French by speaking French all the time, dressing in the French manner, showing wild enthusiasm for de Gaulle, and cultivating French acquaintances. But I might on the other hand attempt to get you to believe that I am French by simply telling you that I am French. Now, what is the difference between these two ways of my attempting to get you to believe that I am French? One crucial difference is that in the second case I attempt to get you to believe that I am French by getting you to recognize that it is my purported intention to get you to believe just that. That is one of the things involved in telling you that I am French. But of course if I try to get you to believe that I am French by putting on the act I described, then your recognition of my intention to produce in you the belief that I am French is not the means I am employing. Indeed in this case you would, I think, become rather suspicious if you recognized my intention.

However valuable this analysis of meaning is, it seems to me to be in certain respects defective. First of all, it fails to distinguish the different kinds of effects—perlocutionary versus illocutionary—that one may intend to produce in one's hearers, and it further fails to show the way in which these different kinds of effects are related to the notion of meaning. A second defect is that it fails to account for the extent to which meaning is a matter of rules or conventions. That is, this account of meaning does not show the connection between one's meaning something by what one says and what that which one says actually means in the language. In order to illustrate this point I now wish to present a counterexample to this analysis of meaning. The point of the counterexample will be to illustrate the connection between what a speaker means and what the words he utters mean.

Suppose that I am an American soldier in the Second World War and that I am captured by Italian troops. And suppose also that I wish to get these troops to believe that I am a German officer in order to get them to release me. What I would like to do is to tell them in German or Italian that I am a German officer. But let us suppose I don't know enough German or Italian to do that. So I, as it were, attempt to put on a show of telling them that I am a German officer by reciting those few bits of German that I know, trusting that they don't know enough German to see through my plan. Let us suppose I know only one line of German, which I remember from a poem I had to memorize in a high school German course. Therefore I, a captured American, address my Italian captors with the following sentence: "Kennst du das Land, wo die Zitronen blühen?" Now, let us describe the situation in Gricean terms. I intend to produce a certain effect in them, namely, the effect of believing that I am a German officer; and I intend to produce this effect by means of their recognition of my intention. I intend that they should think that I am trying to tell them is that I am a German officer. But does it follow from this account that when I say "Kennst du das Land . . ." etc., what I mean is, "I am a German officer"? Not only does it not follow, but in this case it seems plainly false that when I utter the German sentence what I mean is "I am a German officer," or even "Ich bin ein deutscher Offizier," because what the words mean is, "Knowest thou the land where the lemon trees bloom?" Of course, I want my captors to be deceived into thinking that what I mean is "I am a German officer," but part of what is involved in the deception is getting them to think that that is what the words which I utter mean in German. At one point in the *Philosophical Investigations* Wittgenstein says "Say 'it's cold here' and mean 'it's warm here.' "[6] The reason we are unable to do this is that what we can mean is a function of what we are saying. Meaning is more than a matter of intention, it is also a matter of convention.

Grice's account can be amended to deal with counterexamples of this kind. We have here a case where I am trying to produce a certain effect by means of the recognition of my intention to produce that effect, but the device I use to produce this effect is one which is conventionally, by the rules governing the use of that device, used as a means of producing quite different illocutionary effects. We must therefore reformulate the Gricean account of meaning in such a way as to make it clear that one's meaning something when one says something is more than just contingently related to what the sentence means in the language one is speaking. In our analysis of illocutionary acts, we must capture both the intentional and the conventional aspects and especially the relationship between them. In the performance of an illocutionary act the speaker intends to produce a certain effect by means of getting the hearer to recognize his intention to produce that effect, and furthermore, if he is using words literally, he intends this recognition to be achieved in virtue of the fact that the rules for using the expressions he utters associate the expressions with the production of that effect. It is this *combination* of elements which we shall need to express in our analysis of the illocutionary act.

V. HOW TO PROMISE

I shall now attempt to give an analysis of the illocutionary act of promising. In order to do this I shall ask what conditions are necessary and sufficient for the act of promising to have been performed in the utterance of a given sentence. I shall attempt to answer this question by stating these conditions as a set of propositions such that the conjunction of the members of the set entails the proposition that a speaker made a promise, and the proposition that the speaker made a promise entails this conjunction. Thus each condition will be a necessary condition for the performance of the act of promising, and taken collectively the set of conditions will be a sufficient condition for the act to have been performed.

If we get such a set of conditions we can extract from them a set of rules for the use of the function indicating device. The method here is analogous to discovering the rules of chess by asking oneself what are the necessary and sufficient conditions under which one can be said to have correctly moved a knight or castled or checkmated a player, etc. We are in the position of someone who has learned to play chess without ever having the rules formulated and who wants such a formulation. We learned how to play the game of illocutionary acts, but in general it was done without an explicit formulation of the rules, and the first step in getting such a formulation is to set out the conditions for the performance of a particular illocutionary act. Our inquiry will therefore serve a double philosophical purpose. By stating a set of conditions for the performance of a particular illocutionary act we shall have offered a partial explication of that notion and shall also have paved the way for the second step, the formulation of the rules.

I find the statement of the conditions very difficult to do, and I am not entirely satisfied with the list I am about to present. One reason for the difficulty is that the notion of a promise, like most notions in ordinary language, does not have absolutely strict rules. There are all sorts of odd, deviant, and borderline promises; and counterexamples, more or less bizarre, can be produced against my analysis. I am inclined to think we shall not be able to get a set of knockdown necessary and sufficient conditions that will exactly mirror the ordinary use of the word "promise." I am confining my discussion, therefore, to the center of the concept of promising and ignoring the fringe, borderline, and partially defective cases. I also confine my discussion to fullblown explicit promises and ignore promises made by elliptical turns of phrase, hints, metaphors, etc.

Another difficulty arises from my desire to state the conditions without certain forms of circularity. I want to give a list of conditions for the performance of a certain illocutionary act, which do not themselves mention the performance of any illocutionary acts. I need to satisfy this condition in order to offer an explication of the notion of an illocutionary act in general, otherwise I should simply be showing the relation between different illocu-tionary acts. However, although there will be no reference to illocutionary *acts,* certain illocutionary *concepts* will appear in the analysans as well as in the analysandum; and I think this form of circularity is unavoidable because of the nature of constitutive rules.

In the presentation of the conditions I shall first consider the case of a sincere promise and then show how to modify the conditions to allow for insincere promises. As our inquiry is semantical rather than syntactical, I shall simply assume the existence of grammatically well-formed sentences.

Given that a speaker S utters a sentence T in the presence of a hearer H, then, in the utterance of T, S sincerely (and nondefectively) promises that p to H if and only if:

(1) *Normal input and output conditions obtain.* I use the terms 'input' and 'output' to cover the large and indefinite range of conditions under which any kind of serious linguistic communication is possible. 'Output' covers the conditions for intelligible speaking and 'input' covers the conditions for understanding. Together they include such things as that the speaker and hearer both know how to speak the language; both are conscious of what they are doing; the speaker is not acting under duress or threats; they have no physical impediments to communication, such as deafness, aphasia, or laryngitis; they are not acting in a play or telling jokes, etc.

(2) *S expresses that p in the utterance of T.* This condition isolates the propositional content from the rest of the speech act and enables us to concentrate on the peculiarities of promising in the rest of the analysis.

(3) *In expressing that p, S predicates a future act A of S.* In the case of promising the function indicating device is an expression whose scope includes certain features of the proposition. In a promise an act must be predicated of the speaker and it cannot be a past act. I cannot promise to have done something, and I cannot promise that someone else will do something. (Although I can promise to see that he will do it.) The notion of an act, as I am construing it for present purposes, includes refraining from acts, performing series of acts, and may also include states and conditions: I may promise

not to do something, I may promise to do something repeatedly, and I may promise to be or remain in a certain state or condition. I call conditions (2) and (3) the *propositional content conditions.*

(4) *H would prefer S's doing A to his not doing A, and S believes H would prefer his doing A to his not doing A.* One crucial distinction between promises on the one hand and threats on the other is that a promise is a pledge to do something for you, not to you, but a threat is a pledge to do something to you, not for you. A promise is defective if the thing promised is something the promisee does not want done; and it is further defective if the promisor does not believe the promisee wants it done, since a nondefective promise must be intended as a promise and not as a threat or warning. I think both halves of this double condition are necessary in order to avoid fairly obvious counterexamples.

One can, however, think of apparent counterexamples to this condition as stated. Suppose I say to a lazy student "If you don't hand in your paper on time I promise you I will give you a failing grade in the course." Is this utterance a promise? I am inclined to think not; we would more naturally describe it as a warning or possibly even a threat. But why then is it possible to use the locution "I promise" in such a case? I think we use it here because "I promise" and "I hereby promise" are among the strongest function indicating devices for *commitment* provided by the English language. For that reason we often use these expressions in the performance of speech acts which are not strictly speaking promises but in which we wish to emphasize our commitment. To illustrate this, consider another apparent counterexample to the analysis along different lines. Sometimes, more commonly I think in the United States than in England, one hears people say "I promise" when making an emphatic assertion. Suppose, for example, I accuse you of having stolen the money. I say, "You stole that money, didn't you?" You reply "No, I didn't, I promise you I didn't." Did you make a promise in this case? I find it very unnatural to describe your utterance as a promise. This

utterance would be more aptly described as an emphatic denial, and we can explain the occurrence of the function indicating device "I promise" as derivative from genuine promises and serving here as an expression adding emphasis to your denial.

In general the point stated in condition (4) is that if a purported promise is to be nondefective the thing promised must be something the hearer wants done, or considers to be in his interest, or would prefer being done to not being done, etc.; and the speaker must be aware of or believe or know, etc. that this is the case. I think a more elegant and exact formulation of this condition would require the introduction of technical terminology.

(5) *It is not obvious to both S and H that S will do A in the normal course of events.* This condition is an instance of a general condition on many different kinds of illocutionary acts to the effect that the act must have a point. For example, if I make a request to someone to do something which it is obvious that he is already doing or is about to do, then my request is pointless and to that extent defective. In an actual speech situation, listeners, knowing the rules for performing illocutionary acts, will assume that this condition is satisfied. Suppose, for example, that in the course of a public speech I say to a member of my audience "Look here, Smith, pay attention to what I am saying." In order to make sense of this utterance the audience will have to assume that Smith has not been paying attention or at any rate that it is not obvious that he has been paying attention, that the question of his paying attention has arisen in some way; because a condition for making a request is that it is not obvious that the hearer is doing or about to do the thing requested.

Similarly with promises. It is out of order for me to promise to do something that it is obvious I am going to do anyhow. If I do seem to be making such a promise, the only way my audience can make sense of my utterance is to assume that I believe that it is not obvious that I am going to do the thing promised. A happily married man who promises his wife he will not desert her in the next week is likely to provide more anxiety than comfort.

Parenthetically I think this condition is an instance of the sort of phenomenon stated in Zipf's law. I think there is operating in our language, as in most forms of human behavior, a principle of least effort, in this case a principle of maximum illocutionary ends with minimum phonetic effort; and I think condition (5) is an instance of it.

I call conditions such as (4) and (5) *preparatory conditions*. They are *sine quibus non* of happy promising, but they do not yet state the essential feature.

(6) *S intends to do A.* The most important distinction between sincere and insincere promises is that in the case of the insincere promise the speaker intends to do the act promised, in the case of the insincere promise he does not intend to do the act. Also in sincere promises the speaker believes it is possible for him to do the act (or to refrain from doing it), but I think the proposition that he intends to do it entails that he thinks it is possible to do (or refrain from doing) it, so I am not stating that as an extra condition. I call this condition the *sincerity condition*.

(7) *S intends that the utterance of T will place him under an obligation to do A.* The essential feature of a promise is that it is the undertaking of an obligation to perform a certain act. I think that this condition distinguishes promises (and other members of the same family such as vows) from other kinds of speech acts. Notice that in the statement of the condition we only specify the speaker's intention; further conditions will make clear how that intention is realized. It is clear, however, that having this intention is a necessary condition of making a promise; for if a speaker can demonstrate that he did not have this intention in a given utterance, he can prove that the utterance was not a promise. We know, for example, that Mr Pickwick did not promise to marry the woman because we know he did not have the appropriate intention.

I call this the *essential condition*.

(8) *S intends that the utterance of T will produce in H a belief that conditions (6) and (7) obtain by means of the recognition of the intention to produce that belief, and he intends*

this recognition to be achieved by means of the recognition of the sentence as one conventionally used to produce such beliefs. This captures our amended Gricean analysis of what it is for the speaker to mean to make a promise. The speaker intends to produce a certain illocutionary effect by means of getting the hearer to recognize his intention to produce that effect, and he also intends this recognition to be achieved in virtue of the fact that the lexical and syntactical character of the item he utters conventionally associates it with producing that effect.

Strictly speaking this condition could be formulated as part of condition (1), but it is of enough philosophical interest to be worth stating separately. I find it troublesome for the following reason. If my original objection to Grice is really valid, then surely, one might say, all these iterated intentions are superfluous; all that is necessary is that the speaker should seriously utter a sentence. The production of all these effects is simply a consequence of the hearer's knowledge of what the sentence means, which in turn is a consequence of his knowledge of the language, which is assumed by the speaker at the outset. I think the correct reply to this objection is that condition (8) explicates what it is for the speaker to 'seriously' utter the sentence, i.e. to utter it and mean it, but I am not completely confident about either the force of the objection or of the reply.

(9) *The semantical rules of the dialect spoken by S and H are such that T is correctly and sincerely uttered if and only if conditions (1)–(8) obtain.* This condition is intended to make clear that the sentence uttered is one which by the semantical rules of the language is used to make a promise. Taken together with condition (8), it eliminates counterexamples like the captured soldier example considered earlier. Exactly what the formulation of the rules is, we shall soon see.

So far we have considered only the case of a sincere promise. But insincere promises are promises nonetheless, and we now need to show how to modify the conditions to allow for them. In making an insincere promise the speaker does not have all the intentions and beliefs he has when making a sincere promise. However, he purports to have them. Indeed it is because he purports to have intentions and beliefs which he does not have that we describe his act as insincere. So to allow for insincere promises we need only to revise our conditions to state that the speaker takes responsibility for having the beliefs and intentions rather than stating that he actually has them. A clue that the speaker does take such responsibility is the fact that he could not say without absurdity, e.g. "I promise to do A but I do not intend to do A." To say "I promise to do A" is to take responsibility for intending to do A, and this condition holds whether the utterance was sincere or insincere. To allow for the possibility of an insincere promise then we have only to revise condition (6) so that it states not that the speaker intends to do A, but that he takes responsibility for intending to do A, and to avoid the charge of circularity I shall phrase this as follows:

(6*) *S intends that the utterance of T will make him responsible for intending to do A.* Thus amended [and with 'sincerely' dropped from our analysandum and from condition (9)], our analysis is neutral on the question whether the promise was sincere or insincere.

VI. RULES FOR THE USE OF THE FUNCTION INDICATING DEVICE

Our next task is to extract from our set of conditions a set of rules for the use of the function indicating device. Obviously not all of our conditions are equally relevant to this task. Condition (1) and conditions of the forms (8) and (9) apply generally to all kinds of normal illocutionary acts and are not peculiar to promising. Rules for the function indicating device for promising are to be found corresponding to conditions (2)–(7).

The semantical rules for the use of any function indicating device P for promising are:

Rule 1. P is to be uttered only in the context of a sentence (or larger stretch of discourse) the utterance of which predicates some future act A of the speaker S. I call this the *propositional content rule*. It is derived from the propositional content conditions (2) and (3).

Rule 2. P is to be uttered only if the hearer H would prefer S's doing A to his not doing A, and S believes H would prefer S's doing A to his not doing A.

Rule 3. P is to be uttered only if it is not obvious to both S and H that S will do A in the normal course of events. I call rules (2) and (3) *preparatory rules*. They are derived from the preparatory conditions (4) and (5).

Rule 4. P is to be uttered only if S intends to do A. I call this the *sincerity rule*. It is derived from the sincerity condition (6).

Rule 5. The utterance of P counts as the undertaking of an obligation to do A. I call this the *essential rule.*

These rules are ordered: Rules 2–5 apply only if rule 1 is satisfied, and rule 5 applies only if rules 2 and 3 are satisfied as well.

Notice that whereas rules 1–4 take the form of quasi-imperatives, i.e., they are of the form: utter P only if x, rule 5 is of the form: the utterance of P counts as Y. Thus rule 5 is of the kind peculiar to systems of constitutive rules which I discussed in section II.

Notice also that the rather tiresome analogy with games is holding up remarkably well. If we ask ourselves under what conditions a player could be said to move a knight correctly, we would find preparatory conditions, such as that it must be his turn to move, as well as the essential condition stating the actual positions the knight can move to. I think that there is even a sincerity rule for competitive games, the rule that each side tries to win. I suggest that the team which 'throws' the game is behaving in a way closely analogous to the speaker who lies or makes false promises. Of course, there usually are no propositional content rules for games, because games do not, by and large, represent states of affairs.

If this analysis is of any general interest beyond the case of promising then it would seem that these distinctions should carry over into other types of speech act, and I think a little reflection will show that they do. Consider, e.g., giving an order. The preparatory conditions include that the speaker should be in a position of authority over the hearer, the sincerity condition is that the speaker wants the ordered act done, and the essential condition has to do with the fact that the utterance is an attempt to get the hearer to do it. For assertions, the preparatory conditions include the fact that the hearer must have some basis for supposing the asserted proposition is true, the sincerity condition is that he must believe it to be true, and the essential condition has to do with the fact that the utterance is an attempt to inform the hearer and convince him of its truth. Greetings are a much simpler kind of speech act, but even here some of the distinctions apply. In the utterance of "Hello" there is no propositional content and no sincerity condition. The preparatory condition is that the speaker must have just encountered the hearer, and the essential rule is that the utterance indicates courteous recognition of the hearer.

A proposal for further research then is to carry out a similar analysis of other types of speech acts. Not only would this give us an analysis of concepts interesting in themselves, but the comparison of different analyses would deepen our understanding of the whole subject and incidentally provide a basis for a more serious taxonomy than any of the usual facile categories such as evaluative versus descriptive, or cognitive versus emotive.

NOTES

1. Austin, J. L., *How To Do Things With Words* (Oxford: 1962).
2. This distinction occurs in J. Rawls, "Two Concepts of Rules", *Philosophical Review*, 1955, and J. R. Searle, "How to Derive 'Ought' from 'Is'," *Philosophical Review*, 1964.
3. The formulation "X counts as Y" was originally suggested to me by Max Black.
4. In the sentence "I promise that I will come" the function indicating device and the propositional element are separate. In the sentence "I promise to come," which means the same as the first and is derived from it by certain transformations, the two elements are not separate.
5. *Philosophical Review*, 1957.
6. *Philosophical Investigations* (Oxford: 1953), para. 510.

On Saying Something 10

ZENO VENDLER

I

Falling through Austin's prism the concept of saying something spreads out in a spectrum of illocutionary acts. These acts consist in the issuing of an utterance with a certain illocutionary force.[1] All "happy" or "successful" utterances are endowed with such a force in addition to their meaning (i.e., sense and reference, as he puts it). These forces specify how the utterance in question is intended to be taken—that is, what natural effect (cognitive, motive, social or legal) it is intended to have, and, accordingly, in what dimensions (truth, feasibility, propriety, and so on) it is supposed to be assessed; whether, for instance, it has the "force" of a statement, a warning, a promise, an order, and so forth.

In most cases the illocutionary force remains implicit; more often than not, in a given situation, the speaker need not explicitly specify how the utterance is to be taken: the circumstances and the context may be sufficient to decide. In others the speaker may give a hint, or more than a hint, by employing certain linguistic media, such as a suitable intonation pattern, sentence transform, or performative verb.[2] Think of the various ways in which a superior officer might order his subordinate to occupy the city: "You will occupy the city" (only the context and, possibly, the intonation pattern distinguishes this from a mere forecast); "Occupy the city!" (here a transform, the imperative, is used in addition to the intonation); "I order you to occupy the city" (in this case he employs a performative verb). Similar examples could be produced for questions, warnings, promises, and the like.

Among these media, the use of performative verbs is the least ambiguous and the most versatile; transforms and intonation patterns are far more restricted in power and variety. It appears, moreover, that whatever the other devices can do, the use of a suitable performative verb can do, but not the other way around. Consequently, from a methodological point of view, it is profitable to regard the utterance prefixed by such a verb as the "normal form" of a performative utterance, that is, of an utterance endowed with an illocutionary force. Implicit performatives, which lack such verbs, have their force "because, in so far as and when they are linked in 'origin' with these special explicit performative verbs like 'promise,' 'pronounce,' 'find,' etc."[3] Since, as I mentioned above, Austin accords illocutionary forces to all "happy" utterances, his implied doctrine is a sweeping generalization: the normal form of all "happy" utterances of the language will contain a performative verb prefixing the substance of the utterance.[4] If this is so, then the list of performative verbs will amount to the

From *Res Cogitans* (Ithaca: Cornell University Press, 1972).

list of illocutionary forces discernible in a given language. This connection explains why Austin ends the second half of his lectures, in which he is primarily concerned with illocutionary forces, by compiling a catalogue of performative verbs.

II

We may recall that Austin's investigations begin with an attempt to draw a distinction between "performative" and "constative" utterances. As this task cannot be accomplished to his satisfaction, he develops the theory of illocutionary acts, that is, of illocutionary forces accompanying all "happy" or "successful" utterances. In this new perspective the performative-constative distinction fades away and what he previously called "performative" utterances retain no special status except for a stronger emphasis on some illocutionary force or another. Nevertheless, and exactly because of this strong emphasis, the intuitive notion of an illocutionary act remains dependent upon the previously described characteristics of performative utterances. Austin suggests a fair number of such marks, but I select three of them, which are given great weight in his own exposition, in order to provide an intuitive check on results to be obtained in a more formal way later on.

These three can best be expressed in three kinds of "formula" which I shall call the "to say" formula, the "in saying" formula, and the "hereby" formula. The first exhibits the very notion of a "performative" utterance (i.e., to say something is to do something); for example,

> To say (in the appropriate circumstances) "I *promise* to pay you $5.00" is to *promise* to pay somebody $5.00.

In an implicit case:

> To say (in the appropriate circumstances) "The bull is charging" is to *warn* somebody that the bull is charging.

The "in saying" formula is equally central to the notion of an "in-locutionary" act (i.e.,

doing something in saying something); for example:

> In saying that the bull was charging he *warned* his companion.

Finally, the possibility of adjoining the adverb *hereby* to the first person singular present indicative active occurrence of a performative verb gives us the "hereby" formula; for example:

> I hereby *promise* to pay you $5.00.

In spite of the intuitive aid these formulae provide for the understanding of what illocutionary acts are, and how performative verbs function, Austin's own discussion shows that they cannot be relied upon, severally or jointly, to form a criterion for the recognition of performative verbs. (But little imagination is required to make obviously undesirable verbs fit into these formulae, or to find some performatives which would not enter them for some reason or other.) Moreover, from a linguistic point of view, these formulae, even in a suitably generalized form, are ad hoc creations which do not tie in with the system of grammar, and which, accordingly, shed no light on the deeper syntactical function of performative verbs. Hence Austin's persistent quest for a truly "grammatical" criterion.

III

Indeed, he seems to find one. He notices that it is the first person singular form of the present perfect (i.e., nonprogressive) tense of the performative verb that carries the illocutionary force, and, consequently, is a true present in the sense of, roughly, indicating what happens at the moment of the utterance, whereas the progressive tense hardly occurs at all. This is in marked contrast with most other verbs: "I am smoking," for instance, is the usual form of reporting my concurrent smoking; "I smoke" is used to admit a disreputable habit. Hence the possibility of saying "I smoke but I am not smoking now." "I promise to pay on time," on the other hand, is normally used to make a promise (which is made, *ipso dicto,* at that moment) and does not say anything about the speaker's habit of promising. The same thing holds of other typical performatives; think of "I warn," "I order," "I sentence," "I name," and so forth. The progressive tense is quite alien to these verbs, except for some such colloquial emphatic uses as "I am warning you."[5] Having found this interesting and important feature, Austin then proceeds to use "the simple test (with caution) of the first person present indicative active form" in going through the dictionary to hunt for performatives.[6]

Is this test good enough? The obvious answer is that it is not. There are entire families of clearly nonperformative verbs that share the same preference for the present perfect even in the first person singular—for example, the intuitive group of verbs that traditionally have been called "propositional attitude" verbs: "believe," "know," "understand," "doubt," "remember," "expect," "intend," and the like. Then there are other, shall we say, "attitude" verbs, like "love," "hate," "prefer," "detest," and so forth. Not even the best intentions in the world can make these performatives: they certainly do not fit into the formulae discussed above; yet they pass the present perfect test with no trouble, and show the same reluctance toward the progressive form as the genuine performatives. Thus it is not surprising that Austin, employing this supposed criterion, comes to wonder about "know," "believe," and "doubt,"[7] and that such verbs as "value," "understand," "envisage," "favor," "resent," "overlook," "intend," and "regard" turn up unquestioned in his final list. Some of these may have performative uses now and then, but by and large they show a much greater resemblance to the verbs of propositional (or other) attitudes. To anticipate: they are "thinking" verbs rather than "saying" verbs.

IV

The fact that the alleged criterion lets in not just a few unimportant or borderline items, but large families of very common verbs that are not performatives, signals the breakdown of that criterion. Yet, I think, Austin's intu-

ition that performative verbs are akin to propositional attitude verbs spurs us in the right direction. The obvious similarity between these two groups is the following: both kinds normally take, or at least can take, a noun clause rather than a simple noun for verb-object. We know, believe, or think *that something is the case,* we doubt or wonder *whether something is the case,* and we may remember *what we did yesterday.* In a similar way, I may state, predict, or warn you *that something is going to happen,* I may promise *to do something,* and I may apologize *for having done something.* After all, the very name, propositional attitude, suggests that the objects of those verbs are not simple nouns but sentences or propositions. As for performative verbs, we recall that they are like labels attached not to nouns but to utterances to mark their illocutionary force. To use another simile, the performative verb is like a frame or container in which an utterance is enclosed and offered in a particular way. It appears, then, that both performatives and verbs like *"know," "believe,"* and *"doubt"* belong to the same genus of container verbs, verbs, that is, the object of which is a noun-clause or, in modern terminology, a sentence nominalization of a certain type.[8] Thus it is not surprising that they share an added feature, namely, the preference for the present perfect tense. Austin recognized a characteristic of the genus to which the performatives belong, but, owing to his lack of attention to the form of the appropriate verb-object, failed to recognize the genus itself, not to speak of the specific difference that separates the performatives from the other branches of the same genus.

Austin leads us to the gates of the Promised Land, but he himself does not enter. It is up to us to continue the journey, first looking at the performatives in this new perspective and then trying to find the real criteria that set them apart. As we are going to see, this study will yield two unexpected byproducts. First, a natural subdivision of the class of performatives: a result which will vindicate Austin's own intuition in the grouping of illocutionary forces. And, second—a still more important gain—by viewing the performatives in the natural context of other "propositional" verbs, we will obtain the first glimpse of the true relation of speech and thought.

V

Performatives are container verbs of a certain kind. In order to illustrate this point in some detail, I shall give a list of utterances, the production of which, provided it is "happy" in Austin's sense (i.e., not affected by some "infelicities" of context and circumstance), normally amounts to the performance of an illocutionary act. After each utterance I shall add the sentence from which the particular verb-object has been derived by the nominalizing transformation. In this list I purposely include examples from the whole range of illocutionary acts.

(1)   I suggest that Joe committed the crime
(1a)   Joe committed the crime
(2)   I deny having seen the victim
(2a)   I have seen the victim
(3)   I call it murder
(3a)   It is murder
(4)   I urge you to proceed
(4a)   You should proceed
(5)   I appoint you to the presidency
(5a)   You shall become the president
(6)   I promise to pay on time
(6a)   I shall pay on time
(7)   I apologize for having offended you
(7a)   I have offended you.

The morphological details of the nominalizations appearing in this list will be discussed in due course. For the time being I merely call attention to the fact that nominalizations of this kind are to be distinguished from those of another sort, which correspond to entirely different container verbs. Some examples:

> I am watching the sunset
>
> I am listening to his singing
>
> I am observing the passage of Venus
>
> I am imitating his walk.

Elsewhere, I have described in great detail the differences between these two kinds of nominalization.[9] By way of a rough summary,

one can say that the product of the former kind, which I called the "imperfect" nominal, expresses a proposition, whereas the product of this latter kind, called the "perfect" nominal, denotes an event, process, or action. Since these things, unlike propositions, are temporal entities, which occur, go on, or take place somewhere in the world, it is not surprising to find "perceptual" container verbs in the list just given, and these occurring in the progressive tense, indicating temporal succession. The simple present, on the other hand, neatly corresponds to the atemporal nature of propositions.

Nevertheless it is exactly a temporal aspect that will split the class of propositional verbs into performatives and verbs of propositional attitudes, a feature which has escaped Austin's grammar. It is quite clear that whereas the simple present tense, in the case of a performative, singles out the moment at which the illocutionary act occurs, in the case of a propositional attitude verb the same tense does not indicate a unique moment, but an indefinite time-span which includes the moment of the utterance. To use the terminology I introduced in an earlier work, performatives are achievement verbs, but propositional attitude verbs are state verbs according to their time-schema.[10] "When (at what moment) did you promise such and such?" and "For how long did you believe such and such?" are the proper questions, and "At 5 p.m." and "For a year or so," respectively, the appropriate answers, and not the other way around. Again, compare "I still believe" with "I still promise." The first phrase needs no explanation; the second does. It might mean that I have not withdrawn my promise, or that I am still willing to promise, but certainly not that my promising has not yet come to an end.

This difference in their time-schema would be sufficient to distinguish thinking words from saying words, were it not for the fact that there are some propositional verbs with the achievement schema which are nevertheless obviously words of thought and not of saying. "Decide," "realize," "discover," "identify," "recognize," and the like are achievement verbs, yet, typically, are not performatives.

Their behavior with respect to the present tense, however, is very different from that of the performatives. With a performative, the first person singular present form is the most characteristic, and indeed the primary occurrence. Members of the *decide*-group, on the contrary, do not occur in this form except when accompanied by grammatical adjuncts indicating general scope. There is nothing missing in such a sentence as "I promise to pay on time" or "I warn you that the bull is going to charge." On the other hand, the sentence "*I decide to go home," or "*I discover the correct method," is distinctly deviant. "I decide" and "I discover" are only acceptable in such contexts as "I always decide on the spur of the moment" or "I never discover anything without hard work." This feature is not so obvious with the other three verbs just listed. Looking closer we realize, however, that in case they are acceptable in the simple present without a modifier indicating general scope, they occur as a performative or as a propositional attitude verb. "Realize," for example, appears in the role of a propositional attitude verb in the context "I realize that such and such is the case." "Identify" and "recognize," on the other hand, may function as performatives: think of "I hereby identify the accused as the man who . . ." or "I hereby recognize the deputy as the representative of. . . ."

To conclude, performatives belong to the genus of propositional verbs, that is, container verbs corresponding to imperfect nominals, all of which show the symptomatic reluctance toward the progressive form. This genus, however, splits into three main species: (a) performatives, with achievement time-schema and unmodified first person singular present occurrence; (b) the *decide*-group, with the same time-schema but no such present occurrence; (c) propositional attitude verbs with the state time-schema. For the sake of simplicity I shall refer to the last two classes as verbs of mental act and verbs of mental state.

As we see, the correction of Austin's criterion has led us to the recognition of two closely related classes. This relationship will assume great importance later on. Presently,

however, I shall discuss the performatives themselves in some detail. In doing this I am going to follow a generative approach by putting, as it were, our new criteria to work. First I shall enumerate the main types of structure in which imperfect nominals occur; then select the verbs that correspond to each type; and finally weed out state verbs and those achievement verbs that have no unqualified first person present. The residue will be the list of performatives already classified according to structural principles. The fact that these subclasses substantially mirror Austin's own intuitive subdivisions will show not only his acumen, but the correctness and fertility of our improved criteria.

In the following sections I shall restrict myself to the listing of the performative verbs. The rest, the ones I have weeded out in the process, will be taken up in the next chapter.

VI

The simplest, and indeed paradigm form of propositional object is the *that*-clause. The class of performatives that normally take such an object corresponds to Austin's "expositives." This is a very large class comprising many obvious subdivisions, the exact delineation of which, however, would require much more detail than I can here afford to give. Accordingly I shall rely on intuition in giving these subclasses. For my own consolation, I appeal to intuition one step later than Austin.[11]

I begin with the "strong" declaratives: "state," "declare," "assert," "affirm," "claim," "contend," "maintain," and "insist." The next three, "guess," "submit," and "suggest," represent a somewhat weaker commitment. Then there are some special groups: "agree," "disagree," "concede," and "deny" give one's reaction to someone else's word; "report," "testify," "admit," "confess," and "predict," are temporally marked, explicitly invoking the past or the future; "postulate," "argue," and "conclude" operate in a logical context; finally, the obligatory direct object ("you" in the performative case) clearly sets apart the following five: "tell," "assure," "inform," "remind," and "warn."

The *that*-clause is often replaced by such variants as the ones in

I confess having seen her
I admit his superiority
I warn you of his dishonesty.

Yet the *that*-form is always available and remains typical. In a similar way, examples like

He predicted the war
He denied her allegation
He warned me of the bull

require but little sophistication to be recognized as deletion-products of sentences like

He predicted (that) the war (would come)
He denied (that *p*, which) she alleged
He warned me (that) the bull (was dangerous).

Again, *wh*-morphemes may replace some elements in the nominalized sentence leading to such results as

He stated what he found
She told us where he went

and so forth.[12] The grammatical moves behind such derivative surface forms are very common and by this time fairly well known. Thus I shall not pay particular attention to such "standard" deviations, unless they are peculiar to a given structure.

Another point, too, is worth mentioning at least once. Some of the verbs which have an expositive role may have other uses as well. "Warn" and "tell," for instance, can also be followed by the structure which, as we are going to see, defines Austin's "exercitives"; for example:

I tell you to leave the premises
I warn you not to enter the room.

Some other expositives reach beyond the performative domain altogether: one can submit oneself to one's enemy, and the porter can admit the latecomers. These are but the first examples of many performatives that, as it were, play for more than one club, or even outside the league. This fact, however, does not blunt the distinction between the clubs or the leagues.

VII

Austin's "verdictives" are similar to the previous class, except for the fact that the sentence which gets nominalized contains the copula rather than some other verb. This leads to another structure, which obligatorily replaces the *that*-clause: the subject of the nominalized sentence becomes the direct object of the performative and the copula gets deleted or replaced by "as" (occasionally by "to be"). Some examples:

I *call* it murder
I *rank* him second
I *classify* the piece (as) a novel.

This is much smaller class. Yet some subdivisions clearly emerge. First of all, there is a group that measures the objects in question as it were on a scale: "rank," "grade," "place" (e.g. horses after a race), "appraise," and "rate." A broader perspective corresponds to "call," "describe," "characterize," "diagnose," "classify," "define," and "distinguish." With this last verb the nominalized sentence seems to be negative: "I distinguish X from Y" contains "X is not Y." The last group suggests legal context: "plead," "rule," and "find." "Plead" shows an interesting peculiarity: the identity of subject between the performative and the nominalized sentence permits the contraction found in "I plead guilty."

VIII

In the class of "commissives" two new elements enter the picture: a noun-sharing between the subject of the performative and the subject of the nominalized sentence, and an auxiliary (*shall* or *will*) in the latter sentence. "Promise" belongs to this class:

I promise (you) to pay on time

which codes the full form:

I promise (you) that *I shall* pay on time.

Some other commissives are "undertake," "covenant," "contract," "pledge," "guarantee," "vow," "swear," and the negatives "refuse" and "decline." Notice that one can guarantee the future conduct or quality of things other than oneself: "We guarantee the car to last. . . ." This looks like an "exercitive" (see below), but a more careful analysis would reveal something like "We guarantee to recompense you if the car does not last . . ." in the background.

IX

There are two structures corresponding to Austin's "exercitives." The first, for which I shall retain the name, is shown in such sentences as

> I *order* you to proceed
>
> I *advise* you to remain silent.

The infinitive construction in the nominal once more conceals an auxiliary (in this case the "subjunctive equivalent" *should*), and the subject of the nominalized sentence again appears as the direct object of the performative. This, at least in the performative occurrence, is almost always *you*. Spelled out in full:

> I order *you* that *you should* proceed
>
> I advise *you* that *you (should)* remain silent.

This construction picks out a fairly large class of performatives; a subdivision may help us to see their variety. "Order," "command," "demand" (of or from) and the ambivalent "tell" (see section VI, above) are more categorical than "request," "ask," "urge," "counsel," and "advise"; these, in turn, are stronger than "permit" and "allow." Again, whereas "entreat," "pray," "beseech," and "beg" appeal to one's kindness, "dare" and "challenge" provoke one's courage. "Forbid" and "prohibit" have a negative sense by themselves, but the bifurcating "warn" (see section VI) requires a subsequent negation: consider "I forbid you to . . ." versus "I warn you not to. . . ." In this last case what probably happens is that an unspecified threat is deleted: the explicit form would be something like "I warn you that I shall . . ." (or it will . . .) if you. . . ."[13]

X

The next group, which Austin failed to distinguish from the exercitives, shows some similarity both to these and to the verdictives. The subject of the nominalized sentence once again appears as the direct object of the performative. As with the verdictives, the verb-phase of that sentence contains a copulative verb; only here it is more likely to be "become" than "be." Moreover, as with the exercitives, it is affected by the subjunctive or an equivalent modal. But there is a new feature too: if we want to give the full, uncontracted form of the elements entering the construction we feel that the connective "so that" rather than simply "that" should be used. In an example, the derivation goes as follows:

> I appoint *you* so that *you (shall) be (come)* the president
>
> I appoint you to be(come) the president
>
> I appoint you to the presidency.

I shall call the performatives fitting into this slot "operatives." Many members of this very large class conform to the given pattern without hitch. They are the ones that are used to change the status of persons (or other things) in a positive sense: "recommend," "nominate," "appoint," "name," "elect," "hire," "admit," and "promote" (primarily persons); "propose," "dedicate," "proclaim," "assign," "consign," and "relegate" (primarily things). With such negative verbs as "degrade," "demote," "dismiss," "fire," and "suspend," the pattern has to be stretched. Some construction like

> I demote you so that you shall cease to be . . .

must be at the source.

The "so that" instead of "that" is the very soul of an operative utterance. It marks its "efficiency": in issuing an operative I say something and the social, ritual, or legal effect ipso dicto takes place. Compare this with the verdictives. They are used to establish, albeit by a qualified speaker, what is the case; the operatives determine what shall be. Therefore the former speech acts remain, in a sense, in the domain of truth and falsity. Even in the highly ritualistic cases of placing (e.g., horses after the race) or grading (say, students), the assumption remains that these acts "truly" describe or evaluate the performance. This, obviously, is not the case with the operatives. They do not describe or evaluate a given situation: they create a new one. Hence "become" (or "cease to be") rather than "is" in the typical matrix.

In this perspective we can discern whole families of additional operatives: "arrest," "sentence," "condemn," "fine," and "appeal" in the legal sphere; "baptize," "confirm," "ordain," "absolve," "excommunicate," and "canonize" in the religious, "knight" in the feudal domain; perhaps also "offer," "give," "grant," "surrender," "accept," "refuse," and "reject," as well as "greet," "salute," and "welcome." With some of these the general pattern will work only in a seemingly trivial sense. Consider "arrest" and "baptize":

> I arrest you so that you shall be(come) arrested
>
> I baptize you so that you shall be(come) baptized.

This seems to be a travesty of a derivation. For, after all, what prevents one from claiming that, say, behind "I kick you," there must be something like

> I kick you so that you shall be kicked?

This is a serious matter, for if this objection holds up, then our claim that all performatives are propositional verbs goes by the board. Where is the "proposition" in the object of "I arrest you?"

To discuss this problem here would mean a long and distracting digression.

XI

The "behabitives" are an easier matter. They can be collected by using the pattern exhibited by, say,

> I thank you for having helped me
>
> I apologize for having hurt you.

Obviously there is a noun-sharing here between the subject of the contained sentence and either the direct object (as with "thank") or the subject (as with "apologize") of the performative. The contained sentence, however, does not have a modal verb, but a verb usually in the past tense. The verb-phrase of this sentence is brought in by means of a preposition: "for," "upon," or "against." The variety of prepositions suggests a subclassification. The favorable "thank," "praise," and "command" and the unfavorable "apologize," "censure," and "pardon" require "for"; "congratulate," "felicitate," and "compliment" lean toward "upon"; "protest," finally, calls for "against." "Protest," incidentally, is followed by a slightly different structure.

XII

A small but important class of performatives must be added to this list. The verbs "ask," "question," and "inquire" are normally followed by what grammarians call an "indirect question." This is nothing but a nominal formed out of a sentence by either prefixing "whether" or by replacing a noun or adverbial phrase by the appropriate wh-word: "who," "what," "when," "where," "why," "how," etc. Examples:

> I question whether he has succeeded
>
> I ask (you) how he did it.

These, naturally, can be called "interrogatives."

XIII

By way of summary, the results of our discussion are here set out formally. My purpose in doing this is not merely to show the coherence of the preceding classification, but also to prepare the way for a parallel classification to be made in the next chapter. Given the previous discussion, the symbolism will speak for itself.

Expositives:

$$N_i \ V_{ep} \ [NV \ +] \qquad \longrightarrow N_i \ V_{ep} \ that \ N \ V \ +$$

Verdictives:

$$N_i \ V_{vd} \ [N_j \ is \ N_k/A] \qquad \longrightarrow N_i \ V_{vd} \ N_j \ (as) \ N_k/A$$

Commissives:

$N_i \ V_{cm} \ [N_i \ mod(V \ +)] \longrightarrow N_i \ V_{cm} \ to \ V \ +$

Exercitives:

$N_i \ V_{ee} \ [N_j \ mod \ (V \ +)] \longrightarrow N_i \ V_{ee} \ N_j \ to \ V \ +$

Operatives:

$N_i \ V_{op} \ [N_j \ becomes \ N_k] \longrightarrow N_i \ V_{op} \ N_j \ to \ be(come) \ N_k$

Behabitives:

$N_i \ V_{bh} \ [N_j \ past \ (V \ +)] \longrightarrow N_i \ V_{bh} \ N_j \ P \ nom$
$\qquad\qquad\qquad\qquad\qquad (past \ (V \ +))$

Interrogatives:

$N_i \ V_{ir} \ [N \ V \ +] \longrightarrow N_i V_{ir} \ wh\text{-}nom \ (N \ V \ +)$

XIV

Finally, a few words about the verb "say." It often has performative uses: "I say" can introduce statements, orders, promises, apologies, and what not. Again, the question "What did he say?" may be answered by alluding to all sorts of speech-acts: "He stated that . . . ," "He promised to . . . ," "He ordered you to . . . ," "He apologized . . . ," "He asked me whether . . . ," and so forth. It appears, therefore, that "say" is a sort of general performative. The same thing, of course, can also be inferred from its occurrence in the first two Austinian "formulae" given above. These facts are more than enough to show that Austin's discussion, and our own, of illocutionary acts indeed contribute to the analysis of the concept of saying something. To perform an illocutionary act is to say something in the full sense of the word.

Yet this is not the whole story of saying. The same verb can be used in another sense too: one can say words, phrases, and sentences, one can say tongue twisters, rhymes, and rigmaroles, in one's own tongue or in a language otherwise unknown; even parrots and talking dolls can "say" many things in this sense of the word. Yet, obviously, none of these "sayings" will carry an illocutionary force. This weak sense of saying is roughly equivalent to uttering, mouthing, or pronouncing.

Now it is important to realize that these two levels of saying things are radically different. An illocutionary act is not a mere mouthing of a sentence in a certain situation. The circumstances may be right and the sentence well formed, the *I* prefixed and the performative

verb in its due place—nevertheless, no illocutionary act will be performed if, for one thing, the speaker does not understand what he is saying, or, for another, he does not intend to perform such an act, that is, does not intend his audience to take him to be performing one. No matter what the parrot says, it will not make a statement, issue an order, or give a promise; no matter with how serious a mien the child pronounces "Omnia sunt vanitas," he will not say that all things are vanity if he does not know Latin at all; and no matter how much invective I heap upon you, you have no reason to take offence, though you might think you have, if I am but engaged, sincerely from my part yet unbeknownst to you, in rehearsing a play.

Saying in the weak sense falls far short of saying in the full sense; one must understand what one says and one must mean what one says. In this chapter we have surveyed the costumes for the performance, not the actors; we have examined the frames, not the contents.

NOTES

1. J. L. Austin, *How to Do Things with Words.*
2. I shall call all "those verbs which make explicit . . . the illocutionary force of an utterance" (*ibid.*, p. 149) *performative* verbs. My framework is Austin's "general theory," in which the performative–constative distinction of the first half of his book has no special place.
3. *Ibid.*, p. 61.
4. J. R. Ross offers good reasons to think that some performative verb, and the *I*, is actually present even in the deep-structure of simple declarative sentences when they occur in actual use ("On Declarative Sentences," in R. Jacobs and P. Rosenbaum, ed., *Readings in Transformational Grammar*).
5. Notice that such a sentence usually occurs following the warning itself. "I am warning you" is not a warning; it is a reminder of a warning.
6. *How to Do Things with Words*, p. 149.
7. *Ibid.*, pp. 90, 161.
8. See R. B. Lees, *The Grammar of English Nominalizations;* my *Adjectives and Nominalizations;* and my *Linguistics in Philosophy*, ch. 5.
9. *Linguistics in Philosophy*, ch. 5.
10. *Ibid.*, ch. 4.
11. Some very recent work by C. J. Fillmore

promises a more accurate subclassification of the whole performative domain by exposing the various presuppositions behind the use of these verbs. What, for example, does "insist" presuppose, which "state" does not? Obviously, things like past assertion of the same thing, persistent challenge, etc. These are, admittedly, *minutiae,* but if science finds it worthwhile to describe thousands of bugs in a thousand and one details, why should the particulars of our mental habitat deserve less patience or devotion?

12. Interestingly enough, the *wh*-forms cannot occur performatively except in such replies as "I agree with what you said." The sentence "I predict what will happen" is deviant if not actually followed by a prediction. This alone is sufficient to show that "know" is not a performative: "I know what is going to happen" is a knowledge claim even if the speaker does not go on to reveal what he knows.

13. Another way of cutting the pie would involve the notion of presupposed authority. "Order, "command," "permit," "allow," "forbid," and "prohibit," but not the rest, seem to require some authority in the speaker.

Thoughts 11

ZENO VENDLER

I

Performatives, as we have seen in the previous chapter, are but one species of the genus of propositional verbs. We have found two other groups, which I called verbs of mental act and verbs of mental state. The former, exemplified by "decide," are achievement verbs like the performatives, but, unlike them, they lack the unqualified present occurrence. The latter, exemplified by "believe," are easily distinguished from either of the previous classes by their state time-schema.

In this chapter I shall collect these verbs, which were systematically set aside in compiling the catalogue of performatives, and then show that, just as the performatives spell out the various ways of saying something, these verbs display the possible forms of thought. Moreover, as the analogy between the basic frames of speech and thought emerges, together with the identity of their possible content, we will grasp the principles required for the solution of the problems mentioned at the end of the preceding chapter. We are going to realize, with increasing clarity as we go on, the truth and the philosophical importance of the common-sense view that speech is essentially the expression of thought.

The tactical steps to be taken in classifying our two groups of verbs are determined by our previous work with the performatives. With respect to each main type of propositional verb-object, we shall ask the question: are there any verbs taking such an object that conform to the tense-criteria, first of mental-act verbs and second of mental-state verbs? Following Austin's example I shall give a name to each of the non-empty classes thus obtained.

A word of caution: as there were "moonlighting" performatives, there will be two-faced, or even many-faced, verbs in our present domain. As we are going to see, there is a particularly strong tendency to use some original performatives in an extended sense—that is, to denote not a speech act, but a mental act or even state. Owing to the richness of the performative vocabulary, there is a great temptation to borrow some of its items for a different, yet closely related use. We shall encounter some obvious examples of such "leakage" soon enough.

II

What, then, are the mental-act verbs corresponding to the that-clause? There are a few "pure" items: "find out," "discover," "learn," "infer," "deduce," and "establish." These have no performative occurrence and

From *Res Cogitans* (Ithaca: Cornell University Press, 1972).

cannot take on the state-schema: "*I discover that . . . ," "*I still deduce that. . . ." Others, such as "notice," "gather," "understand," "realize," and the temporally marked "recollect," display some symptoms of the state-occurrence: "I notice that . . . ," "I understand that . . . ," "I realize that . . . ," but hardly "*I still realize that . . . ," "*Since when do you understand that . . . ," and so forth. "Guess" and "conclude," on the other hand, are probably borrowed performatives. One can guess or conclude something not only in words, but also without saying anything. This possibility, of course, indicates an extension beyond the performative domain. Finally, I mention the multifarious "see," since one of its uses obviously belongs here, being a near synonym to "realize. . .". I shall call this class "apprehensives."

The corresponding mental-state verbs come in a fair variety. The most typical group once more displays the familiar gamut of "firmness" going from the rather negative "doubt," through the weak "suspect," "surmise," "imagine," "assume," and "suppose," through the stronger "think," "believe," and "hold," up to the categorical, and all important, "know." Needless to say that many of these verbs bifurcate: think of holding candles, assuming duties, and imagining pink rats. The etymology behind these ambivalences is interesting, but we can do without it at this point. There is another group with temporal connotations: "remember," "recall," "expect," "anticipate," and the emotively tinged "hope" and "fear." Then, as we recall, there is some leakage from the apprehensives ("realize," etc.) and some from the performatives: one can maintain things, agree or disagree with people in one's heart as well as in speech. This group of verbs I call "putatives."

III

Turning to the "mental" verbs corresponding to the verdictives, we find but a few achievement verbs: "recognize" and "identify," on the one hand, and "estimate" and "judge,"

on the other, seem to be the natives of this domain, although they all show a tendency to appear in the performative garb now and then. Here, for once, the "leakage" seems to go the other way. The structural similarity to the verdictives is obvious:

I recognized the man as the one who . . .
I estimated its value to be . . .
I judged him incompetent.

The fact that, say, "recognize" might occur in the present tense, even in a nonperformative way, does not change the picture. "I still recognize him" is an ellipsis for "I still can recognize him;" to be able to recognize is, of course, a state. The point is, however, that the "can" version is out of place with respect to a real state verb, for example "regard." "I regard him as a coward" is not an ellipsis for "I can regard him as a coward." To this small class I give a trivial name: "recognitives."

There is a much greater variety in the state equivalents of verdictives. Even the two main semantic groups of the verdictives have their shadows here: "deem," "esteem," "value," and, perhaps, "appreciate" assess worth, whereas "take," "consider," "regard," "look upon," and "see" require a broader semantic frame. The last three (perhaps four) are borrowed from the perceptual domain, yet they transcend it in the present frame, as in "I see it as a crime." So, of course, does "take" transcend the physical domain in, say, "We take it to be self-evident. . . ." I christen this group "assessives."

IV

The commissives, too, have their cognate families. On the achievement side we find our old paradigm "decide" together with "resolve," "choose," and "elect." As you promise or vow to do something, you decide, resolve, choose, or elect to do something. To name these few verbs I resort to the trivial once more and suggest "resolutives."

There is no difficulty in naming the next class, which contains the state equivalents of commissives. It comes naturally to call this rich and important class "conatives." Intuitively, they fall into two groups; whereas "want," "intend," "plan," "mean," and "contemplate" (to do something, of course) do not connote emotions, "wish," "aspire," "desire," "long," "hope," and "covet" clearly do. I am not sure about "prefer" in this respect. The "emotional" group is mainly concerned with becoming something or coming to have something; consequently "be" or "have" are often redundant in the verb object. Hence abbreviated surface forms like

> He aspires to the presidency
> He longs for adulation
> He covets Joe's wife.

Otherwise, the structural similarity between the commissives and resolutives is too obvious to waste words on.

V

To our initial dismay, we find the classes corresponding to the exercitives and operatives almost empty. This stands to reason, however. Exercitives are used, roughly, to cause other people to do something, whereas operatives bring about certain (institutional, legal, or religious) results ipso dicto. Unvoiced thoughts, however, cannot move other people; nor can they be effective in the institutional sphere.

One can wish, of course, that other people do certain things, and one can decide to effect certain institutional changes in one's power. If we do such things, we naturally use the resolutive or conative vocabulary to express it (albeit with a suitably adjusted structure); for example,

> I want him to go home
> I chose him to do the job.

A few originals, namely "select," "pick" and "design," fit into the same structure. In addition, one might resort to metaphorical phrases like "I have him in mind to (or

for). . . ." Think of the Pope actually creating a cardinal "in pectore." Fortunately such real exercitive thinking is the privilege of the exalted few.

VI

Are there mental-act verbs sharing the syntactical slot inhabited by the behabitives? I can think of two: "forgive" and "condone." There are not many state verbs either: we have the favorable "approve of" and "sympathize with" and the unfavorable "blame," "resent," "disapprove of," and "regret." Some of these, notably "condone" and "sympathize," show slight deviations from the behabitive paradigm. "Regret," like the behabitive "apologize," reflects upon the speaker's own past actions. To keep up the naming game I shall call the first small class "remissives" and the second "emotives."

VII

Finally, the interrogatives have the lone "inquisitive," "wonder," for a counterpart. This, of course, is a state verb.

VIII

In order to recapitulate the results of our long, and perhaps tedious, effort at classifying propositional verbs, I shall display them in a series of synoptic tables. The notation will speak for itself. Since the structures given are applicable beyond the performative domain, I shall omit the subscripts marking the propositional verbs. The arrows indicate the direction of "leakage" between the categories. Needless to say that the semantic subclassification is largely intuitive, consequently by no means final and, probably, often wrong. Nevertheless the presence of these semantic factors, and their scope embracing words of speech and thought alike, are certain and are instructive. Owing to the lack of parallelism, I shall omit the operatives and the exercitives.

(a) N_i V that N V +

Expositives	Apprehensives	Putatives
state	find out	know
declare	discover	hold
assert	notice	think
affirm	see⟶	believe
claim	realize	
contend		
maintain⟶		
insist		

agree⟶		
concede		

disagree⟶		
deny		

postulate	infer	
argue	deduce	
conclude⟶	establish	

tell	learn	
assure	gather⟶	
inform	understand⟶	
remind		
warn		

report	recollect	remember
testify		⟵recall
admit		
confess		

predict		expect
		anticipate
		hope
		fear

guess⟶		suspect
submit		⟵surmise
suggest		imagine
		⟵assume
		suppose
		doubt

(b) N V N (*as*) N/A

Verdictives	Recognitives	Assessives
rank	←——estimate	deem
grade	←——judge	←——esteem
place		←——value
appraise		appreciate
rate		

call	←——recognize	←——take
describe	←——identify	consider
characterize		regard
diagnose——→		look upon
classify——→		←——see
define		
distinguish——→		

plead		
rule		
find——→		

(c) N V *to* V +

Commissives	Resolutives	Conatives
promise	←——decide	want
undertake	resolve	intend
covenant	←——choose	plan
contract	elect	mean
pledge		contemplate
guarantee		prefer
vow		
swear		

refuse		
decline		

		wish
		aspire
		desire
		long
		covet

(d) N V N P nom [past (V +)]

Behabitives	Remissives	Emotives
thank		←——approve of
praise		
commend		

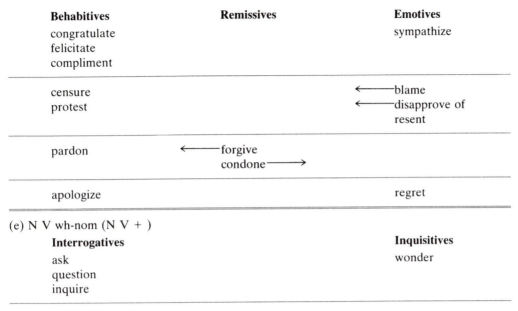

Behabitives	**Remissives**	**Emotives**
congratulate		sympathize
felicitate		
compliment		
censure		←———blame
protest		←———disapprove of
		resent
pardon	←———forgive	
	condone———→	
apologize		regret

(e) N V wh-nom (N V +)

Interrogatives	**Inquisitives**
ask	wonder
question	
inquire	

IX

Thus surveyed, the domain of propositional verbs reveals a staggering perspective: the almost universal identity of the objects of speech and thought. For—to show off some fruits of our hard-earned erudition—the same things that can be asserted, suggested, or denied in words, can be realized, and understood, believed, suspected, or doubted in thought; things regarded, considered, looked upon, and recognized to be such and such in thought, can also be characterized, described, and defined in the same way in words; what one may wish, want, intend, or decide to do in thought, one also can promise, vow, or pledge to do in words; the same things that are worthy of blame, approval, resentment, or forgiveness in thought, deserve to be censured, praised, objected to, and pardoned in words; finally what one wonders about in thought, one can ask about in speech. To put it briefly: you can say whatever you think, and you can think almost whatever you can say. This last qualification is necessary in view of the fact that there are two performative fields, those of the exercitives and the operatives,

that do not have a direct counterpart in the mental domain. Indirectly, of course, via the necessary intention to perform these speech acts, even these fields are related to thought.

Indeed, the use of the very word "thought" is commonly extended to cover what has been said or written, albeit with the exception of exercitive and operative speech. It does not take mind-reading to acquaint oneself with somebody else's thought; ordinary reading or listening is enough; only honesty is required in the writer and understanding in the reader. The *Little Red Book* contains Chairman Mao's thought; yet it is but a book of quotations: it records the statements he made, the promises he gave, the proposals he issued, the challenges he hurled, the praises he offered to his friends, and the condemnations he heaped upon his foes. If he was sincere, these are his thoughts.

For, I repeat, honesty is required: people can lie, dissimulate their intentions, and praise and blame with the tongue but not the heart. What is said, if said with meaning and not merely parrotwise, is a thought, but it may not be the real thought of the speaker. There are thoughts not revealed, not expressed, not given voice; saying and thinking are not the same thing.

X

What, then, is the difference? Is it merely that speech is a noisy form of thinking, and thinking is a silent way of talking to oneself? That the difference is much less trivial can be gathered from the fact that most thinking verbs are state verbs, whereas the performatives are one and all achievement verbs. But there is another, much more illuminating way of approaching the problem. There is a common device of reverbalizing a nominalized verb by using an ad hoc auxiliary. Instead of saying "I kicked," I can say "I gave a kick"; instead of "I looked," "I took a look," and so on. The same move is possible in regard to most propositional verbs. One speaks of giving a promise, holding a belief, or arriving at a decision. The auxiliaries are more or less metaphorical, but this is not a reason for disdaining their aid. For, as we are going to see, the consideration of these auxiliaries casts an extraordinary light on the relation between a person and a proposition, be it the relation of saying or thinking.

To begin with the performatives, the most common auxiliaries are "make," "give," and particularly "issue." One makes a statement, gives a promise, and issues a denial. There are a number of offbeat forms: one offers a proposal, hurls a challenge, pronounces a verdict, hands down a decision, and sounds a warning. The verb "issue" is the most typical: it fits almost all the performatives. This is no surprise; after all, these verbs, as Austin noted, are verbs of issuance: the proposition in question is issued, pronounced (*pronuntio*), given out.

The verbs of thinking call for a totally different set of auxiliaries. With respect to the state verbs, "have" is the most common: one has beliefs, opinions, suspicions, desires, regrets, and what not. The offbeat auxiliaries add color to the picture. Take "belief": like a child, it is conceived, adopted, or embraced; it is nurtured, held, cherished, and entertained; or, if it appears misbegotten, it may be abandoned or given up. The same is true, with less variety, of suspicions, intentions, resentments, and the like. This image is *toto coelo* different from the one evoked by the set corresponding to the performatives; there is no issuance here, the objects of these states being "in" or "with" the person, "held" in one way or another. Moreover, they can be hidden, concealed, or, on the other hand, shown, manifested, expressed, or given voice. What we hold (for a time) in a mental state, we can issue (at a time) in an illocutionary act.

Mental-act verbs share "make" with some performatives: we make decisions, identifications, choices, and so on, just as we make statements, proposals, declarations, and the like. "Make" seems to mark achievement verbs in this domain. Yet the difference remains between the two kinds. Statements, proposals, or declarations can also be issued, which is not true of identifications or choices. As for decisions, they can be issued. But obviously, "decide," in that case, functions as a performative; the counterexample, in fact, works for us. The less standard auxiliaries, such as "reach" (a decision) and "arrive at" (a realization), illustrate the achievement aspect of these verbs. Whereas a mental state is like having or possessing something, a mental act is often like finding or getting hold of something, or, in other cases, like reaching a goal.[1]

The total import of the emerging picture is clear enough. Man lives in two environments, in two worlds: as a "body," an "extended thing," he is among objects and events in the physical, spatio-temporal universe; as a "mind," a "thinking thing," he lives and communes with objects of a different kind, which he also perceives, acquires, holds, and offers in various ways to other citizens of this world, to other minds.

XI

It will be objected that I misrepresent here the concept of thinking; that by focusing exclusively on the sense of the word "thought" which denotes the content or product of the mental processes I ignore these processes themselves or, worse, that by capitalizing on a quirk of the vernacular, I create the impression that by discussing thought in this sense I have exhausted the topic of thinking altogether. "What you are doing"—an opponent might argue—"is a typical case of a process-product confusion; it is like suggesting that the word 'building' denotes only an edifice, forgetting the other sense, which denotes the activity that produces the edifice. For, no doubt, thinking is an activity, a process, something that goes on, which we can pursue, and of which we are aware throughout our conscious life. Thinking is the stream of consciousness, the 'buzzing-blooming confusion' of images, sounds, feelings, and emotions; interspersed, it is true, by words or even sentences dimly 'heard,' subvocally 'pronounced,' or 'glanced at' with the mind's eye. To phrase my objection somewhat differently, you have confined your attention to 'thinking that' . . . and to the objects of 'thinking that . . . ,' while ignoring 'thinking about . . .' and 'thinking of. . . .' And these ways of thinking are indeed processes according to your own criteria. We ask, in the progressive tense, 'What are you thinking about?' and we say 'I was thinking about you all the time. . . .' Moreover, the philosophically interesting sense of 'thinking' is obviously this process sense: the process of thinking constitutes our 'inner life'; and this is the thinking of which we are really aware, the one that remains inaccessible to others. Thinking in the propositional sense, 'thinking that . . . ,' is rather like a disposition to say certain things and to behave in one way rather than another. For, surely, we are not aware, at any given time, of all that we think in the propositional sense. A man sound asleep may be said to 'think' (i.e., to believe, suspect, want, regret, etc.) many things in this sense, without doing any thinking at that moment."

I reply to the second half of the objection first. What the objector says is like claiming that speaking is really "talking about," not "saying that." Talking about something is indeed an activity one pursues, a process that goes on. As we ask "What is he thinking about?" we also ask "What is he talking about?" in the progressive tense. Talking about something is carried on in a process of talking, in producing a patterned sequence of noises. Yet, clearly, the mere utterance of sounds, in no matter what sequence, does not amount to talking about anything. Parrots and dolls may talk in this sense, yet they cannot talk *about* anything. For, as we remarked above, they cannot say anything in the full sense of the word. And no one can talk about anything without saying something in the process, that is, without performing some illocutionary acts. Thinking about (or thinking of) something also involves a process of "thinking." The images, the sounds, the subvocal words, what have you, all may be there, but, again, no such succession of images will constitute the process of thinking about (or of) something, unless these "images" carry some mental acts. Animals, probably, can "think" in the sense of having internal experiences of a similar kind; what they cannot do is to think about something. In talking about something a person performs a series of illocutionary acts: he may assert, suggest, or argue that something is the case; describe and rate a person or a thing; recommend, urge, or advise a certain course of action; and so on. In thinking about something one goes through a series of mental acts, often involving some changes of mental states: one may guess, assume, realize, or conclude that something is the case; regard, consider, or view a certain thing in many ways; contemplate, plan, and decide to do one thing or another; and wonder about consequences. One also might adopt beliefs, give up suspicions, modify intentions—that is, "make up" or "change one's mind" in these and many other ways. The idea that one might be thinking about something without performing any of these or similar acts is as incomprehensible as the idea of talking about something without saying anything at all.

These reflections enable us to answer the first point about the process-product confusion. Between thinking and building *nego paritatem*. Not because buildings are visible and thoughts are not, not even because the result of building, the edifice, is physically distinct from the agent, while the alleged result of thinking, the thought, is not; but simply because the process of thinking, thinking about or thinking of, involves and presupposes thoughts, whereas the process of building does not involve and presuppose edifices already in existence. Remember, once more, the analogy of speech: talking about something is to be understood in terms of saying something, not the other way around; saying something is not the product of talking about something. Similarly, having a thought is not the product of thinking about something; it is rather this latter notion that involves the former: thinking about something consists in conceiving and entertaining a series of thoughts. The builder may stop building without having completed any edifice; the thinker who stops thinking, on the other hand, already must have had some thoughts.

XII

In the reply just given I relied heavily on the parallelism of speech and thought, on the analogy of proportionality between saying something and talking about something on the one hand, and thinking something and thinking about something on the other. I even let myself be lured into suggesting that, speaking somewhat poetically, as external noisemaking is the carrier of speech, internal image-making is the carrier of thought. Yet this cannot be. For whereas speech is the expression of thought in a code—that is, by means of a language—thought is not an expression of anything and is not conceived in a code or via a code.

It may happen that through the ignorance of a particular language I fail to understand what someone else has said, or even what I myself recite in that tongue. It may also happen that a sentence in my native tongue, heard, read, or uttered by myself, escapes my understanding. It is inconceivable, however, that I might fail to understand what I think. Hearing the speaker's voice, or seeing his writing, is indispensable for getting at what he said, but what do I have to see or hear, externally or in my mind, to get at my own thoughts? I do not deny that some inner experiences may accompany our thinking

about something: the confusion of images, sounds, or even of words, phrases, and sentences, mentally heard, seen, or vocalized, in this language or in that, may be there, but their possible presence has nothing in common with the necessity of using a language in talking about something. Such accompaniments of thinking are by no means all internal: postures (like that of Rodin's "Thinker"), frowns ("thoughtful" frowns), mumblings ("thinking aloud"), gestures, and so forth, may go with thinking as well, in much the same way as smiles and grimaces, gestures and posturings, may accompany our speech without affecting what we say. But, in the case of speech, such trappings are to be distinguished from the code-elements, that is, the words, structures, intonation patterns, and the like that convey the message. These, but not the smiles and the sighs, *belong* to the language, are the elements of a highly complex and learned code. With thought, all the things we mentioned, external and internal, are mere accessories; there is no message to encode and no private language to use for the encoding.

If you say something to me, you must know what you want to say. Otherwise, even if your mouth pronounces words, you would merely parrot something but not say anything. I, on the other hand, have nothing but your words to go on; these are the medium through which I have to get the message. Naturally, I might not get it. You may have chosen inappropriate words, I may not know the language well enough, you may have committed a slip of the tongue, or I may have misheard you. Thus it is always possible that I fail to understand you or that I misunderstand you. And this possibility is inherent in any use of any code: encoding and decoding can be correct or incorrect. Now if thinking needed a code, consisting of words or other symbols; if, in other words, thinking were something like talking to oneself silently; then, on the one hand, the thinker would know what he wanted to "say" to himself, but on the other, he could be mistaken about what he did "say." In other words, it would be possible for him to know and not to know what he thinks at the same time.

This is absurd, of course, but the absurdity

crops up earlier still. Concerning speech, which involves encoding—that is, putting thoughts into words—it makes sense to speak of what somebody wanted to say but could not, because, for example, he did not know the language or was affected by aphasia. What would it be, on the other hand, to want to think something yet being unable to do so because of some malfunctioning of the mental "medium" or because of one's deficient command over the same?

XIII

If thinking is not identical with the flux of words and images we perceive in the imagination, then—the question arises—how are we aware of our own thoughts? Or, shall we agree with our objector and admit that our thoughts—our beliefs, suspicions, decisions, intentions, regrets, and so on—are merely dispositions?

In the first place I can see some, but not much, plausibility to the view that beliefs, suspicions, and other mental states are dispositions. A mental state normally has an effect on what people do and say. By observing them and listening to their words we might gather some clues as to what they know, believe, or intend to do, even if they do not explicitly reveal in words what these things are, much as we can gather the condition of muscles, bones, and nerves from the way people walk, limp, or hobble. Of course, in either case, the subject of our observation might choose not to reveal anything or mislead us on purpose: the witness can stand mute or prevaricate, and the patient can lie prone or dance and grin and bear it. If people's knowledge, beliefs, and intentions consisted in some pattern of their overt behavior, the task of poker players, spies, diplomats, detectives, interrogators, and inquisitors would be easy indeed, and thumbscrews and racks would never have been heard of. As a broken bone does not consist in limping and the like, one's intention to go to Paris does not consist in poring over the map of France, or doing similar things.

In order to assess the dispositional account

of mental states, it is illuminating to compare such states with certain human traits that are indeed but dispositions. If we say that a person is generous or mean, patient or irritable, polite or uncouth, we ascribe to him a fairly permanent, and fairly predictable, pattern which marks some relevant domains of his behavior, normally without implying anything about his mental states. After all, a person may be irritable or uncouth without wanting to be, or even without knowing that he is. Thus with respect to these characteristics, it is possible for us to know that a certain person has them, without himself being aware of the fact. Thus there would be no point in "putting him to the question" (on the rack or otherwise) to induce him to reveal what he knows but we do not. All we have to do is to observe him with care. For if a person's urbanity, patience, or generosity never manifests itself, then, whatever he may think of himself, the person is not polite, patient, or generous.

This is obviously not so with mental states. Take, for instance, an expert of Roman history; think of all the information, all the beliefs, assumptions, guesses and suspicions he might have concerning his subject. Then ask yourself whether it is necessary, or even possible, for him to display all these mental states, in word or deed, in order to have them. Again, some people's consciences are burdened with guilty secrets from their past, which they would not reveal in any circumstances. And, speaking of guilty secrets, what about the professional secrecy incumbent upon priests, lawyers and doctors concerning the revelations of their clients? The father confessor must not reveal, either by word or by deed, in any circumstances whatsoever, what he has been told *sub sigillo*. Does the requirement of unconditional secrecy demand something inconceivable? Yet the confessor knows these secrets, and normally believes what he has been told.

"Still, he could tell you what he knows, as the historian too could voice or otherwise manifest his beliefs, if he wanted to." This is the last line of defence for the dispositional account, that so-called mental states are not so much a matter of actual, but rather of hypothetical behavior—what the agent would do and say if. . . . This is like an appeal to sleeping witnesses: what they would have seen had they been awake. Let us consider once more real dispositions. Take Joe, who does not display any courtesy toward his fellow men; he is certainly not polite in anybody's book. Now could one save his reputation by arguing that he would behave otherwise if he wanted to, or if he were placed in circumstances that in fact never occurred? Obviously not, since all this amounts to is that Joe could be polite if he wanted to, or would be polite given such and such. It does not follow at all, however, that he is polite now. Therefore, if mental states were indeed bona fide dispositions, then by merely suggesting what people would do or say in certain possible circumstances one would only account for what they would believe, suspect, or whatever in those circumstances, and not for what they do believe or suspect now. The logic of dispositional terms indeed involves the conditional. The assertion that somebody is polite is not a mere description; it warrants projections too: "Since Jim is polite, he will (or would) yield his seat." But in saying that he is polite we also imply some actual facts. It comes down to this: it makes perfect sense to say that Sherlock Holmes suspected the butler all along, but gave no sign of it; it is nonsense to say, however, that he was polite to the butler all along without showing any sign of it.

It does not help to insist that a dispositional predicate may be true of a subject without any actual manifestation—for example, that a vase may be brittle without ever actually breaking. Granted, but in that case one must have some other ground for saying that it is brittle—for example, that it is made of glass (i.e., has a certain molecular structure). But if, say, Holmes never met the butler, what other reason could there be for claiming that nevertheless he was polite to the man? We have to realize, therefore, that whereas politeness is a "pure" disposition, brittleness is not. In either case the unfulfilled hypotheticals are but a projection from a categorical base. In the case of pure dispositions (politeness, generosity, and the like), that base must be actual behavior (the man did behave politely on a number of occasions); in the case of, let us say, "mixed" dispositions (brittleness, elasticity, and the like), it may be either actual behavior or some actual state (e.g., internal structure).

Hence it is clear that mental states cannot be pure dispositions. Holmes suspected the butler from the beginning without showing any sign of it. For this reason we did not know whom he suspected, but he certainly did know. On the other hand, if he did not show any politeness toward the butler, we cannot say that although we did not know that he was polite toward the butler, he did. His suspicion, therefore, must comprise an actual state, which can subsist and can be known independently of any manifestations.

What then are these mental states? One might wish to cast a final doubt upon their independent existence by pointing out that whereas molecular structures, broken bones, and torn ligaments can be directly observed by means of the electron microscope, the X-ray machine, or the naked eye, beliefs, intentions, and the like cannot. True, but this merely shows that mental states are not observable entities. If I am asked whether I believe that Paris is a beautiful city, or whether I intend to go there next summer, I do not have to observe or recall my conduct to answer truthfully. I do not have to "observe" my beliefs and intentions either; I merely voice them or express them in words. It may happen that I do not know how to answer such questions. Do I think that Madrid is a lively place? If I have no set opinion on this particular matter, I may try to form one, try to "make up my mind" about it. This may take some thinking based on certain facts I can recall about Madrid—and not about my actual or possible behavior.

Notice how different it is with real dispositions. There the subject and the observer are in the same boat. To find out whether you are polite, patient, or generous, you and I have to rely on the same evidence: your conduct in the relevant circumstances. Therefore you too can be mistaken in these matters, and be corrected by other people. As for your mental states, I need evidence (your words and actions); you do not. It would be rather odd to suggest that you yourself should recall your past actions to find out what you believe, whom you suspect, and what you intend to do, and it would be ludicrous to add that you should ask me, or other observers, about it.

If you ask a man whether he is polite, he may answer falsely for two reasons: he may be mistaken, or he may be lying. If, on the other hand, you ask him whether he believes that he is polite, his answer can be false only if he is lying. Thus whereas a man may honestly claim that he is polite, and be in fact impolite, nobody can honestly claim that he believes that he is polite, while in fact not believing that he is. With real dispositions the subject's own claim stands on a par with the verdicts of other observers, that is, it can be challenged for honesty or truth. With mental states his words enjoy a "privileged" status: to challenge them is tantamount to assailing his honesty, since the escape hatch of possible error is barred.

Or consider: if a friend of mine is accused of a crime, I may try to believe that he is innocent, or—if I do not succeed—I may at least try to behave as if I believed that he is innocent. Now if belief were a disposition, these two endeavors would amount to the same thing. And they do not.

With respect to mental acts the dispositional account loses even the initial plausibility. Decisions are often sudden, and recognitions and realizations normally take but a moment. I just decided not to go to the movies tonight. This may be true, no matter what I do afterward, even if I call up the theater for reservations. For I could have changed my mind or decided to fool you. I may be the only one who will ever know what I have decided in my heart.

One final point. I have granted above that mental states often indeed dispose a person to act in one way or another; they are apt to mold one's acts. But, again, these acts themselves may be mental acts; mental states may mold one's mental "behavior." If Joe loves Mary, he will not merely try to please her and seek her company, he will also often think about how to please her and how to find her company. Love, of course, is a "mixed" state, part of it being emotion. But the same is true of purely mental states. Take intentions: my intention to go to France will govern, in part, my thoughts at least as much as my overt acts. Moreover, the implications may be mental altogether. One may resolve not to think about something or other (say a threat, an unworthy suspicion, or the like). As a result, the person will avert or cut off such thoughts when they emerge. So, I ask, what is the point of trying to explain mental states in terms of overt behavior if mental acts, at least, have to be admitted anyway?

XIV

How do I know my own mental acts? How do I know what I just decided; how do I know what I believe, what I suspect, what I intend to do? These are one and all silly questions. But the fact that they are silly is instructive. It indicates that we are aware of these mental acts and states immediately, not less than of the sensations we feel, the pains we suffer, and the mental images we entertain. As it is silly to ask somebody, "How do you know that you are in pain?" it is equally foolish to ask, "How do you know that you want to go to the movies?" We do not conclude the existence of our beliefs or intentions on the basis of observing our own actions any more than we discover the existence of our headache by looking into a mirror. Nor, for that matter, do we have to listen to our own voices to know what we are saying, or watch our limbs to find out what we are doing, except in some abnormal situations.

This common feature of "immediate awareness" may be behind the temptation to confuse thought with sensations, feelings, mental images, and the like. Yet these things, the "buzzing blooming confusion" of consciousness, have very little to do with thought. Much thinking may cause headache, but the headache does not add to the thinking; it is likely to stop it. So are other strong sensations, emotions, compulsive images, feelings of pain, dizziness, nausea, and so forth. These are not thinking, nor do their tamer cousins amount to thinking when they occur in dreams, daydreams, reveries, or mindless contemplations. The process of thinking may be accompanied, however, by all sorts of mental images, as we have conceded above, but this remains accidental. What I say essentially depends upon the words I pronounce; what I think is essentially independent of the play of my imagination. This latter may help or distract; St. Antony in the desert has been disturbed by the lascivious play of his imagination while meditating upon the holy mysteries, yet he carried on bravely; the mathematician and the chess player, on the other hand, are likely to evoke certain images to aid their thinking. It stands to reason, too, that words, or even sentences, are apt to crop up in the imagination, while thinking about something. After all, these are the normal means of expressing the thoughts the thinker entertains; no wonder they are closely linked together. Often such words break into the open: the thinker begins to mumble or even gesticulate.

Yet if, say, a mathematician thinks about a problem, that is what he thinks about no matter what goes on in the background of his fancy. He may see shapes or flashes of lights; he may hear music or human voices. Some of these may help, others hinder; but all are compatible with his thinking about that problem, and so is the absence of any imagery. He is not bound to use any images in his thinking, as he is bound to use certain words in telling us what he found out. Speech needs a language; thought does not.

NOTES

1. It is rather instructive to try the verb "try" (and its cognates, "succeed" and "fail") on performatives and mental verbs. Compare, for instance, "He tried to state (deny, tell) . . . "and "He tried to believe (recall, decide)." . . . In the former case the obstacles the person had to overcome must have affected his speech (sluggish tongue, outside noise, etc.). In the latter case the obstacles must have been "inside" him (prejudice, sluggish memory, etc.). This point I owe to Mr. David Brusegard.

Logic and Conversation   12

H. P. GRICE

It is a commonplace of philosophical logic that there are, or appear to be, divergences in meaning between, on the one hand, at least some of what I shall call the formal devices—$\sim$, $\wedge$, $\vee$, $\supset$, (x), $(\imath x)$, $(\exists x)$ (when these are given a standard two-valued interpretation)—and, on the other, what are taken to be their analogs or counterparts in natural language—such expressions as "not," "and," "or," "if," "all," "some" (or "at least one"), "the." Some logicians may at some time have wanted to claim that there are in fact no such divergences; but such claims, if made at all, have been somewhat rashly made, and those suspected of making them have been subjected to some pretty rough handling.

Those who concede that such divergences exist adhere, in the main, to one or the other of two rival groups, which for the purposes of this article I shall call the formalist and the informalist groups. An outline of a not uncharacteristic formalist position may be given as follows: Insofar as logicians are concerned with the formulation of very general patterns of valid inference, the formal devices possess a decisive advantage over their natural counterparts. For it will be possible to construct in terms of the formal devices a system of very general formulas, a considerable number of which can be regarded as, or are closely related to, patterns of inferences the expres-

sion of which involves some or all of the devices: Such a system may consist of a certain set of simple formulas that must be acceptable if the devices have the meaning that has been assigned to them, and an indefinite number of further formulas, many of them less obviously acceptable, each of which can be shown to be acceptable if the members of the original set are acceptable. We have, thus, a way of handling dubiously acceptable patterns of inference, and if, as is sometimes possible, we can apply a decision procedure, we have an even better way. Furthermore, from a philosophical point of view, the possession by the natural counterparts of those elements in their meaning, which they do not share with the corresponding formal devices, is to be regarded as an imperfection of natural languages; the elements in question are undesirable excrescences. For the presence of these elements has the result that the concepts within which they appear cannot be precisely/ clearly defined, and that at least some statements involving them cannot, in some circumstances, be assigned a definite truth value; and the indefiniteness of these concepts is not only objectionable in itself but leaves open the way to metaphysics—we cannot be certain that none of these natural language expressions is metaphysically 'loaded'. For these reasons, the expressions, as used in natural speech,

From *Syntax and Semantics*, volume 3, Peter Cole and Jerry L. Morgan, eds. (New York: Academic Press, 1975), pp. 41–58. Copyright 1975 by H. Paul Grice.

cannot be regarded as finally acceptable, and may turn out to be, finally, not fully intelligible. The proper course is to conceive and begin to construct an ideal language, incorporating the formal devices, the sentences of which will be clear, determinate in truth value, and certifiably free from metaphysical implications; the foundations of science will now be philosophically secure, since the statements of the scientist will be expressible (though not necessarily actually expressed) within this ideal language. (I do not wish to suggest that all formalists would accept the whole of this outline, but I think that all would accept at least some part of it.)

To this, an informalist might reply in the following vein. The philosophical demand for an ideal language rests on certain assumptions that should not be conceded; these are, that the primary yardstick by which to judge the adequacy of a language is its ability to serve the needs of science, that an expression cannot be guaranteed as fully intelligible unless an explication or analysis of its meaning has been provided, and that every explication or analysis must take the form of a precise definition that is the expression/assertion of a logical equivalence. Language serves many important purposes besides those of scientific inquiry; we can know perfectly well what an expression means (and so a fortiori that it is intelligible) without knowing its analysis, and the provision of an analysis may (and usually does) consist in the specification, as generalized as possible, of the conditions that count for or against the applicability of the expression being analyzed. Moreover, while it is no doubt true that the formal devices are especially amenable to systematic treatment by the logician, it remains the case that there are very many inferences and arguments, expressed in natural language and not in terms of these devices, that are nevertheless recognizably valid. So there must be a place for an unsimplified, and so more or less unsystematic, logic of the natural counterparts of these devices; this logic may be aided and guided by the simplified logic of the formal devices but cannot be supplanted by it; indeed, not only do the two logics differ, but

sometimes they come into conflict; rules that hold for a formal device may not hold for its natural counterpart.

Now, on the general question of the place in philosophy of the reformation of natural language, I shall, in this article, have nothing to say. I shall confine myself to the dispute in its relation to the alleged divergences mentioned at the outset. I have, moreover, no intention of entering the fray on behalf of either contestant. I wish, rather, to maintain that the common assumption of the contestants that the divergences do in fact exist is (broadly speaking) a common mistake, and that the mistake arises from an inadequate attention to the nature and importance of the conditions governing conversation. I shall, therefore, proceed at once to inquire into the general conditions that, in one way or another, apply to conversation as such, irrespective of its subject matter.

IMPLICATURE

Suppose that A and B are talking about a mutual friend, C, who is now working in a bank. A asks B how C is getting on in his job, and B replies, "Oh quite well, I think; he likes his colleagues, and he hasn't been to prison yet." At this point, A might well inquire what B was implying, what he was suggesting, or even what he meant by saying that C had not yet been to prison. The answer might be any one of such things as that C is the sort of person likely to yield to the temptation provided by his occupation, that C's colleagues are really very unpleasant and treacherous people, and so forth. It might, of course, be quite unnecessary for A to make such an inquiry of B, the answer to it being, in the context, clear in advance. I think it is clear that whatever B implied, suggested, meant, etc., in this example, is distinct from what B said, which was simply that C had not been to prison yet. I wish to introduce, as terms of art, the verb "*implicate*" and the related nouns "implicature" (cf. implying) and "implicatum" (cf. what is implied). The point of this maneuver is to avoid having, on each occasion, to choose between this or that member of the family of verbs for which "implicate" is to do general duty. I shall, for the time being at least, have to assume to a considerable extent an intuitive understanding of the meaning of "say" in such contexts, and an ability to recognize particular verbs as members of the family with which "implicate" is associated. I can, however, make one or two remarks that may help to clarify the more problematic of these assumptions, namely, that connected with the meaning of the word "say."

In the sense in which I am using the word "say," I intend what someone has said to be closely related to the conventional meaning of the words (the sentence) he has uttered. Suppose someone to have uttered the sentence "He is in the grip of a vice." Given a knowledge of the English language, but no knowledge of the circumstances of the utterance, one would know something about what the speaker had said, on the assumption that he was speaking standard English, and speaking literally. One would know that he had said, about some particular male person or animal x, that at the time of the utterance (whatever that was), either (1) x was unable to rid himself of a certain kind of bad character trait or (2) some part of x's person was caught in a certain kind of tool or instrument (approximate account, of course). But for a full identification of what the speaker had said, one would need to know (a) the identity of x, (b) the time of utterance, and (c) the meaning, on the particular occasion of utterance, of the phrase "in the grip of a vice" [a decision between (1) and (2)]. This brief indication of my use of "say" leaves it open whether a man who says (today) "Harold Wilson is a great man" and another who says (also today) "The British Prime Minister is a great man" would, if each knew that the two singular terms had the same reference, have said the same thing. But whatever decision is made about this question, the apparatus that I am about to provide will be capable of accounting for any implicatures that might depend on the presence of one rather than another of these singular terms in the sentence uttered. Such implicatures would merely be related to different maxims.

In some cases the conventional meaning of the words used will determine what is implicated, besides helping to determine what is said. If I say (smugly), "He is an Englishman; he is, therefore, brave," I have certainly committed myself, by virtue of the meaning of my words, to its being the case that his being brave is a consequence of (follows from) his being an Englishman. But while I have said that he is an Englishman, and said that he is brave, I do not want to say that I have *said* (in the favored sense) that it follows from his being an Englishman that he is brave, though I have certainly indicated, and so implicated, that this is so. I do not want to say that my utterance of this sentence would be, *strictly speaking*, false should the consequence in question fail to hold. So *some* implicatures are conventional, unlike the one with which I introduced this discussion of implicature.

I wish to represent a certain subclass of nonconventional implicatures, which I shall call *conversational* implicatures, as being essentially connected with certain general features of discourse; so my next step is to try to say what these features are.

The following may provide a first approximation to a general principle. Our talk exchanges do not normally consist of a succession of disconnected remarks, and would not be rational if they did. They are characteristically, to some degree at least, cooperative efforts; and each participant recognizes in them, to some extent, a common purpose or set of purposes, or at least a mutually accepted direction. This purpose or direction may be fixed from the start (e.g., by an initial proposal of a question for discussion), or it may evolve during the exchange; it may be fairly definite, or it may be so indefinite as to leave very considerable latitude to the participants (as in a casual conversation). But at each stage, *some* possible conversational moves would be excluded as conversationally unsuitable. We might then formulate a rough general principle which participants will be expected (ceteris paribus) to observe, namely: Make your conversational contribution such as is required, at the stage at which it occurs, by the accepted purpose or direction of the talk exchange in which you are engaged. One might label this the *Cooperative Principle.*

On the assumption that some such general principle as this is acceptable, one may perhaps distinguish four categories under one or another of which will fall certain more specific maxims and submaxims, the following of which will, in general, yield results in accordance with the Cooperative Principle. Echoing Kant, I call these categories Quantity, Quality, Relation, and Manner. The category of *Quantity* relates to the quantity of information to be provided, and under it fall the following maxims: (1) Make your contribution as informative as is required (for the current purposes of the exchange). (2) Do not make your contribution more informative than is required. (The second maxim is disputable; it might be said that to be overinformative is not a transgression of the Cooperative Principle but merely a waste of time. However, it might be answered that such overinformativeness may be confusing in that it is liable to raise side issues; and there may also be an indirect effect, in that the hearers may be misled as a result of thinking that there is some particular *point* in the provision of the excess of information. However this may be, there is perhaps a different reason for doubt about the admission of this second maxim, namely, that its effect will be secured by a later maxim, which concerns relevance.)

Under the category of *quality* falls a supermaxim—"Try to make your contribution one that is true"—and two more specific maxims:

1. Do not say what you believe to be false.
2. Do not say that for which you lack adequate evidence.

Under the category of *Relation* I place a single maxim, namely, "Be relevant." Though the maxim itself is terse, its formulation conceals a number of problems that exercise me a good deal: questions about what different kinds and focuses of relevance there may be, how these shift in the course of a talk exchange, how to allow for the fact that subjects of conversation are legitimately changed, and so on. I find the treatment of

such questions exceedingly difficult, and I hope to revert to them in a later work.

Finally, under the category of *Manner,* which I understand as relating not (like the previous categories) to what is said but, rather, to *how* what is said is to be said, I include the supermaxim—"Be perspicuous"—and various maxims such as:

1. Avoid obscurity of expression.
2. Avoid ambiguity.
3. Be brief (avoid unnecessary prolixity).
4. Be orderly.

And one might need others.

It is obvious that the observance of some of these maxims is a matter of less urgency than is the observance of others; a man who has expressed himself with undue prolixity would, in general, be open to milder comment than would a man who has said something he believes to be false. Indeed, it might be felt that the importance of at least the first maxim of Quality is such that it should not be included in a scheme of the kind I am constructing; other maxims come into operation only on the assumption that this maxim of Quality is satisfied. While this may be correct, so far as the generation of implicatures is concerned it seems to play a role not totally different from the other maxims, and it will be convenient, for the present at least, to treat it as a member of the list of maxims.

There are, of course, all sorts of other maxims (aesthetic, social, or moral in character), such as "Be polite," that are also normally observed by participants in talk exchanges, and these may also generate nonconventional implicatures. The conversational maxims, however, and the conversational implicatures connected with them, are specially connected (I hope) with the particular purposes that talk (and so, talk exchange) is adapted to serve and is primarily employed to serve. I have stated my maxims as if this purpose were a maximally effective exchange of information; this specification is, of course, too narrow, and the scheme needs to be generalized to allow for such general purposes as influencing or directing the actions of others.

As one of my avowed aims is to see talking

as a special case or variety of purposive, indeed rational, behavior, it may be worth noting that the specific expectations or presumptions connected with at least some of the foregoing maxims have their analogues in the sphere of transactions that are not talk exchanges. I list briefly one such analogue for each conversational category.

1. *Quantity*. If you are assisting me to mend a car, I expect your contribution to be neither more nor less than is required; if, for example, at a particular stage I need four screws, I expect you to hand me four, rather than two or six.

2. *Quality*. I expect your contributions to be genuine and not spurious. If I need sugar as an ingredient in the cake you are assisting me to make, I do not expect you to hand me salt; if I need a spoon, I do not expect a trick spoon made of rubber.

3. *Relation*. I expect a partner's contribution to be appropriate to immediate needs at each stage of the transaction; if I am mixing ingredients for a cake, I do not expect to be handed a good book, or even an oven cloth (though this might be an appropriate contribution at a later stage).

4. *Manner*. I expect a partner to make it clear what contribution he is making, and to execute his performance with reasonable dispatch.

These analogies are relevant to what I regard as a fundamental question about the Cooperative Principle and its attendant maxims, namely, what the basis is for the assumption which we seem to make, and on which (I hope) it will appear that a great range of implicatures depend, that talkers will in general (ceteris paribus and in the absence of indications to the contrary) proceed in the manner that these principles prescribe. A dull but, no doubt at a certain level, adequate answer is that it is just a well-recognized empirical fact that people *do* behave in these ways; they have learned to do so in childhood and not lost the habit of doing so; and, indeed, it would involve a good deal of effort to make a radical departure from the habit. It is much easier, for example, to tell the truth than to invent lies.

I am, however, enough of a rationalist to want to find a basis that underlies these facts, undeniable though they may be; I would like to be able to think of the standard type of conversational practice not merely as something that all or most do *in fact* follow but as something that it is *reasonable* for us to follow, that we *should not* abandon. For a time, I was attracted by the idea that observance of the Cooperative Principle and the maxims, in a talk exchange, could be thought of as a quasi-contractual matter, with parallels outside the realm of discourse. If you pass by when I am struggling with my stranded car, I no doubt have some degree of expectation that you will offer help, but once you join me in tinkering under the hood, my expectations become stronger and take more specific forms (in the absence of indications that you are merely an incompetent meddler); and talk exchanges seemed to me to exhibit, characteristically, certain features that jointly distinguish cooperative transactions:

1. The participants have some common immediate aim, like getting a car mended; their ultimate aims may, of course, be independent and even in conflict—each may want to get the car mended in order to drive off, leaving the other stranded. In characteristic talk exchanges, there is a common aim even if, as in an over-the-wall chat, it is a second-order one, namely, that each party should, for the time being, identify himself with the transitory conversational interests of the other.

2. The contributions of the participants should be dovetailed, mutually dependent.

3. There is some sort of understanding (which may be explicit but which is often tacit) that, other things being equal, the transaction should continue in appropriate style unless both parties are agreeable that it should terminate. You do not just shove off or start doing something else.

But while some such quasi-contractual basis as this may apply to some cases, there are too many types of exchange, like quarreling and letter writing, that it fails to fit comfortably. In any case, one feels that the talker who is irrelevant or obscure has primarily let down not his audience but himself. So I would like to be able to show that observance of the Cooperative Principle and maxims is reasonable (rational) along the following lines: that any one who cares about the goals that are central to conversation/communication (e.g., giving and receiving information, influencing and being influenced by others) must be expected to have an interest, given suitable circumstances, in participating in talk exchanges that will be profitable only on the assumption that they are conducted in general accordance with the Cooperative Principle and the maxims. Whether any such conclusion can be reached, I am uncertain; in any case, I am fairly sure that I cannot reach it until I am a good deal clearer about the nature of relevance and of the circumstances in which it is required.

It is now time to show the connection between the Cooperative Principle and maxims, on the one hand, and conversational implicature on the other.

A participant in a talk exchange may fail to fulfill a maxim in various ways, which include the following:

1. He may quietly and unostentatiously *violate* a maxim; if so, in some cases he will be liable to mislead.

2. He may *opt out* from the operation both of the maxim and of the Cooperative Principle; he may say, indicate, or allow it to become plain that he is unwilling to cooperate in the way the maxim requires. He may say, for example, "I cannot say more; my lips are sealed."

3. He may be faced by a *clash:* He may be unable, for example, to fulfill the first maxim of Quantity (Be as informative as is required) without violating the second maxim of Quality (Have adequate evidence for what you say).

4. He may *flout* a maxim; that is, he may *blatantly* fail to fulfill it. On the assumption that the speaker is able to fulfill the maxim and to do so without violating another maxim (because of a clash), is not opting out, and is not, in view of the blatancy of his performance, trying to mislead, the hearer is faced with a minor problem: How can his saying what he did say be reconciled with the supposition that he is observing the overall Cooperative Principle? This situation is one that characteristically gives rise to a conversational implicature; and when a conversational implicature is generated in this way, I shall say that a maxim is being *exploited.*

I am now in a position to characterize the notion of conversational implicature. A man who, by (in, when) saying (or making as if to say) that *p* has implicated that *q,* may be said to have conversationally implicated that *q, provided that* (1) he is to be presumed to be observing the conversational maxims, or at least the cooperative principle; (2) the supposition that he is aware that, or thinks that, *q* is required in order to make his saying or making as if to say *p* (or doing so in *those* terms) consistent with this presumption; and (3) the speaker thinks (and would expect the hearer to think that the speaker thinks) that it is within the competence of the hearer to work out, or grasp intuitively, that the supposition mentioned in (2) *is* required. Apply this to my initial example, to B's remark that C has not yet been to prison. In a suitable setting A might reason as follows: "(1) B has apparently violated the maxim 'Be relevant' and so may be regarded as having flouted one of the maxims conjoining perspicuity, yet I have no reason to suppose that he is opting out from the operation of the CP; (2) given the circumstances, I can regard his irrelevance as only apparent if, and only if, I suppose him to think that C is potentially dishonest; (3) B knows that I am capable of working out step (2). So B implicates that C is potentially dishonest."

The presence of a conversational implicature must be capable of being worked out; for even if it can in fact be intuitively grasped, unless the intuition is replaceable by an argument, the implicature (if present at all) will not count as a *conversational* implicature; it will be a *conventional* implicature. To work out that a particular conversational implicature is present, the hearer will rely on the following data: (1) the conventional meaning of the words used, together with the identity of any references that may be involved; (2) the Cooperative Principle and its maxims; (3) the context, linguistic or otherwise, of the utterance; (4) other items of background knowledge; and (5) the fact (or supposed fact) that all relevant items falling under the previous headings are available to both participants and both participants know or assume this to be the case. A general pattern for the working out of a conversational implicature might be given as follows: 'He has said that *p;* there is no reason to suppose that he is not observing the maxims, or at least the Cooperative Principle; he could not be doing this unless he thought that *q;* he knows (and knows that I know that he knows) that I can see that the supposition that he thinks that *q is* required; he has done nothing to stop me thinking that *q;* he intends me to think, or is at least willing to allow me to think, that *q;* and so he has implicated that *q.*'

EXAMPLES

I shall now offer a number of examples, which I shall divide into three groups.

Group A.

Examples in which no maxim is violated, or at least in which it is not clear that any maxim is violated:
(1) A is standing by an obviously immobilized car and is approached by B, the following exchange takes place:

> A: I am out of petrol.
> B: There is a garage round the corner.

(Gloss: B would be infringing the maxim "Be relevant" unless he thinks, or thinks it possible, that the garage is open, and has petrol to sell; so he implicates that the garage is, or at least may be open, etc.) In this example, unlike the case of the remark "He hasn't been to prison yet," the unstated connection between B's remark and A's remark is so obvious that, even if one interprets the supermaxim of Manner, "Be perspicuous," as applying not only to the expression of what is said but also to the connection of what is said

with adjacent remarks, there seems to be no case for regarding that supermaxim as infringed in this example.
(2) The next example is perhaps a little less clear in this respect:

> A: Smith doesn't seem to have a girlfriend these days.
> B: He has been paying a lot of visits to New York lately.

B implicates that Smith has, or may have, a girlfriend in New York. (A gloss is unnecessary in view of that given for the previous example.)

In both examples, the speaker implicates that which he must be assumed to believe in order to preserve the assumption that he is observing the maxim of relation.

Group B.

An example in which a maxim is violated, but its violation is to be explained by the supposition of a clash with another maxim:
(3) A is planning with B an itinerary for a holiday in France. Both know that A wants to see his friend C, if to do so would not involve too great a prolongation of his journey:

> A: Where does C live?
> B: Somewhere in the South of France.

(Gloss: There is no reason to suppose that B is opting out; his answer is, as he well knows, less informative than is required to meet A's needs. This infringement of the first maxim of Quantity can be explained only by the supposition that B is aware that to be more informative would be to say something that infringed the maxim of Quality, "Don't say what you lack adequate evidence for," so B implicates that he does not know in which town C lives.)

Group C.

Examples that involve exploitation, that is, a procedure by which a maxim is flouted for the purpose of getting in a conversational implicature by means of something of the nature of a figure of speech:

In these examples, though some maxim is violated at the level of what is said, the hearer is entitled to assume that that maxim, or at least the overall Cooperative Principle, is observed at the level of what is implicated. (1a) A flouting of the first maxim of Quantity. A is writing a testimonial about a pupil who is a candidate for a philosophy job, and his letter reads as follows: "Dear Sir, Mr. X's command of English is excellent, and his attendance at tutorials has been regular. Yours, etc.' (Gloss: A cannot be opting out, since if he wished to be uncooperative, why write at all? He cannot be unable, through ignorance, to say more, since the man is his pupil; moreover, he knows that more information than this is wanted. He must, therefore, be wishing to impart information that he is reluctant to write down. This supposition is tenable only on the assumption that he thinks Mr. X is no good at philosophy. This, then, is what he is implicating.)

Extreme examples of a flouting of the first maxim of Quantity are provided by utterances of patent tautologies like "Women are women" and "War is war." I would wish to maintain that at the level of what is said, in my favored sense, such remarks are totally noninformative and so, at that level, cannot but infringe the first maxim of Quantity in any conversational context. They are, of course, informative at the level of what is implicated, and the hearer's identification of their informative content at this level is dependent on his ability to explain the speaker's selection of this *particular* patent tautology.

(1b) An infringement of the second maxim of Quantity, "Do not give more information than is required," on the assumption that the existence of such a maxim should be admitted. A wants to know whether *p*, and B volunteers not only the information that *p*, but information to the effect that it is certain that *p*, and that the evidence for its being the case that *p* is so-and-so and such-and-such.

B's volubility may be undesigned, and if it is so regarded by A it may raise in A's mind a doubt as to whether B is as certain as he says he is ('Methinks the lady doth protest too much'). But if it is thought of as designed, it would be an oblique way of conveying that it is to some degree controversial whether or not *p*. It is, however, arguable that such an implicature could be explained by reference to the maxim of Relation without invoking an alleged second maxim of Quantity.

(2a) Examples in which the first maxim of Quality is flouted.

(i) Irony: X, with whom A has been on close terms until now, has betrayed a secret of A's to a business rival. A and his audience both know this. A says "X is a fine friend." (Gloss: It is perfectly obvious to A and his audience that what A has said or has made as if to say is something he does not believe, and the audience knows that A knows that this is obvious to the audience. So, unless A's utterance is entirely pointless, A must be trying to get across some other proposition than the one he purports to be putting forward. This must be some obviously related proposition; the most obviously related proposition is the contradictory of the one he purports to be putting forward.)

(ii) Metaphor: Examples like "You are the cream in my coffee" characteristically involve categorial falsity, so the contradictory of what the speaker has made as if to say will, strictly speaking, be a truism; so it cannot be *that* that such a speaker is trying to get across. The most likely supposition is that the speaker is attributing to his audience some feature or features in respect of which the audience resembles (more or less fancifully) the mentioned substance.

It is possible to combine metaphor and irony by imposing on the hearer two stages of interpretation. I say "You are the cream in my coffee," intending the hearer to reach first the metaphor interpretant "You are my pride and joy" and then the irony interpretant "You are my bane."

(iii) Meiosis: Of a man known to have broken up all the furniture, one says "He was a little intoxicated."

(iv) Hyperbole: Every nice girl loves a sailor.

(2b) Examples in which the second maxim of Quality, "Do not say that for which you lack adequate evidence," is flouted are perhaps not easy to find, but the following seems to be a specimen. I say of X's wife, "She is probably deceiving him this evening." In a suitable context, or with a suitable gesture or tone of voice, it may be clear that I have no adequate reason for supposing this to be the case. My partner, to preserve the assumption that the conversational game is still being played, assumes that I am getting at some related proposition for the acceptance of which I *do* have a reasonable basis. The related proposition might well be that she is given to deceiving her husband, or possibly that she is the sort of person who would not stop short of such conduct.

(3) Examples in which an implicature is achieved by real, as distinct from apparent, violation of the maxim of Relation are perhaps rare, but the following seems to be a good candidate. At a genteel tea party, A says "Mrs. X is an old bag." There is a moment of appalled silence, and then B says "The weather has been quite delightful this summer, hasn't it?" B has blatantly refused to make what *he* says relevant to A's preceding remark. He thereby implicates that A's remark should not be discussed and, perhaps more specifically, that A has committed a social gaffe.

(4) Examples in which various maxims falling under the supermaxim "Be perspicuous" are flouted.

(i) Ambiguity. We must remember that we are concerned only with ambiguity that is deliberate, and that the speaker intends or expects to be recognized by his hearer. The problem the hearer has to solve is why a speaker should, when still playing the conversational game, go out of his way to choose an ambiguous utterance. There are two types of cases:

(a) Examples in which there is no difference, or no striking difference, between two interpretations of an utterance with respect to straightforwardness; neither interpretation is notably more sophisticated, less standard, more recondite or more far-fetched than the other. We might consider Blake's lines: "Never seek to tell thy love, Love that never told can be." To avoid the complications introduced by the presence of the imperative

mood, I shall consider the related sentence, "I sought to tell my love, love that never told can be." There may be a double ambiguity here. "My love" may refer to either a state of emotion or an object of emotion, and "love that never told can be" may mean either "Love that cannot be told" or "love that if told cannot continue to exist." Partly because of the sophistication of the poet and partly because of internal evidence (that the ambiguity is kept up), there seems to be no alternative to supposing that the ambiguities are deliberate and that the poet is conveying both what he would be saying if one interpretation were intended rather than the other, and vice versa; though no doubt the poet is not explicitly *saying* any one of these things but only conveying or suggesting them (cf. "Since she [nature] pricked thee out of women's pleasure, mine be thy love, and thy love's use their treasure.")

(b) Examples in which one interpretation is notably less straightforward than another. Take the complex example of the British General who captured the town of Sind and sent back the message *Peccavi*. The ambiguity involved ("I have Sind"/"I have sinned") is phonemic, not morphemic; and the expression actually used is unambiguous, but since it is in a language foreign to speaker and hearer, translation is called for, and the ambiguity resides in the standard translation into native English.

Whether or not the straightforward interpretant ("I have sinned") is being conveyed, it seems that the nonstraightforward must be. There might be stylistic reasons for conveying by a sentence merely its nonstraightforward interpretant, but it would be pointless, and perhaps also stylistically objectionable, to go to the trouble of finding an expression that nonstraightforwardly conveys that p, thus imposing on an audience the effort involved in finding this interpretant, if this interpretant were otiose so far as communication was concerned. Whether the straightforward interpretant is also being conveyed seems to depend on whether such a supposition would conflict with other conversational requirements, for example, would it be relevant, would it be something the speaker could be supposed to accept, and so on. If such requirements are not satisfied, then the straightforward interpretant is not being conveyed. If they are, it is. If the author of *Peccavi* could naturally be supposed to think that he had committed some kind of transgression, for example, had disobeyed his orders in capturing Sind, and if reference to such a transgression would be relevant to the presumed interests of the audience, then he would have been conveying both interpretants; otherwise he would be conveying only the nonstraightforward one.

(ii) Obscurity. How do I exploit, for the purposes of communication, a deliberate and overt violation of the requirement that I should avoid obscurity? Obviously, if the Cooperative Principle is to operate, I must intend my partner to understand what I am saying despite the obscurity I import into my utterance. Suppose that A and B are having a conversation in the presence of a third party, for example, a child, then A might be deliberately obscure, though not too obscure, in the hope that B would understand and the third party not. Furthermore, if A expects B to see that A is being deliberately obscure, it seems reasonable to suppose that, in making his conversational contribution in this way, A is implicating that the contents of his communication should not be imparted to the third party.

(iii) Failure to be brief or succinct. Compare the remarks:

(a) Miss X sang "Home sweet home."
(b) Miss X produced a series of sounds that corresponded closely with the score of "Home sweet home."

Suppose that a reviewer has chosen to utter (b) rather than (a). (Gloss: Why has he selected that rigmarole in place of the concise and nearly synonymous "sang"? Presumably, to indicate some striking difference between Miss X's performance and those to which the word "singing" is usually applied. The most obvious supposition is that Miss X's performance suffered from some hideous defect. The reviewer knows that this supposition is

what is likely to spring to mind, so that is what he is implicating.)

I have so far considered only cases of what I might call particularized conversational implicature—that is to say, cases in which an implicature is carried by saying that *p* on a particular occasion in virtue of special features of the context, cases in which there is no room for the idea that an implicature of this sort is *normally* carried by saying that *p*. But there are cases of generalized conversational implicature. Sometimes one can say that the use of a certain form of words in an utterance would normally (in the *absence* of special circumstances) carry such-and-such an implicature or type of implicature. Noncontroversial examples are perhaps hard to find, since it is all too easy to treat a generalized conversational implicature as if it were a conventional implicature. I offer an example that I hope may be fairly noncontroversial.

Anyone who uses a sentence of the form "X is meeting a woman this evening" would normally implicate that the person to be met was someone other than X's wife, mother, sister, or perhaps even close platonic friend. Similarly, if I were to say "X went into a house yesterday and found a tortoise inside the front door," my hearer would normally be surprised if some time later I revealed that the house was X's own. I could produce similar linguistic phenomena involving the expressions "a garden," "a car," "a college," and so on. Sometimes, however, there would normally be no such implicature ("I have been sitting in a car all morning"), and sometimes a reverse implicature ("I broke a finger yesterday"). I am inclined to think that one would not lend a sympathetic ear to a philosopher who suggested that there are three senses of the form of expression "an X": one in which it means roughly 'something that satisfies the conditions defining the word *X*,' another in which it means approximately 'an X (in the first sense) that is only remotely related in a certain way to some person indicated by the context,' and yet another in which it means 'an X (in the first sense) that is closely related in a certain way to some person indicated by the context.' Would we not much prefer an account on the following lines (which, of course, may be incorrect in detail): When someone, by using the form of expression "an X," implicates that the X does not belong to or is not otherwise closely connected with some identifiable person, the implicature is present because the speaker has failed to be specific in a way in which he might have been expected to be specific, with the consequence that it is likely to be assumed that he is not in a position to be specific. This is a familiar implicature situation and is classifiable as a failure, for one reason or another, to fulfill the first maxim of Quantity. The only difficult question is why it should, in certain cases, be presumed, independently of information about particular contexts of utterance, that specification of the closeness or remoteness of the connection between a particular person or object and a further person who is mentioned or indicated by the utterance should be likely to be of interest. The answer must lie in the following region: Transactions between a person and other persons or things closely connected with him are liable to be very different as regards their concomitants and results from the same sort of transactions involving only remotely connected persons or things; the concomitants and results, for instance, of my finding a hole in *my* roof are likely to be very different from the concomitants and results of my finding a hole in someone else's roof. Information, like money, is often given without the giver's knowing to just what use the recipient will want to put it. If someone to whom a transaction is mentioned gives it further consideration, he is likely to find himself wanting the answers to further questions that the speaker may not be able to identify in advance; if the appropriate specification will be likely to enable the hearer to answer a considerable variety of such questions for himself, then there is a presumption that the speaker should include it in his remark; if not, then there is no such presumption.

Finally, we can now show that, conversational implicature being what it is, it must possess certain features.

1. Since, to assume the presence of a conversational implicature, we have to assume that at least the Cooperative Principle is being observed, and since it is possible to opt out of the observation of this principle, it follows that a generalized conversational implicature can be canceled in a particular case. It may be explicitly canceled, by the addition of a clause that states or implies that the speaker has opted out, or it may be contextually canceled, if the form of utterance that usually carries it is used in a context that makes it clear that the speaker IS opting out.

2. Insofar as the calculation that a particular conversational implicature is present requires, besides contextual and background information, only a knowledge of what has been said (or of the conventional commitment of the utterance), and insofar as the manner of expression plays no role in the calculation, it will not be possible to find another way of saying the same thing, which simply lacks the implicature in question, except where some special feature of the substituted version is itself relevant to the determination of an implicature (in virtue of one of the maxims of Manner). If we call this feature *nondetachability,* one may expect a generalized conversational implicature that is carried by a familiar, nonspecial locution to have a high degree of nondetachability.

3. To speak approximately, since the calculation of the presence of a conversational implicature presupposes an initial knowledge of the conventional force of the expression the utterance of which carries the implicature, a conversational implicatum will be a condition that is not included in the original specification of the expression's conventional force. Though it may not be impossible for what starts life, so to speak, as a conversational implicature to become conventionalized, to suppose that this is so in a given case would require special justification. So, initially at least, conversational implicata are not part of the meaning of the expressions to the employment of which they attach.

4. Since the truth of a conversational implicatum is not required by the truth of what is said (what is said may be true—what is

implicated may be false), the implicature is not carried by what is said, but only by the saying of what is said, or by 'putting it that way.'

5. Since, to calculate a conversational implicature is to calculate what has to be supposed in order to preserve the supposition that the Cooperative Principle is being observed, and since there may be various possible specific explanations, a list of which may be open, the conversational implicatum in such cases will be disjunction of such specific explanations; and if the list of these is open, the implicatum will have just the kind of indeterminacy that many actual implicata do in fact seem to possess.

Indirect Speech Acts　　13

The simplest cases of meaning are those in which the speaker utters a sentence and means exactly and literally what he says. In such cases the speaker intends to produce a certain illocutionary effect in the hearer, and he intends to produce this effect by getting the hearer to recognize this intention to produce it, and he intends to get the hearer to recognize this intention in virtue of the hearer's knowledge of the rules that govern the utterance of the sentence. But notoriously, not all cases of meaning are this simple: In hints, insinuations, irony, and metaphor— to mention a few examples—the speaker's utterance meaning and the sentence meaning come apart in various ways. One important class of such cases is that in which the speaker utters a sentence, means what he says, but also means something more. For example, a speaker may utter the sentence "I want you to do it" by way of requesting the hearer to do something. The utterance is incidentally meant as a statement, but it is also meant primarily as a request, a request made by way of making a statement. In such cases a sentence that contains the illocutionary force indicators for one kind of illocutionary act can be uttered to perform, *in addition*, another type of illocutionary act. There are also cases in which the speaker may utter a sentence and mean what he says and also mean another illocution with a different propositional content. For example, a speaker may utter the sentence "Can you reach the salt?" and mean it not merely as a question but as a request to pass the salt.

In such cases it is important to emphasize that the utterance is meant as a request; that is, the speaker intends to produce in the hearer the knowledge that a request has been made to him, and he intends to produce this knowledge by means of getting the hearer to recognize his intention to produce it. Such cases, in which the utterance has two illocutionary forces, are to be sharply distinguished from the cases in which, for example, the speaker tells the hearer that he wants him to do something; and then the hearer does it because the speaker wants him to, though no request at all has been made, meant, or understood. The cases we will be discussing are indirect speech acts, cases in which one illocutionary act is performed indirectly by way of performing another.

The problem posed by indirect speech acts is the problem of how it is possible for the speaker to say one thing and mean that but also to mean something else. And since meaning consists in part in the intention to produce understanding in the hearer, a large part of that problem is that of how it is possible for the hearer to understand the

From *Syntax and Semantics*, volume 3, Peter Cole and Jerry L. Morgan, eds. (New York: Academic Press, 1975), pp. 59–82. © John R. Searle.

indirect speech act when the sentence he hears and understands means something else. The problem is made more complicated by the fact that some sentences seem almost to be conventionally used as indirect requests. For a sentence like "Can you reach the salt?" or I would appreciate it if you would get off my foot," it takes some ingenuity to imagine a situation in which their utterances would not be requests.

In Searle (1) I suggested that many such utterances could be explained by the fact that the sentences in question concern conditions of the felicitous performance of the speech acts they are used to perform indirectly—preparatory conditions, propositional content conditions, and sincerity conditions—and that their use to perform indirect speech acts consists in indicating the satisfaction of an essential condition by means of asserting or questioning one of the other conditions. Since that time a variety of explanations have been proposed, involving such things as the hypostatization of 'conversational postulates' or alternative deep structures. The answer I originally suggested seems to me incomplete, and I want to develop it further here. The hypothesis I wish to defend is simply this: In indirect speech acts the speaker communicates to the hearer more than he actually says by way of relying on their mutually shared background information, both linguistic and nonlinguistic, together with the general powers of rationality and inference on the part of the hearer. To be more specific, the apparatus necessary to explain the indirect part of indirect speech acts includes a theory of speech acts, certain general principles of cooperative conversation (some of which have been discussed by Grice) and mutually shared factual background information of the speaker and the hearer, together with an ability on the part of the hearer to make inferences. It is not necessary to assume the existence of any conversational postulates (either as an addition to the theory of speech acts or as part of the theory of speech acts) nor any concealed imperative forces or other ambiguities. We will see, however, that in some cases, convention plays a most peculiar role.

Aside from its interest for a theory of meaning and speech acts, the problem of indirect speech acts is of philosophical importance for an additional reason. In ethics it has commonly been supposed that "good" "right", "ought", etc. somehow have an imperative or 'action guiding' meaning. This view derives from the fact that sentences such as "You ought to do it" are often uttered by way of telling the hearer to do something. But from the fact that such sentences can be uttered as directives[1] it no more follows that "ought" has an imperative meaning than from the fact that "Can you reach the salt" can be uttered as a request to pass the salt it follows that "can" has an imperative meaning. Many confusions in recent moral philosophy rest on a failure to understand the nature of such indirect speech acts. The topic has an additional interest for linguists because of its syntactical consequences, but I shall be concerned with these only incidentally.

A SAMPLE CASE

Let us begin by considering a typical case of the general phenomenon of indirection:

(1) Student X: *Let's go to the movies tonight.*
(2) Student Y: *I have to study for an exam.*

The utterance of (1) constitutes a proposal in virtue of its meaning, in particular because of the meaning of "Let's." In general, literal utterances of sentences of this form will constitute proposals, as in:

(3) Let's eat pizza tonight.

or:

(4) Let's go ice skating tonight.

The utterance of (2) in the context just given would normally constitute a rejection of the proposal, but not in virtue of its meaning. In virtue of its meaning it is simply a statement about Y. Statements of this form do not, in general, constitute rejections of proposals, even in cases in which they are made in response to a proposal. Thus, if Y had said:

(5) I have to eat popcorn tonight.

or:

(6) I have to tie my shoes.

in a normal context, neither of these utterances would have been a rejection of the proposal. The question then arises, How does X know that the utterance is a rejection of the proposal? and that question is a part of the question, How is it possible for Y to intend or mean the utterance of (2) as a rejection of the proposal? In order to describe this case, let us introduce some terminology. Let us say that the *primary* illocutionary act performed in Y's utterance is the rejection of the *proposal* made by X, and that Y does that by way of performing a *secondary* illocutionary act of making a statement to the effect that he has to prepare for an exam. He performs the secondary illocutionary act by way of uttering a sentence the *literal* meaning of which is such that its literal utterance constitutes a performance of that illocutionary act. We may, therefore, further say that the secondary illocutionary act is literal; the primary illocutionary act is not literal. Let us assume that we know how X understands the literal secondary illocutionary act from the utterance of the sentence. The question is, How does he understand the nonliteral primary illocutionary act from understanding the literal secondary illocutionary act? And that question is part of the larger question, How is it possible for Y to mean the primary illocution when he only utters a sentence that means the secondary illocution, since to mean the primary illocution is (in large part) to intend to produce in X the relevant understanding?

A brief reconstruction of the steps necessary to derive the primary illocution from the literal illocution would go as follows. (In normal conversation, of course, no one would consciously go through the steps involved in this reasoning.)

Step 1. I have made a proposal to Y, and in response he has made a statement to the effect that he has to study for an exam (facts about the conversation).

Step 2. I assume that Y is cooperating in the conversation and that therefore his remark is intended to be relevant (principles of conversational cooperation).

Step 3. A relevant response must be one of acceptance, rejection, counterproposal, further discussion, etc. (theory of speech acts).

Step 4. But his literal utterance was not one of these, and so was not a relevant response inference from steps 1 and 3).

Step 5. Therefore, he probably means more than he says. Assuming that his remark is relevant, his primary illocutionary point must differ from his literal one (inference from steps 2 and 4).[2] (This step is crucial. Unless a hearer has some inferential strategy for finding out when primary illocutionary points differ from literal illocutionary points, he has no way of understanding indirect illocutionary acts.)

Step 6. I know that studying for an exam normally takes a large amount of time relative to a single evening, and I know that going to the movies normally takes a large amount of time relative to a single evening (factual background information).

Step 7. Therfore, he probably cannot both go to the movies and study for an exam in one evening (inference from step 6).

Step 8. A preparatory condition on the acceptance of a proposal, or on any other commissive, is the ability to perform the act predicated in the propositional content condition (theory of speech acts).

Step 9. Therefore, I know that he has said something that has the consequence that he probably cannot consistently accept the proposal (inference from steps 1, 7, and 8).

Step 10. Therefore, his primary illocutionary point is probably to reject the proposal (inference from steps 5 and 9).

It may seem somewhat pedantic to set all of this out in 10 steps; but if anything, the example is still underdescribed—I have not, for example, discussed the role of the assumption of sincerity, or the ceteris paribus conditions that attach to various of the steps. Notice, also, that the conclusion is probabilistic. It is and ought to be. This is because the reply does not necessarily constitute a rejection of the proposal. Y might have gone on to say:

(7) I have to study for an exam, but let's go to the movies anyhow.

(8) I have to study for an exam, but I'll do it when we get home from the movies.

The inferential strategy is to establish, first, that the primary illocutionary point departs from the literal, and second, what the primary illocutionary point is.

The argument of this chapter will be that the theoretical apparatus used to explain this case will suffice to explain the general phenomenon of indirect illocutionary acts. That apparatus includes mutual background information, a theory of speech acts, and certain general principles of conversation. In particular, we explained this case without having to assume that sentence (2) is ambiguous or that it is 'ambiguous in context' or that it is necessary to assume the existence of any 'conversational postulates' in order to explain X's understanding the primary illocution of the utterance. The main difference between this case and the cases we will be discussing is that the latter all have a generality of *form* that is lacking in this example. I shall mark this generality by using bold type for the formal features in the surface structure of the sentences in question. In the field of indirect illocutionary acts, the area of directives is the most useful to study because ordinary conversational requirements of politeness normally make it awkward to issue flat imperative sentences (e.g., "Leave the room") or explicit performatives (e.g., "I order you to leave the room"), and we therefore seek to find indirect means to our illocutionary ends (e.g., "I wonder if you would mind leaving the room"). In directives, politeness is the chief motivation for indirectness.

SOME SENTENCES 'CONVENTIONALLY' USED IN THE PERFORMANCE OF INDIRECT DIRECTIVES

Let us begin, then, with a short list of some of the sentences that could quite standardly be used to make indirect requests and other directives such as orders. At a pretheoretical level these sentences naturally tend to group themselves into certain categories.[3]

Group 1.

Sentences concerning H's ability to perform A

Can you reach the salt?

Can you pass the salt?

Could you be a little more quiet?

You could be a little more quiet.

You can go now (this may also be a permission = you may go now).

Are you able to reach the book on the top shelf?

Have you got change for a dollar?

Group 2.

Sentences concerning S's wish or want that H will do A

I would like you to go now.

I want you to do this for me, Henry.

I would/should appreciate it if you would/could do it for me.

I would/should be most grateful if you would/could help us out.

I'd rather you didn't do that any more.

I'd be very much obliged if you would pay me the money back soon.

I hope you'll do it.

I wish you wouldn't do that.

Group 3.

Sentences concerning H's doing A

Officers **will** henceforth wear ties at dinner.

Will you quit making that awful racket?

Would you kindly get off my foot?

Won't you stop making that noise soon?

Aren't you going to eat your cereal?

Group 4.

Sentences concerning H's desire or willingness to do A

Would you be willing to write a letter of recommendation for me?

Do you want to hand me that hammer over there on the table?

Would you mind not making so much noise?

Would it be convenient for you to come on Wednesday?

Would it be too much (trouble) for you to pay me the money next Wednesday?

Group 5.

Sentences concerning reasons for doing A

You ought to be more polite to your mother.

You should leave immediately.

Must you continue hammering that way?

Ought you to eat quite so much spaghetti?

Should you be wearing John's tie?

You had better go now.

Hadn't you better go now?

Why not stop here?

Why don't you try it just once?

Why don't you be quiet?

It would be better for you (for us all) if you would leave the room.

It wouldn't hurt if you left now.

It might help if you shut up.

It would be better if you gave me the money now.

It would be a good idea if you left town.

We'd all be better off if you'd just pipe down a bit.

This class also contains many examples that have no generality of form but obviously, in an appropriate context, would be uttered as indirect requests, e.g.,

You're standing on my foot.

I can't see the movie screen while you have that hat on.

Also in this class belong, possibly:

How many times have I told you (must I tell you) not to eat with your fingers?

I must have told you a dozen times not to eat with your mouth open.

If I have told you once I have told you a thousand times not to wear your hat in the house.

Group 6.

Sentences embedding one of these elements inside another; also, sentences embedding an explicit directive illocutionary verb inside one of these contexts

Would you mind awfully if I asked you if you could write me a letter of recommendation?

Would it be too much if I suggested that you could possibly make a little less noise?

Might I ask you to take off your hat?

I hope you won't mind if I ask you if you could leave us alone.

I would appreciate it if you could make less noise.[4]

This is a very large class, since most of its members are constructed by permitting certain of the elements of the other classes.

SOME PUTATIVE FACTS

Let us begin by noting several salient facts about the sentences in question. Not everyone will agree that what follows are facts; indeed, most of the available explanations consist in denying one or more of these statements. Nonetheless, at an intuitive pretheoretical level each of the following would seem to be correct observations about the sentences in question, and I believe we should surrender these intuitions only in the face of very serious counterarguments. I will eventually argue that an explanation can be given that is consistent with all of these facts.

Fact 1: The sentences in question do not have an imperative force as part of their meaning. This point is sometimes denied by philosophers and linguists, but very powerful evidence for it is provided by the fact that it is possible without inconsistency to connect the literal utterance of one of these forms with the denial of any imperative intent, e.g.,

I'd like you to do this for me, Bill, but I am not asking you to do it or requesting that you do it or ordering you to do it or telling you to do it.

I'm just asking you, Bill: Why not eat beans? But in asking you that I want you to understand that I am not telling you to eat beans; I just want to know your reasons for thinking you ought not to.

Fact 2: The sentences in question are not ambiguous as between an imperative illocutionary force and a nonimperative illocutionary force. I think this is intuitively apparent, but in any case, an ordinary application of Occam's razor places the onus of proof on those who wish to claim that these sentences are ambiguous. One does not multiply meanings beyond necessity. Notice, also, that it is no help to say they are 'ambiguous in context,' for all that means is that one cannot always tell from what the sentence means what the speaker means by its utterance, and that is not sufficient to establish sentential ambiguity.

Fact 3: Notwithstanding facts 1 and 2, these are standardly, ordinarily, normally—indeed, I shall argue, conventionally—used to issue directives. There is a systematic relation between these and directive illocutions in a way that there is no systematic relation between "I have to study for an exam" and rejecting proposals. Additional evidence that they are standardly used to issue imperatives is that most of them take "please," either at the end of the sentence or preceding the verb, e.g.,

I want you to stop making that noise, please.

Could you please lend me a dollar?

When "please" is added to one of these sentences, it explicitly and literally marks the primary illocutionary point of the utterance as directive, even though the literal meaning of the rest of the sentence is not directive.

It is because of the combination of facts 1, 2, and 3 that there is a problem about these cases at all.

Fact 4: The sentences in question are not, in the ordinary sense, idioms.[5] An ordinary example of an idiom is "kicked the bucket" in "Jones kicked the bucket." The most powerful evidence I know that these sentences are not idioms is that in their use as indirect directives they admit of literal responses that presuppose that they are uttered literally. Thus, an utterance of "Why don't you be quiet, Henry?" admits as a response an utterance of "Well, Sally, there are several reasons for not being quiet. First, ..." Possible exceptions to this are occurrences of

"would" and "could" in indirect speech acts, and I will discuss them later.

Further evidence that they are not idioms is that, whereas a word-for-word translation of "Jones kicked the bucket" into other languages will not produce a sentence meaning "Jones died," translations of the sentences in question will often, though by no means always, produce sentences with the same indirect illocutionary act potential of the English examples. Thus, e.g., "Pourriez-vous m'aider?" and "Können Sie mir helfen?" can be uttered as indirect requests in French or German. I will later discuss the problem of why some translate with equivalent indirect illocutionary force potential and some do not.

Fact 5: To say they are not idioms is not to say they are not idiomatic. All the examples given are idiomatic in current English, and—what is more puzzling—they are idiomatically used as requests. In general, nonidiomatic equivalents or synonyms would not have the same indirect illocutionary act potential. Thus, "Do you want to hand me the hammer over there on the table?" can be uttered as a request, but "Is it the case that you at present desire to hand me that hammer over there on the table?" has a formal and stilted character that in almost all contexts would eliminate it as a candidate for an indirect request. Furthermore, "Are you able to hand me that hammer?", though idiomatic, does not have the same indirect request potential as "Can you hand me that hammer?" That these sentences are idiomatic and are *idiomatically used as directives* is crucial to their role in indirect speech acts. I will say more about the relations of these facts later.

Fact 6: The sentences in question have literal utterances in which they are not also indirect requests. Thus, "Can you reach the salt?" can be uttered as a simple question about your abilities (say, by an orthopedist wishing to know the medical progress of your arm injury). "I want you to leave" can be uttered simply as a statement about one's wants, without any directive intent. At first sight, some of our examples might not appear to satisfy this condition, e.g.,

Why not stop here?

Why don't you be quiet?

But with a little imagination it is easy to construct situations in which utterances of these would be not directives but straightforward questions. Suppose someone had said "We ought not to stop here." Then "Why not stop here?" would be an appropriate question, without necessarily being also a suggestion. Similarly, if someone had just said "I certainly hate making all this racket," an utterance of "(Well, then) Why don't you be quiet?" would be an appropriate response, without also necessarily being a request to be quiet.

It is important to note that the intonation of these sentences when they are uttered as indirect requests often differs from their intonation when uttered with only their literal illocutionary force, and often the intonation pattern will be that characteristic of literal directives.

Fact 7: In cases where these sentences are uttered as requests, they still have their literal meaning and are uttered with and as having that literal meaning. I have seen it claimed that they have different meanings 'in context' when they are uttered as requests, but I believe that is obviously false. The man who says "I want you to do it" means literally that he wants you to do it. The point is that, as is always the case with indirection, he means not only what he says but something more as well. What is added in the indirect cases is not any additional or different *sentence* meaning, but additional *speaker* meaning. Evidence that these sentences keep their literal meanings when uttered as indirect requests is that responses that are appropriate to their literal utterances are appropriate to their indirect speech act utterances (as we noted in our discussion of fact 4), e.g.,

Can you pass the salt?

No, sorry, I can't, it's down there at the end of the table.

Yes, I can. (Here it is.)

Fact 8: It is a consequence of fact 7 that when one of these sentences is uttered with the primary illocutionary point of a directive, the literal illocutionary act is also performed. In every one of these cases, the speaker issues a directive *by way of* asking a question or making a statement. But the fact that his primary illocutionary intent is directive does not alter the fact that he is asking a question or making a statement. Additional evidence for fact 8 is that a subsequent report of the utterance can truly report the literal illocutionary act.

Thus, e.g., the utterance of "I want you to leave now, Bill" can be reported by an utterance of "He told me he wanted me to leave, so I left." Or, the utterance of "Can you reach the salt?" can be reported by an utterance of "He asked me whether I could reach the salt." Similarly, an utterance of "Could you do it for me, Henry; could you do it for me and Cynthia and the children?" can be reported by an utterance of "He asked me whether I could do it for him and Cynthia and the children."

This point is sometimes denied. I have seen it claimed that the literal illocutionary acts are always defective or are not 'conveyed' when the sentence is used to perform a nonliteral primary illocutionary act. As far as our examples are concerned, the literal illocutions are always conveyed and are sometimes, but not in general, defective. For example, an indirect speech act utterance of "Can you reach the salt?" may be defective in the sense that S may already know the answer. But even this form *need* not be defective. (Consider, e.g., "Can you give me change for a dollar?.") Even when the literal utterance is defective, the indirect speech act does not depend on its being defective.

AN EXPLANATION IN TERMS OF THE THEORY OF SPEECH ACTS

The difference between the example concerning the proposal to go to the movies and all of the other cases is that the other cases are systematic. What we need to do, then, is to describe an example in such a way as to show how the apparatus used on the first example will suffice for these other cases and also will explain the systematic character of the other cases.

I think the theory of speech acts will enable us to provide a simple explanation of how these sentences, which have one illocutionary force as part of their meaning, can be used to perform an act with a different illocutionary force. Each type of illocutionary act has a set of conditions that are necessary for the successful and felicitous performance of the act. To illustrate this, I will present the conditions on two types of acts within the two genuses, directive and commissive [Searle (1)]

A comparison of the list of felicity conditions on the directive class of illocutionary acts and our list of types of sentences used to perform indirect directives show that Groups 1–6 of types can be reduced to three types: those having to do with felicity conditions on the performance of a directive illocutionary act, those having to do with reasons for doing the act, and those embedding one element inside another one. Thus, since the ability of H to perform A (Group 1) is a preparatory condition, the desire of S that H perform A (Group 2) is the sincerity condition, and the predication of A of H (Group 3) is the propositional content condition, all of Groups 1–3 concern felicity conditions on directive illocutionary acts. Since wanting to do something is a reason par excellence for doing it, Group 4 assimilates to Group 5, as both concern reasons for doing A. Group 6 is a special class only by courtesy, since its elements either are performative verbs or are already contained in the other two categories of felicity conditions and reasons.

Ignoring the embedding cases for the moment, if we look at our lists and our sets of conditions, the following generalizations naturally emerge.

Generalization 1: S can make an indirect request (or other directive) by either asking whether or stating that a preparatory condition concerning H's ability to do A obtains.

Generalization 2: S can make an indirect directive by either asking whether or stating that the propositional content condition obtains.

Generalization 3: S can make an indirect directive by stating that the sincerity condition obtains, but not by asking whether it obtains.

Generalization 4: S can make an indirect directive by either stating that or asking whether there are good or overriding reasons for doing A, except where the reason is that H wants or wishes, etc., to do A, in which case he can only ask whether H wants, wishes, etc., to do A.

It is the existence of these generalizations that accounts for the systematic character of the relation between the sentences in Groups 1–6 and the directive class of illocutionary acts. Notice that these are generalizations and not rules. The rules of speech acts (or some of them) are stated in the list of conditions presented earlier. That is, for example, it is a rule of the directive class of speech acts that the directive is defective if the hearer is unable to perform the act, but it is precisely not a rule

	Directive (Request)	Commissive (Promise)
Preparatory condition	H is able to perform A.	S is able to perform A. H wants S to perform A.
Sincerity condition	S wants H to do A.	S intends to do A.
Propositional content condition	S predicates a future act A of H.	S predicates a future act A of S.
Essential condition	Counts as an attempt by S to get H to do A.	Counts as the undertaking by S of an obligation to do A.

of speech acts or of conversation that one can perform a directive by asking whether the preparatory condition obtains. The theoretical task is to show how that generalization will be a consequence of the rule, together with certain other information, namely, the factual background information and the general principles of conversation.

Our next task is to try to describe an example of an indirect request with at least the same degree of pedantry we used in our description of the rejection of a proposal. Let us take the simplest sort of case: At the dinner table, X says to Y, "Can you pass the salt?" by way of asking Y to pass the salt. Now, how does Y know that X is requesting him to pass the salt instead of just asking a question about his abilities to pass the salt? Notice that not everything will do as a request to pass the salt. Thus, if X had said "Salt is made of sodium chloride" or "Salt is mined in the Tatra mountains," without some special stage setting, it is very unlikely that Y would take either of these utterances as a request to pass the salt. Notice further that, in a normal conversational situation, Y does not have to go through any conscious process of inference to derive the conclusion that the utterance of "Can you pass the salt?" is a request to pass the salt. He simply hears it as a request. This fact is perhaps one of the main reasons why it is tempting to adopt the false conclusion that somehow these examples must have an imperative force as part of their meaning or that they are 'ambiguous in context,' or some such. What we need to do is offer an explanation that is consistent with all of facts 1–8 yet does not make the mistake of hypostatizing concealed imperative forces or conversational postulates. A bare-bones reconstruction of the steps necessary for Y to derive the conclusion from the utterance might go roughly as follows:

Step 1: Y has asked me a question as to whether I have the ability to pass the salt (fact about the conversation).

Step 2. I assume that he is cooperating in the conversation and that therefore his utterance has some aim or point (principles of conversational cooperation).

Step 3. The conversational setting is not such as to indicate a theoretical interest in my salt-passing ability (factual background information).

Step 4. Furthermore, he probably already knows that the answer to the question is yes (factual background information). (This step facilitates the move to step 5, but is not essential.)

Step 5. Therefore, his utterance is probably not just a question. It probably has some ulterior illocutionary point (inference from steps 1, 2, 3, and 4). What can it be?

Step 6. A preparatory condition for any directive illocutionary act is the ability of H to perform the act predicated in the propositional content condition (theory of speech acts).

Step 7. Therefore, X has asked me a question the affirmative answer to which would entail that the preparatory condition for requesting me to pass the salt is satisfied (inference from steps 1 and 6).

Step 8: We are now at dinner and people normally use salt at dinner; they pass it back and forth, try to get others to pass it back and forth, etc. (background information).

Step 9: He has therefore alluded to the satisfaction of a preparatory condition for a request whose obedience conditions it is quite likely he wants me to bring about (inference from Steps 7 and 8).

Step 10: Therefore, in the absence of any other plausible illocutionary point, he is probably requesting me to pass him the salt (inference from steps 5 and 9).

The hypothesis being put forth in this chapter is that all the cases can be similarly analyzed. According to this analysis, the reason I can ask you to pass the salt by saying "Can you pass the salt?" but not by saying "Salt is made of sodium chloride" or "Salt is mined in the Tatra mountains" is that your ability to pass the salt is a preparatory condition for requesting you to pass the salt in a way that the other sentences are not related to requesting you to pass the salt. But obviously, that answer is not by itself sufficient, because not all questions about your abilities are requests. The hearer therefore needs some way of finding out when the utterance is just a question about his abilities and when it is a request made by way of asking a question about his abilities. It is at this point that the general principles of conversation (together with factual background information) come into play.

The two features that are crucial, or so I am suggesting, are, first, a strategy for establishing the existence of an ulterior illocutionary point beyond the illocutionary point contained in the meaning of the sentence, and second, a device for finding out what the ulterior illocutionary point is. The first is established by the principles of conversation operating on the information of the hearer and the speaker, and the second is derived from the theory of speech acts together with background information. The generalizations are to be explained by the fact that each of them records a strategy by means of which the hearer can find out how a primary illocutionary point differs from a secondary illocutionary point.

The chief motivation—though not the only motivation—for using these indirect forms is politeness. Notice that, in the example just given, the "Can you" form is polite in at least two respects. Firstly, X does not presume to know about Y's abilities, as he would if he issued an imperative sentence; and, secondly, the form gives—or at least appears to give—Y the option of refusing, since a yes-no question allows *no* as a possible answer. Hence, compliance can be made to appear a free act rather than obeying a command.[6]

SOME PROBLEMS

It is important to emphasize that I have by no means demonstrated the thesis being argued for in this chapter. I have so far only suggested a pattern of analysis that is consistent with the facts. Even supposing that this pattern of analysis could be shown to be successful in many more cases, there are still several problems that remain:

Problem 1

The biggest single problem with the foregoing analysis is this: If, as I have been arguing, the

mechanisms by which indirect speech acts are meant and understood are perfectly general— having to do with the theory of speech acts, the principles of cooperative conversation, and shared background information—and not tied to any particular syntactical form, then why is it that some syntactical forms work better than others. Why can I ask you to do something by saying "Can you hand me that book on the top shelf?" but not, or not very easily, by saying "Is it the case that you at present have the ability to hand me that book on the top shelf?"

Even within such pairs as:

Do you want to do A?
Do you desire to do A?

and:

Can you do A?
Are you able to do A?

there is clearly a difference in indirect illocutionary act potential. Note, for example, that the first member of each pair takes "please" more readily than the second. Granting that none of these pairs are exact synonyms, and granting that all the sentences have some use as indirect requests, it is still essential to explain the differences in their indirect illocutionary act potential. How, in short, can it be the case that some sentences are not imperative idioms and yet function as forms for idiomatic requests?

The first part of the answer is this: The theory of speech acts and the principles of conversational cooperation do, indeed, provide a framework within which indirect illocutionary acts can be meant and understood. However, within this framework certain forms will tend to become conventionally established as the standard idiomatic forms for indirect speech acts. While keeping their literal meanings, they will acquire conventional uses as, e.g., polite forms for requests.

It is by now, I hope, uncontroversial that there is a distinction to be made between meaning and use, but what is less generally recognized is that there can be conventions of usage that are not meaning conventions. I am suggesting that "can you," "could you," "I want you to," and numerous other forms are conventional ways of making requests (and in that sense it is not incorrect to say they are idioms), but at the same time they do not have an imperative meaning (and in that sense it would be incorrect to say they are idioms). Politeness is the most prominent motivation for indirectness in requests, and certain forms naturally tend to become the conventionally polite ways of making indirect requests.

If this explanation is correct, it would go some way toward explaining why there are differences in the indirect speech forms from one language to another. The mechanisms are not peculiar to this language or that, but at the same time the standard forms from one language will not always maintain their indirect speech act potential when translated from one language to another. Thus, "Can you hand me that book?" will function as an indirect request in English, but its Czech translation, "Můžete mi podat tu Knížku?" will sound very odd if uttered as a request in Czech.

A second part of the answer is this: In order to be a plausible candidate for an utterance as an indirect speech act, a sentence has to be idiomatic to start with. It is very easy to imagine circumstances in which: "Are you able to reach that book on the top shelf?" could be uttered as a request. But it is much harder to imagine cases in which "Is it the case that you at present have the ability to reach that book on the top shelf?" could be similarly used. Why?

I think the explanation for this fact may derive from another maxim of conversation having to do with speaking idiomatically. In general, if one speaks unidiomatically, hearers assume that there must be a special reason for it, and in consequence, various assumptions of normal speech are suspended. Thus, if I say, archaically, "Knowest thou him who calleth himself Richard Nixon?," you are not likely to respond as you would to an utterance of "Do you know Richard Nixon?"

Besides the maxims proposed by Grice, there seems to be an additional maxim of conversation that could be expressed as follows: "Speak idiomatically unless there is some special reason not to." For this reason, the normal conversational assumptions on which the possibility of indirect speech acts rests are in large part suspended in the nonidiomatic cases.

The answer, then, to problem 1 is in two parts. In order to be a plausible candidate at all for use as an indirect speech act, a sentence has to be idiomatic. But within the class of idiomatic sentences, some forms tend to become entrenched as conventional devices for indirect speech acts. In the case of directives, in which politeness is the chief motivation for the indirect forms, certain forms are conventionally used as polite requests. Which kinds of forms are selected will, in all likelihood, vary from one language to another.

Problem 2

Why is there an asymmetry between the sincerity condition and the others such that one can perform an indirect request only by asserting the satisfaction of a sincerity condition, not by querying it, whereas one can perform indirect directives by either asserting or querying the satisfaction of the propositional content and preparatory conditions?

Thus, an utterance of "I want you to do it" can be a request, but not an utterance of "Do I want you to do it?" The former can take "please," the latter cannot. A similar asymmetry occurs in the case of reasons: "Do you want to leave us alone?" can be a request, but not "You want to leave us alone."[7] Again, the former can take "please," the latter cannot. How is one to explain these facts?

I believe the answer is that it is odd, in normal circumstances, to ask other people about the existence of one's own elementary psychological states, and odd to assert the existence of other people's elementary psychological states when addressing them. Since normally you are never in as good a position as I am to assert what I want, believe, intend, and so on, and since I am normally not in as good a position as you to assert what you want, believe, intend, and so on, it is, in general, odd for me to ask you about my states or tell you about yours. We shall see shortly that this asymmetry extends to the indirect performance of other kinds of speech acts.

Problem 3

Though this chapter is not intended as being about English syntactical forms, some of the sentences on our lists are of enough interest to deserve special comment. Even if it should turn out that these peculiar cases are really imperative idioms, like "how about . . .?," it would not alter the general lines of my argument; it would simply shift some examples out of the class of indirect speech acts into the class of imperative idioms.

One interesting form is 'why not plus verb,' as in "Why not stop here?" This form, unlike "Why don't you?," has many of the same syntactical constraints as imperative sentences. For example, it requires a voluntary verb. Thus, one cannot say "Why not resemble your grandmother?" unless one believes that one can resemble someone as a voluntary action, whereas one can say "Why not imitate your grandmother?" Furthermore, like imperative sentences, this form requires a reflexive when it takes a second-person direct object, e.g., "Why not wash yourself?" Do these facts prove that the 'Why not . . .?' (and the 'why . . .?') forms are imperative in meaning? I think they are not. On my account, the way an utterance of 'why not?' works is this: In asking "Why not stop here?" as a suggestion to stop here, S challenges H to provide reasons for not doing something on the tacit assumption that the absence of reasons for not doing something is itself a reason for doing it, and the suggestion to do it is therefore made indirectly in accordance with the generalization that alluding to a reason for doing something is a way of making an indirect directive to do it. This analysis is supported by several facts. First, as we have already seen, this form can have a literal utterance in which it is not uttered as a suggestion; second, one can respond to the suggestion with a response appropriate

to the literal utterance, e.g., "Well, there are several reasons for not stopping here. First . . ." And third, one can report an utterance of one of these, without reporting any directive illocutionary forces, in the form "He asked me why we shouldn't stop there." And here the occurrence of the practical "should" or "ought" (not the theoretical "should" or "ought") is sufficient to account for the requirement of a voluntary verb.

Other troublesome examples are provided by occurrences of "would" and "could" in indirect speech acts. Consider, for example, utterances of "Would you pass me the salt?" and "Could you hand me that book?" It is not easy to analyze these forms and to describe exactly how they differ in meaning from "Will you pass me the salt?" and "Can you hand me that book?" Where, for example, are we to find the 'if' clause, which, we are sometimes told, is required by the so-called subjunctive use of these expressions? Suppose we treat the 'if' clause as "if I asked you to." Thus, "Would you pass me the salt?" is short for "Would you pass me the salt if I asked you to?"

There are at least two difficulties with this approach. First, it does not seem at all plausible for "could," since your abilities and possibilities are not contingent on what I ask you to do. But second, even for "would" it is unsatisfactory, since "Would you pass me the salt if I asked you to?" does not have the same indirect illocutionary act potential as the simple "Would you pass me the salt?" Clearly, both forms have uses as indirect directives, but, equally clearly, they are not equivalent. Furthermore, the cases in which "would" and "could" interrogative forms *do* have a nonindirect use seem to be quite different from the cases we have been considering, e.g., "Would you vote for a Democrat?" or "Could you marry a radical?" Notice, for example, that an appropriate response to an utterance of these might be, e.g., "Under what conditions?" or "It depends on the situation." But these would hardly be appropriate responses to an utterance of "Would you pass me the salt?" in the usual dinner table scene we have been envisaging.

"Could" seems to be analyzable in terms of "would" and possibility or ability. Thus, "Could you marry a radical" means something like "Would it be possible for you to marry a radical?" "Would", like "will," is traditionally analyzed either as expressing want or desire or as a future auxiliary.

The difficulty with these forms seems to be an instance of the general difficulty about the nature of the subjunctive and does not necessarily indicate that there is any imperative meaning. If we are to assume that "would" and "could" have an imperative meaning, then it seems we will be forced to assume, also, that they have a commissive meaning as well, since utterances of "Could I be of assistance?" and "Would you like some more wine?" are both normally offers. I find this conclusion implausible because it involves an unnecessary proliferation of meanings. It violates Occam's razor regarding concepts. It is more economical to assume that "could" and "would" are univocal in "Could you pass the salt?," "Could I be of assistance?," Would you stop making that noise?", and "Would you like some more wine?". However, a really satisfactory analysis of these forms awaits a satisfactory analysis of the subjunctive. The most plausible analysis of the indirect request forms is that the suppressed 'if' clause is the polite "if you please" or "if you will."

EXTENDING THE ANALYSIS

I want to conclude this chapter by showing that the general approach suggested in it will work for other types of indirection besides just directives. Obvious examples, often cited in the literature, are provided by the sincerity conditions. In general, one can perform any illocutionary act by asserting (though not by questioning) the satisfaction of the sincerity condition for that act. Thus, for example,

I am sorry I did it. (an apology)
I think/believe he is in the next room. (an assertion)

I am so glad you won. (congratulations)
I intend to try harder next time, coach. (a promise)
I am grateful for your help. (thanks)

I believe, however, that the richest mine for examples other than directives is provided by commissives, and a study of the examples of sentences used to perform indirect commissives (especially offers and promises) shows very much the same patterns that we found in the study of directives. Consider the following sentences, any of which can be uttered to perform an indirect offer (or, in some cases, a promise).

(I) Sentences concerning the preparatory conditions:

(A) that S is able to perform the act:

Can I help you?
I can do that for you.
I could get it for you.
Could I be of assistance?

(B) that H wants S to perform the act:

Would you like some help?
Do you want me to go now, Sally?
Wouldn't you like me to bring some more next time I come?
Would you rather I came on Tuesday?

(II) Sentences concerning the sincerity condition:

I intend to do it for you.
I plan on repairing it for you next week.

(III) Sentences concerning the propositional content condition:

I will do it for you.
I am going to give it to you next time you stop by.
Shall I give you the money now?

(IV) Sentences concerning S's wish or willingness to do A:

I want to be of any help I can.
I'd be willing to do it (if you want me to).

(V) Sentences concerning (other) reasons for S's doing A:

I think I had better leave you alone.

Wouldn't it be better if I gave you some assistance?

You need my help, Cynthia.

Notice that the point made earlier about the elementary psychological states holds for these cases as well: One can perform an indirect illocutionary act by asserting, but not by querying, one's own psychological states; and one can perform an indirect illocutionary act by querying, but not by asserting, the presence of psychological states in one's hearer.

Thus, an utterance of "Do you want me to leave?" can be an offer to leave, but not "You want me to leave." (Though it can be, with the tag question "You want me to leave, don't you?") Similarly, "I want to help you out" can be uttered as an offer, but not "Do I want to help you out?"

The class of indirect commissives also includes a large number of hypothetical sentences:

If you wish any further information, just let me know.

If I can be of assistance, I would be most glad to help.

If you need any help, call me at the office.

In the hypothetical cases, the antecedent concerns either one of the preparatory conditions, or the presence of a reason for doing A, as in "If it would be better for me to come on Wednesday, just let me know." Note also that, as well as hypothetical sentences, there are iterated cases of indirection. Thus, e.g., "I think I ought to help you out" can be uttered as an indirect offer made by way of making an indirect assertion. These examples suggest the following further generalizations.

Generalization 5. S can make an indirect commissive by either asking whether or stating that the preparatory condition concerning his ability to do A obtains.

Generalization 6. S can make an indirect commissive by asking whether, though not by stating that, the preparatory condition concerning H's wish or want that S do A obtains.

Generalization 7. S can make an indirect commissive by stating that, and in some forms by asking whether, the propositional content condition obtains.

Generalization 8. S can make an indirect commissive by stating that, but not by asking whether, the sincerity condition obtains.

Generalization 9. S can make an indirect commissive by stating that or by asking whether there are good or overriding reasons for doing A, except where the reason is that S wants or desires to do A, in which case he can only state but not ask whether he wants to do A.

I would like to conclude by emphasizing that my approach does not fit any of the usual explanatory paradigms. The philosopher's paradigm has normally been to get a set of logically necessary and sufficient conditions for the phenomena to be explained; the linguist's paradigm has normally been to get a set of structural rules that will generate the phenomena to be explained. I am unable to convince myself that either of these paradigms is appropriate for the present problem. The problem seems to me somewhat like those problems in the epistemological analysis of perception in which one seeks to explain how a perceiver recognizes an object on the basis of imperfect sensory input. The question, "How do I know he has made a request when he only asked me a question about my abilities?" may be like the question, "How do I know it was a car when all I perceived was a flash going past me on the highway?" If so, the answer to our problem may be neither "I have a set of axioms from which it can be deduced that he made a request" nor "I have a set of syntactical rules that generate an imperative deep structure for the sentence he uttered."

ACKNOWLEDGMENTS

I am indebted for comments on earlier drafts of this study to Julian Boyd, Charles Fillmore, Dorothea Franck, Georgia Green, George Lakoff, Dagmar Searle, and Alan Walworth.

REFERENCES

Searle, J. R. (1) *Speech Acts.* Cambridge University Press, New York and London: 1969.)

Searle, J. R. (2) A taxonomy of illocutionary acts. In K. Gunderson, ed., *Minnesota studies in the philosophy of language.* (University of Minnesota Press, Minneapolis: 1975).

NOTES

1. The class of 'directive' illocutionary acts includes acts of ordering, commanding, requesting, pleading, begging, praying, entreating, instructing, forbidding, and others. See Searle (2) for an explanation of this notion.

2. For an explanation of the notion of 'illocutionary point' and its relation to illocutionary force, see Searle (2).

3. In what follows, I use the letters *H, S,* and *A* as abbreviations for "hearer," "speaker," and "act" or "action."

4. This form is also included in Group 2.

5. There are some idioms in this line of business, however, for example "How about" as used in proposals and requests: "How about going to the movies tonight?" "How about giving me some more beer?"

6. I am indebted to Dorothea Franck for discussion of this point.

7. This point does not hold for the etymologically prior sense of *want* in which it means 'need.'

Pragmatics   14

ROBERT C. STALNAKER

Until recently, pragmatics—the study of language in relation to the users of language—has been the neglected member of the traditional three-part division of the study of signs; syntax, semantics, pragmatics. The problems of pragmatics have been treated informally by philosophers in the ordinary language tradition, and by some linguists, but logicians and philosophers of a formalistic frame of mind have generally ignored pragmatic problems, or else pushed them into semantics and syntax. My project in this paper is to carve out a subject matter that might plausibly be called pragmatics and which is in the tradition of recent work in formal semantics. The discussion will be programmatic. My aim is not to solve the problems I shall touch on, but to persuade you that the theory I sketch has promise. Although this paper gives an informal presentation, the subject can be developed in a relatively straightforward way as a *formal pragmatics* no less rigorous than present-day logical syntax and semantics. The subject is worth developing, I think, first to provide a framework for treating some philosophical problems that cannot be adequately handled within traditional formal semantics, and second to clarify the relation between logic and formal semantics and the study of natural language.

I shall begin with the second member of the triad, semantics. The boundaries of this subject are not so clear as is sometimes supposed, and since pragmatics borders on semantics, these boundaries will determine where our subject begins. After staking out a claim for pragmatics, I shall describe some of the tasks that fall within its range and try to defend a crucial distinction on which the division between semantics and pragmatics is based.

I. SEMANTICS

If we look at the general characterizations of semantics offered by Morris and Carnap, it will seem an elusive object. Semantics, according to them, concerns the relationship between signs and their *designata*. The *designatum* of a sign, Morris writes, is what is "taken account of in virtue of the presence of the sign." He also says "a *designatum* is not a thing, but a kind of object, or a class of objects."[1] Carnap is equally vague in giving a general characterization. The designatum of an expression, he says, is what he who uses it intends to refer to by it, "e.g., to an object or a property or a state of affairs. . . . (For the moment, no exact definition for 'designatum' is intended; this word is merely to serve as a convenient common term for different cases— object, properties, etc., whose fundamental

From Harman and Davidson, eds., *Semantics of Natural Language*, (Dordrecht, Holland: D. Reidel, 1972), pp. 380–97.

differences in other respects are not hereby denied.)"[2]

Though a clear general definition is hard to come by, the historical development of formal semantics is well delineated. The central problems in semantics have concerned the definition of truth, or truth conditions, for the sentences of certain languages. Formal semantics abstracts the problem of giving truth conditions for sentences away from problems concerning the purposes for which those sentences are uttered. People do many things with language, one of which is to express *propositions* for one reason or another, propositions being abstract objects representing truth conditions. Semantics has studied that aspect of language use in isolation from others. Hence I shall consider semantics to be the study of propositions.

The explication of *proposition* given in formal semantics is based on a very homely intuition: when a statement is made, two things go into determining whether it is true or false. First, what did the statement say: what proposition was asserted? Second, what is the world like; does what was said correspond to it? What, we may ask, must a proposition be in order that this simple account be correct? It must be a rule, or a function, taking us from the way the world is into a truth value. But since our ideas about how the world is change, and since we may wish to consider the statement relative to hypothetical and imaginary situations, we want a function taking not just the actual state of the world, but various possible states of the world into truth values. Since there are two truth values, a proposition will be a way—any way—of dividing a set of possible states of the world into two parts: the ones that are ruled out by the truth of the proposition, and the ones that are not.[3]

Those who find the notion of a *possible world* obscure may feel that this explication of proposition is unhelpful, since formal semantics generally takes that notion, like the notion of an individual, as primitive.[4] Some explanation is perhaps needed, but I am not sure what kind. Even without explanation, the notion has, I think, enough intuitive content to make it fruitful in semantics. I shall say only that one requirement for identifying a possible world is to specify a domain of individuals said to exist in that world.[5]

If we explain propositions as functions from possible worlds into truth values, they will have the properties that have traditionally been ascribed to them. Propositions are things that may be considered in abstraction on the one hand from particular languages and linguistic formulations (the sentences that express them), and on the other hand from the kinds of linguistic acts in which they figure) for example the assertions and commands in which a proposition is asserted or commanded). Thus once the homely intuition mentioned above has done its work, we may forget about assertions and consider propositions themselves, along with similar things such as functions taking individuals into propositions, and functions taking propositions into propositions.

Generally, the study of formal semantics has proceeded by first setting up a language, and then laying down rules for matching up the sentences of that language with propositions or truth values. But the languages are set up usually for no other purpose than to represent the propositions, or at least this is how formalized languages have been used by philosophers. Regimentation or formalization is simply a way to make clearer what the truth conditions are—what proposition is expressed by what is regimented or formalized. But with an adequate theory of propositions themselves, such philosophical analyses can proceed without the mediation of a regimented or formalized object language. Rather than translate a problematic locution into an object language in which it is clear what propositions are expressed by the sentences, one can simply state what proposition is expressed by that locution. The effect is the same. Unless one is concerned with proof theory, he may drop the language out altogether with no loss.

According to this characterization of semantics, then, the subject has no essential connection with languages at all, either natural or artificial. (Of course semantical theories are expressed *in* language, but so are theories about rocks.) This is not to deny the possibility of a *causal* relationship between language and our conception of a proposition. It may be, for example, that the fact that we think of a possible world as a domain of individuals together with the ascription of properties to them is a result of the fact that our language has a subject-predicate structure. It is also not to deny that the study of the grammar of natural language may be a rich source of insight into the nature of propositions and a source of evidence for distinctions among propositions. If we find in grammar a device for marking a distinction of content, we may presume that there is a distinction of content to be marked. But whatever the causal or evidential story, we may still abstract the study of propositions from the study of language. By doing so, I think we get a clearer conception of a relation between them.

Though one may study propositions apart from language, accounting for the relation between language and propositions still falls partly within the domain of semantics. One of the jobs of natural language is to express propositions, and it is a semantical problem to specify the rules for matching up sentences of a natural language with the propositions that they express. In most cases, however, the rules will not match sentences directly with propositions, but will match sentences with propositions relative to features of the context in which the sentence is used. These contextual features are a part of the subject matter of pragmatics, to which I shall now turn.

II. PRAGMATICS

Syntax studies sentences, semantics studies propositions. Pragmatics is the study of linguistic acts and the contexts in which they are performed. There are two major types of problems to be solved within pragmatics: first, to define interesting types of speech acts and speech products; second, to characterize the features of the speech context which help determine which proposition is expressed by a given sentence. The analysis of illocutionary acts is an example of a problem of the first kind; the study of indexical expressions is an example of the second. My primary concern will be with problems of the second kind, but I shall say a few general things about the first before I go on to that.

Assertions, commands, counterfactuals, claims, conjectures and refutations, requests, rebuttals, predictions, promises, pleas, speculations, explanations, insults, inferences, guesses, generalizations, answers, and lies are all kinds of linguistic acts. The problem of analysis in each case is to find necessary and sufficient conditions for the successful (or perhaps in some cases normal) performance of the act. The problem is a pragmatic one since these necessary and sufficient conditions will ordinarily involve the presence or absence of various properties of the context in which the act is performed,[6] for example, the intentions of the speaker, the knowledge, beliefs, expectations, or interests of the speaker and his audience, other speech acts that have been performed in the same context, the time of utterance, the effects of the utterance, the truth-value of the proposition expressed, the semantic relations between the proposition expressed and some others involved in some way.

Almost all of the speech act types mentioned above involve the expression of a proposition, and in the first type of pragmatic problem, the identity of that proposition is taken to be unproblematic. In most cases, however, the context of utterance affects not only the force with which the proposition is expressed, but also the proposition itself. It may be that the semantical rules determine the proposition expressed by a sentence or clause only relative to some feature of the situation in which the sentence is used.

Consider a statement 'everybody is having a good time'. I assume that you understand the *sentence* well enough. Now assume also that you are omniscient with respect to people having a good time: you know for each person that ever lived and for each time up to now whether or not that person was having a good time at that time. Under these conditions, you may still be in doubt about the truth of the statement for at least two reasons: first, you do not know when it was made; second, you do not know what class of people it was made about. It is unlikely that the speaker meant everybody in the universe. He may have meant everybody at some party, or everyone listening to some philosophical lecture, and if so, then we have to know what party, or what lecture before we know even what was said, much less whether what was said is true.

Statements involving personal pronouns and demonstratives furnish the most striking examples of this kind. When you say "We shall overcome," I need to know who you are, and for whom you are speaking. If you say "that is a great painting," I need to know what you are looking at, or pointing to, or perhaps what you referred to in your previous utterance. Modal terms also are notoriously dependent on context for their interpretation. For a sentence using *can, may, might, must* or *ought*, to determine a proposition unambiguously, a domain of 'all possible worlds' must be specified or intended. It need not be *all* conceivable worlds in any absolute sense, if there is such a sense. Sentences involving modals are usually to be construed relative to all possible worlds consistent with the speaker's knowledge, or with some set of presuppositions, or with what is morally right, or legally right, or normal, or what is within someone's power. Unless the relevant domain of possible worlds is clear in the context, the proposition expressed is undetermined.

The formal *semantic* analysis of such concepts as universality and necessity isolates the relevant contextual or pragmatic parameters of an interpretation (as, for example, a domain of discourse in classical first order logic, a set of possible worlds and a relation of relative possibility on them in Kripke's semantics for modal logic), and defines truth conditions relative to these parameters. The second kind of pragmatic problem is to explicate the relation of these parameters to each other and to more readily identifiable features of linguistic contexts.

The scheme I am proposing looks roughly like this: the syntactical and semantic rules for a language determine an interpreted sentence or clause; this, together with some features of the context of use of the sentence or clause determines a proposition; this in turn, together with a possible world, determines a truth-value. An interpreted sentence, then, corresponds to a function from contexts into propositions, and a proposition is a function from possible worlds into truth-values.

According to this scheme, both contexts and possible worlds are partial determinants of the truth-value of what is expressed by a given sentence. One might merge them together, considering a proposition to be a function from context-possible worlds (call them points of reference) into truth-values. Pragmatics-semantics could then be treated as the study of the way in which, not propositions, but truth-values are dependent on context, and part of the context would be the possible world in which the sentence is uttered. This is, I think, the kind of analysis of pragmatics proposed and developed by Richard Montague.[7] It is a simpler analysis than the one I am sketching; I need some argument for the necessity or desirability of the extra step on the road from sentences to truth-values. The step is justified only if the middlemen—the propositions—are of some independent interest, and only if there is some functional difference between contexts and possible worlds.

The independent interest in propositions comes from the fact that they are the objects of illocutionary acts and propositional attitudes. A proposition is supposed to be the common content of statements, judgments, promises, wishes and wants, questions and answers, things that are possible or probable. The meanings of sentences, or rules determining truth-values directly from contexts, cannot plausibly represent these objects.

If O'Leary says "Are you going to the party?" and you answer, "Yes, I'm going," your answer is appropriate because the proposition you affirm is the only one expressed in his question. On the simpler analysis, there is nothing to be the common content of question and answer except a truth-value. The propositions are expressed from different points of reference, and according to the simpler analysis, they are different propositions. A truth-value, of course, is not enough to be the common content. If O'Leary asks "Are you going to the party?" it would be appropriate for you to answer, "Yes, snow is white."

When O'Leary says at the party, "I didn't have to be here you know," he means something like this: it was not necessary that O'Leary be at that party. The words *I* and *here* contribute to the determination of a proposition, and this proposition is what O'Leary declares to be not necessary. Provided he was under no obligation or compulsion to be there, what he says is correct. But if the proposition declared to be not necessary were something like the meaning of the sentence, then O'Leary would be mistaken since the sentence 'I am here' is true from all points of reference, and hence necessarily true on the simpler analysis.

Suppose you say "He is a fool" looking in the direction of Daniels and O'Leary. Suppose it is clear to me that O'Leary is a fool and that Daniels is not, but I am not sure who you are talking about. Compare this with a situation in which you say "He is a fool" pointing unambiguously at O'Leary, but I am in doubt about whether he is one or not. In both cases, I am unsure about the truth of what you say, but the source of the uncertainty seems radically different. In the first example, the doubt is about what proposition was expressed, while in the second there is an uncertainty about the facts.

These examples do not provide any criteria for distinguishing the determinants of truth which are part of the context from those which are part of the possible world, but they do support the claims that there is a point to the distinction, and that we have intuitions about the matter. I certainly do not want to suggest that the distinction is unproblematic, or that it is not sometimes difficult or arbitrary to characterize certain truth determinants as semantic or pragmatic.[8] I want to suggest only that there are clear cases on which to rest the distinction between context and possible world, and differences in language use which depend on how it is made. To lend more detailed support to the suggestion, I shall first discuss a concept of *pragmatic presupposition* which is central to the characterization of contexts, as opposed to possible worlds, and second describe a kind of *pragmatic ambiguity* which depends on the distinction.

III. PRESUPPOSITIONS

The notion of presupposition that I shall try to explicate is a pragmatic concept, and must be distinguished from the semantic notion of presupposition analyzed by van Fraassen.[9] According to the *semantic* concept, a proposition P presupposes a proposition Q if and only if Q is necessitated both by P and by *not-P*. That is, in every model in which P is either true or false, Q is true. According to the *pragmatic* conception, presupposition is a propositional attitude, not a semantic relation. People, rather than sentences or propositions, are said to have, or make, presuppositions in this sense. More generally, any participant in a linguistic content (a person, a group, an institution, perhaps a machine) may be the subject of a presupposition. Any proposition may be the object, or context of one.

There is no conflict between the semantic and pragmatic concepts of presupposition: they are explications of related but different ideas. In general, any semantic presupposition of a proposition expressed in a given context will be a pragmatic presupposition of the people in that context, but the converse clearly does not hold.

To presuppose a proposition in the pragmatic sense is to take its truth for granted, and to assume that others involved in the context do the same. This does not imply that the person need have any particular mental attitude toward the proposition, or that he need assume anything about the mental attitudes of others in the context. Presuppositions are probably best viewed as complex dispositions which are manifested in linguistic behavior. One has presuppositions in virtue of the statements he makes, the questions he asks, the commands he issues. Presuppositions are propositions implicitly *supposed* before the relevant linguistic business is transacted.

The set of all the presuppositions made by a person in a given context determines a class of possible worlds, the ones consistent with all the presuppositions. This class sets the boundaries of the linguistic situation. Thus, for example, if the situation is an inquiry, the question will be, which of the possible worlds consistent with the presupppositions is the actual world? If it is a deliberation then the question is, which of *those* worlds shall we make actual? If it is a lecture, then the point is to inform the audience more specifically about the location of the actual world within that class of possible worlds. Commands and promises are expected to be obeyed and kept within the bounds of the presuppositions. Since the presuppositions play such a large part in determining what is going on in a linguistic situation, it is important that the participants in a single context have the same set of presuppositions if misunderstanding is to be avoided. This is why presupposition involves not only taking the truth of something for granted, but also assuming that others do the same.

The boundaries determined by presuppositions have two sides. One cannot normally assert, command, promise, or even conjecture what is inconsistent with what is presupposed. Neither can one assert, command, promise, or conjecture what is itself presupposed. There is no point in expressing a presupposition unless it distinguishes among the possible worlds which are considered live options in the context.

Presuppositions, of course, need not be true. Where they turn out false, sometimes the whole point of the inquiry, deliberation, lecture, debate, command, or promise is destroyed, but at other times it does not matter much at all. Suppose, for example, we are discussing whether we ought to vote for Daniels or O'Leary for president, presupposing that they are the Democratic and Republican candidates, respectively. If our real interest is in coming to a decision about who to vote for in the presidential election, then the debate will seem a waste of time when we discover that, in reality, the candidates are Nixon and Muskie. However, if our real concern was with the relative merits of the character and executive ability of Daniels and O'Leary, then our false presupposition makes little difference. Minor revisions might bring our debate in line with new presuppositions. The same contrast applies to a scientific experiment performed against the background of a presupposed theoretical framework. It may lose its point when the old theory is rejected, or it may easily be accommodated to the new theory. Sometimes, in fact, puzzlement is resolved and anomalies are explained by the discovery that a presupposition is false, or that a falsehood was presupposed. An experimental result may be more easily accommodated to the new presuppositions than to the old ones.

Normally, presuppositions are at least *believed* to be true. That is one reason that we can often infer more about a person's beliefs from his assertions than he says in them. But in some cases, presuppositions may be things we are unsure about, or even propositions believed or known to be untrue. This may happen in cases of deception: the speaker presupposes things that his audience believes but that he knows to be false in order to get them to believe further false things. More innocently, a speaker may presuppose what is untrue to facilitate communication, as when an anthropologist adopts the presuppositions of his primitive informant in questioning him. Most innocent of all are cases of fiction and pretending: speaker and audience may conspire together in presupposing things untrue, as when the author of a novel presupposes some of what was narrated in earlier chapters. In some contexts, the truth is beside the point. The actual world is, after all, only one possible world among many.

The shared presuppositions of the participants in a linguistic situation are perhaps the most important constituent of a context. The concept of pragmatic presupposition should play a role, both in the definition of various speech acts such as assertion, prediction, or counterfactual statement, and also in specifying semantic rules relating sentences to propositions relative to contexts.

IV. PRAGMATIC AMBIGUITY

The best example of the kind of ambiguity that I shall describe is given in Keith Donnellan's distinction between referential and attributive uses of definite descriptions.[10] After sketching an account of his distinction within the theory of pragmatics, I shall give some examples of other pragmatic ambiguities which have similar explanations.

Consider the following three statements, together with parenthetical comments on the contexts in which they were made:

(1) Charles Daniels is bald (said about a philosopher named Charles Daniels by one of his friends).
(2) I am bald (said by Charles Daniels, the man mentioned above).
(3) The man in the purple turtleneck shirt is bald (said by someone in a room containing one and only one man in a purple turtleneck shirt, that man being Charles Daniels).

The question is, what proposition was expressed in each of these three cases? In the first case, since 'Charles Daniels' is a proper name, and since the speaker knows the intended referent well, there is no problem: the proposition is the one that says that *that* man has the property of being bald. In possible worlds in which that same man, Charles Daniels, is bald, the statement is true; in possible worlds in which he is not bald, the statement is false. What is the truth-value in possible worlds where he does not exist? Perhaps the function is undefined for those arguments. We need not worry about it though, since the existence of Charles Daniels will be presupposed in any context in which that presupposition is expressed.

The second statement expresses exactly the same proposition as the first since it is true in possible worlds where the referent of the pronoun, *I,* Charles Daniels, is bald, and false when he is not. To believe what is expressed in the one statement is to believe what is expressed in the other; the second might be made as a report of what was said in the first. To interpret the second *sentence,* one needs to know different things about the context than one needs to know to interpret the first, but once both statements are understood, there is no difference between them.

In both cases, there is a pragmatic problem of determining from the context which individual is denoted by the similar term. The answer to this question fixes the proposition—the content of what is said. In case (1), a relatively unsystematic convention, the convention of matching proper names to individuals, is involved. In case (2), there is a systematic rule matching a feature of the context (the speaker) with the singular term *I.* Different rules applied

to different sentences in different contexts determine the same proposition.

What about the third case? Here there are two ways to analyze the situation corresponding to the referential and attributive uses of definite descriptions distinguished by Donnellan. We might say that the relation between the singular term "the man in the purple turtleneck shirt" and the referent, Charles Daniels, is determined by the context, and so the proposition expressed is the same as that expressed by statements (1) and (2). As with the term *I,* there are relatively systematic rules for matching up definite descriptions with their denotations in a context: the referent is the one and only one member of the appropriate domain who is *presupposed* to have the property expressed in the description. The rule cannot always be applied, but in the case described, it can be.

Alternatively, we might understand the rule picking out the denotation of the singular term to be itself a part of the proposition. This means that the relation between the definite description and its denotation is a function, not of the context, but of the possible world. In different possible worlds the truth-value of the proposition may depend on different individuals. It also means that we may understand the proposition—the content of the statement—without knowing who the man in the purple turtleneck shirt is, although we may have to know who he is in order to know that it is true.

The simpler account of pragmatics which merges possible worlds with contexts cannot account for Donnellan's distinction. If one goes directly from sentence (together with context) to truth-value, one misses the ambiguity, since the truth conditions for the sentence in a fixed context (in normal cases at least) coincide for the two readings. If one goes from the sentence together with context to proposition, and proposition together with possible world to truth-value, however, the ambiguity comes out in the intermediate step. There are at least three important differences between the referential and attributive uses of descriptions. These differences provide further argument for a theory which allows the distinction to be made and which gives some account of it.

First, in modal contexts and contexts involving propositional attitudes, the distinction makes a difference even for the *truth-value* of statements in which descriptions occur. Compare

(4) The man in the purple turtleneck shirt might have been someone else.
(5) The man in the purple turtleneck shirt might have worn white tie and tails.

Both statements say approximately that a certain proposition was possibly true. But in each case there are two propositions that can be intended, and which one is chosen may make a difference in the truth-value of the ascription of possibility to the proposition. If the first means, roughly, that Daniels might have been someone else, it is false, perhaps contradictory. On the other hand, if it means that someone else might have been the one wearing the turtleneck shirt (perhaps he almost lent it to me), then it may be true. The second statement can mean either that Daniels might have worn white tie and tails, or that it might have been the case that whoever was wearing the purple turtleneck shirt was *also* wearing white tie and tails. Clearly, the truth conditions are different for these two readings.

In a formal language containing modal or epistemic operators and descriptions, the distinction can be interpreted as a *syntactical* distinction. That is, statements (4) and (5) could each be formalized in two syntactically different ways with the description falling inside of the scope of the modal operator in one and outside the scope in the other.[11] But this procedure has two limitations: (a) it would be highly implausible to suggest that the *English* sentences (4) and (5) are syntactically ambiguous. There are no natural syntactical transformations of (4) and (5) which remove the ambiguity. (b) Modal and propositional attitude concepts may be involved, not only as parts of statements, but as comments on them and attitudes toward them. The content of statement (3) above, which cannot be treated as syntactically ambiguous even in a formalized language, may be doubted, affirmed, believed, or lamented. What one is doing in taking these attitudes or actions

depends on which of the two readings is given to the statement.

Second, as Donnellan noted, the distinction makes a difference for the presuppositions required by the context in which the statement is made. In general, we may say that when a simple subject–predicate statement is made, the existence of the subject is normally presupposed. When you say "the man in the purple turtleneck shirt is bald," you presuppose that the man in the purple turtleneck shirt exists. But of course the same ambiguity infects that statement of presupposition; how it is to be taken depends on what reading is given to the original statement. If the statement is given the referential reading, then so must be the presupposition. What is presupposed is that Daniels exists. If the statement is given the attributive reading, then the presupposition is that there is one and only one man (in the appropriate domain) wearing a purple turtleneck shirt. This is exactly the presupposition difference pointed out by Donnellan. Within the framework I am using, the different presuppositions can be seen to be instances of a single principle.

Third, the distinction is important if one considers what happens when the description fails to apply uniquely in the context. In *both* referential and attributive uses of descriptions, it is a presupposition of the context that the description applies uniquely, but if this presupposition is false, the consequences are different. In the case of referential uses, Donnellan has noted, the fact that the presupposition fails may have little effect on the statement. The speaker may still have successfully referred to someone, and successfully said something about him. When the presupposition fails in the attributive sense, however, that normally means that nothing true or false has been said at all. This difference has a natural explanation within our framework.

Where the rules determining the denotation of the singular term are considered as part of the context, what is relevant is not what is true, but what is presupposed. The definite description in statement (3) above, on the referential reading, denotes the person who is *presupposed* to be the one and only one man in a purple turtleneck shirt (in the appropriate domain). If there is no one person who is presupposed to fit the description, then reference fails (even if some person does *in fact* fit the description uniquely). But if there is one, then it makes no difference whether that presupposition is true or false. The presupposition helps to determine the proposition expressed, but once that proposition is determined, it can stand alone. The fact that Daniels is bald in no way depends on the color of his shirt.

On the attributive reading, however, the rule determining the denotation of the description is a part of the proposition, so it is what is true that counts, not what is presupposed. The proposition is about whoever uniquely fits the description, so if no one does, no truth-value is determined.

The points made in distinguishing these two uses of definite descriptions can be generalized to apply to other singular terms. Proper names, for example, are normally used to refer, but can be used in a way resembling the attributive use of definite descriptions. When you ask, "Which one is Daniels?" you are not *referring* to Daniels, since you do not presuppose of any one person that he is Daniels. When I answer "Daniels is the bald one," I am using "the bald one" referentially, and the name Daniels attributively. I am telling you not that Daniels is bald, but that he is Daniels. Using this distinction, we can explain how identity statements can be informative, even when two proper names flank the identity sign.

It has been emphasized by many philosophers that referring is something done by people with terms, and not by terms themselves. That is why reference is a problem of pragmatics, and it is why the role of a singular term depends less on the syntactic or semantic category of the term (proper name, definite description, pronoun) than it does on the speaker, the context, and the presuppositions of the speaker in that context.

The notion of pragmatic ambiguity can be extended to apply to other kinds of cases. In general, a sentence has the potential for pragmatic ambiguity if some rule involved in the interpretation of that sentence may be applied either to the context or to the possible world. Applied to the context, the rule will either contribute to the determination of the proposition (as in the case of the referential use of definite descriptions) or it will contribute to the force with which the proposition is expressed. Applied to the possible world, the rule is incorporated into the proposition itself, contributing to the determination of a truth-value. Conditional sentences, sentences containing certain modal terms, and sentences containing what have been called parenthetical verbs are other examples of sentences which have this potential.

If a person says something of the form 'If *A* then *B*' this may be interpreted either as the categorical assertion of a conditional proposition or as the assertion of the consequent made conditionally on the truth of the antecedent. In the former case, a proposition is determined on the level of semantics as a function of the propositions expressed by antecedent and consequence. In the latter case, the antecedent is an additional presupposition made temporarily, either because the speaker wishes to commit himself to the consequent only should the antecedent be true, or because the assertion of the consequent would not be relevant unless the antecedent is true (as in, for example, "there are cookies in the cupboard if you want some").[12]

A sentence of the form 'It may be that *P*' can be interpreted as expressing a modal proposition, that proposition being a function of *P*, or it may be interpreted as making explicit that the negation of *P* is not presupposed in the context. In the latter case, *P* is the only *proposition* involved. The modal word indicates the force with which it is expressed.

A sentence of the form 'I suppose that *P*' may be meant as a report about a supposition of the speaker, or as a rather tentative assertion of *P*. To read it the second way is to treat *I suppose* as a *parenthetical verb*, since on this reading, the sentence is synonomous with '*P*, I suppose'. The differences between these two readings are explored in Urmson's famous article on parenthetical verbs.[13]

Each of these examples has its own special features and problems. I do not want to suggest that they are instances of a common form. But the ambiguity, in each case, rests on the distinction between context and possible world.

V. CONCLUSION

Let me summarize the main points that I have tried to make. In section one I claimed that semantics is best viewed as the study of propositions, and argued that propositions may be studied independently of language. In section two I defined pragmatics as the study of linguistic acts and the contexts in which they are performed. Two kinds of pragmatic problems were considered; first, the definition of speech acts—the problem of giving necessary and sufficient conditions, not for the truth of a proposition expressed in the act, but for the act being performed; second, the study of the ways in which the linguistic context determines the proposition expressed by a given sentence in that context. The formulation of problems of the second kind depends on a basic distinction between contextual determinants of propositions and propositional determinants of truth. I argued that the distinction has an intuitive basis and is useful in analyzing linguistic situations. In the final two sections, I tried to support this distinction, first by characterizing a pragmatic notion of presupposition that is a central feature of contexts as opposed to possible worlds, and second by describing a kind of pragmatic ambiguity which rests on the distinction.

In this sketch of a theory of pragmatics, I have relied on some undefined and problematic concepts, for example, possible worlds, contexts, and presuppositions. I have given some heuristic account of these concepts, or relied on the heuristic accounts of others, but I have made no attempt to reduce them to each other, or to anything else. It may be charged that these concepts are too unclear to be the basis concepts of a theory, but I think that this objection mistakes the role of basic concepts. It is not assumed that these notions are clear. In fact, one of the points of the theory is to clarify them. So long as certain concepts all have *some* intuitive content, then we can help to explicate them all by relating them to each other. The success of the theory should depend not on whether the concepts can be defined, but on whether or not it provides the machinery to define linguistic acts that seem interesting and to make conceptual distinctions that seem important. With philosophical as well as scientific theories, one may explain one's theoretical concepts, not by defining them, but by using them to account for the phenomena.

ACKNOWLEDGMENTS

The research for and preparation of this paper was supported by the National Science Foundation, grant number GS-2574. I would like to thank Professors David Shwayder and Richmond Thomason for their helpful comments on a draft of this paper.

REFERENCES

1. Charles W. Morris, *Foundations of the Theory of Signs* (Chicago: 1938), pp. 4–5.
2. Rudolf Carnap, *Foundations of Logic and Mathematics* (Chicago, 1939): p. 4.
3. See Dana Scott, "Advice on Modal Logic," in *Philosophical Problems in Logic: Recent Developments*, ed. Karel Lambert (Dordrecht: D. Reidel, 1970), pp. 143–73.
4. This is not an inevitable strategy. Instead of taking individuals and possible worlds as primitive, defining properties and relations as functions from one to the other, one might take individuals, properties, and relations as primitive and define possible worlds in terms of these.
5. A theory of possible worlds and propositions defined in terms of them is not committed to any absolute notion of synonymy or analyticity. Since propositions are functions taking possible worlds as arguments, a domain of possible worlds must be specified as the domain of the function. But the domain need not be *all* possible worlds in any absolute or metaphysical sense. We may leave open the possibility that the domain may be extended as our imaginations develop, or as discoveries are made, or as our interests change. Propositional identity is, of course, relative to the specification of a domain of possible worlds.
6. This is not necessarily so, however. Since speech act types can be *any* way of picking out a class of particular speech acts, one might define one in such a way that the context was irrelevant, and the problem of analysis reduced to a problem of syntax or semantics, as for example the speech act of uttering a grammatical sentence of English, or the speech act of expressing the proposition *X*.

7. R. Montague, "Pragmatics," in *Contemporary Philosophie—La philosophie contemporaine*, ed. R. Klibansky (Florence: La Nuova Italia Editrice, 1968), vol. 1, pp. 102–122. Montague uses the phrase 'point of reference' as does Dana Scott in the paper mentioned in note 3.

8. Tenses and times, for example, are an interesting case. Does a tensed sentence determine a proposition which is sometimes true, sometimes false, or does it express different timeless propositions at different times? I doubt that a single general answer can be given, but I suspect that one's philosophical views about time may be colored by his tendency to think in one of these ways or the other.

9. Bas C. van Fraassen, "Singular Terms, Truth Value Gaps, and Free Logic," *Journal of Philosophy*, 63 (1966), 481–495, and "Presupposition, Implication, and Self Reference," *Journal of Philosophy* 65 (1968), 136–151.

10. Keith Donnellan, "Reference and Definite Descriptions," *The Philosophical Review*, 75 (1966), 281–304.

11. See R. Thomason and R. Stalnaker, "Modality and Reference," *Noûs* 2 (1968): 359–372; and R. Stalnaker and R. Thomason, "Abstraction in First Order Modal Logic," *Theoria*, 34 (1968), 203–207.

12. See R. Stalnaker, "A Theory of Conditionals," in *Studies in Logical Theory*, ed. Nicholas Rescher (Oxford: 1968), pp. 98–112 for a semantical theory of conditional propositions. Nuel Belnap has developed a theory of conditional assertion in "Conditional Assertion and Restricted Quantification," *Noûs* 4 (1970).

13. J. O. Urmson, "Parenthetical Verbs," *Mind*, 61 (1952), 192–212.

SUGGESTED FURTHER READING

Austin, J. L., *How To Do Things With Words,* 2d ed., ed. J. O. Urmson and Marina Sbisa (Cambridge: Harvard University Press, 1975).

Austin, J. L., *Philosophical Essays,* ed. J. O. Urmson and G. J. Warnock (London: Oxford University Press, 1970).

Davis, Steven, Perlocutions, *Linguistics and Philosophy* 3 (1979), 225–43.

Geach, Peter, Assertion, *Philosophical Review* 74 (1965), 449–65.

Ginet, Carl, Performativity, *Linguistics and Philosophy* 3 (1979), 245–65.

Grice, H. P., Further Notes on Logic and Conversation, in *Syntax and Semantics: Pragmatics*, vol. 7, ed. Peter Cole (New York: Academic Press, 1978), pp. 113–127.

Holdcroft, David, *Words and Deeds* (London: Clarendon Press, 1978).

Kartunnen, Lauri and Stanley Peters, Conventional Implicature, in *Syntax and Semantics,* vol. 11, ed. Choon-Kyu Oh and David A. Dinneen (New York: Academic Press, 1979), pp. 1–56.

Lewis, David, Scorekeeping in a Language Game, *Journal of Philosophical Logic* 8 (1979), 339–59.

Martinich, A. P., Conversational Maxims and Some Philosophical Problems, *Philosophical Quarterly* 30 (1980), 215–228.

Martinich, A. P., A Pragmatic Solution to the Liar Paradox, *Philosophical Studies* 43 (1982), 63–67.

Martinich, A. P., *Communication and Reference* (Berlin and New York: Walter de Gruyter, 1984).

Searle, John, Austin on Locutionary and Illocutionary Acts, *Philosophical Review* 77 (1968), 405–24.

Searle, John, *Speech Acts* (Cambridge: Cambridge University Press, 1969).

Searle, John, *Expression and Meaning* (Cambridge: Cambridge University Press, 1979).

Searle, John, *Intentionality* (Cambridge: Cambridge University Press, 1983).

Strawson, P. F. Intention and Convention in Speech Acts, *Philosophical Review* 73 (1964), 439–460.

Vendler, Zeno, *Res Cogitans* (Ithaca: Cornell University Press, 1972).

III

REFERENCE AND DESCRIPTIONS

There is a long philosophical tradition according to which the basic structure of language and the basic structure of reality are the same. The basic linguistic structure is supposed to be that of subjects and predicates while the basic ontological structure is supposed to be particulars and universals.

Consider the sentence

Socrates is wise.

It can be divided into two parts: "Socrates" and "is wise." "Socrates" is the subject and "is wise" is the predicate. The function of "Socrates" and of subject expressions generally, according to this long tradition, is to refer to, pick out, or identify a particular object, in this case the man Socrates. Always, or at least typically, particular objects are individual things that have a position within space and time. So it makes sense to say that Socrates lived in Athens in the fifth century B.C. The function of "is wise" is to express or designate the property of being wise. Properties are things that particulars have and can share with other particulars. Thus, Socrates shares the property of being wise with Plato, Aristotle, and all the other wise human beings who ever lived. Because properties can be shared, they are sometimes called "universals." Thus there is an asymmetry between subjects and predicates. Socrates is one thing; he is not shared by other things; but being wise is shared by many particulars.

As it stands, our explanation of the functions of subjects and predicates is inadequate because it does not give any indication of the purpose of referring or predicating. What is their point? One can understand this only by understanding the function of subject/predicate sentences as a whole; their function is categorization. To categorize something physically is to group objects into different types or sorts. If one sorts coins, then one sorts all the pennies together, all the nickels together, all the dimes together, and so on. One might put each kind of coin into a box or container of some kind. Subject/predicate sentences have the function of mentally or conceptually categorizing things. Subject expressions denote individual objects, like individual coins, and locate them in the category expressed by the predicate, like the containers used for sorting coins. The function of "Socrates is wise," then, is to refer to Socrates for the purpose of categorizing him as having the property of being wise. If he fits into that category, then the statement is true. If he does not fit into that category, then the statement is false.

Of the two terms, 'subject' has exercised philosophers more. The reason is that philosophers have traditionally been concerned with whether anything that humans believe or say is true; and if anything is true then, it seems, language must somehow attach to the world.

Further, language attaches to the world through the relation of reference which holds between subjects and particulars. Although this claim appears to solve a problem, it actually creates many. One of the most basic is the Paradox of Reference and Existence:

(1)   Everything referred to must exist.
(2)   "Hamlet" refers to Hamlet.
(3)   Hamlet does not exist.

These three propositions are inconsistent because (1) and (2) entail

(3')   Hamlet exists.

which contradicts (3). Although most nonphilosophers would try to resolve the paradox by denying (1), most philosophers hold that (1) is true. They take this position because if it were possible to refer to things that did not exist, then reference could not guarantee that language attached to reality. Frege, Russell, and Strawson all agree that it is (2) that is false. The various explanations for why (2) is false are ingenious, if not always plausible.

Another problem is whether subject expressions attach to reality directly or indirectly. Gottlob Frege argued in "On Sense and Nominatum" that subject expressions, whether proper names or descriptions, attach indirectly, through what he calls their sense (*Sinn*)—roughly, their conceptual content.

Bertrand Russell directly opposes Frege and claims that all genuine subject expressions refer directly, that descriptions are neither genuine names nor genuine subjects, and that ordinary proper names are not genuine names and hence not genuine subjects. Most other philosophers interested in this question line up along the basic Fregean and Russellian positions. Strawson is a kind of Fregean and in "On Referring" attacks Russell's position on all the major points: He claims that subject expressions do not refer directly, that descriptions can be genuine subjects, and that ordinary proper names are genuine names and subjects. The most important point Strawson makes against Russell however, is a position opposed to Frege as well, and in this way Strawson contributes something new to the debate. Both Russell and Frege hold that it is words or expressions that refer. Strawson, in contrast, holds that it is speakers who refer primarily; words refer derivatively. His view of this matter is a consequence of his views expressed in "Meaning and Truth," namely, that speakers mean primarily; words mean derivatively.

Although they are seemingly diametrically opposed, Keith Donnellan tries to effect an Hegelian-like synthesis of Russell and Strawson. They are both right and both wrong, and he has something better to offer that incorporates what is correct in his predecessors. For, according to Donnnellan, there are two uses of descriptions. One ("the attributive use") is the focus of Russell's theory; the other ("the referential use") is the focus of Strawson's. Donnellan himself is particularly interested in the referential use of descriptions, which is the same or very close to the way proper names are used. Two important points are left unclear in Donnellan's article. One, which is not resolved decisively in his later work, is whether he thinks the attributive-referential distinction is a semantic or pragmatic one. (Some have argued that it is syntactic, but Donnellan does not agree with this.) The other is what it means for someone to have an object in mind. Donnellan's later articles suggest that he means that the person is linked by an historical or causal chain to the object. (See "Suggestions for Further Reading" in section IV for references.) Donnellan's views about historical or causal chains are also similar to those that Kripke expresses in *Naming and Necessity*.

Kripke's "Speaker Reference and Semantic Reference" is a criticism of Donnellan's criticisms of Russell. One conclusion of Kripke's incisive criticism of Donnellan is that the latter has not shown Russell's theory to be wrong. Some more important results are methodological. As part of his argument Kripke appeals to distinctions Grice drew in "Meaning."

On Sense and Nominatum   15

GOTTLOB FREGE

The idea of Sameness[1] challenges reflection. It raises questions which are not quite easily answered. Is Sameness a relation? A relation between objects? Or between names or signs of objects? I assumed the latter alternative in my *Begriffsschrift*. The reasons that speak in its favor are the following: "a=a" and "a = b" are sentences of obviously different cognitive significance: "a=a" is valid *a priori* and according to Kant is to be called analytic, whereas sentences of the form "a = b" often contain very valuable extensions of our knowledge and cannot always be justified in an *a priori* manner. The discovery that it is not a different and novel sun which rises every morning, but that it is the very same, certainly was one of the most consequential ones in astronomy. Even nowadays the re-cognition (identification) of a planetoid or a comet is not always a matter of self-evidence. If we wished to view identity as a relationship between the objects designated by the names 'a' and 'b' then "a = b" and "a = a" would not seem different if "a = b" is true. This would express a relation of a thing to itself, namely, a relation such that it holds between everything and itself but never between one thing and another. What one wishes to express with "a = b" seems to be that the signs or names 'a' and 'b' name the same thing; and in that case we would be dealing with those signs: a relation between them would be asserted. But this relation could hold only inasmuch as they name or designate something. The relation, as it were, is mediated through the connection of each sign with the same nominatum. This connection, however, is arbitrary. You cannot forbid the use of an arbitrarily produced process or object as a sign for something else. Hence, a sentence like "a = b" would no longer refer to a matter of fact but rather to our manner of designation; no genuine knowledge would be expressed by it. But this is just what we do want to express in many cases. If the sign 'a' differs from the sign 'b' only as an object (here by its shape) but not by its rôle as a sign, that is to say, not in the manner in which it designates anything, then the cognitive significance of "a = a" would be essentially the same as that of "a = b", if "a = b" is true. A difference could arise only if the difference of the signs corresponds to a difference in the way in which the designated objects are given. Let a, b, c be straight lines which connect the corners of a triangle with the midpoints of the opposite sides. The point

Translated by Herbert Feigl from the article "Ueber Sinn und Bedeutung," *Zeitschr. f. Philos. und Philos. Kritik*, 100 (1892). The terminology adopted is largely that used by R. Carnap in *Meaning and Necessity* (Chicago: University of Chicago Press, 1947).

   From *Readings in Philosophical Analysis*, Herbert Feigl and Wilfrid Sellars, eds. (New York: Appleton-Century-Crofts, 1949), pp. 85–102.

of intersection of a and b is then the same as that of b and c. Thus we have different designations of the same point and these names ('intersection of a and b', 'intersection of b and c') indicate also the manner in which these points are presented. Therefore the sentence expresses a genuine cognition.

Now it is plausible to connect with a sign (name, word combination, expression) not only the designated object, which may be called the nominatum of the sign, but also the sense (connotation, meaning) of the sign in which is contained the manner and context of presentation. Accordingly, in our examples the *nominata* of the expressions 'the point of intersection of a and b' and 'the point of intersection of b and c' would be the same—not their senses. The nominata of 'evening star' and 'morning star' are the same but not their senses.

From what has been said it is clear that I here understand by 'sign' or 'name' any expression which functions as a proper name, whose nominatum accordingly is a definite object (in the widest sense of this word). But no concept or relation is under consideration here. These matters are to be dealt with in another essay. The designation of a single object may consist of several words or various signs. For brevity's sake, any such designation will be considered as a proper name.

The sense of a proper name is grasped by everyone who knows the language or the totality of designations of which the proper name is a part;[2] this, however, illuminates the nominatum, if there is any, in a very one-sided fashion. A complete knowledge of the nominatum would require that we could tell immediately in the case of any given sense whether it belongs to the nominatum. This we shall never be able to do.

The regular connection between a sign, its sense and its nominatum is such that there corresponds a definite sense to the sign and to this sense there corresponds again a definite nominatum; whereas not one sign only belongs to one nominatum (object). In different languages, and even in one language, the same sense is represented by different expressions. It is true, there are exceptions to this rule. Certainly there should be a definite sense

to each expression in a complete configuration of signs, but the natural languages in many ways fall short of this requirement. We must be satisfied if the same word, at least in the same context, has the same sense. It can perhaps be granted that an expression has a sense if it is formed in a grammatically correct manner and stands for a proper name. But as to whether there is a denotation corresponding to the connotation is hereby not decided. The words 'the heavenly body which has the greatest distance from the earth' have a sense; but it is very doubtful as to whether they have a nominatum. The expression 'the series with the least convergence' has a sense; but it can be proved that it has no nominatum, since for any given convergent series, one can find another one that is less convergent. Therefore the grasping of a sense does not with certainty warrant a corresponding nominatum.

When words are used in the customary manner then what are talked about are their nominata. But it may happen that one wishes to speak about the words themselves or about their senses. The first case occurs when one quotes someone else's words in direct (ordinary) discourse. In this case one's own words immediately name (denote) the words of the other person and only the latter words have the usual nominata. We thus have signs of signs. In writing we make use of quotes enclosing the word-icons. A word-icon in quotes must therefore not be taken in the customary manner.

If we wish to speak of the sense of an expression 'A' we can do this simply through the locution 'the sense of the expression 'A' '. In indirect (oblique) discourse we speak of the sense, e.g., of the words of someone else. From this it becomes clear that also in indirect discourse words do not have their customary nominata; they here name what customarily would be their sense. In order to formulate this succinctly we shall say: words in indirect discourse are used *indirectly,* or have *indirect* nominata. Thus we distinguish the *customary* from the *indirect* nominatum of a word; and similarly, its *customary* sense from its *indirect* sense. The indirect nominatum of a word is therefore its customary sense. Such exceptions must be kept in mind if one wishes correctly to comprehend the manner of connection between signs, senses, and nominata in any given case.

Both the nominatum and the sense of a sign must be distinguished from the associated image. If the nominatum of a sign is an object of sense perception, my image of the latter is an inner picture[3] arisen from memories of sense impressions and activities of mine, internal or external. Frequently this image is suffused with feelings; the definiteness of its various parts may vary and fluctuate. Even with the same person the same sense is not always accompanied by the same image. The image is subjective; the image of one person is not that of another. Hence, the various differences between the images connected with one and the same sense. A painter, a rider, a zoologist probably connect very different images with the name 'Bucephalus'. The image thereby differs essentially from the connotation of a sign, which latter may well be common property of many and is therefore not a part or mode of the single person's mind; for it cannot well be denied that mankind possesses a common treasure of thoughts which is transmitted from generation to generation.[4]

While, accordingly, there is no objection to speak without qualification of the sense in regard to images, we must, to be precise, add *whose* images they are and at what time they occur. One might say: just as words are connected with different images in two different persons, the same holds of the senses also. Yet this difference would consist merely in the manner of association. It does not prevent both from apprehending the same sense, but they cannot have the same image. *Si duo idem faciunt, non est idem.* When two persons imagine the same thing, each still has his own image. It is true, occasionally we can detect differences in the images or even in the sensations of different persons. But an accurate comparison is impossible because these images cannot be had together in one consciousness.

The nominatum of a proper name is the object itself which is designated thereby; the image which we may have along with it is quite subjective; the sense lies in between, not

subjective as is the image, but not the object either. The following simile may help in elucidating these relationships. Someone observes the moon through a telescope. The moon is comparable with the nominatum; it is the object of the observation which is mediated through the real image projected by the object lens into the interior of the telescope, and through the retinal image of the observer. The first may be compared with the sense, the second with the presentation (or image in the psychological sense). The real image inside the telescope, however, is relative; it depends upon the standpoint, yet, it is objective in that it can serve several observers. Arrangements could be made such that several observers could utilize it. But every one of them would have only his own retinal image. Because of the different structures of the eyes not even geometrical congruence could be attained; a real coincidence would in any case be impossible. One could elaborate the simile by assuming that the retinal image of *A* could be made visible to *B;* or *A* could see his own retinal image in a mirror. In this manner one could possibly show how a presentation itself can be made into an object; but even so, it would never be to the (outside) observer what it is to the one who possesses the image. However, these lines of thought lead too far afield.

We can now recognize three levels of differences of words, expressions and complete sentences. The difference may concern at most the imagery, or else the sense but not the nominatum, or finally also the nominatum. In regard to the first level, we must note that, owing to the uncertain correlation of images with words, a difference may exist for one person that another does not discover. The difference of a translation from the original should properly not go beyond the first level. Among the differences possible in this connection we mention the shadings and colorings which poetry seeks to impart to the senses. These shadings and colorings are not objective. Every listener or reader has to add them in accordance with the hints of the poet or speaker. Surely, art would be impossible without some kinship among human imageries; but just how far the intentions of the poet are realized can never be exactly ascertained.

We shall henceforth no longer refer to the images and picturizations; they were discussed only lest the image evoked by a word be confused with its sense or its nominatum.

In order to facilitate brief and precise expression we may lay down the following formulations:

A proper name (word, sign, sign-compound, expression) expresses its sense, and designates or signifies its nominatum. We let a *sign express* its sense and *designate* its nominatum.

Perhaps the following objection, coming from idealistic or skeptical quarters, has been kept in abeyance for some time: "You have been speaking without hesitation of the moon as an object; but how do you know that the name 'the moon' has in fact a nominatum? How do you know that anything at all has a nominatum?" I reply that it is not our intention to speak of the image of the moon, nor would we be satisfied with the sense when we say 'the moon'; instead, we presuppose a nominatum here. We should miss the meaning altogether if we assumed that we had reference to images in the sentence "the moon is smaller than the earth." Were this intended we would use some such locution as 'my image of the moon'. Of course, we may be in error as regards that assumption, and such errors have occurred on occasion. However, the question whether we could possibly always be mistaken in this respect may here remain unanswered; it will suffice for the moment to refer to our intention in speaking and thinking in order to justify our reference to the nominatum of a sign; even if we have to make the proviso: if there is such a nominatum.

Thus far we have considered sense and nominatum only of such expressions, words, and signs which we called proper names. We are now going to inquire into the sense and the nominatum of a whole declarative sentence. Such a sentence contains a proposition.[5] Is this thought to be regarded as the sense or the nominatum of the sentence? Let us for the moment assume that the sentence has a nominatum! If we then substitute a word in it by another word with the same nominatum but a different sense, then this substitution cannot affect the nominatum of the sentence. But we realize that in such cases the proposition is changed; e.g., the proposition of the sentence "the morning star is a body illuminated by the sun" is different from that of "the evening star is a body illuminated by the sun." Someone who did not know that the evening star is the same as the morning star could consider the one proposition true and the other false. The proposition can therefore not be the nominatum of the sentence; it will instead have to be regarded as its sense. But what about the nominatum? Can we even ask this question? A sentence as a whole has perhaps only sense and no nominatum? It may in any case be expected that there are such sentences, just as there are constituents of sentences which do have sense but no nominatum. Certainly, sentences containing proper names without nominata must be of this type. The sentence "Odysseus deeply asleep was disembarked at Ithaca" obviously has a sense. But since it is doubtful as to whether the name 'Odysseus' occurring in this sentence has a nominatum, so it is also doubtful that the whole sentence has one. However, it is certain that whoever seriously regards the sentence either as true or false also attributes to the name 'Odysseus' a nominatum, not only a sense; for it is obviously the nominatum of this name to which the predicate is either ascribed or denied. He who does not acknowledge the nominatum cannot ascribe or deny a predicate to it. It might be urged that the consideration of the nominatum of the name is going farther than is necessary; one could be satisfied with the sense, if one stayed with the proposition. If all that mattered were only the sense of the sentence (i.e., the proposition) then it would be unnecessary to be concerned with the nominata of the sentence-components, for only the sense of the components can be relevant for the sense of the sentence. The proposition remains the same, no matter whether or not the name 'Odysseus' has a nominatum. The fact that we are at all concerned about the nominatum of a sentence-component indicates that we generally acknowledge or postulate a nominatum for the sentence itself. The proposition loses in interest as soon as we recognize that one of its parts is lacking a nominatum. We may therefore be justified to ask for a nominatum of a sentence, in addition to its sense. But why do we wish that every proper name have not only a sense but also a nominatum? Why is the proposition alone not sufficient? We answer: because what matters to us is the truth-value. This, however, is not always the case. In listening to an epic, for example, we are fascinated by the euphony of the language and also by the sense of the sentences and by the images and emotions evoked. In turning to the question of truth we disregard the artistic appreciation and pursue scientific considerations. Whether the name 'Odysseus' has a nominatum is therefore immaterial to us as long as we accept the poem as a work of art.[6] Thus, it is the striving for truth which urges us to penetrate beyond the sense to the nominatum.

We have realized that we are to look for the nominatum of a sentence whenever the nominata of the sentece-components are the thing that matters; and that is the case whenever and only when we ask for the truth value.

Thus we find ourselves persuaded to accept the *truth-value* of a sentence as its nominatum. By the truth-value of a sentence I mean the circumstances of its being true or false. There are no other truth-values. For brevity's sake I shall call the one the True and the other the False. Every declarative sentence, in which what matters are the nominata of the words, is therefore to be considered as a proper name; and its nominatum, if there is any, is either the True or the False. These two objects are recognized, even if only tacitly, by everyone who at all makes judgments, holds anything as true, thus even by the skeptic. To designate truth-values as objects may thus far appear as a capricious idea or as a mere play on words, from which no important conclusion should be drawn. What I call an object can be discussed only in connection with the nature of concepts and relations. That I will reserve for another essay. But this might be clear even here: in every judgment[7]—no matter how obvious—a step is made from the level of propositions to the level of the nominata (the objective facts).

It may be tempting to regard the relation of a proposition to the True not as that of sense to nominatum but as that of the subject to the predicate. One could virtually say: "the proposition that 5 is a prime number is true." But on closer examination one notices that this does not say any more than is said in the simple sentence "5 is a prime number." This makes clear that the relation of a proposition to the True must not be compared with the relation of subject and predicate. Subject and predicate (interpreted logically) are, after all, components of a proposition; they are on the same level as regards cognition. By joining subject and predicate, we always arrive only at a proposition; in this way we never move from a sense to a nominatum or from a proposition to its truth-value. We remain on the same level and never proceed from it to the next one. Just as the sun cannot be part of a proposition, so the truth-value, because it is not the sense, but an object, cannot be either.

If our conjecture (that the nominatum of a sentence is its truth-value) is correct, then the truth-value must remain unchanged if a sentence-component is replaced by an expression with the same nominatum but with a different sense. Indeed, Leibnitz declares: "*Eadem sunt, quae sibi mutuo substitui possunt, salva veritate.*" What else, except the truth-value, could be found, which quite generally belongs to every sentence and regarding which the nominata of the components are relevant and which would remain invariant for substitutions of the type indicated?

Now if the truth-value of a sentence is its nominatum, then all true sentences have the same nominatum, and likewise all false ones. This implies that all detail has been blurred in the nominatum of a sentence. What interests us can therefore never be merely the nominatum; but the proposition alone does not give knowledge; only the proposition together with its nominatum, i.e., its truth-value, does. Judging may be viewed as a movement from a proposition to its nominatum, i.e., its truth-value. Of course this is not intended as a definition. Judging is indeed something peculiar and unique. One might say that judging consists in the discerning of parts within the truth-value. This discernment occurs through recourse to the proposition. Every sense that belongs to a truth-value would correspond in its own manner to the analysis. I have, however, used the word 'part' in a particular manner here: I have transferred the relation of whole and part from the sentence to its nominatum. This I did by viewing the nominatum of a word as part of the nominatum of a sentence, when the word itself is part of the sentence. True enough, this way of putting things is objectionable since as regards the nominatum the whole and one part of it does not determine the other part; and also because the word 'part' in reference to bodies has a different customary usage. A special expression should be coined for what has been suggested above.

We shall now further examine the conjecture that the truth-value of a sentence is its nominatum. We have found that the truth-value of a sentence remains unaltered if an expression within the sentence is replaced by a synonymous one. But we have as yet not considered the case in which the expression-to-be-replaced is itself a sentence. If our view is correct, then the truth-value of a sentence, which contains another sentence as a part, must remain unaltered when we substitute for the part another of the same truth-value. Exceptions are to be expected if the whole or the part are either in direct or indirect discourse; for, as we have seen, in that case the nominata of the words are not the usual ones. A sentence in direct discourse nominates again a sentence but in indirect discourse it nominates a proposition.

Our attention is thus directed to subordinate sentences (i.e., dependent clauses). These present themselves of course as parts of a sentence-structure which from a logical point of view appears also as a sentence, and indeed as if it were a main clause. But here we face the question whether in the case of dependent clauses it also holds that their nominata are truth-values. We know already that this is not the case with sentences in indirect discourse. The grammarians view clauses as representatives of sentence-parts and divide them accordingly into subjective, relative, and adverbial clauses. This might suggest that the nominatum of a clause is not a truth-value but rather it is of similar nature as that of a noun or of an adjective or of an adverb; in short, of a

sentence-part whose sense is not a proposition but only part thereof. Only a thorough investigation can provide clarity in this matter. We shall herein not follow strictly along grammatical lines, but rather group together what is logically of comparable type. Let us first seek out such instances in which, as we just surmised, the sense of a clause is not a self-sufficient proposition.

Among the abstract clauses beginning with 'that' there is also the indirect discourse, of which we have seen that in it the words have their indirect (oblique) nominata which coincide with what are ordinarily their senses. In this case then the clause has as its nominatum a proposition, not a truth-value; its sense is not a proposition but it is the sense of the words 'the proposition that . . .", which is only a part of the proposition corresponding to the total sentence-structure. This occurs in connection with 'to say', 'to hear', 'to opine', 'to be convinced', 'to infer', and similar words.[8] The situation is different, and rather complicated in connection with such words as 'to recognize', 'to know', 'to believe', a matter to be considered later.

One can see that in these cases the nominatum of the clause indeed consists in the proposition, because whether that proposition is true or false is immaterial for the truth of the whole sentence. Compare, e.g., the following two sentences: "Copernicus believed that the planetary orbits are circles" and "Copernicus believed that the appearance of the sun's motion is produced by the real motion of the earth." Here the one clause can be substituted for the other without affecting the truth. The sense of the principal sentence together with the clause is the single proposition; and the truth of the whole implies neither the truth nor the falsity of the clause. In cases of this type it is not permissible to replace in the clause one expression by another of the same nominatum. Such replacement maybe made only by expressions of the same indirect nominatum, i.e., of the same customary sense. If one were to infer: the nominatum of a sentence is not its truth-value ("because then a sentence could always be replaced by another with the same truth-value"), he would prove too much; one could just as well maintain that the nominatum of the word 'morning star' is not Venus, for one cannot always substitute 'Venus' for 'morning star'. The only correct conclusion is that the nominatum of a sentence is *not always* its truth-value, and that 'morning star' does not always nominate the planet Venus; for this is indeed not the case when the word is used with its indirect nominatum. Such an exceptional case is before us in the clauses just considered, whose nominatum is a proposition.

When we say "it seems that . . ." then we mean to say "it seems to me that . . ." or "I opine that . . . ." This is the same case over again. Similarly with the expressions such as: 'to be glad', 'to regret', 'to approve', 'to disapprove', 'to hope', 'to fear'. When Wellington, toward the end of the battle of Belle-Alliance was glad that the Prussians were coming, the ground of his rejoicing was a conviction. Had he actually been deceived, he would not have been less glad, as long as his belief persisted; and before he arrived at the conclusion that the Prussians were coming he could not have been glad about it, even if in fact they were already approaching.

Just as a conviction or a belief may be the ground of a sentiment, so it can also be the ground of another conviction such as in inference. In the sentence "Columbus inferred from the roundness of the earth that he could, traveling westward, reach India" we have, as nominata of its parts two propositions: that the earth is round, and that Columbus traveling westward could reach India. What matters here is only that Columbus was convinced of the one as well as of the other and that the one conviction furnishes the ground for the other. It is irrelevant for the truth of our sentence whether the earth is really round and whether Columbus could have reached India in the manner he fancied. But it is not irrelevant whether for 'the earth' we substitute 'the planet accompanied by one satellite whose diameter is larger than one-fourth of its own diameter'. Here also we deal with the indirect nominata of the words.

Adverbial clauses of purpose with 'so that' likewise belong here; obviously the purpose is a proposition; therefore: indirect nominata of the words, expressed in subjunctive form.

The clause with 'that' after 'to command',

'to request', 'to forbid' would appear in imperative form in direct discourse. Imperatives have no nominata; they have only sense. It is true, commands or requests are not propositions, but they are of the same type as propositions. Therefore the words in the dependent clauses after 'to command', 'to request', etc. have indirect nominata. The nominatum of such a sentence is thus not a truth-value but a command, a request, and the like.

We meet a similar situation in the case of dependent questions in phrases like 'to doubt if', 'not to know what'. It is easy to see that the words, here too, have to be interpreted in terms of their indirect nominata. The dependent interrogatory clauses containing 'who', 'what', 'where', 'when', 'how', 'whereby', etc. often apparently approximate closely adverbial clauses in which the words have their ordinary nominata. These cases are linguistically distinguished through the mode of the verb. In the subjunctive we have a dependent question and the indirect nominata of the words, so that a proper name cannot generally be replaced by another of the same object.

In the instances thus far considered the words in the clause had indirect nominata; this made it intelligible that the nominatum of the clause itself is indirect, i.e., not a truth-value, but a proposition, a command, a request, a question. The clause could be taken as a noun; one might even say, as a proper name of that proposition, command, etc., in whose rôle it functions as the context of the sentence-structure.

We are now going to consider clauses of another type, in which the words do have their customary nominata although there does not appear a proposition as the sense or a truth-value as the nominatum. How this is possible will best be elucidated by examples.

"He who discovered the elliptical shape of the planetary orbits, died in misery."

If, in this example, the sense of the clause were a proposition, it would have to be expressible also in a principal sentence. But this cannot be done because the grammatical subject 'he who' has no independent sense. It merely mediates the relations to the second part of the sentence: 'died in misery'. There-fore the sense of the clause is not a complete proposition and its nominatum is not a truth-value, but Kepler. It might be objected that the sense of the whole does include a proposi-tion as its part; namely, that there was someone who first recognized the elliptical shape of the planetary orbits; for if we accept the whole as true we cannot deny this part. Indubitably so; but only because otherwise the clause "he who discovered the elliptical shape, etc." would have no nominatum. Whenever something is asserted then the presupposition taken for granted is that the employed proper names, simple or com-pound, have nominata. Thus, if we assert "Kepler died in misery" it is presupposed that the name 'Kepler' designates something. How-ever, the proposition that the name 'Kepler' designates something is, the foregoing notwith-standing, not contained in the sense of the sentence "Kepler died in misery." If that were the case the denial would not read "Kepler did not die in misery" but "Kepler did not die in misery, or the name 'Kepler' is without nominatum." That the name 'Kepler' desig-nates something is rather the presupposition of the assertion "Kepler died in misery" as well as of its denial. Now, it is a defect of languages that expressions are possible within them, which, in their grammatical form, seemingly determined to designate an object, do not fulfill this condition in special cases; because this depends on the truth of the sentence. Thus it depends upon the truth of the sentence "there was someone who discov-ered the ellipticity of the orbits" whether the clause 'he who discovered the ellipticity of the orbits' really designates an object, or else merely evokes the appearance thereof, while indeed being without nominatum. Thus it may seem as if our clause, as part of its sense, contained the proposition that there existed someone who discovered the ellipticity of the orbits. If this were so, then the denial would have to read "he who first recognized the ellipticity of the orbits did not die in misery, or there was no one who discovered the ellip-ticity of the orbits." This, it is obvious, hinges upon an imperfection of language of which, by the way, even the symbolic language of

analysis is not entirely free; there, also, sign compounds may occur which appear as if they designated something, but which at least hitherto are without nominatum, e.g., diver-gent infinite series. This can be avoided, e.g., through the special convention that the nominatum of divergent infinite series be the number 0. It is to be demanded that in a logically perfect language (logical symbolism) every expression constructed as a proper name in a grammatically correct manner out of already introduced symbols, in fact desig-nate an object; and that no symbol be intro-duced as a proper name without assurance that it have a nominatum. It is customary in logic texts to warn against the ambiguity of expressions as a source of fallacies. I deem it at least as appropriate to issue a warning against apparent proper names that have no nominata. The history of mathematics has many a tale to tell of errors which originated from this source. The demagogic misuse is close (perhaps closer) at hand as in the case of ambiguous expressions. 'The will of the peo-ple' may serve as an example in this regard; for it is easily established that there is no generally accepted nominatum of that expres-sion. Thus it is obviously not without impor-tance to obstruct once for all the source of these errors, at least as regards their occur-rence in science. Then such objections as the one discussed above will become impossible, for then it will be seen that whether a proper name has a nominatum can never depend upon the truth of a proposition.

Our considerations may be extended from these subjective clauses to the logically related relative and adverbial clauses.

Relative clauses, too, are employed in the formation of compound proper names—even if, in contradistinction to subjective clauses, they are not sufficient by themselves for this purpose. These relative clauses may be re-garded as equivalent to appositions. Instead of 'the square root of 4 which is smaller than 0' we can also say 'the negative square root of 4'. We have here a case in which out of a conceptual expression a compound proper name is formed, with the help of the definite article in the singular. This is at any rate permissible when one and only one object is comprised by the concept.[9] Conceptual expression can be formed in such a fashion that their characteristics are indicated through relative clauses as in our example through the clause 'which is smaller than 0'. Obviously, such relative clauses, just as the subjective clauses above, do not refer to a proposition as their sense nor to a truth-value as their nominatum. Their sense is only a part of a proposition, which in many cases, can be expressed by a simple apposition. As in the subjective clauses an independent subject is missing and it is therefore impossible to represent the sense of the clause in an independent principal sentence.

Places, dates and time-intervals are objects from a logical point of view; the linguistic symbol of a definite place, moment, or span of time must therefore be viewed as a proper name. Adverbial clauses of space or time can then be used in the formation of such proper names in a fashion analogous to the one we have just remarked in the case of subjective and relative clauses. Similarly, expressions for concepts which comprise places, etc., can be formed. Here too, it is to be remarked, the sense of the subordinate clauses cannot be rendered in a principal clause, because an essential constituent, namely the determination of place and time, is missing and only alluded to by a relative pronoun or a conjunction.[10]

In conditional clauses also, there is, just as we have realized in the case of subjective, relative, and adverbial clauses, a constituent with indeterminate indication corresponding to which there is a similar one in the concluding clause. In referring to one another the two clauses combine into a whole which expresses, as a rule, only one proposition. In the sentence "if a number is smaller than 1 and greater than 0, then its square is also smaller than 1 and greater than 0" this constituent in the conditional clause is 'a number' and in the concluding clause it is 'its'. Just through this indeterminacy the sense acquires the universal character which one expects of a law. But it is in this way also that it comes about that the conditional clause alone does not possess a complete proposition as its sense, and that together with the concluding clause it ex-

presses a single proposition whose parts are no longer propositions. It is not generally the case that a hypothetical judgment correlates two judgments. Putting it in that (or a similar) manner would amount to using the word 'judgment' in the same sense that I have attributed to the word 'proposition'. In that case I would have to say: in a hypothetical proposition two propositions are related to each other. But this could be the case only if an indeterminately denoting constituent were absent;[11] but then universality would also be missing.

If a time point is to be indeterminately indicated in a conditional and a concluding clause, then this is not infrequently effected by *tempus praesens* of the verb, which in this case does not connote the present time. It is this grammatical form which takes the place of the indeterminately indicating constituent in the main and the dependent clause. "When the sun is at the Tropic of Cancer, the northern hemisphere has its longest day" is an example. Here, too, it is impossible to express the sense of the dependent clause in a main clause. For this sense is not a complete proposition; if we said: "the sun is at the Tropic of Cancer" we would be referring to the present time and thereby alter the sense. Similarly, the sense of the main clause is not a proposition either, only the whole consisting of main and dependent clause contains a proposition. Further, it may occur that several constituents common to conditional and concluding clause are indeterminately indicated.

It is obvious that subjective clauses containing 'who', 'what', and adverbial clauses with 'where', 'when' 'wherever' 'whenever' are frequently to be interpreted, inasmuch as their sense is concerned, as conditional sentences, e.g., "He who touches pitch soils himself."

Conditional clauses can also be replaced by relative clauses. The sense of the previously mentioned sentence can also be rendered by "the square of a number which is smaller than 1 and larger than 0, is smaller than 1 and larger than 0."

Quite different is the case in which the common constituent of main and dependent clause is represented by a proper name. In the sentence: "Napoleon who recognized the danger to his right flank, personally led his troops against the enemy's position" there are expressed two propositions:

(1) Napoleon recognized the danger to his right flank.
(2) Napoleon personally led his troops against the enemy's position.

When and where this happened can indeed be known only from the context, but is to be viewed as thereby determined. If we pronounce our whole sentence as an assertion we thereby assert simultaneously its two component sentences. If one of the components is false the whole is false. Here we have a case in which the dependent clause by itself has a sense in a complete proposition (if supplemented by temporal and spatial indications). The nominatum of such a clause is therefore a truth-value. We may therefore expect that we can replace it by a sentence of the same truth value without altering the truth of the whole. This is indeed the case; but it must be kept in mind that for a purely grammatical reason, its subject must be 'Napoleon'; because only then can the sentence be rendered in the form of a relative clause attached to 'Napoleon'. If the demand to render it in this form and if the conjunction with 'and' is admitted, then this limitation falls away.

Likewise, in dependent clauses with 'although' complete propositions are expressed. This conjunction really has no sense and does not affect the sense of the sentence; rather, it illuminates it in a peculiar fashion.[12] Without affecting the truth of the whole the implicate may be replaced by one of the same truth-value; but the illumination might then easily appear inappropriate, just as if one were to sing a song of sad content in a cheerful manner.

In these last instances the truth of the whole implied the truth of the component sentences. The situation is different if a conditional sentence expresses a complete proposition; namely, when in doing so it contains instead of a merely indicating constituent a proper name or something deemed equivalent to a proper name. In the sentence: "if the sun has already risen by now, the sky is heavily overcast," the tense is the present—

therefore determinate. The place also is to be considered determinate. Here we can say that a relation is posited such that the case does not arise in which the antecedent sentence nominates the True and the consequent sentence nominates the False. Accordingly the given (whole) sentence is true if the sun has not as yet risen (no matter whether or not the sky be heavily overcast), and also if the sun has risen and the sky is heavily overcast. Since all that matters are only the truth-values, each of the component sentences can be replaced by another one of the same truth-value, without altering the truth-value of the whole sentence. In this case also, the illumination would usually seem inappropriate; the proposition could easily appear absurd; but this has nothing to do with the truth-value of the sentence. It must always be remembered that associated thoughts are evoked on the side; but these are not really expressed and must therefore not be taken account of; their truth-values cannot be relevant.[13]

We may hope we have considered the simple types of sentences. Let us now review what we have found out!

The sense of a subordinate clause is usually not a proposition but only part of one. Its nominatum is therefore not a truth-value. The reason for this is *either:* that the words in the subordinate clause have only indirect nominata, so that the nominatum, not the sense, of the clause is a proposition, *or,* that the clause, because of a contained indeterminately indicating constituent, is incomplete, such that only together with the principal clause does it express a proposition. However, there are also instances in which the sense of the dependent clause is a complete proposition, and in this case it can be replaced by another clause of the same truth-value without altering the truth-value of the whole, that is, inasmuch as there are no grammatical obstacles in the way.

In a survey of the various occurrent clauses one will readily encounter some which will not properly fit within any of the considered divisions. As far as I can see, the reason for that is that these clauses do not have quite so simple a sense. It seems that almost always we connect associated propositions with the main proposition which we express; these associated propositions, even if unexpressed, are associated with our words according to psychological laws also by the listener. And because they appear as associated automatically with our words (as in the case of the main proposition) we seem to wish, after all, to express such associated propositions along with the main propositions. The sense of the sentence thereby becomes richer and it may well happen that we may have more simple propositions than sentences. In some cases the sentence may be interpreted in this way, in others, it may be doubtful whether the associated proposition belongs to the sense of the sentence or whether it merely accompanies it.[14] One might find that in the sentence: "Napoleon, who recognized the danger to his right flank, personally led his troops against the enemy's position" there are not only the previously specified two propositions, but also the proposition that the recognition of the danger was the reason why he led his troops against the enemy. One may indeed wonder whether this proposition is merely lightly suggested or actually expressed. Consider the question whether our sentence would be false if Napoleon's resolution had been formed before the recognition of the danger. If our sentence were true even despite this, then the associated proposition should be regarded as part of the sense of the sentence. In the alternative case the situation is rather complicated: we should then have more simple propositions than sentences. Now if we replace the sentence "Napoleon recognized the danger for his right flank" by another sentence of the same truth-value, e.g., by: "Napoleon was over forty-five years old" this would change not only our first but also our third proposition; and this might thereby change also the truth-value of the third proposition—namely, if his age was not the reason for his resolution to lead the troops against the enemy. Hence, it is clear that in such instances sentences of the same truth-value cannot always be substituted for one another. The sentence merely by virtue of its connection with another expresses something more than it would by itself alone.

Let us now consider cases in which this occurs regularly. In the sentence: "Bebel imagines that France's desire for vengeance could be assuaged by the restitution of Alsace-Lorraine" there are expressed two propositions which, however, do not correspond to the main and the dependent clause—namely:

(1) Bebel believes that France's desire for vengeance could be assuaged by the restitution of Alsace-Lorraine;
(2) France's desire for vengeance cannot be assuaged by the restitution of Alsace-Lorraine.

In the expression of the first proposition the words of the dependent clause have indirect nominata; while the same words, in the expression of the second proposition, have their usual nominata. Hence, we see that the dependent clause of our original sentence really is to be interpreted in a twofold way; i.e., with different nominata, one of which is a proposition and the other a truth-value. An analogous situation prevails with expressions like 'to know', 'to recognize', 'it is known'.

A condition clause and its related main clause express several propositions which, however, do not correspond one-to-one to the clauses. The sentence: "Since ice is specifically lighter than water, it floats on water" asserts:

(1) Ice is specifically lighter than water.
(2) If something is specifically lighter than water, it floats on water.
(3) Ice floats on water.

The third proposition, being implied by the first two, would perhaps not have to be mentioned expressly. However, neither the first and the third, nor the second and the third together would completely render the sense of our sentence. Thus we see that the dependent clause 'since ice is specifically lighter than water' expresses both our first proposition and part of the second. Hence, our clause cannot be replaced by another of the same truth-value; for thereby we are apt to alter our second proposition and could easily affect its truth-value.

A similar situation holds in the case of the sentence: "If iron were lighter than water it would float on water." Here we have the two propositions that iron is not lighter than water and that whatever is lighter than water floats on water. The clause again expresses the one proposition and part of the other. If we interpret the previously discussed sentence: "After Schleswig-Holstein was separated from Denmark, Prussia and Austria fell out with one another" as containing the proposition that Schleswig-Holstein once was separated from Denmark, then we have: firstly, the proposition, secondly, the proposition that, at a time more precisely determined by the dependent clause, Prussia and Austria fell out with one another. Here, too, the dependent clause expresses not only one proposition but also part of another. Therefore, it may not generally be replaced by another clause of the same truth-value.

It is difficult to exhaust all possibilities that present themselves in language; but I hope, in essence at least, to have disclosed the reasons why, in view of the invariance of the truth of a whole sentence, a clause cannot always be replaced by another of the same truth-value. These reasons are:

(1) that the clause does not denote a truth-value in that it expresses only a part of a proposition;

(2) that the clause, while it does denote a truth-value, is not restricted to this function in that its sense comprises, beside one proposition, also a part of another.

The first case holds

(a) with the indirect nominata of the words;

(b) if a part of the sentence indicates only indirectly without being a proper name.

In the second case the clause is to be interpreted in a twofold manner; namely, once with its usual nominatum; the other time with its indirect nominatum; or else, the sense of a part of the clause may simultaneously be a constituent of another proposition which, together with the sense expressed in the dependent clause, amounts to the total sense of the main and the dependent clause.

This makes it sufficiently plausible that instances in which a clause is not replaceable by another of the same truth-value do not disprove our view that the nominatum of a sentence is its truth-value and its sense a proposition.

Let us return to our point of departure now.

When we discerned generally a difference in cognitive significance between "a = a" and "a = b" then this is now explained by the fact that for the cognitive significance of a sentence the sense (the proposition expressed) is no less relevant than its nominatum (the truth-value). If a = b, then the nominatum of 'a' and of 'b' is indeed the same and therefore also the truth-value of "a = b" is the same as that of "a = a". Nevertheless, the sense of 'b' may differ from the sense of 'a'; and therefore the proposition expressed by "a = b" may differ from the proposition expressed by "a = a"; in that case the two sentences do not have the same cognitive significance. Thus, if, as above, we mean by 'judgment' the transition from a proposition to its truth-value, then we can also say that the judgments differ from one another.

NOTES

1. I use this word in the sense of identity and understand "a = b" in the sense of "a is the same as b" or "a and b coincide".

2. In the case of genuinely proper names like 'Aristotle' opinions as regards their sense may diverge. As such may, e.g., be suggested: Plato's disciple and the teacher of Alexander the Great. Whoever accepts this sense will interpret the meaning of the statement "Aristotle was born in Stagira" differently from one who interpreted the sense of 'Aristotle' as the Stagirite teacher of Alexander the Great. As long as the nominatum remains the same, these fluctuations in sense are tolerable. But they should be avoided in the system of a demonstrative science and should not appear in a perfect language.

3. With the images we can align also the percepts in which the sense impressions and activities themselves take the place of those traces left in the mind. For our purposes the difference is unimportant, especially since besides sensations and activities recollections of such help in completing the intuitive presentation. 'Percept' may also be understood as the object, inasmuch as it is spatial or capable of sensory apprehension.

4. It is therefore inexpedient to designate fundamentally different things by the one word 'image' (or 'idea').

5. By 'proposition' I do not refer to the subjective

activity of thinking but rather to its objective content which is capable of being the common property of many.

6. It would be desirable to have an expression for signs which have sense only. If we call them 'icons' then the words of an actor on stage would be icons; even the actor himself would be an icon.

7. A judgment is not merely the apprehension of a thought or proposition but the acknowledgment of its truth.

8. In "*A* lied, that he had seen *B*" the clause denotes a proposition of which it is said, firstly, that *A* asserted it as true, and, secondly, that *A* was convinced of its falsity.

9. According to our previous remarks such an expression should always be assured of a nominatum, e.g., through the special convention that the nomination be the number 0 if there is no object or more than one object denoted by the expression.

10. Regarding these sentences, however, several interpretations are easily conceivable. The sense of the sentence "after Schleswig-Holstein was torn away from Denmark, Prussia and Austria fell out with one another" could also be rendered by "after the separation of Schl.-H. from Denmark, Prussia and Austria fell out with one another." In this formulation it is sufficiently clear that we should not regard it as part of this sense that Schleswig-Holstein once was separated from Denmark; but rather that this is the necessary presupposition for the very existence of a nominatum of the expression 'after the separation of Schl.-H. from D.' Yet, our sentence could also be interpreted to the effect that Sch.-H. was once separated from D. This case will be considered later. In order to grasp the difference more clearly, let us identify ourselves with the mind of a Chinese who, with his trifling knowledge of European history, regards it as false that Schl.-H. was ever separated from D. This Chinese would regard as neither true nor false the sentence as interpreted in the first manner. He would deny to it any nominatum becuase the dependent clause would be lacking a nominatum. The dependent clause would only apparently indicate a temporal determination. But if the Chinese interprets our sentence in the second manner, then he will find it expressing a proposition which he would consider false, in addition to a component which, for him, would be without nominatum.

11. Occasionally there is no explicit linguistic indication and the interpretation has to depend upon the total context.

12. Similarly in the cases of 'but', 'yet'.

13. The proposition of the sentence could also be formulated thus: "either the sun has not as yet risen or the sky is heavily overcast." This shows how to interpret this type of compound sentence.

14. This may be of importance in the question as to whether a given assertion be a lie, an oath, or a perjury.

On Denoting   16

BERTRAND RUSSELL

By a 'denoting phrase' I mean a phrase such as any one of the following: a man, some man, any man, every man, all men, the present King of England, the present King of France, the center of mass in the solar system at the first instant of the twentieth century, the revolution of the earth round the sun, the revolution of the sun round the earth. Thus a phrase is denoting solely in virtue of its *form*. We may distinghish three cases: (1) A phrase may be denoting, and yet not denote anything; e.g., 'the present King of France'. (2) A phrase may denote one definite object, e.g., 'the present King of England' denotes a certain man. (3) A phrase may denote ambiguously; e.g., 'a man' denotes not many men, but an ambiguous man. The interpretation of such phrases is a matter of considerable difficulty; indeed, it is very hard to frame any theory not susceptible of formal refutation. All the difficulties with which I am acquainted are met, so far as I can discover, by the theory which I am about to explain.

The subject of denoting is of very great importance, not only in logic and mathematics, but also in theory of knowledge. For example, we know that the center of mass of the solar system at a definite instant is some definite point, and we can affirm a number of propositions about it; but we have no immedi-ate *acquaintance* with this point, which is only known to us by description. The distinction between *acquaintance* and *knowledge about* is the distinction between the things we have presentations of, and the things we can only reach by denoting phrases. It often happens that we know that a certain phrase denotes unambiguously, although we have no acquain-tance with what it denotes; this occurs in the above case of the center of mass. In percep-tion we have acquaintance with the objects of perception, and in thought we have acquain-tance with objects of a more abstract logical character; but we do not necessarily have acquaintance with the objects denoted by phrases composed of words with whose mean-ings we are acquainted. To take a very important instance: there seems no reason to believe that we are ever acquainted with other people's minds, seeing that these are not directly perceived; hence what we know about them is obtained through denoting. All think-ing has to start from acquaintance, but it succeeds in thinking *about* many things with which we have no acquaintance.

The course of my argument will be as follows. I shall begin by stating the theory I intend to advocate;[1] I shall then discuss the theories of Frege and Meinong, showing why neither of them satisfies me; then I shall give

From *Logic and Knowledge,* ed. Robert C. Marsh (London: Allen and Unwin, 1956), pp. 41–56.

the grounds in favor of my theory; and finally I shall briefly indicate the philosophical consequences of my theory.

My theory, briefly, is as follows. I take the notion of the *variable* as fundamental; I use '$C(x)$' to mean a proposition[2] in which x is a constituent, where x, the variable, is essentially and wholly undetermined. Then we can consider the two notions '$C(x)$ is always true' and '$C(x)$ is sometimes true.'[3] Then *everything* and *nothing* and *something* (which are the most primitive of denoting phrases) are to be interpreted as follows:

> C (everything) means '$C(x)$ is always true';
>
> C (nothing) means ' "$C(x)$ is false" is always true';
>
> C (something) means 'It is false that "$C(x)$ is false" is always true'.[4]

Here the notion '$C(x)$ is always true' is taken as ultimate and indefinable, and the others are defined by means of it. *Everything, nothing,* and *something* are not assumed to have any meaning in isolation, but a meaning is assigned to *every* proposition in which they occur. This is the principle of the theory of denoting I wish to advocate: that denoting phrases never have any meaning in themselves, but that every proposition in whose verbal expression they occur has a meaning. The difficulties concerning denoting are, I believe, all the result of a wrong analysis of propositions whose verbal expressions contain denoting phrases. The proper analysis, if I am not mistaken, may be further set forth as follows.

Suppose now we wish to interpret the proposition, 'I met a man'. If this is true, I met some definite man; but that is not what I affirm. What I affirm is, according to the theory I advocate:

> ' "I met x, and x is human" is not always false'.

Generally, defining the class of men as the class of objects having the predicate *human*, we say that:

> 'C (a man)' means ' "$C(x)$ and x is human" is not always false'. This leaves 'a man', by itself, wholly destitute of meaning, but gives a meaning to every proposition in whose verbal expression 'a man' occurs.

Consider next the proposition 'all men are mortal'. This proposition[5] is really hypothetical and states that *if* anything is a man, it is mortal. That is, it states that if x is a man, x is mortal, whatever x may be. Hence, substituting 'x is human' for 'x is a man', we find:

> 'All men are mortal' means ' "If x is human, x is mortal" is always true'.

This is what is expressed in symbolic logic by saying that 'all men are mortal' means ' "x is human" implies "x is mortal" for all values of x'. More generally, we say:

> 'C (all men)' means ' "If x is human, then C (x) is true" is always true'.

Similarly

> 'C (no men)' means ' "If x is human, then C (x) is false" is always true'.
>
> 'C (some men)' will mean the same as 'C (a man)',[6] and
>
> 'C (a man)' means 'It is false that "C (x) and x is human" is always false'.
>
> 'C (every man)' will mean the same as 'C (all men)'.

It remains to interpret phrases containing *the.* These are by far the most interesting and difficult of denoting phrases. Take as an example 'the father of Charles II was executed'. This asserts that there was an x who was the father of Charles II and was executed. Now, *the,* when it is strictly used, involves uniqueness; we do, it is true, speak of '*the son* of So-and-so' even when So-and-so has several sons, but it would be more correct to say '*a* son of So-and-so". Thus for our purposes we take *the* as involving uniqueness. Thus when we say 'x was *the* father of Charles II' we not only assert that x had a certain relation to Charles II, but also that nothing else had this relation. The relation in question, without the assumption of uniqueness, and without any denoting phrases, is expressed by 'x begat Charles II'. To get an equivalent of 'x was the father of Charles II', we must add, 'If y is other than x, y did not beget Charles II', or what is equivalent, 'If y begat Charles II, y is identical with x'. Hence, 'x is the father of Charles II' becomes: 'x begat Charles II; and 'if y begat Charles II, y is identical with x' is always true of y'.

Thus 'the father of Charles II was executed' becomes:

'It is not always false of x that x begat Charles II and that x was executed and that "if y begat Charles II, y is identical with x" is always true of y'.

This may seem a somewhat incredible interpretation; but I am not at present giving reasons, I am merely *stating* the theory.

To interpret 'C (the father of Charles II)', where C stands for any statement about him, we have only to substitute C (x) for 'x was executed' in the above. Observe that, according to the above interpretation C may be, "C (the father of Charles II)' implies:

'It is not always false of x that "if y begat Charles II, y is identical with x" is always true of y',

which is what is expressed in common language by 'Charles II had one father and no more'. Consequently if this condition fails, *every* proposition of the form 'C (the father of Charles II)' is false. Thus e.g. every proposition of the form 'C (the present King of France)' is false. This is a great advantage in the present theory. I shall show later that it is not contrary to the law of contradiction, as might be at first supposed.

The above gives a reduction of all propositions in which denoting phrases occur to forms in which no such phrases occur. Why it is imperative to effect such a reduction, the subsequent discussion will endeavor to show.

The evidence for the above theory is derived from the difficulties which seem unavoidable if we regard denoting phrases as standing for genuine constituents of the propositions in whose verbal expressions they occur. Of the possible theories which admit such constituents the simplest is that of Meinong.[7] This theory regards any grammatically correct denoting phrase as standing for an *object*. Thus 'the present King of France', 'the round square', etc., are supposed to be genuine objects. It is admitted that such objects do not *subsist,* but nevertheless they are supposed to be objects. This is in itself a difficult view; but the chief objection is that such objects, admittedly, are apt to infringe the law of contradiction. It is contended, for example, that the existent present King of France exists,

and also does not exist; that the round square is round, and also not round, etc. But this is intolerable; and if any theory can be found to avoid this result, it is surely to be preferred.

The above breach of the law of contradiction is avoided by Frege's theory. He distinguishes, in a denoting phrase, two elements, which we may call the *meaning* and the *denotation.*[8] Thus 'the center of mass of the solar system at the beginning of the twentieth century' is highly complex in *meaning,* but its *denotation* is a certain point, which is simple. The solar system, the twentieth century, etc., are constituents of the *meaning;* but the *denotation* has no constituents at all.[9] One advantage of this distinction is that it shows why it is often worthwhile to assert identity. If we say 'Scott is the author of *Waverley*', we assert an identity of denotation with a difference of meaning. I shall, however, not repeat the grounds in favor of this theory, as I have urged its claims elsewhere (loc. cit.), and am now concerned to dispute those claims.

One of the first difficulties that confronts us, when we adopt the view that denoting phrases *express* a meaning and *denote* a denotation,[10] concerns the cases in which the denotation appears to be absent. If we say 'the King of England is bald', that is, it would seem, not a statement about the complex *meaning* 'the King of England', but about the actual man denoted by the meaning. But now consider 'the King of France is bald'. By parity of form, this also ought to be about the denotation of the phrase 'the King of France'. But this phrase, though it has a *meaning* provided 'the King of England' has a meaning, has certainly no denotation, at least in any obvious sense. Hence one would suppose that 'the King of France is bald' ought to be nonsense; but it is not nonsense, since it is plainly false. Or again consider such a proposition as the following: 'If u is a class which has only one member, then that one member is a member of u', or, as we may state it, 'If u is a unit class, the u is a u'. This proposition ought to be *always* true, since the conclusion is true whenever the hypothesis is true. But 'the u is a denoting phrase, and it is the denotation, not the meaning, that is said to be a u. Now if u is *not* a unit class, "the u" seems to denote nothing; hence our proposition would seem to become nonsense as soon as *u* is not a unit class.

Now it is plain that such propositions do *not* become nonsense merely because their hypotheses are false. The king in *The Tempest* might say, 'If Ferdinand is not drowned, Ferdinand is my only son'. Now 'my only son' is a denoting phrase, which, on the face of it, has a denotation when, and only when, I have exactly one son. But the above statement would nevertheless have remained true if Ferdinand had been in fact drowned. Thus we must either provide a denotation in cases in which it is at first sight absent, or we must abandon the view that the denotation is what is concerned in propositions which contain denotating phrases. The latter is the course that I advocate. The former course may be taken, as by Meinong, by admitting objects which do not subsist, and denying that they obey the law of contradiction; this, however, is to be avoided if possible. Another way of taking the same course (so far as our present alternative is concerned) is adopted by Frege, who provides by definition some purely conventional denotations for the cases in which otherwise there would be none. Thus 'the King of France', is to denote the null-class; 'the only son of Mr. So-and-so' (who has a fine family of ten), is to denote the class of all his sons; and so on. But this procedure, though it may not lead to actual logical error, is plainly artificial, and does not give an exact analysis of the matter. Thus if we allow that denoting phrases, in general, have the two sides of meaning and denotation, the cases where there seems to be no denotation cause difficulties both on the assumption that there really is a denotation and on the assumption that there really is none.

A logical theory may be tested by its capacity for dealing with puzzles, and it is a wholesome plan, in thinking about logic, to stock the mind with as many puzzles as possible, since these serve much the same purpose as is served by experiments in physical science. I shall therefore state three puzzles which a theory as to denoting ought to be able to solve; and I shall show later that my theory solves them.

(1) If *a* is identical with *b*, whatever is true of the one is true of the other, and either may be substituted for the other in any proposition without altering the truth or falsehood of that proposition. Now George IV wished to know whether Scott was the author of *Waverley;* and in fact Scott *was* the author of *Waverley.* Hence we may substitute *Scott* for *the author of 'Waverley'*, and thereby prove that George IV wished to know whether Scott was Scott. Yet an interest in the law of identity can hardly be attributed to the first gentleman of Europe.

(2) By the law of excluded middle, either '*A* is *B*' or '*A* is not *B*' must be true. Hence either 'the present King of France is bald' or 'the present King of France is not bald' must be true. Yet if we enumerated the things that are bald, and then the things that are not bald, we should not find the present King of France in either list. Hegelians, who love a synthesis, will probably conclude that he wears a wig.

(3) Consider the proposition '*A* differs from *B*'. If this is true, there is a difference between *A* and *B,* which fact may be expressed in the form 'the difference between *A* and *B* subsists'. But if it is false that *A* differs from *B*, then there is no difference between *A* and *B*, which fact may be expresssed in the form 'the difference between *A* and *B* does not subsist'. But how can a non-entity be the subject of a proposition? 'I think, therefore I am' is no more evident than 'I am the subject of a proposition, therefore I am', provided 'I am' is taken to assert subsistence or being,[11] not existence. Hence, it would appear, it must always be self-contradictory to deny the being of anything; but we have seen, in connection with Meinong, that to admit being also sometimes leads to contradictions. Thus, if *A* and *B* do not differ, to suppose either that there is, or that there is not, such an object as 'the difference between *A* and *B*' seems equally impossible.

The relation of the meaning to the denotation involves certain rather curious difficulties, which seem in themselves sufficient to prove that the theory which leads to such difficulties must be wrong.

When we wish to speak about the *meaning* of a denoting phrase, as opposed to its *denotation,* the natural mode of doing so is by inverted commas. Thus we say:

> The center of mass of the solar system is a point, not a denoting complex;
> 'The center of mass of the solar system' is a denoting complex, not a point.

Or again,

> The first line of Gray's Elegy states a proposition.

"The first line of Gray's Elegy" does not state a proposition. Thus taking any denoting phrase, say *C,* we wish to consider the relation between *C* and '*C*', where the difference of the two is the kind exemplified in the above two instances.

We say, to begin with, that when *C* occurs it is the *denotation* that we are speaking about; but when '*C*'occurs, it is the *meaning.* Now the relation of meaning and denotation is not merely linguistic through the phrase: there must be a logical relation involved, which we express by saying that the meaning denotes the denotation. But the difficulty which confronts us is that we cannot succeed in *both* preserving the connection of meaning and denotation *and* preventing them from being one and the same; also that the meaning cannot be got at except by means of denoting phrases. This happens as follows.

The one phrase *C* was to have both meaning and denotation. But if we speak of 'the meaning of *C*', that gives us the meaning (if any) of the denotation. 'The meaning of the first line of Gray's Elegy' is the same as 'The meaning of "The curfew tolls the knell of parting day",' and is not the same as 'The meaning of "the first line of Gray's Elegy".' Thus in order to get the meaning we want, we must speak not of 'the meaning of *C*', but of 'the meaning of "*C*",' which is the same as '*C*' by itself. Similarly 'the denotation of *C*' does not mean the denotation we want, but means something which, if it denotes at all, denotes what is denoted by the denotation we want. For example, let '*C*' be 'the denoting complex occurring in the second of the above instances'. Then *C* = 'the first line of Gray's Elegy', and the denotation of *C* = The curfew tolls the knell of parting day. But what we *meant* to have as the denotation was 'the first line of Gray's Elegy'. Thus we have failed to get what we wanted.

The difficulty in speaking of the meaning of a denoting complex may be stated thus: The moment we put the complex in a proposition, the proposition is about the denotation; and if we make a proposition in which the subject is 'the meaning of *C*', then the subject is the meaning (if any) of the denotation, which was not intended. This leads us to say that, when we distinguish meaning and denotation, we must be dealing with the meaning: the meaning has denotation and is a complex, and there is not something other than the meaning, which can be called the complex, and be said to *have* both meaning and denotation. The right phrase, on the view in question, is that some meanings have denotations.

But this only makes our difficulty in speaking of meanings more evident. For suppose *C* is our complex; then we are to say that *C is* the meaning of the complex. Nevertheless, whenever *C* occurs without inverted commas, what is said is not true of the meaning, but only of the denotation, as when we say: 'The center of mass of the solar system is a point. Thus to speak of *C* itself, i.e., to make a proposition about the meaning, our subject must not be *C,* but something which denotes *C.* Thus '*C*', which is what we use when we want to speak of the meaning, must be not the meaning, but something which denotes the meaning. And *C* must not be a constituent of this complex (as it is of 'the meaning of *C*'); for if *C* occurs in the complex, it will be its denotation, not its meaning, that will occur, and there is no backward road from denotations to meanings, because every object can be denoted by an infinite number of different denoting phrases.

Thus it would seem that '*C*' and *C* are different entities, such that '*C*' denotes *C;* but this cannot be an explanation, because the relation of '*C*' to *C* remains wholly mysterious; and where we are to find the denoting complex '*C*' which is to denote *C?* Moreover, when *C* occurs in a proposition, it is not *only* the denotation that occurs (as we shall see in the next paragraph); yet, on the view in question, *C* is only the denotation, the meaning being wholly relegated to '*C*'. This is an inextricable tangle and seems to prove that the whole distinction of meaning and denotation has been wrongly conceived.

That the meaning is relevant when a denoting phrase occurs in a proposition is formally proved by the puzzle about the author of *Waverley.* The proposition 'Scott was the author of *Waverley*' has a property not possessed by 'Scott was Scott', namely the property that George IV wished to know whether it was true. Thus the two are not identical propositions; hence the meaning of 'the author of *Waverley*' must be relevant as well as the denotation, if we adhere to the point of view to which this distinction belongs. Yet, as we have just seen, so long as we adhere to this point of view, we are compelled to hold that only the denotation can be relevant. Thus the point in question must be abandoned.

It remains to show how all the puzzles we have been considering are solved by the theory explained at the beginning of this article.

According to the view which I advocate, a denoting phrase is essentially *part* of a sentence, and does not, like most single words, have any significance on its own account. If I say 'Scott was a man', that is a statement of the form '*x* was a man', and it has 'Scott' for its subject. But if I say 'the author of *Waverley* was a man', that is not a statement of the form '*x* was a man', and does not have 'the author of *Waverley*' for its subject. Abbreviating the statement made at the beginning of this article, we may put, in place of 'the author of *Waverley* was a man', the following: 'One and only one entity wrote *Waverley,* and that one was a man'. (This is not so strictly what is meant as what was said earlier; but it is easier to follow.) And speaking generally, suppose we wish to say that the author of *Waverley* had the property ϕ, what we wish to say is equivalent to 'One and only one entity wrote *Waverley,* and that one had the property ϕ'.

The explanation of *denotation* is now as follows. Every proposition in which 'the author of *Waverley*' occurs being explained as above, the proposition "Scott was the author of *Waverley*' (i.e., 'Scott was identical with the author of *Waverley*') becomes 'One and only one entity wrote *Waverley,* and Scott was identical with that one'; or, reverting to the wholly explicit form: 'It is not always false of *x* that *x* wrote *Waverley,* that it is always true of *y* that if *y* wrote *Waverley, y* is identical with *x,* and that Scott is identical with *x*'. Thus if '*C*' is a denoting phrase, it may happen that there is one entity *x* (there cannot be more than one) for which the proposition '*x* is identical with *C*' is true, this proposition being interpreted as above. We may then say that the entity *x* is the denotation of the phrase '*C*'. Thus Scott is the denotation of 'the author of *Waverley*'. The '*C*' in inverted commas will be merely the *phrase,* not anything that can be called the *meaning.* The phrase *per se* has no meaning, because in any proposition in which it occurs the proposition, fully expressed, does not contain the phrase, which has been broken up.

The puzzle about George IV's curiosity is now seen to have a very simple solution. The proposition 'Scott was the author of *Waverley*', which was written out in its unabbreviated form in the preceding paragraph, does not contain any constituent 'the author of *Waverley*' for which we could substitute 'Scott'. This does not interfere with the truth of inferences resulting from making what is *verbally* the substitution of 'Scott' for 'the author of *Waverley*', so long as 'the author of *Waverley*' has what I call a *primary* occurrence in the proposition considered. The difference of primary and secondary occurrences of denoting phrases is as follows:

When we say: 'George IV wished to know whether so-and-so', or when we say 'So-and-so is surprising' or 'So-and-so is true', etc., the 'so-and-so' must be a proposition. Suppose now that 'so-and-so' contains a denoting phrase. We may either eliminate this denoting phrase from the subordinate proposition 'so-and-so', or from the whole proposition in which 'so-and-so' is a mere constituent. Different propositions result according to which we do. I have heard of a touchy owner of a yacht to whom a guest, on first seeing it, remarked, 'I thought your yacht was larger than it is'; and the owner replied, 'No, my yacht is not larger than it is'. What the guest meant was, 'The size that I thought your yacht was is greater than the size your yacht is'; the meaning attributed to him is, 'I thought the size of your yacht was greater than the size of your yacht'.

To return to George IV and *Waverley,* when we say 'George IV wished to know whether Scott was the author of *Waverley*', we normally mean 'George IV wished to know whether one and only one man wrote *Waverley* and Scott was that man'; but we *may* also mean: 'One and only one man wrote *Waverley,* and George IV wished to know whether Scott was that man'. In the latter, 'the author of *Waverley*' has a *primary* occurrence; in the former, a *secondary.* The latter might be expressed by 'George IV wished to know, concerning the man who in fact wrote *Waverley,* whether he was Scott'. This would be true, for example, if George IV had seen Scott at a distance, and had asked 'Is that Scott?'. A *secondary* occurrence of a denoting phrase may be defined as one in which the phrase occurs in a proposition *p* which is a mere constituent of the proposition we are considering, and the substitution for the denoting phrase is to be effected in *p,* not in the whole proposition concerned. The ambiguity as between primary and secondary occurrences is hard to avoid in language; but it does no harm if we are on our guard against it. In symbolic logic it is of course easily avoided.

The distinction of primary and secondary occurrences also enables us to deal with the question whether the present King of France is bald or not bald, and generally with the logical status of denoting phrases that denote nothing. If '*C*' is a denoting phrase, say 'the term having the property *F*', then

'*C* has the property ϕ' means 'one and only one term has the property *F,* and that one has the property ϕ'.[12]

If now the property *F* belongs to no terms, or to several, it follows that '*C* has the property ϕ' is false for *all* values of ϕ. Thus 'the present King of France is bald' is certainly false; and 'the present King of France is not bald' is false if it means

'There is an entity which is now King of France and is not bald'.

but is true if it means

'It is false that there is an entity which is now King of France and is bald'.

That is, 'the King of France is not bald' is false if the occurrence of 'the King of France' is *primary,* and true if it is *secondary.* Thus all propositions in which 'the King of France' has a primary occurrence are false; the denials of such propositions are true, but in them 'the King of France' has a secondary occurrence. Thus we escape the conclusion that the King of France has a wig.

We can now see also how to deny that there is such an object as the difference between *A* and *B* in the case when *A* and *B* do not differ. If *A* and *B* do differ, there is one and only one entity *x* such that '*x* is the difference between *A* and *B*' is a true proposition; if *A* and *B* do not differ, there is no such entity *x*. Thus according to the meaning of denotation lately explained, 'the difference between *A* and *B*' has a denotation when *A* and *B* differ, but not otherwise. This difference applies to true and false propositions generally. If '*a R b*' stands for '*a* has the relation *R* to *b*', then when *a R b* is true, there is such an entity as the relation *R* between *a* and *b;* when *a R b* is false, there is no such entity. Thus out of any proposition we can make a denoting phrase, which denotes an entity if the proposition is true, but does not denote an entity if the proposition is false. E.g., it is true (at least we will suppose so) that the earth revolves around the sun, and false that the sun revolves around the earth; hence 'the revolution of the earth round the sun' denotes an entity, while 'the revolution of the sun round the earth' does not denote an entity.[13]

The whole realm of non-entities, such as 'the round square', 'the even prime other than 2', 'Apollo', 'Hamlet', etc., can now be satisfactorily dealt with. All these are denoting phrases which do not denote anything. A proposition about Apollo means what we get by substituting what the classical dictionary tells us is meant by Apollo, say 'the sun-god'. All propositions in which Apollo occurs are to be interpreted by the above rules for denoting phrases. If 'Apollo' has a primary occurrence, the proposition containing the occurrence is false; if the occurrence is secondary, the proposition may be true. So again 'the round square is round' means 'there is one and only one entity *x* which is round and square, and that entity is round', which is a false proposition, not, as Meinong maintains, a true one. 'The most perfect Being has all perfections; existence is a perfection; therefore the most perfect Being exists' becomes:

'There is one and only one entity x which is most perfect; that one has all perfections; existence is a perfection; therefore that one exists'. As a proof, this fails for want of a proof of the premise 'there is one and only one entity x which is most perfect'.[14]

Mr. MacColl (*Mind,* N.S., No. 54, and again No. 55, page 401) regards individuals as of two sorts, real and unreal; hence he defines the null-class as the class consisting of all unreal individuals. This assumes that such phrases as 'the present King of France', which do not denote a real individual, do, nevertheless, denote an individual, but an unreal one. This is essentially Meinong's theory, which have seen reason to reject because it conflicts with the law of contradiction. With our theory of denoting, we are able to hold that there are no unreal individuals; so that the null-class is the class containing no members, not the class containing as members all unreal individuals.

It is important to observe the effect of our theory on the interpretation of definitions which proceed by means of denoting phrases. Most mathematical definitions are of this sort: for example '$m - n$ means the number which, added to n, gives m'. Thus $m - n$ is defined as meaning the same as a certain denoting phrase; but we agreed that denoting phrases have no meaning in isolation. Thus what the definition really ought to be is: 'Any proposition containing $m-n$ is to mean the proposition which results from substituting for "$m - n$" "the number which, added to n, gives m".' The resulting proposition is interpreted according to the rules already given for interpreting propositions whose verbal expression contains a denoting phrase. In the case where m and n are such that there is one and only one number x which, added to n, gives m, there is a number x which can be substituted for $m - n$ in any proposition containing $m - n$ without altering the truth or falsehood of the proposition. But in other cases, all propositions in which '$m - n$' has a primary occurrence are false.

The usefulness of *identity* is explained by the above theory. No one outside a logic-book ever wishes to say 'x is x', and yet assertions of identity are often made in such forms as 'Scott was the author of *Waverley*' or 'thou art the man'. The meaning of such propositions cannot be stated without the notion of identity, although they are not simply statements that Scott is identical with another term, the author of *Waverley,* or that thou art identical with another term, the man. The shortest statement of 'Scott is the author of *Waverley*' seems to be 'Scott wrote *Waverley;* and it is always true of y that if y wrote *Waverley*, y is identical with Scott'. It is in this way that identity enters into 'Scott is the author of *Waverley*'; and it is owing to such uses that identity is worth affirming.

One interesting result of the above theory of denoting is this: when there is anything with which we do not have immediate acquaintance, but only definition by denoting phrases, then the propositions in which this thing is introduced by means of a denoting phrase do not really contain this thing as a constituent, but contain instead the constituents expressed by the several words of the denoting phrase. Thus in every proposition that we can apprehend (i.e. not only in those whose truth or falsehood we can judge of, but in all that we can think about), all the constituents are really entities with which we have immediate acquaintance. Now such things as matter (in the sense in which matter occurs in physics) and the minds of other people are known to us only by denoting phrases, i.e. we are not *acquainted* with them, but we know them as what has such and such properties. Hence, although we can form propositional functions $C(x)$ which must hold of such and such a material particle, or of So-and-so's mind, yet we are not acquainted with the propositions which affirm these things that we know must be true, because we cannot apprehend the actual entities concerned. What we know is 'So-and-so has a mind which has such and such properties', where A is the mind in question. In such a case, we know the properties of a thing without having acquaintance with the thing itself, and without, consequently, knowing any single proposition of which the thing itself is a constituent.

Of the many other consequences of the view I have been advocating, I will say nothing. I will only beg the reader not to make up his mind against the view—as he might be tempted to do, on account of its apparently excessive complication—until he has attempted to construct a theory of his own on the subject of denotation. This attempt, I believe, will convince him that, whatever the true theory may be, it cannot have such a simplicity as one might have expected beforehand.

NOTES

1. I have discussed this subject in *Principles of Mathematics,* Chap. V, and § 476. The theory there advocated is very nearly the same as Frege's, and is quite different from the theory to be advocated in what follows.
2. More exactly, a propositional function.
3. The second of these can be defined by means of the first, if we take it to mean, 'It is not true that "C (x) is false" is always true'.
4. I shall sometimes use, instead of this complicated phrase, the phrase 'C (x) is not always false', or 'C (x) is sometimes true', supposed *defined* to mean the same as the complicated phrase.
5. As has been ably argued in Mr. Bradley's *Logic,* Book I, Chap. II.
6. Psychologically 'C (a man)' has a suggestion of *only* one, and 'C (some men)' has a suggestion of *more than one;* but we may neglect these suggestions in a preliminary sketch.
7. See *Untersuchungen zur Gegenstandstheorie und Psychologie* (Leipzig, 1904) the first three articles (by Meinong, Ameseder, and Mally respectively).
8. See his "Ueber Sinn und Bedeutung," *Zeitschrift für Phil. und Phil. Kritik,* 100. [*Reprinted in this volume.*]
9. Frege distinguishes the two elements of meaning and denotation everywhere, and not only in complex denoting phrases. Thus it is the *meanings* of the constituents of a denoting complex that enter into its *meaning,* not their *denotation.* In the proposition 'Mont Blanc is over 1,000 metres high', it is, according to him the *meaning* of 'Mont Blanc', not the actual mountain, that is a constituent of the *meaning* of the proposition.
10. In this theory, we shall say that the denoting phrase *expresses* a meaning; and we shall say both of the phrase and of the meaning that they *denote* a denotation. In the other theory, which I advocate, there is no *meaning,* and only sometimes a *denotation.*
11. I use these as synonyms.
12. This is the abbreviated, not the stricter, interpretation.
13. The propositions from which such suppositions are derived are not identical either with these entities or with the propositions that these entities have being.
14. The argument can be made to prove validly that all members of the class of most perfect Beings exist; it can also be proved formally that this class cannot have *more* than one member; but, taking the definition of perfection as possession of all positive predicates, it can be proved almost equally formally that the class does not have even one member.

Descriptions 17

BERTRAND RUSSELL

We dealt in the preceding chapter with the words *all* and *some;* in this chapter we shall consider the word *the* in the singular, and in the next chapter we shall consider the word *the* in the plural. It may be thought excessive to devote two chapters to one word, but to the philosophical mathematician it is a word of very great importance: like Browning's Grammarian with the enclitic δε, I would give the doctrine of this word if I were "dead from the waist down" and not merely in a prison.

We have already had occasion to mention "descriptive functions," i.e. such expressions as "the father of x" or "the sine of x." These are to be defined by first defining "descriptions."

A "description" may be of two sorts, definite and indefinite (or ambiguous). An indefinite description is a phrase of the form "a so-and-so," and a definite description is a phrase of the form "the so-and-so" (in the singular). Let us begin with the former.

"Who did you meet?" "I met a man." "That is a very indefinite description." We are therefore not departing from usage in our terminology. Our question is: What do I really assert when I assert "I met a man"? Let us assume, for the moment, that my assertion is true, and that in fact I met Jones. It is clear that what I assert is *not* "I met Jones." I may say "I met a man, but it was not Jones"; in that case, though I lie, I do not contradict myself, as I should do if when I say I met a man I really mean that I met Jones. It is clear also that the person to whom I am speaking can understand what I say, even if he is a foreigner and has never heard of Jones.

But we may go further: not only Jones, but no actual man, enters into my statement. This becomes obvious when the statement is false, since then there is no more reason why Jones should be supposed to enter into the proposition than why anyone else should. Indeed the statement would remain significant, though it could not possibly be true, even if there were no man at all. "I met a unicorn" or "I met a sea-serpent" is a perfectly significant assertion, if we know what it would be to be a unicorn or a sea-serpent, i.e. what is the definition of these fabulous monsters. Thus it is only what we may call the *concept* that enters into the proposition. In the case of "unicorn," for example, there is only the concept: there is not also, somewhere among the shades, something unreal which may be called "a unicorn." Therefore, since it is significant (though false) to say "I met a unicorn," it is clear that this proposition, rightly analyzed, does not contain a constituent "a unicorn," though it does contain the concept "unicorn."

The question of "unreality," which con-

From *Introduction to Mathematical Philosophy* (London: George Allen and Unwin Ltd., 1919), pp. 167–180.

fronts us at this point, is a very important one. Misled by grammar, the great majority of those logicians who have dealt with this question have dealt with it on mistaken lines. They have regarded grammatical form as a surer guide in analysis than, in fact, it is. And they have not known what differences in grammatical form are important. "I met Jones" and "I met a man" would count traditionally as propositions of the same form, but in actual fact they are of quite different forms: the first names an actual person, Jones; while the second involves a propositional function, and becomes, when made explicit: "The function 'I met x and x is human' is sometimes true." (It will be remembered that we adopted the convention of using "sometimes" as not implying more than once.) This proposition is obviously not of the form "I met x," which accounts for the existence of the proposition "I met a unicorn" in spite of the fact that there is no such thing as "a unicorn."

For want of the apparatus of propositional functions, many logicians have been driven to the conclusion that there are unreal objects. It is argued, e.g. by Meinong,[1] that we can speak about "the golden mountain," "the round square," and so on; we can make true propositions of which these are the subjects; hence they must have some kind of logical being, since otherwise the propositions in which they occur would be meaningless. In such theories, it seems to me, there is a failure of that feeling for reality which ought to be preserved even in the most abstract studies. Logic, I should maintain, must no more admit a unicorn than zoology can; for logic is concerned with the real world just as truly as zoology, though with its more abstract and general features. To say that unicorns have an existence in heraldry, or in literature, or in imagination, is a most pitiful and paltry evasion. What exists in heraldry is not an animal, made of flesh and blood, moving and breathing of its own initiative. What exists is a picture, or a description in words. Similarly, to maintain that Hamlet, for example, exists in his own world, namely, in the world of Shakespeare's imagination, just as truly as

(say) Napoleon existed in the ordinary world, is to say something deliberately confusing, or else confused to a degree which is scarcely credible. There is only one world, the "real" world: Shakespeare's imagination is part of it, and the thoughts that he had in writing Hamlet are real. So are the thoughts that we have in reading the play. But it is of the very essence of fiction that only the thoughts, feelings, etc., in Shakespeare and his readers are real, and that there is not, in addition to them, an objective Hamlet. When you have taken account of all the feelings roused by Napoleon in writers and readers of history, you have not touched the actual man; but in the case of Hamlet you have come to the end of him. If no one thought about Hamlet, there would be nothing left of him; if no one had thought about Napoleon, he would have soon seen to it that some one did. The sense of reality is vital in logic, and whoever juggles with it by pretending that Hamlet has another kind of reality is doing a disservice to thought. A robust sense of reality is very necessary in framing a correct analysis of propositions about unicorns, golden mountains, round squares, and other such pseudo-objects.

In obedience to the feeling of reality, we shall insist that, in the analysis of propositions, nothing "unreal" is to be admitted. But, after all, if there *is* nothing unreal, how, it may be asked, *could* we admit anything unreal? The reply is that, in dealing with propositions, we are dealing in the first instance with symbols, and if we attribute significance to groups of symbols which have no significance, we shall fall into the error of admitting unrealities, in the only sense in which this is possible, namely, as objects described. In the proposition "I met a unicorn," the whole four words together make a significant proposition, and the word "unicorn" by itself is significant, in just the same sense as the word "man." But the *two* words "a unicorn" do not form a subordinate group having a meaning of its own. Thus if we falsely attribute meaning to these two words, we find ourselves saddled with "a unicorn," and with the problem how there can be such a thing in a world where there are no unicorns. "A unicorn" is an indefinite description which describes nothing. It is not an indefinite description which describes something unreal. Such a proposition as "x is unreal" only has meaning when "x" is a description, definite or indefinite; in that case the proposition will be true if "x" is a description which describes nothing. But whether the description "x" describes something or describes nothing, it is in any case not a constituent of the proposition in which it occurs; like "a unicorn" just now, it is not a subordinate group having a meaning of its own. All this results from the fact that, when "x" is a description, "x is unreal" or "x does not exist" is not nonsense, but is always significant and sometimes true.

We may now proceed to define generally the meaning of propositions which contain ambiguous descriptions. Suppose we wish to make some statement about "a so-and-so," where "so-and-so's" are those objects that have a certain property ϕ, i.e. those objects x for which the propositional function ϕx is true. (E.g. if we take "a man" as our instance of "a so-and-so," ϕx will be "x is human.") Let us now wish to assert the property ψ of "a so-and-so," i.e. we wish to assert that "a so-and-so" has that property which x has when ψx is true. (E.g. in the case of "I met a man," ψx will be "I met x.") Now the proposition that "a so-and-so" has the property ψ is *not* a proposition of the form "ψx." If it were, "a so-and-so" would have to be identical with x for a suitable x; and although (in a sense) this may be true in some cases, it is certainly not true in such a case as "a unicorn." It is just this fact, that the statement that a so-and-so has the property ψ is not of the form ψx, which makes it possible for "a so-and-so" to be, in a certain clearly definable sense, "unreal." The definition is as follows:

The statement that "an object having the property ϕ has the property ψ"

means:

"The joint assertion of ϕx and ψx is not always false."

So far as logic goes, this is the same proposition as might be expressed by "some

ϕ's are ψ's"; but rhetorically there is a difference, because in the one case there is a suggestion of singularity, and in the other case of plurality. This, however, is not the important point. The important point is that, when rightly analyzed, propositions verbally about "a so-and-so" are found to contain no constituent represented by this phrase. And that is why such propositions can be significant even when there is no such thing as a so-and-so.

The definition of *existence*, as applied to ambiguous descriptions, results from what was said at the end of the preceding chapter [chapter 15 of *Introduction to Mathematical Philosophy*]. We say that "men exist" or "a man exists" if the propositional function "x is human" is sometimes true; and generally "a so-and-so" exists if "x is so-and-so" is sometimes true. We may put this in other language. The proposition "Socrates is a man" is no doubt *equivalent* to "Socrates is human," but it is not the very same proposition. The *is* of "Socrates is human" expresses the relation of subject and predicate; the *is* of "Socrates is a man" expresses identity. It is a disgrace to the human race that it has chosen to employ the same word "is" for these two entirely different ideas—a disgrace which a symbolic logical language of course remedies. The identity in "Socrates is a man" is identity between an object named (accepting "Socrates" as a name, subject to qualifications explained later) and an object ambiguously described. An object ambiguously described will "exist" when at least one such proposition is true, i.e. when there is at least one true proposition of the form "x is a so-and-so," where "x" is a name. It is characteristic of ambiguous (as opposed to definite) descriptions that there may be any number of true propositions of the above form—Socrates is a man, Plato is a man, etc. Thus "a man exists" follows from Socrates, or Plato, or anyone else. With definite descriptions, on the other hand, the corresponding form of proposition, namely, "x is the so-and-so" (where "x" is a name), can only be true for one value of x at most. This brings us to the subject of definite descriptions, which are to be defined in a way analogous to that employed for ambiguous descriptions, but rather more complicated.

We come now to the main subject of the present chapter, namely, the definition of the word *the* (in the singular). One very important point about the definition of "a so-and-so" applies equally to "the so-and-so"; the definition to be sought is a definition of propositions in which this phrase occurs, not a definition of the phrase itself in isolation. In the case of "a so-and-so," this is fairly obvious: no one could suppose that "a man" was a definite object, which could be defined by itself. Socrates is a man, Plato is a man, Aristotle is a man, but we cannot infer that "a man" means the same as "Socrates" means and also the same as "Plato" means and also the same as "Aristotle" means, since these three names have different meanings. Nevertheless, when we have enumerated all the men in the world, there is nothing left of which we can say, "This is a man, and not only so, but it is *the* 'a man,' the quintessential entity that is just an indefinite man without being anybody in particular." It is of course quite clear that whatever there is in the world is definite: if it is a man it is one definite man and not any other. Thus there cannot be such an entity as "a man" to be found in the world, as opposed to specific men. And accordingly it is natural that we do not define "a man" itself, but only the propositions in which it occurs.

In the case of "the so-and-so" this is equally true, though at first sight less obvious. We may demonstrate that this must be the case, by a consideration of the difference between a *name* and a *definite description*. Take the proposition, "Scott is the author of *Waverley*." We have here a name, "Scott," and a description, "the author of *Waverley*," which are asserted to apply to the same person. The distinction between a name and all other symbols may be explained as follows:

A name is a simple symbol whose meaning is something that can only occur as subject, i.e. something of the kind that we defined as an "individual" or a "particular." And a "simple" symbol is one which has no parts that are symbols. Thus "Scott" is a simple symbol, because, though it has parts (namely, separate letters), these parts are not symbols. On the other hand, "the author of *Waverley*" is not a simple symbol, because the separate words that compose the phrase are parts which are symbols. If, as may be the case, whatever *seems* to be an "individual" is really capable of further analysis, we shall have to content ourselves with what may be called "relative individuals," which will be terms that, throughout the context in question, are never analyzed and never occur otherwise than as subjects. And in that case we shall have correspondingly to content ourselves with "relative names." From the standpoint of our present problem, namely, the definition of descriptions, this problem, whether these are absolute names or only relative names, may be ignored, since it concerns different stages in the hierarchy of "types," whereas we have to compare such couples as "Scott" and "the author of *Waverley*," which both apply to the same object, and do not raise the problem of types. We may, therefore, for the moment, treat names as capable of being absolute; nothing that we shall have to say will depend upon this assumption, but the wording may be a little shortened by it.

We have, then, two things to compare: (1) a *name,* which is a simple symbol, directly designating an individual which is its meaning, and having this meaning in its own right, independently of the meanings of all other words; (2) a *description,* which consists of several words, whose meanings are already fixed, and from which results whatever is to be taken as the "meaning" of the description.

A proposition containing a description is not identical with what that proposition becomes when a name is substituted, even if the name names the same object as the description describes. "Scott is the author of *Waverley*" is obviously a different proposition from "Scott is Scott": the first is a fact in literary history, the second a trivial truism. And if we put anyone other than Scott in place of "the author of *Waverley*," our proposition would become false, and would therefore certainly no longer be the same proposition. But, it may be said, our proposition is essentially of the same form as (say) "Scott is Sir Walter," in which two names are said to apply to the same person. The reply is that, if "Scott is Sir Walter" really means "the person named 'Scott' is the person named 'Sir Walter,' " then the names are being used as descriptions: i.e. the individual, instead of being named, is being described as the person having that name. This is a way in which names are frequently used in practice, and there will, as a rule, be nothing in the phraseology to show whether they are being used in this way or *as* names. When a name is used directly, merely to indicate what we are speaking about, it is no part of the *fact* asserted, or of the falsehood if our assertion happens to be false: it is merely part of the symbolism by which we express our thought. What we want to express is something which might (for example) be translated into a foreign language; it is something for which the actual words are a vehicle, but of which they are no part. On the other hand, when we make a proposition about "the person called 'Scott,' " the actual name "Scott" enters into what we are asserting, and not merely into the language used in making the assertion. Our proposition will now be a different one if we substitute "the person called 'Sir Walter.' " But so long as we are using names *as* names, whether we say "Scott" or whether we say "Sir Walter" is as irrelevant to what we are asserting as whether we speak English or French. Thus so long as names are used *as* names, "Scott is Sir Walter" is the same trivial proposition as "Scott is Scott." This completes the proof that "Scott is the author of *Waverley*" is not the same proposition as results from substituting a name for "the author of *Waverley*," no matter what name may be substituted.

When we use a variable, and speak of a propositional function, ϕx say, the process of applying general statements about x to particular cases will consist in substituting a name for the letter "x," assuming that ϕ is a function which has individuals for its arguments. Suppose, for example, that ϕx is "always true"; let it be, say, the "law of identity," $x=x$. Then we may substitute for "x" any name we choose, and we shall obtain a true proposition. Assuming for the moment

that "Socrates," "Plato," and "Aristotle" are names (a very rash assumption), we can infer from the law of identity that Socrates is Socrates, Plato is Plato, and Aristotle is Aristotle. But we shall commit a fallacy if we attempt to infer, without further premisses, that the author of *Waverley* is the author of *Waverley*. This results from what we have just proved, that, if we substitute a name for "the author of *Waverley*" in a proposition, the proposition we obtain is a different one. That is to say, applying the result to our present case: If "x" is a name, "$x=x$" is not the same proposition as "the author of *Waverley* is the author of *Waverley*," no matter what name "x" may be. Thus from the fact that all propositions of the form "$x=x$" are true we cannot infer, without more ado, that the author of *Waverley* is the author of *Waverley*. In fact, propositions of the form "the so-and-so is the so-and-so" are not always true: it is necessary that the so-and-so should *exist* (a term which will be explained shortly). It is false that the present King of France is the present King of France, or that the round square is the round square. When we substitute a description for a name, propositional functions which are "always true" may become false, if the description describes nothing. There is no mystery in this as soon as we realize (what was proved in the preceding paragraph) that when we substitute a description the result is not a value of the propositional function in question.

We are now in a position to define propositions in which a definite description occurs. The only thing that distinguishes "the so-and-so" from "a so-and-so" is the implication of uniqueness. We cannot speak of "*the* inhabitant of London," because inhabiting London is an attribute which is not unique. We cannot speak about "the present King of France," because there is none; but we can speak about "the present King of England." Thus propositions about "the so-and-so" always imply the corresponding propositions about "a so-and-so," with the addendum that there is not more than one so-and-so. Such a proposition as "Scott is the author of Waverley" could not be true if *Waverley* had never been written, or if several people had written it; and no more could any other proposition resulting from a propositional function x by the substitution of "the author of *Waverley*" for "x." We may say that "the author of *Waverley*" means "the value of x for which 'x wrote *Waverley*' is true." Thus the proposition "the author of *Waverley* was Scotch," for example, involves:

(1) "x wrote *Waverley*" is not always false
(2) "if x and y wrote *Waverley*, x and y are identical" is always true
(3) "if x wrote *Waverley*, x was Scotch" is always true

These three propositions, translated into ordinary language, state:

(1) at least one person wrote *Waverley*
(2) at most one person wrote *Waverley*
(3) whoever wrote *Waverley* was Scotch

All these three are implied by "the author of *Waverley* was Scotch." Conversely, the three together (but no two of them) imply that the author of *Waverley* was Scotch. Hence the three together may be taken as defining what is meant by the proposition "the author of *Waverley* was Scotch."

We may somewhat simplify these three propositions. The first and second together are equivalent to: "There is a term c such that 'x wrote *Waverley*' is true when x is c and is false when x is not c." In other words, "There is a term c such that 'x wrote *Waverley*' is always equivalent to 'x is c.' " (Two propositions are "equivalent" when both are true or both are false.) We have here, to begin with, two functions of x, "x wrote *Waverley*" and "x is c," and we form a function of c by considering the equivalence of these two functions of x for all values of x; we then proceed to assert that the resulting function of c is "sometimes true," i.e. that it is true for at least one value of c. (It obviously cannot be true for more than one value of c.) These two conditions together are defined as giving the meaning of "the author of *Waverley* exists."

We may now define "the term satisfying the function ϕx exists." This is the general form of which the above is a particular case. "The author of *Waverley*" is "the term satisfying the

function 'x wrote *Waverley*.' " And "the so-and-so" will always involve reference to some propositional function, namely, that which defines the property that makes a thing a so-and-so. Our definition is as follows:

"The term satisfying the function ϕx exists" means:
"There is a term c such that ϕx is always equivalent to 'x is c.' "

In order to define "the author of *Waverley* was Scotch," we have still to take account of the third of our three propositions, namely, "Whoever wrote *Waverley* was Scotch." This will be satisfied by merely adding that the c in question is to be Scotch. Thus "the author of *Waverley* was Scotch" is:

"There is a term c such that (1) 'x wrote *Waverley*' is always equivalent to 'x is c,' (2) c is Scotch."

And generally: "the term satisfying ϕx satisfies ψx" is defined as meaning:

"There is a term c such that (1) ϕx is always equivalent to 'x is c,' (2) ψx is true."

This is the definition of propositions in which descriptions occur.

It is possible to have much knowledge concerning a term described, i.e. to know many propositions concerning "the so-and-so," without actually knowing what the so-and-so is, i.e. without knowing any proposition of the form "x is the so-and-so," where "x" is a name. In a detective story propositions about "the man who did the deed" are accumulated, in the hope that ultimately they will suffice to demonstrate that it was A who did the deed. We may even go so far as to say that, in all such knowledge as can be expressed in words—with the exception of "this" and "that" and a few other words of which the meaning varies on different occasions—no names, in the strict sense, occur, but what seem like names are really descriptions. We may inquire significantly whether Homer existed, which we could not do if "Homer" were a name. The proposition "the so-and-so exists" is significant, whether true or false; but if a is the so-and-so (where "a" is a name), the words "*a* exists" are meaning-less. It is only of descriptions—definite or indefinite—that existence can be significantly asserted; for, if "*a*" is a name, it *must* name something: what does not name anything is not a name, and therefore, if intended to be a name, is a symbol devoid of meaning, whereas a description, like "the present King of France," does not become incapable of occurring significantly merely on the ground that it describes nothing, the reason being that it is a *complex* symbol, of which the meaning is derived from that of its constituent symbols. And so, when we ask whether Homer existed, we are using the word "Homer" as an abbreviated description: we may replace it by (say) "the author of the *Iliad* and the *Odyssey*." The same considerations apply to almost all uses of what look like proper names.

When descriptions occur in propositions, it is necessary to distinguish what may be called "primary" and "secondary" occurrences. The abstract distinction is as follows. A description has a "primary" occurrence when the proposition in which it occurs results from substituting the description for "*x*" in some propositional function ϕ*x;* a description has a "secondary" occurrence when the result of substituting the description for *x* in ϕ*x* gives only *part* of the proposition concerned. An instance will make this clearer. Consider "the present King of France is bald." Here "the present King of France" has a primary occurrence, and the proposition is false. Every proposition in which a description which describes nothing has a primary occurrence is false. But now consider "the present King of France is not bald." This is ambiguous. If we are first to take "*x* is bald," then substitute "the present King of France" for "*x*," and then deny the result, the occurrence of "the present King of France" is secondary and our proposition is true; but if we are to take "*x* is not bald" and substitute "the present King of France" for "*x*," then "the present King of France" has a primary occurrence and the proposition is false. Confusion of primary and secondary occurrences is a ready source of fallacies where descriptions are concerned.

Descriptions occur in mathematics chiefly in the form of *descriptive functions*, i.e. "the term having the relation R to *y*," or "the R of *y*" as we may say, on the analogy of "the father of *y*" and similar phrases. To say "the father of *y* is rich," for example, is to say that the following propositional function of *c:* "*c* is rich, and '*x* begat *y*' is always equivalent to '*x* is *c*,' " is "sometimes true," i.e. is true for at least one value of *c*. It obviously cannot be true for more than one value.

The theory of descriptions, briefly outlined in the present chapter, is of the utmost importance both in logic and in theory of knowledge. But for purposes of mathematics, the more philosophical parts of the theory are not essential, and have therefore been omitted in the above account, which has confined itself to the barest mathematical requisites.

REFERENCES

1. *Untersuchungen zur Gegenstandstheorie und Psychologie*, 1904.

On Referring   18

P. F. STRAWSON

We very commonly use expressions of certain kinds to mention or refer to some individual person or single object or particular event or place or process, in the course of doing what we should normally describe as making a statement about that person, object, place, event, or process. I shall call this way of using expressions the 'uniquely referring use'. The classes of expressions which are most commonly used in this way are: singular demonstrative pronouns ("this" and "that"); proper names e.g. "Venice," "Napoleon," "John"); singular personal and impersonal pronouns ("he," "she," "I," "you," "it"); and phrases beginning with the definite article followed by a noun, qualified or unqualified, in the singular (e.g. "the table," "the old man," "the king of France"). Any expression of any of these classes can occur as the subject of what would traditionally be regarded as a singular subject-predicate sentence; and would, so occurring, exemplify the use I wish to discuss.

I do not want to say that expressions belonging to these classes never have any other use than the one I want to discuss. On the contrary, it is obvious that they do. It is obvious that anyone who uttered the sentence, "The whale is a mammal," would be using the expression "the whale" in a way quite different from the way it would be used by anyone who had occasion seriously to utter the sentence, "The whale struck the ship." In the first sentence one is obviously *not* mentioning, and in the second sentence one obviously *is* mentioning, a particular whale. Again if I said, "Napoleon was the greatest French soldier," I should be using the word "Napoleon" to mention a certain individual, but I should not be using the phrase, "the greatest French soldier," to mention an individual, but to say something about an individual I had already mentioned. It would be natural to say that in using this sentence I was talking *about* Napoleon and that what I was *saying* about him was that he was the greatest French soldier. But of course I *could* use the expression, "the greatest French soldier," to mention an individual; for example, by saying: "The greatest French soldier died in exile." So it is obvious that at least some expressions belonging to the classes I mentioned *can* have uses other than the use I am anxious to discuss. Another thing I do not want to say is that in any given sentence there is never more than one expression used in the way I propose to discuss. On the contrary, it is obvious that there may be more than one. For example, it would be natural to say that, in seriously using the sentence, "The whale struck the ship," I was saying something about both a certain whale and a certain ship, that I

From *Essays in Conceptual Analysis*, Anthony Flew, ed. (London: Macmillan and Company Ltd., 1956), pp. 21–52. Author's notes in brackets added in 1956.

219

was using each of the expressions "the whale" and "the ship" to mention a particular object; or, in other words, that I was using each of these expressions in the uniquely referring way. In general, however, I shall confine my attention to cases where an expression used in this way occurs as the grammatical subject of a sentence.

I think it is true to say that Russell's theory of descriptions, which is concerned with the last of the four classes of expressions I mentioned above (i.e. with expressions of the form "the so-and-so"), is still widely accepted among logicians as giving a correct account of the use of such expressions in ordinary language. I want to show in the first place, that this theory, so regarded, embodies some fundamental mistakes.

What question or questions about phrases of the form "the so-and-so" was the theory of descriptions designed to answer? I think that at least one of the questions may be illustrated as follows. Suppose someone were now to utter the sentence, "The king of France is wise." No one would say that the sentence which had been uttered was meaningless. Everyone would agree that it was significant. But everyone knows that there is not at present a king of France. One of the questions the theory of descriptions was designed to answer was the question: How can such a sentence as "The king of France is wise" be significant even when there is nothing which answers to the description it contains, i.e., in this case, nothing which answers to the description "The king of France"? And one of the reasons why Russell thought it important to give a correct answer to this question was that he thought it important to show that another answer which might be given was wrong. The answer that he thought was wrong, and to which he was anxious to supply an alternative, might be exhibited as the conclusion of either of the following two fallacious arguments. Let us call the sentence "The king of France is wise" the sentence S. Then the first argument is as follows:

(1) The phrase, "the king of France," is the subject of the sentence S.

Therefore (2) if S is a significant sentence, S is a sentence *about* the king of France.

But (3) if there in no sense exists a king of France, the sentence is not about anything, and hence not about the king of France.

Therefore (4) since S is significant, there must in some sense (in some world) exist (or subsist) the king of France.

And the second argument is as follows:

(1) If S is significant, it is either true or false.

(2) S is true if the king of France is wise and false if the king of France is not wise.

(3) But the statement that the king of France is wise and the statement that the king of France is not wise are alike true only if there is (in some sense, in some world) something which is the king of France.

Hence (4) since S is significant, there follows the same conclusion as before.

These are fairly obviously bad arguments, and, as we should expect, Russell rejects them. The postulation of a world of strange entities, to which the king of France belongs, offends, he says, against "that feeling for reality which ought to be preserved even in the most abstract studies." The fact that Russell rejects these arguments is, however, less interesting than the extent to which, in rejecting their conclusion, he concedes the more important of their principles. Let me refer to the phrase, "the king of France," as the phrase D. Then I think Russell's reasons for rejecting these two arguments can be summarized as follows. The mistake arises, he says, from thinking that D, which is certainly the *grammatical* subject of S, is also the *logical* subject of S. But D is not the logical subject of S. In fact S, although grammatically it has a singular subject and a predicate, is not logically a subject-predicate sentence at all. The proposition it expresses is a complex kind of *existential* proposition, part of which might be described as a "uniquely existential" proposition. To exhibit the logical form of the proposition, we should rewrite the sentence in a logically appropriate grammatical form, in such a way that the deceptive similarity of S to a sentence expressing a subject-predicate proposition would disappear, and we should be safeguarded against arguments such as the bad ones I outlined above. Before recalling the details of Russell's analysis of S, let us notice what his answer, as I have so far given it, seems to imply. His answer seems to imply that in the case of a sentence which is similar to S in that (1) it is grammatically of the subject-predicate form and (2) its grammatical subject does not refer to anything, then the only alternative to its being meaningless is that it should not really (i.e. logically) be of the subject-predicate form at all, but of some quite different form. And this in its turn seems to imply that if there are any sentences which are genuinely of the subject-predicate form, then the very fact of their being significant, having a meaning, guarantees that there *is* something referred to by the logical (and grammatical) subject. Moreover, Russell's answer seems to imply that there are such sentences. For if it is true that one may be misled by the grammatical similarity of S to other sentences into thinking that it is logically of the subject-predicate form, then surely there must be other sentences grammatically similar to S, which *are* of the subject-predicate form. To show not only that Russell's answer seems to imply these conclusions, but that he accepted at least the first two of them, it is enough to consider what he says about a class of expressions which he calls "logically proper names" and contrasts with expressions, like D, which he calls "definite descriptions." Of logically proper names Russell says or implies the following things:

(1) That they and they alone can occur as subjects of sentences which are genuinely of the subject-predicate form.

(2) That an expression intended to be a logically proper name is *meaningless* unless there is some single object for which it stands: for the *meaning* of such an expression just is the individual object which the expression designates. To be a name at all, therefore, it *must* designate something.

It is easy to see that if anyone believes these two propositions, then the only way for him to

save the significance of the sentence S is to deny that it is a logically subject-predicate sentence. Generally, we may say that Russell recognizes only two ways in which sentences which seem, from their grammatical structure, to be about some particular person or individual object or event, can be significant:

(1) The first is that their grammatical form should be misleading as to their logical form, and that they should be analyzable, like S, as a special kind of existential sentence.

(2) The second is that their grammatical subject should be a logically proper name, of which the meaning is the individual thing it designates.

I think that Russell is unquestionably wrong in this, and that sentences which are significant, and which begin with an expression used in the uniquely referring way, fall into neither of these two classes. Expressions used in the uniquely referring way are never either logically proper names or descriptions, if what is meant by calling them "descriptions" is that they are to be analyzed in accordance with the model provided by Russell's theory of descriptions.

There are no logically proper names and there are no descriptions (in this sense).

Let us now consider the details of Russell's analysis. According to Russell, anyone who asserted S would be asserting that:

(1) There is a king of France
(2) There is not more than one king of France
(3) There is nothing which is king of France and is not wise

It is easy to see both how Russell arrived at this analysis, and how it enables him to answer the question with which we began, viz. the question: How can the sentence S be significant when there is no king of France? The way in which he arrived at the analysis was clearly by asking himself what would be the circumstances in which we would say that anyone who uttered the sentence S had made a true assertion. And it does seem pretty clear, and I have no wish to dispute, that the sentences (1)–(3) above do describe circumstances which are at least *necessary* conditions of anyone making a true assertion by uttering the sentence S. But, as I hope to show, to say this is not at all the same thing as to say that Russell has given a correct account of the use of the sentence S or even that he has given an account which, though incomplete, is correct as far as it goes; and is certainly not at all the same thing as to say that the model translation provided is a correct model for all (or for any) singular sentences beginning with a phrase of the form "the so-and-so."

It is also easy to see how this analysis enables Russell to answer the question of how the sentence S can be significant, even when there is no king of France. For, if this analysis is correct, anyone who utters the sentence S today would be jointly asserting three propositions, one of which (viz. that there is a king of France) would be false; and since the conjunction of three propositions, of which one is false, is itself false, the assertion as a whole would be significant, but false. So neither of the bad arguments for subsistent entities would apply to such an assertion.

II

As a step towards showing that Russell's solution of his problem is mistaken, and towards providing the correct solution, I want now to draw certain distinctions. For this purpose I shall, for the remainder of this section, refer to an expression which has a uniquely referring use as "an expression" for short; and to a sentence beginning with such an expression as "a sentence" for short. The distinctions I shall draw are rather rough and ready, and, no doubt, difficult cases could be produced which would call for their refinement. But I think they will serve my purpose. The distinctions are between:

(A1)   a sentence
(A2)   a use of a sentence
(A3)   an utterance of a sentence

and, correspondingly, between:

(B1)   an expression
(B2)   a use of an expression
(B3)   an utterance of an expression

Consider again the sentence, "The king of France is wise." It is easy to imagine that this sentence was uttered at various times from, say, the beginning of the seventeenth century onwards, during the reigns of each successive French monarch; and easy to imagine that it was also uttered during the subsequent periods in which France was not a monarchy. Notice that it was natural for me to speak of "the sentence" or "this sentence" being uttered at various times during this period; or, in other words, that it would be natural and correct to speak of *one and the same* sentence being uttered on all these various occasions. It is in the sense in which it would be correct to speak of one and the same sentence being uttered on all these various occasions that I want to use the expression (A1) "a sentence." There are, however, obvious differences between different *occasions of the use* of this sentence. For instance, if one man uttered it in the reign of Louis XIV and another man uttered it in the reign of Louis XV, it would be natural to say (to assume) that they were respectively talking about different people; and it might be held that the first man, in using the sentence, made a true assertion, while the second man, in using the same sentence, made a false assertion. If on the other hand two different men simultaneously uttered the sentence (e.g. if one wrote it and the other spoke it) during the reign of Louis XIV, it would be natural to say (assume) that they were both talking about the same person, and, in that case, in using the sentence, they *must* either both have made a true assertion or both have made a false assertion. And this illustrates what I mean by *a use* of a sentence. The two men who uttered the sentence, one in the reign of Louis XV and one in the reign of Louis XIV, each made a different use of the same sentence; whereas the two men who uttered the sentence simultaneously in the reign of Louis XIV, made the same use[1] of the same sentence. Obviously in the case of this sentence, and equally obviously in the case of many others, we cannot talk of *the sentence* being true or false, but only of its being used to make a true or false assertion or (if this is preferred) to express a true or a false proposition. And equally obviously we cannot talk of *the sentence* being *about* a particular person, for the same sentence may be used at different times to talk about quite different particular persons, but only of *a use* of the sentence to talk about a particular person. Finally it will make sufficiently clear what I mean by an utterance of a sentence if I say that the two men who simultaneously uttered the sentence in the reign of Louis XIV made two different utterances of the same sentence, though they made the same *use* of the sentence.

If we now consider not the whole sentence, "The king of France is wise," but that part of it which is the expression, "the king of France," it is obvious that we can make analogous, though not identical distinctions between (1) the expression, (2) a use of the expression, and (3) an utterance of the expression. The distinctions will not be identical; we obviously cannot correctly talk of the expression "the king of France" being used to express a true or false proposition, since in general only sentences can be used truly or falsely; and similarly it is only by using a sentence and not by using an expression alone, that you can talk about a particular person. Instead, we shall say in this case that you *use* the expression to *mention* or *refer to* a particular person in the course of using the sentence to talk about him. But obviously in this case, and a great many others, the *expression* (B1) cannot be said to mention, or refer to, anything, any more than the *sentence* can be said to be true or false. The same expression can have different mentioning-uses, as the same sentence can be used to make statements with different truth-values. 'Mentioning', or 'referring', is not something an expression does; it is something that someone can use an expression to do. Mentioning, or referring to, something is a characteristic of *a use* of an expression, just as 'being about' something, and truth-or-falsity, are characteristics of *a use* of a sentence.

A very different example may help to make these distinctions clearer. Consider another case of an expression which has a uniquely referring use, viz. the expression "I"; and consider the sentence, "I am hot." Countless

people may use this same sentence; but it is logically impossible for two different people to make *the same use* of this sentence: or, if this is preferred, to use it to express the same proposition. The expression "I" may correctly be used by (and only by) any one of innumerable people to refer to himself. To say this is to say something about the expression "I": it is, in a sense, to give its meaning. This is the sort of thing that can be said about *expressions*. But it makes no sense to say of the *expression* "I" that it refers to a particular person. This is the sort of thing that can be said only of a particular use of the expression.

Let me use "type" as an abbreviation for "sentence or expression." Then I am not saying that there are sentences and expressions (types), *and* uses of them, *and* utterances of them, as there are ships *and* shoes *and* sealing-wax. I am saying that we cannot say *the same things* about types, uses of types, and utterances of types. And the fact is that we do talk about types; and that confusion is apt to result from the failure to notice the differences between what we can say about these and what we can say only about the *uses* of types. We are apt to fancy we are talking about sentences and expressions when we are talking about the uses of sentences and expressions.

This is what Russell does. Generally, as against Russell, I shall say this. Meaning (in at least one important sense) is a function of the sentence or expression; mentioning and referring and truth or falsity, are functions of the use of the sentence or expression. To give the meaning of an expression (in the sense in which I am using the word) is to give *general directions* for its use to refer to or mention particular objects or persons; to give the meaning of a sentence is to give *general directions* for its use in making true or false assertions. It is not to talk about any particular occasion of the use of the sentence or expression. The meaning of an expression cannot be identified with the object it is used, on a particular occasion, to refer to. The meaning of a sentence cannot be identified with the assertion it is used, on a particular occasion, to make. For to talk about the meaning of an expression or sentence is not to talk about its use on a particular occasion, but about the rules, habits, conventions governing its correct use, on all occasions, to refer or to assert. So the question of whether a sentence or expression *is significant or not* has nothing whatever to do with the question of whether the sentence, *uttered on a particular occasion,* is, on that occasion, being used to make a true-or-false assertion or not, or of whether the expression is, on that occasion, being used to refer to, or mention, anything at all.

The source of Russell's mistake was that he thought that referring or mentioning, if it occurred at all, must be meaning. He did not distinguish (B1) from (B2); he confused expressions with their use in a particular context; and so confused meaning with mentioning, with referring. If I talk about my handkerchief, I can, perhaps, produce the object I am referring to out of my pocket. I cannot produce the meaning of the expression, "my handkerchief," out of my pocket. Because Russell confused meaning with mentioning, he thought that if there were any expressions having a uniquely referring use, which were what they seemed (i.e. logical subjects) and not something else in disguise, their meaning must *be* the particular object which they were used to refer to. Hence the troublesome mythology of the logically proper name. But if someone asks me the meaning of the expression "this"—once Russell's favorite candidate for this status—I do not hand him the object I have just used the expression to refer to, adding at the same time that the meaning of the word changes every time it is used. Nor do I hand him all the objects it ever has been, or might be, used to refer to. I explain and illustrate the conventions governing the use of the expression. This *is* giving the meaning of the expression. It is quite different from giving (in any sense of giving) the object to which it refers; for the expression itself does not refer to anything; though it can be used, on different occasion, to refer to innumerable things. Now as a matter of fact there is, in English, a sense of the word "mean" in which this word does approximate to "indicate, mention or refer to"; e.g. when

somebody (unpleasantly) says, "I mean you"; or when I point and say, "That's the one I mean." But *the one I meant* is quite different from *the meaning of the expression* I used to talk of it. In this special sense of "mean," it is people who mean, not expressions. People use expressions to refer to particular things. But the meaning of an expression is not the set of things or the single thing it may correctly be used to refer to: the meaning is the set of rules, habits, conventions for its use in referring.

It is the same with sentences: even more obviously so. Everyone knows that the sentence, "The table is covered with books," is significant, and everyone knows what it means. But if I ask, "What object is that sentence about?" I am asking an absurd question—a question which cannot be asked about the sentence, but only about some use of the sentence: and in this case the sentence has not been used to talk about something, it has only been taken as an example. In knowing what it means, you are knowing how it could correctly be used to talk about things: so knowing the meaning has nothing to do with knowing about any particular use of the sentence to talk about anything. Similarly, if I ask: "Is the sentence true or false?" I am asking an absurd question, which becomes no less absurd if I add, "It must be one or the other since it is significant." The question is absurd, because the *sentence* is neither true nor false any more than it is *about* some object. Of course the fact that it is significant is the same as the fact that it *can* correctly be used to talk about something and that, in so using it, someone will be making a true or false assertion. And I will add that it will be used to make a true or false assertion *only* if the person using it *is* talking about something. If, when he utters it, he is not talking about anything, then his use is not a genuine one, but a spurious or pseudo-use: he is not making either a true or a false assertion, though he may think he is. And this points the way to the correct answer to the puzzle to which the theory of descriptions gives a fatally incorrect answer. The important point is that the question of whether the sentence is significant or not is quite independent of the question that can be raised about a particular use of it, viz. the question whether it is a genuine or a spurious use, whether it is being used to talk about something, or in make-believe, or as an example in philosophy. The question whether the sentence is significant or not is the question whether there exist such language habits, conventions or rules that the sentence logically could be used to talk about something; and is hence quite independent of the question whether it is being so used on a particular occasion.

III

Consider again the sentence, "The king of France is wise," and the true and false things Russell says about it.

There are at least two true things which Russell would say about the sentence:

(1) The first is that it is significant; that if anyone were now to utter it, he would be uttering a significant sentence.

(2) The second is that anyone now uttering the sentence would be making a true assertion only if there in fact at present existed one and only one king of France, and if he were wise.

What are the false things which Russell would say about the sentence? They are:

(1) That anyone now uttering it would be making a true assertion or a false assertion.

(2) That part of what he would be asserting would be that there at present existed one and only one king of France.

I have already given some reasons for thinking that these two statements are incorrect. Now suppose someone were in fact to say to you with a perfectly serious air: "The king of France is wise." Would you say, "That's untrue"? I think it is quite certain that you would not. But suppose he went on to *ask* you whether you thought that what he had just said was true, or was false; whether you agreed or disagreed with what he had just said. I think you would be inclined, with some hesitation, to say that you did not do either; that the question of whether his statement was true or false simply *did not arise,* because

there was no such person as the king of France. You might, if he were obviously serious (had a dazed astray-in-the-centuries look), say something like: "I'm afraid you must be under a misapprehension. France is not a monarchy. There is no king of France." And this brings out the point that if a man seriously uttered the sentence, his uttering it would in some sense be *evidence* that he *believed* that there was a king of France. It would not be evidence for his believing this simply in the way in which a man's reaching for his raincoat is evidence for his believing that it is raining. But nor would it be evidence for his believing this in the way in which a man's saying, "It's raining," is evidence for his believing that it is raining. We might put it as follows. To say "The king of France is wise" is, in some sense of 'imply', to *imply* that there is a king of France. But this is a very special and odd sense of 'imply'. 'Implies' in this sense is certainly not equivalent to 'entails' (or 'logically implies'). And this comes out from the fact that when, in response to his statement, we say (as we should) "There is no king of France," we should certainly *not* say we were *contradicting* the statement that the king of France is wise. We are certainly not saying that it is false. We are, rather, giving a reason for saying that the question of whether it is true or false simply does not arise.

And this is where the distinction I drew earlier can help us. The sentence, "The king of France is wise," is certainly significant; but this does not mean that any particular use of it is true or false. We use it truly or falsely when we use it to talk about someone; when, in using the expression, "The king of France," we are in fact mentioning someone. The fact that the sentence and the expression, respectively, are significant just is the fact that the sentence *could* be used, in certain circumstances, to say something true or false, that the expression *could* be used, in certain circumstances, to mention a particular person; and to know their meaning is to know what sort of circumstances these are. So when we utter the sentence without in fact mentioning anybody by the use of the phrase, "The king of France," the sentence does not cease to be significant: We simply *fail* to say anything true or false because we simply fail to mention anybody by this particular use of that perfectly significant phrase. It is, if you like, a spurious use of the sentence, and a spurious use of the expression; though we may (or may not) mistakenly think it a genuine use.

And such spurious uses[2] are very familiar. Sophisticated romancing, sophisticated fiction,[3] depend upon them. If I began, "The king of France is wise," and went on, "and he lives in a golden castle and has a hundred wives", and so on, a hearer would understand me perfectly well, without supposing *either* that I was talking about a particular person, *or* that I was making a false statement to the effect that there existed such a person as my words described. (It is worth adding that where the use of sentences and expressions is overtly fictional, the sense of the word "about" may change. As Moore said, it is perfectly natural and correct to say that some of the statements in *Pickwick Papers* are *about* Mr. Pickwick. But where the use of sentences and expressions is not overtly fictional, this use of "about" seems less correct; i.e. it would not *in general* be correct to say that a statement was about Mr. X or the so-and-so, unless there were such a person or thing. So it is where the romancing is in danger of being taken seriously that we might answer the question, "Who is he talking about?" with "He's not talking about anybody"; but, in saying this, we are not saying that what he is saying is either false or nonsense.)

Overtly fictional uses apart, however, I said just now that to use such an expression as "The king of France" at the beginning of a sentence was, in some sense of 'imply', to imply that there was a king of France. When a man uses such an expression, he does not *assert,* nor does what he says *entail,* a uniquely existential proposition. But one of the conventional functions of the definite article is to act as a *signal* that a unique reference is being made—a signal, not a disguised assertion. When we begin a sentence with "the such-and-such" the use of "the" shows, but does not state, that we are, or intended to be,

referring to one particular individual of the species "such-and-such." *Which* particular individual is a matter to be determined from context, time, place, and any other features of the situation of utterance. Now, whenever a man uses any expression, the presumption is that he thinks he is using it correctly: so when he uses the expression, "the such-and-such," in a uniquely referring way, the presumption is that he thinks both that there is *some* individual of that species, and that the context of use will sufficiently determine which one he has in mind. To use the word "the" in this way is then to imply (in the relevant sense of 'imply') that the existential conditions described by Russell are fulfilled. But to use "the" in this way is not to *state* that those conditions are fulfilled. If I begin a sentence with an expression of the form, "the so-and-so," and then am prevented from saying more, I have made no statement of any kind; but I may have succeeded in mentioning someone or something.

The uniquely existential assertion supposed by Russell to be part of any assertion in which a uniquely referring use is made of an expression of the form "the so-and-so" is, he observes, a compound of two assertions. To say that there is a φ is to say something compatible with there being several φs; to say there is not more than one φ is to say something compatible with there being none. To say there is one φ and one only is to compound these two assertions. I have so far been concerned mostly with the alleged assertion of existence and less with the alleged assertion of uniqueness. An example which throws the emphasis on the latter will serve to bring out more clearly the sense of 'implied' in which a uniquely existential assertion is implied, but not entailed, by the use of expressions in the uniquely referring way. Consider the sentence, "The table is covered with books." It is quite certain that in any normal use of this sentence, the expression "the table" would be used to make a unique reference, i.e. to refer to some one table. It is a quite strict use of the definite article, in the sense in which Russell talks on p. 30 of *Principia Mathematica,* of using the article "*strictly,* so as to imply uniqueness." On the same page Russell says that a phrase of the form "the so-and-so," used strictly, "will only have an application in the event of there being one so-and-so and no more." Now it is obviously quite false that the phrase "the table" in the sentence "the table is covered with books," used normally, will "only have an application in the event of there being one table and no more." It is indeed tautologically true that, in such a use, the phrase will have an application only in the event of there being one table and no more *which is being referred to,* and that it will be understood to have an application only in the event of there being one table and no more which it is understood as being used to refer to. To use the sentence is not to assert, but it is (in the special sense discussed) to imply, that there is only one thing which is *both* of the kind specified (i.e. a table) *and is being referred to* by the speaker. It is obviously not to assert this. To refer is not to say you are referring. To say there is *some table or other* to which you are referring is not the same as referring to a particular table. We should have no use for such phrases as "the individual I referred to" unless there were something which counted as referring. (It would make no sense to say you had pointed if there were nothing which counted as pointing.) So once more I draw the conclusion that referring to or mentioning a particular thing cannot be dissolved into any kind of assertion. To refer is not to assert, though you refer in order to go on to assert.

Let me now take an example of the uniquely referring use of an expression not of the form, "the so-and-so." Suppose I advance my hands, cautiously cupped, towards someone, saying, as I do so, "This is a fine red one." He, looking into my hands and seeing nothing there, may say: "What is? What are you talking about?" Or perhaps, "But there's nothing in your hands." Of course it would be absurd to say that, in saying "But you've got nothing in your hands," he was *denying* or *contradicting* what I said. So "this" is not a disguised description in Russell's sense. Nor is it a logically proper name. For one must know what the sentence means in order to react in that way to the utterance of it. It is precisely because the significance of the word "this" is independent of any particular reference it may be used to make, though not independent of the way it may be used to refer, that I can, as in this example, use it to *pretend* to be referring to something.

The general moral of all this is that communication is much less a matter of explicit or disguised assertion than logicians used to suppose. The particular application of this general moral in which I am interested is its application to the case of making a unique reference. It is a part of the significance of expressions of the kind I am discussing that they can be used, in an immense variety of contexts, to make unique references. It is no part of their significance to assert that they are being so used or that the conditions of their being so used are fulfilled. So the wholly important distinction we are required to draw is between

(1) using an expression to make a unique reference; and
(2) asserting that there is one and only one individual which has certain characteristics (e.g. is of a certain kind, or stands in a certain relation to the speaker, or both).

This is, in other words, the distinction between

(1) sentences containing an expression used to indicate or mention or refer to a particular person or thing; and
(2) uniquely existential sentences.

What Russell does is progressively to assimilate more and more sentences of class (1) to sentences of class (2), and consequently to involve himself in insuperable difficulties about logical subjects, and about values for individual variables generally: difficulties which have led him finally to the logically disastrous theory of names developed in the *Enquiry into Meaning and Truth* and in *Human Knowledge.* That view of the meaning of logical-subject-expressions which provides the whole incentive to the Theory of Descriptions at the same time precludes the possibility of Russell's ever finding any satisfactory substitutes for those expressions which, beginning with substantival phrases, he progressively degrades from the status of logical subjects.[4] It is not simply, as is sometimes said, the fascination of the relation between a name and its bearer, that is the root of the trouble. Not even names come up to the impossible standard set. It is rather the combination of two more radical misconceptions: first, the failure to grasp the importance of the distinction (section II above) between what may be said of an expression and what may be said of a particular use of it; second, a failure to recognize the uniquely referring use of expressions for the harmless, necessary thing it is, distinct from, but complementary to, the predicative or ascriptive use of expressions. The expressions which can in fact occur as singular logical subjects are expressions of the class I listed at the outset (demonstratives, substantival phrases, proper names, pronouns): to say this is to say that these expressions, together with context (in the widest sense), are what one uses to make unique references. The point of the conventions governing the uses of such expressions is, along with the situation of utterance, to secure uniqueness of reference. But to do this, enough is enough. We do not, and we cannot, while referring, attain the point of complete explicitness at which the referring function is no longer performed. The actual unique reference made, if any, is a matter of the particular use in the particular context; the significance of the expression used is the set of rules or conventions which permit such references to be made. Hence we can, using significant expressions, pretend to refer, in make-believe or in fiction, or mistakenly think we are referring when we are not referring to anything.[5]

This shows the need for distinguishing two kinds (among many others) of linguistic conventions or rules: rules for referring, and rules for attributing and ascribing; and for an investigation of the former. If we recognize this distinction of use for what it is, we are on the way to solving a number of ancient logical and metaphysical puzzles.

My last two sections are concerned, but only in the barest outline, with these questions.

IV

One of the main purposes for which we use language is the purpose of stating facts about things and persons and events. If we want to fulfill this purpose we must have some way of forestalling the question, "What (who, which one) are you talking about?" as well as the question, "What are you saying about it (him, her)?" The task of forestalling the first question is the referring (or identifying) task. The task of forestalling the second is the attributive (or descriptive or classificatory or ascriptive) task. In the conventional English sentence which is used to state, or to claim to state, a fact about an individual thing or person or event, the performance of these two tasks can be roughly and approximately assigned to separable expressions.[6] And in such a sentence, this assigning of expressions to their separate rôles corresponds to the conventional grammatical classification of subject and predicate. There is nothing sacrosanct about the employment of separable expressions for these two tasks. Other methods could be, and are, employed. There is, for instance, the method of uttering a single word or attributive phrase in the conspicuous presence of the object referred to; or that analogous method exemplified by, e.g., the painting of the words "unsafe for lorries" on a bridge, or the tying of a label reading "first prize" on a vegetable marrow. Or one can imagine an elaborate game in which one never used an expression in the uniquely referring way at all, but uttered only uniquely existential sentences, trying to enable the hearer to identify what was being talked of by means of an accumulation of relative clauses. (This description of the purposes of the game shows in what sense it would be a game: this is not the normal use we make of existential sentences.) Two points require emphasis. The first is that the necessity of performing these two tasks in order to state particular facts requires no transcendental explanation: To call attention to it is partly to elucidate the meaning of the phrase, "stating a fact." The second is that even this elucidation is made in terms derivative from the grammar of the conventional singular sentence; that even the overtly functional, linguistic distinction between the identifying and attributive rôles that words may play in language is prompted by the fact that ordinary speech offers us separable expressions to which the different functions may be plausibly and approximately assigned. And this functional distinction has cast long philosophical shadows. The distinctions between particular and universal, between substance and quality, are such pseudo-material shadows, cast by the grammar of the conventional sentence, in which separable expressions play distinguishable rôles.[7]

To use a separate expression to perform the first of these tasks is to use an expression in the uniquely referring way. I want now to say something in general about the conventions of use for expressions used in this way, and to contrast them with conventions of ascriptive use. I then proceed to the brief illustration of these general remarks and to some further applications of them.

What in general is required for making a unique reference is, obviously, some device, or devices, for showing both *that* a unique reference is intended and *what* unique reference it is; some device requiring and enabling the hearer or reader to identify what is being talked about. In securing this result, the context of utterance is of an importance which it is almost impossible to exaggerate; and by "context" I mean, at least, the time, the place, the situation, the identity of the speaker, the subjects which form the immediate focus of interest, and the personal histories of both the speaker and those he is addressing. Besides context, there is, of course, convention—linguistic convention. But, except in the case of genuine proper names, of which I shall have more to say later, the fulfillment of more or less precisely stateable contextual conditions is *conventionally* (or, in a wide sense of the word, *logically*) required for the correct referring use of expressions in a sense in which this is not true of correct ascriptive uses. The requirement for

the correct application of an expression in its ascriptive use to a certain thing is simply that the thing should be of a certain kind, have certain characteristics. The requirement for the correct application of an expression in its referring use to a certain thing is something over and above any requirement derived from such ascriptive meaning as the expression may have; it is, namely, the requirement that the thing should be in a certain relation to the speaker and to the context of utterance. Let me call this the contextual requirement. Thus, for example, in the limiting case of the word "I" the contextual requirement is that the thing should be identical with the speaker; but in the case of most expressions which have a referring use this requirement cannot be so precisely specified. A further, and perfectly general, difference between conventions for referring and conventions for describing is one we have already encountered, viz. that the fulfillment of the conditions for a correct ascriptive use of an expression is a part of what is stated by such a use; but the fulfillment of the conditions for a correct referring use of an expression is never part of what is stated, though it is (in the relevant sense of 'implied') implied by such a use.

Conventions for referring have been neglected or misinterpreted by logicians. The reasons for this neglect are not hard to see, though they are hard to state briefly. Two of them are, roughly: (1) the preoccupation of most logicians with definitions; (2) the preoccupation of some logicians with formal systems.

(1) A definition, in the most familiar sense, is a specification of the conditions of the correct ascriptive or classificatory use of an expression. Definitions take no account of contextual requirements. So that in so far as the search for the meaning or the search for the analysis of an expression is conceived as the search for a definition, the neglect or misinterpretation of conventions other than ascriptive is inevitable. Perhaps it would be better to say (for I do not wish to legislate about "meaning" or "analysis") that logicians have failed to notice that problems of use are wider than problems of analysis and meaning.

(2) The influence of the preoccupation with mathematics and formal logic is most clearly seen (to take no more recent examples) in the cases of Leibniz and Russell. The constructor of calculuses, not concerned or required to make factual statements, approaches applied logic with a prejudice. It is natural that he should assume that the types of convention with whose adequacy in one field he is familiar should be really adequate, if only one could see how, in a quite different field—that of statements of fact. Thus we have Leibniz striving desperately to make the uniqueness of unique references a matter of logic in the narrow sense, and Russell striving desperately to do the same thing, in a different way, both for the implication of uniqueness and for that of existence.

It should be clear that the distinction I am trying to draw is primarily one between different roles or parts that expressions may play in language, and not primarily one between different groups of expressions; for some expressions may appear in either role. Some of the kinds of words I shall speak of have predominantly, if not exclusively, a referring role. This is most obviously true of pronouns and ordinary proper names. Some can occur as wholes or parts of expressions which have a predominantly referring use, and as wholes or parts of expressions which have a predominantly ascriptive or classificatory use. The obvious cases are common nouns; or common nouns preceded by adjectives, including participial adjectives; or, less obviously, adjectives or participial adjectives alone. Expressions capable of having a referring use also differ from one another in at least the three following, not mutually independent, ways.

(1) They differ in the extent to which the reference they are used to make is dependent on the context of their utterance. Words like "I" and "it" stand at one end of this scale—the end of maximum dependence—and phrases like "the author of *Waverley*" and "the eighteenth king of France" at the other.

(2) They differ in the degree of 'descriptive meaning' they possess: by 'descriptive meaning' I intend 'conventional limitation, in application, to things of a certain general kind, or possessing certain general characteristics'. At one end of this scale stand the proper names we most commonly use in ordinary discourse; men, dogs, and motor-bicycles may be called "Horace." The pure name has no descriptive meaning (except such as it may acquire *as a result of* some one of its use as a name). A word like "he" has minimal descriptive meaning, but has some. Substantival phrases like "the round table" have the maximum descriptive meaning. An interesting intermediate position is occupied by 'impure' proper names like "The Round Table"—substantival phrases which have grown capital letters.

(3) Finally, they may be divided into the following two classes: (i) those of which the correct referring use is regulated by some *general* referring-cum-ascriptive conventions; (ii) those of which the correct referring use is regulated by no general conventions, either of the contextual or the ascriptive kind, but by conventions which are ad hoc for each particular use (though not for each particular utterance). To the first class belong both pronouns (which have the least descriptive meaning) and substantival phrases (which have the most). To the second class belong, roughly speaking, the most familiar kind of proper names. Ignorance of a man's name is not ignorance of the language. This is why we do not speak of the meaning of proper names. (But it won't do to say they are meaningless.) Again an intermediate position is occupied by such phrases as "The Old Pretender." Only an old pretender may be so referred to; but to know which old pretender is not to know a general, but an ad hoc, convention.

In the case of phrases of the form "the so-and-so" used referringly, the use of "the" together with the position of the phrase in the sentence (i.e. at the beginning, or following a transitive verb or preposition) acts as a signal *that* a unique reference is being made; and the following noun, or noun and adjective, together with the context of utterance, shows *what* unique reference is being made. In general the functional difference between common nouns and adjective is that the former are naturally and commonly used referringly, while the latter are not commonly, or so naturally, used in this way, except as qualifying nouns; though they can be, and are, so used alone. And of course this functional difference is not independent of the descriptive force peculiar to each word. In general we should expect the descriptive force of nouns to be such that they are more efficient tools for the job of showing what unique reference is intended when such a reference is signalized; and we should also expect the descriptive force of the words we naturally and commonly use to make unique references to mirror our interest in the salient, relatively permanent and behavioral characteristics of things. These two expectations are not independent of one another; and, if we look at the differences between the commoner sort of common nouns and the commoner sort of adjectives, we find them both fulfilled. These are differences of the kind that Locke quaintly reports, when he speaks of our ideas of substances being *collections* of simple ideas; when he says that "powers make up a great part of our ideas of substances"; and when he goes on to contrast the identity of real and nominal essence in the case of simple ideas with their lack of identity and the shiftingness of the nominal essence in the case of substances. 'Substance' itself is the troublesome tribute Locke pays to his dim awareness of the difference in predominant linguistic function that lingered even when the noun had been expanded into a more or less indefinite string of adjectives. Russell repeats Locke's mistake with a difference when, admitting the inference from syntax to reality to the extent of feeling that he can get rid of this metaphysical unknown only if he can purify language of the referring function altogether, he draws up his program for "abolishing particulars"; a programme, in fact, for abolishing the distinction of logical use which I am here at pains to emphasize.

The contextual requirement for the referring use of pronouns may be stated with the greatest precision in some cases (e.g. "I" and "you") and only with the greatest vagueness in others ("it" and "this"). I propose to say nothing further about pronouns, except to

point to an additional symptom of the failure to recognize the uniquely referring use for what it is; the fact, namely, that certain logicians have actually sought to elucidate the nature of a variable by offering such *sentences* as "he is sick," "it is green," as examples of something in ordinary speech like a *sentential function*. Now of course it is true that the word "he" may be used on different occasions to refer to different people or different animals: so may the word "John" and the phrase "the cat." What deters such logicians from treating these two expressions as quasi-variables is, in the first case, the lingering superstition that a name is logically tied to a single individual, and, in the second case, the descriptive meaning of the word "cat." But "he," which has a wide range of applications and minimal descriptive force, only acquires a use as a referring word. It is this fact, together with the failure to accord to expressions, used referringly, the place in logic which belongs to them (the place held open for the mythical logically proper name), that accounts for the misleading attempt to elucidate the nature of the variable by reference to such words as "he," "she," "it."

Of ordinary proper names it is sometimes said that they are essentially words each of which is used to refer to just one individual. This is obviously false. Many ordinary personal names—names *par excellence*—are correctly used to refer to numbers of people. An ordinary personal name is, roughly, a word, used referringly, of which the use is *not* dictated by any descriptive meaning the word may have, and is *not* prescribed by any such general rule for use as a referring expression (or a part of a referring expression) as we find in the case of such words as "I," "this" and "the," but is governed by ad hoc conventions for each particular set of applications of the word to a given person. The important point is that the correctness of such applications does not follow from any *general* rule or convention for the use of the word as such. (The limit of absurdity and obvious circularity is reached in the attempt to treat names as disguised description in Russell's sense; for what is in the special sense implied, but not entailed, by my now referring to someone by name is simply the existence of someone, *now being referred to,* who is *conventionally referred to* by that name) Even this feature of names, however, is only a symptom of the purpose for which they are employed. At present our choice of names is partly arbitrary, partly dependent on legal and social observances. It would be perfectly possible to have a thorough-going *system* of names, based e.g. on dates of birth, or on a minute classification of physiological and anatomical differences. But the success of any such system would depend entirely on the convenience of the resulting name-allotments for the purpose of making unique references; and this would depend on the multiplicity of the classifications used and the degree to which they cut haphazardly across normal social groupings. Given a sufficient degree of both, the selectivity supplied by context would do the rest; just as in the case with our present naming habits. Had we such a system, we could use name-words descriptively (as we do at present, to a limited extent and in a different way, with some famous names) as well as referringly. But it is by criteria derived from consideration of the requirements of the referring task that we should assess the adequacy of any system of naming. From the naming point of view, no kind of classification would be better or worse than any other simply because of the kind of classification—natal or anatomical—that it was.

I have already mentioned the class of quasi-names, of substantival phrases which grow capital letters, and of which such phrases as "the Glorious Revolution," "the Great War," "the Annunciation," "the Round Table" are examples. While the descriptive meaning of the words which follow the definite article is still relevant to their referring role, the capital letters are a sign of that extralogical selectivity in their referring use, which is characteristic of pure names. Such phrases are found in print or in writing when one member of some class of events or things is of quite outstanding interest in a certain society. These phrases are embryonic names. A phrase may, for obvious reasons, pass into, and out of, this class (e.g. "the Great War").

V

I want to conclude by considering, all too briefly, three further problems about referring uses.

(a) *Indefinite references:* Not all referring uses of singular expressions forestall the question "What (who, which one) are you talking about?" There are some which either invite this question, or disclaim the intention or ability to answer it. Examples are such sentence-beginnings as "A man told me that . . . ," "Someone told me that . . . " The orthodox (Russellian) doctrine is that such sentences are existential, but not uniquely existential. This seems wrong in several ways. It is ludicrous to suggest that part of what is asserted is that the class of men or persons is not empty. Certainly this is *implied* in the by now familiar sense of implication; but the implication is also as much an implication of the *uniqueness* of the particular object of reference as when I begin a sentence with such a phrase as "the table." The difference between the use of the definite and indefinite articles is, very roughly, as follows. We use "the" either when a previous reference has been made, and when "the" signalizes that the same reference is being made; or when, in the absence of a previous indefinite reference, the context (including the hearer's assumed knowledge) is expected to enable the hearer to tell *what* reference is being made. We use "a" either when these conditions are not fulfilled, or when, although a definite reference *could* be made, we wish to keep dark the identity of the individual to whom, or to which, we are referring. This is the *arch* use of such a phrase as "a certain person" or "someone"; where it could be expanded, not into "someone, but you wouldn't (or I don't) know who" but into "someone, but I'm not telling you who."

(b) *Identification statements:* By this label I intend statements like the following:

(i*a*)   That is the man who swam the channel twice on one day.

(ii*a*) Napoleon was the man who ordered the execution of the Duc d'Enghien.

The puzzle about these statements is that their grammatical predicates do not seem to be used in a straightforwardly ascriptive way as are the grammatical predicates of the statements:

(i*b*) That man swam the channel twice in one day.

(ii*b*) Napoleon ordered the execution of the Duc d'Enghien.

But if, in order to avoid blurring the difference between (i*a*) and (i*b*) and (ii*a*) and (ii*b*), one says that the phrases which form the grammatical complements of (i*a*) and (ii*a*) are being used referringly, one becomes puzzled about what is being said in these sentences. We seem then to be referring to the same person twice over and either saying nothing about him and thus making no statement, or identifying him with himself and thus producing a trivial identity.

The bogy of triviality can be dismissed. This only arises for those who think of the object referred to by the use of an expression as its meaning, and thus think of the subject and complement of these sentences as meaning the same because they could be used to refer to the same person.

I think the differences between sentences in the (*a*) group and sentences in the (*b*) group can best be understood by considering the differences between the circumstances in which you would say (i*a*) and the circumstances in which you would say (i*b*). You would say (i*a*) instead of (i*b*) if you knew or believed that your hearer knew or believed that *someone* had swum the channel twice in one day. You say (i*a*) when you take your hearer to be in the position of one who can ask: "Who swam the channel twice in one day?" (And in asking this, he is not saying that anyone did, though his asking it implies—in the relevant sense—that someone did.) Such sentences are like answers to such questions. They are better called 'identification-statements' than 'identities'. Sentence (i*a*) does not assert more or less than sentence (i*b*). It is just that you say (i*a*) to a man whom you take to know certain things that you take to be unknown to the man to whom you say (i*b*).

This is, in the barest essentials, the solution to Russell's puzzle about 'denoting phrases' joined by "is"; one of the puzzles which he claims for the theory of descriptions the merit of solving.

(3) *The logic of subjects and predicates:* Much of what I have said of the uniquely referring use of expressions can be extended, with suitable modifications, to the non-uniquely referring use of expressions; i.e. to some uses of expressions consisting of "the," "all the," "all," "some," "some of the," etc. followed by a noun, qualified or unqualified, in the *plural;* to some uses of "they," "them," "those," "these"; and to conjunctions of names. Expressions of the first kind have a special interest. Roughly speaking, orthodox modern criticism, inspired by mathematical logic, of such traditional doctrines as that of the Square of Opposition and of some of the forms of the syllogism traditionally recognized as valid, rests on the familiar failure to recognize the special sense in which existential assertions may be implied by the referring use of expressions. The universal propositions of the fourfold schedule, it is said, must *either* be given a negatively existential interpretation (e.g. for A, "there are no Xs which are not Ys") *or* they must be interpreted as conjunctions of negatively and positively existential statements of, e.g., the form (for A) "there are no Xs which are not Ys, and there are Xs." The I and O forms are normally given a positively existential interpretation. It is then seen that, whichever of the above alternatives is selected, some of the traditional laws have to be abandoned. The dilemma, however, is a bogus one. If we interpret the propositions of the schedule as neither positively, nor negatively, nor positively *and* negatively, existential, but as sentences such that *the question of whether they are being used to make true or false assertions does not arise except when the existential condition is fulfilled for the subject term,* then all the traditional laws hold good together. And this interpretation is far closer to the most common uses of expressions beginning with "all" and "some" than is any Russellian alternative. For these expressions are most commonly used in the referring way.

A literal-minded and childless man asked whether all his children are asleep will certainly not answer "Yes" on the ground that he has none; but nor will he answer "No" on this ground. Since he has no children, the question does not arise. To say this is not to say that I may not use the sentence, "All my children are asleep," with the intention of letting someone know that I have children, or of deceiving him into thinking that I have. Nor is it any weakening of my thesis to concede that singular phrases of the form "the so-and-so" may sometimes be used with a similar purpose. Neither Aristotelian nor Russellian rules give the exact logic of any expression of ordinary language; for ordinary language has no exact logic.

NOTES

1. This usage of "use" is, of course, different from (a) the current usage in which 'use' (of a particular word, phrase, sentence) = (roughly) 'rules for using' = (roughly) 'meaning'; and from (b) my own usage in the phrase "uniquely referring use of expressions" in which "use" = (roughly) 'way of using'.

[2. The choice of the word "spurious" now seems to me unfortunate, at least for some nonstandard uses. I should now prefer to call some of these "secondary" uses.]

3. The unsophisticated kind begins: "Once upon time there was . . ."

4. And this in spite of the danger-signal of that phrase, "*misleading* grammatical form."

[5. This sentence now seems to me objectionable in a number of ways, notably because of an unexplicitly restrictive use of the word 'refer'. It could be more exactly phrased as follows: 'Hence we can, using significant expressions, refer in secondary ways, as in make-believe or in fiction, or mistakenly think we are referring to something in the primary way when we are not, in that way, referring to anything'.]

6. I neglect relational sentences; for these require, not a modification in the principle of what I say, but a complication of the detail.

[7. What is said or implied in the last two sentences of this paragraph no longer seems to me true, unless considerably qualified.]

Reference
and Definite Descriptions
19

KEITH DONNELLAN

Definite descriptions, I shall argue, have two possible functions. They are used to refer to what a speaker wishes to talk about, but they are also used quite differently. Moreover, a definite description occurring in one and the same sentence may, on different occasions of its use, function in either way. The failure to deal with this duality of function obscures the genuine referring use of definite descriptions. The best-known theories of definite descriptions, those of Russell and Strawson, I shall suggest, are both guilty of this. Before discussing this distinction in use, I will mention some features of these theories to which it is especially relevant.

On Russell's view a definite description may denote an entity: "if 'C' is a denoting phrase [as definite descriptions are by definition], it may happen that there is one entity x (there cannot be more than one) for which the proposition 'x is identical with C' is true. . . . We may then say that the entity x is the denotation of the phrase 'C.' "[1] In using a definite description, then, a speaker may use an expression which denotes some entity, but this is the only relationship between that entity and the use of the definite description recognized by Russell. I shall argue, however, that there are two uses of definite descriptions. The definition of denotation given by Russell is applicable to both, but in one of

these the definite description serves to do something more. I shall say that in this use the speaker uses the definite description to *refer* to something, and call this use the "referential use" of a definite description. Thus, if I am right, referring is not the same as denoting and the referential use of definite descriptions is not recognized on Russell's view.

Furthermore, on Russell's view the type of expression that comes closest to performing the function of the referential use of definite descriptions turns out, as one might suspect, to be a proper name (in "the narrow logical sense"). Many of the things said about proper names by Russell can, I think, be said about the referential use of definite descriptions without straining senses unduly. Thus the gulf Russell thought he saw between names and definite descriptions is narrower than he thought.

Strawson, on the other hand, certainly does recognize a referential use of definite definitions. But what I think he did not see is that a definite description may have a quite different role—may be used nonreferentially, even as it occurs in one and the same sentence. Strawson, it is true, points out nonreferential uses of definite descriptions,[2] but which use a definite description has seems to be for him a function of the kind of sentence in which it occurs; whereas, if I am right, there can be

From *Philosophical Review*, 75 (1966), pp. 281–304.

two possible uses of a definite description in the same sentence. Thus, in "On Referring," he says, speaking of expressions used to refer, "Any expression of any of these classes [one being that of definite descriptions] can occur as the subject of what would traditionally be regarded as a singular subject-predicate sentence; and would, so occurring, exemplify the use I wish to discuss."[3] So the definite description in, say, the sentence "The Republican candidate for president in 1968 will be a conservative" presumably exemplifies the referential use. But if I am right, we could not say this of the sentence in isolation from some particular occasion on which it is used to state something; and then it might or might not turn out that the definite description has a referential use.

Strawson and Russell seem to me to make a common assumption here about the question of how definite descriptions function: that we can ask how a definite description functions in some sentence independently of a particular occasion upon which it is used. This assumption is not really rejected in Strawson's arguments against Russell. Although he can sum up his position by saying, " 'Mentioning' or 'referring' is not something an expression does; it is something that someone can use an expression to do,"[4] he means by this to deny the radical view that a "genuine" referring expression *has* a referent, functions to refer, independent of the context of some use of the expression. The denial of this view, however, does not entail that definite descriptions cannot be identified as referring expressions in a sentence unless the sentence is being used. Just as we can speak of a function of a tool that is not at the moment performing its function, Strawson's view, I believe, allows us to speak of the referential function of a definite description in a sentence even when it is not being used. This, I hope to show, is a mistake.

A second assumption shared by Russell's and Strawson's account of definite descriptions is this. In many cases a person who uses a definite descriptions can be said (in some sense) to presuppose or imply that something fits the description.[5] If I state that the king is

on his throne, I presuppose or imply that there is a king. (At any rate, this would be a natural thing to say for anyone who doubted that there is a king.) Both Russell and Strawson assume that where the presupposition or implication is false, the truth value of what the speaker says is affected. For Russell the statement made is false; for Strawson it has no truth value. Now if there are two uses of definite descriptions, it may be that the truth value is affected differently in each case by the falsity of the presupposition or implication. This is what I shall in fact argue. It will turn out, I believe, that one or the other of the two views, Russell's or Strawon's, may be correct about the nonreferential use of definite descriptions, but neither fits the referential use. This is not so surprising about Russell's view, since he did not recognize this use in any case, but it is surprising about Strawson's since the referential use is what he tries to explain and defend. Furthermore, on Strawson's account, the result of there being nothing which fits the description is a failure of reference.[6] This too, I believe, turns out not to be true about the referential use of definite descriptions.

II

There are some uses of definite descriptions which carry neither any hint of a referential use nor any presupposition or implication that something fits the description. In general, it seems, these are recognizable from the sentence frame in which the description occurs. These uses will not interest us, but it is necessary to point them out if only to set them aside.

An obvious example would be the sentence "The present King of France does not exist," used, say, to correct someone's mistaken impression that de Gaulle is the King of France.

A more interesting example is this. Suppose someone were to ask, "Is de Gaulle the King of France?" This is the natural form of words for a person to use who is in doubt as to whether de Gaulle is King or President of France. Given this background to the question, there seems to be no presupposition or implication that someone is the King of France. Nor is the person attempting to refer to someone by using the definite description. On the other hand, reverse the name and description in the question and the speaker probably would be thought to presuppose or imply this. "Is the King of France de Gaulle?" is the natural question for one to ask who wonders whether it is de Gaulle rather than someone else who occupies the throne of France.[7]

Many times, however, the use of a definite description does carry a presupposition or implication that something fits the description. If definite descriptions do have a referring role, it will be here. But it is a mistake, I think, to try, as I believe both Russell and Strawson do, to settle this matter without further ado. What is needed, I believe, is the distinction I will now discuss.

III

I will call the two uses of definite descriptions I have in mind the attributive use and the referential use. A speaker who uses a definite description attributively in an assertion states something about whoever or whatever is the so-and-so. A speaker who uses a definite description referentially in an assertion, on the other hand, uses the description to enable his audience to pick out whom or what he is talking about and states something about that person or thing. In the first case the definite description might be said to occur essentially, for the speaker wishes to assert something about whatever or whoever fits that description; but in the referential use the definite description is merely one tool for doing a certain job—calling attention to a person or thing—and in general any other device for doing the same job, another description or a name, would do as well. In the attributive use, the attribute of being the so-and-so is all important, while it is not in the referential use.

To illustrate this distinction, in the case of a single sentence, consider the sentence, "Smith's murderer is insane." Suppose first

that we come upon poor Smith foully murdered. From the brutal manner of the killing and the fact that Smith was the most lovable person in the world, we might exclaim, "Smith's murderer is insane." I will assume, to make it a simpler case, that in a quite ordinary sense we do not know who murdered Smith (though this is not in the end essential to the case). This, I shall say, is an attributive use of the definite description.

The contrast with such a use of the sentence is one of those situations in which we expect and intend our audience to realize whom we have in mind when we speak of Smith's murderer and, most importantly, to know that it is this person about whom we are going to say something.

For example, suppose that Jones has been charged with Smith's murder and has been placed on trial. Imagine that there is a discussion of Jones's odd behavior at his trial. We might sum up our impression of his behavior by saying, "Smith's murderer is insane." If someone asks to whom we are referring, by using this description, the answer here is "Jones." This, I shall say, is a referential use of the definite description.

That these two uses of the definite description in the same sentence are really quite different can perhaps best be brought out by considering the consequences of the assumption that Smith had no murderer (for example, he in fact committed suicide). In both situations, in using the definite description "Smith's murderer," the speaker in some sense presupposes or implies that there is a murderer. But when we hypothesize that the presupposition or implication is false, there are different results for the two uses. In both cases we have used the predicate "is insane," but in the first case, if there is no murderer, there is no person of whom it could be correctly said that we attributed insanity to him. Such a person could be identified (correctly) only in case someone fitted the description used. But in the second case, where the definite description is simply a means of identifying the person we want to talk about, it is quite possible for the correct identification to be made even though no one fits the description we used.[8] We were speaking about Jones even though he is not in fact Smith's murderer and, in the circumstances imagined, it was his behavior we were commenting upon. Jones might, for example, accuse us of saying false things of him in calling him insane and it would be no defense, I should think, that our description, "the murderer of Smith," failed to fit him.

It is, moreover, perfectly possible for our audience to know to whom we refer, in the second situation, even though they do not share our presupposition. A person hearing our comment in the context imagined might know we are talking about Jones even though he does not think Jones guilty.

Generalizing from this case, we can say, I think, that there are two uses of sentences of the form, "The φ is ψ." In the first, if nothing is the φ then nothing has been said to be ψ. In the second, the fact that nothing is the φ does not have this consequence.

With suitable changes the same difference in use can be formulated for uses of language other than assertions. Suppose one is at a party and, seeing an interesting-looking person holding a martini glass, one asks, "Who is the man drinking a martini?" If it should turn out that there is only water in the glass, one has nevertheless asked a question about a particular person, a question that it is possible for someone to answer. Contrast this with the use of the same question by the chairman of the local Teetotalers Union. He has just been informed that a man is drinking a martini at their annual party. He responds by asking his informant, "Who is the man drinking a martini?" In asking the question the chairman does not have some particular person in mind about whom he asks the question; if no one is drinking a martini, if the information is wrong, no person can be singled out as the person about whom the question was asked. Unlike the first case, the attribute of being the man drinking a martini is all-important, because if it is the attribute of no one, the chairman's question has no straight-forward answer.

This illustrates also another difference between the referential and the attributive use of definite descriptions. In the one case we have asked a question about a particular person or thing even though nothing fits the description we used; in the other this is not so. But also in the one case our question can be answered; in the other it cannot be. In the referential use of a definite description we may succeed in picking out a person or thing to ask a question about even though he or it does not really fit the description; but in the attributive use if nothing fits the description, no straightforward answer to the question can be given.

This further difference is also illustrated by commands or orders containing definite descriptions. Consider the order, "Bring me the book on the table." If "the book on the table" is being used referentially, it is possible to fulfill the order even though there is no book on the table. If, for example, there is a book *beside* the table, though there is none *on* it, one might bring that book back and ask the issuer of the order whether this is "the book you meant." And it may be. But imagine we are told that someone has laid a book on our prize antique table, where nothing should be put. The order, "Bring me the book on the table" cannot now be obeyed unless there is a book that has been placed on the table. There is no possibility of bringing back a book which was never on the table and having it be the one that was meant, because there is no book that in that sense was "meant." In the one case the definite description was a device for getting the other person to pick the right book; if he is able to pick the right book even though it does not satisfy the description, one still succeeds in his purpose. In the other case, there is, antecedently, no "right book" except one which fits the description; the attribute of being the book on the table is essential. Not only is there no book about which an order was issued, if there is no book on the table, but the order itself cannot be obeyed. When a definite description is used attributively in a command or question and nothing fits the description, the command cannot be obeyed and the question cannot be answered. This suggests some analogous consequence for assertions containing definite descriptions used attributively. Perhaps the analogous result is that the assertion is neither true nor false: this is Strawson's view of what happens when the presupposition of the use of a definite description is false. But if so, Strawson's view works not for definite descriptions used referentially, but for the quite different use, which I have called the attributive use.

I have tried to bring out the two uses of definite descriptions by pointing out the different consequences of supposing that nothing fits the description used. There are still other differences. One is this: when a definite description is used referentially, not only is there in some sense a presupposition or implication that someone or something fits the description, as there is also in the attributive use, but there is a quite different presupposition; the speaker presupposes of some *particular* someone or something that he or it fits the description. In asking, for example, "Who is the man drinking a martini?" where we mean to ask a question about that man over there, we are presupposing that that man over there is drinking a martini—not just that *someone* is a man drinking a martini. When we say, in a context where it is clear we are referring to Jones, "Smith's murderer is insane," we are presupposing that Jones is Smith's murderer. No such presupposition is present in the attributive use of definite descriptions. There is, of course, the presupposition that someone *or other* did the murder, but the speaker does not presuppose of someone in particular— Jones or Robinson, say—that he did it. What I mean by this second kind of presupposition that someone or something in particular fits the description—which is present in a referential use but not in an attributive use—can perhaps be seen more clearly by considering a member of the speaker's audience who believes that Smith was not murdered at all. Now in the case of the referential use of the description, "Smith's murderer," he could accuse the speaker of mistakenly presupposing both that someone or other is the murderer and that also Jones is the murderer, for even though he believes Jones not to have done the deed, he knows that the speaker was referring to Jones. But in the case of the

attributive use, he can accuse the speaker of having only the first, less specific presupposition; he cannot pick out some person and claim that the speaker is presupposing that that person is Smith's murderer. Now the more particular presuppositions that we find present in referential uses are clearly not ones we can assign to a definite description in some particular sentence in isolation from a context of use. In order to know that a person presupposes that Jones is Smith's murderer in using the sentence "Smith's murderer is insane," we have to know that he is using the description referentially and also to whom he is referring. The sentence by itself does not tell us any of this.

IV

From the way in which I set up each of the previous examples it might be supposed that the important difference between the referential and the attributive use lies in the beliefs of the speaker. Does he believe of some particular person or thing that he or it fits the description used? In the Smith murder example, for instance, there was in the one case no belief as to who did the deed, whereas in the contrasting case it was believed that Jones did it. But this is, in fact, not an essential difference. It is possible for a definite description to be used attributively even though the speaker (and his audience) believes that a certain person or thing fits the description. And it is possible for a definite description to be used referentially where the speaker believes that nothing fits the description. It is true—and this is why, for simplicity, I set up the examples the way I did—that if a speaker does not believe that anything fits the description or does not believe that he is in a position to pick out what does fit the description, it is likely that he is not using it referentially. It is also true that if he and his audience would pick out some particular thing or person as fitting the description, then a use of the definite description is very likely referential. But these are only presumptions and not entailments.

To use the Smith murder case again,

suppose that Jones is on trial for the murder and I and everyone else believe him guilty. Suppose that I comment that the murderer of Smith is insane, but instead of backing this up, as in the example previously used, by citing Jone's behavior in the dock, I go on to outline reasons for thinking that *anyone* who murdered poor Smith in that particularly horrible way must be insane. If now it turns out that Jones was not the murderer after all, but someone else was, I think I can claim to have been right if the true murderer is after all insane. Here, I think, I would be using the definite description attributively, even though I believe that a particular person fits the description.

It is also possible to think of cases in which the speaker does not believe that what he means to refer to by using the definite description fits the description, or to imagine cases in which the definite description is used referentially even though the speaker believes *nothing* fits the description. Admittedly, these cases may be parasitic on a more normal use; nevertheless, they are sufficient to show that such beliefs of the speaker are not decisive as to which use is made of a definite description.

Suppose the throne is occupied by a man I firmly believe to be not the king, but a usurper. Imagine also that his followers as firmly believe that he is the king. Suppose I wish to see this man. I might say to his minions, "Is the king in his countinghouse?" I succeed in referring to the man I wish to refer to without myself believing that he fits the description. It is not even necessary, moreover, to suppose that his followers believe him to be the king. If they are cynical about the whole thing, know he is not the king, I may still succeed in referring to the man I wish to refer to. Similarly, neither I nor the people I speak to may suppose that *anyone* is the king and, finally, each party may know that the other does not so suppose and yet the reference may go through.

V

Both the attributive and the referential use of definite descriptions seem to carry a presup-

position or implication that there is something which fits the description. But the reasons for the existence of the presupposition or implication are different in the two cases.

There is a presumption that a person who uses a definite description referentially believes that what he wishes to refer to fits the description. Because the purpose of using the description is to get the audience to pick out or think of the right thing or person, one would normally choose a description that he believes the thing or person fits. Normally a misdescription of that to which one wants to refer would mislead the audience. Hence, there is a presumption that the speaker believes *something* fits the description— namely, that to which he refers.

When a definite description is used attributively, however, there is not the same possibility of misdescription. In the example of "Smith's murderer" used attributively, there was not the possibility of misdescribing Jones or anyone else; we were not referring to Jones nor to anyone else by using the description. The presumption that the speaker believes *someone* is Smith's murderer does not arise here from a more specific presumption that he believes Jones or Robinson or someone else whom he can name or identify is Smith's murderer.

The presupposition or implication is borne by a definite description used attributively because if nothing fits the description the linguistic purpose of the speech act will be thwarted. That is, the speaker will not succeed in saying something true, if he makes an assertion; he will not succeed in asking a question that can be answered, if he has asked a question; he will not succeed in issuing an order that can be obeyed, if he has issued an order. If one states that Smith's murderer is insane, when Smith has no murderer, and uses the definite description nonreferentially, then one fails to say anything *true*. If one issues the order "Bring me Smith's murderer" under similar circumstances, the order cannot be obeyed; nothing would count as obeying it.

When the definite description is used referentially, on the other hand, the presupposition or implication stems simply from the fact that normally a person tries to describe correctly what he wants to refer to because normally this is the best way to get his audience to recognize what he is referring to. As we have seen, it is possible for the linguistic purpose of the speech act to be accomplished in such a case even though nothing fits the description; it is possible to say something true or to ask a question that gets answered or to issue a command that gets obeyed. For when the definite description is used referentially, one's audience may succeed in seeing to what one refers even though neither it nor anything else fits the description.

VI

The result of the last section shows something to be wrong with the theories of both Russell and Strawson; for though they give differing accounts of the implication or presupposition involved, each gives only one. Yet, as I have argued, the presupposition or implication is present for a quite different reason, depending upon whether the definite description is used attributively or referentially, and exactly what presuppositions or implications are involved is also different. Moreover, neither theory seems a correct characterization of the referential use. On Russell's there is a logical entailment: "The ϕ is ψ" entails "There exists one and only one ϕ." Whether or not this is so for the attributive use, it does not seem true of the referential use of the definite description. The "implication" that something is the ϕ, as I have argued, does not amount to an entailment; it is more like a presumption based on what is *usually* true of the use of a definite description to refer. In any case, of course, Russell's theory does not show—what is true of the referential use—that the implication that *something* is the ϕ comes from the more specific implication that *what is being referred to* is the ϕ. Hence, as a theory of definite descriptions, Russell's view seems to apply, if at all, to the attributive use only.

Russell's definition of denoting (a definite description denotes an entity if that entity fits the description uniquely) is clearly applicable to either use of definite descriptions. Thus whether or not a definite description is used referentially or attributively, it may have a denotation. Hence, denoting and referring, as I have explicated the latter notion, are distinct and Russell's view recognizes only the former. It seems to me, moreover, that this is a welcome result, that denoting and referring should not be confused. If one tried to maintain that they are the same notion, one result would be that a speaker might be referring to something without knowing it. If someone said, for example, in 1960 before he had any idea that Mr. Goldwater would be the Republican nominee in 1964, "The Republican candidate for president in 1964 will be a conservative," (perhaps on the basis of an analysis of the views of party leaders) the definite description here would *denote* Mr. Goldwater. But would we wish to say that the speaker had referred to, mentioned, or talked about Mr. Goldwater? I feel these terms would be out of place. Yet if we identify referring and denoting, it ought to be possible for it to turn out (after the Republican Convention) that the speaker had, unknown to himself, referred in 1960 to Mr. Goldwater. On my view, however, while the definite description used did *denote* Mr. Goldwater (using Russell's definition), the speaker used it *attributively* and did not *refer* to Mr. Goldwater.

Turning to Strawson's theory, it was supposed to demonstrate how definite descriptions are referential. But it goes too far in this direction. For there are nonreferential uses of definite descriptions also, even as they occur in one and the same sentence. I believe that Strawson's theory involves the following propositions:

(1) If someone asserts that the ϕ is ψ he has not made a true or false statement if there is no ϕ.[9]

(2) If there is no ϕ then the speaker has failed to refer to anything.[10]

(3) The reason he has said nothing true or false is that he has failed to refer.

Each of these propositions is either false or, at best, applies to only one of the two uses of definite descriptions.

Proposition (1) is possibly true of the

attributive use. In the example in which "Smith's murderer is insane" was said when Smith's body was first discovered, an attributive use of the definite description, there was no person to whom the speaker referred. If Smith had no murderer, nothing true was said. It is quite tempting to conclude, following Strawson, that nothing true *or* false was said. But where the definite description is used referentially, something true may well have been said. It is possible that something true was said of the person or thing referred to.[11]

Proposition (2) is, as we have seen, simply false. Where a definite description is used referentially it is perfectly possible to refer to something though nothing fits the description used.

The situation with proposition (3) is a bit more complicated. It ties together, on Strawson's view, the two strands given in (1) and (2). As an account of why, when the presupposition is false, nothing true or false has been stated, it clearly cannot work for the attributive use of definite descriptions, for the reason it supplies is that reference has failed. It does not then give the reason why, if indeed this is so, a speaker using a definite description attributively fails to say anything true or false if nothing fits the description. It does, however, raise a question about the referential use. Can reference fail when a definite description is used referentially?

I do not fail to refer merely because my audience does not correctly pick out what I am referring to. I can be referring to a particular man when I use the description "the man drinking a martini," even though the people to whom I speak fail to pick out the right person or any person at all. Nor, as we have stressed, do I fail to refer when nothing fits the description. But perhaps I fail to refer in some extreme circumstances, when there is nothing that *I* am willing to pick out as that to which I referred.

Suppose that I think I see at some distance a man walking and ask, "Is the man carrying a walking stick the professor of history?" We should perhaps distinguish four cases at this point. (a) There is a man carrying a walking stick; I have then referred to a person and asked a question about him that can be answered if my audience has the information. (b) The man over there is not carrying a walking stick, but an umbrella; I have still referred to someone and asked a question that can be answered, though if my audience sees that it is an umbrella and not a walking stick, they may also correct my apparently mistaken impression. (c) It is not a man at all, but a rock that looks like one; in this case, I think I still have referred to something, to the thing over there that happens to be a rock but that I took to be a man. But in this case it is not clear that my question can be answered correctly. This, I think, is not because I have failed to refer, but rather because, given the true nature of what I referred to, my question is not appropriate. A simple "No, that is not the professor of history" is at least a bit misleading if said by someone who realizes that I mistook a rock for a person. It may, therefore, be plausible to conclude that in such a case I have not asked a question to which there is a straightforwardly correct answer. But if this is true, it is not because nothing fits the description I used, but rather because what I referred to is a rock and my question has no correct answer when asked of a rock. (d) There is finally the case in which there is nothing at all where I thought there was a man with a walking stick; and perhaps here we have a genuine failure to refer at all, even though the description was used for the purpose of referring. There is no rock, nor anything else, to which I meant to refer; it was, perhaps, a trick of light that made me think there was a man there. I cannot say of anything, "That is what I was referring to, though I now see that it's not a man carrying a walking stick." This failure of reference, however, requires circumstances much more radical than the mere nonexistence of anything fitting the description used. It requires that there be nothing of which it can be said, "That is what he was referring to." Now perhaps also in such cases, if the speaker has asserted something, he fails to state anything true or false if there is nothing that can be identified as that to which he referred. But if so, the failure of reference and truth value does not come about merely because nothing fits the description he used. So (3) may be true of some cases of the referential use of definite descriptions; it may be true that a failure of reference results in a lack of truth value. But these cases are of a much more extreme sort than Strawson's theory implies.

I conclude, then, that neither Russell's nor Strawson's theory represents a correct account of the use of definite descriptions—Russell's because it ignores altogether the referential use, Strawson's because it fails to make the distinction between the referential and the attributive and mixes together truths about each (together with some things that are false).

VII

It does not seem possible to say categorically of a definite description in a particular sentence that it is a referring expression (of course, one could say this if he meant that it *might* be used to refer). In general, whether or not a definite description is used referentially or attributively is a function of the speaker's intentions in a particular case. "The murderer of Smith" may be used either way in the sentence "The murderer of Smith is insane." It does not appear plausible to account for this, either, as an ambiguity in the sentence. The grammatical structure of the sentence seems to me to be the same whether the description is used referentially or attributively: that is, it is not syntactically ambiguous. Nor does it seem at all attractive to suppose an ambiguity in the meaning of the words; it does not appear to be semantically ambiguous. (Perhaps we could say that the sentence is pragmatically ambiguous: the distinction between roles that the description plays is a function of the speaker's intentions.) These, of course, are intuitions; I do not have an argument for these conclusions. Nevertheless, the burden of proof is surely on the other side.

This, I think, means that the view, for example, that sentences can be divided up into predicates, logical operators, and refer-

ring expressions is not generally true. In the case of definite descriptions one cannot always assign the referential function in isolation from a particular occasion on which it is used.

There may be sentences in which a definite description can be used only attributively or only referentially. A sentence in which it seems that the definite description could be used only attributively would be "Point out the man who is drinking my martini," I am not so certain that any can be found in which the definite description can be used only referentially. Even if there are such sentences, it does not spoil the point that there are many sentences, apparently not ambiguous either syntactically or semantically, containing definite descriptions that can be used either way.

If it could be shown that the dual use of definite descriptions can be accounted for by the presence of an ambiguity, there is still a point to be made against the theories of Strawson and Russell. For neither, so far as I can see, has anything to say about the possibility of such an ambiguity and, in fact, neither seems compatible with such a possibility. Russell's does not recognize the possibility of the referring use, and Strawson's, as I have tried to show in the last section, combines elements from each use into one unitary account. Thus the view that there is an ambiguity in such sentences does not seem any more attractive to these positions.

VIII

Using a definite description referentially, a speaker may say something true even though the description correctly applies to nothing. The sense in which he may say something true is the sense in which he may say something true about someone or something. This sense is, I think, an interesting one that needs investigation. Isolating it is one of the byproducts of the distinction between the attributive and referential uses of definite descriptions.

For one thing, it raises questions about the notion of a statement. This is brought out by considering a passage in a paper by Leonard

Linsky in which he rightly makes the point that one can refer to someone although the definite description used does not correctly describe the person:

. . . said of a spinster that "Her husband is kind to her" is neither true nor false. But a speaker might very well be referring to someone using these words, for he may think that someone is the husband of the lady (who in fact is a spinster). Still, the statement is neither true nor false, for it presupposes that the lady has a husband, which she has not. This last refutes Strawson's thesis that if the presupposition of existence is not satisfied, the speaker has failed to refer.[12]

There is much that is right in this passage. But because Linsky does not make the distinction between the referential and the attributive uses of definite descriptions, it does not represent a wholly adequate account of the situation. A perhaps minor point about this passage is that Linsky apparently thinks it sufficient to establish that the speaker in his example is referring to someone by using the definite description "her husband," that he *believe* that someone is her husband. This will only approximate the truth provided that the "someone" in the description of the belief means "someone in particular" and is not merely the existential quantifier, "there is someone or other." For in both the attributive and the referential use the belief that someone *or other* is the husband of the lady is very likely to be present. If, for example, the speaker has just met the lady and, noticing her cheerfulness and radiant good health, makes his remark from his conviction that these attributes are always the result of having good husbands, he would be using the definite description attributively. Since she has no husband, there is no one to pick out as the person to whom he was referring. Nevertheless, the speaker believed that *someone or other* was her husband. On the other hand, if the use of "her husband" was simply a way of referring to a man speaker has just met whom he assumed to be the lady's husband, he would have referred to that man even though neither he nor anyone else fits the description. I think it is likely that in this passage Linsky did mean by

"someone," in his description of the belief, "someone in particular." But even then, as we have seen, we have neither a sufficient nor a necessary condition for a referential use of the definite description. A definite description can be used attributively even when the speaker believes that some particular thing or person fits the description, and it can be used referentially in the absence of this belief.

My main point, here, however, has to do with Linsky's view that because the presupposition is not satisfied, the *statement* is neither true nor false. This seems to me possibly correct *if* the definite description is thought of as being used attributively (depending upon whether we go with Strawson or Russell). But when we consider it as used referentially, this categorical assertion is no longer clearly correct. For the man the speaker referred to may indeed be kind to the spinster; the speaker may have said something true about that man. Now the difficulty is in the notion of "the statement." Suppose that we know that the lady is a spinster, but nevertheless know that the man referred to by the speaker is kind to her. It seems to me that we shall, on the one hand, want to hold that the speaker said something true, but be reluctant to express this by "It is true that her husband is kind to her."

This shows, I think, a difficulty in speaking simply about "the statement" when definite descriptions are used referentially. For the speaker stated something, in this example, about a particular person, and his statement, we may suppose, was true. Nevertheless, we should not like to agree with his statement by using the sentence he used; we should not like to identify the true statement via the speaker's words. The reason for this is not so hard to find. If we say, in this example, "It is true that her husband is kind to her," *we* are now using the definite description either attributively or referentially. But we should not be subscribing to what the original speaker truly said if we use the description attributively, for it was only in its function as referring to a particular person that the definite description yields the possibility of saying something true (since the lady has no husband). Our reluctance, however, to endorse the original speaker's statement by using the definite description referentially to refer to the same person stems from quite a different consideration. For if we too were laboring under the mistaken belief that this man was the lady's husband, we could agree with the original speaker using his exact words. (Moreover, it is possible, as we have seen, deliberately to use a definite description to refer to someone we believe not to fit the description.) Hence, our reluctance to use the original speaker's words does not arise from the fact that if we did we should not succeed in stating anything true or false. It rather stems from the fact that when a definite description is used referentially there is a presumption that the speaker believes that what he refers to fits the description. Since we, who know the lady to be a spinster, would not normally want to give the impression that we believe otherwise, we would not like to use the original speaker's way of referring to the man in question.

How then would we express agreement with the original speaker without involving ourselves in unwanted impressions about our beliefs? The answer shows another difference between the referential and attributive uses of definite descriptions and brings out an important point about genuine referring.

When a speaker says, "The ϕ is ψ," where "the ϕ" is used attributively, if there is no ϕ, we cannot correctly report the speaker as having said *of* this or that person or thing that it is ψ. But if the definite description is used referentially we can report the speaker as having attributed ψ to something. And *we* may refer to what the speaker referred to, using whatever description or name suits our purpose. Thus, if a speaker says, "Her husband is kind to her," referring to the man he was just talking to, and if that man is Jones, we may report him as having said *of Jones* that he is kind to her. If Jones is also the president of the college, we may report the speaker as having said *of the president of the college* that he is kind to her. And finally, if we are talking to Jones, we may say, referring to the original speaker, "He said of you that *you* are kind to

her." It does not matter here whether or not the woman has a husband or whether, if she does, Jones is her husband. If the original speaker referred to Jones, he said of him that he is kind to her. Thus where the definite description is used referentially, but does not fit what was referred to, we can report what a speaker said and agree with him by using a description or name which does fit. In doing so we need not, it is important to note, choose a description or name which the original speaker would agree fits what he was referring to. That is, we can report the speaker in the above case to have said truly of Jones that he is kind to her even if the original speaker did not know that the man he was referring to is named Jones or even if he thinks he is not named Jones.

Returning to what Linsky said in the passage quoted, he claimed that, were someone to say "Her husband is kind to her," when she has no husband, *the statement* would be neither true nor false. As I have said, this is a likely view to hold if the definite description is being used attributively. But if it is being used referentially it is not clear what is meant by "the statement." If we think about what the speaker said about the person he referred to, then there is no reason to suppose he has not said something true or false about him, even though he is not the lady's husband. And Linsky's claim would be wrong. On the other hand, if we do not identify the statement in this way, what is the statement that the speaker made? To say that the statement he made was that her husband is kind to her lands us in difficulties. For we have to decide whether in using the definite description here in the identification of the statement, we are using it attributively or referentially. If the former, then we misrepresent the linguistic performance of the speaker; if the latter, then we are ourselves referring to someone and reporting the speaker to have said something of that person, in which case we are back to the possibility that he did say something true or false of that person.

I am thus drawn to the conclusion that when a speaker uses a definite description referentially he may have stated something true or false even if nothing fits the description, and that there is not a clear sense in which he has made a statement which is neither true nor false.

IX

I want to end by a brief examination a picture of what a genuine referring expression is that one might derive from Russell's views. I want to suggest that this picture is not so far wrong as one might suppose and that strange as this may seem, some of the things we have said about the referential use of definite descriptions are not foreign to this picture.

Genuine proper names, in Russell's sense, would refer to something without ascribing any properties to it. They would, one might say, refer to the thing itself, not simply the thing in so far as it falls under a certain description.[13] Now this would seem to Russell something a definite description could not do, for he assumed that if definite descriptions were capable of referring at all, they would refer to something only in so far as that thing satisfied the description. Not only have we seen this assumption to be false, however, but in the last section we saw something more. We saw that when a definite description is used referentially, a speaker can be reported as having said something *of* something. And in reporting what it was of which he said something we are not restricted to the description he used, or synonyms of it; we may ourselves refer to it using any descriptions, names, and so forth, that will do the job. Now this seems to give a sense in which we are concerned with the thing itself and not just the thing under a certain description, when we report the linguistic act of a speaker using a definite description referentially. That is, such a definite description comes closer to performing the function of Russell's proper names than certainly he supposed.

Secondly, Russell thought, I believe, that whenever we use descriptions, as opposed to proper names, we introduce an element of generality which ought to be absent if what we are doing is referring to some particular thing. This is clear from his analysis of sentences containing definite descriptions. One of the conclusions we are supposed to draw from that analysis is that such sentences express what are in reality completely general propositions: there is a φ and only one such and any φ is ψ. We might put this in a slightly different way. If there is anything which might be identified as reference here, it is reference in a very weak sense—namely, reference to *whatever* is the one and only one φ, if there is any such. Now this is something we might well say about the attributive use of definite descriptions, as should be evident from the previous discussion. But this lack of particularity is absent from the referential use of definite descriptions precisely because the description is here merely a device for getting one's audience to pick out or think of the thing to be spoken about, a device which may serve its function even if the description is incorrect. More importantly perhaps, in the referential use as opposed to the attributive, there is a *right* thing to be picked out by the audience and its being the right thing is not simply a function of its fitting the description.

ACKNOWLEDGMENTS

I should like to thank my colleagues, John Canfield, Sydney Shoemaker, and Timothy Smiley, who read an earlier draft and gave me helpful suggestions. I also had the benefit of the valuable and detailed comments of the referee for the paper, to whom I wish to express my gratitude.

NOTES

1. "On Denoting," reprinted in *Logic and Knowledge,* ed. Robert C. Marsh (London: 1956), p. 51.
2. 'On Referring,' reprinted in *Philosophy and Ordinary Language,* ed. Charles C. Caton (Urbana: 1963), pp. 162–163.
3. *Ibid.,* p. 162.
4. *Ibid.,* p. 170.
5. Here and elsewhere I use the disjunction "presuppose or imply" to avoid taking a stand that would side me with Russell or Strawson on the issue of what the relationship involved is. To take a stand here would be beside my main point as well as being misleading, since later on I shall argue that the presupposition or implication arises in a different way depending upon the use to which the definite description is put.

This last also accounts for my use of the vagueness indicator, "in some sense."

6. In a footnote added to the original version of "On Referring" (*op. cit.*, p. 181) Strawson seems to imply that where the presupposition is false, we still succeed in referring in a "secondary" way, which seems to mean "as we could be said to refer to fictional or make-believe things." But his view is still that we cannot refer in such a case in the "primary" way. This is, I believe, wrong. For a discussion of this modification of Strawson's view see Charles E. Caton, "Strawson on Referring," *Mind*, LXVIII (1959), 539–544.

7. This is an adaptation of an example (used for a somewhat different purpose) given by Leonard Linsky in "Reference and Referents," in *Philosophy and Ordinary Language*, p. 80.

8. In "Reference and Referents" (pp. 74–75, 80), Linsky correctly points out that one does not fail to refer simply because the description used does not in fact fit anything (or fits more than one thing). Thus he pinpoints one of the difficulties in Strawson's view. Here, however, I use this fact about referring to make a distinction I believe he does not draw, between two uses of definite descriptions. I later discuss the second passage from Linsky's paper.

9. In "A Reply to Mr. Sellars," *Philosophical Review*, LXIII (1954), 216–121, Strawson admits that we do not always refuse to ascribe truth to what a person says when the definite description he uses fails to fit anything (or fits more than one thing). To cite one of his examples, a person who said, "The United States Chamber of Deputies contains representatives of two major parties," would be allowed to have said something true even though he had used the wrong title. Strawson thinks this does not constitute a genuine problem for his view. He thinks that what we do in such cases, "where the speaker's intended reference is pretty clear, is simply to amend his statement in accordance with his guessed intentions and assess the amended statement for truth or falsity; we are not awarding a truth value at all to the original statement" (p. 230).

The notion of an "amended statement," however, will not do. We may note, first of all, that the sort of case Strawson has in mind could arise only when a definite description is used referentially. For the "amendment" is made by seeing the speaker's intended reference. But this could happen only if the speaker had an intended reference, a particular person or thing in mind, independent of the description he

used. The cases Strawson has in mind are presumably not cases of slips of the tongue or the like; presumably they are cases in which a definite description is used because the speaker believes, though he is mistaken, that he is describing correctly what he wants to refer to. We supposedly amend the statement by knowing to what he intends to refer. But what description is to be used in the amended statement? In the example, perhaps, we could use "the United States Congress." But this description might be one the speaker would not even accept as correctly describing what he wants to refer to, because he is misinformed about the correct title. Hence, this is not a case of deciding what the speaker meant to say as opposed to what he in fact said, for the speaker did not mean to say "the United States Congress." If this is so, then there is no bar to the "amended" statement containing any description that does correctly pick out what the speaker intended to refer to. It could be, e.g., "The lower house of the United States Congress." But this means that there is no one unique "amended" statement to be assessed for truth value. And, in fact, it should now be clear that the notion of the amended statement really plays no role anyway. For if we can arrive at the amended statement only by first knowing to what the speaker intended to refer, we can assess the truth of what he said simply by deciding whether what he intended to refer to has the properties he ascribed to it.

10. As noted earlier (note 6), Strawson may allow that one has possibly referred in a "secondary" way, but, if I am right, the fact that there is no ϕ does not preclude one from having referred in the same way one does if there is a ϕ.

11. For a further discussion of the notion of saying something true *of* someone or something, see section VIII.

12. "Reference and Referents," p. 80. It should be clear that I agree with Linsky in holding that a speaker may refer even though the "presupposition of existence" is not satisfied. And I agree in thinking this an objection to Strawson's view. I think, however, that this point, among others, can be used to define two distinct uses of definite descriptions which, in turn, yields a more general criticism of Strawson. So, while I develop here a point of difference, which grows out of the distinction I want to make, I find myself in agreement with much of Linsky's article.

13. Cf. "The Philosophy of Logical Atomism," reprinted in *Logic and Knowledge*, p. 200.

SAUL KRIPKE

I am going to discuss some issues inspired by a well-known paper of Keith Donnellan, "Reference and Definite Descriptions,"[2] but the interest—to me—of the contrast mentioned in my title goes beyond Donnellan's paper: I think it is of considerable constructive as well as critical importance to the philosophy of language. These applications, however, and even everything I might want to say relative to Donnellan's paper, cannot be discussed in full here because of problems of length.

Moreover, although I have a considerable interest in the substantive issues raised by Donnellan's paper, and by related literature, my own conclusions will be methodological, not substantive. I can put the matter this way: Donnellan's paper claims to give decisive objections both to Russell's theory of definite descriptions (taken as a theory about English) and to Strawson's. My concern is *not* primarily with the question: is Donnellan right, or is Russell (or Strawson)? Rather, it is with the question: do the considerations *in Donnellan's paper* refute Russell's theory (or Strawson's)? For definiteness, I will concentrate on Donnellan versus Russell, leaving Strawson aside. And about this issue I will draw a definite conclusion, one which I think will illuminate a few methodological maxims about language. Namely, I will conclude that the considera-

tions in Donnellan's paper, *by themselves,* do *not* refute Russell's theory.

Any conclusions about Russell's views *per se,* or Donnellan's, must be tentative. If I were to be asked for a tentative stab about Russell, I would say that although his theory does a far better job of handling ordinary discourse than many have thought, and although many popular arguments against it are inconclusive, probably it ultimately fails. The considerations I have in mind have to do with the existence of "improper" definite descriptions, such as "the table," where uniquely specifying conditions are not contained in the description itself. Contrary to the Russellian picture, I doubt that such descriptions can always be regarded as elliptical with some uniquely specifying conditions added. And it may even be the case that a true picture will resemble various aspects of Donnellan's in important respects. But such questions will largely be left aside here.

I will state my preference for one substantive conclusion (although I do not feel completely confident of it either): that unitary theories, like Russell's, are preferable to theories that postulate an ambiguity. And much, though not all, of Donnellan's paper seems to postulate a (semantic) ambiguity between his "referential" and "attributive"

From *Contemporary Perspectives in the Philosophy of Language,* Peter A. French, Theodore E. Uehling, Jr. and Howard K. Wettstein, eds. (Minneapolis: University of Minnesota Press, 1977), pp. 6–27. © 1977 by Saul Kripke.

uses. But—as we shall see—Donnellan is not entirely consistent on this point, and I therefore am not sure whether I am expressing disagreement with him even here.[3]

1. PRELIMINARY CONSIDERATIONS

Donnellan claims that a certain linguistic phenomenon argues against Russell's theory. According to Russell, if someone says, "The x such that $\phi(x)$ ψ's," he means that there is an x which uniquely satisfies "$\phi(x)$" and that any such x satisfies "$\psi(x)$." [I.e., $(\exists x)$ $(\phi!(x) \wedge \psi(x))$, where "$\phi!(x)$" abbreviates "$\phi(x) \wedge (y)(\phi(y) \supset y = x)$"]. Donnellan argues that some phenomenon of the following kind tells against Russell: Suppose someone at a gathering, glancing in a certain direction, says to his companion,

(1) "The man over there drinking champagne is happy tonight."

Suppose both the speaker and hearer are under a false impression, and that the man to whom they refer is a teetotaler, drinking sparkling water. He may, nevertheless, be happy. Now, if there is no champagne drinker over there, Russell would regard (1) as false, and Frege and Strawson would give it a truth-value gap. Nevertheless, as Donnellan emphasizes, we have a substantial intuition that the speaker said something true of the man to whom he referred in spite of his misimpression.

Since no one is really drinking champagne, the case involves a definite description that is empty, or vacuous, according to both Russell and Frege. So as to avoid any unnecessary and irrelevant entanglements of the present question with the issues that arise when definite descriptions are vacuous, I shall modify this case (and all other cases where, in Donnellan's paper, the description was vacuous).[4] Suppose that "over there," exactly one man *is* drinking champagne, although his glass is not visible to the speaker (nor to his hearer). Suppose that he, unlike the teetotaler to whom the speaker refers, has been driven to drink precisely by his misery. Then *all* the classical theories (both Russellian and Fre-

gean) would regard (1) as false (since exactly one man over there is drinking champagne, and he is *not* happy tonight). Now the speaker has spoken *truly* of the man to whom he refers (the teetotaler), yet this dimension is left out in all the classical analyses, which would assign falsehood to his assertion solely on the basis of the misery of *someone else* whom *no one* was talking about (the champagne drinker). Previously Linsky had given a similar example. He gave it as an empty case; once again I modify it to make the description nonvacuous. Someone sees a woman with a man. Taking the man to be her husband, and observing his attitude towards her, he says, "Her husband is kind to her," and someone else may nod, "Yes, he seems to be." Suppose the man in question is not her husband. Suppose he is her lover, to whom she has been driven precisely by her husband's cruelty. Once again both the Russellian analysis and the Fregean analysis would assess the statement as false, and both would do so on the basis of the cruelty of a man neither participant in the dialogues was talking about.

Again, an example suggested to me by a remark of L. Crocker: suppose a religious narrative (similar, say, to the Gospels) consistently refers to its main protagonist as "The Messiah." Suppose a historian wishes to assess the work for *historical accuracy*—that is, he wishes to determine whether it gives an accurate account of the life of its hero (whose identity we assume to be established). Does it matter to this question whether the hero really was the Messiah, as long as the author took him to be so, and addressed his work to a religious community that shared this belief? Surely not. And note that it is no mere "principle of charity" that is operating here. On the contrary, if someone other than the person intended were really the Messiah, and if, by a bizarre and unintended coincidence, the narrative gave a fairly true account of *his* life, we would not for that reason call it "historically true." On the contrary, we would regard the work as historically *false* if the events mentioned were false of its intended protagonist. Whether the story happened to fit the true Messiah—who may have been totally unknown to the author and even have lived after the time the work was composed—would be irrelevant. Once again, this fact seems inconsistent with the positions both of Frege and of Russell.

On the basis of such examples, Donnellan distinguishes two uses of definite descriptions. In the "attributive" use, a speaker "states something about whoever or whatever is the so-and-so." In the "referential" use, a speaker "uses the description to enable his audience to pick out whom or what he is talking about and states something about that person or thing. In the first [attributive] case, the definite description might be said to occur essentially, for the speaker wishes to assert something about whatever or whoever fits that description; but in the referential use the definite description is merely one tool for . . . calling attention to a person or thing . . . and . . . any other device for doing the same job, another description or name, would do as well."[5] For example, suppose I come upon Smith foully murdered. The condition of Smith's body moves me to say, "Smith's murderer is (must be) insane." Then we have an *attributive* use: we speak of the murderer, whoever he may be. On the other hand, suppose that Jones is on trial for Smith's murder and that I am among the spectators in the courtroom. Observing the wild behavior of the defendant at the dock, I may say, "Smith's murderer is insane." (I forgot the defendant's name, but am firmly convinced of his guilt.) Then my use is referential: whether or not Jones was the real murderer, and even if someone else was, if Jones accused me of libel, his failure to fit my description would give me no defense. All of the previous cases, (the teetotaling "champagne" drinker, the lover taken for a husband, the false Messiah), are all referential in Donnellan's sense.

An intuitive mark of the attributive use is the legitimacy of the parenthetical comment, "whoever he is." In the first case, we may say "Smith's murderer, whoever he is, is insane," but not in the second. But we should not be misled: a definite description may be used attributively even if the speaker believes that a certain person, say, Jones, fits it, provided

that he is talking about *whoever* fits, and his belief that Jones in fact fits is not relevant. In the case where I deduce the murderer's insanity from the condition of Smith's body, I use the description attributively even if I suspect, or even am firmly convinced, that Jones is the culprit.

I have no doubt that the distinction Donnellan brings out exists and is of fundamental importance, though I do not regard it as exclusive or exhaustive. But Donnellan also believes that Russell's theory applies, if at all, only to attributive uses, and that referential uses of definite descriptions are close to proper names, even to Russell's "logically proper" names. And he appears to believe that the examples of the referential uses mentioned above are inexplicable on Russell's theory. It is these views that I wish to examine.

2. SOME ALLEGED APPLICATIONS OF THE DISTINCTION

Some alleged applications of Donnellan's distinction have entered the oral tradition, and even to an extent, the written tradition, that are not in Donnellan's paper. I will mention some that I find questionable. Unfortunately I will have to discuss these applications more briefly than the issues in question really deserve, since they are ancillary to the main theme.

2a. De Dicto–De Re

Many able people, in and out of print, have implied that Donnellan's distinction has something to do with, can be identified with, or can replace, the *de dicto-de re* distinction, or the small scope–large scope distinction in modal or intensional contexts.

"The number of planets is necessarily odd" can mean two things, depending on whether it is interpreted *de dicto* or *de re*. If it is interpreted *de dicto,* it asserts that the proposition that the number of planets is odd is a necessary truth—something I take to be false (there might have been eight planets). If it is interpreted *de re,* it asserts that the actual number of planets (nine) has the property of necessary oddness (essentialists like me take this to be true). Similarly, if we say, "Jones believes that the richest debutante in Dubuque will marry him," we may mean that Jones's belief has a certain content, viz., that the richest debutante in Dubuque will marry him; or we may mean that he believes, *of* a girl who is (in fact) the richest in Dubuque, that she will marry him. The view in question suggests that the *de dicto* case is to be identified with Donnellan's *attributive* use, the *de re* with the *referential*.

Any such assimilation, in my opinion, is confused. (I don't think Donnellan makes it.) There are many objections; I will mention a few. First, the *de dicto* use of the definite description cannot be identified with either the *referential* or the *attributive* use. Here the basic point was already noticed by Frege. If a description is embedded in a (*de dicto*) intensional context, we cannot be said to be talking *about* the thing described, either *qua* its satisfaction of the description or *qua* anything else. Taken *de dicto*, "Jones believes that the richest debutante in Dubuque will marry him," can be asserted by someone who thinks (let us suppose, wrongly) that there are *no* debutantes in Dubuque; certainly then, he is in no way talking about the richest debutante, even "attributively." Similarly, "It is possible that (France should have a monarchy in 1976, and that) the King of France in 1976 should have been bald" is true, if read *de dicto;* yet we are not using "the King of France in 1976" attributively to speak of the King of France in 1976, for there is none. Frege concluded that "the King of France in 1976" refers, in these contexts, to its ordinary sense; at any rate, if we wish to speak of "reference" here, it cannot be to the nonexistent king. Even if there were such a king, the quoted assertion would say nothing about *him,* if read *de dicto:* to say that *he* might have been bald, would be *de re* (indeed, this *is* the distinction in question).

Second, and even more relevantly, Donnellan's referential use cannot be identified with the *de re* use. (I think Donnellan would agree.) Suppose I have no idea how many

planets there are, but (for some reason) astronomical theory dictates that that number must be odd. If I say, "The number of planets (whatever it may be) is odd," my description is used attributively. If I am an essentialist, I will also say, "The number of planets (whatever it may be) is necessarily odd," on the grounds that all odd numbers are necessarily odd; and my usage is just as attributive as in the first case. In "Smith's murderer, whoever he may be, is known to the police, but they're not saying," or, more explicitly, "The police know concerning Smith's murderer, whoever he is, that he committed the murder; but they're not saying who he is," "Smith's murderer" is used attributively, but is *de re*.

Finally: Russell wished to handle the *de dicto–de re* distinction by his notion of the *scope* of a description. Some have suggested that Donnellan's referential–attributive distinction can replace Russell's distinction of scope. But *no* twofold distinction can do this job. Consider:

(2) The number of planets might have been necessarily even.

In a natural use, (2) can be interpreted as true; for example, there might have been exactly eight planets, in which case the number of planets would have been even, and hence necessarily even. (2), interpreted as true, is neither *de re* nor *de dicto;* that is, the definite description neither has the largest nor the smallest possible scope. Consider:

(2a) $\Diamond \Box (\exists x)$ (There are exactly x planets and x is even)

(2b) $(\exists x)$ (There are exactly x planets and $\Diamond \Box (x$ is even)).

(2c) $\Diamond (\exists x)$ (There are exactly x planets and $\Box (x$ is even)).

(2a)–(2c) give three alternative Russellian analyses of (2). (2a) gives the description the smallest possible scope (*de dicto*); it says, presumably falsely, that it might have been necessary that there was an even number of planets. (2b) gives the description the largest possible scope (*de re*); it says, still falsely, of the actual number of planets (viz., nine) that it might have been necessarily even. (2c) is the interpretation which makes (2) true. When intensional operators are iterated, intermediate scopes are possible. Three analogous interpretations are possible, say, for "Jones doubts that Holmes believes that Smith's murderer is insane"; or (using an indefinite description) for "Hoover charged that the Berrigans plotted to kidnap a high American official." (I actually read something like this last in a newspaper and wondered what was meant.)[6] This may mean: (a) there is a particular high official such that Hoover charged that the Berrigans plotted to kidnap him (largest scope, *de re,* this was the interpretation intended); or (b) Hoover charged that the Berrigans plotted as follows: let's kidnap a high official (smallest scope, *de dicto*); or (c) Hoover charged that there was a high official (whose identity may have been unknown to Hoover) whom the Berrigans planned to kidnap (intermediate scope).

As intensional (or other) constructions are iterated, there are more and more possible scopes for a definite description. No *twofold* distinction can replace Russell's notion of scope.[7] In particular, neither the *de dicto–de re* distinction nor the referential–attributive distinction can do so.

2b. Rigid Definite Descriptions

If definite descriptions, $\iota x \phi(x)$, are taken as primitive and assigned reference, then the conventional nonrigid assignment assigns to such a description, with respect to each possible world, the unique object, if any, which would have ϕ'd in that world. (Forget the vacuous case, which requires a further convention.) For example, "the number of planets" denotes eight, speaking of a counterfactual situation where there would have been eight planets (and "the number of planets is even" is true of such a situation). Another type of definite description, $\iota x \phi x$, a "rigid" definite description, could be introduced semantically by the following stipulation: let $\iota x \phi x$ denote, with respect to all possible worlds, the unique object that (actually) ϕ's (then "the number of planets is odd," as interpreted, expresses a necessary truth).

Both kinds of definite descriptions can obviously be introduced, theoretically, into a single formal language, perhaps by the notations just given. Some have suggested that definite descriptions, in English, are *ambiguous* between the two readings. It has further been suggested that the two types of definite descriptions, the nonrigid and the rigid, are the source of the *de dicto–de re* distinction and should replace Russell's notion of scope for the purpose. Further, it has been suggested that they amount to the same thing as Donnellan's attributive–referential distinction.[8]

My comments will be brief, so as to avoid too much excursus. Although I have an open mind on the subject, I am not yet convinced that there is any clear evidence for such an ambiguity. Being a twofold distinction, the ambiguity alleged cannot replace Russell's notion of scope, for the reasons given above. Once Russell's notion is available, it can be used to handle the *de dicto–de re* distinction; a further ambiguity seems unnecessary. More relevant to the present context, the "rigid" sense of a definite description, if it exists, cannot be identified with Donnellan's "referential" use. I take it that the identification of the referential use with the rigid definite description was inspired by some line of reasoning like this: Donnellan holds that referential descriptions are those close to proper names, even to Russell's "logically proper names." But surely proper names, or at least, Russellian "logically proper names," are rigid. Hence Donnellan's referential descriptions are just the rigid definite descriptions.

If we assume that Donnellan thinks of names as rigid, as I think of them, his referential definite descriptions *would* most plausibly be taken to refer rigidly to their referents. But it is not clear that he does agree with me on the rigidity of such reference.[9] More important, a rigid definite description, as defined above, still determines its referent via its unique satisfaction of the associated property—and this fact separates the notion of such a description from that of a referential description, as Donnellan defines it. David Kaplan has suggested that a demonstrative "that" can be used, in English, to make any definite description rigid. "That bastard—the man who killed Smith, whoever he may be—is surely insane!" The subject term rigidly designates Smith's murderer, but it is still attributive in Donnellan's sense.[10]

2c. Referential Descriptions

In Naming and Necessity,"[11] one argument I presented against the description (or cluster-of-descriptions) theory of proper names concerned cases where the referent of a name, the person named by the name, did not satisfy the descriptions usually associated with it, and someone else did. For example, the name "Gödel" might be taken to mean "the man who proved the incompleteness of arithmetic"; but even if Gödel had been a fraud, who had proved nothing at all and had misappropriated his work from an unknown named "Schmidt," our term "Gödel" would refer to the fraud, not to the man who really satisfied the definite description. Against this it has been said that although the argument does succeed in its main purpose of refuting the description theory as a theory of reference (that is, it shows that the descriptive properties cited do not determine the referent), it does nothing to show that names are not abbreviated definite descriptions, because we could take the descriptions in question to be referential in Donnellan's sense. Referential descriptions can easily refer to things that fail to satisfy the descriptions; nothing in my argument shows that names are not synonymous with such descriptions.[12]

My reaction to such an argument may become clearer later. For the moment, (too) briefly: In the case of "Her husband is kind to her," and similar cases, "her husband" can refer to her lover, as long as we are under the misapprehension that the man to whom we refer (the lover) *is* her husband. Once we are apprised of the true facts, we will no longer so refer to him. Similarly, someone can use "the man who proved the incompleteness of arithmetic," as a referential definite description, to refer to Gödel; it might be so used, for example, by someone who had forgotten his

name. If the hypothetical fraud were discovered, however, the description is no longer usable as a device to refer to Gödel; henceforth it can be used only to refer to Schmidt. We would withdraw any previous assertions using the description to refer to Gödel (unless they also were true of Schmidt). We would *not* similarly withdraw the *name* "Gödel," even after the fraud was discovered; "Gödel" would still be used to name Gödel, not Schmidt. The name and the description, therefore, are not synonymous. (See also note 27 below.)

3. THE MAIN PROBLEM

3a. A Disagreement with Russell?

Do Donnellan's observations provide an argument against Russell's theory? Do his *views* contradict Russell's? One might think that if Donnellan is right, Russell must be wrong, since Donnellan's truth conditions for statements containing referential definite descriptions differ from Russell's. Unfortunately, this is not so clear. Consider the case of "Her husband is kind to her," mistakenly said of the lover. If Donnellan had roundly asserted that the quoted statement is true if and only if the *lover* is kind to her, regardless of the kindness of the husband, the issue between him and Russell would be clearly joined. But Donnellan doesn't say this: rather he says that the speaker has referred to a certain person, the lover, and said *of him* that he is kind to her. But if we ask, "Yes, but was the statement he made true?", Donnellan would hedge. For if *we* are not under the misimpression that the man the speaker referred to was her husband, *we* would not express the same assertion by "Her husband is kind to her." "If it ['her husband'] is being used referentially, it is not clear what is meant by 'the statement.' . . . To say that the statement he made was that her husband is kind to her lands us in difficulties. For we [in so reporting what the speaker said must use the definite description] either attributively or referentially. If the former, then we misrepresent the linguistic performance of the speaker; if the latter, then we ourselves are referring to someone," and ordinarily we can refer to someone as "her husband" only if we take him to be her husband.[13]

Since Donnellan does not clearly assert that the statement "her husband is kind to her" ever has non-Russelian truth conditions, he has *not,* so far, clearly contradicted Russell's theory. His argument, as he presents it, that there is a problem in reporting "the statement" is questionable, in two ways.

First, it uses the premise that if we say, "Jones said that her husband is kind to her," we ourselves must use the description attributively or referentially; but, as we saw, a definite description in indirect discourse is *neither* referential nor attributive.[14]

Second, there is an important problem about the nature of the referential–attributive distinction. Donnellan says that his distinction is neither syntactic nor semantic:

The grammatical structure of the sentence seems to me to be the same whether the description is used referentially or attributively: that is, it is not syntactically ambiguous. Nor does it seem at all attractive to suppose an ambiguity in the meaning of the words; it does not appear to be semantically ambiguous. (Perhaps we could say that the sentence is pragmatically ambiguous: the distinction between roles that the description plays is a function of the speaker's intentions.) These, of course, are intuitions; I do not have an argument for these conclusions. Nevertheless, the burden of proof is surely on the other side.[15]

Suppose for the moment that this is so. Then if the referential–attributive distinction is pragmatic, rather than syntactic or semantic, it is presumably a distinction about speech acts. There is no reason to suppose that in making an indirect discourse report on what someone else has said I myself must have similar intentions, or be engaged in the same kind of speech act; in fact, it is clear that I am not. If I say "Jones said the police were around the corner," Jones may have said it as a warning, but *I* need not say it as a warning. If the referential–attributive distinction is neither syntactic nor semantic, there is no reason, without further argument, to suppose that my usage, in indirect discourse, should match the man on whom I report, as referen-

tial or attributive. The case is quite different for a genuine semantic ambiguity. If Jones says, "I have never been at a bank," and I report this, saying, "Jones denied that he was ever at a bank," the sense I give to "bank" must match Jones's if my report is to be accurate.

Indeed, the passage seems inconsistent with the whole trend of Donnellan's paper. Donnellan suggests that there is no syntactic or semantic ambiguity in the statement, "Her husband is kind to her." He also suggests that Russell may well give a correct analysis of the attributive use but not of the referential use. Surely this is not coherent. It is not "uses," in some pragmatic sense, but *senses* of a sentence which can be analyzed. If the sentence is *not* (syntactically or) semantically ambiguous, it has only *one* analysis; to say that it has two distinct analyses is to attribute a syntactic or semantic ambiguity to it.

Donnellan's arguments for his refusal to give a truth value to the speaker's assertion, "Her husband is kind to her," seem to be fallacious. My own suggested account of the matter below—in terms of a theory of speech acts—creates no problem about "the statement"; it is simply the statement that her husband is kind to her. But Donnellan's cautious refusal to say, under the circumstances mentioned, that "Her husband is kind to her" is true, seems nevertheless to be intuitively correct. The man to whom the speaker refers is—let us suppose—kind to her. But it seems hard for us to say that when he uttered, "Her husband is kind to her," it expressed a truth, if *we* believe that her husband is unkind to her.

Now Donnellan thinks that he has refuted Russell. But all he has clearly claimed, let alone established, is that a speaker can refer to the lover and say, of him, that he is kind to her by saying "Her husband is kind to her." So, first, we can ask: If this claim is correct, does it conflict with Russell's views?

Second, since Donnellan's denial that he advocates a semantic ambiguity in definite descriptions seems inconsistent with much of his paper, we can try ignoring the denial, and take his paper to be arguing for such an ambiguity. Then we may ask: has Donnellan established a (semantic) ambiguity inconsistent with Russell's theory?

3b. General Remarks: Apparatus

We need a general apparatus to discuss these questions. Some of the apparatus is well known, but I review it for its intrinsic importance and interest. First, let us distinguish, following Grice,[16] between what *the speaker's words meant,* on a given occasion, and what *he meant,* in saying these words, on that occasion. For example, one burglar says to another, "The cops are around the corner." What *the words meant* is clear: the police were around the corner. But *the speaker may well have meant,* "We can't wait around collecting any more loot: Let's split!" That is not *the meaning of the words,* even on that occasion, though that is *what he meant in saying those words, on that occasion.* Suppose he had said, "The cops are inside the bank." Then on that occasion, "bank" meant a commercial bank, not a river bank, and this is relevant to what the *words* meant, on that occasion. (On other occasions, the same words might mean that the police were at a river bank.) But, if the speaker *meant* "Let's split," this is no part of the *meaning of his words,* even on that occasion.

Again (inspired by an example of Grice)[17] A magician makes a handkerchief change color. Someone says, recalling the trick, "Then he put the red handkerchief on the side of the table"; and someone else interjects, cautiously, "It *looked* red." The words meant, on that occasion, that the object referred to (the handkerchief) looked red. What we speak of when we speak of the meaning of his words, on that occasion, includes a disambiguation of the utterance. (Perhaps, on some occasions, where "it" refers to a book, a phonetically identical utterance might mean, "it looked read," well-thumbed and well-perused). But the speaker meant, on this occasion, to suggest that perhaps the handkerchief wasn't really red, that perhaps the trick relied on some kind of illusion. (Note that, on this occasion,

not only do the *words* "it looked red" mean what they mean, but also the *speaker* means that it looked red, as well as that it may not have been red. On the other hand, the speaker has no intention of producing a belief in the hearer that the handkerchief looked red, or a belief in the hearer that he (the speaker) believed it looked red. Both facts are common knowledge. The same *could* hold for "The cops are around the corner."[18] Do these examples contradict Grice's analysis of "meaning"? Grice's theory has become very complex and I am not quite sure.)

The notion of what words can mean, in the language, is semantical: it is given by the conventions of our language. What they mean, on a given occasion, is determined, on a given occasion, by these conventions, together with the intentions of the speaker and various contextual features. Finally what the speaker meant, on a given occasion, in saying certain words, derives from various further special intentions of the speaker, together with various general principles, applicable to all human languages regardless of their special conventions. (Cf. Grice's "conversational maxims.") For example, "It looks red" replaced a categorical affirmation of redness. A plausible general principle of human discourse would have it that if a second speaker insists that a stronger assertion should be replaced by a weaker one, he thereby wishes to cast doubt on the stronger assertion; whence, knowing the semantics of English, and the meaning of the speaker's words on this occasion, we can deduce what was meant (the Gricean "conversational implicature").[19]

Let us now speak of speaker's reference and semantic reference: these notions are special cases of the Gricean notions discussed above. If a speaker has a designator in his idiolect, certain conventions of his idiolect[20] (given various facts about the world) determine the referent in the idiolect: that I call the *semantic referent* of the designator. (If the designator is ambiguous, or contains indexicals, demonstratives, or the like, we must speak of the semantic referent on a given occasion. The referent will be determined by the conventions of the language plus the speaker's intentions and various contextual features.)

Speaker's reference is a more difficult notion. Consider, for example, the following case, which I have mentioned elsewhere.[21] Two people see Smith in the distance and mistake him for Jones. They have a brief colloquy: "What is Jones doing?" "Raking the leaves." "Jones," in the common language of both, is a name of Jones; it *never* names Smith. Yet, in some sense, on this occasion, clearly both participants in the dialogue have referred to Smith, and the second participant has said something true about the man he referred to if and only if Smith was raking the leaves (whether or not Jones was). How can we account for this? Suppose a speaker takes it that a certain object *a* fulfills the conditions for being the semantic referent of a designator, "*d*." Then, wishing to say something about *a,* he uses "*d*" to speak about *a;* say, he says "ϕ(*d*)." Then, he said, of *a,* on that occasion, that it ϕ'd; in the appropriate Gricean sense (explicated above), he *meant* that *a* ϕ'd. This is true even if *a* is not really the semantic referent of "d." If it is not, then *that a* ϕ's is included in what he meant (on that occasion), but not in the meaning of his words (on that occasion).

So, we may tentatively define the speaker's referent of a designator to be that object which the speaker wishes to talk about, on a given occasion, and believes fulfills the conditions for being the semantic referent of the designator. He uses the designator with the intention of making an assertion about the object in question (which may not really be the semantic referent, if the speaker's belief that it fulfills the appropriate semantic conditions is in error). The speaker's referent is the thing the speaker referred to by the designator, though it may not be the referent of the designator, in his idiolect. In the example above, Jones, the man named by the name, is the semantic referent. Smith is the speaker's referent, the correct answer to the question, "To whom were you referring?"[22]

Below, the notion of speaker's reference will be extended to include more cases where existential quantification rather than designation is involved.

In a given idiolect, the semantic referent of a designator (without indexicals) is given by a *general* intention of the speaker to refer to a certain object whenever the designator is used. The speaker's referent is given by a *specific* intention, on a given occasion, to refer to a certain object. If the speaker believes that the object he wants to talk about, on a given occasion, fulfills the conditions for being the semantic referent, then he believes that there is no clash between his general intentions and his specific intentions. My hypothesis is that Donnellan's referential-attributive distinction should be generalized in this light. For the speaker, on a given occasion, may believe that his specific intention coincides with his general intention for one of two reasons. In one case (the "simple" case), his specific intention is simply to refer to the semantic referent: that is, his specific intention *is* simply his general semantic intention. (For examples, he uses "Jones" as a name of Jones—elaborate this according to your favorite theory of proper names—and, on this occasion, simply wishes to use "Jones" to refer to Jones.) Alternatively—the "complex" case—he has a specific intention, which is distinct from his general intention, but which he believes, as a matter of fact, to determine the same object as the one determined by his general intention. (For example, he wishes to refer to the man "over there" but believes that he *is* Jones.) In the "simple" case, the speaker's referent is, *by definition,* the semantic referent. In the "complex" case, they may coincide, if the speaker's belief is correct, but they need not. (The man "over there" may be Smith and not Jones.) To anticipate, my hypothesis will be that Donnellan's "attributive" use is nothing but the "simple" case, specialized to definite descriptions, and that the "referential" use is, similarly, the "complex" case. If such a conjecture is correct, it would be wrong to take Donnellan's "referential" use, as he does, to be a use of a description as if it were a proper name. For the distinction of simple and complex cases will apply to proper names just as much as to definite descriptions.

3c. Donnellan's Argument Against Russell: Methodological and Substantive Considerations

In the light of the notions just developed, consider the argument Donnellan adduces against Russell. Donnellan points to a phenomenon which he alleges to be inexplicable on a Russellian account of English definite descriptions. He accounts for it by positing an ambiguity. Alternatively, we wish to account for the phenomenon on pragmatic grounds, encapsulated in the distinction between speaker's reference and semantic reference. How can we see whether Donnellan's phenomenon conflicts with a Russellian account?

I propose the following test for any alleged counterexample to a linguistic proposal: If someone alleges that a certain linguistic phenomenon in English is a counterexample to a given analysis, consider a hypothetical language which (as much as possible) is like English except that the analysis is *stipulated* to be correct. Imagine such a hypothetical language introduced into a community and spoken by it. *If the phenomenon in question would still arise in a community that spoke such a hypothetical language (which may not be English), then the fact that it arises in English cannot disprove the hypothesis that the analysis is correct for English.* An example removed from the present discussion: Some have alleged that identity cannot be the relation that holds between, and only between, each thing and itself, for if so, the nontriviality of identity statements would be inexplicable. If it is conceded, however, that such a relation makes sense, and if it can be shown that a hypothetical language involving such a relation would generate the same problems, it will follow that the existence of these problems does not refute the hypothesis that "identical to" stands for this same relation in English.[23]

By "the weak Russell language," I will mean a language similar to English except that the truth conditions of sentences with definite descriptions are *stipulated* to coincide with Russell's: for example, "The present King of France is bald" is to be true iff exactly one person is King of France, and that person is bald. On the weak Russell language, this effect can be achieved by assigning semantic reference to definite descriptions: the semantic referent of a definite description is the unique object that satisfies the description, if any; otherwise there is no semantic referent. A sentence of the simple subject-predicate form will be true if the predicate is true of the (semantic) referent of its subject; false, if either the subject has no semantic referent or the predicate is not true of the semantic referent of the subject.

Since the weak Russell language takes definite descriptions to be primitive designators, it is not fully Russellian. By "the intermediate Russell language," I mean a language in which sentences containing definite descriptions are taken to be abbreviations or paraphrases of their Russellian analyses: for example, "The present King of France is bald" *means* (or has a "deep structure" like) "Exactly one person is at present King of France, and he is bald," or the like. Descriptions are not terms, and are not assigned reference or meaning in isolation. The "strong Russell language" goes further: definite descriptions are actually *banned* from the language and Russellian paraphrases are used in their place. Instead of saying "Her husband is kind to her," a speaker of this language must say "Exactly one man is married to her, and he is kind to her," or even (better), "There is a unique man who is married to her, and every man who is married to her is kind to her," or the like. If Russell is right, long-windedness is the only defect of these versions.

Would the phenomenon Donnellan adduces arise in communities that spoke these languages? Surely speakers of these languages are no more infallible than we. They too will find themselves at a party and mistakenly think someone is drinking champagne even though he is actually drinking sparkling water. If they are speakers of the weak or intermediate Russell languages, they will say, "The man in the corner drinking champagne is happy tonight." They will say this precisely because *they think, though erroneously, that the Russellian truth conditions are satisfied.* Wouldn't

we say of these speakers that they are referring to the teetotaler, under the misimpression that he is drinking champagne? And, if
he is happy, are they not saying of him, *truly*,
that he is happy? Both answers seem obviously affirmative.

In the case of the weak Russell language,
the general apparatus previously developed
seems fully adequate to account for the
phenomenon. The semantic referent of a
definite description is given by the conditions
laid down above: it is a matter of the specific
conventions of the (weak) Russell language,
in this case that the referent is the unique
object satisfying the descriptive conditions.
The speaker's referent, on the other hand, is
determined by a general theory of speech acts,
applicable to all languages: it is the object to
which the speaker wishes to refer, and which
he believes fulfills the Russellian conditions
for being the semantic referent. Again, in
asserting the sentence he does, the speaker
means that the speaker's referent (the teetotaler) satisfied the predicate (is happy). Thus
the rough theoretical apparatus above accounts fully for our intuitions about this case.

What about the other Russellian languages? Even in the strong Russell language,
where explicit descriptions are outlawed, the
same phenomena can occur. In fact, they
occur in English in "arch" uses of existential
quantification: "Exactly *one person* (or: *some*
person or other) is drinking champagne in that
corner, and I hear he is romantically linked
with Jane Smith." The circumlocution, in
English, expresses the delicacy of the topic,
but the speaker's reference (in quite an
ordinary sense) may well be clear, even if he
in fact is drinking sparkling water. In English
such circumlocutions are common only when
the speaker wishes to achieve a rather arch
and prissy effect, but in the strong Russell
language (which of course isn't English), they
would be made more common because the
definite article is prohibited.

This example leads to an extension of the
notion of speaker's reference. When a
speaker asserts an existential quantification,
$(\exists x)(\phi x \wedge \psi x)$, it may be clear which thing he
has in mind as satisfying "ϕx," and he may

wish to convey to his hearers that that thing
satisfies "ψx." In this case, the thing in
question (which may or may not actually
satisfy "ϕx") is called the "speaker's referent"
when he makes the existential assertion. In
English, as I have mentioned, such cases
("arch" uses) are rather rare; but they can be
carried off even if the existential quantification is expressed in a highly roundabout and
apparently nonreferring fashion. "Not *everyone* in this room is abstaining from champagne, and any such nonabstainer. . . ."[24]

If the notion of speaker's reference applies
to the strong Russell language, it can apply to
the intermediate Russell language as well,
since the speaker's referent of "$\psi(\imath x \phi)(x))$" is
then the thing he has in mind as uniquely
instantiating "$\phi(x)$" and about which he
wishes to convey that it ψ's.

Since the phenomenon Donnellan cites
would arise in all the Russell languages, if
they *were* spoken, the fact that they *do* arise in
English, as *actually* spoken, can be no argument that English is not a Russell language.

We may contrast the Russell languages with
what may be called the D-languages. In the
D-languages the apparent ambiguity between
referential and attributive definite descriptions is explicitly built into the semantics of
the language and affects truth conditions.
(The D-languages are meant to suggest "Donnellan," but are not called the "Donnellan
languages," since Donnellan, as we have
seen, is "ambiguous" as to whether he posits a
semantic ambiguity.) The *unambiguous D-
language* contains two distinct words, "the"
and "ze" (rhymes with "the"). A statement of
the form ". . . the F . . ." is true iff the
predicate represented by the dots is true of the
unique object fulfilling F (we need not specify
what happens if there is no such thing; if we
wish to follow Russell, take it to be false). A
statement of the form ". . . ze F . . ." is to be
true iff the predicate represented by the dots
is true of the unique thing the speaker thinks F
is true of. (Once again, we leave free what
happens if there is no such thing.) *The
ambiguous D-language* is like the unambiguous D-language except that "the," ambiguously, can be interpreted according to the

semantics either of "the" *or* of "ze." The general impression conveyed by Donnellan's paper, in spite of his statement at one point to the contrary, is that English is the ambiguous D-language; only on such a hypothesis could we say that the "referential use" (really, referential *sense*) diverges from Russell's theory. The truth-conditions of statements containing "ze," and therefore of one sense of "the" in the ambiguous D-language, *are* incompatible with Russell's theory.[25]

We have two hypotheses: one says that English is a Russell language, while the other says that English is the ambiguous D-language. Which hypothesis is preferable? Since, as we have argued, the phenomena Donnellan adduces would arise in a hypothetical society that spoke any of the Russell languages, the existence in English of such phenomena provides no argument against the hypothesis that English is a Russell language. If Donnellan had possessed a clear intuition that "Her husband is kind to her," uttered in reference to the kind lover of a woman married to a cruel husband, expressed the literal truth, then he *would* have adduced a phenomenon that conforms to the ambiguous D-language but is incompatible with any Russell language. But Donnellan makes no such assertion: he cautiously, and correctly, confines himself to the weaker claim that the speaker spoke truly of the man to whom he referred. This weaker claim, we have seen, *would* hold for a speaker of a Russell language.

So Donnellan's examples provide, in themselves, no evidence that English is the ambiguous D-language rather than a Russell language. Granting that this is so, we can ask whether there is any reason to favor the Russell language hypothesis over the D-language hypothesis. I think there are several general methodological considerations that are relevant.

The Russell language theory, or any other unitary account (that is, any account that postulates no semantic ambiguity), accounts for Donnellan's referential–attributive phenomenon by a general pragmatic theory of speech acts, applicable to a very wide range of languages; the D-language hypothesis ac-counts for these same phenomena by positing a semantic ambiguity. The unitary account appeals to a general apparatus that applies to cases, such as the "Smith-Jones" case, where it is completely implausible that a semantic ambiguity exists. According to the unitary account, far from the referential use constitut-ing a special namelike use of definite descrip-tions, the referential–attributive distinction is simply a special case of a general distinction, applicable to proper names as well as to definite descriptions, and illustrated in prac-tice by the (leaf-raking) Smith-Jones case. And anyone who compares the Smith-Jones case, where presumably no one is tempted to posit a special semantic ambiguity, with Don-nellan's cases of definite descriptions, must surely be impressed by the similarity of the phenomena.[26]

Under these circumstances, surely general methodological principles favor the existing account. The apparatus of speaker's reference and semantic reference, and of simple and complex uses of designators, is needed *any-way,* to explain the Smith-Jones case; it is applicable to all languages.[27] Why posit a semantic ambiguity when it is both insufficient in general and superfluous for the special case it seeks to explain?[28] And why are the phenomena regarding proper names so similar to those for definite descriptions, if the one case involves no semantic ambiguity while the other does?

It is very much the lazy man's approach in philosophy to posit ambiguities when in trouble. If we face a putative counterexample to our favorite philosophical thesis, it is always open to us to protest that some key term is being used in a special sense, different from its use in the thesis. We may be right, but the ease of the move should counsel a policy of caution: Do not posit an ambiguity unless you are really forced to, unless there are really compelling theoretical or intuitive grounds to suppose that an ambiguity really is present.

Let me say a bit more in defense of this. Many philosophers, for example, have advo-cated a "strong" account of knowledge ac-cording to which it is very hard to know anything; stiff requirements must be satisfied.

When such philosophers have been confronted with intuitive counterexamples to such strong requirements for knowledge they either have condemned them as popular and loose usages or they have asserted that "know" is being used in a different "weak" sense. The latter move—distinguishing two or more "strong" and "weak" senses of "know"—strikes me as implausible. There *are* different senses of "know," distinguished in German as "kennen" and "wissen," and in French as "connaître" and "savoir"; a person is usually known in the one sense, a fact in the other. It is no surprise that other languages use distinct words for these various senses of "know"; there is no reason for the ambiguity to be preserved in languages unrelated to our own. But what about the uses of "know" that characteristically are followed by that-clauses, knowing that *p?* Are these ambiguous? I would be very surprised to be told that the Eskimos have two separate words, one for (say) Hintikka's "strong" sense of "know," another for his "weak" sense. Perhaps this indicates that we think of knowledge as a unitary concept, unlikely to be "disambiguated" by two separate words in any language.

We thus have two methodological considerations that can be used to test any alleged ambiguity. "Bank" is ambiguous; we would expect the ambiguity to be disambiguated by separate and unrelated words in some other languages. Why should the two separate senses be reproduced in languages unrelated to English? First, then, we can consult our linguistic intuitions, independently of any empirical investigation. Would we be surprised to find languages that used two separate words for the two alleged senses of a given word? If so, then, to that extent our linguistic intuitions are really intuitions of a unitary concept, rather than of a word that expresses two distinct and unrelated senses. Second, we can ask empirically whether languages are in fact found that contain distinct words expressing the allegedly distinct senses. If no such language is found, once again this is evidence that a unitary account of the word or phrase in question should be sought.

As far as our main question is concerned, the first of these two tests, that of our intuitive expectation, seems to me overwhelmingly to favor a unitary account of descriptions, as opposed to the ambiguity postulated in the ambiguous D-language. If English really is the ambiguous D-language, we should expect to find other languages where the referential and attributive uses are expressed by two separate words, as in the *unambiguous* D-language. I at least would find it quite surprising to learn that say, the Eskimo, used two separate words "the" and "ze," for the attributive and referential uses. To the extent that I have this intuition, to that extent I think of "the" as a unitary concept. I should have liked to be able to report that I have reinforced this guess by an actual empirical examination of other languages—the second test—but as of now I haven't done so.[29]

Several general methodological considerations favor the Russell language (or some other unitary account) against the ambiguous D-language as a model for English. First, the unitary account conforms to considerations of economy in that it does not "multiply senses beyond necessity." Second, the metalinguistic apparatus invoked by the unitary account to explain the referential–attributive distinction is an apparatus that is needed in *any case* for other cases, such as proper names. The separate referential sense of descriptions postulated by the D-language hypothesis, is an idle wheel that does no work: if it were absent, we would be able to express everything we wished to express, in the same way. Further, the resemblance between the case of descriptions and that of proper names (where presumably no one would be tempted to postulate an ambiguity) is so close that any attempt to explain the cases differently is automatically suspect. Finally, we would not expect the alleged ambiguity to be disambiguated in other languages, and this means we probably regard ourselves as possessing a unitary concept.

Aside from methodological considerations, is there any direct evidence that would favor one of our two rival accounts? As I remarked above, if we had a direct intuition that "Her husband is kind to her" could be true even when her actual husband is cruel, then we would have decisive evidence for the D-language model; but Donnellan rightly disclaims any such intuition. On the other hand, I myself feel that such a sentence expresses a falsehood, even when "her husband" is used referentially to refer to a kind man; but the popularity of Donnellan's view has made me uncertain that this intuition should be pressed very far. In the absence of such direct intuitions that would settle the matter conclusively, it would seem that the actual practice of English speakers is compatible with either model, and that only general methodological considerations favor one hypothesis rather than another. Such a situation leaves me uneasy. If there really is no direct evidence to distinguish the two hypotheses, how are they different hypotheses? If two communities, one of whom spoke the ambiguous D-language and the other of whom spoke the (weak) Russell language, would be able to intermingle freely without detecting any linguistic difference, do they really speak two different languages? If so, wherein is the difference?

Two hypothetical communities, one of which was explicitly taught the ambiguous D-language and the other of which was taught the (weak) Russell language (say, in school), would have direct and differing intuitions about the truth-value of "Her husband was kind to her"; but it is uncertain whether English speakers have any such intuitions. If they have none, is this a respect in which English differs from both the Russell languages and the D-languages, and thus differentiates it from both? Or, on the contrary, is there a pragmatic consideration, deriving no doubt from the fact that the relevant rules of language are not explicitly taught, that will explain why we lack such intuitions (if we do) without showing that neither the D-language nor the Russell language is English?

Some commentators on the dispute between Russell and Frege and Strawson over sentences containing vacuous definite descriptions have held that no direct linguistic phenomena conclusively decide between the two

views: we should therefore choose the most economical and theoretically satisfying model. But if this is so, are there really two views, and if there are, shouldn't we perhaps say that neither is correct? A hypothetical community that was explicitly taught Russellian or Frege-Strawsonian truth-conditions for sentences containing vacuous definite descriptions would have no difficulty producing direct intuitions that decide the Russell-Strawson dispute. If the commentators in question are correct, speakers of English have no such intuitions. Surely this fact, too, would be a significant fact about English, for which linguistic theory should give an account. Perhaps pragmatic considerations suffice for such an account; or, perhaps, the alleged lack of any such intuition must be accounted for by a feature built into the semantics of English itself. In the latter case, neither the Russellian nor the Frege-Strawsonian truth-conditions would be appropriate for English. Similar considerations would apply to the issue between Donnellan and Russell.[30]

I am uncertain about these questions. Certainly it would be best if there were directly observable phenomena that differentiated between the two hypotheses. Actually I can think of one rather special and localized phenomenon that may indeed favor the Russellian hypothesis, or some other unitary hypothesis. Consider the following two dialogues:

Dialogue I: A: "Her husband is kind to her."

B: "No, he isn't. The man you're referring to isn't her husband."

Dialogue II: A: "Her husband is kind to her."

B: "He is kind to her, but he isn't her husband."

In the first dialogue the respondent (B) uses "he" to refer to the semantic referent of "her husband" as used by the first speaker (A); in the second dialogue the respondent uses "he" to refer to the speaker's referent. My tendency is to think that both dialogues are proper. The unitary account can explain this fact, by saying that pronominalization can pick up *either* a previous semantic reference or a previous speaker's reference.[31,32] In the case of the two contrasting dialogues, these diverge.

If English were the ambiguous D-language, the second dialogue would be easy to explain. "He" refers to the object that is both the semantic referent and the speaker's referent of "her husband." (Recall that the notions of speaker's reference and semantic reference are general notions applicable to all languages, even to the D-languages.[33]) The first dialogue, however, would be much more difficult, perhaps impossible, to explain. When A said "her husband," according to the D-language hypothesis he was using "her husband" in the referential sense. Both the speaker's referent and the semantic referent would be the kind lover; only if B had misunderstood A's use as attributive could he have used "he" to refer to the husband, but such a misunderstanding is excluded by the second part of B's utterance. If the first dialogue is proper, it seems hard to fit it into the D-language model.[34]

4. CONCLUSION

I said at the beginning that the main concern of this paper was methodological rather than substantive. I do think that the considerations in this paper make it overwhelmingly probable that an ultimate account of the phenomena behind Donnellan's distinction will make use of the pragmatic ambiguity between "simple" and "complex" uses, as I defined them above, rather than postulating an ambiguity of the D-language type. But any ultimate substantive conclusion on the issue requires a more extensive and thorough treatment than has been given here. First, I have not here examined theories that attempt to explain Donnellan's distinction as a *syntactic* ambiguity, either of scope or of restrictive and nonrestrictive clauses in deep structure.[35] Both these views, like the line suggested in the present paper, are compatible with a unitary hypothesis such as the hypothesis that English is a Russell language. Although I am not inclined to accept either of these views, some

others have found them plausible and unless they are rebutted, they too indicate that Donnellan's observations cannot be taken as providing a conclusive argument against Russell without further discussion.

Second, and most important, no treatment of definite descriptions can be complete unless it examines the complete range of uses of the definite article and related linguistic phenomena. Such a treatment should attempt, as I have argued above, to make it clear why the same construction with a definite article is used for a wide range of cases. It would be wrong for me not to mention the phenomena most favorable to Donnellan's intuitions. In a demonstrative use such as "that table," it seems plausible, as I have mentioned above,[36] that the term rigidly designates its referent. It also seems plausible that the reference of such a demonstrative construction can be an object to which the descriptive adjectives in the construction do not apply (for example, "that scoundrel" may be used to refer to someone who is not, in fact, a scoundrel) and it is not clear that the distinction between speaker's reference and semantic reference should be invoked to account for this. As I also said above, it seems to me to be likely that "indefinite" definite descriptions[37] such as "the table" present difficulties for a Russellian analysis. It is somewhat tempting to assimilate such descriptions to the corresponding demonstratives (for example, "that table") and to the extent that such a temptation turns out to be plausible, there may be new arguments in such cases for the intuitions of those who have advocated a rigid vs. nonrigid ambiguity in definite descriptions, or for Donnellan's intuitions concerning the referential case, or for both.[38]

Because I have not yet worked out a complete account that satisfies me, and because I think it would be wrong to make any definitive claim on the basis of the restricted class of phenomena considered here, I regard the primary lessons of this paper as methodological. They illustrate some general methodological considerations and apparatus that I think should be applied to the problems discussed here and to other linguistic problems. They show in the present case that the argument Donnellan actually presents in his original paper shows nothing against a Russellian or other unitary account, and they make it highly probable to me that the problems Donnellan handles by semantic ambiguity should instead be treated by a general theory of speech acts. But at this time nothing more definitive can be said. I think that the distinction between semantic reference and speaker's reference will be of importance not only (as in the present paper) as a critical tool to block postulation of unwarranted ambiguities, but also will be of considerable constructive importance for a theory of language. In particular, I find it plausible that a diachronic account of the evolution of language is likely to suggest that what was originally a mere speaker's reference may, if it becomes habitual in a community, evolve into a semantic reference. And this consideration may be *one* of the factors needed to clear up some puzzles in the theory of reference.[39,40]

ACKNOWLEDGMENTS

I should like to thank Margaret Gilbert and Howard Wettstein for their assistance in the preparation of this paper.

NOTES

1. Versions of this paper—not read from the present manuscript—were given from 1971 onward to colloquia at New York University, M.I.T., the University of California (Los Angeles), and elsewhere. The present version was written on the basis of a transcript of the M.I.T. version prepared by the editors of this volume. Donnellan himself heard the talk at U.C.L.A., and his "Speaker Reference, Descriptions, and Anaphora," to a large extent appears to be a comment on considerations of the type mentioned here. (He does not, however, specifically refer to the present paper.) I decided *not* to alter the paper I gave in talks to take Donnellan's later views into account: largely I think the earlier version stands on its own, and the issues Donnellan raises in the later paper can be discussed elsewhere. Something should be said here, however, about the pronominalization phenomena. In his paper, Donnellan seems to think that these phenomena are incompatible with the suggestion that speaker's reference is a pragmatic notion. On the contrary, at the end of the present paper (and of the talk Donnellan heard), I emphasize these very phenomena and argue that they support this suggestion. See also note 31 below.

2. [Reprinted in this volume.] See also Keith S. Donnellan, "Putting Humpty Dumpty Together Again," *The Philosophical Review*, 77 (1968): 203–215.

3. In his later paper mentioned above in note 1, Donnellan seems more clearly to advocate a semantic ambiguity; but he hedges a bit even in the later paper.

4. I will also avoid cases of "improper" descriptions, where the uniqueness condition fails. Such descriptions may or may not be important for an ultimate evaluation of Donnellan's position, but none of the arguments in his paper rest on them.

5. "Reference and Definite Descriptions," p. 285. My discussion in this paragraph and the next is based on Donnellan's paper, pp. 285, 289–90.

6. At the time, it had not yet been revealed that Kissinger was the official in question.

7. In fact, no n-fold distinction can do so, for any fixed n. Independently of the present writer, L. Kartunnen has argued similarly that no dual or n-fold distinction can replace scope distinctions. I discussed the matter briefly in "Identity and Necessity," *Identity and Individuation*, ed. M. Munitz (New York: 1972), p. 149, n. 10.

8. See the papers of Stalnaker and Partee in *The Semantics of Natural Language*, eds. D. Davidson and G. Harman (Dordrecht: 1971) for such suggestions and also for some of the views mentioned in the previous section. I should emphasize that most of the stimulating discussion in these papers can be made independent of any of the identifications of Donnellan's distinction with others which are rejected here.

9. See his paper "The Contingent *A Priori* and Rigid Designators," [in which] Donnellan asks whether I think proper names (in natural language) are *always* rigid: obviously, he thinks, proper names *could* be introduced to abbreviate nonrigid definite descriptions. My view is that proper names (except perhaps, for some quirky and derivative uses, that are not uses as *names*) *are* always rigid. In particular this applies to "Neptune." It would be logically possible to have single words that abbreviated nonrigid definite descriptions, but these would not be *names*. The point is not merely terminological: I mean that such abbreviated nonrigid definite descriptions would differ in an important semantical feature from (what we call) typical proper names in our actual speech. I merely state my position and do not argue it; nor can I digress to comment on the other points raised in Donnellan's paper in this volume.

10. See Kaplan's paper "Dthat." [Reprinted in this volume.] In that paper, however, he also has some tendency to confuse rigidity with Donnellan's referentiality.
11. In the Davidson-Harman volume mentioned in note 8. [Partially reprinted in this volume.]
12. For this view, see Jerrold J. Katz, "Logic and Language: An Examination of Recent Criticisms of Intensionalism," in *Minnesota Studies in the Philosophy of Science*, vol. VII (Minneapolis: 1975), pp. 36–130. See especially sections 5.1 and 5.2. As far as proper names are concerned, Katz thinks that *other* arguments tell against the description theory even as a theory of meaning.
13. See Donnellan, "Reference and Definite Descriptions," [p. 245, this volume].
14. So I argued in the talks, and rightly, if Donnellan is taken literally. See note 25 below, however, for a more charitable reading, which probably corresponds to Donnellan's intent. We must, however, take descriptions to be *semantically* ambiguous if we are to maintain the reading in question: see the point raised immediately after this one.
15. "Reference and Definite Descriptions" [p. 243].
16. For Grice, see the following papers, which I follow loosely in a good deal of the discussion at the beginning of this section: "The Causal Theory of Perception," *Proceedings of the Aristotelian Society,* supplementary vol. 35 (1961); "Logic and Conversation" [reprinted in this volume]; "Meaning," *Philosophical Review* 66 (1957), 337–88; [reprinted in this volume] "Utterer's Meaning, Sentence-Meaning and Word-Meaning," *Foundations of Language* 4 (1968), 225–42; "Utterer's Meaning and Intentions, *Philosophical Review* 78 (1969), 144–77."
17. In "The Causal Theory of Perception."
18. Suppose the second burglar is well aware of the proximity of the police, but procrastinates in his greed for more loot. Then the first burglar imparts no *information* by saying what he does, but simply urges the second burglar to "split."
19. Although conversational principles are applicable to *all languages,* they may apply differently to *different societies.* In a society where blunt statement was considered rude, where "it looks red" replaced "it is red" just because of such a custom, "it looks red" might carry different conversational implicatures from our own. This might be the case even though the members of the society spoke *English,* just as we do. Conversational principles are matters for the psychology, sociology, and anthropology of linguistic communities; they are applicable to these communities no matter what language they may speak, though the applicable principles may vary somewhat with the communities (and may even, to some extent, be conditioned by the fact that they speak languages with

certain structures.) Often, of course, we can state widely applicable, "cross-cultural," general conversational principles. Semantic and syntactic principles, on the other hand, are matters of the conventions of a language, in whatever cultural matrix it may be spoken. *Perhaps* sometimes it is difficult to draw the line, but it exists in general nonetheless.
20. If the views about proper names I have advocated in "Naming and Necessity" are correct (Donnellan, in fact, holds similar views), the conventions regarding names in an idiolect usually involve the fact that the idiolect is no mere idiolect, but part of a common language, in which reference may be passed from link to link.

    As the present paper attests, my views on proper names in "Naming and Necessity" have no special connection with the referential–attributive distinction.
21. "Naming and Necessity," p. 343, n. 3.
22. Donnellan shows in his paper that there are "referential" uses, of a somewhat exceptional kind, where the speaker, or even both the speaker and the hearer, are aware that the description used does not apply to the thing they are talking about. For example, they use "the King," knowing him to be a usurper, but fearing the secret police. Analogous cases can be given for proper names: if Smith is a lunatic who thinks he is Napoleon, they may humor him. Largely for the sake of simplicity of exposition, I have excluded such both from the notion of speaker's reference and from Donnellan's "referential" use (and the "D-languages" below). I do not think that the situation would be materially altered if both notions were revised so as to admit these cases, in a more refined analysis. In particular, it would probably *weaken* the case for a semantic ambiguity if these cases were allowed: for they shade into ironical and "inverted commas" cases. "He is a 'fine friend'," may be ironical (whether or not inverted commas are used in the transcription). " 'The King' is still in power"; " 'Napoleon' has gone to bed" are similar, whether or not explicit inverted commas are used. It is fairly clear that "fine friend," "brilliant scholar," etc., do not have ironical and inverted commas *senses:* irony is a certain form of speech act, to be accounted for by pragmatic considerations. The case for a semantic ambiguity in definite descriptions is similarly *weakened* if we include such cases as referential uses.

    In ordinary discourse, we say that the speaker was referring to someone under a wide variety of circumstances, including linguistic errors, verbal slips, and deliberate misuses of language. (If Mrs. Malaprop says, "The geography teacher said that equilateral triangles are equiangular," she *refers* to the geometry teacher.) The more such phenomena one includes in the notion of speaker's reference, the further one gets from any connection of the notion with semantical matters.

23. See the discussion of "schmidentity" in "Naming and Necessity."

24. Or, using variables explicitly, "There is a person x such that . . ." Notice that in an utterance of "$(\exists x)\ (\phi x \wedge \psi x)$," as long as it is clear *which* thing allegedly satisfying "ϕx" the speaker has in mind, there can be a speaker's referent, even if both the speaker and the hearer are aware that many things satisfy "ϕx."

25. This description of the D-languages specifies nothing about semantical features more "intensional" than truth conditions. It is plausible to assume that "ze F" is a *rigid* designator of the thing believed to be uniquely F, but this is not explicitly included in the extensional truth conditions. Nor has anything been said about the behavior of "ze F" in belief and indirect discourse contexts. *If* we stipulate that "ze F," even in such contexts, designates the thing the speaker believes uniquely F's, then indeed "Jones said that ze man she married is kind to her," will not be a proper way of reporting Jones's utterance "Ze man she married is kind to her" (even if Jones and the speaker happen to have the same belief as to who her husband is; the difficulty is more obvious if they do not.) No doubt it is this fact that lies behind Donnellan's view that, in the referential case, it is hard to speak of "the statement," even though his exposition of the matter seems to be defective. Such implications, which are not present in the Russell language, lend only further implausibility to the supposition that English is the ambiguous D-language.

To repeat note 22, actually there are many other ways, other than taking something uniquely to satisfy "F," that might be included under referential uses of "the F." The best short way to specify the semantics of "ze F" would seem to be this: "ze F" refers, in the unambiguous D-language, to what would have been the speaker's referent of "the F" in the weak Russell language (under the same circumstances)! But this formulation makes it very implausible that the ambiguous D-language is anything but a chimerical model for English.

26. There is one significant difference between the case of proper names and that of definite descriptions. If someone uses "Jones" to refer to Smith, he has *misidentified* Smith as Jones, taken Smith for someone else. To some extent I *did* think that *Jones* was raking the leaves. (I assume that "Jones" is already in his idiolect as a name of Jones. If I am introduced to an impostor and am told, "This man is none other than Albert Einstein," if I am fooled I will have *taken* him, falsely, to be Einstein. Someone else, who has never heard of Einstein before,

may merely be mistaken as to the impostor's name.) On the other hand, if I think that someone is "her husband" and so refer to him, I need not at all have confused two people. I merely think that one person possesses a property—that of being married to her—that in fact he lacks. The real husband is irrelevant.

27. In terms of this apparatus, I can sharpen the reply to Katz, note 12 above. If Schmidt had discovered the incompleteness of arithmetic but I had thought it was Gödel who did so, a complex ("referential") use of the description has a semantic reference to Schmidt but a speaker's reference to Gödel. Once I am apprised of the true facts, speaker's reference and semantic reference will coincide thereafter and I will no longer use the description to refer to Gödel. The name "Gödel," on the other hand, has Gödel as its *semantic* referent: the name will always be applied to Gödel in the presence of correct information. Whether a term would be withdrawn in the presence of correct information (without changing the language) is a good intuitive test for divergence of semantic reference and speaker's reference (disregarding the cases in note 22).

28. There is another problem for any theory of semantic ambiguity. Donnellan says that if I say "Smith's murderer is insane," solely on the basis of the grisly conditions of Smith's body, my use of "Smith's murderer" is attributive (even if I in fact have a belief as to who the murderer is), but if I say it on the basis of the supposed murderer's behavior at the dock, my use is referential. Surely, however, my reasons can be mixed: perhaps neither consideration would have sufficed by itself, but they suffice jointly. What is my use then? A user of the unambiguous D-language would have to choose between "the" and "ze." It seems very implausible to suppose that the speaker is confused and uncertain about what sense he gives to his description; but what else can we say if we suppose that English is the ambiguous D-language? (This problem arises even if the man at the dock is guilty, so that in fact there is no conflict. It is more obvious if he is innocent.)

A pragmatic theory of the referential–attributive distinction can handle such cases much more easily. Clearly there can be borderline cases between the simple and the complex use—where, to some extent the speaker wishes to speak of the semantic referent and to some extent he wishes to speak of something he believes to be the semantic referent. He need not sort out his motives carefully, since he thinks these things are one and the same!

Given such mixed motives, the speaker's reference may be partially to one thing and partially to another, even when the semantic reference is unambiguous. This is especially likely in the case of proper names, since divergences between speaker's referent and semantic referent are characteristically *misidentifications* (see note 26). Even if the speaker's referent of "Jones" in "Jones is raking the leaves" is Smith, to some extent I have said *of Jones* that he is raking the leaves. There are gradations, depending on the speaker's interests and intentions, as to what extent the speaker's reference was to Jones and to what extent it was to Smith. The problem is less common in the case of descriptions, where misidentification need not have occurred.

29. Of course these tests must be used with some caution. The mere fact that some language subdivides the extension of an English word into several subclasses, with their own separate words, and has no word for the whole extension, does not show that the English word was ambiguous (think of the story that the Eskimos have different words for different kinds of snow). If many unrelated languages preserve a single word, this in itself is evidence for a unitary concept. On the other hand, a word may have different senses that are obviously related. One sense may be metaphorical for another (though in that case, it may not really be a separate sense, but simply a common metaphor.) "Statistics" can mean both statistical data and the science of evaluating such data. And the like. The more we can explain relations among senses, and the more "natural" and "inevitable" the relationship, the more we will expect the different senses to be preserved in a wide variety of other languages.

The test, therefore, needs further exploration and refinement. It is certainly wrong to postulate an ambiguity without any explanation of some connection between the "senses" that explains why they occur in a wide variety of languages. In the referential–attributive case, I feel that any attempt to explain the connection between the referential and the attributive uses will be so close to the kind of pragmatic account offered here as to render any assumptions of distinct senses inplausible and superfluous.

30. That is, the *concept* of truth conditions is somehow inappropriate for the semantics of English. The vague uneasiness expressed in these paragraphs expresses my own rather confused occasional doubts and is ancillary to the main theme. Moore's "paradox of analysis" may be a related problem.

Quine's philosophy of language characteristically is based on a naturalistic doubt about building any "rules" or "conventions" into a language that are not recoverable from actual linguistic practices, even if such rules may be necessary to stipulate the language. In this sense, the uneasiness expressed is Quinean in spirit. I find Quine's emphasis on a naturalistic approach to some extent salutary. But I also

feel that our intuitions of semantic rules as speakers should not be ignored cavalierly.

31. Geach, in his book "Reference and Generality," emended ed. (Ithaca: 1970), and elsewhere, has argued vigorously against speaking of pronominalization as picking up a previous reference. I do not wish to argue the extent to which he is right here. I use the terminology given in the text for convenience, but to the extent Geach's views are correct I think the example could presumably be reformulated to fit his scheme. I think the views expressed in this paper are very much in the spirit of Geach's remarks on definite descriptions and speaker's reference in the book just cited. See Geach's discussion, e.g., on p. 8.

32. Donnellan, in "Speaker Reference, Descriptions, and Anaphora," thinks that the fact that pronouns can pick up a previous semantic reference somehow casts doubt on a view that makes speaker's reference a nonsemantical notion. I don't see why: "he," "she," "that," etc., can, under various circumstances, refer to anything salient in an appropriate way. Being physically distinguished against its background is a property that may make an object salient; having been referred to by a previous speaker is another. In "Naming and Necessity," note 3, I suggested tentatively that Donnellan's "remarks about reference have little to do with semantics or truth conditions." The point would be put more exactly if I had said that Donnellan's distinction is not itself a semantical one, though it is relevant to semantics through pronominalization, as many other nonsemantical properties are.

Pronominalization phenomena are relevant to another point. Often one hears it argued against Russell's existential analysis of *indefinite* descriptions that an indefinite description may be anaphorically referred to by a pronoun that seems to preserve the reference of the indefinite description. I am not sure that these phenomena do conflict with the existential analysis. (I am not completely sure there are some that don't, either.) In any event, many cases can be accounted for (given a Russellian theory) by the facts that: (i) existential statements can carry a speaker's reference; (ii) pronouns can refer to the speaker's referent.

33. The use of "ze" in the unambiguous D-language is such that the semantic reference automatically coincided with the speaker's reference, but nevertheless, the notions are applicable. So are the notions of simple and complex uses of designators. However, speakers of the unambiguous D-language might be less likely ever to use "the" in a complex case: for, one might be inclined to argue, if such are their intentions, why not use "ze"?

34. Various moves might be tried, but none that I can think of seem to me to be plausible. It has

been suggested to me that sometimes the respondent in a dialogue deliberately feigns to misunderstand an ambiguous phrase used by the first speaker, and that, given the supposed ambiguity of "her husband" in the ambiguous D-language, the first dialogue can be interpreted as such a case. For example, the following dialogue: "Jones put the money in a bank." "He put the money in one all right, but it wasn't a commercial bank; he was so much afraid it would be discovered that he hid it near the river." It seems implausible to me that the first dialogue in the text fits into such a very jocular model. But notice further that the joke consists in a mock *confirmation* of the first speaker's assertion. It would be rather bizarre to respond, "He didn't put the money in the bank, and it wasn't a commercial bank." The first dialogue would have to conform to such a bizarre pattern on the hypothesis in question.

Alternatively, it might be suggested that B uses "he" as a pronoun of laziness for A's "her husband," taken in the supposed referential sense. This move seems to be excluded, since B may well be in no position to use "her husband" referentially. He may merely have heard that she is married to a cruel man.

35. I believe that Kartunnen has advocated the view that the referential–attributive distinction arises from a scope ambiguity; I do not know whether this has been published. Since the referential–attributive "ambiguity" arises even in simple sentences such as "Smith's murderer is insane," where there appears to be no room for any scope ambiguity, such a view seems forced to rely on acceptance of Ross's suggestion that all English assertive utterances begin with an initial "I say that," which is suppressed in "surface structure" but present in "deep structure."

For the view that derives the referential–attributive "ambiguity" from a distinction of restrictive and nonrestrictive clauses in "deep structure," see J. M. Bell, "What is Referential Opacity?", *The Journal of Philosophical Logic*, 2 (1973): 155–180. See also the work of Emmon Bach on which Bell's paper is based, "Nouns and Noun Phrases," in *Universals in Linguistic Theory*, ed. E. Bach and R. T. Harms (New York: 1968), pp. 91–122. For reasons of space I have not treated these views here. But some of my arguments that Donnellan's distinction is pragmatic apply against them also.

36. See p. 260 above; also see note 10 above.

37. The term is Donnellan's. See "Putting Humpty Dumpty Together Again," p. 204, footnote 5.

38. I believe that when Donnellan heard the present paper, he too mentioned considerations of this kind. The cases are mentioned briefly in Donnellan's paper, "Putting Humpty Dumpty Together Again," *ibid*. Donnellan's paper "Speaker Reference, Descriptions and Anaphora" mentioned above also makes use of the existence of such incomplete descriptions but I do not find his arguments conclusive.

39. See the Santa Claus and Madagascar cases in "Naming and Necessity."

40. It seems likely that the considerations in this paper will also be relevant to the concept of a supposed "± Specific" distinction for indefinite descriptions, as advocated by many linguists.

SUGGESTED FURTHER READING

Donnellan, Keith, Putting Humpty Dumpty Together Again, *Philosophical Review* 77 (1967), 203–215.

Donnellan, Keith, Speaker Reference, Descriptions, and Anaphora, in *Contemporary Perspectives in the Philosophy of Language*, ed. Peter A. French, Theodore E. Uehling, Jr. and Howard K. Wettstein (Minneapolis: University of Minnesota Press, 1979), pp. 28–44.

Gareth Evans, *Varieties of Reference* (Oxford: Oxford University Press, 1982).

Geach, Peter, *Reference and Generality* emended ed. (Ithaca: Cornell University Press, 1965).

Kaplan, David, What is Russell's Theory of Descriptions? in *Bertrand Russell*, ed. D. F. Pears (Garden City, N.Y.: Anchor Books, 1972), pp. 227–44.

Linsky, Leonard, *Referring* (London: Routledge & Kegan Paul, 1967).

MacKay, Alfred F., Mr. Donnellan and Humpty Dumpty on Referring, *Philosophical Review*, 77 (1968), 197–202.

Martinich, A. P., The Attributive Use of Proper Names, *Analysis*, 37 (1979), 159–163.

Martinich, A. P., Referring, *Philosophy and Phenomenological Research* 40 (1979), 157–172.

Martinich, A.P. *Communication and Reference* (Berlin and New York: Walter de Gruyter, 1984), pp. 133–199.

Russell, Bertrand, Denoting, in *Principles of Mathematics*, 2d ed. (New York: W. W. Norton & Company, Inc., 1937), pp. 53–65.

Searle, John R., *Expression and Meaning* (Cambridge: Cambridge University Press, 1979), pp. 137–161.

Searle, John R., *Intentionality* (Cambridge University Pres, Cambridge: 1983), pp. 197–261.

Strawson, P. F., *Subject and Predicate in Logic and Grammar* (London: Methuen & Company, 1974).

Stroll, Avrum, On "The," *Philosophy and Phenomenological Research* 16 (1955–56), 496–504.

Vendler, Zeno, Singular Terms, in *Linguistics in Philosophy* (Ithaca: Cornell University Press, 1967), pp. 33–69.

IV

NAMES AND DEMONSTRATIVES

Bertrand Russell argued that descriptions are not names. It might seem that this would need no argument at all unless one knows something about the history of philosophical views about names. Russell was in effect arguing against the great nineteenth century philosopher John Stuart Mill, who held that descriptions are "many-worded names" (*System of Logic,* book I, chapter 2, section 2). His own example of a many-worded name is "the king who succeeded William the Conqueror."

Although philosophers have concentrated on understanding how names of individuals function or what their meanings are, the function and meaning of general names is equally important, and Mill treated both equally. He says that names can be divided into two types: connotative and nonconnotative. The historical importance of Mill's view justifies quoting from him at length:

A non-connotative term is one which signifies a subject only, or an attribute only. A connotative term is one which denotes a subject and implies an attribute. By a subject is here meant anything which possesses attributes. Thus John, or London, or England are names which signify a subject only. Whiteness, length, virtue, signify an attribute only. None of these names, therefore, are connotative. But *white, long, virtuous,* are connotative. The word *white* denotes all white things, as snow, paper, the foam of the sea, etc., and implies, or in the language of the schoolmen, *connotes,* the attribute *whiteness.* The word *white* is not predicated of the attribute, but of the subjects, snow, etc.; but when we predicate it of them, we convey the meaning that the attribute whiteness now belongs to them. . . .

All concrete general names are connotative. The word *man,* for example, denotes Peter, Jane, John, and an indefinite number of other individuals of whom, taken as a class, it is the name. But it is applied to them because they possess, and to signify that they possess, certain attributes. These seem to be corporeity, animal life, rationality, and a certain external form which, for distinction, we call the human. Every existing thing which possessed all these attributes would be called a man; and anything which possessed none of them, or only one, or two, or even three of them without the fourth, would not be so called. For example, if in the interior of Africa there were to be discovered a race of animals possessing reason equal to that of human beings but with the form of an elephant, they would not be called men. Swift's Houyhnhnms would not be so called. Or if such newly-discovered beings possessed the form of man without any vestige of reason, it is probable that some other name than that of man would be found for them. How it happens that there can be any doubt about the matter will appear hereafter. The word *man*, therefore, signifies all these attributes and all subjects which possess these attributes. But it can be predicated only of the subjects. What we call men are the subjects, the individual Stiles and Nokes, not the qualities by which their humanity is constituted. The name, therefore, is said to signify the subjects *directly,* the attributes *indirectly;* it *denotes* the subjects and implies, or involves, or indicates, or, as we shall say henceforth, *connotes*, the attributes. It is a connotative name.

Proper names are not connotative; they denote the individuals who are called by them, but they do not indicate or imply any attributes as belonging to those individuals. When we name a child by the name Paul or a dog by the name Caesar, these names are simply marks used to enable those individuals to be made subjects of discourse. It may be said, indeed, that we must have had some reason for giving them those names rather than any others, and this is true, but the name, once given, is independent of the reason. A man may have been named John because that was the name of his father; a town may have been named Dartmouth because it is situated at the mouth of the Dart. But it is no part of the signification of the word John that the father of the person so called bore the same name, nor even of the word Dartmouth to be situated at the mouth of the Dart. If sand should choke up the mouth of the river or an earthquake change its course and remove it to a distance from the town, the name of the town would not necessarily be changed. . . . Proper names are attached to the objects themselves and are not dependent on the continuance of any attribute of the object.

But there is another kind of names, which, although they are individual names—that is, predicable only of one subject—are really connotative. For, though we may give to an individual a name utterly unmeaning, unmeaningful which we call a proper name—a word which answers the purpose of showing what thing it is we are talking about, but not of telling anything about it; yet a name peculiar to an individual is not necessarily of this description. It may be significant of some attribute or some union of attributes which, being possessed by no object but one, determines the name exclusively to that individual. "The sun" is a name of this description; "God," when used by a monotheist, is another. These, however, are scarcely examples of what we are now attempting to illustrate, being, in strictness of language, general, not individual names, for, however they may be *in fact* predicable only of one object, there is nothing in the meaning of the words themselves which implies this; and, accordingly, when we are imagining and not affirming, we may speak of many suns; and the majority of mankind have believed, and still believe, that there are many gods. But it is easy to produce words which are real instances of connotative individual names. It may be part of the meaning of the connotative name itself, that there can exist but one individual possessing the attribute which it connotes, as, for instance, "the *only* son of John Stiles"; "the *first* emperor of Rome." Or the attribute connoted may be a connection with some determinate event, and the connection may be of such a kind as only one individual could have, or may, at least, be such as only one individual actually had, and this may be implied in the form of the expression. "The father of Socrates" is an example of the one kind (since Socrates could not have had two fathers), "the author of the *Iliad*," "the murderer of Henri Quatre," of the second. For, though it is conceivable that more persons than one might have participated in the authorship of the Iliad or in the murder of Henri Quatre, the employment of the article *the* implies that, in fact, this was not the case. What is here done by the word *the* is done in other cases by the context; thus, "Caesar's army" is an individual name if it appears from the context that the army meant is that which Caesar commanded in a particular battle. The still more general expressions, "the Roman army," or "the Christian army," may be individualized in a similar manner. Another case of frequent occurrence has already been noticed; it is the following: The name, being a many-worded one, may consist, in the first place, of a *general* name, capable therefore, in itself, of being affirmed of more things than one, but which is, in the second place, so limited by other words joined with it that the entire expression can only be predicated of one object, consistently with the meaning of the general term. This is exemplified in such an instance as the following: "the present Prime Minister of England." "Prime Minister of England" is a general name; the attributes which it connotes may be possessed by an indefinite number of persons, in succession, however, not simultaneously, since the meaning of the name itself imports (among other things) that there can be only one such person at a time. This being the case, and the application of the name being afterward limited, by the article and the word *present,* to such individuals as possess the attributes at one indivisible point in time, it becomes applicable only to one individual. And, as this appears from the meaning of the name without any extrinsic proof, it is strictly an individual name.

From the preceding observations it will easily be collected that whenever the names given to objects convey any information—that is, whenever they have properly any meaning—the meaning resides not in what they *denote* but in what they *connote.* The only names of objects which connote nothing are *proper* names, and these have, strictly speaking, no signification.

. . . A proper name is but an unmeaning mark which we connect in our minds with the idea of the object, in order that, whenever the mark meets our eyes or occurs to our thoughts, we may think of that individual object. Not being attached to the thing itself, it does not, like the chalk, enable us to distinguish the object when we see it, but it enables us to distinguish the object when it is spoken of, either in the records of our own experience or in the discourse of others, to know that what we find asserted in any proposition of which it is the subject is asserted of the individual thing with which we were previously acquainted (*System of Logic,* book I, chapter 2, section 5).

Notice that Mill holds all concrete general names, such as "man," "human," "cat," and "white," are connotative and that proper names such as "John Jones," "Sarah Smith," and "World War II," are nonconnotative. Frege in "On Sense and Nominatum" developed his theory of "*Sinn*" (meaning) as an alternative to Mill's view.

John Searle in "Proper Names" presents a Fregean theory of names, according to which every proper name is associated with a more or less determinate set of descriptions that determines what object is designated by a name. Names, in short, designate indirectly.

Saul Kripke's book *Naming and Necessity* has a critique of the Fregean view espoused by Searle. In the sections reprinted here, Kripke espouses a kind of Russellian view, arguing that names are directly correlated with their nominatum (what they name). He infers that proper names ensure that the same individual is picked out in every possible world.

While most discussions of names prior to 1970 concentrated on proper names, that is, names of individuals or particulars, whether the object was a substance like a person or an animal, or an event, like a war or a walk. Kripke showed that the same or very similar things could be said about names of natural kinds of things: human, dog, gold, and water. Contrary to previous widespread belief, such names are not descriptive; they are directly denotative. Hilary Putnam independently of Kripke came to much the same conclusion. In "Meaning and Reference" he argues that "natural kind" terms are immediately denotative.

Gareth Evans in "The Causal Theory of Names" criticizes aspects of both the description theory and the causal theory of names before presenting his own view, which preserves what he takes to be the underlying intuitions of those superseded theories. Evans distinguishes two kinds of description theories: one a theory about what a speaker denotes by a name and one a theory about what a name itself denotes. Both are defective. It is important to note that both the description theory and the causal theory answer the question, "Given that reference occurs, what determines what object is referred to?" This question presupposes that there is an answer to the question, "Under what conditions does reference occur?"

Evans points out that an adequate answer to the former question and hence the latter one involves an intentional account of names.

In "Proper Names and Intentionality," John Searle defends his view of proper names against Kripke's criticisms. He also points out that what is correct about Kripke's views was always part of his descriptivist views.

Proper Names   21

Do proper names have senses? Frege[1] argues that they must have senses, for, he asks, how else can identity statements be other than trivially analytic. How, he asks, can a statement of the form "a = b," if true, differ in cognitive value from "a = a"? His answer is that though "a" and "b" have the same referent they have or may have different *senses*, in which case the statement is true, though not analytically so. But this solution seems more appropriate where "a" and "b" are both nonsynonymous definite descriptions, or where one is a definite description and one is a proper name, than where both are proper names. Consider, for example, statements made with the following sentences:

(a) "Tully = Tully" is analytic.

But is

(b) "Tully = Cicero" synthetic?

If so, then each name must have a different sense, which seems at first sight most implausible, for we do not ordinarily think of proper names as having a sense at all in the way that predicates do; we do not, e.g. give definitions of proper names. But of course (b) gives us information not conveyed by (a). But is this information about words? The statement is not about words.

For the moment let us consider the view that (b) is, like (a), analytic. A statement is

analytic if and only if it is true in virtue of linguistic rules alone, without any recourse to empirical investigation. The linguistic rules for using the name "Cicero" and the linguistic rules for using the name "Tully" are such that both names refer to, without describing, the same identical object; thus it seems the truth of the identity can be established solely by recourse to these rules and the statement is analytic. The sense in which the statement is informative is the sense in which any analytic statement is informative; it illustrates or exemplifies certain contingent facts about words, though it does not of course describe these facts. On this account the difference between (a) and (b) above is not as great as might at first seem. Both are analytically true, and both illustrate contingent facts about our use of symbols. Some philosophers claim that (a) is fundamentally different from (b) in that a statement using this form will be true for any arbitrary substitution of symbols replacing "Tully".[2] This, I wish to argue, is not so. The fact that the same mark refers to the same object on two different occasions of its use is a convenient but contingent usage, and indeed we can easily imagine situations where this would not be the case. Suppose, e.g. we have a language in which the rules for using symbols are correlated not simply with a type-word, but with the order of its token appearances in the discourse. Some codes are

From *Mind*, volume 67 (1958), pp. 166–173.

like this. Suppose the first time an object is referred to in our discourse it is referred to by "x", the second time by "y", etc. For anyone who knows this code "x = y" is trivially analytic, but "x = x" is senseless. This example is designed to illustrate the similarity of (a) and (b) above; both are analytic and both give us information, though each gives us different information, about the use of words. The truth of the statements that Tully = Tully and Tully = Cicero both follow from linguistic rules. But the fact that the words "Tully = Tully" are used to express this identity is just as contingent as, though more universally conventional in our language than, the fact that the words "Tully = Cicero" are used to express the identity of the same object.

This analysis enables us to see how both (a) and (b) could be used to make analytic statements and how in such circumstances we could acquire different information from them, without forcing us to follow either of Frege's proposed solutions, i.e. that the two propositions are in some sense about words (*Begriffsschrift*) or his revised solution, that the terms have the same reference but different senses (*Sinn und Bedeutung*). But though this analysis enables us to see how a sentence like (b) *could* be used to make an analytic statement it does not follow that it could not also be used to make a synthetic statement. And indeed some identity statements using two proper names are clearly synthetic; people who argue that Shakespeare was Bacon are not advancing a thesis about language. In what follows I hope to examine the connection between proper names and their referents in such a manner as to show how both kinds of identity statement are possible and in so doing to show in what sense a proper name has a sense.

I have so far considered the view that the rules governing the use of a proper name are such that it is used to refer to and not to describe a particular object, that it has reference but not sense. But now let us ask how it comes about that we are able to refer to a particular object by using its name. How, for example, do we learn and teach the use of proper names? This seems quite simple—we

identify the object, and, assuming that our student understands the general conventions governing proper names, we explain that this word is the name of that object. But unless our student already knows another proper name of the object, we can only *identify* the object (the necessary preliminary to teaching the name) by ostension or description; and, in both cases, we identify the object in virtue of certain of its characteristics. So now it seems as if the rules for a proper name must somehow be logically tied to particular characteristics of the object in such a way that the name has a sense as well as a reference; indeed, it seems it could not have a reference unless it did have a sense, for how, unless the name has a sense, is it to be correlated with the object?

Suppose someone answers this argument as follows: "The characteristics located in teaching the name are not the rules for using the proper name: they are simply pedagogic devices employed in teaching the name to someone who does not know how to use it. Once our student has identified the object to which the name applies he can forget or ignore these various descriptions by means of which he identified the object, for they are not part of the sense of the name; the name does not have a *sense*. Suppose, for example, that we teach the name 'Aristotle' by explaining that it refers to a Greek philosopher born in Stagira, and suppose that our student continues to use the name correctly, that he gathers more information about Aristotle, and so on. Let us suppose it is discovered later on that Aristotle was not born in Stagira at all, but in Thebes. We will not now say that the meaning of the name has changed, or that Aristotle did not really exist at all. In short, explaining the use of a name by citing characteristics of the object is not giving the rules for the name, for the rules contain no descriptive content at all. They simply correlate the name to the object independently of any descriptions of it."

But is the argument convincing? Suppose most or even all of our present factual knowledge of Aristotle proved to be true of no one at all, or of several people living in scattered countries and in different centuries? Would we not say for this reason that Aristotle did not exist after all, and that the name, though it has a conventional sense, refers to no one at all? On the above account, if anyone said that Aristotle did not exist, this must simply be another way of saying that "Aristotle" denoted no objects, and nothing more; but if anyone did say that Aristotle did not exist he might mean much more than simply that the name does not denote anyone.[3] If, for example, we challenged his statement by pointing out that a man named "Aristotle" lived in Hoboken in 1903, he would not regard this as a relevant countercharge. We say of Cerberus and Zeus that neither of them ever existed, without meaning that no object ever bore these names, but only that certain kinds (descriptions) of objects never existed and bore these names. So now it looks as though proper names do have a sense necessarily but have a reference only contingently. They begin to look more and more like shorthand and perhaps vague descriptions.

Let us summarize the two conflicting views under consideration: the first asserts that proper names have essentially a reference but not a sense—proper names denote but do not connote; the second asserts that they have essentially a sense and only contingently a reference—they refer only on the condition that one and only one object satisfies their sense.

These two views are paths leading to divergent and hoary metaphysical systems. The first leads to ultimate objects of reference, the substances of the scholastics and the *Gegenstände* of the *Tractatus*. The second leads to the identity of indiscernibles, and variables of quantification as the only referential terms in the language. The subject-predicate structure of the language suggests that the first must be right, but the way we use and teach the use of proper names suggests that it cannot be right: a philosophical problem.

Let us begin by examining the second. If it is asserted that every proper name has a sense, it must be legitimate to demand of any name, "What is its sense?" If it is asserted that a proper name is a kind of shorthand description then we ought to be able to present the description in place of the proper name. But how are we to proceed with this? If we try to present a complete description of the object as

the sense of a proper name, odd consequences would ensue, e.g. that any true statement about the object using the name as subject would be analytic, any false one self-contradictory, that the meaning of the name (and perhaps the identity of the object) would change every time there was any change at all in the object, that the name would have different meanings for different people, etc. So suppose we ask what are the necessary and sufficient conditions for applying a particular name to a particular object. Suppose for the sake of argument that we have independent means for locating an object; then what are the conditions for applying a name to it; what are the conditions for saying, e.g. "This is Aristotle"? At first sight these conditions seem to be simply that the object must be identical with an object originally christened by this name, so the sense of the name would consist in a statement or set of statements asserting the characteristics which constitute this identity. The sense of "This is Aristotle" might be, "This object is spatio-temporally continuous with an object originally named 'Aristotle'." But this will not suffice, for, as was already suggested, the force of "Aristotle" is greater than the force of "identical with an object named 'Aristotle'," for not just any object named "Aristotle" will do. "Aristotle" here refers to a particular object named "Aristotle," not to any. "Named 'Aristotle' " is a universal term, but "Aristotle," is a proper name, so "This is named 'Aristotle' " is at best a necessary but not a sufficient condition for the truth of "This is Aristotle"? Briefly and trivially, it is not the identity of this with any object named "Aristotle," but rather its identity with Aristotle that constitutes the necessary and sufficient conditions for the truth of "This is Aristotle."

Perhaps we can resolve the conflict between the two views of the nature of proper names by asking what is the unique function of proper names in our language. To begin with, they mostly refer or purport to refer to particular objects; but of course other expressions, definite descriptions and demonstratives, perform this function as well. What then is the difference between proper names and other singular referring expressions? Unlike demonstratives, a proper name refers without presupposing any stage settings or any special contextual conditions surrounding the utterance of the expression. Unlike definite descriptions, they do not in general *specify* any characteristics at all of the objects to which they refer. "Scott" refers to the same object as does "the author of *Waverley*," but "Scott" specifies none of its characteristics, whereas "the author of *Waverley*" refers only in virtue of the fact that it does specify a characteristic. Let us examine this difference more closely. Following Strawson[4] we may say that referring uses of both proper names and definite descriptions presuppose the existence of one and only one object referred to. But as a proper name does not in general specify any characteristics of the object referred to, how then does it bring the reference off? How is a connection between name and object ever set up? This, which seems the crucial question, I want to answer by saying that though proper names do not normally assert or specify any characteristics, their referring uses nonetheless presuppose that the object to which they purport to refer has certain characteristics. But which ones? Suppose we ask the users of the name "Aristotle" to state what they regard as certain essential and established facts about him. Their answers would be a set of uniquely referring descriptive statements. Now what I am arguing is that the descriptive force of "This is Aristotle" is to assert that a sufficient but so far unspecified number of these statements are true of this object. Therefore, referring uses of "Aristotle" presuppose the existence of an object of whom a sufficient but so far unspecified number of these statements are true. To use a proper name referringly is to presuppose the truth of certain uniquely referring descriptive statements, but it is not ordinarily to assert these statements or even to indicate which exactly are presupposed. And herein lies most of the difficulty. The question of what constitutes the criteria for "Aristotle" is generally left open, indeed it seldom in fact arises, and when it does arise it is we, the users of the name, who decide more or less arbitrarily what these criteria shall be. If, for example, of the characteristics agreed to be true of Aris-

totle, half should be discovered to be true of one man and half true of another, which would we say was Aristotle? Neither? The question is not decided for us in advance.

But is this imprecision as to what characteristics exactly constitute the necessary and sufficient conditions for applying a proper name a mere accident, a product of linguistic slovenliness? Or does it derive from the functions which proper names perform for us? To ask for the criteria for applying the name "Aristotle" is to ask in the formal mode what Aristotle is; it is to ask for a set of identity criteria for the object Aristotle. "What is Aristotle?" and "What are the criteria for applying the name 'Aristotle'?" ask the same question, the former in the material mode, and the latter in the formal mode of speech. So if we came to agreement in advance of using the name on precisely what characteristics constituted the identity of Aristotle, our rules for using the name would be precise. But this precision would be achieved only at the cost of entailing some specific predicates by any referring use of the name. Indeed, the name itself would become superfluous for it would become logically equivalent to this set of descriptions. But if this were the case we would be in the position of only being able to refer to an object by describing it. Whereas in fact this is just what the institution of proper names enables us to avoid and what distinguishes proper names from descriptions. If the criteria for proper names were in all cases quite rigid and specific then a proper name would be nothing more than a shorthand for these criteria, a proper name would function exactly like an elaborate definite description. But the uniqueness and immense pragmatic convenience of proper names in our language lie precisely in the fact that they enable us to refer publicly to objects without being forced to raise issues and come to agreement on what descriptive characteristics exactly constitute the identity of the object. They function not as descriptions, but as pegs on which to hang descriptions. Thus the looseness of the criteria for proper names is a necessary condition for isolating the referring function from the describing function of language.

To put the same point differently, suppose

we ask, "Why do we have proper names at all?" Obviously, to refer to individuals. "Yes, but descriptions could do that for us." But only at the cost of specifying identity conditions every time reference is made: suppose we agree to drop "Aristotle" and use, say, "the teacher of Alexander," then it is a necessary truth that the man referred to is Alexander's teacher—but it is a contingent fact that Aristotle ever went into pedagogy (though I am suggesting it is a necessary fact that Aristotle has the logical sum, inclusive disjunction, of properties commonly attributed to him: any individual not having at least some of these properties could not be Aristotle).

Of course it should not be thought that the only sort of looseness of identity criteria for individuals is that which I have described as peculiar to proper names. Referring uses of definite descriptions may raise problems concerning identity of quite different sorts. This is especially true of past tense definite descriptions. "This is the man who taught Alexander" may be said to entail, e.g. that this object is spatio-temporally continuous with the man teaching Alexander at another point in space-time: but someone might also argue that this man's spatio-temporal continuity is a contingent characteristic and not an identity criterion. And the logical nature of the connection of such characteristics with the man's identity may again be loose and undecided in advance of dispute. But this is quite another dimension of looseness than that which I cited as the looseness of the criteria for applying proper names and does not affect the distinction in function between definite descriptions and proper names, *viz.* that definite descriptions refer only in virtue of the fact that the criteria are not loose in the original sense, for they refer by telling us what the object is. But proper names refer without so far raising the issue of what the object is.

We are now in a position to explain how it is that "Aristotle" has a reference but does not describe, and yet the statement "Aristotle never existed" says more than that "Aristotle" was never used to refer to any object. The statement asserts that a sufficient number of the conventional presuppositions, descriptive statements, of referring uses of "Aristotle" are false. Precisely which statements are asserted to be false is not yet clear, for what precise conditions constitute the criteria for applying "Aristotle" is not yet laid down by the language.

We can now resolve our paradox: does a proper name have a sense? If this asks whether or not proper names are used to describe or specify characteristics of objects, the answer is "no." But if it asks whether or not proper names are logically connected with characteristics of the object to which they refer, the answer is "yes, in a loose sort of way." (This shows in part the poverty of a rigid sense–reference, denotation–connotation approach to problems in the theory of meaning.)

We might clarify these points by comparing paradigmatic proper names with degenerate proper names like "The Bank of England." For these latter, it seems the sense is given as straightforwardly as in a definite description; the presuppositions, as it were, rise to the surface. And a proper name may acquire a rigid descriptive use without having the verbal form of a description: God is just, omnipotent, omniscient, etc., *by definition* for believers. Of course the form may mislead us; the Holy Roman Empire was neither holy, nor Roman, etc., but it was nonetheless the Holy Roman Empire. Again it may be conventional to name only girls "Martha," but if I name my son "Martha" I may mislead, but I do not lie.

Now reconsider our original identity, "Tully = Cicero." A statement made using this sentence would, I suggest, be analytic for most people; the same descriptive presuppositions are associated with each name. But of course if the descriptive presuppositions were different it might be used to make a synthetic statement; it might even advance a historical discovery of the first importance.

NOTES

1. *Translations from the Philosophical Writings of Gottlob Frege*, ed. Geach and Black, pp. 56ff.
2. W. V. Quine, *From a Logical Point of View*, esp. chapter 2.
3. *Cf.* Wittgenstein, *Philosophical Investigations*, para. 79.
4. "On Referring," *Mind*, 1950.

Naming and Necessity 22

SAUL KRIPKE

LECTURE I

. . . The first topic in the pair of topics is naming. By a name here I will mean a proper name, i.e., the name of a person, a city, a country, etc. It is well known that modern logicians also are very interested in definite descriptions: phrases of the form "the x such that ϕx," such as "the man who corrupted Hadleyburg." Now, if one and only one man ever corrupted Hadleyburg, then that man is the referent, in the logician's sense, of that description. We will use the term 'name' so that it does *not* include definite descriptions of that sort, but only those things which in ordinary language would be called 'proper names'. If we want a common term to cover names and descriptions, we may use the term 'designator'.

It is a point, made by Donnellan,[1] that under certain circumstances a particular speaker may use a definite description to refer, not to the proper referent, in the sense that I've just defined it, of that description, but to something else which he wants to single out and which he thinks is the proper referent of the description, but which in fact isn't. So you may say, "The man over there with the champagne in his glass is happy," though he actually only has water in his glass. Now, even though there is no champagne in his glass, and there may be another man in the room who

does have champagne in his glass, the speaker *intended* to refer, or maybe, in some sense of 'refer', *did* refer, to the man he thought had the champagne in his glass. Nevertheless, I'm just going to use the term 'referent of the description' to mean the object uniquely satisfying the conditions in the definite description. This is the sense in which it's been used in the logical tradition. So, if you have a description of the form "the x such that ϕx," and there is exactly one x such that ϕx, that is the referent of the description. . . .

Many people have said that the theory of Frege and Russell is false, but, in my opinion, they have abandoned its letter while retaining its spirit, namely, they have used the notion of a cluster concept. Well, what is this? The obvious problem for Frege and Russell, the one which comes immediately to mind, is already mentioned by Frege himself. He said,

In the case of genuinely proper names like "Aristotle" opinions as regards their sense may diverge. As such may, e.g., be suggested: Plato's disciple and the teacher of Alexander the Great. Whoever accepts this sense will interpret the meaning of the statement "Aristotle was born in Stagira," differently from one who interpreted the sense of "Aristotle" as the Stagirite teacher of Alexander the Great. As long as the nominatum remains the same, these fluctuations in sense are tolerable. But they should be avoided in the system of a demonstrative science and should not appear in a perfect language.[2]

From *Naming and Necessity* (Cambridge: Harvard University Press, 1980).

So, according to Frege, there is some sort of looseness or weakness in our language. Some people may give one sense to the name "Aristotle," others may give another. But of course it is not only that; even a single speaker when asked "What description are you willing to substitute for the name?" may be quite at a loss. In fact, he may know many things about him; but any particular thing that he knows he may feel clearly expresses a contingent property of the object. If "Aristotle" meant *the man who taught Alexander the Great,* then saying "Aristotle was a teacher of Alexander the Great" would be a mere tautology. But surely it isn't; it expresses the fact that Aristotle taught Alexander the Great, something we could discover to be false. So, *being the teacher of Alexander the Great* cannot be part of [the sense of] the name.

The most common way out of this difficulty is to say "really it is not a weakness in ordinary language that we can't substitute a *particular* description for the name; that's all right. What we really associate with the name is a *family* of descriptions." A good example of this is in *Philosophical Investigations,* where the idea of family resemblances is introduced and with great power.

Consider this example. If one says "Moses did not exist," this may mean various things. It may mean: the Israelites did not have a *single* leader when they withdrew from Egypt—or: their leader was not called Moses—or: there cannot have been anyone who accomplished all that the Bible relates of Moses— . . . But when I make a statement about Moses,—am I always ready to substitute some *one* of those descriptions for "Moses"? I shall perhaps say: by "Moses" I understand the man who did what the Bible relates of Moses, or at any rate, a good deal of it. But how much? Have I decided how much must be proved false for me to give up my proposition as false? Has the name "Moses" got a fixed and unequivocal use for me in all possible cases?[3]

According to this view, and a *locus classicus* of it is Searle's article on proper names,[4] the referent of a name is determined not by a single description but by some cluster or family. Whatever in some sense satisfies enough or most of the family is the referent of the name. I shall return to this view later. It may seem, as an analysis of ordinary language, quite a bit more plausible than that of Frege and Russell. It may seem to keep all the virtues and remove the defects of this theory.

Let me say (and this will introduce us to another new topic before I really consider this theory of naming) that there are two ways in which the cluster concept theory, or even the theory which requires a single description, can be viewed. One way of regarding it says that the cluster or the single description actually gives the meaning of the name; and when someone says "Walter Scott," he means *the man such that such and such and such and such.*

Now another view might be that even though the description in some sense doesn't give the *meaning* of the name, it is what *determines its reference* and although the phrase "Walter Scott" isn't *synonymous* with "the man such that such and such and such and such," or even maybe with the family (if something can be synonymous with a family), the family or the single description is what is used to determine to whom someone is referring when he says "Walter Scott." Of course, if when we hear his beliefs about Walter Scott we find that they are actually much more nearly true of Salvador Dali, then according to this theory the reference of this name is going to be Mr. Dali, not Scott. There are writers, I think, who explicitly deny that names have meaning at all even more strongly than I would but still use this picture of how the referent of the name gets determined. A good case in point is Paul Ziff, who says, very emphatically, that names don't have meaning at all, [that] they are not a part of language in some sense. But still, when he talks about how we determine what the reference of the name was, then he gives this picture. Unfortunately I don't have the passage in question with me, but this is what he says.[5]

The difference between using this theory as a theory of meaning and using it as a theory of reference will come out a little more clearly later on. But some of the attractiveness of the theory is lost if it isn't supposed to give the meaning of the name; for some of the solutions of problems that I've just mentioned will not be right, or at least won't clearly be right, if the description doesn't give the meaning of the name. For example, if someone said "Aristotle does not exist" *means* "there is no man doing such and such," or in the example from Wittgenstein, "Moses does not exist," *means* "no man did such and such," that might depend (and in fact, I think, does depend) on taking the theory in question as a theory of the meaning of the name "Moses," not just as a theory of its reference. Well, I don't know. Perhaps all that is immediate now is the other way around: if "Moses" means the same as "the man who did such and such" then to say that Moses did not exist is to say that the man who did such and such did not exist, that is, that no one person did such and such. If, on the other hand, "Moses" is not synonymous with any description, then even if its reference is in some sense determined by a description, statements containing the name cannot in general be *analyzed* by replacing the name by a description, though they may be materially equivalent to statements containing a description. So the analysis of singular existence statements mentioned above will have to be given up, unless it is established by some special argument, independent of a general theory of the meaning of names; and the same applies to identity statements. In any case, I think it's false that "Moses exists" means that at all. So we won't have to see if such a special argument can be drawn up.[6]

Before I go any further into this problem, I want to talk about another distinction which will be important in the methodology of these talks. Philosophers have talked (and, of course, there has been considerable controversy in recent years over the meaningfulness of these notions) [about] various categories of truth, which are called 'a priori', 'analytic', 'necessary'—and sometimes even 'certain' is thrown into this batch. The terms are often used as if *whether* there are things answering to these concepts is an interesting question, but we might as well regard them all as meaning the same thing. Now, everyone remembers Kant (a bit) as making a distinction between 'a priori' and 'analytic'. So

maybe this distinction is still made. In contemporary discussion very few people, if any, distinguish between the concepts of statements being a priori and their being necessary. At any rate I shall *not* use the terms 'a priori' and 'necessary' interchangeably here.

Consider what the traditional characterizations of such terms as 'a priori' and 'necessary' are. First the notion of a prioricity is a concept of epistemology. I guess the traditional characterization from Kant goes something like: a priori truths are those which can be known independently of any experience. This introduces another problem before we get off the ground, because there's another modality in the characterization of 'a priori', namely, it is supposed to be something which *can* be known independently of any experience. That means that in some sense it's *possible* (whether we do or do not in fact know it independently of any experience) to know this independently of any experience. And possible for whom? For God? For the Martians? Or just for people with minds like ours? To make this all clear might [involve] a host of problems all of its own about what sort of possibility is in question here. It might be best therefore, instead of using the phrase 'a priori truth', to the extent that one uses it at all, to stick to the question of whether a particular person or knower knows something a priori or believes it true on the basis of a priori evidence.

I won't go further too much into the problems that might arise with the notion of a prioricity here. I will say that some philosophers somehow change the modality in this characterization from *can* to *must*. They think that if something belongs to the realm of *a priori* knowledge, it couldn't possibly be known empirically. This is just a mistake. Something may belong in the realm of such statements that *can* be known *a priori* but still may be known by particular people on the basis of experience. To give a really common sense example: anyone who has worked with a computing machine knows that the computing machine may give an answer to whether such and such a number is prime. No one has calculated or proved that the number is prime;

but the machine has given the answer: this number is prime. We, then, if we believe that the number is prime, believe it on the basis of our knowledge of the laws of physics, the construction of the machine, and so on. We therefore do not believe this on the basis of purely a priori evidence. We believe it (if anything is a posteriori at all) on the basis of a posteriori evidence. Nevertheless, maybe this could be known a priori by someone who made the requisite calculations. So 'can be known a priori' doesn't mean 'must be known a priori'.

The second concept which is in question is that of necessity. Sometimes this is used in an epistemological way and might then just mean a priori. And of course, sometimes it is used in a physical way when people distinguish between physical and logical necessity. But what I am concerned with here is a notion which is not a notion of epistemology but of metaphysics, in some (I hope) nonpejorative sense. We ask whether something might have been true, or might have been false. Well, if something is false, it's obviously not necessarily true. If it is true, might it have been otherwise? Is it possible that, in this respect, the world should have been different from the way it is? If the answer is "no," then this fact about the world is a necessary one. If the answer is "yes," then this fact about the world is a contingent one. This in and of itself has nothing to do with anyone's knowledge of anything. It's certainly a philosophical thesis, and not a matter of obvious definitional equivalence, either that everything a priori is necessary or that everything necessary is a priori. Both concepts may be vague. That may be another problem. But at any rate they are dealing with two different domains, two different areas, the epistemological and the metaphysical. Consider, say, Fermat's last theorem—or the Goldbach conjecture. The Goldbach conjecture says that an even number greater than 2 must be the sum of two prime numbers. If this is true, it is presumably necessary, and, if it is false, presumably necessarily false. We are taking the classical view of mathematics here and assume that in mathematical reality it is either true or false.

If the Goldbach conjecture is false, then there is an even number, n, greater than 2, such that for no primes p_1 and p_2, both $< n$, does $n = p_1 + p_2$. This fact about n, if true, is verifiable by direct computation, and thus is necessary if the results of arithmetical computations are necessary. On the other hand, if the conjecture is true, then every even number exceeding 2 is the sum of two primes. Could it then be the case that, although in fact every such even number is the sum of two primes, there might have been such an even number which was not the sum of two primes? What would that mean? Such a number would have to be one of 4, 6, 8, 10, . . . ; and, by hypothesis, since we are assuming Goldbach's conjecture to be true, each of these can be shown, again by direct computation, to be the sum of two primes. Goldbach's conjecture, then, cannot be contingently true or false; whatever truth-value it has belongs to it by necessity.

But what we can say, of course, is that right now, as far as we know, the question can come out either way. So, in the absence of a mathematical proof deciding this question, none of us has any a priori knowledge about this question in either direction. We don't know whether Goldbach's conjecture is true or false. So right now we certainly don't know anything a priori about it. . . .

Let's use some terms quasi-technically. Let's call something a 'rigid designator' if in every possible world it designates the same object, a 'nonrigid' or 'accidental designator' if that is not the case. Of course we don't require that the objects exist in all possible worlds. Certainly Nixon might not have existed if his parents had not gotten married, in the normal course of things. When we think of a property as essential to an object we usually mean that it is true of that object in any case where it would have existed. A rigid designator of a necessary existent can be called 'strongly rigid.'

One of the intuitive theses I will maintain in these talks is that *names* are rigid designators. Certainly they seem to satisfy the intuitive test mentioned above: although someone other than the U.S. President in 1970 might have been the U.S. President in 1970 (e.g., Humphrey might have), no one other than Nixon might have been Nixon. In the same way, a designator rigidly designates a certain object if it designates that object wherever the object exists; if, in addition, the object is a necessary existent, the designator can be called 'strongly rigid.' For example, "the President of the U.S. in 1970" designates a certain man, Nixon; but someone else (e.g., Humphrey) might have been the President in 1970, and Nixon might not have; so this designator is not rigid.

In these lectures, I will argue, intuitively, that proper names are rigid designators, for although the man (Nixon) might not have been the President, it is not the case that he might not have been Nixon (though he might not have been *called* "Nixon"). Those who have argued that to make sense of the notion of rigid designator, we must antecedently make sense of "criteria of transworld identity" have precisely reversed the cart and the horse; it is *because* we can refer (rigidly) to Nixon, and stipulate that we are speaking of what might have happened to *him* (under certain circumstances), that "transworld identifications" are unproblematic in such cases.[7]

The tendency to demand purely qualitative descriptions of counterfactual situations has many sources. One, perhaps, is the confusion of the epistemological and the metaphysical, between a prioricity and necessity. If someone identifies necessity with a prioricity, and thinks that objects are named by means of uniquely identifying properties, he may think that it is the properties used to identify the object which, being known about it a priori, must be used to identify it in all possible worlds, to find out which object is Nixon. As against this, I repeat: (1) Generally, things aren't 'found out' about a counterfactual situation, they are stipulated; (2) possible worlds need not be given purely qualitatively, as if we were looking at them through a telescope. And we will see shortly that the properties an object has in every counterfactual world have nothing to do with properties used to identify it in the actual world. . . .

LECTURE II

Last time we ended up talking about a theory of naming which is given by a number of theses:

(1) To every name or designating expression "X," there corresponds a cluster of properties, namely the family of those properties φ such that A believes "φX."

(2) One of the properties, or some conjointly, are believed by A to pick out some individual uniquely.

(3) If most, or a weighted most, of the φ's are satisfied by one unique object y, then y is the referent of "X."

(4) If the vote yields no unique object, "X" does not refer.

(5) The statement, "If X exists, then X has most of the φ's" is known a priori by the speaker.

(6) The statement, "If X exists, then X has most of the φ's" expresses a necessary truth (in the idiolect of the speaker).

(C) For any successful theory, the account must not be circular. The properties which are used in the vote must not themselves involve the notion of reference in such a way that it is ultimately impossible to eliminate.

(C) is not a thesis but a condition on the satisfaction of the other theses. In other words, theses (1)–(6) cannot be satisfied in a way which leads to a circle, in a way which does not lead to any independent determination of reference. The example I gave last time of a blatantly circular attempt to satisfy these conditions was a theory of names mentioned by William Kneale. I was a little surprised at the statement of the theory when I was reading what I had copied down, so I looked it up again. I looked it up in the book to see if I'd copied it down accurately. Kneale *did* use the past tense. He said that though it is not trifling to be told that Socrates was the greatest philosopher of ancient Greece, it is trifling to be told that Socrates was called "Socrates." Therefore, he concludes, the name "Socrates" must simply mean "the individual called 'Socrates'." Russell, as I've said, in some places gives a similar analysis. Anyway, as stated using the past tense, the condition wouldn't be circular, because one certainly could decide to use the term "Socrates" to refer to whoever was called "Socrates" by the Greeks. But, of course, in that sense it's not at all trifling to be told that Socrates was called "Socrates." If this is any kind of fact, it might be false. Perhaps we know that *we* call him "Socrates"; that hardly shows that the Greeks did so. In fact, of course, they may have pronounced the name differently. It may be, in the case of this particular name, that transliteration from the Greek is so good that the English version is not pronounced *very* differently from the Greek. But that won't be so in the general case. Certainly it is not trifling to be told that Isaiah was called "Isaiah." In fact, it is false to be told that Isaiah was called "Isaiah"; the prophet wouldn't have recognized this name at all. And of course the Greeks didn't call their country anything like "Greece." Suppose we amend the thesis so that it reads: it's trifling to be told that Socrates is called "Socrates" by us, or at least, by me, the speaker. Then in some sense this is fairly trifling. I don't think it is necessary or analytic. In the same way, it is trifling to be told that horses are called "horses," without this leading to the conclusion that the word "horse" simply *means* "the animal called a 'horse'." As a theory of the reference of the name "Socrates" it will lead immediately to a vicious circle. If one was determining the referent of a name like 'Glunk' to himself and made the following decision, "I shall use the term 'Glunk' to refer to the man that I call 'Glunk'," this would get one nowhere. One had better have some independent determination of the referent of "Glunk." This is a good example of a blatantly circular determination. Actually sentences like "Socrates is called 'Socrates' " are very interesting and one can spend, strange as it may seem, hours talking about their analysis. I actually did, once, do that. I won't do that, however, on this occasion. (See how high the seas of language can rise. And at the lowest points too.) Anyway this is a useful example of a violation of the noncircularity condition. The theory will satisfy all of these statements, perhaps, but it satisfies them only because there is some independent way of determining the reference independently of the particular condition: being the man called "Socrates."

I have already talked about, in the last lecture, thesis (6). Theses (5) and (6), by the way, have converses. What I said for thesis (5) is that the statement that if X exists, X has most of the φ's, is a priori true for the speaker. It will also be true under the given theory that certain converses of this statement hold true also a priori for the speaker, namely: if any unique thing has most of the properties φ in the properly weighted sense, it is X. Similarly a certain converse to this will be *necessarily* true, namely: if anything has most of the properties φ in the properly weighted sense, it is X. So really one can say that it is both a priori and necessary that something is X if and only if it uniquely has most of the properties φ. This really comes from the previous theses (1)–(4), I suppose. And (5) and (6) really just say that a sufficiently reflective speaker grasps this theory of proper names. Knowing this, he therefore sees that (5) and (6) are true. The objections to theses (5) and (6) will *not* be that some speakers are unaware of this theory and therefore don't know these things.

What I talked about in the last lecture is thesis (6). It's been observed by many philosophers that, if the cluster of properties associated with a proper name is taken in a very narrow sense, so that only one property is given any weight at all, let's say one definite description to pick out the referent—for example, Aristotle was the philosopher who taught Alexander the Great—then certain things will seem to turn out to be necessary truths which are not necessary truths—in this case, for example, that Aristotle taught Alexander the Great. But as Searle said, it is not a necessary truth but a contingent one that Aristotle ever went into pedagogy. Therefore, he concludes that one must drop the original paradigm of a single description and turn to that of a cluster of descriptions.

To summarize some things that I argued last time, this is not the correct answer (whatever it may be) to this problem about necessity. For Searle goes on to say,

Suppose we agree to drop "Aristotle" and use, say, "the teacher of Alexander," then it is a necessary truth that the man referred to is Alexander's teacher—but it is a contingent fact that Aristotle ever went into pedagogy, though I am suggesting that it is a necessary fact that Aristotle has the logical sum, inclusive disjunction, of properties commonly attributed to him. . . .[8]

This is what is not so. It just is not, in any intuitive sense of necessity, a necessary truth that Aristotle had the properties commonly attributed to him. There is a certain theory, perhaps popular in some views of the philosophy of history, which might both be deterministic and yet at the same time assign a great role to the individual in history. Perhaps Carlyle would associate with the meaning of the name of a great man his achievements. According to such a view it will be necessary, once a certain individual is born, that he is destined to perform various great tasks and so it will be part of the very nature of Aristotle that he should have produced ideas which had a great influence on the western world. Whatever the merits of such a view may be as a view of history or the nature of great men, it does not seem that it should be trivially true on the basis of a theory of proper names. It would seem that it's a contingent fact that Aristotle ever did *any* of the things commonly attributed to him today, *any* of these great achievements that we so much admire. . . .

To clear up one thing which some people have asked me: When I say that a designator is rigid, and designates the same thing in all possible worlds, I mean that, as used in *our* language, it stands for that thing, when *we* talk about counterfactual situations. I don't mean, of course, that there mightn't be counterfactual situations in which in the other possible worlds people actually spoke a different language. One doesn't say that "two plus two equals four" is contingent because people might have spoken a language in which "two plus two equals four" meant that seven is even. Similarly, when we speak of a counterfactual situation, we speak of it in English, even if it is part of the description of that counterfactual situation that we were all speaking German in that counterfactual situa-

tion. We say, "suppose we had all been speaking German" or "suppose we had been using English in a nonstandard way." Then we are describing a possible world or counterfactual situation in which people, including ourselves, did speak in a certain way different from the way we speak. But still, in describing that world, we use *English* with *our* meanings and *our* references. It is in this sense that I speak of a rigid designator as having the same reference in all possible worlds. I also don't mean to imply that the thing designated exists in all possible worlds, just that the name refers rigidly to that thing. If you say "suppose Hitler had never been born" then "Hitler" refers here, still rigidly, to something that would not exist in the counterfactual situation described.

Given these remarks, this means we must cross off thesis (6) as incorrect. The other theses have nothing to do with necessity and can survive. In particular thesis (5) has nothing to do with necessity and it can survive. If I use the name "Hesperus" to refer to a certain planetary body when seen in a certain celestial position in the evening, it will not therefore be a necessary truth that Hesperus is ever seen in the evening. That depends on various contingent facts about people being there to see and things like that. So even if I should say to myself that I will use "Hesperus" to name the heavenly body I see in the evening in yonder position of the sky, it will not be necessary that Hesperus was ever seen in the evening. But it may be a priori in that this is how I have determined the referent. If I have determined that Hesperus is the thing that I saw in the evening over there, then I will know, just from making that determination of the referent, that if there is any Hesperus at all it's the thing I saw in the evening. This at least survives as far as the arguments we have given up to now go.

How about a theory where thesis (6) is eliminated? Theses (2), (3), and (4) turn out to have a large class of counterinstances. Even when theses (2)–(4) are true, thesis (5) is usually false; the truth of theses (3) and (4) is an empirical 'accident', which the speaker hardly knows a priori. That is to say, other principles really determine the speaker's reference, and the fact that the referent coincides with that determined by (2)–(4) is an 'accident', which we were in no position to know a priori. Only in a rare class of cases, usually initial baptisms, are all of (2)–(5) true.

What picture of naming do these Theses [(1)–(5)] give you? The picture is this. I want to name an object. I think of some way of describing it uniquely and then I go through, so to speak, a sort of mental ceremony: By "Cicero" I shall mean the man who denounced Catiline; and that's what the reference of "Cicero" will be. I will use "Cicero" to designate rigidly the man who (in fact) denounced Catiline, so I can speak of possible worlds in which he did not. But still my intentions are given by first, giving some condition which uniquely determines an object, then using a certain word as a name for the object determined by this condition. Now there may be some cases in which we actually do this. Maybe, if you want to stretch and call it description, when you say: I shall call that heavenly body over there "Hesperus."[9] That is really a case where the theses not only are true but really even give a correct picture of how the reference is determined. Another case, if you want to call this a name, might be when the police in London use the name "Jack" or "Jack the Ripper" to refer to the man, whoever he is, who committed all these murders, or most of them. Then they are giving the reference of the name by a description.[10] But in many or most cases, I think the theses are false. So let's look at them.[11]

Thesis (1), as I say, is a definition. Thesis (2) says that one of the properties believed by A of the object, or some conjointly, are believed to pick out some individual uniquely. A sort of example people have in mind is just what I said: I shall use the term "Cicero" to denote the man who denounced Catiline (or first denounced him in public, to make it unique). This picks out an object uniquely in this particular reference. Even some writers such as Ziff in *Semantic Analysis,* who don't believe that names have meaning in any sense, think that this is a good picture of the way reference can be determined.

Let's see if thesis (2) is true. It seems, in some a priori way, that it's got to be true, because if you don't think that the properties you have in mind pick out anyone uniquely— let's say they're all satisfied by two people— then how can you say which one of them you're talking about? There seem to be no grounds for saying you're talking about the one rather than about the other. Usually the properties in question are supposed to be some famous deeds of the person in question. For example, Cicero was the man who denounced Catiline. The average person, according to this, when he refers to Cicero, is saying something like "the man who denounced Catiline" and thus has picked out a certain man uniquely. It is a tribute to the education of philosophers that they have held this thesis for such a long time. In fact, most people, when they think of Cicero, just think of a *famous Roman orator,* without any pretension to think either that there was only one famous Roman orator or that one must know something else about Cicero to have a referent for the name. Consider Richard Feynman, to whom many of us are able to refer. He is a leading contemporary theoretical physicist. Everyone *here* (I'm sure!) can state the contents of one of Feynman's theories so as to differentiate him from Gell-Mann. However, the man in the street, not possessing these abilities, may still use the name "Feynman." When asked he will say: well he's a physicist or something. He may not think that this picks out anyone uniquely. I still think he uses the name "Feynman" as a name for Feynman.

But let's look at some of the cases where we do have a description to pick out someone uniquely. Let's say, for example, that we know that Cicero was the man who first denounced Catiline. Well, that's good. That really picks someone out uniquely. However, there is a problem, because this description contains another name, namely "Catiline." We must be sure that we satisfy the conditions in such a way as to avoid violating the noncircularity condition here. In particular, we must not say that Catiline was the man denounced by Cicero. If we do this, we will really not be picking out anything uniquely, we will simply be picking out a pair of objects A and B, such that A denounced B. We do not think that this was the only pair where such denunciations ever occurred; so we had better add some other conditions in order to satisfy the uniqueness condition.

If we say Einstein was the man who discovered the theory of relativity, that certainly picks out someone uniquely. One can be sure, as I said, that everyone *here* can make a compact and independent statement of this theory and so pick out Einstein uniquely; but many people actually don't know enough about this stuff, so when asked what the theory of relativity is, they will say: "Einstein's theory," and thus be led into the most straightforward sort of vicious circle.

So thesis (2), in a straightforward way, fails to be satisfied when we say Feynman is a famous physicist without attributing anything else to Feynman. In another way it may not be satisfied in the proper way even when it is satisfied: If we say Einstein was "the man who discovered relativity theory," that does pick someone out uniquely; but it may not pick him out in such a way as to satisfy the noncircularity condition, because the theory of relativity may in turn be picked out as "Einstein's theory." So thesis (2) seems to be false. . . .

Let's go on to thesis (3): If most of the φ's, suitably weighted, are satisfied by a unique object γ, then γ is the referent of the name for the speaker. Now, since we have already established that Thesis (2) is wrong, why should any of the rest work? . . . Suppose most of the φ's are in fact satisfied by a unique object. Is that object necessarily the referent of "X" for A? Let's suppose someone says that Gödel is the man who proved the incompleteness of arithmetic, and this man is suitably well educated and is even able to give an independent account of the incompleteness theorem. He doesn't just say, "Well, that's Gödel's theorem," or whatever. He actually states a certain theorem, which he attributes to Gödel as the discoverer. Is it the case, then, that if most of the φ's are satisfied by a unique object γ, then γ is the referent of the name

"X" for A? Let's take a simple case. In the case of Gödel that's practically the only thing many people have heard about him—that he discovered the incompleteness of arithmetic. Does it follow that whoever discovered the incompleteness of arithmetic is the referent of "Gödel"?

Imagine the following blatantly fictional situation. (I hope Professor Gödel is not present.) Suppose that Gödel was not in fact the author of this theorem. A man named "Schmidt," whose body was found in Vienna under mysterious circumstances many years ago, actually did the work in question. His friend Gödel somehow got hold of the manuscript and it was thereafter attributed to Gödel. On the view in question, then, when our ordinary man uses the name "Gödel," he really means to refer to Schmidt, because Schmidt is the unique person satisfying the description, "the man who discovered the incompleteness of arithmetic." Of course you might try changing it to "the man who *published* the discovery of the incompleteness of arithmetic." By changing the story a little further one can make even this formulation false. Anyway, most people might not even know whether the thing was published or got around by word of mouth. Let's stick to "the man who discovered the incompleteness of arithmetic." So, since the man who discovered the incompleteness of arithmetic is in fact Schmidt, we, when we talk about "Gödel," are in fact always referring to Schmidt. But it seems to me that we are not. We simply are not. One reply, which I will discuss later, might be: You should say instead, "the man to whom the incompleteness of arithmetic is commonly attributed," or something like that. Let's see what we can do with that later.

But it may seem to many of you that this is a very odd example, or that such a situation occurs rarely. This also is a tribute to the education of philosophers. Very often we use a name on the basis of considerable misinformation. The case of mathematics used in the fictive example is a good case in point. What do we know about Peano? What many people in this room may 'know' about Peano is that he was the discoverer of certain axioms which characterize the sequence of natural numbers, the so-called "Peano axioms." Probably some people can even state them. I have been told that these axioms were not first discovered by Peano but by Dedekind. Peano was of course not a dishonest man. I am told that his footnotes include a credit to Dedekind. Somehow the footnote has been ignored. So on the theory in question the term "Peano," as we use it, really refers to—now that you've heard it you see that you were really all the time talking about—Dedekind. But you were not. Such illustrations could be multiplied indefinitely.

Even worse misconceptions, of course, occur to the layman. In a previous example I supposed people to identify Einstein by reference to his work on relativity. Actually, I often used to hear that Einstein's most famous achievement was the invention of the atomic bomb. So when we refer to Einstein, we refer to the inventor of the atomic bomb. But this is not so. Columbus was the first man to realize that the earth was round. He was also the first European to land in the western hemisphere. Probably none of these things are true, and therefore, when people use the term "Columbus" they really refer to some Greek if they use the roundness of the earth, or to some Norseman, perhaps, if they use the "discovery of America." But they don't. So it does not seem that if most of the φ's are satisfied by a unique object γ, then γ is the referent of the name. This seems simply to be false.[12]

Thesis (4): If the vote yields no unique object the name does not refer. Really this case has been covered before—has been covered in my previous examples. First, the vote may not yield a *unique* object, as in the case of Cicero or Feynman. Secondly, suppose it yields *no* object, that nothing satisfies most, or even any, substantial number, of the φ's. Does that mean the name doesn't refer? No: in the same way that you may have false beliefs about a person which may actually be true of someone else, so you may have false beliefs which are true of absolutely no one. And these may constitute the totality of your beliefs. Suppose, to vary the example about Gödel, no one had discovered the incomplete-

ness of arithmetic—perhaps the proof simply materialized by a random scattering of atoms on a piece of paper—the man Gödel being lucky enough to have been present when this improbable event occurred. Further, suppose arithmetic is in fact complete. One wouldn't really expect a random scattering of atoms to produce a correct proof. A subtle error, unknown through the decades, has still been unnoticed—or perhaps not actually unnoticed, but the friends of Gödel. . . . So even if the conditions are not satisfied by a unique object the name may still refer. I gave you the case of Jonah last week. Biblical scholars, as I said, think that Jonah really existed. It isn't because they think that someone ever was swallowed by a big fish or even went to Nineveh to preach. These conditions may be true of no one whatsoever and yet the name "Jonah" really has a referent. In the case above of Einstein's invention of the bomb, possibly no one really deserves to be called the "inventor" of the device.

Thesis 5 says that the statement "If X exists, then X has most of the φ's," is a priori true for A. Notice that even in a case where (3) and (4) *happen* to be true, a typical speaker hardly knows a priori that they are, as required by the theory. I *think* that my belief about Gödel *is* in fact correct and that the "Schmidt" story is just a fantasy. But the belief hardly constitutes a priori knowledge. . . .

Someone, let's say, a baby, is born; his parents call him by a certain name. They talk about him to their friends. Other people meet him. Through various sorts of talk the name is spread from link to link as if by a chain. A speaker who is on the far end of this chain, who has heard about, say Richard Feynman, in the marketplace or elsewhere, may be referring to Richard Feynman even though he can't remember from whom he first heard of Feynman or from whom he ever heard of Feynman. He knows that Feynman is a famous physicist. A certain passage of communication reaching ultimately to the man himself does reach the speaker. He then is referring to Feynman even though he can't identify him uniquely. He doesn't know what a Feynman diagram is, he doesn't know what the Feynman theory of pair production and annihilation is. Not only that: he'd have trouble distinguishing between Gell-Mann and Feynman. So he doesn't have to know these things, but, instead, a chain of communication going back to Feynman himself has been established, by virtue of his membership in a community which passed the name on from link to link, not by a ceremony that he makes in private in his study: "By 'Feynman' I shall mean the man who did such and such and such and such." . . . On our view, it is not how the speaker thinks he got the reference, but the actual chain of communication, which is relevant.

I think I said the other time that philosophical theories are in danger of being false, and so I wasn't going to present an alternative theory. Have I just done so? Well, in a way; but my characterization has been far less specific than a real set of necessary and sufficient conditions for reference would be. Obviously the name is passed on from link to link. But of course not every sort of causal chain reaching from me to a certain man will do for me to make a reference. There may be a causal chain from our use of the term "Santa Claus" to a certain historical saint, but still the children, when they use this, by this time probably do not refer to that saint. So other conditions must be satisfied in order to make this into a really rigorous theory of reference. I don't know that I'm going to do this because, first, I'm sort of too lazy at the moment; secondly, rather than giving a set of necessary and sufficient conditions which will work for a term like reference, I want to present just a *better picture* than the picture presented by the received views.

Haven't I been very unfair to the description theory? Here I have stated it very precisely—more precisely, perhaps, than it has been stated by any of its advocates. So then it's easy to refute. Maybe if I tried to state mine with sufficient precision in the form of six or seven or eight theses, it would also turn out that when you examine the theses one by one, they will all be false. That might even be so, but the difference is this. What I think the examples I've given show is not

simply that there's some technical error here or some mistake there, but that the whole picture given by this theory of how reference is determined seems to be wrong from the fundamentals. It seems to be wrong to think that we give ourselves some properties which somehow qualitatively uniquely pick out an object and determine our reference in that manner. What I am trying to present is a better picture—a picture which, if more details were to be filled in, might be refined so as to give more exact conditions for reference to take place.

One might never reach a set of necessary and sufficient conditions. I don't know, I'm always sympathetic to Bishop Butler's "Everything is what it is and not another thing'—in the nontrivial sense that philosophical analyses of some concept like reference, in completely different terms which make no mention of reference, are very apt to fail. Of course in any particular case when one is given an analysis one has to look at it and see whether it is true or false. One can't just cite this maxim to oneself and then turn the page. But more cautiously, I want to present a better picture without giving a set of necessary and sufficient conditions for reference. Such conditions would be very complicated, but what is true is that it's in virtue of our connection with other speakers in the community, going back to the referent himself, that we refer to a certain man.

There may be some cases where the description picture is true, where some man really gives a name by going into the privacy of his room and saying that the referent is to be the unique thing with certain identifying properties. "Jack the Ripper" was a possible example which I gave. Another was "Hesperus." Yet another case which can be forced into this description is that of meeting someone and being told his name. Except for a belief in the description theory, in its importance in other cases, one probably wouldn't think that that was a case of giving oneself a description, i.e., "the guy I'm just meeting now." But one can put it in these terms if one wishes, and if one has never heard the name in any other way. Of course, if you're introduced to a man and told, "That's Einstein," you've heard of him before, it may be wrong, and so on. But maybe in some cases such a paradigm works—especially for the man who first gives someone or something a name. Or he points to a star and says, "That is to be Alpha Centauri." So he can really make himself this ceremony: "By 'Alpha Centauri' I shall mean the star right over there with such and such coordinates." But in general this picture fails. In general our reference depends not just on what we think ourselves, but on other people in the community, the history of how the name reached one, and things like that. It is by following such a history that one gets to the reference. . . .

A rough statement of a theory might be the following: An initial "baptism" takes place. Here the object may be named by ostension, or the reference of the name may be fixed by a description.[13] When the name is "passed from link to link," the receiver of the name must, I think, intend when he learns it to use it with the same reference as the man from whom he heard it. If I hear the name "Napoleon" and decide it would be a nice name for my pet aardvark, I do not satisfy this condition.[14] (Perhaps it is some such failure to keep the reference fixed which accounts for the divergence of present uses of "Santa Claus" from the alleged original use.)

Notice that the preceding outline hardly *eliminates* the notion of reference; on the contrary, it takes the notion of intending to use the same reference as a given. There is also an appeal to an initial baptism which is explained in terms either of fixing a reference by a description, or ostension (if ostension is not to be subsumed under the other category).[15] (Perhaps there are other possibilities for initial baptisms.) Further, the George Smith case casts some doubt as to the sufficiency of the conditions. Even if the teacher does refer to his neighbor, is it clear that he has passed on his reference to the pupils? Why shouldn't their belief be about any other man named "George Smith"? If he says that Newton was hit by an apple, somehow his task of transmitting a reference is easier, since he has communicated a common misconception about Newton.

To repeat, I may not have presented a theory, but I do think that I have presented a better picture than that given by description theorists.

I think the next topic I shall want to talk about is that of statements of identity. Are these necessary or contingent? The matter has been in some dispute in recent philosophy. First, everyone agrees that descriptions can be used to make contingent identity statements. If it is true that the man who invented bifocals was the first Postmaster General of the United States—that these were one and the same— it's contingently true. That is, it might have been the case that one man invented bifocals and another was the first Postmaster General of the United States. So certainly when you make identity statements using descriptions— when you say "the x such that φx and the x such that ψx are one and the same"—that can be a contingent fact. But philosophers have been interested also in the question of identity statements between names. When we say "Hesperus is Phosphorus" or "Cicero is Tully," is what we are saying necessary or contingent? Further, they've been interested in another type of identity statement, which comes from scientific theory. We identify, for example, light with electromagnetic radiation between certain limits of wavelengths, or with a stream of photons. We identify heat with the motion of molecules; sound with a certain sort of wave disturbance in the air; and so on. Concerning such statements the following thesis is commonly held. First, that these are obviously contingent identities: we've found out that light is a stream of photons, but of course it might not have been a stream of photons. Heat is in fact the motion of molecules; we found that out, but heat might not have been the motion of molecules. Secondly, many philosophers feel damned lucky that these examples are around. Now, why? These philosophers, whose views are expounded in a vast literature, hold to a thesis called "the identity thesis" with respect to some psychological concepts. They think, say, that pain is just a certain material state of the brain or of the body, or what have you—say the stimulation of C-fibers. (It doesn't matter what.) Some people have then objected, "Well, look, there's perhaps a *correlation* between pain and these states of the body; but this must just be a contingent correlation between two different things, because it was an empirical discovery that this correlation ever held. Therefore, by 'pain' we must mean something different from this state of the body or brain; and, therefore, they must be two different things."

Then it's said, "Ah, but you see, this is wrong! Everyone knows that there can be contingent identities." First, as in the bifocals and Postmaster General case, which I have mentioned before. Second, in the case, believed closer to the present paradigm, of theoretical identifications, such as light and a stream of photons, or water and a certain compound of hydrogen and oxygen. These are all contingent identities. They might have been false. It's no surprise, therefore, that it can be true as a matter of contingent fact and not of any necessity that feeling pain, or seeing red, is just a certain state of the human body. Such psychophysical identifications can be contingent facts just as the other identities are contingent facts. And of course there are widespread motivations—ideological, or just not wanting to have the 'nomological dangler' of mysterious connections not accounted for by the laws of physics, one to one correlations between two different kinds of thing, material states, and things of an entirely different kind, which lead people to want to believe this thesis.

I guess the main thing I'll talk about first is identity statements between names. . . .

Let's suppose we refer to the same heavenly body twice, as "Hesperus" and "Phosphorus." We say: Hesperus is that star over there in the evening; Phosphorus is that star over there in the morning. Actually, Hesperus is Phosphorus. Are there really circumstances under which Hesperus wouldn't have been Phosphorus? Supposing that Hesperus is Phosphorus, let's try to describe a possible situation in which it would not have been. Well, it's easy. Someone goes by and he calls two *different* stars "Hesperus" and "Phospho-

rus." It may even be under the same conditions as prevailed when we introduced the names "Hesperus" and "Phosphorus." But are those circumstances in which Hesperus is not Phosphorus or would not have been Phosphorus? It seems to me that they are not.

Now, of course I'm committed to saying that they're not, by saying that such terms as "Hesperus" and "Phosphorus," when used as names, are rigid designators. They refer in every possible world to the planet Venus. Therefore, in that possible world too, the planet Venus is the planet Venus and it doesn't matter what any other person has said in this other possible world. How should *we* describe this situation? He can't have pointed to Venus twice, and in the one case called it "Hesperus" and in the other "Phosphorus," as we did. If he did so, then "Hesperus is Phosphorus" would have been true in that situation too. He pointed maybe neither time to the planet Venus—at least one time he didn't point to the planet Venus, let's say when he pointed to the body he called "Phosphorus." Then in that case we can certainly say that the name "Phosphorus" might not have referred to Phosphorus. We can even say that in the very position when viewed in the morning that we found Phosphorus, it might have been the case that Phosphorus was not there—that something else was there, and that even, under certain circumstances it would have been *called* "Phosphorus." But that still is not a case in which Phosphorus was not Hesperus. There might be a possible world in which, a possible counterfactual situation in which, "Hesperus" and "Phosphorus" weren't names of the things they in fact are names of. Someone, if he did determine their reference by identifying descriptions, might even have used the very identifying descriptions we used. But still that's not a case in which Hesperus wasn't Phosphorus. For there couldn't have been such a case, given that Hesperus is Phosphorus.

Now this seems very strange because in advance, we are inclined to say, the answer to the question whether Hesperus is Phosphorus might have turned out either way. So aren't there really two possible worlds—one in which Hesperus was Phosphorus, the other in which Hesperus wasn't Phosphorus—in advance of our discovering that these were the same? First, there's one sense in which things might turn out either way, in which it's clear that that doesn't imply that the way it finally turns out isn't necessary. For example, the four color theorem might turn out to be true and might turn out to be false. It might turn out either way. It still doesn't mean that the way it turns out is not necessary. Obviously, the 'might' here is purely 'epistemic'—it merely expresses our present state of ignorance, or uncertainty.

But it seems that in the Hesperus–Phosphorus case, something even stronger is true. The evidence I have before I know that Hesperus is Phosphorus is that I see a certain star or a certain heavenly body in the evening and call it "Hesperus," and in the morning and call it "Phosphorus." I know these things. There certainly is a possible world in which a man should have seen a certain star at a certain position in the evening and called it "Hesperus" and a certain star in the morning and called it "Phosphorus"; and should have concluded—should have found out by empirical investigation—that he names two different stars, or two different heavenly bodies. At least one of these stars or heavenly bodies was not Phosphorus, otherwise it couldn't have come out that way. But that's true. And so it's true that given the evidence that someone has antecedent to his empirical investigation, he can be placed in a sense in exactly the same situation, that is a qualitatively identical epistemic situation, and call two heavenly bodies "Hesperus" and "Phosphorus," without their being identical. So in that sense we can say that it might have turned out either way. Not that it might have turned out either way as to Hesperus's being Phosphorus. Though for all we knew in advance, Hesperus wasn't Phosphorus, that couldn't have turned out any other way, in a sense. But being put in a situation where we have exactly the same evidence, qualitatively speaking, it could have turned out that Hesperus was not Phosphorus; that is, in a counterfactual world in which "Hesperus" and "Phosphorus" were not used

in the way that we use them, as names of this planet, but as names of some other objects, one could have had qualitatively identical evidence and concluded that "Hesperus" and "Phosphorus" named two different objects.[16] But we, using the names as we do right now, can say in advance, that if Hesperus and Phosphorus are one and the same, then in no other possible world can they be different. We use "Hesperus" as the name of a certain body and "Phosphorus" as the name of a certain body. We use them as names of those bodies in all possible worlds. If, in fact, they are the *same* body, then in any other possible world we have to use them as a name of that object. And so in any other possible world it will be true that Hesperus is Phosphorus. So two things are true: first, that we do not know a priori that Hesperus is Phosphorus, and are in no position to find out the answer except empirically. Second, this is so because we could have evidence qualitatively indistinguishable from the evidence we have and determine the reference of the two names by the positions of two planets in the sky, without the planets being the same.

Of course, it is only a contingent truth (not true in every other possible world) that the star seen over there in the evening is the star seen over there in the morning, because there are possible worlds in which Phosphorus was not visible in the morning. But that contingent truth shouldn't be identified with the statement that Hesperus is Phosphorus. It could only be so identified if you thought that it was a necessary truth that Hesperus is visible over there in the evening or that Phosphorus is visible over there in the morning. But neither of those are necessary truths even if that's the way we pick out the planet. These are the contingent marks by which we identify a certain planet and give it a name.

NOTES

1. Keith Donnellan, "Reference and Definite Descriptions," *Philosophical Review* 75 (1966), pp. 281–304, [reprinted in this volume]. See also Leonard Linsky, "Reference and Referents," in *Philosophy and Ordinary Language*,

ed. Caton (University of Illinois Press, Urbana: 1963.) Donnellan's distinction seems applicable to names as well as to descriptions. Two men glimpse someone at a distance and think they recognize him as Jones. "What is Jones doing?' Raking the leaves." If the distant leaf-raker is actually Smith, then in some sense they are *referring* to Smith, even though they both use "Jones" *as a name of* Jones. In the text, I speak of the 'referent' of a name to mean the thing named by the name— e.g., Jones, not Smith—even though a speaker may sometimes properly be said to use the name to refer to someone else. Perhaps it would have been less misleading to use a technical term, such as 'denote' rather than 'refer'. My use of 'refer' is such as to satisfy the schema, "The referent of 'X' is X," where "X" is replaceable by any name or description. I am tentatively inclined to believe, in opposition to Donnellan, that his remarks about reference have little to do with semantics or truth-conditions, though they may be relevant to a theory of speech acts. Space limitations do not permit me to explain what I mean by this, much less defend the view, except for a brief remark: Call the referent of a name or description in my sense the 'semantic referent'; for a name, this is the thing named, for a description, the thing uniquely satisfying the description.

Then the speaker may *refer* to something other than the semantic referent if he has appropriate false beliefs. I think this is what happens in the naming (Smith-Jones) cases and also in the Donnellan 'champagne' case; the one requires no theory that names are ambiguous, and the other requires no modification of Russell's theory of descriptions.

2. Gottlob Frege, "On Sense and Nominatum," translated by Herbert Feigl in *Readings in Philosophical Analysis*, ed. Herbert Feigl and Wilfrid Sellars (Appleton Century Crofts: 1949), p. 86.
3. Ludwig Wittgenstein, *Philosophical Investigations*, trans. G. E. M. Anscombe (MacMillan: 1953), §79.
4. John R. Searle, "Proper Names," *Mind* 67 (1958), 166–73. [Reprinted in this volume.]
5. Ziff's most detailed statement of his version of the cluster-of-descriptions theory of the reference of names is in "About God," reprinted in *Philosophical Turnings* (Cornell University Press, Ithaca, and Oxford University Press, London: 1966) pp. 94–96. A briefer statement is in his *Semantic Analysis,* (Cornell University Press, Ithaca: 1960) pp. 102–05 (esp. pp. 103–04). The latter passage suggests that names of things with which we are acquainted should be treated somewhat differently (using ostension and baptism) from names of historical figures,

where the reference is determined by (a cluster of) associated descriptions. On p. 93 of *Semantic Analysis* Ziff states that "simple strong generalization(s) about proper names" are impossible; "one can only say what is so for the most part . . ." Nevertheless Ziff clearly states that a cluster-of-descriptions theory is a reasonable such rough statement, at least for historical figures. For Ziff's view that proper names ordinarily are not words of the language and ordinarily do not have meaning, see pp. 85–89 and 93–94 of *Semantic Analysis.*
6. Those determinists who deny the importance of the individual in history may well argue that had Moses never existed, someone else would have arisen to achieve all that he did. Their claim cannot be refuted by appealing to a correct philosophical theory of the meaning of 'Moses exists'.
7. Of course I don't imply that language contains a name for every object. Demonstratives can be used as rigid designators, and free variables can be used as rigid designators of unspecified objects. Of course when we specify a counterfactual situation, we do not describe the whole possible world, but only the portion which interests us.
8. Searle, "Proper Names," in Caton, op. cit., p. 160. [Reprinted in this volume.]
9. An even better case of determining the reference of a name by description, as opposed to ostension, is the discovery of the planet Neptune. Neptune was hypothesized as the planet which caused such and such discrepancies in the orbits of certain other planets. If Leverrier indeed gave the name "Neptune" to the planet before it was ever seen, then he fixed the reference of "Neptune" by means of the description just mentioned. At that time he was unable to see the planet even through a telescope. At this stage, an a priori material equivalence held between the statements "Neptune exists" and "some one planet perturbing the orbit of such and such other planets exists in such and such a position," and also such statements as "if such and such perturbations are caused by a planet, they are caused by Neptune" had the status of a priori truths. Nevertheless, they were not *necessary* truths, since "Neptune" was introduced as a name rigidly designating a certain planet. Leverrier could well have believed that if Neptune had been knocked off its course one million years earlier, it would have caused no such perturbations and even that some other object might have caused the perturbations in its place.
10. Following Donnellan's remarks on definite descriptions, we should add that in some cases, an object may be identified, and the reference of a name fixed, using a description which may turn

out to be false of its object. The case where the reference of "Phosphorus" is determined as the "morning star," which later turns out not to be a star, is an obvious example. In such cases, the description which fixes the reference clearly is in no sense known a priori to hold of the object, though a more cautious substitute may be. If such a more cautious substitute is available, it is really the substitute which fixes the reference in the sense intended in the text.

11. Some of the theses are sloppily stated in respect of fussy matters like use of quotation marks and related details. (For example, theses (5) and (6), as stated, presuppose that the speaker's language is English.) Since the purport of the theses is clear, and they are false anyway, I have not bothered to set these things straight.

12. The cluster-of-descriptions theory of naming would make "Peano discovered the axioms for number theory" express a trivial truth, not a misconception, and similarly for other misconceptions about the history of science. Some who have conceded such cases to me have argued that there are *other* uses of the same proper names satisfying the cluster theory. For example, it is argued, if we say, "Gödel proved the incompleteness of arithmetic," we are, of course, referring to Gödel, not to Schmidt. But, if we say, "Gödel relied on a diagonal argument in this step of the proof," don't we here, perhaps, refer to *whoever proved the theorem?* Similarly, if someone asks, "What did Aristotle (or Shakespeare) have in mind here?", isn't he talking about the author of the passage in question, whoever he is? By analogy to Donnellan's usage for descriptions, this might be called an "attributive" use of proper names. If this is so, then assuming the Gödel-Schmidt story, the sentence "Gödel proved the incompleteness theorem" is false, but "Gödel used a diagonal argument in the proof" is (at least in some contexts) true, and the reference of the name 'Gödel' is ambiguous. Since some counterexamples remain, the cluster-of-descriptions theory would still, in general, be false, which was my main point in the text; but it would be applicable in a wider class of cases than I thought. I think, however, that no such ambiguity need be postulated. It is, perhaps, true that sometimes when someone uses the name "Gödel," his main interest is in whoever proved the theorem, and *perhaps*, in some sense, he 'refers' to him. I do not think that this case is different from the case of Smith and Jones. If I mistake Jones for Smith, I may *refer* (in an appropriate sense) to Jones when I say that Smith is raking the leaves; nevertheless I do not use "Smith" ambiguously, as a name sometimes of Smith and sometimes of Jones, but univocally as a name of Smith.

Similarly, if I erroneously think that Aristotle wrote such-and-such passage, I may perhaps sometimes use "Aristotle" to *refer* to the actual author of the passage, even though there is no ambiguity in my use of the name. In both cases, I will withdraw my original statement, and my original use of the name, if apprised of the facts. Recall that, in these lectures, 'referent' is used in the technical sense of the thing named by a name (or uniquely satisfying a description), and there should be no confusion.

13. A good example of a baptism whose reference was fixed by means of a description was that of naming Neptune in n. 9. The case of a baptism by ostension can perhaps be subsumed under the description concept also. Thus the primary applicability of the description theory is to cases of initial baptism. Descriptions are also used to fix a reference in cases of designation which are similar to naming except that the terms introduced are not usually called 'names'. The terms "one meter," "100 degrees Centigrade," have already been given as examples, and other examples will be given later in these lectures. Two things should be emphasized concerning the case of introducing a name via a description in an initial baptism. First, the description used is not synonymous with the name it introduces but rather fixes its reference. Here we differ from the usual description theorists. Second, most cases of initial baptism are far from those which originally inspired the description theory. Usually a baptizer is acquainted in some sense with the object he names and is able to name it ostensively. Now the inspiration of the description theory lay in the fact that we can often use names of famous figures of the past who are long dead and with whom no living person is acquainted; and it is precisely these cases which, on our view, cannot be correctly explained by a description theory.

14. I can transmit the name of the aardvark to other people. For each of these people, as for me, there will be a certain sort of causal or historical connection between my use of the name and the Emperor of the French, but not one of the required type.

15. Once we realize that the description used to fix the reference of a name is not synonymous with it, then the description theory can be regarded as presupposing the notion of naming or reference. The requirement I made that the description used not itself involve the notion of reference in a circular way is something else and is crucial if the description theory is to have any value at all. The reason is that the description theorist supposes that each speaker essentially uses the description he gives in an initial act of naming to determine his reference. Clearly, if he introduces the name "Cicero" by the deter-

mination, "By 'Cicero' I shall refer to the man I call 'Cicero'," he has by this ceremony determined no reference at all.

Not all description theorists thought that they were eliminating the notion of reference altogether. Perhaps some realized that some notion of ostension, or primitive reference, is required to back it up. Certainly Russell did.

16. There is a more elaborate discussion of this point in the third lecture, where its relation to a certain sort of counterpart theory is also mentioned.

The Causal Theory of Names   23

I

1. In a paper which provides the starting point of this enquiry Saul Kripke opposes what he calls the description theory of names and makes a counterproposal of what I shall call the causal theory.[1] To be clear about what is at stake and what should be the outcome in the debate he initiated seems to me important for our understanding of talk and thought about the world in general as well as for our understanding of the functioning of proper names. I am anxious therefore that we identify the profound bases and likely generalizations of the opposing positions and do not content ourselves with counterexamples.

I should say that Kripke deliberately held back from presenting his ideas as a theory. I shall have to tighten them up, and I may suggest perhaps unintended directions of generalization; therefore his paper should be checked before the causal theory I consider is attributed to him.

There are two related but distinguishable questions concerning proper names. The first is about what the name denotes upon a particular occasion of its use when this is understood as being partly determinative of what the speaker strictly and literally said. I shall use the faintly barbarous coinage: *what the speaker denotes* (upon an occasion) for this notion. The second is about *what the name denotes;* we want to know what conditions have to be satisfied by an expression and an item for the first to be the, or a, name of the second. There is an entirely parallel pair of questions concerning general terms. In both cases it is ambiguity which prevents an easy answer of the first in terms of the second; to denote X it is not sufficient merely to utter something which is X's name.

Consequently there are two description theories, not distinguished by Kripke.[2] The description theory of speaker's denotation holds that a name "N.N." denotes X upon a particular occasion of its use by a speaker S just in case X is uniquely that which satisfies all or most of the descriptions ϕ such that S would assent to "N.N. is ϕ" (or "*That* N.N. is ϕ"). Crudely: the cluster of information S has associated with the name determines its denotation upon a particular occasion by *fit*. If the speaker has no individuating information he will denote nothing.

The description theory of what a name denotes holds that, associated with each name as used by a group of speakers who believe and intend that they are using the name with the same denotation, is a description or set of descriptions cullable from their beliefs which an item has to satisfy to be the bearer of the name. This description is used to explain the role of the name in existential, identity and opaque contexts. The theory is by no means

From *Aristotelian Society: Supplementary Volume 47* (1973), pp. 187–208.

committed to the thesis that every user of the name must be in possession of the description; just as Kripke is not committed to holding that every user of the expression "one meter" knows about the meter rod in Paris by saying that its reference is fixed by the description "Length of stick S in Paris." Indeed if the description is arrived at in the manner of Strawson[3]—averaging out the different beliefs of different speakers—it is most unlikely that the description will figure in every user's name-associated cluster.

The direct attack in Kripke's paper passes this latter theory by; most conspicuously the charge that the description theory ignores the social character of naming. I shall not discuss it explicitly either, though it will surface from time to time and the extent to which it is right should be clear by the end of the paper.

Kripke's direct attacks are unquestionably against the first description theory. He argues:

(a) An ordinary man in the street can denote the physicist Feynman by using the name "Feynman" and say something true or false of him even though there is no description uniquely true of the physicist which he can fashion. (The conditions aren't necessary.)

(b) A person who associated with the name "Gödel" merely the description "prover of the incompleteness of arithmetic" would nonetheless be denoting Gödel and saying something false of him in uttering "Gödel proved the incompleteness of arithmetic" even if an unknown Viennese by the name of Schmidt had in fact constructed the proof which Gödel had subsequently broadcast as his own. (If it is agreed that the speaker does not denote Schmidt the conditions aren't sufficient; if it is also agreed that he denotes Gödel, again they are not necessary.)

The strong thesis (that the description theorist's conditions are sufficient) is outrageous. What the speaker denotes in the sense we are concerned with is connected with saying in that strict sense which logicians so rightly prize, and the theory's deliverances of strict truth conditions are quite unacceptable. They would have the consequence, for example, that if I was previously innocent of knowledge or belief regarding Mr. *Y, and X* is wrongly introduced to me as Mr. *Y,* then I must speak the truth in uttering "Mr. *Y* is here" since *X* satisfies the overwhelming majority of descriptions I would associate with the name and *X* is there. I have grave doubts as to whether anyone has ever seriously held this thesis.

It is the weaker thesis—that some descriptive identification is necessary for a speaker to denote something—that it is important to understand. Strictly, Kripke's examples do not show it to be false since he nowhere provides a convincing reason for not taking into account speakers' possession of descriptions like "man bearing such-and-such a name"; but I too think it is false. It can be seen as the fusion of two thoughts. First: that in order to be saying something by uttering an expression one must utter the sentence with certain intentions; this is felt to require, in the case of sentences containing names, that one be aiming at something with one's use of the name. Secondly—and this is where the underpinning from a certain Philosophy of Mind becomes apparent—to have an intention or belief concerning some item (which one is not in a position to demonstratively identify) one must be in possession of a description uniquely true of it. Both strands deserve at least momentary scrutiny.

We are prone to pass too quickly from the observation that neither parrots nor the wind *say* things to the conclusion that to say that *p* requires that one must intend to say that *p* and therefore, so to speak, be able to identify *p* independently of one's sentence. But the most we are entitled to conclude is that to say something one must intend to say something by uttering one's sentence (one normally will intend to say what it says). The application of the stricter requirement would lead us to relegate too much of our discourse to the status of mere mouthing. We constantly use general terms of whose satisfaction conditions we have but the dimmest idea. "Microbiologist," "chlorine" (the stuff in swimming pools), "nicotine" (the stuff in cigarettes); these (and countless other words) we cannot define nor offer remarks which would distinguish their meaning from that of closely related words. It is wrong to say that we say nothing by uttering sentences containing these expressions, even if we recoil from the strong thesis, from saying that what we do say is determined by those hazy ideas and half-identifications we would offer if pressed.

The Philosophy of Mind is curiously popular but rarely made perfectly explicit.[4] It is held by anyone who holds that S believes that a is F if and only if

$$\exists\phi[(S \text{ believes } \exists x(\phi x \& (\forall y) (\phi y \to x = y) \& Fx)) \& \phi a \& (\forall y) (\phi y \to y = a)]$$

Obvious alterations would accommodate the other psychological attitudes. The range of the property quantifier must be restricted to exclude such properties as "being identical with a" otherwise the criterion is trivial.[5] The situation in which a thinking planning or wanting human has some item which is the object of his thought, plan or desire is represented as a species of essentially the same situation as that which holds when there is no object and the thought, plan or desire is, as we might say, purely general. There are thoughts, such as the thought that there are 11-fingered men, for whose expression general terms of the language suffice. The idea is that when the psychological state involves an object, a general term believed to be uniquely instantiated and in fact uniquely instantiated by the item which is the object of the state will figure in its specification. This idea may be coupled with a concession that there are certain privileged objects to which one may be more directly related; indeed such a concession appears to be needed if the theory is to be able to allow what appears an evident possibility: object-directed thoughts in a perfectly symmetrical or cyclical universe.

This idea about the nature of object-directed psychological attitudes obviously owes much to the feeling that there must be something we can say about what is believed or wanted even when there is no appropriate object actually to be found in the world. But it can also be seen as deriving support from a principle of charity: so attribute objects to beliefs that true belief is maximized. (I do not think this is an acceptable principle; the acceptable principle enjoins minimizing the attribution of *inexplicable* error and therefore cannot be operated without a theory of the causation of belief for the creatures under investigation.)

We cannot deal comprehensively with this Philosophy of Mind here. My objections to it are essentially those of Wittgenstein. For an item to be the object of some psychological attitude of yours may be simply for you to be placed in a context which relates you to that thing. What makes it one rather than the other of a pair of identical twins that you are in love with? Certainly not some specification blue printed in your mind; it may be no more than this: it was one of them and not the other that you have met. The theorist may gesture to the description "the one I have met" but can give no explanation for the impossibility of its being outweighed by other descriptions which may have been acquired as a result of error and which may in fact happen to fit the other, unmet, twin. If God had looked into your mind, he would not have seen there with whom you were in love, and of whom you were thinking.

With that I propose to begin considering the causal theory.

2. The causal theory as stated by Kripke goes something like this. A speaker, using a name "NN" on a particular occasion will denote some item x if there is a causal chain of *reference-preserving links* leading back from his use on that occasion ultimately to the item x itself being involved in a name-acquiring transaction such as an explicit dubbing or the more gradual process whereby nick names stick. I mention the notion of a reference-preserving link to incorporate a condition that Kripke lays down; a speaker S's transmission of a name "NN" to a speaker S' constitutes a reference-preserving link only if S intends to be using the name with the same denotation as he from whom he in his turn learned the name.

Let us begin by considering the theory in answer to our question about speaker's denotation (i.e., at the level of the individual speaker). In particular, let us consider the thesis that it is *sufficient* for someone to denote x on a particular occasion with the name that this use of the name on that occasion be a causal consequence of his exposure to other speakers using the expression to denote x.

An example which might favorably dispose one towards the theory is this. A group of people are having a conversation in a pub, about a certain Louis of whom S has never heard before. S becomes interested and asks: "What did Louis do then?" There seems to be no question but that S denotes a particular man and asks about him. Or on some subsequent occasion S may use the name to offer some new thought to one of the participants: "Louis was quite right to do that." Again he clearly denotes whoever was the subject of conversation in the pub. This is difficult to reconcile with the description theory since the scraps of information which he picked up during the conversation might involve some distortion and fit someone else much better. Of course he has the description "the man they were talking about" but the theory has no explanation for the impossibility of its being outweighed.

The causal theory can secure the right answer in such a case but I think deeper reflection will reveal that it too involves a refusal to recognize the insight about contextual determination I mentioned earlier. For the theory has the following consequence: that at any future time, no matter how remote or forgotten the conversation, no matter how alien the subject matter and confused the speaker, S will denote one particular Frenchman—perhaps Louis XIII—so long as there is a causal connection between his use at that time and the long distant conversation.

It is important in testing your intuitions against the theory that you imagine the predicate changed—so that he says something like "Louis was a basketball player" which was not heard in the conversation and which arises as the result of some confusion. This is to prevent the operation of what I call the "mouthpiece syndrome" by which we attach sense and reference to a man's remarks only because we hear someone else speaking

through him; as we might with a messenger, carrying a message about matters of which he was entirely ignorant.

Now there is no knock-down argument to show this consequence unacceptable; with pliant enough intuitions you can swallow anything in philosophy. But notice how little *point* there is in saying that he denotes one French King rather than any other, or any other person named by the name. There is now nothing that the speaker is prepared to say or do which relates him differentially to that one King. This is why it is so outrageous to say that he believes that Louis XIII is a basketball player. The notion of saying has simply been severed from all the connections that made it of interest. Certainly we did not think we were letting ourselves in for this when we took the point about the conversation in the pub. What has gone wrong?[6]

The causal theory again ignores the importance of surrounding context, and regards the capacity to denote something as a magic trick which has somehow been passed on, and once passed on cannot be lost. We should rather say: in virtue of the context in which the man found himself the man's dispositions were bent towards one particular man—Louis XIII—whose states and doings alone he would count as serving to verify remarks made in that context using the name. And of course that context can persist, for the conversation can itself be adverted to subsequently. But it can also disappear so that the speaker is simply not sensitive to the outcome of any investigations regarding the truth of what he is said to have said. And at this point saying becomes detached, and uninteresting.

(It is worth observing how ambivalent Kripke is on the relation between denoting and believing; when the connection favors him he uses it; we are reminded for example that the ordinary man has a false belief about Gödel and not a true belief about Schmidt. But it is obvious that the results of the 'who are they believing about?' criterion are bound to come dramatically apart from the results of the 'who is the original bearer of the name?' criterion, if for no other reason than that the former must be constructed to give results in cases where there is no name and where the latter cannot apply. When this happens we are sternly reminded that "X refers" and "X says" are being used in *technical* senses.[7] But there are limits. One could regard the aim of this paper to restore the connection which must exist between strict truth conditions and the beliefs and interests of the users of the sentences if the technical notion of strict truth conditions is to be of interest to us.)

Reflection upon the conversation in the pub appeared to provide one reason for being favorably disposed towards the causal theory. There is another connected reason we ought to examine briefly. It might appear that the causal theory provides the basis for a general nonintentional answer to the problem of ambiguity. The problem is clear enough: What conditions have to be satisfied for a speaker to have said that *p* when he utters a sentence which may appropriately be used to say that *q* and that *r* and that *s* in addition? Two obvious alternative answers are (a) the extent to which it is reasonable for his audience to conclude that he was saying that *p,* and (b) his intending to say that *p*.

Neither is without its difficulties. We can therefore imagine someone hoping for a natural extension of the causal theory to general terms which would enable him to explain for example how a child who did not have determinative intentions because of the technical nature of the subject matter may still say something determinate using a sentence which is in fact ambiguous.

I touch upon this to ensure that we are keeping the range of relevant considerations to be brought to bear upon the debate as wide as it must be. But I think little general advantage can accrue to the causal theory from thus broadening the considerations. The reason is that it simply fails to have the generality of the other two theories; it has no obvious application, for example, to syntactic ambiguity or to ambiguity produced by attempts to refer with nonunique descriptions, or pronouns. It seems inconceivable that the general theory of disambiguation required for such cases would be inadequate to deal with the phenomenon of shared names and would

require ad hoc supplementation from the causal theory.

I want to stress how, precisely because the causal theory ignores the way context can be determinative of what gets *said,* it has quite unacceptable consequences. Suppose for example on a T.V. quiz program I am asked to name a capital city and I say "Kingston is the capital of Jamaica"; I should want to say that I had said something strictly and literally true even though it turns out that the man from whom I had picked up this scrap of information was actually referring to Kingston-upon-Thames and making a racist observation.

It may begin to appear that what gets said is going to be determined by what name is used, what items bear the name, and general principles of contextual disambiguation. The causal origin of the speaker's familiarity with the name, save in certain specialized "mouthpiece cases," does not seem to have a critical role to play.

This impression may be strengthened by the observation that a causal connection between my use of the name and use by others (whether or nor leading back ultimately to the item itself) is simply not necessary for me to use the name to say something. Amongst the Wagera Indians, for example, "newly born children receive the names of deceased members of their family according to fixed rules . . . the first born takes on the name of the paternal grandfather, the second that of the father's eldest brother, the third that of the maternal grandfather."[8] In these and other situations (names for streets in U.S. cities etc.,) a knowledgeable speaker may excogitate a name and use it to denote some item which bears it without any causal connection whatever with the use by others of that name.

These points might be conceded by Kripke while maintaining the general position that the denotation of a name in a community is still to be found by tracing a causal chain of reference preserving links back to some item. It is to this theory that I now turn.

3. Suppose a parallel theory were offered to explain the sense of general terms (not just terms for natural kinds). One would reply as

follows: "There aren't two fundamentally different mechanisms involved in a word's having a meaning: one bringing it about that a word acquires a meaning, and the other—a causal mechanism—which operates to ensure that its meaning is preserved. The former processes are operative all the time; whatever explains how a word gets its meaning also explains how it preserves it, if preserved it is. Indeed such a theory could not account for the phenomenon of a word's changing its meaning. It is perfectly possible for this to happen without anyone's intending to initiate a new practice with the word; the causal chain would then lead back too far."

Change of meaning would be decisive against such a theory of the meaning of general terms. Change of denotation is similarly decisive against the causal theory of names. Not only are changes of denotation imaginable, but it appears that they actually occur. We learn from Isaac Taylor's book: *Names and their History,* 1898:

In the case of 'Madagascar' a hearsay report of Malay or Arab sailors misunderstood by Marco Polo . . . has had the effect of transferring a corrupt form of the name of a portion of the African mainland to the great African Island.

A simple imaginary case would be this: Two babies are born, and their mothers bestow names upon them. A nurse inadvertently switches them and the error is never discovered. It will henceforth undeniably be the case that the man universally known as "Jack" is so called because a woman dubbed some other baby with the name.

It is clear that the causal theory unamended is not adequate. It looks as though, once again, the intentions of the speakers to use the name to refer to something must be allowed to count in determination of what it denotes.

But it is not enough to say that and leave matters there. We must at least sketch a theory which will enable "Madagascar" to be the name of the island yet which will not have the consequence that "Gödel" would become a name of Schmidt in the situation envisaged by Kripke nor "Goliath" a name of the Philistine killed by David. (Biblical scholars

now suggest that David did not kill Goliath, and that the attribution of the slaying to Elhannan the Bethlehemite in 2 *Samuel* 21 xix is correct. David is thought to have killed a Philistine but not Goliath[9].) For although this has never been explicitly argued I would agree that even if the 'information' connected with the name in possession of an entire community was merely that "Goliath was the Philistine David slew" this would still not mean that "Goliath" referred in that community to that man, and therefore that the sentence expressed a truth. And if we simultaneously thought that the name *would* denote the Philistine slain by Elhannan then both the necessity and sufficiency of the conditions suggested by the description theory of the denotation of a name are rejected. This is the case Kripke should have argued but didn't.

4. Before going on to sketch such a theory in the second part of this paper let me survey the position arrived at and use it to make a summary statement of the position I wish to adopt.

We can see the undifferentiated description theory as the expression of two thoughts.

(a) the denotation of a name is determined by what speakers intend to refer to by using the name

(b) the object a speaker intends to refer to by his use of a name is that which satisfies or fits the majority of descriptions which make up the cluster of information which the speaker has associated with the name.

We have seen great difficulties with (a) when this is interpreted as a thesis at the micro level. But consideration of the phenomenon of a name's getting a denotation, or changing it, suggests that there being a community of speakers using the name with such and such as the intended referent is likely to be a crucial constituent in these processes. With names, as with other expressions in the language, what they signify depends upon what we use them to signify—a truth whose recognition is compatible with denying the collapse of saying into meaning at the level of the individual speaker.

It is in (b) that the real weakness lies: the bad old Philosophy of Mind which we momentarily uncovered. Not so much in the idea that the intended referent is determined in a more or less complicated way by the associated information, but the specific form the determination was supposed to take: *fit*. There is something absurd in supposing that the intended referent of some perfectly ordinary use of a name by a speaker could be some item utterly isolated (causally) from the user's community and culture simply in virtue of the fact that it fits better than anything else the cluster of descriptions he associates with the name. I would agree with Kripke in thinking that the absurdity resides in the absence of any causal relation between the item concerned and the speaker. But it seems to me that he has mislocated the causal relation; the important causal relation lies between that item's states and doings and the speaker's body of information—not between the item's being dubbed with a name and the speaker's contemporary use of it.

Philosophers have come increasingly to realize that major concepts in epistemology and the philosophy of mind have causality embedded within them. Seeing and knowing are both good examples.

The absurdity in supposing that the denotation of our contemporary use of the name "Aristotle" could be some unknown (*n.b.*) item whose doings are causally isolated from our body of information is strictly parallel to the absurdity in supposing that one might be seeing something one has no causal contact with solely upon the ground that there is a splendid match between object and visual impression.

There probably is some *degree of fit* requirement in the case of seeing which means that after some amount of distortion or fancy we can no longer maintain that the causally operative item was still being seen. And I think it is likely that there is a parallel requirement for referring. We learn for example from E. K. Chambers' *Arthur of Britain* that Arthur had a son Anir "whom legend has perhaps confused with his burial place." If Kripke's notion of reference fixing is such that those who said Anir was a burial place of Arthur might be denoting a person, it

seems that it has little to commend it, and is certainly not justified by the criticisms he makes against the description theory. But the existence or nature of this 'degree of fit' requirement will not be something I shall be concerned with here.

We must allow then that the denotation of a name in the community will depend in a complicated way upon what those who use the term intend to refer to, but we will so understand 'intended referent' that typically a *necessary* (but not sufficient) condition for *x*'s being the intended referent of *S*'s use of a name is that *x* should be the source of causal origin of the body of information that *S* has associated with the name.

II

5. The aim I have set myself, then, is modest; it is not to present a complete theory of the denotation of names. Without presenting a general theory to solve the problem of ambiguity I cannot present a theory of speaker's denotation, although I will make remarks which prejudice that issue. I propose merely to sketch an account of what makes an expression into a name for something that will allow names to change their denotations.

The enterprise is more modest yet for I propose to help myself to an undefined notion of speaker's reference by borrowing from the theory of communication. But a word of explanation.

A speaker may have succeeded in *getting it across* or in *communicating* that *p* even though he uses a sentence which may not appropriately be used to say that *p*. Presumably this success consists in his audience's having formed a belief about him. This need not be the belief that the speaker intended to say in the strict sense that *p*, since the speaker may succeed in getting something across despite using a sentence which he is known to know cannot appropriately be used to say that *p*. The speaker will have referred to *a*, in the sense I am helping myself to, only if he has succeeded in getting it across that *Fa* (for some substitution *F*). Further stringent conditions are required. Clearly this notion is quite different from the notion of denotation which I have been using, tied as denotation is to saying in the strict sense. One may refer to x by using a description that x does not satisfy; one may not thus denote x.

Now a speaker may know or believe that there is such-and-such an item in the world and intend to refer to it. And this is where the suggestion made earlier must be brought to bear, for *that* item is not (in general) the satisfier of the body of information the possession by the speaker of which makes it true that he knows of the existence of the item; it is rather that item which is causally responsible for the speaker's possession of that body of information, or dominantly responsible if there is more than one. (The point is of course not specific to this intention, or to intention as opposed to other psychological attitudes.) Let us then, very briefly, explore these two ideas: source and dominance.

Usually our knowledge or belief about particular items is derived from information-gathering transactions, involving a causal interaction with some item or other, conducted ourselves, or is derived, maybe through a long chain, from the transactions of others. Perception of the item is the main but by no means the only way an item can impress itself on us; for example, a man can be the source of things we discover by rifling through his suitcase or by reading his works.

A causal relation is of course not sufficient; but we may borrow from the theory of knowledge and say something like this. X is the source of the belief S expresses by uttering "Fa" if there was an episode which caused S's belief in which X and S were causally related in a type of situation apt for producing knowledge that something F-s $(\exists x(Fx))$—a type of situation in which the belief that something F-s would be caused by something's F-ing. That it is a way of producing knowledge does not mean that it cannot go wrong; that is why X, by smoking French cigarettes can be the source of the belief S expresses by "a smokes Greek cigarettes."

Of course some of our information about the world is not so based; we may deduce that there is a tallest man in the world and deduce that he is over six feet tall. No man is the source of this information; a name introduced in relation to it might function very much as the unamended description theory suggested.

Legend and fancy can create new characters, or add bodies of sourceless material to other dossiers; restrictions on the causal relation would prevent the inventors of the legends turning out to be the sources of the beliefs their legends gave rise to. Someone other than the ϕ can be the source of the belief S expresses by "a is the ϕ"; Kripke's Gödel, by claiming the proof, was the source of the belief people manifested by saying "Gödel proved the incompleteness of arithmetic," not Schmidt.

Misidentification can bring it about that the item which is the source of the information is different from the item about which the information is believed. I may form the belief about the wife of some colleague that she has nice legs upon the basis of seeing someone else—but the girl I saw is the source.

Consequently a cluster or dossier of information can be dominantly of[10] an item though it contains elements whose source is different. And we surely want to allow that persistent misidentification can bring it about that a cluster is dominantly of some item other than that it was dominantly of originally.

Suppose I get to know a man slightly. Suppose then a suitably primed identical twin takes over his position, and I get to know him fairly well, not noticing the switch. Immediately after the switch my dossier will still be dominantly of the original man, and I falsely believe, as I would acknowledge if it was pointed out, that *he* is in the room. Then I would pass through a period in which neither was dominant; I had not misidentified one as the other, an asymmetrical relation, but rather confused them. Finally the twin could take over the dominant position; I would not have false beliefs about who is in the room, but false beliefs about, e.g., when I first met the man in the room. These differences seem to reside entirely in the differences in the believer's reactions to the various discoveries, and dominance is meant to capture those differences.

Dominance is not simply a function of *amount* of information (if that is even intelligible). In the case of persons, for example, each man's life presents a skeleton and the dominant source may be the man who contributed to covering most of it rather than the man who contributed most of the covering. Detail in a particular area can be outweighed by spread. Also the believer's reasons for being interested in the item at all will weigh.

Consider another example. If it turns out that an impersonator had taken over Napoleon's role from 1814 onwards (post-Elba) the cluster of the typical historian would still be dominantly of the man responsible for the earlier exploits (α in diagram 1) and we would say that they had false beliefs about who fought at Waterloo. If however the switch had occurred much earlier, it being an unknown army officer being impersonated, then their information would be dominantly of the later man (β in diagram 2). They did not have false beliefs about who was the general at Waterloo, but rather false beliefs about that general's early career.

I think we can say that *in general* a speaker intends to refer to the item that is the dominant source of his associated body of information. It is important to see that this will not change from occasion to occasion

depending upon subject matter. Some have proposed[11] that if in case 1 the historian says "Napoleon fought skillfully at Waterloo" it is the imposter β who is the intended referent, while if he had said in the next breath ". . . unlike his performance in the Senate" it would be α. This seems a mistake; not only was what the man said false, what he intended to say was false too, as he would be the first to agree; it wasn't Napoleon who fought skilfully at Waterloo.

With this background then we may offer the following tentative definition: "NN" is a name of x if there is a community C—

1. in which it is common knowledge that members of C have in their repertoire the procedure of using "NN" to refer to x (with the intention of referring to x);

2. the success in reference in any particular case being intended to rely on common knowledge between speaker and hearer that "NN" has been used to refer to x by members of C and not upon common knowledge of the satisfaction by x of some predicate embedded in "NN"[12]

(In order to keep the definition simple no attempt is made to cover the sense in which an unused institutionally approved name is a name.)

This distinction (between use-because-(we

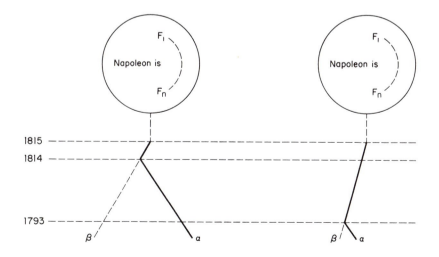

know)-we-use-it and use upon other bases) is just what is needed to distinguish dead from live metaphors; it seems to me the only basis on which to distinguish the referential functioning of names, which may grammatically be descriptions, from that of descriptions.[13]

The definition does not have the consequence that the description "the man we call 'NN' " is a name, for *its* success as a referential device does not rely upon common knowledge that *it* is or has been used to refer to *x*.

Intentions alone don't bring it about that a name gets a denotation; without the intentions being manifest there cannot be the common knowledge required for the practice.

Our conditions are more stringent than Kripke's since for him an expression becomes a name just so long as someone has dubbed something with it and thereby caused it to be in common usage. This seems little short of magical. Suppose one of a group of villagers dubbed a little girl on holiday in the vicinity "Goldilocks" and the name caught on. However suppose that there were two identical twins the villagers totally failed to distinguish. I should deny that "Goldilocks" is the name of either—even if by some miracle each villager used the name consistently but in no sense did they fall into two coherent subcommunities. (The name might denote the girl first dubbed if for some peculiar reason the villagers were deferential to the introducer of the name—of this more below.)

Consider the following case. An urn is discovered in the Dead Sea containing documents in which are found fascinating mathematical proofs. Inscribed at the bottom is the name "Ibn Khan" which is quite naturally taken to be the name of the constructor of the proofs. Consequently it passes into common usage amongst mathematicians concerned with that branch of mathematics. "Khan conjectured here that . . ." and the like. However suppose the name was the name of the scribe who had transcribed the proofs much later; a small "*id scripsit*" had been obliterated.

Here is a perfect case where there is a coherent community using the name with the mathematician as the intended referent and a consequence of the definition would be that "Ibn Khan" would be one of his names. Also, "Malachai" would have been the name of the author of the Biblical work of the same name despite that its use was based upon a misapprehension ("Malachai" means my messenger).[14]

Speakers within such traditions use names under the misapprehension that their use is in conformity with the use of other speakers referring to the relevant item. The names would probably be withdrawn when that misapprehension is revealed, or start a rather different life as "our" names for the items (cf., "Deutero Isaiah" etc.) One might be impressed by this, and regard it as a reason for denying that those within these traditions spoke the literal truth in using the names. It is very easy to add a codicil to the definition which would have this effect.

Actually it is not a very good reason for denying that speakers within such traditions are speaking the literal truth.[15] But I do not want to insist upon any decision upon this point. This is because one can be concessive and allow the definition to be amended without giving up anything of importance. First: the definition with its codicil will still allow many names to change their denotation. Secondly: it obviously fails to follow from the fact that, in our example, the community of mathematicians were not denoting the mathematician [but] that they were denoting the scribe and were engaged in strictly speaking massive falsehood of him.

Let me elaborate the first of these points.

There is a fairly standard way in which people get their names. If we use a name of a man we expect that it originated in the standard manner and this expectation may condition our use of it. But consider names for people which are obviously nicknames, or names for places or pieces of music. Since there is no standard way in which these names are bestowed subsequent users will not in general use the name under any view as to its origin, and therefore when there is a divergence between the item involved in the name's origin and the speakers' intended referent there will be no *mis*apprehension, no latent motive for withdrawing the name, and thus no bar to the name's acquiring a new denotation even by the amended definition. So long as they have no reason to believe that the name has dragged any information with it, speakers will treat the revelation that the name had once been used to refer to something different with the same sort of indifference as that with which they greet the information that "meat" once meant groceries in general.

We can easily tell the story in case 2 of our Napoleon diagram so that α was the original bearer of the name "Napoleon" and it was transferred to the counterfeit because of the similarity of their appearances and therefore without the intention on anyone's part to initiate a new practice. Though this is not such a clear case I should probably say that historians have used the name "Napoleon" to refer to β. They might perhaps abandon it, but that of course fails to show that they were all along denoting α. Nor does the fact that someone in the know might come along and say "Napoleon was a fish salesman and was never at Waterloo" show anything. The relevant question is: "Does this contradict the assertion that was made when the historians said "Napoleon was at Waterloo?" To give an affirmative answer to this question requires the prior determination that they have all along been denoting α.

We need one further and major complication. Although standardly we use expressions with the intention of conforming with the general use made of them by the community, sometimes we use them with the *overriding* intention to conform to the use made of them by some other person or persons. In that case I shall say that we use the expression *deferentially* (with respect to that other person or group of persons). This is true of some general terms too: "viol," "minuet" would be examples.

I should say, for example, that the man in the conversation in the pub used "Louis" deferentially. This is not just a matter of his ignorance; he could, indeed, have an opinion as to who this Louis is (the man he met earlier

perhaps) but still use the expression deferentially. There is an important gap between

intending to refer to the ϕ and believing that α = the ϕ

and

intending to refer to *a*

for even when he has an opinion as to who they are talking about I should say that it was the man they were talking about, and not the man he met earlier, that he intended to refer to.

Archaeologists might find a tomb in the desert and claim falsely that it is the burial place of some little known character in the Bible. They could discover a great deal about the man in the tomb so that he and not the character in the Bible was the dominant source of their information. But, given the nature and point of their enterprise, the archaeologists are using the name deferentially to the authors of the Bible. I should say, then, that they denote that man, and say false things about him. Notice that in such a case there is some point to this characterization.

The case is in fact no different with any situation in which a name is used with the overriding intention of referring to something satisfying such and such a description. Kripke gives the example of "Jack the Ripper." Again, after the arrest of a man *a* not in fact responsible for the crimes, *a* can be the dominant source of speakers' information but the intended referent could well be the murderer and not *a*. Again this will be productive of a whole lot of falsehood.

We do not use all names deferentially, least of all deferentially to the person from whom we picked them up. For example the mathematicians did not use the name "Ibn Khan" with the *overriding* intention of referring to whoever bore that name or was referred to by some other person or community.

We must thus be careful to distinguish two reasons for something that would count as "withdrawing sentences containing the name":

(a) the item's not bearing the name "NN" ("Ibn Khan," "Malachai"), and

(b) the item's not being NN (the biblical archaeologists).

I shall end with an example that enables me to draw these threads together and summarize where my position differs from the causal theory.

A youth A leaves a small village in the Scottish highlands to seek his fortune having acquired the nickname "Turnip" (the reason for choosing a nickname is I hope clear). Fifty or so years later a man B comes to the village and lives as a hermit over the hill. The three or four villagers surviving from the time of the youth's departure believe falsely that this is the long-departed villager returned. Consequently they use the name "Turnip" among themselves and it gets into wider circulation among the younger villagers who have no idea how it originated. I am assuming that the older villagers, if the facts were pointed out would say: "It isn't Turnip after all" rather than "It appears after all that Turnip did not come from this village." In that case I should say that they use the name to refer to A, and in fact, denoting him, say false things about him (even by uttering "Here is Turnip coming to get his coffee again.")

But they may die off, leaving a homogeneous community using the name to refer to the man over the hill. I should say the way is clear to its becoming his name. The story is not much affected if the older villagers pass on some information whose source is A by saying such things as "Turnip was quite a one for the girls," for the younger villagers' clusters would still be dominantly of the man over the hill. But it is an important feature of my account that the information that the older villagers gave the younger villagers could be so rich, coherent and important to them that A could be the dominant source of their information, so that they too would acknowledge "That man over the hill isn't Turnip after all."

A final possibility would be if they used the name deferentially towards the older villagers, for some reason, with the consequence that no matter who was dominant they denote whoever the elders denote.

CONCLUSION

6. Espousers of both theories could reasonably claim to be vindicated by the position we have arrived at. We have secured for the description theorist much that he wanted. We have seen for at least the most fundamental case of the use of names (nondeferentially used names) the idea that their denotation is fixed in a more or less complicated way by the associated bodies of information that one could cull from the users of the name turns out not to be so wide of the mark. But of course that the fix is by causal origin and not by fit crucially affects the impact this idea has upon the statement of the truth conditions of existential or opaque sentences containing names. The theorist can also point to the idea of dominance as securing what he was trying, admittedly crudely, to secure with his talk of the "majority of" the descriptions, and to the 'degree of fit requirement' as blocking consequences he found objectionable.

The causal theorist can also look with satisfaction upon the result, incorporating as it does his insight about the importance of causality into a central position. Further, the logical doctrines he was concerned to establish, for example the noncontingency of identity statements made with the use of names, are not controverted. Information is individuated by source; if *a* is the source of a body of information nothing else could have been. Consequently nothing else could have been *that a*.

The only theorists who gain no comfort are those who, ignoring Kripke's explicit remarks to the contrary,[16] supposed that the causal theory could provide them with a totally *nonintentional* answer to the problem posed by names. But I am not distressed by their distress.

Our ideas also point forwards; for it seems that they, or some close relative, must be used in explaining the functioning of at least some demonstratives. Such an expression as "That mountaineer" in "That mountaineer is coming to town tonight" may advert to a body of information presumed in common possession, perhaps through the newspapers, which fixes its denotation. No one can be *that* mountaineer unless he is the source of that information no matter how perfectly he fits it, and of course someone can be that mountaineer and fail to fit quite a bit of it. It is in such generality that defense of our ideas must lie.

But with these hints I must leave the subject.

REFERENCES

1. S. A. Kripke, "Naming and Necessity," in Davidson and Harman, eds. *Semantics of Natural Languages,* pp. 253–355. [Reprinted in this volume.]
2. This can be seen in the way the list of theses defining the Description Theory alternate between those mentioning a speaker and those that don't, culminating in the uneasy idea of an idiolect of one. The description theorists of course do not themselves distinguish them clearly either, and many espouse both.
3. P. F. Strawson, *Individuals* (Methuen), p. 191.
4. For example see J. R. Searle, *Speech Acts,* p. 87; E. Gellner, "Ethics and Logic," *Proceedings of the Aristotelian Society* (1954–5), B. Russell *Problems of Philosophy,* p. 29. E. Sosa criticizes it in "Quantifiers, Belief, and Sellars," in Davis, Hockney, and Wilson, eds., *Philosophical Logic,* p. 69.
5. I owe this observation to G. Harman.
6. Kripke expresses doubts about the sufficiency of the conditions for this sort of reason [see p. 289, this volume].
7. *Id.* [p. 293, this volume].
8. E. Delhaise, "Les Wagera," *Monogr. Ethnogr.* 1909.
9. Robinson, *History of Israel,* p. 187.
10. The term is D. Kaplan's, see "Quantifying In" [reprinted in this volume], in Davidson and Hintikka, eds., *Words and Objections:* I think there are clear similarities between my notion of a dominant source and notions he is there sketching. However I want nothing to do with vividness. I borrow the term "dossier" from H. P. Grice's paper "Vacuous Names" in the same volume.
11. K. S. Donnellan, "Proper Names and Identifying Descriptions" in Davidson and Harman, eds., p. 371.
12. For the notion of "common knowledge" see D. K. Lewis, *Convention* and the slightly different notion in S. Schiffer, *Meaning* (Oxford, Oxford University Press: 1972). For the notion of "a procedure in the repertoire" see H. P. Grice "Utterer's Meaning, Sentence Meaning, Word Meaning," *Foundations of Language* (1968). Clearly the whole enterprise owes to Grice but no commitment is here made to any specific version of the theory of communication.
13. And if Schiffer is right much more as well—see *Meaning,* chapter V.
14. See Otto Eissfeldt, *The Old Testament,* p. 441.
15. John McDowell has persuaded me of this, as of much else. He detests my conclusions.
16. Kripke [p. 289, this volume].

Meaning and Reference   24

HILARY PUTNAM

Unclear as it is, the traditional doctrine that the notion "meaning" possesses the extension/intension ambiguity has certain typical consequences. The doctrine that the meaning of a term is a concept carried the implication that meanings are mental entities. Frege, however, rebelled against this "psychologism." Feeling that meanings are *public* property—that the *same* meaning can be "grasped" by more than one person and by persons at different times—he identified concepts (and hence "intensions" or meanings) with abstract entities rather than mental entities. However, "grasping" these abstract entities was still an individual psychological act. None of these philosophers doubted that understanding a word (knowing its intension) was just a matter of being in a certain psychological state (somewhat in the way in which knowing how to factor numbers in one's head is just a matter of being in a certain very complex psychological state).

Secondly, the timeworn example of the two terms 'creature with a kidney' and 'creature with a heart' does show that two terms can have the same extension and yet differ in intension. But it was taken to be obvious that the reverse is impossible: two terms cannot differ in extension and have the same intension. Interestingly, no argument for this impossibility was ever offered. Probably it reflects the tradition of the ancient and medieval philosophers, who assumed that the concept corresponding to a term was just a conjunction of predicates, and hence that the concept corresponding to a term must *always* provide a necessary and sufficient condition for falling into the extension of the term. For philosophers like Carnap, who accepted the verifiability theory of meaning, the concept corresponding to a term provided (in the ideal case, where the term had "complete meaning") a *criterion* for belonging to the extension (not just in the sense of "necessary and sufficient condition," but in the strong sense of *way of recognizing* whether a given thing falls into the extension or not). So theory of meaning came to rest on two unchallenged assumptions:

(1) That knowing the meaning of a term is just a matter of being in a certain psychological state (in the sense of "psychological state," in which states of memory and belief are "psychological states"; no one thought that knowing the meaning of a word was a continuous state of consciousness, of course).

From *The Journal of Philosophy*, volume 70 (1973), pp. 699–711. Presented in an APA symposium on Reference, December 28, 1973. A very much expanded version of this paper appeared under the title "The Meaning of 'Meaning' " in *Language, Mind, and Knowledge*, Keith Gunderson, ed. (Minneapolis: University of Minnesota Press, 1975), pp. 131–93.

(2) That the meaning of a term determines its extension (in the sense that sameness of intension entails sameness of extension).

I shall argue that these two assumptions are not jointly satisfied by *any* notion, let alone any notion of meaning. The traditional concept of meaning is a concept which rests on a false theory.

ARE MEANINGS IN THE HEAD?

For the purpose of the following science-fiction examples, we shall suppose that somewhere there is a planet we shall call Twin Earth. Twin Earth is very much like Earth: in fact, people on Twin Earth even speak *English*. In fact, apart from the differences we shall specify in our science-fiction examples, the reader may suppose that Twin Earth is *exactly* like Earth. He may even suppose that he has a *Doppelganger*—an identical copy—on Twin Earth, if he wishes, although my stories will not depend on this.

Although some of the people on Twin Earth (say, those who call themselves "Americans" and those who call themselves "Canadians" and those who call themselves "Englishmen," etc.) speak English, there are, not surprisingly, a few tiny differences between the dialects of English spoken on Twin Earth and standard English.

One of the peculiarities of Twin Earth is that the liquid called "water" is not H_2O but a different liquid whose chemical formula is very long and complicated. I shall abbreviate this chemical formula simply as XYZ. I shall suppose that XYZ is indistinguishable from water at normal temperatures and pressures. Also, I shall suppose that the oceans and lakes and seas of Twin Earth contain XYZ and not water, that it rains XYZ on Twin Earth and ·not water, etc.

If a space ship from Earth ever visits Twin Earth, then the supposition at first will be that 'water' has the same meaning on Earth and on Twin Earth. This supposition will be corrected when it is discovered that "water" on Twin Earth is XYZ, and the Earthian space ship will report somewhat as follows.

"On Twin Earth the word 'water' means XYZ."

Symmetrically, if a space ship from Twin Earth ever visits Earth, then the supposition at first will be that the word 'water' has the same meaning on Twin Earth and on Earth. This supposition will be corrected when it is discovered that "water" on Earth is H_2O, and the Twin Earthian space ship will report:

"On Earth the word 'water' means H_2O."

Note that there is no problem about the extension of the term 'water': the word simply has two different meanings (as we say); in the sense in which it is used on Twin Earth, the sense of water$_{TE}$, what *we* call "water" isn't water, while in the sense in which it is used on Earth, the sense of water$_E$, what the Twin Earthians call "water" simple isn't water. The extension of 'water' in the sense of water$_E$ is the set of all wholes consisting of H_2O molecules, or something like that; the extension of water in the sense of water$_{TE}$ is the set of all wholes consisting of XYZ molecules, or something like that.

Now let us roll the time back to about 1750. The typical Earthian speaker of English did not know that water consisted of hydrogen and oxygen, and the typical Twin-Earthian speaker of English did not know that "water" consisted of XYZ. Let Oscar$_1$ be such a typical Earthian English speaker, and let Oscar$_2$ be his counterpart on Twin Earth. You may suppose that there is no belief that Oscar$_1$ had about water that Oscar$_2$ did not have about "water." If you like, you may even suppose that Oscar$_1$ and Oscar$_2$ were exact duplicates in appearance, feelings, thoughts, interior monologue, etc. Yet the extension of the term 'water' was just as much H_2O on Earth in 1750 as in 1950; and the extension of the term 'water' was just as much XYZ on Twin Earth in 1750 as in 1950. Oscar$_1$ and Oscar$_2$ understood the term 'water' differently in 1750 *although they were in the same psychological state,* and although, given the state of science at the time, it would have taken their scientific communities about fifty years to discover that they understood the term 'water' differently. Thus the extension of the term 'water' (and, in fact, its "meaning" in the intuitive preanalytical usage of that term) is *not* a function of the psychological state of the speaker by itself.[1]

But, it might be objected, why should we accept it that the term 'water' had the same extension in 1750 and in 1950 (on both Earths)? Suppose I point to a glass of water and say "this liquid is called water." My "ostensive definition" of water had the following empirical presupposition: that the body of liquid I am pointing to bears a certain sameness relation (say, *x is the same liquid as y*, or *x is the same$_L$ as y*) to most of the stuff I and other speakers in my linguistic community have on other occasions called "water." If this presupposition is false because, say, I am—unknown to me—pointing to a glass of gin and not a glass of water, then I do not intend my ostensive definition to be accepted. Thus the ostensive definition conveys what might be called a "defeasible" necessary and sufficient condition: the necessary and sufficient condition for being water is bearing the relation *same$_L$* to the stuff in the glass; but this is the necessary and sufficient condition only if the empirical presupposition is satisfied. If it is not satisfied, then one of a series of, so to speak, "fallback" conditions becomes activated.

The key point is that the relation *same$_L$* is a *theoretical* relation: whether something is or is not the same liquid as *this* may take an indeterminate amount of scientific investigation to determine. Thus, the fact that an English speaker in 1750 might have called XYZ "water," whereas he or his successors would not have called XYZ water in 1800 or 1850 does not mean that the "meaning" of 'water' changed for the average speaker in the interval. In 1750 or in 1850 or in 1950 one might have pointed to, say, the liquid in Lake Michigan as an example of "water." What changed was that in 1750 we would have mistakenly thought that XYZ bore the relation *same$_L$* to the liquid in Lake Michigan, whereas in 1800 or 1850 we would have known that it did not.

Let us now modify our science-fiction story. I shall suppose that molybdenum pots and pans *can't* be distinguished from aluminum pots and pans save by an expert. (This could be true for all I know, and, *a fortiori*, it could be true for all I know by virtue of "knowing the meaning" of the words *aluminum* and *molybdenum*.) We will now suppose that molybdenum is as common on Twin Earth as aluminum is on Earth, and that aluminum is as rare on Twin Earth as molybdenum is on Earth. In particular, we shall assume that "aluminum" pots and pans are made of molybdenum on Twin Earth. Finally, we shall assume that the words 'aluminum' and 'molybdenum' are *switched* on Twin Earth: 'aluminum' is the name of *molybdenum*, and 'molybdenum' is the name of *aluminum*. If a space ship from Earth visited Twin Earth, the visitors from Earth probably would not suspect that the "aluminum" pots and pans on Twin Earth were not made of aluminum, especially when the Twin Earthians *said* they were. But there is one important difference between the two cases. An Earthian metallurgist could tell very easily that "aluminum" was molybdenum, and a Twin Earthian metallurgist could tell equally easily that aluminum was "molybdenum." (The shudder quotes in the preceding sentence indicate Twin Earthian usages.) Whereas in 1750 no one on either Earth or Twin Earth could have distinguished water from "water," the confusion of aluminum with "aluminum" involves only a part of the linguistic communities involved.

This example makes the same point as the preceding example. If Oscar$_1$ and Oscar$_2$ are standard speakers of Earthian English and Twin Earthian English, respectively, and neither is chemically or metallurgically sophisticated, then there may be no difference at all in their psychological states when the use the world 'aluminum'; nevertheless, we have to say that 'aluminum' has the extension *aluminum* in the idiolect of Oscar$_1$ and the extension *molybdenum* in the idiolect of Oscar$_2$. (Also we have to say that Oscar$_1$ and Oscar$_2$ mean different things by 'aluminum'; that 'aluminum' has a different meaning on Earth than it does on Twin Earth, etc.) Again we see that the psychological state of the speaker does *not* determine the extension (*or* the "meaning," speaking preanalytically) of the word.

Before discussing this example further, let me introduce a *non*-science-fiction example. Suppose you are like me and cannot tell an elm from a beech tree. We will say that the extension of 'elm' in my idiolect is the same as the extension of 'elm' in anyone else's, viz., the set of all elm trees, and that the set of all beech trees is the extension of 'beech' in *both* of our idiolects. Thus 'elm' in my idiolect has a different extension from 'beech' in your idiolect (as it should). Is it really credible that this difference in extension is brought about by some difference in our *concepts?* My *concept* of an elm tree is exactly the same as my concept of a beech tree (I blush to confess). If someone heroically attempts to maintain that the difference between the extension of 'elm' and the extension of 'beech' in *my* idiolect is explained by a difference in my psychological state, then we can always refute him by constructing a "Twin Earth" example—just let the worlds 'elm' and 'beech' be switched on Twin Earth (the way 'aluminum' and 'molybdenum' were in the previous example). Moreover, suppose I have a *Doppelganger* on Twin Earth who is molecule for molecule "identical" with me. If you are a dualist, then also suppose my *Doppelganger* thinks the same verbalized thoughts I do, has the same sense data, the same dispositions, etc. It is absurd to think *his* psychological state is one bit different from mine: yet he 'means' *beech* when he says "elm," and *I* "mean" *elm* when I say "elm." Cut the pie any way you like, "meanings" just ain't in the *head!*

A SOCIOLINGUISTIC HYPOTHESIS

The last two examples depend upon a fact about language that seems, surprisingly, never to have been pointed out: that there is *division of linguistic labor.* We could hardly use such words as 'elm' and 'aluminum' if no one possessed a way of recognizing elm trees and aluminum metal; but not everyone to whom the distinction is important has to be able to make the distinction. Let us shift the example; consider *gold*. Gold is important for many reasons: it is a precious metal; it is a monetary metal; it has symbolic value (it is important to most people that the "gold" wedding ring they wear *really* consist of gold and not just *look* gold); etc. Consider our community as a "factory": in this "factory" some people have

the "job" of *wearing gold wedding rings;* other people have the "job" of selling gold wedding rings; still other people have the job of *telling whether or not something is really gold.* It is not at all necessary or efficient that every one who wears a gold ring (or a gold cufflink, etc.), or discusses the "gold standard," etc., engage in buying and selling gold. Nor is it necessary or efficient that every one who buys and sells gold be able to tell whether or not something is really gold in a society where this form of dishonesty is uncommon (selling fake gold) and in which one can easily consult an expert in case of doubt. And it is *certainly* not necessary or efficient that every one who has occasion to buy or wear gold be able to tell with any reliability whether or not something is really gold.

The foregoing facts are just examples of mundane division of labor (in a wide sense). But they engender a division of linguistic labor: every one to whom gold is important for any reason has to *acquire* the word 'gold'; but he does not have to acquire the *method of recognizing* whether something is or is not gold. He can rely on a special subclass of speakers. The features that are generally thought to be present in connection with a general name—necessary and sufficient conditions for membership in the extension, ways of recognizing whether something is in the extension, etc.—are all present in the linguistic community *considered as a collective body;* but that collective body divides the "labor" of knowing and employing these various parts of the "meaning" of 'gold'.

This division of linguistic labor rests upon and presupposes the division of *non*linguistic labor, of course. If only the people who know how to tell whether some metal is really gold or not have any reason to have the word 'gold' in their vocabulary, then the word 'gold" will be as the word 'water' was in 1750 with respect to that subclass of speakers, and the other speakers just won't acquire it at all. And some words do not exhibit any division of linguistic labor: 'chair', for example. But with the increase of division of labor in the society and the rise of science, more and more words begin to exhibit this kind of division of labor. 'Water', for example, did not exhibit it at all before the rise of chemistry. Today it is obviously necessary for every speaker to be able to recognize water (reliably under normal conditions), and probably most adult speakers even know the necessary and sufficient condition "water is H_2O," but only a few adult speakers could distinguish water from liquids that superficially resembled water. In case of doubt, other speakers would rely on the judgment of these "expert" speakers. Thus the way of recognizing possessed by these "expert" speakers is also, through them, possessed by the collective linguistic body, even though it is not possessed by each individual member of the body, and in this way the most *recherché* fact about water may become part of the *social* meaning of the word although unknown to almost all speakers who acquire the word.

It seems to me that this phenomenon of division of linguistic labor is one that it will be very important for sociolinguistics to investigate. In connection with it, I should like to propose the following hypothesis:

HYPOTHESIS OF THE UNIVERSALITY OF THE DIVISION OF LINGUISTIC LABOR: Every linguistic community exemplifies the sort of division of linguistic labor just described; that is, it possesses at least some terms whose associated "criteria" are known only to a subset of the speakers who acquire the terms, and whose use by the other speakers depends upon a structured cooperation between them and the speakers in the relevant subsets.

It is easy to see how this phenomenon accounts for some of the examples given above of the failure of the assumptions (1 and 2). When a term is subject to the division of linguistic labor, the "average" speaker who acquires it does not acquire anything that fixes its extension. In particular, his individual psychological state *certainly* does not fix its extension; it is only the sociolinguistic state of the collective linguistic body to which the speaker belongs that fixes the extension.

We may summarize this discussion by pointing out that there are two sorts of tools in the world: there are tools like a hammer or a screwdriver which can be used by one person; and there are tools like a steamship which require the cooperative activity of a number of persons to use. Words have been thought of too much on the model of the first sort of tool.

INDEXICALITY AND RIGIDITY

The first of our science-fiction examples—'water' on Earth and on Twin Earth in 1750—does not involve division of linguistic labor, or at least does not involve it in the same way the examples of 'aluminum' and 'elm' do. There were not (in our story, anyway) any "experts" on water on Earth in 1750, nor any experts on "water" on Twin Earth. The example *does* involve things which are of fundamental importance to the theory of reference and also to the theory of necessary truth, which we shall now discuss.

Let W_1 and W_2 be two possible worlds in which I exist and in which this glass exists and in which I am giving a meaning explanation by pointing to this glass and saying "This is water." Let us suppose that in W_1 the glass is full of H_2O and in W_2 the glass is full of XYZ. We shall also suppose that W_1 is the *actual* world, and that XYZ is the stuff typically called "water" in the world W_2 (so that the relation between English speakers in W_1 and English speakers in W_2 is exactly the same as the relation between English speakers on Earth and English speakers on Twin Earth). Then there are two theories one might have concerning the meaning of 'water':

(1) One might hold that 'water' was *world-relative* but *constant* in meaning (i.e., the word has a constant relative meaning). On this theory, 'water' means the same in W_1 and W_2; it's just that water is H_2O in W_1, and water is XYZ in W_2.
(2) One might hold that water is H_2O in all worlds (the stuff called "water" in W_2 isn't water), but 'water' doesn't have the same meaning in W_1 and W_2.

If what was said before about the Twin Earth case was correct, then (2) is clearly the correct theory. When I say "*this* (liquid) is water," the "this" is, so to speak, a *de re* "this"—i.e., the force of my explanation is that "water" is whatever bears a certain equivalence relation (the relation we called "*same*$_L$" above) to the piece of liquid referred to as "this" *in the actual world.*

We might symbolize the difference between the two theories as a "scope" difference in the following way. On theory (1), the following is true:

(1') (For every world W) (for every x in W) (x is water ≡ x bears *same*$_L$ to the entity referred to as "this" in W)

while on theory (2):

(2') (For every world W) (For every x in W) (x is water ≡ x bears *same*$_L$ to the entity referred to as "this" *in the actual world W_1*)

I call this a "scope" difference because in (1') 'the entity referred to as "this" ' is within the scope of 'For every world W'—as the qualifying phrase 'in W' makes explicit—whereas in (2') 'the entity referred to as "this" ' means "the entity referred to as 'this' *in the actual world,*" and has thus a reference *independent* of the bound variable 'W'.

Kripke calls a designator "rigid" (in a given sentence) if (in that sentence) it refers to the same individual in every possible world in which the designator designates. If we extend this notion of rigidity to substance names, then we may express Kripke's theory and mine by saying that the term 'water' is *rigid.*

The rigidity of the term 'water' follows from the fact that when I give the "ostensive definition": "*this* (liquid) is water," I intend (2') and not (1').

We may also say, following Kripke, that when I give the ostensive definition "*this* (liquid) is water," the demonstrative 'this' is *rigid.*

What Kripke was the first to observe is that this theory of the meaning (or "use," or whatever) of the word 'water' (and other natural-kind terms as well) has startling consequences for the theory of necessary truth.

To explain this, let me introduce the notion of a *cross-world relation.* A two-term relation R will be called *cross-world* when it is understood in such a way that its extension is a set of ordered pairs of individuals *not all in the same possible world.* For example, it is easy to understand the relation *same height as* as a

cross-world relation: just understand it so that, e.g., if x is an individual in a world W_1 who is 5 feet tall (in W_1) and y is an individual in W_2 who is 5 feet tall (in W_2), then the ordered pair x,y belongs to the extension of *same height as.* (Since an individual may have different heights in different possible worlds in which that same individual exists, strictly speaking, it is not the ordered pair x,y that constitutes an element of the extension of *same height as,* but rather the ordered pair *x-in-world-W_1, y-in-world-W_2.*)

Similarly, we can understand the relation *same*$_L$ (same liquid as) as a cross-world relation by understanding it so that a liquid in world W_1 which has the same important physical properties (in W_1) that a liquid in W_2 possesses (in W_2) bears *same*$_L$ to the latter liquid.

Then the theory we have been presenting may be summarized by saying that an entity x, in an arbitrary possible world, is *water* if and only if it bears the relation *same*$_L$ (construed as a cross-world relation) to the stuff *we* call "water" in the actual world.

Suppose, now, that I have not yet discovered what the important physical properties of water are (in the actual world)—i.e., I don't yet know that water is H_2O. I may have ways of *recognizing* water that are successful (of course, I may make a small number of mistakes that I won't be able to detect until a later stage in our scientific development), but not know the microstructure of water. If I agree that a liquid with the superficial properties of "water" but a different microstructure *isn't really water,* then my ways of recognizing water cannot be regarded as an analytical specification of what *it is to be* water. Rather, the operational definition, like the ostensive one, is simply a way of pointing out a standard—pointing out the stuff *in the actual world* such that, for x to be water, in *any* world, is for x to bear the relation *same*$_L$ to the *normal* members of the class of *local* entities that satisfy the operational definition. "Water" on Twin Earth is not water, even if it satisfies the operational definition, because it doesn't bear *same*$_L$ to the *local* stuff that satisfies the operational definition, and local stuff that satisfies the operational definition but has a microstructure different from the rest of the local stuff that satisfies the operational definition isn't water either, because it doesn't bear $same_L$ to the *normal* examples of the local "water."

Suppose, now, that I discover the microstructure of water—that water is H_2O. At this point I will be able to say that the stuff on Twin Earth that I earlier *mistook* for water isn't really water. In the same way, if you describe, not another planet in the actual universe, but another possible universe in which there is stuff with the chemical formula XYZ which passes the "operational test" for *water,* we shall have to say that that stuff isn't water but merely XYZ. You will not have described a possible world in which "water is XYZ," but merely a possible world in which there are lakes of XYZ, people drink XYZ (and not water), or whatever. In fact, once we have discovered the nature of water, nothing counts as a possible world in which water doesn't have that nature. Once we have discovered that water (in the actual world) is H_2O, *nothing counts as a possible world in which water isn't H_2O.*

On the other hand, we can perfectly well imagine having experiences that would convince us (and that would make it rational to believe that) water *isn't* H_2O. In that sense, it is conceivable that water isn't H_2O. It is conceivable but it isn't possible! Conceivability is no proof of possibility.

Kripke refers to statements that are rationally unrevisble (assuming there are such) as *epistemically necessary.* Statements that are true in all possible worlds he refers to simply as necessary (or sometimes as "metaphysically necessary"). In this terminology, the point just made can be restated as: a statement can be (metaphysically) necessary and epistemically contingent. Human intuition has no privileged access to metaphysical necessity.

In this paper, our interest is in theory of meaning, however, and not in theory of necessary truth. Words like 'now', 'this', 'here' have long been recognized to be *indexical,* or *token-reflexive*—i.e., to have an extension which varies from context to context or token to token. For these words, no one has ever suggested the traditional theory

that "intension determines extension." To take our Twin Earth example: if I have a *Doppelganger* on Twin Earth, then when I think "I have a headache," *he* thinks "I have a headache." But the extension of the particular token of 'I' in his verbalized thought is himself (or his unit class, to be precise), while the extension of the token of 'I' in *my* verbalized thought is *me* (or my unit class, to be precise). So the same word, 'I', has two different extensions in two different idiolects; but it does not follow that the concept I have of myself is in any way different from the concept my *Doppelganger* has of himself.

Now then, we have maintained that indexicality extends beyond the *obviously* indexical words and morphemes (e.g., the tenses of verbs). Our theory can be summarized as saying that words like 'water' have an unnoticed indexical component: "water" is stuff that bears a certain similarity relation to the water *around here.* Water at another time or in another place or even in another possible world has to bear the relation $same_L$ to *our* "water" *in order to be water.* Thus the theory that (1) words have "intensions," which are something like concepts associated with the words by speakers; and (2) intension determines extension—cannot be true of natural-kind words like 'water' for the same reason it cannot be true of obviously indexical words like 'I'.

The theory that natural-kind words like 'water' are indexical leaves it open, however, whether to say that 'water' in the Twin Earth dialect of English has the same *meaning* as 'water' in the Earth dialect and a different extension—which is what we normally say about 'I' in different idiolects—thereby giving up the doctrine that "meaning (intension) determines extension," or to say, as we have chosen to do, that difference in extension is *ipso facto* a difference in meaning for natural-kind words, thereby giving up the doctrine that meanings are concepts, or, indeed, mental entities of *any* kind.[2]

It should be clear, however, that Kripke's doctrine that natural-kind words are rigid designators and our doctrine that they are indexical are but two ways of making the same point.

We have now seen that the extension of a term is not fixed by a concept that the individual speaker has in his head, and this is true both because extension is, in general, determined *socially*—there is division of linguistic labor as much as of "real" labor—and because extension is, in part, determined *indexically*. The extension of our terms depends upon the actual nature of the particular things that serve as paradigms, and this actual nature is not, in general, fully known to the speaker. Traditional semantic theory leaves out two contributions to the determination of reference—the contribution of society and the contribution of the real world; a better semantic theory must encompass both.

NOTES

1. See note 2 and the corresponding text.
2. Our reasons for rejecting the first option—to say that 'water' has the same meaning on Earth and on Twin Earth, while giving up the doctrine that meaning determines reference—are presented in "The Meaning of 'Meaning'." They may be illustrated thus: Suppose 'water' has the same meaning on Earth and on Twin Earth. Now, let the word 'water' become phonemically different on Twin Earth—say, it becomes 'quaxel'. Presumably, this is not a change in meaning per se, on any view. So 'water' and 'quaxel' have the same meaning (although they refer to different liquids). But this is highly counterintuitive. Why not say, then, that 'elm' in my idiolect has the same meaning as 'beech' in your idiolect, although they refer to different trees?

Donnellan, in "Reference and Definite Descriptions" says, "Using a definite description referentially a speaker may say something true even though the description correctly applies to nothing."[1] His example—taken from Linsky[2]—has someone saying of a spinster:

Her husband is kind to her

after having had Mr. Jones—actually the spinster's brother—misintroduced as the spinster's husband. And—to fill it out—having noticed Jones' solicitous attention to his sister. The speaker used the nondenoting description "Her husband" to refer to Mr. Jones. And so, what he said was true.

There are a lot of entities associated with the utterance of "Her husband is kind to her" which are commonly said to have been said: tokens, types, sentences, propositions, statements, etc. The something-true-said, Donnellan calls a *statement*.

On the other hand, "If . . . the speaker has just met the lady and, noticing her cheerfulness and radiant good health, made his remark from his conviction that these attributes are always the result of having good husbands, he would be using the definite description attributively."[3]

After pointing out that "in general, whether or not a definite description is used referentially or attributively is a function of the speaker's intentions in a particular case,"[4] he mentions that according to Russell's theory of descriptions, the use of *the* φ might be thought of as involving reference "in a very weak sense . . . to *whatever* is the one and only one φ, if there is any such."[5] Donnellan then concludes:

Now this is something we might well say about the attributive use of definite descriptions. . . . But this lack of particularity is absent from the referential use of definite descriptions precisely because the description is here merely a device for getting one's audience to pick out or think

Do not partake of this article before reading the following Warning: This paper was prepared for and read at the 1970 Stanford Workshop on Grammar and Semantics. Peter Cole has persuaded me—against my better judgment—that it has aged long enough to be digestible. The paper has not been revised other than to remove the subtitle comment "[Stream of Consciousness Draft: Errors, confusions, and disorganizations are not to be taken seriously]." That injunction must still be strictly obeyed. Some parts of this ramble are straightened out in the excessive refinements of "Bob and Carol and Ted and Alice" (which appeared in the proceedings for which this was destined). A more direct presentation of the resulting theory along with some of its applications is to be found in my *Demonstratives* An intermediate progress report occurs in "On the Logic of Demonstratives." "DTHAT" is pronounced as a single syllable.

From *Syntax and Semantics*, volume 9, Peter Cole, ed. (New York: Academic Press, 1978), pp. 221–253. © 1978 by David Kaplan.

of the thing to be spoken about, a device which may serve its function even if the description is incorrect. More importantly perhaps, in the referential use as opposed to the attributive, there is a right thing to be picked out by the audience, and its being the right thing is not simply a function of its fitting the description.[6]

Donnellan develops his theory by adducing a series of quite plausible examples to help him answer certain theoretical questions, e.g., are there sentences in which the contained definite description can only be used referentially (or only attributively)? Can reference fail when a definite description is used referentially?, etc.

In my own reading and rereading of Donnellan's article I always find it both fascinating and maddening. Fascinating, because the fundamental distinction so clearly reflects an accurate insight into language use, and maddening, because: first, the examples seem to me to alternate between at least two clearly discriminable concepts of *referential use;* second, the notion of *having someone in mind* is not analyzed but used; and third, the connections with the developed body of knowledge concerning intensional logics—their syntax and semantics—are not explicitly made, so we cannot immediately see what Donnellan and intensional logic have to offer each other, if anything.

As one of the body developers, I find this last snub especially inexcusable. This is not a divergent perception for those of my ilk. Hintikka remarks (plaintively?), "The only thing I miss in Donnellan's excellent paper is a clear realization that the distinction he is talking about is only operative in contexts governed by propositional attitudes or other modal terms."[7]

Hintikka's remark is at first surprising, since none of Donnellan's examples seem to have this form. But the remark falls into place when we recognize that Donnellan is concerned essentially with a given speaker who is *asserting* something, *asking* something, or *commanding* something. And thus if we pull back and focus our attention on the sentence *describing* the speech act:

John asserted that Mary's husband is kind to her

the intensional operator appears.

Probably Hintikka wanted to argue that the sentence:

Her husband is kind to her

is not itself ambiguous in the way that, say:

Every boy kissed a girl

is. The fact that an ambiguous sentence is produced by embedding ϕ in some sentential context (for example, an intensional or temporal operator) should not be construed to indicate an ambiguity in ϕ. For were it so, (almost?) all sentences would be ambiguous.

Donnellan's distinction is a contribution to the redevelopment of an old and commonsensical theory about language which—at least in the philosophical literature—has rather been in a decline during the ascendency of semantics over epistemology of the 1930s, '40s, and '50s. The commonsense theory is one that Russell wrestled with in *The Principles of Mathematics*[8] but seemed to reject in "On Denoting."[9] This theory asserts roughly that the correct analysis of a typical speech act, for example,

John is tall

distinguishes *who* is being talked about, i.e. the individual under consideration—here, John—from *how* he is being characterized—here, as tall.

Russell's analysis of the proposition expressed by

John is tall

provides it with two components: the property expressed by the predicate is tall, and the individual John. That's right, John himself, right there, trapped in a proposition.

During the Golden Age of Pure Semantics we were developing a nice homogeneous theory, with language, meanings, and entities of the world each properly segregated and related one to another in rather smooth and comfortable ways. This development probably came to its peak in Carnap's *Meaning and Necessity.*[10] Each *designator* has both an intension and an extension. Sentences have truth-values as extensions and propositions as intentions, predicates have classes as extensions and properties as intensions, terms have individuals as extensions and *individual concepts* as intensions, and so on. The intension of a compound is a function of the intensions of the parts and similarly the extension (except when intensional operators appear). There is great beauty and power in this theory.

But there remained some nagging doubts: proper names, demonstratives, and quantification into intensional contexts.

Proper names may be a practical convenience in our mundane transactions, but they are a theoretician's nightmare. They are like bicycles. Everyone easily learns to ride, but no one can correctly explain how he does it. Completely new theories have been proposed within the last few years, in spite of the fact that the subject has received intense attention throughout this century, and in some portions of Tibet people have had proper names for even longer than that.

The main difficulty has to do, I believe, with the special intimate relationship between a proper name and its bearer. Russell said that in contrast with a common noun, like "unicorn," a proper name *means* what it names. And if it names nothing, it means nothing. In the case of "unicorn" we have a meaning, perhaps better a *descriptive meaning,* which we make use of in looking for such things. But in the case of the name "Moravcsik" there is just Moravcsik. There is no basis on which to ask whether Moravcsik exists. Such a question is—for Russell—meaningless. But people persist in asking this question. Maybe not this very question, but analogous ones like:

> Does Santa Claus exist?

There were other apparent difficulties in Russell's theory. The astronomical discovery that Hesperus was identical with Phosphorus became a triviality. The sentence expressing it expressed the same proposition as "Hesperus is identical with Hesperus." Furthermore, although the bearer of a given proper name is the be-all and end-all of the name's semantic

relata, almost every proper name has dozens of bearers.

And then there are the unforgivable distortions of the minimal descriptive content of proper names. We all know of butchers named "Baker" and dogs named "Sir Walter." The ultimate in such perversity occurs in titles of the top administrative officers at UCLA. We have four vice-chancellors at UCLA, one of whom has the title "The Vice-Chancellor."

All in all, proper names are a mess and if it weren't for the problem of how to get the kids to come in for dinner, I'd be inclined to just junk them.

At any rate, the attempt during the Golden Age was to whip proper names into line. In fact into the line of common nouns. People do ask:

> Does Santa Claus exist?

So that must mean something like:

> Does a unicorn exist?

They do ask:

> Is Hesperus identical with Phosphorus?

So that must mean something like:

> Are bachelors identical with college graduates?

Thus was waged a war of attrition against proper names. Many were unmasked as disguised descriptions, e.g. "Aristotle" means *the student of Plato and teacher of Alexander who. . . .*—not an unreasonable proposal.

However, some of these exposés did seem a bit oppressive, e.g. Russell's suggestion that:

> Scott is Sir Walter

really means:

> The person named "Scott" is the person named "Sir Walter"

followed by his nonchalant remark: "This is a way in which names are frequently used in practice, and there will, as a rule, be nothing in the phraseology to show whether they are being used in this way or as names."[11] But at least they isolated the few real troublemakers—who turned out not to be our good old proper names at all but a handful of determined outside demonstratives: "this," "that," etc.

In summary, the technique was first to expose a proper name as a disguised description (sometimes on tenuous and unreliable evidence) and then ruthlessly to eliminate it.

We thus reduce the exciting uncertainties of:

Socrates is a man

to the banality of:

All men are mortal

The demonstratives were still there, but they were so gross they could be ignored.

Lately, under the pressure of the new interest in singular propositions generated by intensional logic, the verities of the Golden Age are breaking down. Once logicians became interested in formalizing a logic of necessity, belief, knowledge, assertion, etc., traditional syntactical ways quickly led to formulas like

John asserted that x is a spy

with free 'x' and then with 'x' bound to an anterior operator. Under what circumstances does a given individual, taken as value of 'x', satisfy this formula? Answer: If the appropriate singular proposition was the content of John's assertive utterance.

It seems that in at least certain speech acts, what I am trying to express can't quite be put into words. It is that proposition of Russell's with John trapped in it.

The property of being tall is exactly expressed by "is tall," and the concept of the unique spy who is shorter than all other spies is exactly expressed by "the shortest spy"; but no expression exactly expresses John. An expression may express a concept or property that, in reality, only John satisfies. There are many such distinct concepts; none of which is John himself.

I would like to distinguish between the kind of propositions which were considered by Aristotle (*all S is P, some S is not P*, etc.) and the kind of proposition considered by the early Russell. I call the former *general propositions* and the latter *singular propositions*.

Suppose, just for definiteness, that we fix attention on sentences of simple subject-predicate form. The following are examples:

(1) A spy is suspicious.
(2) Every spy is suspicious.
(3) The spy is suspicious.
(4) John is suspicious.

Now let us think of the proposition associated with each sentence as having two components. Corresponding to the predicate we have the property of being suspicious; and corresponding to the subject we have either what Russell in 1903 called a *denoting concept* or an individual. Let us take the proposition to be the ordered couple of these two components.

Again, to fix ideas, let us provide a possible-world style of interpretation for these notions. We think of each total or complete possible state of affairs as a possible world. The possible worlds are each continuants through time and may in fact overlap at certain times. For example, a possible world may agree with the actual world up to the time at which some individual made a particular decision; the possible world may then represent an outcome of a decision other than the one actually taken. (In science fiction, such cases are called *alternate time lines*.)

Within this framework we can attempt to represent a number of the semantic notions in question. We might represent the property of *being suspicious* by that function P which assigns to each possible world w and each time t the set of all those individuals of w which, in w, are suspicious at t. We might represent the denoting concepts expressed by the denoting phrases 'A spy', 'Every spy', and 'The spy' as, say, the ordered couples: $\langle$'A',$S\rangle$, $\langle$'Every',$S\rangle$, $\langle$'The',$S\rangle$ where S is the property (represented as above) of *being a spy*.[12] The fact that the logical words 'A', 'Every', and 'The' are just carried along reflects our treatment of them as *syncategorematic*, i.e. as having no independent meaning but as indicators of how to combine the meaning-bearing parts (here "spy" and the predicate) in determining the meaning of the whole. For (1), (2), and (3) the corresponding propositions are now represented by:

(5) $\langle\langle\text{'A'},S\rangle P\rangle$

(6) $\langle\langle\text{'Every'},S\rangle P\rangle$

(7) $\langle\langle\text{'The'},S\rangle P\rangle$

It should be clear that each of (5)–(7) will determine a function which assigns to each possible world w and time t a truth value. And in fact the truth value so assigned to any w and t will be exactly the truth value in w at t of the corresponding sentence. For example: (6) determines that function which assigns truth to a given w and t if and only if every member of $S(w,t)$ is a member of $P(w,t)$. Notice that the function so determined by (6) also correctly assigns to each w and t the truth value in w at t of (2). (For the purpose of (7), let us take $*$ to be a "truth value" which is assigned to w and t when $S(w,t)$ contains other than a single member.)

The proposition corresponding to (4) would be:

(8) $\langle\text{John},P\rangle$

not $\langle\text{'John'},P\rangle$ mind you, but $\langle\text{John},P\rangle$. And (8) will determine that function F which assigns Truth to w and t if and only if John is a member of $P(w,t)$. If John is an individual of w at the time t (i.e. John exists in w and is alive at t) but is not a member of $P(w,t)$, then $F(w,t)$ is falsehood; and if John is not an individual of w at the time t, then $F(w,t)$ is $*$.

This brief excursion into possible-world semantics is only to fix ideas in a simple way within that framework (I will later make further use of the framework) and is not put forward as an ideal (in any sense: generalizability, elegance, etc.) representation of the semantic notions of property, proposition, denoting concept, etc. My main motivation is to present a representation which will clearly distinguish singular and general propositions.

It would, of course, have been possible to supply a representation of the proposition expressed by (4) which is, in a sense, formally equivalent to (8) and which blurs the distinction I wish to emphasize. I do it now lest anyone think that the possibility is a relevant refutation of my later remarks. Let us clearly depart from Russell by associating a denoting concept:

(9) $\langle\text{'Proper Name'},J\rangle$

where J is what we might call *John's essence*, the property of *being John*, namely, that function which assigns to each possible world w and time t the set {John} if John is an individual of w and is alive in w at t and the empty set otherwise. The analogue to (8) is now

(10) $\langle\langle\text{'Proper Name'},J\rangle\ P\rangle$

It will be noted that we have now treated the proper name "John" rather like the definite description "The John," in which the proper name plays the role of a common noun. Accordingly the function from possible worlds and times to truth values which is determined by (10) is identical with that determined by:

(11) $\langle\langle\text{'The'},J\rangle\ P\rangle$

There are certainly other representations of these propositions which ally various subgroups. In fact, once any formal structure is established, the production of isomorphic structures satisfying specified "internal" conditions is largely a matter of logical ingenuity of the "pure" kind.[13]

To return to the point, I have represented propositions in a way which emphasizes the singular–general distinction, because I want to revive a view of language alternate to that of the Golden Age. The view of the Golden Age is, I believe, undoubtedly correct for a large portion of language behavior, in particular, communication by means of general propositions. But the alternate view accounts for a portion of language behavior not accommodated by the view of the Golden Age.

The alternate view is: *that some or all of the denoting phrases used in an utterance should not be considered part of the content of what is said but should rather be thought of as contextual factors which help us interpret the actual physical utterance as having a certain content.* The most typical of such contextual factors is the fact that the speaker's utterance is to be taken as an utterance of some specific language, say, English. When I utter "yes," which means *yes* in English and *no* in Knoh, you must know I am speaking Knoh to know I have said *no*. It is no *part* of what I have said that I am speaking Knoh, though Knoh being a complete tongue, I could add that by uttering "I am speaking English." Such an utterance is of doubtful utility in itself; but, fortunately, there are other means by which this fact can be ascertained by my auditor, e.g. by my general physical appearance, or, if I am not a native Knoh, by my pointing to Knoh on a celestial globe. A homelier example has a haberdasher utter to a banker, "I am out of checks." Whether the utterance takes place in the store or at the bank will help the banker determine what the haberdasher has said. In either case it is no *part* of what was said that the haberdasher used "checks" to mean bank checks rather than suits with a checkered pattern. Of course the haberdasher could go on, if he desired, to so comment on his past performance, but that would be to say something else. Still closer to home is my wife's utterance: "It's up to you to punish Jordan for what happened today." It is by means of various subtle contextual clues that I understand her to be charging me to administer discipline to our son and not to be calling on me to act where the United Nations has failed. Again, should I exhibit momentary confusion she might, by a comment, a gesture, or simply some more discourse on the relevant naughtiness, assist me in properly decoding her first utterance so that I could understand what she was, in fact, saying. There are other ways—more controversial than the intentional resolution of the reference of a proper name among the many persons so dubbed—in which contextual factors determine the content of an utterance containing a proper name; but I am reserving all but the most blatantly obvious remarks for later.

Now let us narrow our attention to utterances containing *singular denoting phrases* (i.e. denoting phrases which purport to stand for a unique individual, such as "the spy," "John", "$\sqrt{2}$," etc.).[14]

How can contextual factors determine that part of the content of an utterance which corresponds to a singular denoting phrase?

Two ways have already been mentioned: by determining what language is being spoken and by determining which of the many persons so dubbed a proper name stands for. But the most striking way in which such contextual factors enter is in connection with *demonstratives:* "this," "this spy," "that book," etc. In at least some typical uses of these phrases, it is required that the utterance be accompanied by a *demonstration*—paradigmatically, a pointing—which indicates the object for which the phrase stands.[15] I will speak of a *demonstrative use* of a singular denoting phrase when the speaker intends that the object for which the phrase stands be designated by an associated demonstration.[16]

Now we can add another example of a subject-predicate sentence to those of (1)–(4):

(12)   He [the speaker points at John] is suspicious.

I am adopting the convention of enclosing a description of the relevant demonstration in square brackets immediately following each denoting phrase which is used demonstratively.[17]

What shall we take as the proposition corresponding to (12) (which I also call the *content* of the *utterance* (12))? In line with our program of studying contextual factors which are not *part* of what is said but whose role is rather to help us interpret the utterance as *having* a certain content, we shall take the component of the proposition which corresponds to the demonstrative to be the individual demonstrated. Thus the varying *forms* which such a demonstration can take are not reflected in the content of the utterance (i.e. the proposition). The demonstration "gives us" the element of the proposition corresponding to the demonstrative. But *how* the demonstration gives that individual to us is here treated as irrelevant to the content of the utterance; just as the different *ways* by which I might have come to understand which Jordan was relevant to my wife's utterance, or the different *ways* by which one might come to understand that a speaker is speaking Knoh rather than English, do not alter the content of those utterances. Thus, for example, the utterances (in English):

(13) He [the speaker points at John, as John stands on the demonstration platform nude, clean shaven, and bathed in light] is suspicious.

(14) He [the speaker points at John, as John lurks in shadows wearing a trenchcoat, bearded, with his hat pulled down over his face] is suspicious.

are taken, along with other refinements of (12), as expressing the same proposition, namely:

(15) ⟨John, P⟩.

It should immediately be apparent that we are in store for some delightful anomalies. Erroneous beliefs may lead a speaker to put on a demonstration which does not demonstrate what he thinks it does, with the result that he will be under a misapprehension as to *what* he has said. Utterances of identity sentences containing one or more demonstratives may express necessary propositions, though neither the speaker nor his auditors are aware of it. In fact, we get extreme cases in which linguistic competence is simply insufficient to completely determine the content of what is said. Of course this was already established by the case of the Knoh-English translation problem, but the situation is more dramatic using the demonstratives.

The present treatment is not inevitable. An alternative is to incorporate the demonstration in the proposition. We would argue as follows: Frege's *sense and denotation* distinction[18] can be extended to all kinds of indicative devices. In each case we have the object indicated (the "denotation") and the manner of indication (the "sense"). It is interesting to note that (at least in Feigl's translation) Frege wrote of "the sense (connotation, meaning) of the sign in which is contained the *manner and context* of presentation of the denotation of the sign."[19] I think it reasonable to interpret Frege as saying that the sense of a sign is what is grasped by the linguistically competent auditor, and it seems natural to generalize and say that it is the "sense" of the demonstration that is grasped by the competent auditor of utterances containing demonstratives. Thus we see how the drawn-out English utterance:

(16) That [the speaker points at Phosphorus in early morning] is the same planet as that [the speaker points at Hesperus in the early evening].

could be both informative and true.

Let us call the preceding a *Fregean treatment of demonstratives*. It is worth developing (which means primarily working on the ontology (metaphysics?) of demonstrations and the semantics of demonstration descriptions) but, I believe, will ultimately be unsatisfactory. For now I'll just outline some of the reasons. The demonstrative use of demonstratives plays an important role in language learning, in general, in the learning and use of proper names, in our misty use of *de re* modalities, in our better grounded use of what Quine calls the *relational* senses of epistemic verbs (i.e. the senses of those intensional verbs that permit quantification in).[20] And, in general, I believe that we can sharpen our epistemological insights in a number of areas by taking account of what I call the demonstrative use of expression. Such uses are far more widespread than one imagined.

I earlier called the Fregean treatment of demonstratives "unsatisfactory." I would be more cautious in saying that it was wrong. (However I do think an empirical argument from linguistic behavior could be developed to show that it is wrong. I take Donnellan's study of the phenomenology of what he calls referential use to be an excellent start in that direction.) What I am confident of is that if we force all phenomena that suggest a special *demonstrative* use of language, along with what I regard as a corresponding feature—a special *singular* form of proposition—into the Fregean mold of linguistic elements with a sense and a denotation, the sense being the element which appears in the proposition (thus leaving us with only general propositions), then important insights will be lost. I don't deny that on a phenomenon-by-phenomenon basis we can (in some sense) keep stretching Frege's brilliant insights to cover. With a little ingenuity I think we *can* do that. But we shouldn't.

Now let me offer a slightly different and somewhat a priori justification for studying the phenomena of demonstrative uses of expressions and singular propositions. I leave aside the question whether we have correctly analyzed any actual linguistic behavior, whether concerned with the so-called demonstrative *phrases* or otherwise.

Having explained so clearly and precisely what such a use of language would amount to, in terms of a possible-world semantics, I can simply resolve to so use the word "that" in the future. At a minimum I could introduce the *new* word "dthat" for the demonstrative use of "that." Couldn't I? I can, and I will. In fact, I do.

I like this intentional (i.e. stipulative) way of looking at the use of "dthat" because I believe that in many cases where there are competing Fregean and demonstrative analyses of some utterances or class of utterances the matter can be resolved simply by the intentions of the speaker (appropriately conveyed to the auditor?). Thus in the case of proper names (to which I will return below) I might simply resolve to use them demonstratively (i.e. as demonstrating the individual whom they are a name *of* in the nomenclature of an earlier paper[21]) on certain occasions and in a Fregean way[22] on other occasions. Of course one who did not have a clear understanding of the alternatives might have difficulty in characterizing his own use, but once we have explored each choice there is nothing to prevent us from choosing either, "unnatural" though the choice may be.

It should probably be noted that despite the accessibility of the semantics of "dthat" our *grasp* of the singular propositions so expressed is, in John Perry's apt phrase, a bit of *knowledge by description* as compared with our rather more direct acquaintance with the general propositions expressed by nondemonstrative utterances.

Armed with "dthat" we can now explore and possibly even extend the frontiers of demonstrations.

When we considered the Fregean analysis of demonstrations, we attempted to establish parallels between demonstrations and descriptions.[23] Insofar as this aspect of the Fregean program is successful, it suggests the possibility

of a demonstrative analysis of descriptions. *If pointing can be taken as a form of describing, why not take describing as a form of pointing?* Note that our demonstrative analysis of demonstrations need not, indeed should not, deny or even ignore the fact that demonstrations have both a sense and a demonstratum. It is just that according to the demonstrative analysis the sense of the demonstration does not appear in the proposition. Instead the sense is used only to fix the demonstratum which itself appears directly in the proposition. I propose now to do the same for descriptions. Instead of taking the sense of the description as subject of the proposition, we use the sense only to fix the denotation which we then take directly as subject component of the proposition. I now take the utterance of the description as a demonstration and describe it with the usual quotation devices, thus:

(17)   Dthat ["the spy"] is suspicious.

For fixity of ideas, let us suppose, what is surely false, that in fact, actuality, and reality there is one and only one spy, and John is he. We might express this so:

(18)   "the spy" denotes John.[24]

In the light of (18), (17) expresses:

(19)   ⟨John, *P*⟩

(also known as '(8)' and '(15)').

Recollecting and collecting we have:

(3)   The spy is suspicious.
(4)   John is suspicious.
(7)   ⟨⟨'The',*S*⟩ *P*⟩
(12)   He [the speaker points at John] is suspicious.

or as we might now write (12):

(20)   Dhe [the speaker points at John] is suspicious.[25]

Earlier we said that an utterance of (3) expresses (7), and only an utterance of (12) [i.e. (20)] or possibly (4) expresses (19). I have already suggested that an utterance of (4) may sometimes be taken in a Fregean way to express something like (7), and now I want to point out that for want of "dthat" some speakers may be driven to utter (3) when they intend what is expressed by (17).

If an utterance of (3) may indeed some-times express (19), then Donnellan was essen-tially correct in describing his referential and attributive uses of definite descriptions as a "duality of function." And it might even be correct to describe this duality as an *ambiguity* in the sentence type (3). I should note right here that my demonstrative use is not quite Donnellan's referential use—a deviation that I will expatiate on below—but it is close enough for present purposes.

The ambiguity in question here is of a rather special kind. For under no circum-stances could the choice of disambiguation for an utterance of (3) affect the truth-value. Still there are two distinct propositions involved, and even two distinct functions from possible worlds and times to truth-values, determined by the two propositions.

Before continuing with the ambiguity in (3), it would be well to interject some remarks on sentence types and sentence tokens (of which utterances are one kind) especially as they relate to demonstratives.

Sentence types vary considerably in the degree to which they contain implicit and explicit references to features of the context of utterance. The references I have in mind here are those that affect the truth-value of the sentence type on a particular occasion of utterance. At one extreme stand what Quine (in *Word and Object*) called *eternal sentences:* those in which the feature linguists call *tense* does not really reflect a perspective from some point in time, which contain no *indexi-cals* such as "now," "here," "I," etc., and whose component names and definite de-scriptions are not understood to require contextual determination as did the "Jordan" of our earlier example. Quine describes such sentences as "those whose truth value stays fixed through time and from speaker to speaker."[26] But I prefer my own vaguer formulation: *those sentences which do not express a perspective from within space-time.* Quine and I would both count "In 1970 American women exceed American men in wealth" as eternal; he would (presumably) also count "The UCLA football team always has, does, and will continue to outclass the

Stanford football team" as eternal. I would not.

Truth values are awarded directly to eternal sentences without any relativization to time, place, etc.[27] But for the fugitive sentence no stable truth value can be awarded. Let us consider first tensed sentences, e.g.:

(21)   American men will come to exceed Ameri-can women in intelligence.

Without disputing the facts, if (21) were true at one time, it would fail to be true at some later time. (Since one doesn't come to exceed what one already exceeds.)

Now let's dredge up the possible worlds. We associated with (21) a function which assigns to each possible world and time a truth value. Such a function seems to represent, for reasons which have been much discussed, at least part of the meaning of (21) or part of what we grasp when we understand (21).[28] There is another kind of "content" associated with a fugitive sentence like (21), namely, the content of a particular utterance of (21). In a sense, any particular utterance (token) of a fugitive sentence (type) is an *eternalization* of the fugitive sentence. The relativization to time is fixed by the time of utterance. We can associate with each utterance of a fugitive sentence the same kind of function from possible worlds to truth values that we asso-ciate directly with eternal sentences.

Before becoming completely lost in a vague nomenclature, let me make some stipulations. I will call the function which assigns to a time and a possible world the truth value of a given fugitive sentence (type) at that time in that world the *meaning* of the given sentence. The meaning of a sentence is what a person who is linguistically competent grasps, it is common to all utterances of the sentence, and it is one of the components which goes into determin-ing the *content* of any particular utterance of the sentence. The *content* of an utterance is that function which assigns to each possible world the truth value which the utterance would take if it were evaluated with respect to that world. There is some unfortunate slack in the preceding characterizations, which I will try to reduce.[29]

Let φ be a fugitive sentence like (21); let φ̄ be the meaning of φ, let W be the set of possible worlds; let T be the set of times (I assume that all possible worlds have the same temporal structure and, in fact, the very same times, i.e. a given time in one world has a unique counterpart in all others); let U be the set of possible utterances; for $u \varepsilon U$ let $S(u)$ be the sentence uttered in u; let $T(u)$ be the time of u (when only $S(u)$ and $T(u)$ are relevant; we might identify u with $\langle S(u), T(u) \rangle$ and let $\bar{u}$ be the content of u. The relation between the meaning of a sentence (whose only fugitive aspect is its temporality) and the content of one of its possible utterances can now be concisely expressed as follows:

(22) $\Lambda u \varepsilon U \Lambda w \varepsilon W (\bar{u}(w) = \overline{S(u)} \ (T(u), w))$

or, identifying u with $\langle S(u), T(u) \rangle$:

(23) $\Lambda w \varepsilon W \Lambda t \varepsilon T \ (\overline{\langle \bar{\phi}, t \rangle}(w) = \bar{\phi}(t, w))$

To put it another way, an utterance of φ fixes a time, and the content of the utterance takes account of the truth value of φ in all possible worlds but *only at that time.*

From (22) and (23) it would appear that the notions of meaning and content are interdefinable. Therefore, since we already have begun developing the theory of meaning for fugitive sentences (see especially the work of Montague),[30] why devote any special attention to the theory of content? Is it not simply a subtheory of a definitional extension of the theory of meaning? I think not. But the reasons go beyond simple examples like (21) and take us, hopefully, back to the main track of this paper. It is worth looking more deeply into the structure of utterances than a *simple* definition of that notion within the theory of meaning would suggest. (I stress *simple* because I have not yet really investigated sophisticated definitions.)

First we have problems about the counterfactual status of possible utterances: Are utterances *in* worlds, are they assumed to occur in worlds in which their content is being evaluated, or are they extraworldly, with their content evaluated independent of their occurrence? Consider the infamous 'I am here now', or perhaps more simply:

(24) An utterance is occurring.

Is the meaning of (24) to assign to a time and world the truth-value which an utterance of (24) *would* take *were* it to occur in that world at that time? Or does it assign simply the truth value of (24) in that world at that time? Presumably the latter. But this is to assume that utterances come complete, with the value of all their contextually determined features filled in (otherwise the utterance alone—without being set in a world—would not have a content). I do not want to make this assumption since I am particularly interested in the *way* in which a demonstration, for example, picks out its demonstratum.

And now we are back to the ambiguity in (3). I would like to count my *verbal* demonstration, as in (17), as part of the sentence type. Then it seems that an utterance of such a sentence either must include a world, or else, what is more plausible, must be in a world. I guess what I want to say, what I should have said, is that an utterance has to occur *somewhere,* in some world, and the world in which it occurs is a crucial factor in determining what the content is. This really says something about how (I think) I want to treat (possible) demonstrations. I want the same (possible) demonstrations (e.g. ["the spy"]) to determine different demonstrata in different worlds (or possibly even at different times in the same world). Now I see why I was so taken with the Fregean treatment of demonstrations. We should be able to represent demonstrations as something like functions from worlds, times, etc., to demonstrata. Thus, *just like the meaning of a definite description!* The difference lies in how the content of a particular utterance is computed.

I realize that the foregoing is mildly inconsistent, but let us push on. Let u be an utterance of (17) in w at t, and let u' be an utterance of (3) in w at t. Let's not worry, for now, about the possibility of a clash of utterances. If we look at the content of u and the content of u' we will see that they differ—though they will always agree in w. The content of u is like what I earlier called a singular proposition (except that I should have fixed the time), whereas the content of *u'* is like what I earlier called a general proposition. For the content of *u* to assign truth to a given world *w'*, the individual who must be suspicious in *w'* at *t* is not the denotation of "the spy" in *w'* at *t*, but rather the denotation of "the spy" in *w* at *t*. The *relevant individual* is determined in the world in which the utterance takes place, and then that same individual is checked for suspicion in all other worlds, whereas for the content of *u'*, we determine a (possibly) new relevant individual in each world.[31]

What is especially interesting is that these two contents must agree in the world *w*, the world in which the utterance took place.

Now note that the verbal form of (3) might have been adopted by one who lacked "dthat" to express what is expressed by (17). We seem to have here a kind of *de dicto-de re* ambiguity in the verbal form of (3) and without benefit of any intensional operator. No question of an utterer's intentions has been brought into play. *There is no question of an analysis in terms of scope, since there is no operator.* The two sentence types (3) and (17) are such that when uttered in the same context they have different contents but always the same truth value where uttered. Donnellan vindicated! (Contrary to my own earlier expectations.)

I am beginning to suspect that I bungled things even worse than I thought in talking about meanings, contents, etc. The meaning of a sentence type should probably be a function from utterances to *contents* rather than from something like utterances to truth values. If this correction were made, then we could properly say that (13) and (17) differ in meaning.

It would also give a more satisfactory analysis of a sentence type like:

(25)   Dthat ['the morning star'] is identical with dthat ['the evening star'].

Although (25) expresses a true content on some possible occasions of use and a false content on others, it is not simply contingent, since on all possible occasions its content is either necessary or impossible. (I am assuming that distinct individuals don't merge.)

Even one who grasped the meaning of (25) would not of course know its truth value simply on witnessing an utterance. Thus we answer the question how an utterance of an identity sentence can be informative though *necessary!*

Another example on the question of necessity. Suppose I now utter:

(26)   I am more than thirty-six years old.

What I have said is true. Is it necessary? This may be arguable. (*Could* I be younger than I am at this very same time?) But the fact that the sentence, if uttered at an earlier time or by another person, could express something false is certainly irrelevant. The point is: simply to look at the spectrum of *truth-values* of different utterances of (25) and (26) and not at the spectrum of *contents* of different utterances of (25) and (26) is to miss something interesting and important.

I earlier said that my demonstrative use is not quite Donnellan's referential use, and I want now to return to that point. When a speaker uses an expression demonstratively he *usually* has in mind—so to speak—an intended demonstratum, and the demonstration is thus *teleological*. Donnellan and I disagree on how to bring the intended demonstratum into the picture. To put it crudely, Donnellan believes that for most purposes we should take the demonstratum to be the intended demonstratum. I believe that these are different notions that may well involve different objects.

From my point of view the situation is interesting precisely because we have a case here in which a person can fail to say what he intended to say, and the failure is not a linguistic error (such as using the wrong word) but a factual one. It seems to me that such a situation can arise only in the demonstrative mode.

Suppose that without turning and looking I point to the place on my wall which has long been occupied by a picture of Rudolf Carnap and I say:

(27)   Dthat [I point as above] is a picture of one of the greatest philosophers of the twentieth century.

But unbeknownst to me, someone has replaced my picture of Carnap with one of Spiro Agnew. I think it would simply be wrong to argue an "ambiguity" in the demonstration, so great that it can be bent to my intended demonstratum. I have said of a picture of Spiro Agnew that it pictures one of the greatest philosophers of the twentieth century. And my speech and demonstration suggest no other natural interpretation to the linguistically competent public observer.

Still, it would be perhaps equally wrong not to pursue the notion of the intended demonstratum. Let me give three reasons for that pursuit:

1. The notion is epistemologically interesting in itself.

2. It may well happen—as Donnellan has pointed out—that we succeed in communicating what we intended to say in spite of our failure to say it. (E.g. the mischievous fellow who switched pictures on me would understand full well what I was intending to say.)

3. There are situations where the demonstration is sufficiently ill-structured in itself so that we would regularly take account of the intended demonstratum as, *within limits,* a legitimate disambiguating or vagueness-removing device.

I have two kinds of examples for this third point. First, there are the cases of vague demonstrations by a casual wave of the hand. I suppose that ordinarily we would allow that a demonstration had been successful if the intended object were *roughly* where the speaker pointed. That is, we would not bring out surveying equipment to help determine the content of the speaker's assertion; much more relevant is what he intended to point at. Second, whenever I point at something, from the surveyor's point of view I point at many things. When I point at my son (and say "I love dthat"), I may also be pointing at a book he is holding, his jacket, a button on his jacket, his skin, his heart, and his dog standing behind him—from the surveyor's point of view. *My* point is that if I intended to point at my son and it is true that I love him, then what I said is true. And the fact that I do

not love his jacket does not make it equally false. There are, of course, limits to what can be accomplished by intentions (even the best of them). No matter how hard I intend Carnap's picture, in the earlier described case, I do not think it reasonable to call the content of my utterance true.

Another example where I would simply distinguish the content asserted and the content intended is in the use of "I."[32] A person might utter:

(28) I am a general.

intending—that is "having in mind"—de Gaulle, and being under the delusion that he himself was de Gaulle. But the linguistic constraints on the possible demonstrata of "I" will not allow anyone other than de Gaulle to so demonstrate de Gaulle, no matter how hard they try.

All this familiarity with demonstratives has led me to believe that I was mistaken in "Quantifying In" in thinking that the most fundamental cases of what I might now describe as a person having a propositional attitude (believing, asserting, etc.) toward a singular proposition required that the person be *en rapport* with the subject of the proposition. It is now clear that I can assert *of* the first child to be born in the twenty-first century that *he* will be bald, simply by assertively uttering,

(29) Dthat ['the first child to be born in the twenty-first century'] will be bald.

I do not now see exactly how the requirement of being *en rapport* with the subject of a singular proposition fits in. Are there two kinds of singular propositions? Or are there just two different ways to know them?

EXCITING FUTURE EPISODES

1. Making sense out of the foregoing.

2. Showing how nicely (3) and (17) illustrate an early point about the possibility of incorporating contextual factors (here, a demonstration) as part of the content of the utterance. Another example compares uses of 'the person at whom I am pointing' as demonstration and as subject.

3. Justifying calling (17) a *de re* form by showing how it can be used to explicate the notion of modality *de re* without depending on scope.

4. Extending the demonstrative notion to *in*definite descriptions to see if it is possible to so explicate the ± specific idea. (It isn't.)

5. Improving (by starting all over) the analysis of the relation between Montague's treatment of indexicals and my treatment of demonstratives.

6. Showing how the treatment of proper names in the Kripke-Kaplan-Donnellan way (if there is such) is akin (?) to demonstratives.

7. Discussing the role of common noun phrases in connection with demonstratives, as in:

(30)   Dthat coat [the speaker points at a boy wearing a coat] is dirty.

8. Quine's contention that the content of any utterance can also be expressed by an eternal sentence. Is it true?

9. Much more to say about the phenomenology of intending to demonstrate *x,* and also about the truth-conditions of '*y* intends to demonstrate *x*'.

10. Demonstratives, dubbings, definitions, and other forms of language learning. Common nouns: what they mean and how we learn it. This section will include such pontifications as the following:

It is a mistake to believe that normal communication takes place through the encoding and decoding of general propositions, by means of our grasp of *meanings*. It is a more serious mistake, because more pernicious, to believe that other aspects of communication can be accounted for by a vague reference to "contextual features" of the utterance. Indeed, we first learn the meanings of almost all parts of our language by means quite different from those of the formal definitions studied in metamathematics; and the means used for first teaching the meanings of words, rather than withering away, are regularly and perhaps even essentially employed thereafter in all forms of communication.

ACKNOWLEDGMENTS

This work was supported by the National Science Foundation.

NOTES

1. Keith S. Donnellan, "Reference and Definite Descriptions," *The Philosophical Review*, 75 (1966): 298. [Reprinted in this volume.]
2. Leonard Linsky, "Reference and Referents," in *Philosophy and Ordinary Language*, ed. C. Caton (Urbana: 1963).
3. Donnellan, "Reference and Definite Descriptions," p. 299.
4. *Ibid.,* p. 297.
5. *Ibid.,* p. 303.
6. *Ibid.*
7. Jaakko Hintikka, "Individual, Possible Worlds, and Epistemic Logic," *Noûs*, 1 (1967): 47.
8. Bertrand Russell, *The Principles of Mathematics* (Cambridge, England: 1903).
9. Bertrand Russell, "On Denoting," *Mind*, 14 (1905): 479–93.
10. Rudolf Carnap, *Meaning and Necessity* (Chicago: 1947).
11. Bertrand Russell, *Introduction to Mathematical Philosophy* (London: 1920), p. 174.
12. Both 'denoting concept' and 'denoting phrase' are Russell's terms used in Russell's way.
13. An example is the possibility of producing set theoretical representations of the system of natural numbers which make all even numbers alike in certain set theoretical features (distinct from such numerical features as divisibility by two) and all odd numbers alike in other set theoretical features, or which provide simple and elegant definitions (i.e. representations) of certain basic numerical operations and relations such as *less than* or *plus*, etc.
14. It is not too easy to single out such phrases without the help of some theory about logical form or some semantical theory. I suppose what I am after is what linguists call syntactical criteria. But I have had difficulty in finding one which will not let in phrases like "a spy." Another difficulty is concerned with phrases like "John's brother" which seem to vary in their uniqueness suppositions. "John's brother is the man in dark glasses" carries, for me, the supposition that John has just one brother; whereas "The man in dark glasses is John's brother" does not. In fact the latter seems the most natural formulation when suppositions about the number of John's brothers are completely absent, since both "The man in dark glasses is one of John's brothers" and "The man in dark glasses is a brother of John" suppose, for me, that John has more than one brother.
15. The question whether all uses of demonstratives are accompanied by demonstrations depends on a number of factors, some empirical, some stipulative, and some in the twilight zone of theoretical ingenuity. The stipulative question is whether we use 'demonstrative' to describe certain phrases which might also be

described by enumeration or some such syntactical device, e.g. all phrases beginning with either "this" or "that" and followed by a common noun phrase; or whether we use 'demonstrative' to describe a certain characteristic *use* of such phrases. In the latter case it may be stipulatively true that an utterance containing a demonstrative must be accompanied by a demonstration. In the former case, the question turns both on how people in fact speak and on how clever our theoretician is in producing *recherché* demonstrations to account for apparent counterexamples.

16. This formulation probably needs sharpening. Don't take it as a definition.

17. It should not be supposed that my practice indicates any confidence as to the nature and structure of what I call *demonstrations* or the proper form for a *demonstration-description* to take. Indeed, these are difficult and important questions which arise repeatedly in what follows.

18. Gottlob Frege, "Ueber Sinn und Bedeutung," *Zeitschrift Fur Philosophie und Philosophische Kritik*. Translated (by Feigl) in *Readings in Philosophical Analysis*, eds. H. Feigl and W. Sellars (New York: 1949). [Reprinted in this volume.] Also translated (by Black) in *Translations from the Writings of Gottlob Frege*, eds. P. Geach and M. Black (Oxford: 1966).

19. *Ibid.*, emphasis added.

20. W. V. Quine, "Quantifiers and Propositional Attitudes," *Journal of Philosophy*, 53 (1955): 177–87. [Reprinted in this volume.]

21. David Kaplan, "Quantifying In," *Synthese*, 19 (1968): 178–214. [Reprinted in this volume.] I will attempt later to press the case that this use of proper names, which involves no waving of hands or fixing of glance, may be assimilated to the more traditional forms of demonstrative use.

22. "In the case of genuinely proper names like 'Aristotle' opinions as regards their sense may diverge. As such may, e.g., be suggested: Plato's disciple and the teacher of Alexander the Great. Whoever accepts this sense will interpret the meaning of the statement 'Aristotle was born in Stagira' differently from one who interpreted the sense of 'Aristotle' as the Stagirite teacher of Alexander the Great" (from Feigl's translation of Frege's "Ueber Sinn und Bedeutung").

23. A third kind of indicative device is the picture. Consideration of pictures, which to me lie somewhere between pointing and describing, may help drive home the parallels—in terms of the distinction between the object indicated and the manner of indication—between description, depiction, and demonstration.

24. That all utterances are in English is a general and implicit assumption except where it is explicitly called into question.

25. "Dhe" is really a combination of the demonstrative with a common noun phrase. It stands for "dthat male." More on such combinations later.

26. W. V. Quine, *Word and Object* (Cambridge, Mass.: 1960), p. 193.

27. There are, of course, two hidden relativizations involved even for eternal sentences. One is to a *language*, i.e. an association of meanings with words. The Knoh-English example was meant to dramatize this relativization. The other is to a possible world. There is always the implicit reference to the actual world when we use just the expression 'true'. If the analogy between moments of time and possible worlds holds—as some philosophers think—then maybe we should begin our classification of sentences not with explicitly dated eternal sentences like "in 1970 . . ." but with 'perfect' sentences like "In the possible world Charlie in 1970 . . .".

28. Rather than talking directly to these functions, I should really talk of entities like ⟨⟨'The',S)P⟩ and only derivatively of the functions.

29. This is aside from the inadequacy mentioned in the previous note, which continues to bother me.

30. The most relevant works are "Pragmatics" (1968) and "Pragmatics and Intensional Logic" (1970), both reprinted in Richard Montague, *Formal Philosophy* (New Haven, 1974).

31. I am still bothered by the notion of an utterance at t in w, where there is no utterance at t in w.

32. "I" is, of course, a demonstrative; as opposed, e.g. to "the person who is uttering this utterance," which contains only the demonstrative 'this utterance'. Let us compare utterances of:

> (i) I am exhausted

> (ii) The person who is uttering this utterance is exhausted

both uttered by s on the same occasion (!): To find the truth value of the content of (ii) in w' we must first locate the same utterance in w' (if it exists there at all) and see who, if anyone, is uttering it. Since s could well be exhausted silently in w', the two contents are not the same.

Proper Names and Intentionality   26

John R. Searle

1. THE NATURE OF THE PROBLEM

The problem of proper names ought to be easy, and at one level I think it is: we need to make repeated references to the same object, even when the object is not present, and so we give the object a name. Henceforward this name is used to refer to that object. However, puzzles arise when we reflect on the following sorts of considerations: objects are not given to us prior to our system of representation; what counts as one object or the same object is a function of how we divide up the world. The world does not come to us already divided up into objects; we have to divide it; and how we divide it is up to our system of representation, and in that sense is up to us, even though the system is biologically, culturally, and linguistically shaped. Furthermore, in order that someone can give a name to a certain object or know that a name is the name of that object, he has to have some *other* representation of that object independently of just having the name.

For the purposes of this study we need to explain how the use of proper names fits in with our general account of Intentionality. Both definite descriptions and indexicals serve to express at least a certain chunk of Intentional content. The expression may not by itself be sufficient to identify the object referred to, but in cases where the reference succeeds there is enough other Intentional content available to the speaker to nail down the reference. This thesis holds even for "referential" uses of definite descriptions, where the Intentional content that is actually expressed in the utterance may not even be true of the object referred to.[1] But what about proper names? They obviously lack an explicit Intentional content, but do they serve to focus the speaker's and hearer's Intentionality in some way; or do they simply refer to objects without any intervening Intentional content? On my account the answer is obvious. Since linguistic reference is always dependent on or is a form of mental reference and since mental reference is always in virtue of Intentional content including Background and Network,[2] proper names must in some way depend on Intentional content, and it is now time to make that way—or those ways—fully explicit.

The problem of proper names used to be put in the form, "Do proper names have sense?", and in contemporary philosophy there are supposed to be two competing answers to that question: an affirmative answer given by the "descriptivist" theory, according to which a name refers by being associated with a description or perhaps a cluster of descriptions, and a negative answer given by the "causal" theory according to

From *Intentionality* (Cambridge: Cambridge University Press, 1983), pp. 231–61.

which a name refers because of a "causal chain" connecting the utterance of the name to the bearer of the name or at least to the naming ceremony in which the bearer of the name got the name. I believe that neither side should be satisfied with these labels. The causal theory would be better described as the external causal chain of communication theory,[3] and the descriptivist theory would be better described as the Intentionalist or internalist theory, for reasons which will emerge in this discussion.

Labels apart, it is important to get clear at the start about what exactly is at issue between these two theories. Almost without exception, the accounts I have seen of the descriptivist theory are more or less crude distortions of it, and I want to make explicit four of the most common misconceptions of the issues in order to set them aside so that we can get at the real issues.

First, the issue is most emphatically not about whether proper names must be exhaustively analyzed in completely general terms. I do not know of any descriptivist theorist who has ever maintained that view, though Frege sometimes talks as if he might be sympathetic to it. In any case it has never been my view, nor, I believe, has it ever been the view of Strawson or Russell.

Second, as far as I am concerned the issue is not really about analyzing proper names in *words* at all. In my earlier writings on this subject[4] I pointed out that in some cases the only "identifying description" a speaker might have that he associates with the name is simply the ability to recognize the object.

Third, some authors[5] think that the descriptivist holds that proper names are associated with a 'dossier' in the speaker's mind and that the issue is between this dossier conception and the conception of the use of a proper name as analogous to pointing. But that again is a misconception of descriptivism. On the descriptivist account, pointing is precisely an example that fits his thesis, since pointing succeeds only in virtue of the intentions of the pointer.

Fourth, Kripke claims that on the descriptivist picture "some man really gives a name by going into the privacy of his own room and

saying that the referent is to be the unique thing with certain identifying properties."[6] But that is not the view any descriptivist known to me ever espoused and it is not surprising that Kripke gives no source for this strange view.

But if these four accounts misrepresent descriptivism and the issues between descriptivist and causal theories, what exactly are these views and the issues between them? The issue is simply this: Do proper names refer by setting *internal* conditions of satisfaction in a way that is consistent with the general account of Intentionality that I have been providing, or do proper names refer in virtue of some *external* causal relation? Let us try to state this issue a little more precisely. The descriptivist is committed to the view that in order to account for how a proper name refers to an object we need to show how the object *satisfies* or *fits* the "descriptive" Intentional content that is associated with the name in the minds of speakers; some of this Intentionality will normally be expressed or at least be expressible in words. The causal theorist is committed to the view that no such Intentionalist analysis will ever do the job and that in order to account for the relation of successful reference between the utterance of a name and the object referred to we need to show some sort of external causal connection between the utterance of a name and the object. Both theories are attempts to answer the question, "How in the utterance of a name does the speaker succeed in referring to an object?" The answer given by the descriptivist is that the speaker refers to the object because and only because the object satisfies the Intentional content associated with the name. The causal theorist answers that the speaker refers to an object because and only because there is a causal chain of communication connecting the speaker's utterance with the object or at least with the baptism of the object—an important qualification we will come to later.

II. THE CAUSAL THEORY

There are different versions of the causal theory and I shall not try to discuss all of them. The most influential have been those of Kripke and Donnellan, and I shall confine most of my discussion to their views. They are not identical, but I will call attention to the differences between them only when necessary to avoid confusion.

I begin with Kripke's version.

A rough statement of a theory might be the following. An initial baptism takes place. Here the object may be named by ostension, or the reference of the name may be fixed by a description. When the name is "passed from link to link", the receiver of the name must, I think, intend when he hears it to use it with the same reference as the man from whom he heard it.[7]

There are several things to notice about this passage. First, the account of the introduction of the name in the baptism is entirely descriptivist. The baptism either gives us an Intentional content in verbal form, a definite description (Kripke gives the example of the introduction of the name "Neptune" for a then as yet unperceived planet), or it gives the Intentional content of a perception when a object is named ostensively. In the perceptual case, there is indeed a causal connection, but as it is Intentional causation, internal to the perceptual content, it is useless to the causal theorist in his effort to give an external causal account of the relation of name to object. Of course, in such cases there will also be an external causal account in terms of the impact of the object on the nervous system, but the external causal phenomena will not by themselves give an ostensive definition of the name. To get the ostensive definition the perceiver has to perceive the object, and that involves more than the physical impact of the object on his nervous system. So it is an odd feature of Kripke's version of the causal theory that the external causal chain does not actually reach up to the object, it only reaches to the baptism of the object, to the name introduction ceremony, and from that point on what fixes the reference is an Intentional content which may or may not also have an external causal connection to the object. Many, perhaps most, philosophers think of the causal theory of names as asserting a causal connection between the referring use of names and the object they name, but in

Kripke's case at least that isn't really true. An interesting point and one we will come back to later.

Some authors, e.g. Devitt,[8] are disappointed with this aspect of Kripke's account and want to reserve the notion of genuinely "designational" names to those that are causally connected to the object itself. But this seems quite arbitrary. There is nothing to prevent us from introducing a name by description and using it to refer, even as a "rigid designator"; and in any case, there are lots of proper names of abstract entities, e.g., numerals are names of numbers, and abstract entities are incapable of initiating physical causal chains.

A second feature to notice about Kripke's account is that the causal chain isn't, so to speak, *pure*. In addition to causation and baptism, an extra Intentionalistic element is allowed to creep in: each speaker must intend to refer to the same object as the person from whom he learned the name. So this does give us some Intentional content associated with each use of a name 'N' in the causal chain, viz., 'N is the object referred to by the person from whom I got the name." Now this is an odd requirement for the following reason: if everybody in the chain actually had this restricted intention, and if the Intentional content were in fact satisfied, i.e., if each speaker really did succeed in referring to the same object, then it would follow trivially that the reference would go right back to the target of the initial baptism and the talk about causation would be redundant. But that is presumably not Kripke's idea, since that would have no explanatory power and would in fact be circular. We would explain successful reference in virtue of a chain of successful references. Kripke's idea is clearly this: you will account for how the Intentional content is satisfied, that is, how the reference is successful, in terms of external causation plus the intention that it should be successful. So Kripke sets three conditions to account for how each token utterance refers to the initial target: initial baptism, causal chain, restricted Intentional content. And the account is still external in this sense: though each link in the chain of communication is perceived by both speaker and hearer, "It is not how the speaker thinks he got the reference but the actual chain of communication which is relevant."[9]

Before criticizing Kripke's account let us turn to Donnellan's.

The main idea is that when a speaker uses a name intending to refer to an individual and predicate something of it, successful reference will occur when there is an individual that enters into the historically correct explanation of who [sic] it is that the speaker intended to predicate something of. That individual will then be the referent and the statement made will be true or false depending on whether it has the property designated by the predicate.[10]

The passage has two key elements: (a) "historically correct explanation of" (b) "who it is that the speaker intended to predicate something of." To help us with (a) Donellan introduces the idea of an "omniscient observer of history." The omniscient observer will see whom or what we meant even if we can't give any Intentional content that fits whom or what we meant. But then in what did our satisfying (b) consist? What fact about *us* makes it the case that when we said, for example, "Socrates is snub nosed", it was *Socrates* that we "intended to predicate something of"? Evidently, on Donnellan's account, no fact about us at all—except for the causal chain connecting our utterance to Socrates. But, then, what is the nature of this chain; what does the omniscient observer look for and why? Rorty assures us that the causal theory needs only "ordinary physical causation," the banging of object against object, as it were. I think Donnellan's observer is going to have to look for Intentional causation and Intentional content. I will come back to this point.

Kripke insists, and I take it that Donnellan would agree, that the causal theory is not intended as a complete theory but rather as a "picture" of how proper names work. Still, we want to know if it is an accurate picture, and one way to proceed is to try to get counterexamples, examples of names that don't work according to the picture. Does the causal theory (or picture) as stated, for example, by Kripke give us sufficient conditions of successful reference using proper names? The answer, I think, is clearly no. There are numerous counterexamples in the literature, but

perhaps the most graphic is from Gareth Evans.[11] "Madagascar" was originally the name of a part of Africa. Marco Polo, though he presumably satisfied Kripke's condition of intending to use the name with the same reference as "the man from whom he heard it," nonetheless referred to an island off the coast of Africa, and that island is now what we mean by "Madagascar". So, the use of the name "Madagascar" satisfies a causal condition that connects it with the African mainland, but that is not sufficient to enable it to refer to the African mainland. The question we need to come back to is how and why does it refer to Madagascar instead of the African mainland, given that the causal chain goes to the mainland?

If a Kripkean causal chain picture does not give us a sufficient condition does it at least give us a necessary condition? Here again the answer seems to me clearly no. In general it is a good idea to use examples that have been presented against one as examples that actually work in one's favor, so let us consider the following from Kaplan.[12] He writes that the description theory couldn't be right because, for example, it says in the *Concise Biographical Dictionary* (Concise Publications: Walla Walla, Washington) that "Rameses VIII" is "One of a number of ancient pharaohs about whom nothing is known." But surely we can refer to him even though we do not satisfy the description theory for using his name. Actually what the example shows is that a great deal is known about Rameses VIII, and indeed he is a rather ideal case even for the most naive version of the description theory since we seem to have a perfect identifying description. Rameses VIII is the pharaoh named "Rameses" who ruled Egypt after a pharaoh named "Rameses VII."[13] That is, imagine, as I suppose is the case, that we have at least some knowledge of the history of ancient Egypt, including the knowledge that pharaohs with the same name are numbered sequentially. Suppose for the sake of argument that we know quite a bit about Rameses VII and Rameses IX. We could then use, without any hesitation, the name "Rameses VIII" to refer to the Rameses who came between Rameses VII and Rameses IX, even though the various causal chains stretching back from us to ancient Egypt miss Rameses VIII. What we have in this case is an example of the Network in operation; in this case, it is that part of the Network containing knowledge about the past.

In general one can say that the whole Network of Intentionality is nailed down causally, *via* Intentional causation, to the real world at various points, but it would be a serious mistake to suppose that the Network must nail down, by any kind of causation, at every single point that reference is made using a proper name.[14] I believe the reason that causal theorists make this mistake is that they overdraw the analogy between reference and perception, an analogy that is made explicitly by Donnellan.[15] Perception does nail down to the world in this way at every point, because every perceptual experience has the causal self-referentiality of Intentional content that we have discussed earlier. But proper names do not carry that kind of causation, even of Intentional causation. It is possible to satisfy the conditions for successfully using a proper name even though there is no causal connection, either Intentional or external, between the utterance of the name and the object referred to. Indeed, this will be the use for any system of names where one can identify the bearer of the name from the position of the name in the system. I can, for example, refer to M Street in Washington simply because I know that there is in that city an alphabetical sequence of street names, "A", "B", "C", etc. I needn't have any causal connection with M Street in order to do that.[16] And the point is even clearer if we consider names of abstract entities: if I count up to 387, the numeral names the number without any causal chain connecting me and any alleged baptismal ceremony of that number.

There are plenty of acknowledged counterexamples to the claim that the causal theory gives us either necessary or sufficient conditions for the use of a proper name to refer to its bearer. Why are the authors of these theories not impressed by these examples? There is, by the way, an odd asymmetry in the role of counterexamples in these discussions:

alleged counterexamples to the descriptivist theory are generally regarded as disastrous for the theory; counterexamples to the causal theory are cheerfully accepted as if they did not matter. The reason why the causal theorists are not impressed, I suspect, is that they feel that, as Kripke says explicitly, the causal theory offers a more adequate *picture* of how names work even if it cannot account for every case. After all, the counterexamples may just be odd and marginal cases and what we really want to know is what is central and essential to the operation of the institution of proper names. Furthermore, the counterexamples are not really very important to us theoretically unless they are backed by some independently motivated theory, some account of why they are counterexamples. I am in sympathy with both of these impulses and I believe we should look for the essential character of the institution and not be too impressed by odd examples, and I believe the counterexamples are only interesting if backed by a theory that explains them. Indeed, I would like to see counterexamples to both the causal and descriptivist theory treated with these same attitudes. The difficulty is that counterexamples I have presented do seem to raise serious difficulties for the causal theory (or picture) and they are backed by a theory of Intentionality. In the Madagascar case the Intentionality that attaches to the name shifts the reference from the terminus of the causal chain to the object that satisfies the associated Intentional content, and in the case of locating names in systems of names the position of a name as an element in the Network gives sufficient Intentionality to secure reference for the name without any causal chain.

Let us then turn to the more important question: Does the causal theory or picture give the essential character of the institution of proper names? I think the answer is clearly no. To see this, imagine a primitive hunter-gatherer community with a language containing proper names. (And it is not at all implausible to imagine a language used by a primitive community; as far as we know it was in such communities that human languages evolved in the first place.) Imagine that everybody in the tribe knows everybody else and that newborn members of the tribe are baptized at ceremonies attended by the entire tribe. Imagine, furthermore, that as the children grow up they learn the names of people as well as the local names of mountains, lakes, streets, houses, etc., by ostension. Suppose also that there is a strict taboo in this tribe against speaking of the dead, so that no one's name is ever mentioned after his death. Now the point of the fantasy is simply this: As I have described it, this tribe has an institution of proper names used for reference in exactly the same way that our names are used for reference, but *there is not a single use of a name in the tribe that satisfies the causal chain of communication theory*. As I have described it there is not a single chain of communication of the sort favored by Kripke, Donnellan, and others. Every use of the name in this tribe as I described it satisfies the descriptivist claim that there is an Intentional content associating the name with the object. In this case we are to suppose that the people are taught the names by ostension and that they learn to recognize their fellow tribe members, mountains, houses, etc. The teaching sets up an Intentional content which the object satisfies.[17]

It seems to me that the causal theorist might make the following reply: The spirit of the causal theory is kept in this example, because though there is no chain of *communication* there is nonetheless a *causal* connection between the acquisition of the name and the object named because the object is presented ostensively. The answer to that is twofold. First, the kind of causal connection that teaches the use of the name is straightforward Intentional causation; it is not externalist at all. That is, the kind of causal connection that is set up in these cases is a descriptivist causal connection. When I say "Baxter", I mean the man I am able to *recognize as* Baxter or the man to whom I was *introduced as* Baxter, or the man whom I *saw* baptized as Baxter, and in each of these cases the causal element implied by the italicized term is Intentional causation. In every case the causal condition is part of the Intentional content associated with

the name. And notice that what counts is not the fact that I give a *verbal* description, but that there is an Intentional content.

If the causal theory is to be an alternative to the descriptivist theory, the causation in question must not be descriptivist, it must not be internal, otherwise the causal theory is just a variant of the descriptivist theory. It just amounts to the claim that descriptivism includes some, e.g., perceptual, elements in the Intentional content associated with the use of the name. But, secondly, we needn't even suppose that all of the names in the community are introduced by ostension. As Kripke concedes, there may be names in the community that are introduced purely by description. Suppose that the astronomers and meteorologists of the community are able to predict storms and astronomical events in the future and that they attach proper names to these future events and phenomena. These names are taught to all the members of the community purely by description and there isn't any question of the events causing the names because the events are in the future. Now here it seems to me is a community that satisfies all of the conditions essential for having proper names and having the institution of proper names that function to refer in the way that our proper names function to refer, but there is not a single use of a proper name that satisfies the story, picture, or theory of the causal theorists.

If we so easily describe an example of an entire community that satisfies the conditions for using proper names but does not satisfy the conditions laid down by the causal theory, how are we to account for the fact that the theory has seemed so plausible to so many philosophers? What are we to make of this dispute? Notice that in neither Donnellan nor in Kripke was the causal theory presented as the result of some independently motivated account of the use of names, rather it was presented as a briefly sketched alternative to the descriptivist theory. The main thrust of both arguments was in attempting to refute descriptivism, and if we are to understand what is going on in this dispute we must now turn to that theory.

III. THE DESCRIPTIVIST ACCOUNT OF PROPER NAMES

You will not understand the descriptivist theories unless you understand the views they were originally opposed to. At the time I wrote "Proper names"[18] in 1955 there were three standard views of names in the philosophical literature: Mill's view that names have no connotation at all but simply a denotation, Frege's view that the meaning of a name is given by a single associated definite description, and what might be called the standard logic textbook view that the meaning of a name "*N*" is simply "called N". Now the first and third of these views seem to be obviously inadequate. If the problem of a theory of proper names is to answer the question, "In virtue of what does the speaker in the utterance of a name succeed in referring to a particular object?", then Mill's account is simply a refusal to answer the question; it simply says that the name refers to the object, and that's that. But the third answer is also defective. As I wrote in *Speech Acts,*

the description, "The man called *X*" will not do, or at any rate will not do by itself, as a satisfaction of the principle of identification. For if you ask me, "Whom do you mean by *X?*" and I answer, "The man called *X*", even if it were true that there is only one man who is called *X,* I am simply saying that he is the man whom other people refer to by the name "*X*". But if they refer to him by the name "*X*" then they must also be prepared to substitute an identifying description for "*X*" and if they in turn substitute "the man called *X*", the question is only carried a stage further and cannot go on indefinitely without circularity or infinite regress. My reference to an individual may be parasitic on someone else's but this parasitism cannot be carried on indefinitely if there is to be any reference at all.

For this reason it is no answer at all to the question of what if anything is the sense of a proper name "*X*" to say its sense or part of its sense is "called *X*". One might as well say that part of the meaning of "horse" is "called a horse". It is really quite amazing how often this mistake is made.[19]

Perhaps equally amazing is that Kripke makes this same point,[20] even using the same example of "horse" as if it were an objection or difficulty for the description theory, when

in fact it was one of the fundamental theses of the theory, at least in its recent formulations. Notice, however, that the above passage does not imply that one cannot refer to an object by a name "*N*" when the only identifying description one has of the object is "called '*N*' ", rather it says that this by itself cannot be a complete account of how proper names refer, for such identifying descriptions are dependent on there being some other identifying descriptions of a completely different sort. The polemical aim of the passage was to attack the standard logic textbook view, not for giving a false account of how reference is secured but for giving an account which is incomplete and lacking in explanatory power. Often, in fact, one does make what I called parasitic references using a proper name: often the only identifying description one associates with a name "*N*" is simply the "object called *N* in my community or by my interlocutors". In such a case, my use of the name is parasitic on other speakers' use of the name in the sense that my reference, using a name to which I can attach only the Intentional content "called *N*", is successful only if there are now or have been other people who use or have used the name "*N*" and attach a semantic or Intentional content of a completely different sort. (And remember, "identifying description" does not imply "in words", it simply means: Intentional content, including Network and Background, sufficient to identify the object, and that content may or may not be in words.) Thus, for example, if all I know about Plotinus is that I have heard other people talk about somebody using the name "Plotinus", I can still refer to Plotinus using "Plotinus", but my ability to do that is parasitic on other speakers.

Frege's account, then, is the most promising, and it was that account I sought to develop. Its chief merit is that Frege sees that with proper names, as with any term capable of referring, there must be some Intentional content in virtue of which it refers. Its chief demerits are that he seems to have thought that semantic content was always in words, specifically definite descriptions, and that the description gave a definition or sense of the name. One additional virtue of the Fregean account, and the account I tried to develop, is that they enable us to answer certain puzzling questions concerning the occurrence of proper names in identity statements, in existential statements, and in intensional-with-an-s statements about Intentional states, and, as far as I can see, no causal theorist to date has given a satisfactory answer to these questions.

Now in the light of this brief sketch of the motivations for the descriptivist theory let us have another look at the causal theory. From the point of view of the descriptivist theory, what the causal analysis amounts to is the following: *the "causal chain of communication" is simply a characterization of the parasitic cases seen from an external point of view.* Let me try to make this clear. Kripke says that at each link in the chain of communication the speaker must have the intention, "when I utter '*N*' I mean to refer to the same object as the person from whom I got the name '*N*' ". The descriptivist says that one sort of identifying description that one can attach to a name "*N*" is "the person referred to by others in my linguistic community as '*N*' ". Both sides agree that this is not enough by itself: Kripke insists that the chain must terminate in an initial baptism; the descriptivist allows for a variety of ways in which it can terminate, of which an initial baptism is one. Where is the difference? As far as the issue between descriptivism and the causal theory is concerned there is no difference: Kripke's theory is just a variant form of descriptivism. But what about the causal chain? Doesn't the causal theory require an external causal chain that guarantees successful reference? *The external causal chain plays no explanatory role whatever in either Kripke's or Donnellan's account,* as I will explain shortly. The only chain that matters is a transfer of Intentional content from one use of an expression to the next; in every case reference is secured in virtue of descriptivist Intentional content in the mind of the speaker who uses the expression. This will become clearer when we turn to the alleged counterexamples, but you can see it already in Kripke's characterization: Suppose that there is an initial baptism of a mountain with the name "*N*" and then a chain with ten links, each of a person who utters

"*N*" intending to use it to refer to whatever the person he got it from used it. Assuming there is no intervening Intentionality, no other beliefs, etc., about *N,* this by itself is sufficient to guarantee that each person refers to the initial target of the baptism solely in virtue of the fact that there is one and only one object that satisfies or fits his or her Intentional content. After the speaker who made the initial baptism, subsequent Intentional contents are parasitic on the prior ones for achieving reference. Of course there will be an external causal characterization of the chain, and an omniscient observer could observe Mr. One talking to Mrs. Two and so on down to Mr. Ten, and he could describe a sequence of events without mentioning any Intentionality, without any mention of descriptive content. But the sequence of features characterized by the external observer are not what secures reference. Reference, for Kripke, is secured entirely by descriptive content.

The way to test which feature is doing the work, descriptive content or causal chain, is to vary one while holding the other constant and see what happens. Suppose that Miss Seven decides to use the name not to refer to the same thing as the person from whom she got it but to refer to her pet poodle instead. Externally described, the chain of communication can be exactly the same: the name "*N*" goes from One to Ten, but the shift in Intentional content means that Seven, Eight, Nine, and Ten are referring to a poodle and not a mountain, solely because the poodle and not the mountain satisfies their identifying description (this is much like the Madagascar example). Or, conversely, imagine that the chain is one of constant descriptive content, each parasitic on the prior speaker back to the initial baptism, but vary the external causal story in any way you like and this still will not affect the reference. Now which is doing the work, Intentionality or "ordinary physical causation"?

In response to the suggestion that the descriptivist can easily accommodate their account, Kripke, Donnellan, and Devitt all insist that on the descriptivist view the speaker would have to remember from whom he got the name. But this seems to me plainly false. I can (and do), for example, make parasitic references using the name "Plotinus" in the manner I considered above without remembering from whom I got the name. I just intend to refer to the same person as the person (whoever that may be) from whom I got the name, in accordance with Kripke's version of descriptivism.

But why does it matter? What difference does it make whether the chain is described by way of Intentional content or external physical causation? Because the issue, to repeat, is whether reference succeeds in virtue of the fact that the object referred to fits or satisfies some associated description or whether reference is achieved by virtue of some facts about the world quite independently of how those facts are represented in the mind: some condition which the utterance of the expression meets which is independent of the contents of any associated description. Kripke and Donnellan claim to be arguing against the conception of reference by way of associated Intentional content and in favor of external causal conditions. I am arguing that to the extent that their account works, it works because it is descriptivist; the external causal chain plays no explanatory role. And I am not saying that their account can be forced into the descriptivist mould, but that when closely scrutinized the very account they offer is descriptivist on its face. We should not be surprised that they have so little to say about causation. It plays no role in their accounts. To see this further let us turn to Donnellan.

Suppose someone says 'Socrates was snub-nosed', and we ask to whom he is referring. The central idea is that this calls for a historical explanation; we search not for an individual who might best fit the speaker's descriptions of the individual to whom he takes himself to be referring . . . but rather for an individual *historically related* to his use of the name 'Socrates' on this occasion. It might be that an omniscient observer of history would see an individual related to an author of dialogues, that one of the central charaters of these dialogues was *modelled* upon that individual, that these dialogues have been handed down and that the speaker has read translations of them, that the speaker's now predicating snub-nosedness of something is *explained by* his having read these translations. . . . 'What individual, if any, would the speaker describe in this way, even perhaps mistakenly?' (my italics).[21]

This passage seems to me to give a very reasonable account—the question it leaves us is: What is the omniscient observer supposed to look for and why? What considerations does he make in deciding "what individual, if any, would the speaker describe in this way"? Since there are an indefinite number of "historical relations" there must be some principle for selecting those that are relevant. What is it? I think that the answer is implicit in the passage. We are to take two sets of Intentional contents as decisive. First, the author of the dialogues *modelled* one of the central characters on an actual individual, that is, the author had a representation of the individual in question and intended the name "Socrates" in the dialogue to refer to him. Second, the speaker, having read the dialogues, intended his use of "Socrates" to refer to the same person that the author of the dialogues referred to. The speaker in his turn will pick up a lot of extra descriptions from the dialogues and these may or may not be true of the man he is referring to.

Now, if we ask the man, "Whom do you mean by 'Socrates'?", he might give us some of these descriptions, and, as Donnellan points out, these descriptions might not be true of the man referred to as "Socrates" by the author of the dialogues but true of someone else, say the author himself. Suppose the man says, "By 'Socrates' I mean the man who invented the method of dialogue", and suppose the author of the dialogues invented it himself and modestly attributed it to Socrates. Now if we then say, "All the same the man was really referring to the person referred to by the author as 'Socrates' and not to the man who *in fact* invented the dialogue method," we are committed to the view that the speaker's Intentional content, "I am referring to the same man as the author of the dialogues referred to," takes precedence over his content, "I am referring to the inventor of the dialogue method." When he gave us the latter answer, he gave it to us on the assumption that one and the same man satisfied both. If they come apart, that is, if each Intentional content is satisfied by a different person, it is up to the speaker which one takes precedence. The speaker expressed a fragment of his

Network of Intentional contents. If that fragment doesn't fit the object which satisfies the rest of the Network, the omniscient observer will, quite reasonably, suppose that the rest of the Network takes precedence. He is referring to the historical Socrates even if he gave a false description, but that supposition is a supposition about how the man's Intentional content determines reference. Thus on both Kripke's and Donnellan's accounts the conditions of successful reference are descriptivist right down to the ground.

IV. DIFFERENCES BETWEEN THE TWO ACCOUNTS

Though both the "descriptivist" and the "causal" theories are at bottom descriptivist, there are still several important differences between them.

1. According to the causal theory the transfer of Intentionality in the chain of communication is really the essence of the institution of proper names. According to the descriptivist it is just an incidental feature. It is not the essential or defining trait of the institution at all. And the purpose of the parable of the hunter-gatherer community was to make just this point: the tribe has the institution of proper names to refer, but there are no chains of communication, no parasistic references. Another way to make the same point is to see that though parasitic reference is always possible for proper names this sort of parasitism is also possible for any word at all that expresses an Intentional content, including general terms. Consider, for example, the words "structuralism" and "structuralist". For a long time I had only the haziest of ideas what these words meant. I knew that structuralism was some kind of fashionable theory, but that was about the limit of my knowledge. Still, given my Network and Background, I could use the word "structuralism" in a parasitic way; I could, for example, ask, "Are there still a lot of structuralists in France?", or, "Is Pierre a structuralist?" And notice that this parasitism is not restricted to natural kind terms of the sort Putnam talks about. It wasn't a case of identifying passing structuralists ostensively by their surface appearance and hoping that one

day scientific investigation would reveal their true nature. As far as this difference between the descriptivist and causal theory is concerned, the argument would appear to favor the descriptivist claim that chains of communication are not the essential feature of the institution of proper names, though both sides would agree that they do in fact commonly occur.

2. The descriptivist finds it very implausible to suppose that in the chains of communication, when they do occur, the only Intentionality which secures reference is that each speaker intends to refer to the same object as the previous speaker. In real life a whole lot of information gets transferred in the chain of communication and some of this information will be relevant to securing reference. For example, the *type* of thing named by the name—whether it is a mountain or a man or a moose or whatever—is generally associated with the name even in the parasitic cases; and if the speaker is wildly mistaken about this we are disinclined to say that he really succeeded in referring. Suppose, for example, that he hears a discussion about Socrates's philosophy of mathematics and he confusedly supposes that "Socrates" is the name of an odd number. Suppose he says "I think Socrates is not a prime but is divisible by 17." He satisfies Kripke's version of the causal theory, but he is not successful in referring to Socrates. Furthermore, where the initial target of the baptism is not identical with the object that satisfies the associated nonparasitic content we don't always construe the reference as going to the initial target. In the Madagascar case, each speaker we suppose intended to refer to the same object as the previous speaker, but Marco Polo introduced some new Intentional content that took precedence over the chain of communication. He identified an island and not a portion of the African continent.

It is a little-noticed but absurd consequence of Kripke's view that it sets no constraints at all on what the name might turn out to refer to. Thus, for example, it might turn out that by "Aristotle" I am referring to a bar stool in Joe's Pizza Place in Hoboken in 1957 if that is what the causal chain happened to lead to. I want to say: by "Aristotle" I couldn't be referring to a bar stool, because that is not what I mean by "Aristotle". And Kripke's remarks about essentialism are not enough to block this result for they are all *de re* necessities attaching to objects themselves but not attaching any restrictive Intentional content to the use of the name. Thus, even if it is a *de re* metaphysical necessity that the actual man had a certain mother and father, that tells us nothing at all about how the name refers to that man and not to a bar stool.

3. In general the descriptivist is inclined to prefer the first-order Intentional content and see the parasitic cases as less important; the causal theorist emphasizes the parasitic identifying description. The germ of truth in the causal theory seems to me this: For names of objects where we are not directly acquainted with the object we will often tend to give precedence to the parasitic Intentional content. For example, for names of remote historical figures, e.g., Napoleon or Socrates, or famous people, e.g., Nixon, given a conflict between the first-order Intentional content and the parasitic we will usually prefer the latter. Why? Because the chain of parasitic Intentionality will get us back to the original target of the baptism and that we are usually, though not always, inclined to think is what matters. In this respect, proper names differ from general terms. Since the point of having proper names is just to refer to objects, not to describe them, it often doesn't really matter to us much what descriptive content is used to identify the object as long as it identifies the right object, where the "right object" is just the one that other people use the name to refer to.

V. ALLEGED COUNTEREXAMPLES TO DESCRIPTIVISM

With this discussion in mind let us turn to the counterexamples. The counterexamples I have seen to the descriptivist theory fail in general because the authors look only at what the agent might *say* and not at the *total Intentional content* he has in his head, and also because they neglect the role of the Network and the Background. Each counterexample is designed to show that a speaker will refer to an object in

the utterance of a name even though the associated definite description is not satisfied by that object or is satisfied by something else or by nothing. I will show that in each case reference is achieved only because the object satisfies the Intentional content in the mind of the speaker.

Example 1: The Gödel/Schmidt Case (Kripke)

The only thing Jones knows or thinks he knows about Kurt Gödel is that he is the author of the famous incompleteness proof. But suppose, in fact, that the proof was written by another man, Schmidt. Now when we ask Jones for an identifying description of "Gödel" he says, "the author of the proof of the incompleteness of arithmetic". But in fact when Jones uses "Gödel" he is referring to Gödel and not to the man who satisfies his description.

It is obvious from what I have said that the correct account of this case is that Jones has quite a bit more Intentional content than just the description he gives. At the very least he has "the man called 'Gödel' in my linguistic community or at least by those from whom I got the name". The reason he doesn't give this as an answer when asked for an identifying description is that he assumes that something more than this is wanted. This much Intentionality is already possessed by whoever asked him for the identifying description.

It is characteristic of these discussions that the authors too seldom give us the sentences in which we are supposed to imagine the same occurring, but if we consider actual sentences, this example could go in either direction. Suppose Jones says, "On line 17 of his proof, Gödel makes what seems to me to be a fallacious inference", and suppose we ask him who he means by "Gödel". He responds, "I mean the author of the famous incompleteness theorem", and we, then, say, "Well, in fact, Gödel did not prove that theorem, it was originally proven by Schmidt". Now what does Jones say? It seems to me that he might well say that by "Gödel" he just means the author of the incompleteness proof regardless of what he is, in fact, called. Kripke concedes that there could be such uses. They involve what I have called secondary aspect uses of proper names.[22] But Jones needn't say that. He might say, "I was referring to the man whom I have heard called 'Kurt Gödel', regardless of whether or not he proved the incompleteness of arithmetic". On the other hand suppose Jones says, "Kurt Gödel lived in Princeton". In this case, it seems to me much more likely that if he finds that Gödel does not satisfy the nonparasitic definite description that he attached to the name he would simply fall back on the parasitic Intentional content that he attaches to the name. But in either case it is the speaker's Intentional content that determines reference. It is not enough to look just as what a speaker says in response to a particular question, one has to look at his total Intentional content, as well as Background capacities associated with a name and at what he would say if informed that different parts of that content were satisfied by different objects. There seems to me nothing in this example that need bother the descriptivist.

Example 2: Thales the Well Digger (Donnellan)[23]

Suppose that all that a certain speaker knows or thinks he knows about Thales is that he is the Greek philosopher who said that all is water. But suppose there never was a Greek philosopher who said such a thing. Suppose that Aristotle and Herodotus were referring to a well digger who said, "I wish all were water so I wouldn't have to dig these damned wells". In such a case, according to Donnellan, when the speaker uses the name "Thales" he is referring to that well digger. Furthermore, suppose there was a hermit who never had any dealings with anyone, who actually held that all was water. Still, when we say "Thales" we are plainly not referring to that hermit.

There are really two aspects to this argument: one about the hermit, the other about the well digger. On the surface, the well digger case is formally similar to the Gödel/Schmidt case. The speaker always has his parasitic Intentional content to fall back on if his associated description is satisfied by some object that doesn't fit the rest of his Inten-

tional content. However, this case also raises the separate issue of how the Network of the speaker's beliefs will set some further constraints on the chain of parasitic Intentionality. Suppose that Herodotus had heard a frog at the bottom of a well making croaking noises that sounded like the Greek for "all is water"; suppose further that this frog is a family pet named "Thales", and that this incident is the origin of the view that somebody held that all is water. When I use the name "Thales", taking myself to be referring to a Greek philosopher, am I referring to that frog? I think not. Similar doubts could be raised about the well digger: I can think of sentences where I would be inclined to say that I was referring to the well digger and other sentences in which I would be inclined to say that I failed to refer to anyone because there was no such person as Thales the philosopher. But in the cases in which I am referring to a well digger I do so because the well digger satisfies enough of my descriptive content; in particular, he satisfies the content, "The person referred to as 'Thales' by the people from whom I got this use of the name", that is, he satisfies the parasitic Intentional content of the sort we mentioned before. In the case of the hermit, the reason we feel no inclination at all to say we are referring to him with the name "Thales" is that he does not satisfy the condition of fitting into the relevant Network of Intentionality. When we say "Thales is the Greek philosopher who held that all is water", we don't just mean *anybody* who held that all is water, we mean that person who was known to other Greek philosophers as arguing that all is water, who was referred to in his time or subsequently by some Greek variant or predecessor of the expression we now pronounce as "Thales", whose works and ideas have come down to us posthumously through the writings of other authors, and so on. Now, to repeat, in all these cases there will be an external causal account of how we got that information, but what secures reference is not the external causal chain, but the sequence of the transfer of Intentional contents. The reason we are not tempted to allow the hermit to qualify as Thales is that he simply does not fit into the Network and the Background. This example is somewhat analogous to the example of the humanoid who invented bifocals eighty billion years before Benjamin Franklin was ever alive. When he said Franklin invented bifocals, we meant: relative to our Network and Background.

Example 3: The Two Patches (Donnellan)[24]

Suppose a man sees two identical colored patches on a screen, one above the other. Suppose he names the top one "*A*" and the bottom one "*B*". The only identifying description he can give for *A* is "the one on top". But suppose that, unknown to him, we have given him inverting lenses so that the one he thinks is on top is really on the bottom and vice versa. In such a case the identifying description he can give is actually false of the object referred to, yet his reference to *A* is nonetheless successful.

I will deal with this example rather swiftly. *A* is the one he actually sees right *there*. It is the one causing *this* visual experience. You couldn't ask for a better 'identifying description' than that. Expressions like "the one on top" are strictly for public consumption, and though one can imagine cases in which they would take precedence over the Intentional presentation, in most cases the presentational content either in perception or in memory is sufficient to pick out *A*. But suppose that he forgets that he saw it. Suppose he even forgets that he thought it was on top. He just remembers that the name named a patch. Can't he still use the name to refer to the patch? Of course. There is no reason why a parasitic Intentional content might not depend on one's own earlier Intentional contents. Now *A* is just identified as "the one I was previously able to identify as '*A*' ", a limiting case, perhaps, but nonetheless a possible one.

Example 4: The Twin Earth (Putnam et al.)[25]

The correct account of how a name secures reference for us here on earth cannot be that it does it by way of an associated descriptive content, because if there were a twin earth our

names would still refer to objects on our earth and not to objects on twin earth, even though any description of an object on earth would equally well fit its *Doppelgänger* on twin earth. In order to account for how reference thus succeeds unambiguously on earth we have to recognize the role of external causal links between utterances and objects.

I have already answered this sort of objection in Chapter 2 [of *Intentionality*] concerning perception and in Chapter 8 concerning indexical expressions. For the case of proper names it suffices to say that the causal self-referentiality of all perceptual forms of Intentionality, the self-referentiality of indexical forms of Intentionality, and in general the way we are indexically related to our own Intentional contents, including the Network and Background, is sufficient to block any possible twin earth ambiguities. We can see this even in the parasitic cases. When, for example, I say that the only description I associate with "Plotinus" is "called Plotinus", I don't mean just any object ever called "Plotinus" by someone. I mean, inter alia, rather the *person* that *I* have heard and read referred to as Plotinus. The fact that a *Doppelgänger* on twin earth could also be called "Plotinus" is as irrelevant as the fact that somebody might have (and no doubt somebody has) named his dog "Plotinus", or that many other people have been called "Plotinus".

VI. MODAL ARGUMENTS

This book is about Intentionality and not about modality, and I have therefore avoided the modal issues up to this point. However, some philosophers think that Kripke's modal arguments are decisive against any version of descriptivism, so I will therefore digress at least briefly to consider them.

Frege had argued that the definite description that a speaker associated with a proper name provided the "sense", in his technical meaning of that word, of the proper name for that speaker. I argued against Frege that the associated definite description couldn't provide a sense or definition of the proper name because that would have as consequence that, for example, it was an analytic necessity that

Aristotle was the most famous teacher of Alexander, if a speaker associated the definite description, "the most famous teacher of Alexander the Great", as the sense of the proper name "Aristotle". I argued that the associated cluster of Intentional contents that speakers associate with a proper name is related to the name by some much weaker relation than definition, and that this approach would preserve the virtues of Frege's account while avoiding its absurd consequences. Kripke begins his criticism of my account by distinguishing descriptivism construed as a theory of reference from descriptivism construed as a theory of meaning, and by claiming that if descriptivism is construed only as a theory of reference, a theory of how reference with proper names is secured, then it is unable to provide a Fregean solution to the puzzles concerning proper names in identity statements, existential statements, and statements concerning propositional attitudes. He doesn't say anything in support of this latter claim, and in any case it seems to me plainly false. I try to show that proper names don't have definitions in the usual sense but that reference is secured by an associated Intentional content. Thus, in Kripke's terms I am providing a theory of reference but not a theory of meaning. However, the distinction is not as sharp as he suggests, for the following reason: the Intentional content associated with a proper name can figure as part of the *propositional content* of a statement made by a speaker using that name, even though the speaker's associated Intentional content is not part of the *definition* of the name. And that is why one can provide a descriptivist theory of how proper names secure reference (and hence give a theory of reference and not a theory of meaning for proper names) while at the same time showing that the methods by which proper names secure reference explain how the meaning of utterances made using those names contains descriptive content (and hence give an account of names which has consequences for the meanings of propositions containing those names). For example, on the descriptivist account a speaker can believe that Hesperus shines near the horizon while not believing that Phosphorus shines

near the horizon, even though Hesperus and Phosphorus are identical. A speaker can consistently believe this if he associates independent Intentional contents with each name, even though in neither case does the Intentional content provide a definition of the name. The cluster theory, so-called, is able to account for such puzzles while at the same time advancing the theory as an account of how reference is secured and not as an account of meaning in the strict and narrow Fregean sense.

Indeed the account I am providing suggests the direction for a solution to Kripke's "puzzle about belief".[26] Here is the puzzle: Suppose a bilingual speaker, not knowing that "Londres" and "London" name the same city, sincerely asserts in French "Londres est jolie" and yet also sincerely asserts in English "London is not pretty". Does he or does he not believe that London is pretty? The first step in solving the puzzle is to note that because the speaker associates different Intentional contents with "Londres" and "London" the contribution that each word makes to the proposition in the man's head is different and therefore he believes two propositions which, though they cannot both be true (because they refer to the same object and attribute inconsistent properties to it), are not contradictories. The case is analogous to the Hesperus-Phosphorus example.[27]

The main modal argument used against my account is the rigid designator argument. In its crudest versions the argument goes as follows:

(1) Proper names are rigid designators.
(2) Definite descriptions are not rigid designators; and, by parity of reasoning, Intentional contents are not rigid designators.

Therefore:

(3) Proper names are not equivalent in meaning or sense or functioning to definite descriptions or Intentional contents of any sort.

Even if we grant the first premise for the sake of the discussion, it seems to me the argument fails for two reasons. First, some definite descriptions are indeed rigid designators. Indeed, any definite description that expresses identity conditions for the object, that is, any description which specifies features which determine the identity of the object will be a rigid designator. Any description expressing properties necessary and sufficient for, for example, being identical with Aristotle, will be a rigid designator. Indeed, it was this feature that I was trying to get at in my earliest discussion of proper names when I said the question of the rule for using a name must be connected to the question of the *identity* of the object.[28] But second, and more important for this discussion, any definite description at all can be treated as a rigid designator by indexing it to the actual world. I can, by simple fiat, decide to use the expression "The inventor of bifocals" in such a way that it refers to the actual person who invented bifocals and continues to refer to that very person in any possible world, even in a possible world in which he did not invent bifocals.[29] Such a use of the definite description will always take wide scope or will be in a sense scopeless in the way that is characteristic of proper names. Since any definite description whatever can be made into a rigid designator, it does not show that the functioning of proper names differs from the function of definite descriptions to show that proper names are always (or almost always) rigid designators and definite descriptions are in general not rigid designators.

VII. HOW DO PROPER NAMES WORK?

I said at the beginning that the answer to this question ought to be fairly easy, and I think it is provided that we keep certain principles in mind. The facts we seek to explain are: Names are used to refer to objects. In general, the contribution that a name makes to the truth conditions of statements is simply that it is used to refer to an object. But there are some statements where the contribution of the name is not, or is not solely, that it is used to refer to an object: in identity statements, in existential statements, and in statements about Intentional states. Furthermore, a name is used to refer to the same object in different possible

worlds where it has different properties from those it has in the actual world.

The principles we need to keep in mind when we explain these facts are:

1. In order that a name should ever come to be used to refer to an object in the first place there must be some independent representation of the object. This may be by way of perception, memory, definite description, etc., but there must be enough Intentional content to identify which object the name is attached to.

2. Once the connection between name and object has been set up, speakers who have mastered the Background practice of using names may make use of the fact that the connection between name and object has been set up, without knowing anything more about the object. Provided they don't have any Intentional content wildly inconsistent with the facts about the object, their only Intentional content might be that they are using the name to refer to what others are using it to refer to, but such cases are parasitic on the nonparasitic forms of identification of the object.

3. All reference is in virtue of Intentional content (broadly construed), whether the reference is by way of names, descriptions, indexicals, tags, labels, pictures, or whatever. The object is referred to only if it fits or satisfies some condition or set of conditions expressed by or associated with the device that is used to refer to it. In the limiting case these conditions may be simple Background capacities for recognition, as, for example, in the case we considered in Chapter 2 where the only Intentional content that a man had associated with the name was simply his capacity to recognize the bearer, or they may be parasitic Intentional contents of the sort described in principle 2. Principles 1 and 2 are simply applications of principle 3.

4. What counts as an object and hence as a possible target for naming and referring is always determined relative to a system of representation. Given that we have a system rich enough to individuate objects (e.g., rich enough to count one horse, a second horse, a third horse . . .), and to identify and reidentify objects (e.g., rich enough to determine

what must be the case if that is to be the *same horse* as the one we saw yesterday), we can then attach names to objects in such a way as to preserve the attachment of the same names to the same objects, even in counterfactual situations where the Intentional content associated with the name is no longer satisfied by the object. Principles 1, 2, and 3 only have application in a representational system which satisfies principle 4.

I believe these principles explain the facts we mentioned above. The whole purpose of having the institution of proper names is to enable us to refer to objects, but since there will be some Intentional content associated with a name, this Intentional content can figure as part of the propositional content of a statement made using a name in identity statements, in existential statements, and in statements about Intentional states, even though the normal and primary function is not to express Intentional content but just to refer to objects, and even though the associated Intentional content is not part of the definition of the name. And the explanation of the fact that names can be introduced by and used with an Intentional content which is not a rigid designator, and still the name can be used as a rigid designator, is simply that we have a notion of the identity of an object which is separable from those particular Intentional contents which are used to identify the object. Thus, for example, we have a notion of *the same man* which is independent of such descriptions as the author of the *Odyssey*. We can then use the name "Homer" to refer to the man who was the actual author of the *Odyssey* even in possible worlds where Homer did not write the *Odyssey*.

Part of the appearance that there is something especially problematic about these rather simple explanations is that there is a family of different sorts of cases in which these principles operate. First, the central cases. The most important and extensive use of names for each of us is of people, places, etc., with which we are in daily, or at least frequent, personal contact. Baptism apart, one originally learns these names from other people, but, once learned, the name is associated with such a rich collection of Intentional contents in the Net-

work that one does not depend on other people to determine which object one is referring to. Think, for example, of the names of your close friends and family members, of the town where you live or the streets in your neighborhood. Here there is no question of any chain of communication. Examples of such names for me would be "Berkeley, California" or "Alan Code".

Second, there are names which have prominent uses, where the uses are not based on acquaintance with the object. The Intentional content associated with these names is for the most part derived from other people, but it is rich enough to qualify as *knowledge about* the object. Examples for me would be such names as "Japan" or "Charles de Gaulle". In such cases, the Intentional content is rich enough so that it sets very strong constraints on the sort of things that could be referred to by my uses of the names. For example, regardless of the chain of communication, it couldn't turn out that by "de Gaulle" I am referring to a Florentine tapestry, or by "Japan" I am referring to a butterfly.

Third, there are uses of names where one is almost totally dependent on other people's prior usage to secure reference. It is these cases that I have described as parasitic, for in these cases the speaker does not have enough Intentional content to qualify as knowledge about the object. The object may not even be generally referred to by the name that he has acquired for it. For me such a name would be "Plotinus". Even in these cases the limited Intentional content places some constraints on the type of object named. In my use, Plotinus couldn't have turned out to be a prime number.

NOTES

1. See John R. Searle, "Referential and Attributive," in *Expression and Meaning* (Cambridge: Cambridge University Press, 1979), pp. 137–61.
2. In what follows in this chapter I will use "Intentional content" broadly so as to include relevant elements of the Network and Background.
3. Keith Donnellan recognizes the inappropriateness of the label for his views. Cf. "Speaking of Nothing," *The Philosophical Review*, 83 (January 1974), pp. 3–32; reprinted in S. P.

Schwartz, ed., *Naming, Necessity and Natural Kinds* (Ithaca and London: Cornell University Press, 1977), pp. 216–44.

4. In, e.g., *Speech Arts* (Cambridge: Cambridge University Press, 1969), p. 90.

5. The term, I believe, was first used by H. P. Grice in "Vacuous Names," in Davidson and Hintikka, eds., *Words and Objections* (Dordrecht: Reidel, 1969), pp. 118–45.

6. Saul Kripke, "Naming and Necessity," in G. Harman and D. Davidson, eds., *Semantics of Natural Language* (Dordrecht: Reidel, 1972), p. 300.

7. Kripke, *op. cit.* p. 302.

8. M. Devitt, *Designation* (Chicago: University of Chicago Press, 1981), esp. chapter 2, pp. 25–64.

9. Kripke, *op. cit.*, p. 300.

10. Donnellan, *op. cit.*, p. 229.

11. Gareth Evans, "The Causal Theory of Names," *Proceedings of the Aristotelian Society,* suppl. vol. 47, pp. 187–208; reprinted in Schwartz, ed., *op. cit.*, pp. 192–215. [Reprinted in this volume.]

12. David Kaplan, "Bob and Carol and Ted and Alice," in K. J. Hintikka et al., eds., *Approaches to Natural Language* (Dordrecht and Boston: Reidel, 1973), pp. 490–518.

13. For reasons we will shortly investigate, this description is parasitic on other speakers, but it is nonetheless sufficient to identify about whom we are talking.

14. I am indebted to Jim Stone for discussion of this point.

15. In Schwartz, ed., *op. cit.*, p. 232.

16. Evans, *op. cit.*, gives several examples of this sort.

17. It does not, of course, set up a definition, for reasons I gave in "Proper Names," *Mind,* 67 (1958), pp. 166–73. [Reprinted in this volume.]

18. *Op. cit.*

19. *Op. cit.*, pp. 170–171.

20. Kripke, *op. cit.*, pp. 283–84.

21. Donnellan, *op. cit.*, pp. 229–30.

22. "Referential and Attributive," in *Expression and Meaning*, p. 148.

23. Keither Donnellan, "Proper Names and Identifying Descriptions," *Synthese,* 21 (1970), pp. 335–58.

24. Ibid., pp. 347ff.

25. Hilary Putnam, "The Meaning of 'Meaning'," in *Philosophical Papers,* vol. 2, *Mind, Language and Reality* (Cambridge: Cambridge University Press, 1975), pp. 215–71.

26. Saul Kripke, "A Puzzle about Belief," in A. Margalit, ed., *Meaning and Use* (Dordrecht: Reidel, 1976), pp. 239–83.

27. Kripke considers the approach I suggest but rejects it on what I believe are inadequate grounds. He thinks that the same puzzle could arise if the speaker associated the same "identifying properties" with each name without knowing that they were the same. The speaker thinks, for example, in English "London is in England", and in French "Londres est en Angleterre", without knowing that England is Angleterre. But once again if we look at the total Intentional content we suppose is in the man's head in order to imagine him saying "Londres est jolie" and simultaneously "London is not pretty", we must suppose that he has different Intentional contents associated with "London" and "Londres". At the very least we must suppose that he thinks they are two *different cities* and that, by itself, has all sorts of ramifications in his network: e.g., he thinks "is identical with Londres" to be false of the town he refers to as "London", while true of that town he refers to as "Londres"; he thinks London and Londres have different locations on the surface of the earth, different inhabitants, etc. The moral as usual is: to resolve the puzzle don't just look at the sentences he utters, look at the total Intentional content in the man's head.

28. In *Mind* (1958), *op. cit.*

29. A similar point is made by D. Kaplan with his notion of "Dthat" ('Dthat', in P. Cole, ed., *Syntax and Semantics,* vol. 9 (New York: 1978) [reprinted in this volume], and by A. Plantinga with his notion of an "Alpha transform," in 'The Boethian Compromise', *American Philosophical Quarterly,* 15, (April 1978), pp. 129–38.

SUGGESTED FURTHER READING

Altham, J. E. J., The Causal Theory of Names, *The Aristotelian Society Supplementary Volume* 47 (1973), 209–225.

Bilgrami, Akeel, Realism without Internalism: A Critique of Searle on Intentionality, *Journal of Philosophy* 86 (1989), 57–72.

Donnellan, Keith, Speaking of Nothing, *The Philosophical Review* 83 (1974), 3–32.

Donnellan, Keith, Proper Names and Identifying Descriptions, in *Semantics of Natural Languages,* ed. Donald Davidson and Gilbert Harman (New York: Humanities Press, Inc., 1972), pp. 356–379.

Donnellan, Keith, Speaker Reference, Descriptions and Anaphora, in *Syntax and Semantics,* vol. 9, ed. Peter Cole (New York: Academic Press, 1978), pp. 47–68.

Donnellan, Keith, The Contingent A Priori and Rigid Designators, in *Contemporary Perspectives in the Philosophy of Language,* ed. Peter French, Theodore Uehling, Jr., and Howard Wettstein (Minneapolis: University of Minnesota Press, 1979), pp. 45–60.

Evans, Gareth, *The Varieties of Reference* (Oxford: Clarendon Press, 1982).

Devitt, Michael, *Designation* (New York: Columbia University Press, 1980).

Kaplan, David, The Logic of Demonstratives, in *Contemporary Perspectives in the Philosophy of Language,* ed. Peter A. French, Theodore Uehling, Jr., and Howard Wettstein (Minneapolis: University of Minnesota Press, 1979), pp. 401–410.

Kraut, Richard, Indiscernibility and Ontology, *Synthese* 44 (1980), 113–35.

Linsky, Leonard, *Names and Descriptions* (Chicago: University of Chicago Press, 1977).

Mill, John Stuart, *A System of Logic,* Book I, chapters 1 and 2.

Putnam, Hilary, Is Semantics Possible? in *Language, Belief, and Metaphysics,* ed. H. E. Kiefer and M. K. Munitz (Albany: State University of New York Press, 1970), pp. 50–63.

Russell, The Philosophy of Logical Atomism, in *Logic and Knowledge,* ed. Robert C. Marsh (London: George Allen and Unwin, 1956), pp. 177–281.

V

PROPOSITIONAL ATTITUDES

Almost everyone, before they investigate the problem carefully, will agree that most sentences or statements refer to the situation they describe. "The cat is on the mat" seems to refer to the situation or state of affairs in which a cat is on a mat. It is natural to think that the sentence would refer to such a situation even if it occurs in a longer sentence. For example, the sentence "It is raining and the cat is on the mat" seems to refer in part to the situation in which a cat is on the mat.

So, why shouldn't "The cat is on the mat" refer to the very same situation in sentences like, "John believed that the cat is on the mat" and "Mary sees the cat is on the mat"? The issue is complicated because there are situations in which people are reluctant to draw the consequences one would expect them to draw when a sentence follows a phrase like "believes" or "sees." For consider this sequence of propositions:

> John believes that the cat is on the mat.
>
> The cat is Tabby.
>
> John believes that Tabby is on the mat.

Suppose that the first two propositions are true. Further suppose that John does not know that "Tabby" is the name of the cat or that Tabby is the cat. Then he would very likely deny that Tabby is on the mat if he were asked about the matter. And this is good evidence that he does not believe that Tabby is on the mat. If this is correct, then it seems that the first two propositions may be true and the third false. This is good, though not decisive, evidence that the first two propositions do not entail the third, and one plausible explanation for why the entailment does not hold is that in the first sentence "the cat is on the mat" refers to something other than the situation of a cat being on the mat. More particularly, "the cat" in "the cat is on the mat" does not refer to Tabby the cat even though the cat is Tabby.

The same kind of argument could be constructed for a great number of verbs such as "think," "know," "doubt," "see," and "hear," which Bertrand Russell called "propositional attitude verbs" because they seem to express some attitude that a person might take with respect to a proposition. Thus, the proposition that the cat is on the mat might be thought, known, or doubted. (Although it is not obvious that one sees or hears propositions, verbs like "see" and "hear" are included by extension because they seem to have the same logic as the others.)

W. V. Quine in "Quantifiers and Propositional Attitudes" explores the differences between sentences like "Ralph believes that someone is a spy" and "There is someone whom Ralph believes is a spy." The latter sentence seems to entail that a person exists who is the object of Ralph's belief. The former does not: it might be true even if Ralph is benighted and there is no one who exists that he believes to be a spy.

Donald Davidson in "Saying That" is concerned with another problem involving "that" clauses: what do they mean or refer to? It is natural to think that "Jocasta" in the sentence "Oedipus does not believe that Jocasta is his mother" refers to Jocasta. This becomes dubious, however, once one considers the apparent consequences of that view. For example, since Jocasta is his mother, "Jocasta" and "his mother" refer to the same person and hence "Jocasta" should be replaceable in "Oedipus does not believe that Jocasta is his mother." But, if the replacement is made, the result is the sentence "Oedipus does not believe that his mother is his mother." And this sentence seems false.

Davidson's solution to this problem is to treat the word "that" in "that"-clauses in the same way it is treated in a sentence like "That is a dog," namely, as a demonstrative pronoun. What "that" in "that"-clauses demonstrates or points out is the clause or sentence immediately following it. That is, the clause or sentence following the word "that" in "that"-clauses should be understood as displayed, not used. Thus, "Oedipus does not believe that Jocasta is his mother" should be construed as "Oedipus does not believe that:

Jocasta is his mother."

David Kaplan's "Quantifying In" develops the problems raised by both Quine and Davidson. After explicating Quine's and Frege's views, Kaplan gives a kind of Fregean treatment of "that"-clauses. "Jocasta" does not have its normal reference to Jocasta; but it need not be construed as referring to its normal sense either. Rather, "Jocasta" can be held tentatively to refer to itself, namely, the name "Jocasta." Kaplan also draws valuable distinctions between the descriptive content of a name, its genetic content (i.e., the origin of the name) and introduces the notion of a vivid name.

Jon Barwise and John Perry in "Semantic Innocence and Uncompromising Situations" sketch a semantic theory that is motivated or inspired by the belief that the clauses that complete expressions like "John believes that" or "Mary sees that" refer to the very same things that they do when they occur alone. That is, they refer to situations, which are complexes of objects and properties. "The cat is on the mat" refers to the complex of a cat, a mat, and the relation of being on something. They call this "pre-Fregean semantic innocence," because they think that Frege corrupted philosophers by his argument to establish that the reference of a sentence or statement is its truth-value. Their own view is summarized in these two paragraphs:

Our approach is to treat the sentence as embedded and the semantics as innocent, and to deny that the problems that Frege and others have seen with this approach amount to much of anything.

For example, we take a statement of the form *X sees S* to embed a statement *S*, and to be true just in case *X* sees a scene (a specific kind of situation) that belongs to some type in the interpretation of *S*. We take *X believes that S,* in its most central and ordinary uses, to say that *X* has a certain complex relational property built of the objects and properties that are constituents of the proposition that *S*. In both cases, the parts of the embedded statement have their usual interpretations in the whole. What can be wrong with this innocent approach?

Jon Barwise and John Perry reject or at least have serious reservations about the line of reasoning that was described at the beginning of this section. Contrary to the standard view, they hold that "John sees the cat on the mat" and "Tabby is the cat on the mat" at least sometimes entail "John sees Tabby on the mat." If the entailment does not seem to hold, it is only because one is confusing what a speaker says by uttering the sentence with what the speaker sometimes conversationally implies. In certain situations, to say "John sees that Tabby is on the mat" conversationally implies that John knows that the cat's name is "Tabby" or that John would assent to the question, "Is Tabby on the mat?" But not in all situations. Suppose that Tabby is owned by Adam and Beth, both of whom are concerned that Tabby be watched at all times; that they ask John, who has never seen or heard of Tabby before, to watch the cat ("John, please watch the cat"). Since they never mention Tabby's name to him, he does not know it. If sometime later Adam asks Beth whether John is watching the cat, Beth may truly, precisely and nonmisleadingly say, "John sees that Tabby is on the mat" without implying or leading Adam to think that John could answer affirmatively to the question, "Is Tabby on the mat?"

Analogous explanations could be given for other situations like these in which substitution of co-referential expressions appear to break down in the so-called opaque contexts of verbs like "believe," "think," "see," and "hear."

Barwise and Perry would agree with most of this, I believe. Their one reservation is that substitution does break down when a singular term is used attributively rather than referentially, as Donnellan describes the distinction in "Reference and Definite Descriptions." Nonetheless, one should question whether this is a proper distinction or whether it does not also arise from confusing the reference achieved through the use of singular terms with conversationally implied reference. (See my *Communication and Reference,* pp. 169–179.)

Most philosophers accept Church's argument or something like it. Church's argument uses the following four statements:

(5)   Sir Walter Scott is the author of *Waverley.*

(6)   Sir Walter Scott is the man who wrote the twenty-nine *Waverley* novels altogether.

(7)   The number, such that Sir Walter Scott is the man that wrote that many *Waverley* novels altogether, is twenty-nine.

(8)   The number of counties in Utah is twenty-nine.

Church claims that since each statement clearly entails the next, (5) entails (8); and since (5) and (8) have nothing in common except their truth-value, if reference is preserved when one statement entails another, the reference of a statement must be its truth-value.

In order to make their own view plausible, it is important for Barwise and Perry to explain why Church's argument is not cogent. They accomplish this with great insight. Roughly, their general claim is that Church's argument takes two incompatible views or perspectives of reference. According to the first perspective, all that is important in referring is the object that eventually gets picked out by an expression, no matter how complex the expression is and no matter what descriptive words are used in order to help pick it out. From this perspective, it is not important whether Cicero is picked out by "the Roman orator" or "the statesman that condemned Catiline." Thus, statements (5)–(8) all have the same logical form: a=b. And each can be rendered in effect as follows:

(5') Scott is Scott.

(6') Scott is Scott.

(7') 29 is 29.

(8') 29 is 29.

The number twenty-nine of course is not mentioned in (5') because it is not designated in any way in (5). But it is not mentioned in (6') either because its designation in (6) is not relevant to the ultimate reference of the terms flanking the "is" of identity. What is identified in (5) is Scott with Scott; and the same holds for (6). The fact that "twenty-nine" occurs in (6) is not significant since its occurence is subordinate to and not essential to the ultimate reference to Scott. In (7) and (8), the situation is reversed. Scott is not mentioned in (8') because he is not designated in any way in (8). And he is not mentioned in (7') either because his designation is not relevant to the ultimate reference of the terms flanking the "is" of identity. What is identified in (7) is the number twenty-nine with the number twenty-nine. The name "Sir Walter Scott" occurs in (7) only in a subordinate clause and is not essential to the reference to the number at issue. But, seen from this perspective, the inference from (6') to (7') and hence from (6) to (7) is invalid.

The second way of looking at reference is to count those concepts and references that are intermediate to the ultimate reference as significant to the form of the statement. From this perspective, it is important how one refers to an object, just as it is important to ordinary people whether they are referred to as "that lovable darling" or "that S.O.B." Roughly, from this second perspective, the meaning of the sentence is important to the way it refers. From this perspective, the inference from (6) to (7) is acceptable because they mean roughly the same thing. But from this same perspective, the inference from (5) to (6) is illicit because they do not have the same meaning, as is the inference from (7) to (8) for the same reason. It is only by conflating the two different perspectives on referring that Church's argument looks plausible.

Barwise and Perry think that Donnellan's distinction between the attributive and referential uses of definite descriptions captures these two perspectives of "reference" in a very broad sense. My own view is that both perspectives ought to be part of a complete theory of reference and that Donnellan in effect strips the referential use of all descriptive content but keeps it in the attributive use.

In addition to its other merits, Barwise and Perry's article is important because it promises to formalize certain informal claims made by J. L. Austin and criticizes certain formal treatments of Frege, Quine, and Davidson.

Quantifiers
and Propositional Attitudes   27

W. V. QUINE

I

The incorrectness of rendering 'Ctesias is hunting unicorns' in the fashion:

$(\exists x)$ (x is a unicorn · Ctesias is hunting x)

is conveniently attested by the nonexistence of unicorns, but is not due simply to that zoological lacuna. It would be equally incorrect to render "Ernest is hunting lions" as:

(1) $(\exists x)$ (x is a lion · Ernest is hunting x),

where Ernest is a sportsman in Africa. The force of (1) is rather that there is some individual lion (or several) which Ernest is hunting; stray circus property, for example.

The contrast recurs in "I want a sloop." The version:

(2) $(\exists x)$ (x is a sloop · I want x)

is suitable insofar only as there may be said to be a certain sloop that I want. If what I seek is mere relief from slooplessness, then (2) gives the wrong idea.

The contrast is that between what may be called the *relational* sense of lion-hunting or sloop-wanting, viz., (1)–(2), and the likelier or *notional* sense. Appreciation of the difference is evinced in Latin and Romance languages by a distinction of mood in subordinate clauses; thus "*Procuro un perro que habla*" has the relational sense:

$(\exists x)$ (x is a dog · x talks · I seek x)

as against the notional "*Procuro un perro que hable*":

I strive that $(\exists x)$ (x is a dog · x talks · I find x).

Pending considerations to the contrary in later pages, we may represent the contrast strikingly in terms of permutations of components. Thus (1) and (2) may be expanded (with some violence to both logic and grammar) as follows:

(3) $(\exists x)$ (x is a lion · Ernest strives that Ernest finds x),

(4) $(\exists x)$ (x is a sloop · I wish that I have x),

whereas "Ernest is hunting lions" and "I want a sloop" in their notional senses may be rendered rather thus:

(5)   Ernest strives that $(\exists x)$ (x is a lion · Ernest finds x),

(6)   I wish that $(\exists x)$ (x is a sloop · I have x).

The contrasting versions (3)–(6) have been wrought by so paraphrasing "hunt" and "want" as to uncover the locutions "strive that" and "wish that," expressive of what Russell has called *propositional attitudes*. Now of all examples of propositional attitudes, the first and foremost is *belief*; and, true to form, this example can be used to point up the contrast between relational and notional

From *The Journal of Philosophy*, volume 53 (1956), pp. 177–187. It is reprinted here minus fifteen lines.

senses still better than (3)–(6) do. Consider the relational and notional senses of believing in spies:

(7) $(\exists x)$ (Ralph believes that x is a spy),
(8) Ralph believes that $(\exists x)$ (x is a spy).

Both may perhaps be ambiguously phrased as "Ralph believes that someone is a spy," but they may be unambiguously phrased respectively as "There is someone whom Ralph believes to be a spy" and "Ralph believes there are spies." The difference is vast; indeed, if Ralph is like most of us, (8) is true and (7) false.

In moving over to propositional attitudes, as we did in (3)–(6), we gain not only the graphic structural contrast between (3)–(4) and (5)–(6) but also a certain generality. For we can now multiply examples of striving and wishing, unrelated to hunting and wanting. Thus we get the relational and notional senses of wishing for a president:

(9) $(\exists x)$ (Witold wishes that x is president),
(10) Witold wishes that $(\exists x)$ (x is president).

According to (9), Witold has his candidate; according to (10) he merely wishes the appropriate form of government were in force. Also we open other propositional attitudes to similar consideration—as witness (7)–(8).

However, the suggested formulations of the relational senses—viz., (3), (4), (7), and (9)—all involve quantifying into a propositional-attitude idiom from outside. This is a dubious business, as may be seen from the following example.

There is a certain man in a brown hat whom Ralph has glimpsed several times under questionable circumstances on which we need not enter here; suffice it to say that Ralph suspects he is a spy. Also there is a gray-haired man, vaguely known to Ralph as rather a pillar of the community, whom Ralph is not aware of having seen except once at the beach. Now Ralph does not know it, but the men are one and the same. Can we say of this *man* (Bernard J. Ortcutt, to give him a name) that Ralph believes him to be a spy? If so, we find ourselves accepting a conjunction of the type:

(11) w sincerely denies '. . .' $\cdot$ w believes that . . .

as true, with one and the same sentence in both blanks. For, Ralph is ready enough to say, in all sincerity, "Bernard J. Ortcutt is no spy." If, on the other hand, with a view to disallowing situations of the type (11), we rule simultaneously that

(12) Ralph believes that the man in the brown hat is a spy,
(13) Ralph does not believe that the man seen at the beach is a spy,

then we cease to affirm any relationship between Ralph and any man at all. Both of the component "that"-clauses are indeed about the man Ortcutt; but the "that" must be viewed in (12) and (13) as sealing those clauses off, thereby rendering (12) and (13) compatible because not, as wholes, about Ortcutt at all. It then becomes improper to quantify as in (7); "believes that" becomes, in a word, referentially opaque.[1]

No question arises over (8); it exhibits only a quantification *within* the "believes that" context, not a quantification *into* it. What goes by the board, when we rule (12) and (13) both true, is just (7). Yet we are scarcely prepared to sacrifice the relational construction "There is someone whom Ralph believes to be a spy," which (7) as against (8) was supposed to reproduce.

The obvious next move is to try to make the best of our dilemma by distinguishing two senses of belief: *belief₁*, which disallows (11), and *belief₂*, which tolerates (11) but makes sense of (7). For belief₁, accordingly, we sustain (12)–(13) and ban (7) as nonsense. For belief₂, on the other hand, we sustain (7); and for *this* sense of belief we must reject (13) and acquiesce in the conclusion that Ralph believes₂ that the man at the beach is a spy even though he *also* believes₂ (and believes₁) that the man at the beach is not a spy.

II

But there is a more suggestive treatment. Beginning with a single sense of belief, viz., belief₁ above, let us think of this at first as a relation between the believer and a certain *intension,* named by the "that"-clause. Intentions are creatures of darkness, and I shall rejoice with the reader when they are exorcised, but first I want to make certain points with the help of them. Now intensions named thus by "that"-clauses, without free variables, I shall speak of more specifically as intensions of degree 0, or propositions. In addition I shall (for the moment) recognize intensions of degree 1, or attributes. These are to be named by prefixing a variable to a sentence in which it occurs free; thus $z(z$ is a spy) is spyhood. Similarly we may specify intensions of higher degrees by prefixing multiple variables.

Now just as we have recognized a dyadic relation of belief between a believer and a proposition, thus:

(14)   Ralph believes that Ortcutt is a spy,

so we may recognize also a triadic relation of belief among a believer, an object, and an attribute, thus:

(15)   Ralph believes $z(z$ is a spy) of Ortcutt.

For reasons which will appear, this is to be viewed not as dyadic belief between Ralph and the proposition *that* Ortcutt has $z(z$ is a spy), but rather as an irreducibly triadic relation among the three things Ralph, $z(z$ is a spy), and Ortcutt. Similarly there is tetradic belief:

(16)   Tom believes $yz(y$ denounced $z)$ of Cicero and Catiline,

and so on.

Now we can clap on a hard and fast rule against quantifying into propositional-attitude idioms; but we give it the form now of a rule against quantifying into names of intensions. Thus, though (7) as it stands becomes unallowable, we can meet the needs which prompted (7) by quantifying rather into the triadic belief construction, thus:

(17) $(\exists x)$ (Ralph believes $z(z$ is a spy) of x).

Here then, in place of (7), is our new way of saying that there is someone whom Ralph believes to be a spy.

Belief$_1$ was belief so construed that a proposition might be believed when an object was specified in it in one way, and yet not believed when the same object was specified in another way; witness (12)–(13). Hereafter we can adhere uniformly to this narrow sense of belief, both for the dyadic case and for triadic and higher; in each case the term which names the intension (whether proposition or attribute or intension of higher degree) is to be looked on as referentially opaque.

The situation (11) is thus excluded. At the same time the effect of belief$_2$ can be gained, simply by ascending from dyadic to triadic belief as in (15). For (15) does relate the men Ralph and Ortcutt precisely as belief$_2$ was intended to do. (15) does remain true of Ortcutt under any designation; and hence the legitimacy of (17).

Similarly, whereas from:

Tom believes that Cicero denounced Catiline

we cannot conclude:

Tom believes that Tully denounced Catiline,

on the other hand we can conclude from:

Tom believes $y(y$ denounced Catiline) of Cicero

that

Tom believes $y(y$ denounced Catiline) of Tully,

and also that

(18) $(\exists x)$(Tom believes $y(y$ denounced Catiline) of x).

From (16), similarly, we may infer that

(19) $(\exists w)(\exists x)$(Tom believes $zy(y$ denounced $z)$ of w and x).

Such quantifications as:

$(\exists x)$ (Tom believes that x denounced Catiline),
$(\exists x)$ (Tom believes $y(y$ denounced $x)$ of Cicero)

still count as nonsense, along with (7); but such legitimate purposes as these might have served are served by (17)–(19) and the like. Our names of intensions, and these only, are what count as referentially opaque.

Let us sum up our findings concerning the seven numbered statements about Ralph. (7) is now counted as nonsense, (8) as true, (12)–

(13) as true, (14) as false, and (15) and (17) as true. Another that is true is:

(20)   Ralph believes that the man seen at the beach is not a spy,

which of course must not be confused with (13).

The kind of exportation which leads from (14) to (15) should doubtless be viewed in general as implicative. Under the terms of our illustrative story, (14) happens to be false; but (20) is true, and it leads by exportation to:

(21)   Ralph believes $z(z$ is not a spy) of the man seen at the beach.

The man at the beach, hence Ortcutt, does not receive reference in (20), because of referential opacity; but he does in (21), so we may conclude from (21) that

(22)   Ralph believes $z(z$ is not a spy) of Ortcutt.

Thus (15) and (22) both count as true. This is not, however, to charge Ralph with contradictory beliefs. Such a charge might reasonably be read into:

(23)   Ralph believes $z(z$ is a spy·z is not a spy) of Ortcutt,

but this merely goes to show that it is undesirable to look upon (15) and (22) as implying (23).

It hardly needs be said that the barbarous usage illustrated in (15)–(19) and (21)–(23) is not urged as a practical reform. It is put forward by way of straightening out a theoretical difficulty, which, summed up, was as follows: Belief contexts are referentially opaque; therefore it is prima facie meaningless to quantify into them; how then to provide for those indispensable relational statements of belief, like "There is someone whom Ralph believes to be a spy"?

Let it not be supposed that the theory which we have been examining is just a matter of allowing unbridled quantification into belief contexts after all, with a legalistic change of notation. On the contrary, the crucial choice recurs at each point: quantify if you will, but pay the price of accepting near-contraries like (15) and (22) at each point at which you choose to quantify. In other words: distinguish as you please between referential and non-referential positions, but keep track, so as to treat each kind appropriately. The notation of intensions, of degree one and higher, is in effect a device for inking in a boundary between referential and nonreferential occurrences of terms.

III

Striving and wishing, like believing, are propositional attitudes and referentially opaque. (3) and (4) are objectionable in the same way as (7), and our recent treatment of belief can be repeated for these propositional attitudes. Thus, just as (7) gave way to (17), so (3) and (4) give way to:

(24) $(\exists x)$ $(x$ is a lion · Ernest strives z(Ernest finds z) of x),

(25) $(\exists x)$ $(x$ is a sloop · I wish z(I have z) of x),

a certain breach of idiom being allowed for the sake of analogy in the case of "strives."

These examples came from a study of hunting and wanting. Observing in (3)–(4) the quantification into opaque contexts, then, we might have retreated to (1)–(2) and forborne to paraphrase them into terms of striving and wishing. For (1)–(2) were quite straightforward renderings of lion-hunting and sloopwanting in their relational senses; it was only the notional senses that really needed the breakdown into terms of striving and wishing, (5)–(6).

Actually, though, it would be myopic to leave the relational senses of lion-hunting and sloop-wanting at the unanalyzed stage (1)–(2). For, whether or not we choose to put these over into terms of wishing and striving, there are other relational cases of wishing and striving which require our consideration anyway—as witness (9). The untenable formulations (3)–(4) may indeed be either corrected as (24)–(25) or condensed back into (1)–(2); on the other hand we have no choice but to correct the untenable (9) on the pattern of (24)–(25), viz., as:

$(\exists x)$ (Witold wishes $y(y$ is president) of x).

The untenable versions (3)–(4) and (9) all had to do with wishing and striving in the relational sense. We see in contrast that (5)–(6) and (10), on the notional side of wishing and striving, are innocent of any illicit quantification into opaque contexts from outside. But now notice that exactly the same trouble begins also on the notional side, as soon as we try to say not just that Ernest hunts lions and I want to sloop, but that *someone* hunts lions or wants a sloop. This move carries us, ostensibly, from (5)–(6) to:

(26) ($\exists w$) (w strives that ($\exists x$) (x is a lion $\cdot$ w finds x)),

(27) ($\exists w$) (w wishes that ($\exists x$) (x is a sloop $\cdot$ w has x)),

and these do quantify unallowably into opaque contexts.

We know how, with help of the attribute apparatus, to put (26)–(27) in order; the pattern, indeed, is substantially before us in (24)–(25). Admissible versions are:

($\exists w$) (w strives $y(\exists x)$ (x is a lion $\cdot$ y finds x) of w),

($\exists w$) (w wishes $y(\exists x)$ (x is a sloop $\cdot$ y has x) of w),

or briefly:

(28) ($\exists w$) (w strives $y(y$ finds a lion) of w),

(29) ($\exists w$) (w wishes $y(y$ has a sloop) of w).

Such quantification of the subject of the propositional attitude can of course occur in belief as well; and, if the subject is mentioned in the belief itself, the above pattern is the one to use. Thus "Someone believes he is Napoleon" must be rendered·

($\exists w$) (w believes $y(y =$ Napoleon) of w).

For concreteness I have been discussing belief primarily, and two other propositional attitudes secondarily: striving and wishing. The treatment is, we see, closely parallel for the three; and it will pretty evidently carry over to other propositional attitudes as well—e.g., hope, fear, surprise. In all cases my concern is, of course, with a special technical aspect of the propositional attitudes: the problem of quantifying in.

IV

There are good reasons for being discontent with an analysis that leaves us with propositions, attributes, and the rest of the intensions. Intensions are less economical than extensions (truth values, classes, relations), in that they are more narrowly individuated. The principle of their individuation, moreover, is obscure.

Commonly logical equivalence is adopted as the principle of individuation of intensions. More explicitly: if S and S' are any two sentences with n ($\geqq 0$) free variables, the same in each, then the respective intensions which we name by putting the n variables (or "that," if $n = 0$) before S and S' shall be one and the same intension if and only if S and S' are logically equivalent. But the relevant concept of logical equivalence raises serious questions in turn.[2] The intensions are at best a pretty obscure lot.

Yet it is evident enough that we cannot, in the foregoing treatment of propositional attitudes, drop the intensions in favor of the corresponding extensions. Thus, to take a trivial example, consider "w is hunting unicorns." On the analogy of (28), it becomes:

w strives $y(y$ finds a unicorn) of w.

Correspondingly for the hunting of griffins. Hence, if anyone w is to hunt unicorns without hunting griffins, the attributes

$y(y$ finds a unicorn),

$y(y$ finds a griffin)

must be distinct. But the corresponding classes are identical, being empty. So it is indeed the attributes, and not the classes, that were needed in our formulation. The same moral could be drawn, though less briefly, without appeal to empty cases.

But there is a way of dodging the intensions which merits serious consideration. Instead of speaking of intensions we can speak of sentences, naming these by quotation. Instead of:

w believes that . . .

we may say:

w believes-true '. . .'.

Instead of:

(30)   *w* believes *y*(. . . *y* . . .) of *x*

we may say:

(31)   *w* believes '. . . y . . .' satisfied by *x*.

The words "believes satisfied by" here, like "believes of" before, would be viewed as an irreducibly triadic predicate. A similar shift can be made in the case of the other propositional attitudes, of course, and in the tetradic and higher cases.

This semantical reformulation is not, of course, intended to suggest that the subject of the propositional attitude speaks the language of the quotation, or any language. We may treat a mouse's fear of a cat as his fearing true a certain English sentence. This is unnatural without being therefore wrong. It is a little like describing a prehistoric ocean current as clockwise.

How, where, and on what grounds to draw a boundary between those who believe or wish or strive that *p*, and those who do not quite believe or wish or strive that *p*, is undeniably a vague and obscure affair. However, if anyone does approve of speaking of belief of a proposition at all and of speaking of a proposition in turn as meant by a sentence, then certainly he cannot object to our semantical reformulation "*w* believes-true *S*" on any special grounds of obscurity; for "*w* believes-true *S*" is explicitly definable in *his* terms as "*w* believes the proposition meant by *S*." Similarly for the semantical reformulation (31) of (30); similarly for the tetradic and higher cases; and similarly for wishing, striving, and other propositional attitudes.

Our semantical versions do involve a relativity to language, however, which must be made explicit. When we say that *w* believes-true *S*, we need to be able to say what language the sentence *S* is thought of as belonging to; not because *w* needs to understand *S*, but because *S* might by coincidence exist (as a linguistic form) with very different meanings in two languages.[3] Strictly, there-

fore, we should think of the dyadic "believes-true *S*" as expanded to a triadic "*w* believes-true *S* in *L*"; and correspondingly for (31) and its suite.

As noted two paragraphs back, the semantical form of expression:

(32)   *w* believes-true ' . . . ' in *L*

can be explained in intensional terms, for persons who favor them, as:

(33)   *w* believes the proposition meant by ' . . . '
         in *L*,

thus leaving no cause for protest on the score of relative clarity. Protest may still be heard, however, on a different score: (32) and (33), though equivalent to each other, are not strictly equivalent to the "*w* believes that . . ." which is our real concern. For, it is argued, in order to infer (33) we need not only the information about *w* which "*w* believes that . . ." provides, but also some extraneous information about the language *L*. Church[4] brings the point out by appeal to translations, substantially as follows. The respective statements:

> *w* believes that there are unicorns,
>
> *w* believes the proposition meant by "There are unicorns" in English

go into German as:

(34)   *w* glaubt, dass es Einhörne gibt,

(35)   *w* glaubt diejenige Aussage, die „There are
         unicorns" auf Englisch bedeutet,

and clearly (34) does not provide enough information to enable a German ignorant of English to infer (35).

The same reasoning can be used to show that "There are unicorns" is not strictly or analytically equivalent to:

> "There are unicorns" is true in English.

Nor, indeed, was Tarski's truth paradigm intended to assert analytic equivalence. Similarly, then, for (32) in relation to "*w* believes that . . ."; a systematic agreement in truth value can be claimed, and no more. This limitation will prove of little moment to persons who share my skepticism about analyticity.

What I find more disturbing about the semantical versions, such as (32), is the need of dragging in the language concept at all. What is a language? What degree of fixity is supposed? When do we have one language and not two? The propositional attitudes are dim affairs to begin with, and it is a pity to have to add obscurity to obscurity by bringing in language variables too. Only let it not be supposed that any clarity is gained by restituting the intensions.

NOTES

1. See *From a Logical Point of View* (Cambridge, Mass.: Harvard University Press: 1953, 2d ed., 1961), pp. 142–159; also "Three grades of modal involvement," Essay 13 of *Ways of Paradox* (Random House, New York: 1966).
2. See my "Two dogmas of empiricism," in *From a Logical Point of View*, op. cit.; also "Carnap and logical truth," Essay 10 in *Ways of Paradox*, op. cit.
3. This point is made by Church, "On Carnap's analysis of statements of assertion and belief," *Analysis*, 10 (1950), 97–99.
4. Ibid., with an acknowledgment to Langford.

On Saying That　　28

DONALD DAVIDSON

"I wish I had said that," said Oscar Wilde in applauding one of Whistler's witticisms. Whistler, who took a dim view of Wilde's originality, retorted, "You will, Oscar; you will." The function of this tale (from Holbrook Jackson's *The Eighteen-Nineties*) is to remind us that an expression like "Whistler said that" may on occasion serve as a grammatically complete sentence. Here we have, I suggest, the key to a correct analysis of indirect discourse, an analysis that opens a lead to an analysis of psychological sentences generally (sentences about propositional attitudes, so-called), and even, though this looks beyond anything to be discussed in the present paper, a clue to what distinguishes psychological concepts from others.

But let us begin with sentences usually deemed more representative of *oratio obliqua*, for example "Galileo said that the earth moves" or "Scott said that Venus is an inferior planet." One trouble with such sentence is that we do not know their logical form. And to admit this is to admit that, whatever else we may know about them, we do not know the first thing. If we accept surface grammar as guide to logical form, we will see "Galileo said that the earth moves" as containing the sentence "the earth moves," and this sentence in turn as consisting of the singular term 'the earth', and a predicate, 'moves'. But if 'the earth' is, in this context, a singular term, it can be replaced, so far as the truth or falsity of the containing sentence is concerned, by any other singular term that refers to the same thing.

The notorious apparent invalidity of this rule can only be apparent, for the rule no more than spells out what is involved in the idea of a (logically) singular term. Only two lines of explanation, then, are open: we are wrong about the logical form, or we are wrong about the reference of the singular term.

What seems anomalous behavior on the part of what seem singular terms dramatizes the problem of giving an orderly account of indirect discourse, but the problem is more pervasive. For what touches singular terms touches what they touch, and that is everything: quantifiers, variables, predicates, connectives. Singular terms refer, or pretend to refer, to the entities over which the variables of quantification range, and it is these entities of which the predicates are or are not true. So it should not surprise us that if we can make trouble for the sentence "Scott said that Venus is an inferior planet" by substituting "the Evening Star" for "Venus," we can equally make trouble by substituting "is identical with Venus or with Mercury" for the coextensive "is an inferior planet." The difficulties with indirect discourse cannot be solved simply by abolishing singular terms.

What should we ask of an adequate account

From *Synthese*, volume 19 (1968–69), pp. 130–146.

of the logical form of a sentence? Above all, I would say, such an account must lead us to see the semantic character of the sentence—its truth or falsity—as owed to how it is composed, by a finite number of applications of some of a finite number of devices that suffice for the language as a whole, out of elements drawn from a finite stock (the vocabulary) that suffices for the language as a whole. To see a sentence in this light is to see it in the light of a theory for its language, a theory that gives the form of every sentence in that language. A way to provide such a theory is by recursively characterizing a truth-predicate, along the lines suggested by Tarski, that satisfies this criterion: the theory entails, for each sentence *s* (when described in a standardized way), that the truth-predicate holds of *s* if and only if _____.— Here the blank is to be filled by a sentence in the metalanguage that is true if and only if *s* is true in the object language.[1] If we accept Tarski's further requirement that no undefined semantical notions be used in characterizing a truth-predicate, then no theory can satisfy the criterion except by describing every sentence in terms of a semantically significant structure.

A satisfactory theory of meaning for a language must, then, give an explicit account of the truth-conditions of every sentence, and this can be done by giving a theory that satisfies Tarski's criteria; nothing less should count as showing how the meaning of every sentence depends on its structure.[2] Two closely linked considerations support the idea that the structure with which a sentence is endowed by a theory of truth in Tarski's style deserves to be called the logical form of the sentence. By giving such a theory, we demonstrate in a persuasive way that the language, though it consists in an indefinitely large number of sentences, can be comprehended by a creature with finite powers. A theory of truth may be said to supply an effective explanation of the semantic role of each significant expression in any of its appearances. Armed with the theory, we can always answer the question, "What are these familiar words doing here?" by saying how

they contribute to the truth-conditions of the sentence. (This is not to assign a 'meaning', much less a reference, to every significant expression.)

The study of the logical form of sentences is often seen in the light of another interest, that of expediting inference. From this point of view, to give the logical form of a sentence is to catalogue the features relevant to its place on the logical scene, the features that determine what sentences it is a logical consequence of, and what sentences it has as logical consequences. A canonical notation graphically encodes the relevant information, making theory of inference simple, and practice mechanical where possible.

Obviously the two approaches to logical form cannot yield wholly independent results, for logical consequence is defined in terms of truth. To say a second sentence is a logical consequence of a first is to say, roughly, that the second is true if the first is no matter how the nonlogical constants are interpreted. Since what we count as a logical constant can vary independently of the set of truths, it is clear that the two versions of logical form, though related, need not be identical. The relation, in brief, seems this. Any theory of truth that satisfies Tarski's criteria must take account of all truth-affecting iterative devices in the language. In the familiar languages for which we know how to define truth the basic iterative devices are reducible to the sentential connectives, the apparatus of quantification, and the description operator if it is primitive. Where one sentence is a logical consequence of another on the basis of quantificational structure alone, a theory of truth will therefore entail that if the first sentence is true, the second is. There is no point, then, in not including the expressions that determine quantificational structure among the logical constants, for when we have characterized truth, on which any account of logical consequence depends, we have already committed ourselves to all that calling such expressions logical constants could commit us. Adding to this list of logical constants will increase the inventory of logical truths and consequence-relations beyond anything a truth definition demands, and will therefore yield richer versions of logical form. For the purposes of the present paper, however, we can cleave to the most austere interpretations of logical consequence and logical form, those that are forced on us when we give a theory of truth.

We are now in a position to explain our aporia over indirect discourse: what happens is that the relation between truth and consequence just sketched appears to break down. In a sentence like "Galileo said that the earth moves" the eye and mind perceive familiar structure in the words "the earth moves." And structure there must be if we are to have a theory of truth at all, for an infinite number of sentences (all sentences in the indicative, apart from some trouble over tense) yield sense when plugged into the slot in "Galileo said that _____." So if we are to give conditions of truth for all the sentences so generated, we cannot do it sentence by sentence, but only by discovering an articulate structure that permits us to treat each sentence as composed of a finite number of devices that make a stated contribution to its truth conditions. As soon as we assign familiar structure, however, we must allow the consequences of that assignment to flow, and these, as we know, are in the case of indirect discourse consequences we refuse to buy. In a way, the case is even stranger than that. Not only do familiar consequences fail to flow from what looks to be familiar structure, but our common sense of language feels little assurance in any inferences based on the words that follow the 'said that' of indirect discourse (there are exceptions).

So the paradox is this: on the one hand, intuition suggests, and theory demands, that we discover semantically significant structure in the 'content-sentences' of indirect discourse (as I shall call sentences following "said that"). On the other hand, the failure of consequence-relations invites us to treat contained sentences as semantically inert. Yet logical form and consequence relations cannot be divorced in this way.

One proposal at this point is to view the words that succeed the "said that" as operating within concealed quotation marks, their sole function being to help refer to a sentence, and their semantic inertness explained by the usual account of quotation. One drawback of this proposal is that no usual account of quotation is acceptable, even by the minimal standards we have set for an account of logical form. For according to most stories, quotations are singular terms without significant semantic structure, and since there must be an infinite number of different quotations, no language that contains them can have a recursively defined truth-predicate. This may be taken to show that the received accounts of quotation must be mistaken—I think it does. But then we can hardly pretend that we have solved the problem of indirect discourse by appeal to quotation.[3]

Perhaps it is not hard to invent a theory of quotation that will serve: the following theory is all but explicit in Quine. Simply view quotations as abbreviations for what you get if you follow these instructions: to the right of the first letter that has opening quotation-marks on its left write right-hand quotation marks, then the sign for concatenation, and then left-hand quotation marks, in that order; do this after each letter (treating punctuation signs as letters) until you reach the terminating right-hand quotation marks. What you now have is a complex singular term that gives what Tarski calls a structural description of an expression. There is a modest addition to vocabulary: names of letters and of punctuation signs, and the sign for concatenation. There is a corresponding addition to ontology: letters and punctuation signs. And finally, if we carry out the application to sentences in indirect discourse, there will be the logical consequences that the new structure dictates. For two examples, each of the following will be entailed by "Galileo said that the earth moves":

($\exists x$) (Galileo said that "the ea"⌢x⌢"th moves")

and (with the premise "r=the 18th letter in the alphabet"):

Galileo said that "the ea"⌢the 18th letter in the alphabet⌢"th moves"

(I have clung to abbreviations as far as possible.) These inferences are not meant in themselves as criticism of the theory of quotation; they merely illuminate it.

Quine discusses the quotational approach to indirect discourse in *Word and Object*,[4] and abandons it for what seems, to me, a wrong reason. Not that there is not a good reason; but to appreciate *it* is to be next door to a solution, as I shall try to show.

Let us follow Quine through the steps that lead him to reject the quotational approach. The version of the theory he considers is not the one once proposed by Carnap to the effect that "said that" is a two-place predicate true of ordered pairs of people and sentences.[5] The trouble with this idea is not that it forces us to assimilate indirect discourse to direct, for it does not. The "said that" of indirect discourse, like the "said" of direct, may relate persons and sentences, but be a different relation; the former, unlike the latter, may be true of a person, and a sentence he never spoke in a language he never knew. The trouble lies rather in the chance that the same sentence may have different meanings in different languages—not too long a chance either if we count ideolects as languages.

Not that it is impossible to find words (as written or sounded) which express quite different ideas in different languages. For example, "Empedokles liebt" do fairly well as a German or an English sentence, in one case saying what Empedokles loved and in the other telling us what he did from the top of Etna. We can scoff at the notion that if we analyze "Galileo said that the earth moves" as asserting a relation between Galileo and the sentence "The earth moves" we must assume Galileo spoke English, but we cannot afford to scoff at the assumption that on this analysis the words of the content-sentence are to be understood as an English sentence.[6]

Calling the relativity to English an assumption may be misleading; perhaps the reference to English is explicit, as follows. A long-winded version of our favorite sentence might be "Galileo spoke a sentence that meant in his language what 'The earth moves' means in English." Since in this version it takes everything save "Galileo" and "The earth moves"

to do the work of "said that," we must count the reference to English as explicit in the "said that." To see how odd this is, however, it is only necessary to reflect that the English words "said that," with their built-in reference to English, would no longer translate (by even the roughest extensional standards) the French "dit que."

We can shift the difficulty over translation away from the "said that" or "dit que" by taking these expressions as three-place predicates relating a speaker, a sentence, and a language, the reference to a language to be supplied either by our (in practice nearly infallible) knowledge of the language to which the quoted material is to be taken as belonging, or by a demonstrative reference to the language of the entire sentence. Each of these suggestions has its own appeal, but neither leads to an analysis that will pass the translation test. To take the demonstrative proposal, translation into French will carry "said that" into "dit que," the demonstrative reference will automatically, and hence perhaps still within the bounds of strict translation, shift from English to French. But when we translate the final singular term, which names an English sentence, we produce a palpably false result.

These exercises help bring out important features of the quotational approach. But now it is time to remark that there would be an anomaly in a position, like the one under consideration, that abjured reference to propositions in favor of reference to languages. For languages (as Quine remarks in a similar context in *Word and Object*) are at least as badly individuated, and for much the same reasons, as propositions. Indeed, an obvious proposal linking them is this: languages are identical when identical sentences express identical propositions. We see, then, that quotational theories of indirect discourse, those we have discussed anyway, cannot claim an advantage over theories that frankly introduce intensional entities from the start; so let us briefly consider theories of the latter sort.

It might be thought, and perhaps often is, that if we are willing to welcome intensional entities without stint—properties, propositions, individual concepts, and whatever else—then no further difficulties stand in the way of giving an account of the logical form of sentences in *oratio obliqua*. This is not so. Neither the languages Frege suggests as models for natural languages nor the languages described by Church are amenable to theory in the sense of a truth-definition meeting Tarski's standards.[7] What stands in the way in Frege's case is that every referring expression has an infinite number of entities it may refer to, depending on the context, and there is no rule that gives the reference in more complex contexts on the basis of the reference in simpler ones. In Church's languages, there is an infinite number of primitive expressions; this directly blocks the possibility of recursively characterizing a truth-predicate satisfying Tarski's requirements.

Things might be patched up by following a leading idea of Carnap's *Meaning and Necessity* and limiting the semantic levels to two: extensions and (first-level) intensions.[8] An attractive strategy might then be to turn Frege, thus simplified, upside down by letting each singular term refer to its sense or intension, and providing a reality function (similar to Church's delta function) to map intensions onto extensions. Under such treatment our sample sentence would emerge like this: "The reality of Galileo said that the earth moves." Here we must suppose that "the earth" names an individual concept which the function referred to by "moves" maps onto the proposition that the earth moves; the function referred to by "said that" in turn maps Galileo and the proposition that the earth moves onto a truth value. Finally, the name, "Galileo" refers to an individual concept which is mapped, by the function referred to by "the reality of" onto Galileo. With ingenuity, this theory can accommodate quantifiers that bind variables both inside and outside contexts created by verbs like "said" and "believes." There is no special problem about defining truth for such a language: everything is on the up and up, purely extensional save in ontology. This seems to be a theory that might do all we have asked. Apart from nominalistic qualms, why not accept it?

My reasons against this course are essentially Quine's. Finding right words of my own to communicate another's saying is a problem in translation (216–217). The words I use in the particular case may be viewed as products of my total theory (however vague and subject to correction) of what the originating speaker means by anything he says: such a theory is indistinguishable from a characterization of a truth-predicate, with his language as object language and mine as metalanguage. The crucial point is that within limits there is no choosing between alternative theories which differ in assigning clearly nonsynonymous sentences of mine as translations of his same utterance. This is Quine's thesis of the indeterminacy of translation (218–221).[9] An example will help bring out the fact that the thesis applies not only to translation between speakers of conspicuously different languages, but also to cases nearer home.

Let someone say (and now discourse is direct), "There's a hippopotamus in the refrigerator"; am I necessarily right in reporting him as having said that there is a hippopotamus in the refrigerator? Perhaps; but under questioning he goes on, "It's roundish, has a wrinkled skin, does not mind being touched. It has a pleasant taste, at least the juice, and it costs a dime. I squeeze two or three for breakfast." After some finite amount of such talk we slip over the line where it is plausible or even possible to say correctly that he said there was a hippopotamus in the refrigerator, for it becomes clear he means something else by at least some of his words than I do. The simplest hypothesis so far is that my word "hippopotamus" no longer translates his word "hippopotamus"; my word "orange" might do better. But in any case, long before we reach the point where homophonic translation must be abandoned, charity invites departures. Hesitation over whether to translate a saying of another by one or another of various nonsynonymous sentences of mine does not necessarily reflect a lack of information: it is just that beyond a point there is no deciding, even in principle, between the view that the Other has used words as we do but has more or less weird beliefs, and the view that we have translated him wrong. Torn between the need to make sense of a speaker's words and the need to make sense of the pattern of his beliefs, the best we can do is choose a theory of translation that maximizes agreement. Surely there is no future in supposing that in earnestly uttering the words "There's a hippopotamus in the refrigerator" the Other has disagreed with us about what can be in the refrigerator if we also must then find ourselves disagreeing with him about the size, shape, color, manufacturer, horsepower, and wheelbase of hippopotami.

None of this shows there is no such thing as correct reporting, through indirect discourse, what another said. All that the indeterminacy shows is that if there is one way of getting it right there are other ways that differ substantially in that nonsynonymous sentences are used after "said that." And this is enough to justify our feeling that there is something bogus about the sharpness questions of meaning must in principle have if meanings are entities.

The lesson was implicit in a discussion started some years ago by Benson Mates. Mates claimed that the sentence "Nobody doubts that whoever believes that the seventh consulate of Marius lasted less than a fortnight believes that the seventh consulate of Marius lasted less than a fortnight" is true and yet might well become false if the last word were replaced by the (supposed synonymous) words "period of fourteen days," and that this could happen no matter what standards of synonymy we adopt short of the question-begging "substitutable everywhere *salva veritate*."[10] Church and Sellars responded by saying the difficulty could be resolved by firmly distinguishing between substitutions based on the speaker's use of language and substitutions colored by the use attributed to others.[11] But this is a solution only if we think there is some way of telling, in what another says, what is owed to the meanings he gives his words and what to his beliefs about the world. According to Quine, this is a distinction not there to be drawn.

The detour has been lengthy; I return now to Quine's discussion of the quotational approach in *Word and Object*. As reported above, Quine rejects relativization to a language on the grounds that the principle of the individuation of languages is obscure, and the issue when languages are identical irrelevant to indirect discourse (214). He now suggests that instead of interpreting the content-sentence of indirect discourse as occurring in a language, we interpret it as voiced by a speaker at a time. The speaker and time relative to which the content-sentence needs understanding is, of course, the speaker of that sentence, who is thereby indirectly attributing a saying to another. So now "Galileo said that the earth moves" comes to mean something like "Galileo spoke a sentence that in his mouth meant what 'The earth moves' now means in mine." Quine makes no objection to this proposal because he thinks he has something simpler and at least as good in reserve. But in my opinion the present proposal deserves more serious consideration, for I think it is nearly right, while Quine's preferred alternatives are seriously defective.

The first of these alternatives is Scheffler's inscriptional theory.[12] Scheffler suggests that sentences in indirect discourse relate a speaker and an utterance: the role of the content-sentence is to help convey what sort of utterance it was. What we get this way is, "Galileo spoke a that-the-earth-moves utterance." The predicate "x is-a-that-the-earth-moves-utterance" has, so far as theory of truth and of inference are concerned, the form of an unstructured one-place predicate. Quine does not put the matter quite this way, and he may resist my appropriation of the terms 'logical form' and 'structure' for purposes that exclude application to Scheffler's predicate. Quine calls the predicate "compound" and describes it as composed of an operator and a sentence (214, 215). These are matters of terminology; the substance, about which there may be no disagreement, is that on Scheffler's theory sentences in *oratio obliqua* have no logical relations that depend on structure in the predicate, and a truth-predicate that applies to all such sentences cannot be characterized in Tarski's style. The reason is plain: there is an infinite number of predicates with the syntax "*x* is-a-_____-utterance" each of which is, in the eyes of semantic theory, unrelated to the rest.

Quine has seized one horn of the dilemma. Since attributing semantic structure to content-sentences in indirect discourse apparently forces us to endorse logical relations we do not want, Quine gives up the structure. The result is that another desideratum of theory is neglected, that truth be defined.

Consistent with his policy of renouncing structure that supports no inferences worth their keep, Quine contemplates one further step; he says, ". . . a final alternative that I find as appealing as any is simply to dispense with the objects of the propositional attitudes" (216). Where Scheffler still saw "said that" as a two-place predicate relating speakers and utterances, though welding content-sentences into one-piece one-place predicates true of utterances, Quine now envisions content-sentence and "said that" welded directly to form the one-place predicate "*x* said-that-the-earth-moves," true of persons. Of course some inferences inherent in Scheffler's scheme now fall away: we can no longer infer "Galileo said something" from our sample sentence, nor can we infer from it and "Someone denied that the earth moves" the sentence "Someone denied what Galileo said." Yet as Quine reminds us, inferences like these may fail on Scheffler's analysis too when the analysis is extended along the obvious line to belief and other propositional attitudes, since needed utterances may fail to materialize (215). The advantages of Scheffler's theory over Quine's "final alternative" are therefore few and uncertain; this is why Quine concludes that the view that invites the fewest inferences is "as appealing as any."

This way of eliminating unwanted inferences unfortunately abolishes most of the structure needed by the theory of truth. So it is worth returning for another look at the earlier proposal to analyze indirect discourse in terms of a predicate relating an originating speaker, a sentence, and the present speaker of the sentence in indirect discourse. For that proposal did not cut off any of the simple entailments we have been discussing, and it

alone of recent suggestions promised, when coupled with a workable theory of quotation, to yield to standard semantic methods. But there is a subtle flaw.

We tried to bring out the flavor of the analysis to which we have returned by rewording our favorite sentence as "Galileo uttered a sentence that meant in his mouth what 'The earth moves' means now in mine." We should not think ill of this verbose version of "Galileo said that the earth moves" because of apparent reference to a meaning ("what 'The earth moves' means"); this expression is not treated as a singular term in the theory. We are indeed asked to make sense of a judgment of synonymy between utterances, but not as the foundation of a theory of language, merely as an unanalyzed part of the content of the familiar idiom of indirect discourse. The idea that underlies our awkward paraphrase is that of *samesaying*: when I say that Galileo said that the earth moves, I represent Galileo and myself as samesayers.

And now the flaw is this. If I merely *say* we are samesayers, Galileo and I, I have yet to *make* us so; and how am I to do this? Obviously, by saying what he said; not by using his words (necessarily), but by using words the same in import here and now as his then and there. Yet this is just what, on the theory, I cannot do. For the theory brings the content-sentence into the act sealed in quotation marks, and on any standard theory of quotation, this means the content-sentence is mentioned and not used. In uttering the words "The earth moves" I do not, according to this account, say anything remotely like what Galileo is claimed to have said; I do not, in fact, say anything. My words in the frame provided by "Galileo said that _____" merely help refer to a sentence. There will be no missing the point if we expand quotation in the style we recently considered. Any intimation that Galileo and I are samesayers vanishes in this version:

Galileo said that 'T' ⌢ 'h' ⌢ 'e' ⌢ '' ⌢ 'e' ⌢ 'a' ⌢ 'r' ⌢ 't' ⌢ 'h' ⌢ '' ⌢ 'm' ⌢ 'o' ⌢ 'v' ⌢ 'e' ⌢ 's'

We seem to have been taken in by a notational accident, a way of referring to expressions that when abbreviated produces framed pictures of the very words referred to. The difficulty is odd; let's see if we can circumvent it. Imagine an altered case. Galileo utters his words "Eppur si muove," I utter my words, "The earth moves." There is no problem yet in recognizing that we are samesayers; an utterance of mine matches an utterance of his in purport. I am not now using my words to help refer to a sentence; I speak for myself, and my words refer in their usual way to the earth and to its movement. If Galileo's utterance "Eppur si muove" made us samesayers, then some utterance or other of Galileo's made us samesayers. The form "($\exists x$) (Galileo's utterance x and my utterance y make us samesayers)" is thus a way of attributing any saying I please to Galileo provided I find a way of replacing 'y' by a word or phrase that refers to an appropriate utterance of mine. And surely there is a way I can do this: I need only produce the required utterance and replace 'y' by a reference to it. Here goes:

> The earth moves.
> ($\exists x$) (Galileo's utterance x and my last utterance make us samesayers).

Definitional abbreviation is all that is needed to bring this little skit down to:

> The earth moves.
> Galileo said that.

Here the "that" is a demonstrative singular term referring to an utterance (not a sentence).

This form has a small drawback in that it leaves the hearer up in the air about the purpose served by saying "The earth moves" until the act has been performed. As if, say, I were first to tell a story and then add, "That's how it was once upon a time." There's some fun to be had this way, and in any case no amount of telling what the illocutionary force of our utterances is is going to insure that they have that force. But in the present case nothing stands in the way of reversing the order of things, thus:

> Galileo said that.
> The earth moves.

Perhaps it is now safe to allow a tiny orthographic change, a change without semantic significance, but suggesting to the eye the relation of introducer and introduced: we may suppress the stop after "that" and the consequent capitalization:

> Galileo said that the earth moves.

Perhaps it should come as no surprise to learn that the form of psychological sentences in English apparently evolved through about the stages our ruminations have just carried us. According to the *Oxford English Dictionary*,

The use of *that* is generally held to have arisen out of the demonstrative pronoun pointing to the clause which it introduces. Cf. (1) He once lived here: we all know *that*; (2) *That* (now *this*) we all know: he once lived here; (3) We all know *that* (or *this*): he once lived here; (4) We all know *that* he once lived here . . . [13]

The proposal then is this: sentences in indirect discourse, as it happens, wear their logical form on their sleeves (except for one small point). They consist of an expression referring to a speaker, the two-place predicate "said," and a demonstrative referring to an utterance. Period. What follows gives the content of the subject's saying, but has no logical or semantic connection with the original attribution of a saying. This last point is no doubt the novel one, and upon it everything depends: from a semantic point of view the content-sentence in indirect discourse is not contained in the sentence whose truth counts.

We would do better, in coping with this subject, to talk of inscriptions and utterances and speech acts, and avoid reference to sentences.[14] For what an utterance of "Galileo said that" does is announce a further utterance. Like any utterance, this first may be serious or silly, assertive or playful; but if it is true, it must be followed by an utterance synonymous with some other. The second utterance, the introduced act, may also be true or false, done in the mode of assertion or of play. But if it is as announced, it must serve at least the purpose of conveying the content of what someone said. The role of the introducing utterance is not unfamiliar: we do the same with words like "This is a joke," "This is an order," "He commanded that," "Now hear this." Such expressions might be called performatives, for they are used to usher in performances on the part of the speaker. A certain interesting reflexive effect sets in when performatives occur in the first-person present tense, for then the speaker utters words which if true are made so exclusively by the content and mode of the performance that follows, and the mode of this performance may well be in part determined by that same performative introduction. Here is an example that will also provide the occasion for a final comment on indirect discourse.

"Jones asserted that Entebbe is equatorial" would, if we parallel the analysis of indirect discourse, come to mean something like, "An utterance of Jones' in the assertive mode had the content of this utterance of mine. Entebbe is equatorial." The analysis does not founder because the modes of utterance of the two speakers may differ; all that the truth of the performative requires is that my second utterance, in whatever mode (assertive or not) match in content an assertive utterance of Jones. Whether such an asymmetry is appropriate in indirect discourse depends on how much of assertion we read into saying. Now suppose I try: "I assert that Entebbe is equatorial." Of course by saying this I may not assert anything; mood of words cannot guarantee mode of utterance. But if my utterance of the performative is true, then I do say something in the assertive mode that has the content of my second utterance—I do, that is, assert that Entebbe is equatorial. If I do assert it, an element in my success is no doubt my utterance of the performative, which announces an assertion; thus performatives tend to be self-fulfilling. Perhaps it is this feature of performatives that has misled some philosophers into thinking that performatives, or their utterances, are neither true nor false.

On the analysis of indirect discourse just proposed, standard problems seem to find a just solution. The appearance of failure of the laws of extensional substitution is explained as due to our mistaking what are really two sentences for one: we make substitutions in one sentence, but it is the other (the utterance of) which changes in truth. Since an utterance of "Galileo said that" and any utterance following it are semantically independent, there is no reason to predict, on grounds of form alone, any *particular* effect on the truth of the first from a change in the second. On the other hand, if the second utterance had been different in any way at all, the first utterance *might* have had a different truth value, for the reference of the "that" would have changed.

The paradox, that sentences (utterances) in *oratio obliqua* do not have the logical consequences they should if truth is to be defined, is resolved. What follows the verb "said" has only the structure of a singular term, usually the demonstrative "that." Assuming the "that" refers, we can infer that Galileo said something from "Galileo said that"; but this is welcome. The familiar words coming in the train of the performative of indirect discourse do, on my account, have structure, but it is familiar structure and poses no problem for theory of truth not there before indirect discourse was the theme.

Since Frege, philosophers have become hardened to the idea that content-sentences in talk about propositional attitudes may strangely refer to such entities as intensions, propositions, sentences, utterances and inscriptions. What is strange is not the entities, which are all right in their place (if they have one), but the notion that ordinary words for planets, people, tables and hippopotami in indirect discourse may give up these pedestrian references for the exotica. If we could recover our pre-Fregean semantic innocence, I think it would seem to us plainly incredible that the words "The earth moves," uttered after the words "Galileo said that," mean anything different, or refer to anything else, than is their wont when they come in other environments. No doubt their role in *oratio obliqua* is in some sense special; but that is another story. Language is the instrument it is because the same expression, with semantic features (meaning) unchanged, can serve countless purposes. I have tried to show how our understanding of indirect discourse does not strain this basic insight.

ACKNOWLEDGMENTS

I am indebted to W. V. Quine and John Wallace for suggestions and criticisms. My research was in part supported by the National Science Foundation.

REFERENCES

1. Alfred Tarski, "The Concept of Truth in Formalized Languages," in *Logic, Semantics, Metamathematics* (Oxford: 1956), pp. 152–278. The criterion is roughly Tarski's Convention *T* that defines the concept of a truth-predicate.
2. The view that a characterization of a truth-predicate meeting Tarski's criteria is the core of a theory of meaning is defended in my "Truth and Meaning," [reprinted in this volume] *Synthese* 17 (1967) 304–323.
3. For documentation and details see my "Theories of Meaning and Learnable Languages," in *Logic, Methodology and Philosophy of Science, Proceedings of the 1964 International Congress,* ed. Yehoshua Bar-Hillel (Amsterdam: 1965), pp. 388–390.
4. *Word and Object* (Cambridge, Mass.: 1960) chapter VI. Hereafter numerals in parentheses refer to pages of this book.
5. R. Carnap, *The Logical Syntax of Language* (London: 1937), p. 248. The same was in effect proposed by P. T. Geach, *Mental Acts* (London: 1957).
6. The point is due to A. Church, "On Carnap's Analysis of Statements of Assertion and Belief," *Analysis* 10 (1950) 97–99.
7. G. Frege, "On Sense and Reference," [reprinted in this volume] in *Philosophical Writings,* ed. P. Geach and M. Black (Oxford: 1952) and A. Church, "A Formulation of the Logic of Sense and Denotation," in *Structure, Method,*

and Meaning: Essays in Honor of H. M. Sheffer ed. Henle, Kallen and Langer (New York: 1951).
8. R. Carnap, *Meaning and Necessity* (Chicago: 1947). The idea of an essentially Fregean approach limited to two semantic levels has also been suggested by Michael Dummett (in an unpublished manuscript). Neither of these proposals is in detail entirely satisfactory in the light of present concerns, for neither leads to a language for which a truth-predicate can be characterized.
9. My assimilation of a translation manual to a theory of truth is not in Quine. For more on this, see the article in reference 2.
10. B. Mates, "Synonymity," in *Meaning and Interpretation* (Berkeley: 1950), pp. 201–226. The example is Church's.
11. A. Church, "Intensional Isomorphism and Identity of Belief," *Philosophical Studies* 5 (1954) 65–73; W. Sellars, "Putnam on Synonymity and Belief," *Analysis* 15 (1955) 117–20.
12. I. Scheffler, "An Inscriptional Approach to Indirect Quotation," *Analysis* 14 (1954) 83–90.
13. J. A. H. Murray et al., eds., *The Oxford English Dictionary* (Oxford: 1933) vol. XI, p. 253. Cf. C. T. Onions, *An Advanced English Syntax* (New York: 1929), pp. 154–156. I first learned that "that" in such contexts evolved from an explicit demonstrative in J. Hintikka, *Knowledge and Belief* (Ithaca: 1962), p. 13. Hintikka remarks that a similar development has taken place in German and Finnish. I owe the reference to the *O.E.D.* to Eric Stiezel.
14. I assume that a theory of truth for a language containing demonstratives must strictly apply to utterances and not to sentences, or will treat truth as a relation between sentences, speakers, and times. The point is discussed in "Truth and Meaning," (see ref. 2) [p. 88, this volume].

Quantifying In[1]   29

DAVID KAPLAN

I

Expressions are used in a variety of ways. Two radically different ways in which the expression "nine" can occur are illustrated by the paradigms:

(1) Nine is greater than five,

(2) Canines are larger than felines.

Let us call the kind of occurrence illustrated in (1) a *vulgar* occurrence, and that in (2) an *accidental* occurrence (or, following Quine, an orthographic accident). For present purposes we need not try to define either of these notions; but presumably there are no serious logical or semantical problems connected with occurrences of either kind. The first denotes, is open to substitution and existential generalization, and contributes to the meaning of the sentence which contains it. To the second, all such concerns are inappropriate.

There are other occurrences of the word "nine," illustrated in

(3) "Nine is greater than five" is a truth of arithmetic,

(4) It is necessary that nine is greater than five,

(5) Hegel believed that nine is greater than five.

These diverge from the paradigm of vulgar occurrence (they fail the substitution test, the existential generalization test, and probably others as well), but they are not, at least to the untutored mind, clearly orthographic accidents either: for in them, the meaning of "nine" seems, somehow, relevant. Let us call them *intermediate occurrences* and their contexts *intermediate contexts*.

These intermediate occurrences have come in for considerable discussion lately. Two kinds of analyses which have been proposed can be conveniently characterized as: (a) assimilating the intermediate occurrences to the accidental occurrences, and (b) assimilating the intermediate occurrences to the vulgar occurrences.

The former view, that the intermediate occurrences are to be thought of like accidental ones, I identify with Quine. Such a charge is slightly inaccurate; I make it chiefly for the sake of dramatic impact. My evidence, carefully selected, is that he has proposed in a few places that quotation contexts, as in (3), be thought of as single words and that "believes that nine is greater than five" be thought of as a simple predicate. And that after introducing a dichotomous classification of occurrences of names into those which he terms 'purely referential' (our vulgar—his criterion is substitutivity) and those which he terms 'nonreferential' (our intermediate and accidental) he writes, "We are not unaccustomed to passing over occurrences that somehow 'do not count'—'mary' in 'summary', 'can' in 'canary'; and we can allow similarly for all

From *Synthese*, volume 19 (1968–69), pp. 178–214. © D. Reidel Publishing Co., Dordrecht, Holland.

370

non-referential occurrences of terms, once we know what to look out for." Further, his very terminology: "opaque" for a context in which names occur nonreferentially, seems to suggest an indissoluble whole, unarticulated by semantically relevant components.[2] But be that as it may, I shall put forward this analysis—the assimilation of intermediate occurrence to accidental ones—primarily in order to contrast its defeatist character with the sanguine view of Frege (and his followers) that we can assimilate the intermediate occurrences to vulgar ones.

II

The view that the occurrences of "nine" in (3), (4), and (5) are accidental may be elaborated, as Quine has done, by contrasting (3), (4), and (5) with:

(6) Nine is such that the result of writing it followed by 'is greater than five' is a theorem of Arithmetic,

(7) Nine is such that necessarily it is greater than five,

(8) Nine is such that Hegel believed it to be greater than five,

in which we put, or attempt to put, "nine" into purely referential position. Quine would still term the occurrences of "five" as nonreferential; thus, the "necessarily it is greater than five" in (7) might be thought of as an atomic predicate expressing some property of the number of baseball positions (assuming (7) to be true). And similarly for (6) and (8). I am not trying to say how we would "ordinarily" understand (6)–(8). I merely use these forms, in which the occurrence of "nine" does not stand within the so-called opaque construction, as a kind of canonical form to express what must be carefully explained, namely that here we attribute a property to a certain number, and that the correctness of this attribution is independent of the manner in which we refer to the number. Thus (6), (7), and (8) are to be understood in such a way that the result of replacing the occurrence of "nine" by any other expression denoting that number would not affect the truth value of the

sentence. This includes replacement by a variable, thus validating existential generalization. In these respects (6)–(8) do indeed resemble (1).

But (3)–(5), which are to be understood in the natural way, are such that the result of substituting "the number of planets" for the occurrences of "nine" would lead from truth to falsehood (didn't Hegel "prove" that the number of planets=5?). Thus, for Quine, these contexts are opaque, and the result of replacing the occurrences of "nine" by the variable "x" and prefixing "$\exists x$" would lead from truth to formulas of, at best, questionable import. In fact, Quine deems such quantification into an opaque context flatly "improper."[3] In these respects (3)–(5) resemble (2). Although the impropriety of substituting or quantifying on the occurrence of "nine" in (2) is gross compared with that involved in applying the corresponding operations to (3)–(5), the view I am here characterizing would make this difference a matter of degree rather than of kind.

I will not expatiate on the contrast between (3)–(5) and (6)–(8), since Quine and others have made familiarity with this contrast a part of the conventional wisdom of our philosophical times. But note that (6)–(8) are not introduced as defined forms whose nonlogical apparatus is simply that of (3)–(5), in the way in which

Exactly one thing is greater than five

can be defined in terms of the non-logical apparatus of (1). Instead (6)–(8) are introduced as new primitive forms.

Earlier I said that (3)–(5) should be understood in the natural way, whereas careful explanation was required for (6)–(8). But will careful explanation suffice? Will anything suffice? What we have done, or rather what we have sketched, is this: a certain skeletal language structure has been given, here using fragments of English, so of course an English reading is at once available, and then certain logical transformations have been pronounced valid. Predicate logic was conducted in this way before Gödel and Tarski, and modal logic was so conducted before Carnap and others began to supply semantical foundations. The earlier method, especially as applied to modal logic (we might call it the run-it-up-the-axiom-list-and-see-if-anyone-deduces-a-contradiction method), seems to me to have been stimulated more by a compulsive permutations-and-combinations mentality than by the true philosophical temperament.

Thus, it just is not enough to describe the form (6) and say that the predicate expresses a property of numbers so that both Leibniz' law, and existential generalization apply. What property of numbers is this? It makes no sense to talk of the result of writing a number. We can write numerals and various other names of numbers but such talk as (6), in the absence of a theory of standard names, is surely based on confusion of mention and use.[4] One is tempted to make the same remark about (7), but in this case an alternative explanation is possible in a metaphysical tradition connected with so-called "Aristotelian essentialism." It is claimed that among the properties of a thing, e.g. being greater than 5, and numbering the planets, some hold of it necessarily, others only contingently. Quine has ably expounded the inevitability of this view of (7).[5]

In contrast to (6) and (7), we can put a strong prima facie case for the sensicalness of (8) by way of illustrative examples which indicate important uses of the form exemplified in (8) as compared with that of the form exemplified in (5). Russell mentions, in a slightly different context, the man who remarked to an acquaintance "I thought that your yacht was longer than it is." The correct rendering here is clearly in the style of (8), viz:

The length of your yacht is such that I thought that your yacht was longer than that.

not in the style of (5);

I thought that your yacht was longer than the length of your yacht.

In "Quantifiers and Propositional Attitudes," Quine supports the use of (8) as against (5) by an ingenious use of existential quantification. He contrasts:

(9)   Ralph believes that someone is a spy,

in which the quantifier occurs within the opaque construction, as does the term in (5), with:

(10)   Someone is such that Ralph believes that he is a spy,

which is an existential generalization of a formula of the form (8). After pointing out that (9) may be rephrased as:

Ralph believes that there are spies,

Quine remarks, "The difference is vast; indeed, if Ralph is like most of us, [(9)] is true and [(10)] is false." In this connection recall that according to Quine's theory of referential opacity, (10) can not be obtained by existential generalization directly from a formula of the form (5) say,

Ralph believes that Ortcutt is a spy,

since the occurrence of the term to be generalized on is here assimilated to that of the orthographic accident and thus is not immediately open to such a move.

Let me sum up what I have called Quine's elaboration of the view that intermediate occurrences are to be assimilated to accidental ones. For those cases in which it is desired to make connections between what occurs within the opaque construction and what occurs without, a special new primitive form is introduced, parallel to the original, but containing one (or more than one) of the crucial terms in a purely referential position. Quine refers to the new form as expressing the *relational* sense of belief. The possibility of introducing such forms always exists and the style of their introduction seems uniform, but since they are primitive each such introduction must be supplied with an ad hoc justification (to the effect that the predicate or operator being introduced makes sense).

III

Let me turn now to the Fregean view that assimilates intermediate occurrences to vulgar ones. The brilliant simplicity of Frege's leading idea in the treatment of intermediate occurrences has often been obscured by a failure to separate that idea from various turgid details involved in carrying the program through in particular interesting cases. But theory must be served.

Frege's main idea, as I understand it, was just this. There are no *real* intermediate occurrences; the appearance of intermediacy created by apparent failures of substitutivity and the like is due to confusion about what is denoted by the given occurrence. Frege here calls our attention to an implicit assumption made in testing for substitutivity and the like. Namely, that a denoting expression must *always* have its usual denotation, and, a fortiori, that two expressions must have the same denotation in a given context if they usually (i.e. in most contexts) have the same denotation.

But we are all familiar with many counter-examples to the assumption that a name always has its usual denotation. Consider:

(11) Although F.D.R. ran for office many times, F.D.R. ran on television only once.

The natural analysis of (11) involves pointing out that the name "F.D.R." is ambiguous, and that in the second clause it denotes a television show rather than a man. Substitutions or any other logical operations based on the assumption that the name has here its usual denotation are pointless and demonstrate nothing. But transformations based on a *correct* analysis of the name's denotation *in this context* will reveal the occurrence to be vulgar. I call this the natural analysis, but it is of course possible for a fanatical mono-denotationalist to insist that his transformations have shown the context:

. . . ran on television only once

to be opaque, and so to conclude that the second occurrence of "F.D.R." in (11) is not purely referential. This view may be expressed moderately, resulting only in an insistence that (11) is improper unless the second clause is rewritten as:

the television show named "F.D.R." ran on television only once.

Often when there is a serious possibility of confusion, we conform to the practice (even if

not the theory) of the fanatical mono-denotationalist and do introduce a new word, add a subscript, or put the original in bold face, italics, or quotation marks. It is often good practice to continue to so mark the different uses of an expression, even when there is little possibility of confusion. Discovering and marking such ambiguities plays a considerable and useful role in philosophy (some, not I, would say it is the essence of philosophy), and much of what has proved most engaging and at the same time most fruitless in logical theory might have been avoided had the first 25 years of this century not seen a lapse from Frege's standards of mention and use. It would be unwary of us to suppose that we have now caught all such ambiguities. Thus, we should not leap to conclusions of opacity.

I indicated in the case of the fanatical mono-denotationalist how it is possible to trade a finding of opacity for one of ambiguity. Frege attempts his assimilation of intermediate occurrences to vulgar ones by indicating (some would say, postulating) ambiguities where others have seen only opacity. It is not denied that the ambiguities involved in the Fregean analysis are far more subtle than that noted in (11), but on his analysis the difference is seen as a matter of degree rather than of kind.

Frege referred to intermediate occurrences as *ungerade* (indirect, oblique). And the terminology is a natural one, for on his conception such an occurrence does not refer directly to its usual denotation but only, at best, indirectly by way of some intermediate *entity* such as a sense or an expression. I will return to this subject later. For now just notice that occurrences which Quine would call purely referential, Frege might call standardly referential; and those in contexts Quine would call referentially opaque, Frege might call nonstandardly referential, but in either case for Frege the occurrences are fully referential. So we require no special nonextensional logic, no restrictions on Leibniz' law, on existential generalization, etc., except those attendant upon consideration of a language containing ambiguous expressions. And even these can be avoided if we follow the practice of the fanatical mono-denotationalist and require linguistic reform so that distinct uses of expressions are marked by some distinction in the expressions themselves. This feature of a development of Frege's doctrine has been especially emphasized by Church.[6]

This then is Frege's treatment of intermediate contexts—obliquity indicates ambiguity. This doctrine accounts in a very natural way for the well-known logical peculiarities of intermediate contexts, such as the failure of substitutivity, existential generalization, etc.

IV

The difficulties in Frege's treatment appear in attempting to work out the details—details of the sort: exactly what *does* "nine" denote in (3)–(5)? Frege's treatment of oblique contexts is often described as one according to which expressions in such contexts denote their ordinary sense or meaning or intension (I here use these terms interchangeably). But this is a bad way of putting the matter for three reasons. (1) It is, I believe, historically inaccurate. It ignores Frege's remarks about quotation marks (see below) and other special contexts. (2) It conflates two separate principles: (a) expressions in oblique contexts don't have their ordinary denotation (which is true), and (b) expressions in oblique contexts denote their ordinary sense (which is not, in general, true). And (3) in focussing attention too rapidly on the special and separate problems of intensional logic, we lose sight of the beauty and power of Frege's general method of treating oblique contexts. We may thus lose the motivation that that general theory might provide for an attack on the problems of the special theory. My own view is that Frege's explanation, by way of ambiguity, of what appears to be the logically deviant behavior of terms in intermediate contexts is so theoretically satisfying that if we have not yet discovered or satisfactorily grasped the peculiar intermediate objects in question, then we should simply continue looking.

There is, however, a method which may assist in the search. Look for something denoted by a compound, say, a sentence, in the oblique context. (In ordinary contexts sentences are taken to denote their own truth values and to be intersubstitutable on that basis.) And then using the fundamental principle: the denotation of the compound is a function of the denotation of the parts, look for something denoted by the parts. It was the use of this principle which, I believe, led to Carnap's discovery of individual concepts,[7] and also led Frege to the view that quotation marks produce an oblique context within which each component expression denotes itself[8] (it is clear in quotation contexts what the whole compound denotes).

Frege's view of quotation contexts would allow for quantification into such contexts, but of course we would have to quantify over expressions (since it is expressions that are denoted in such contexts), and we would have to make some provision to distinguish when a given symbol in such a context is being used as a variable and when it is being used as a constant, i.e. to denote itself. This might be done by taking some distinctive class of symbols to serve as variables.

Let us symbolize Frege's understanding of quotation marks by using forward and backward capital F's. (Typographical limitations have forced elimination of the center horizontal bar of the capital F's.) Then, using Greek letters for variables ranging over expressions we can express such truths as:

(12) $\exists\alpha[\ulcorner\alpha$ is greater than five$\urcorner$ is a truth of arithmetic].[9]

Such is Frege's treatment of quotation marks: it seems to me more interesting and certainly much more fruitful (for the development of any theory in which quotation contexts are at all common) than the usual orthographic accident treatment according to which the quotation marks seal off the context, which is treated as a single indissoluble word. And it is well known that for serious theoretical purposes, quotation marks (under the conventional treatment) are of little use.

The ontological status of meanings or senses is less well settled than that of expressions. But we can again illustrate the principle involved in searching for the intermediate entities, and perhaps even engender an illusion of understanding, by introducing some symbolic devices. First, in analogy to the conventional use of quotation marks, I introduce meaning marks. Their use is illustrated in the following:

(13)   The meaning of "brother" = ^{M}male sibling^M.

Now we can adapt the idea used in producing (12) to meaning marks, so as to produce a Fregean interpretation of them. The context produced by the meaning marks will then not be thought of as referentially opaque but rather such that each expression in such a context will denote its own meaning. Quantification in is permitted, but restricted of course to quantification over meanings. Following the earlier pattern, let us symbolize the new meaning marks with forward and backward capital M's. Using italic letters for variables ranging over meanings, we can express such truths as:

(14) $\exists a \exists b [^M a$ kicked $b^M = {}^M b$ was kicked by $a^M]$

I leave to the reader the problem of making sense of (12)–(14).

This comparison of meaning marks with quotation marks also allows me to make another point relevant to Quine's "Quantifiers and Propositional Attitudes." In his section IV, Quine suggests that by a harmless shift in idiom we can replace talk of meanings by talk of expressions, thus achieving ontological security. I agree, but the parallel can be exploited in either direction: as suggested by the introduction of meaning marks, we might also try to replace talk of expressions by talk of meanings, thus achieving ontological insight. These structural parallels are most helpful in constructing a logic of intensions.[10]

V

We have finished comparing the treatments of (3)–(5) with respect to the two main analyses of intermediate occurrences: assimilation to orthographic accident versus assimilation to vulgar occurrence. The forms involved in (6)–(8) were introduced in connection with what I called Quine's elaboration of the first line. Now what can be done in this direction following Frege's line? The purpose of the new forms in (6)–(8) is to get an expression out from an accidental position to a vulgar one; or, in Quine's terminology, to move a term from an opaque context to a purely referential position. There should be no problem here on Frege's theory, because what is opaque for Quine is already fully referential for Frege. Thus the term is in a fully referential position in the first place. But this will not quite satisfy the demands of (6)–(8), because the term in question does not denote the right thing.

At this point it will be useful to reformulate (3)–(8) [or at least (4), (5), (7), and (8)] so as to make explicit what the objects of belief and necessity are. In so doing we take a step along Frege's path, for the nonsubstitutability of one true sentence for another in such contexts would indicate to Frege an ambiguity in both of them: the sentences lack their usual denotation, a truth value, and instead denote some other entity. Before saying what, note that the necessity symbol will stand for a property—of something or other—and the belief symbol will stand for a two-place relation—between a person and something or other. (This in contrast to treating the necessity symbol simply as a 1-place referentially opaque sentential connective and similarly for belief.) Quine takes the step in Frege's direction in the article under discussion and favors it in the sister article "Three Grades of Modal Involvement." So I take it here. Now what shall the sentences denote? For my present purposes it will suffice to take the ontologically secure position and let them denote expressions, in particular, themselves.[11] Making this explicit, we rewrite (4) and (5) as:

(15)   N "nine is greater than five"

(16)   Hegel B "nine is greater than five"

On the usual reading of quotation marks, (15) and (16) still basically formulate the non-Fregean view, with the referential opacity now charged against the quotes. Keeping in mind that the shift to (7) and (8) was for the purpose of moving "nine" to a purely referential position, we can rewrite (7) and (8) as:

(17)   Nec ("x is greater than five," nine)

(which may be read: '**x** is greater than 5' is necessarily true of nine), and

(18)   Hegel **Bel** ("**x** is greater than five," nine).

Here the symbol for necessity becomes a two-place predicate and that for belief a three-place predicate. "**x** is greater than five" stands for a compound predicate, with the bold face letter "**x**" used only as a *place holder* to indicate subject position. The opacity of quotation marks deny such place holders a referential position in any **Nec** or **Bel** context. '**Nec**' and '**Bel**' are intended to express Quine's relational sense of necessity and belief.[12]

Frege would reformulate (15) and (16) as:

(19)   **N** ⌜nine is greater than five⌝.

(20)   Hegel **B** ⌜nine is greater than five⌝.

Notice that we can use the same predicates as in (15) and (16) since

⌜nine is greater than five⌝ = "nine is greater than five"

just as

$$(3 \times 10^2) + (6 \times 10^1) + (8 \times 10^0) = 368.$$

It should now be clear that although the occurrences of "nine" in (19) and (20) are fully referential, (19) and (20) won't do for the purposes of (17) and (18), because the occurrences of "nine" in (17) and (18) refer to quite a different entity. Combining (17) with:

(21)   Nine numbers the planets,

we derive:

(22) $\exists y[y$ numbers the planets & **Nec** ("**x** is greater than five," $y)]$.

But (19) and (21) seem to yield only:

$\exists y[y$ numbers the planets & **N** ⌜nine is greater than five⌝],

in which the quantifier binds nothing in the necessity context, or:

$\exists \alpha [\alpha$ numbers the planets & **N** ⌜α is greater than five⌝],

which is false because the planets are not numbered by an expression (recall our conventions about Greek variables).

Thus the Fregean formulations appear to lack the kind of recurrence of a variable both within and without the necessity context that is characteristic of quantified modal logic and that appears in (22). But this difficulty can be considerably mitigated by taking note of the fact that though the number nine and the expression 'nine' are distinct entities, there is an important relationship between them. The second denotes the first. We can follow Church[6] by introducing a denotation predicate, 'Δ', into our language, and so restore, at least in an *indirect* way (recall Frege's indirect reference by way of intermediate entities) the connection between occurrences of an expression within and without the modal context, as in:

(23) $\exists y$ [y numbers the planets & $\exists \alpha (\Delta(\alpha y)$ & **N** ⌜α is greater than five⌝)].

I propose (23), or some variant, as Frege's version of (22); and

(24) $\exists \alpha [\Delta(\alpha,$ nine) & **N** ⌜α is greater than five⌝),

or some variant, as Frege's version of (17). (We shall return later to the variants.) (23) and (24) may not be as exciting as (22) and (17), but neither do they commit us to essentialism. It may well be that (24), and its variants, supply all the connection between occurrences of expressions within and without modal contexts as can sensibly be allowed.

When I summed up Quine's elaboration of the orthographic accident theory of intermediate occurrences I emphasized the fact that to move an expression in an opaque construction to referential position, a new *primitive* predicate (such as '**Nec**' and '**Bel**' of (17) and (18)) had to be introduced and supplied with an interpretation. In contrast, the same effect is achieved by Frege's method using only the original predicates plus logical signs, including 'Δ', and of course the ontological decomposition involved in the use of the Frege quotes.

Turning now to belief I propose:

(25) $\exists \alpha[\Delta(\alpha,$ nine) & Hegel **B** ⌜α is greater than five⌝],

or some variant, as Frege's version of Quine's (18).

VI

If we accept (25) as the interpretation of Quine's (18), we can justify a crucial form of inference he seems to consider valid and explain certain seemingly paradoxical results which he accepts.

Quine recites the following story.

There is a certain man in a brown hat whom Ralph has glimpsed several times under questionable circumstances on which we need not enter here; suffice it to say that Ralph suspects he is a spy. Also there is a gray-haired man, vaguely known to Ralph as rather a pillar of the community, whom Ralph is not aware of having seen except once at the beach. Now Ralph does not know it, but the men are one and the same.

Quine then poses the question, "Can we say of this *man* (Bernard J. Ortcutt, to give him a name) that Ralph believes him to be a spy?" The critical facts of the story are summarized in what we would write as:

(26) Ralph **B** "the man in the brown hat is a spy,"
(27) Ralph **B** "the man seen at the beach is not a spy,"
(28) the man in the brown hat = the man seen at the beach = Ortcutt.

Quine answers his own query by deriving what we would write as:

(29) Ralph **Bel** ("x is a spy," the man in the brown hat)

from (26). He says of this move, "The kind of exportation which leads from [(26)] to [(29)] should doubtless be viewed in general as implicative."[13] Now our versions of (26) and (29) are:

(30) Ralph **B** ⌜the man in the brown hat is a spy⌝,
(31) $\exists\alpha[\Delta(\alpha,$ the man in the brown hat$)$ & Ralph **B** ⌜α is a spy⌝$]$.

And (31) certainly is implied by (30) and the nearly analytic truth:

$\Delta($"the man in the brown hat," the man in the brown hat$)$.[14]

We thus justify exportation.

In discussing a seeming paradox Quine notes that exportation will also lead from (27) to:

Ralph **Bel** ("x is not a spy," the man seen at the beach)

and hence, by (28), to:

(32) Ralph **Bel** ("x is not a spy," Ortcutt).

Whereas (29) and (28) yield:

(33) Ralph **Bel** ("x is a spy," Ortcutt).

Thus, asserts Quine,

[(32)] and [(33)] both count as true. This is not, however, to charge Ralph with contradictory beliefs. Such a charge might reasonably be read into:

[(34)] Ralph **Bel** ("x is a spy and x is not a spy," Ortcutt),]

but this merely goes to show that it is undesirable to look upon [(32)] and [(33)] as implying [(34)].

At first blush it may appear that avoidance of that undesirable course [looking upon (32) and (33) as implying (34)] calls for the most intense kind of concentration and focus of interest. In fact one may be pessimistically inclined to take the easy way out and simply dispose of (32), (33), (34) and any other assertions involving **Bel** as nonsense. But, as Quine says, "How then to provide for those indispensable relational statements of belief, like 'There is someone whom Ralph believes to be a spy'.?"

Fortunately our versions of **Bel** again conform to Quine's intuitions. (32), (33) and (34) go over respectively into:

(35) $\exists\alpha[\Delta(\alpha,$ Ortcutt$)$ & Ralph **B** ⌜α is not a spy⌝$]$,
(36) $\exists\alpha[\Delta(\alpha,$ Ortcutt$)$ & Ralph **B** ⌜α is a spy⌝$]$,
(37) $\exists\alpha[\Delta(\alpha,$ Ortcutt$)$ & Ralph **B** ⌜α is a spy and α is not a spy⌝$]$

which clearly verify Quine's claims, even in the presence of the suppressed premise:

$\forall\alpha\forall\beta[$Ralph **B** ⌜ is a spy⌝ & Ralph **B**⌜β is not a spy⌝$\rightarrow$ Ralph **B** ⌜α is a spy and β is not a spy⌝$]$

VII

So far so good. But further exploration with our version of **Bel** suggests that the rule of exportation fails to mesh with the intuitive ideas that originally led Quine to the introduction of **Bel**. And I believe that our version will also allow us to see more clearly exactly what problems lay before us if we are to supply a notion answering to these motivating intuitions. As I hope later developments will show, there are a number of different kinds of counter-cases which could be posed. I will only develop one at this point.

Suppose that the situation is as stated in (9). We would now express (9) as:

(38)   Ralph **B** "∃y y is a spy."

Believing that spies differ widely in height, Ralph believes that one among them is shortest. Thus,

(39)   Ralph **B** "the shortest spy is a spy."

Supposing that there is in fact one shortest spy, by exportation (39) yields:

(40)   Ralph **Bel** ("**x** is a spy," the shortest spy)

which, under the same supposition, by existential generalization yields:

(41)   ∃y Ralph **Bel** ("**x** is a spy," y).

And (41) currently expresses (10). But (10) was originally intended to express a fact which would interest the F.B.I. (recall Quine's comment that if Ralph is like most of us, (10) is false), and we would not expect the interest of that organization to be piqued by Ralph's conviction that no two spies share a size.

Two details of this case can be slightly improved. First, the near analyticity of Ralph's crucial belief, as expressed in (39), can be eliminated by taking advantage of Ralph's belief that all members of the C.P.U.S.A. (none of which are known to him) are spies. Second, we can weaken the assumption of Ralph's special ideas about spy sizes by using only the well-known fact that two persons can not be born at exactly the same time at exactly the same place (where

the place of birth is an interior point of the infant's body). Given any four spatial points a, b, c, d not in a plane, we can use the relations: t_1 is earlier than t_2, and p_1 is closer to $a(b, c, d)$ than p_2 is, to order all space time points. We can then form such names as "the least spy" with the meaning: ^{m}that spy whose spatio-temporal location at birth precedes that of all other spies^m.

Details aside, the point is that exportation, as represented in our current version of **Bel,** conflicts with the intention that there be a 'vast' difference between (9) and (10). Still, I am convinced that we are on the right track. That track, roughly speaking, is this: instead of trying to introduce a new primitive relation like Quine's **Bel,** we focus on trying to define it (or something as close to it as we can sensibly come, remember modal logic) using just the dyadic **B** plus other logical and semi-logical apparatus such as quantifiers, Δ, etc. and also possibly other seemingly more fundamental epistemological notions.

Some years ago I thought that this task was hopeless and took basically the same attitude toward such quantified belief contexts as Quine takes toward quantified modal logic.[15] At that earlier time I used to argue with my colleague, Montgomery Furth, who shares my attitude toward Frege's theory, about the meaningfulness of such quantifications in as in (10). (This was after noticing the difficulty, indicated above, in our current analysis.[16]) Furth suggested that a solution might lie in somehow picking out certain kinds of names as being required for the exportation. But this just seemed essentialism all over again and we gave up. Although still uncertain that (10) makes sense, I think I can show that it comes to something like what Furth had in mind. Indeed, the analogies between the relational senses of belief and necessity are so strong that I have often wondered why Quine's scepticism with regard to **Nec** did not extend to **Bel**.

There is even an inadequacy in our proposed analysis, (24), of **Nec** parallel to that displayed for our proposed analysis, (25), of **Bel**. Although our analysis of **Nec** avoids essentialism, it also avoids rejecting:

(42)   **Nec** ("x = the number of planets," nine),

which comes out true on the understanding:

(43) $\exists\alpha(\Delta(\alpha,\ \text{nine})\ \&\ N\ \ulcorner\alpha\ =\ \text{the number of planets}\urcorner)$

in view of the facts that

> $N\ \ulcorner$the number of planets = the number of planets$\urcorner$

and

> Δ("the number of planets," nine).

In a sense, we have not avoided essentialism but only inessentialism, since so many of nine's properties become essential. Small consolation to know of our essential rationality if each blunder and error is equally ingrained.

The parallel inadequacies of our versions of **Nec** and **Bel** are now apparent. Our analyses credit nine with an excess of essence and put Ralph *en rapport* with an excess of individuals.

VIII

What is wanted is "a frankly inequalitarian attitude toward various ways of specifying the number [nine]".[17] This suggests to me that we should restrict our attention to a smaller class of names; names which are so intimately connected with what they name that they could not but name it. I shall say that such a name *necessarily denotes* its object, and I shall use 'Δ_N' to symbolize this more discriminating form of denotation.

Such a relation is available; based on the notion of a *standard name*. A standard name is one whose denotation is fixed on logical, or perhaps I should say linguistic, grounds alone. Numerals and quotation names are prominent among the standard names.[18] Such names do, in the appropriate sense, necessarily denote their denotations.

Russell and some others who have attempted to treat proper names of persons as standard names have emphasized the purely referential function of such names and their apparent lack of descriptive content. But consideration of the place value system of arabic numerals and our conventions for the construc-

tion of quotation names of expressions should convince us that what is at stake is not pure reference in the absence of any descriptive structure, but rather reference freed of *empirical* vicissitudes. Numbers and expressions, like every other kind of entity, can be named by names which are such that empirical investigation is required to determine their denotations. "The number of planets" and "9" happen to denote the same number. The former might, under other circumstances or at some other time, denote a different number, but so long as we hold constant our conventions of language, "9" will denote the same number under all possible circumstances. To wonder what number is named by the German "die Zahl der Planeten" may betray astronomical ignorance, but to wonder what number is named by the German "Neun" can indicate only linguistic incompetence.[19]

$\Delta_N(\alpha,\ x)$ cannot be analyzed in terms of the analyticity of some sentence of the form $\Delta(\text{---},\ .\ .\ .)$;
since:

> Δ("the number of planets," the number of planets)

is analytic, but "the number of planets" is not a standard name of the number of planets (viz: nine), and

> Δ("9," the number of planets)

is not analytic, although "9" is a standard name of that number. We have in Δ_N a relation that holds between the standard name and the number itself, independent of any particular way of specifying the number. Thus there is a certain intimacy between "9" and 9, lacking between "the number of planets" and the number of planets, which allows "9" to go proxy for 9 in assertions of necessity.

There is a sense in which the finite ordinals (which we can take the entities here under discussion to be) find their essence in their ordering. Thus, names which reflect this ordering in an a priori way, as by making true statements of order analytic, capture all that is essential to these numbers. And our careless attitude toward any intrinsic features of these numbers (e.g. whether zero is a set, and if so whether it has any members) suggests that such names may have captured all there is to these numbers.[20] I am less interested in urging an explanation of the special intimacy between "nine" and nine, than in noting the fact. The phenomenon is widespread, extending to expressions, pure sets of finite rank, and others of their ilk. I would require any adequate explanation to generalize so as to handle all such cases, and I should hope that such an explanation would also support the limitations which I suggest below on the kinds of entities eligible for standard names.[21]

The foregoing considerations suggest simple variants for our current Fregean versions of (17) and (42). We replace (24) with:

$\exists\alpha(\Delta_N(\alpha, \text{nine})\&N \ulcorner\alpha$ is greater than five$\urcorner$

as our analysis of (17), and we replace (43) with:

$\exists\alpha(\Delta_N(\alpha, \text{nine})\&N \ulcorner\alpha =$ the number of planets$\urcorner)$

as our analysis of (42). According to the reformed analyses, (17) and (42) come out respectively as true and false, which accords much better with our intuitions and may even satisfy the essentialist.[22] All, it is hoped, without a lapse into irreducible (though questionable) metaphysical assumptions.

There are, however, limitations on the resort to standard names. Only abstract objects can have standard names, since only they (and not all of them) lack that element of contingency which makes the rest of us liable to failures of existence. Thus, Quine can have no standard name, for he might not be. And then what shall his standard name name? Quine's singleton, {Quine}, though abstract, is clearly no better off.

Numerals are reliable; they always pick out the same number. But to suppose a standard name for Quine would presuppose a solution to the more puzzling problem of what features to take into account in determining that an individual of one possible world is 'the same person' as that of another. Often when the worlds have a common part, as when we consider alternative futures to the present, the individual(s) can be traced back to the common part by the usual continuity conditions and there compared. But for individuals not extant during an overlap such techniques are unavailing. It seems that such radically disjoint worlds are sometimes contemplated by modal logicians. I am not here passing final judgment but only remarking the relevance of a second difference between Quine and Nine: namely, that he presents a very real problem of transworld identification while it does not.

Thus the device of using standard names, which accounts nicely for my own intuitions regarding the essential properties of numbers, appears to break down when set to discriminating essential properties of persons. I am consoled by the fact that my own intuitions do not assign essential properties to persons in any broad metaphysical sense, which is not to say that quantified modal logic can have no interesting interpretation when trans-world identifications are made from the point of view of a frankly special interest.

IX

All this on **Nec** was aimed toward analogy with **Bel** and a charge of inconsistent scepticism against Quine. We have patched our first version of **Nec** with a more discriminating sense of denotation. The same trick would work for **Bel,** if Ralph would confine his cogitations to numbers and expressions. If not, we must seek some other form of special intimacy between name and object which allows the former to go proxy for the latter in Ralph's cognitive state.

I believe that the fundamental difficulty with our first version of **Bel** is that Δ gave us a relation between name and object in which Ralph played no significant role. Supposing all speakers of English to have available approximately the same stock of names (i.e. singular terms), this puts us all *en rapport* with the same persons. But the interesting relational sense of belief, and the one which I suppose Quine to have been getting at with (10), is one which provides Ralph with access to some but not all persons of whom he can frame names. What we are after this time is a three-place relation between Ralph, a name (which I here use in the broad sense of singular term) α, and a person x. For this purpose I will introduce two special notions: that of a name α being *of* x for Ralph, and that of a name being *vivid,* both of which I will compare with the notion of a name *denoting* x.

Let us begin by distinguishing the *descriptive content* of a name from the *genetic character* of the name as used by Ralph. The first goes to user-independent features of the name, the second to features of a particular user's acquisition of certain beliefs involving the name. It is perhaps easiest to make the distinction in terms not of names but of pictures, with consideration limited to pictures which show a single person. Those features of a picture, in virtue of which we say it resembles or is a likeness of a particular person, comprise the picture's descriptive content. The genetic character of a picture is determined by the causal chain of events leading to its production. In the case of photographs and portraits we say that the picture is *of* the person who was photographed or who sat for the portrait. The same relation presumably holds between a perception and the perceived object.[23] This relation between picture and person clearly depends entirely on the genetic character of the picture. Without attempting a definition, we can say that for a picture to be *of* a person, the person must serve significantly in the causal chain leading to the picture's production and also serve as object for the picture. The second clause is to prevent all of an artist's paintings from being *of* the artist. I will shortly say a bit more about how I understand this relation, which I designate with the italicized '*of*'.

The "user-independence" of the descriptive content of a picture lies in the fact that "identical" pictures, such as two prints made from a single negative, will resemble all the same persons. In this sense, the descriptive content of a picture is a function of what we might call the picture-type rather than the picture-token. The "user-dependent" nature of the genetic character of a picture lies in the fact that "identical" paintings can be such that they are *of* different persons (e.g. twins sitting separately for portraits). Thus the genetic character of a picture is a function only of the picture-token. In order to accommodate genesis, I use 'picture' throughout in the sense of 'picture-token'.

Armed with *resemblance* and *of*-ness, let me recite just a few of the familiar facts of portraiture. First, not all pictures *of* a person resemble that person. Of two recent pictures taken of me, one resembles Steve Allen and the other resembles nothing on earth. Secondly, not all pictures which resemble a person are *of* that person. It is obvious that a picture *of* one twin will, if it resembles the twin it is *of,* also resemble the other twin. What is more interesting is that a picture which resembles a person may not be *of* any person at all. My camera may have had a hallucination due to light leaks in its perceptual system. Similarly, if I have drawn my conception of how the typical man will look in one million years, even if a man looking like that now exists, my picture is not *of* him (unless he sat as a model or played some other such role). Thirdly, a picture may be *of* more than one person, as when, by the split mirror technique, we obtain a composite photograph showing one man's head on another man's body. Indeed, in summary, a single picture may be *of* no one, one person, or many persons, while resembling no one, one person, or many persons, with any degree of overlap between those whom it is *of* and those whom it resembles. Of course, if photographs did not frequently, indeed usually, resemble their subjects, they could not serve many of the purposes for which we use them. Still, on occasion, things can and do go awry, and a bad photograph of one is yet a photograph *of* one.

I turn now to cases in which the causal chain from object to picture is relatively indirect. If one or several witnesses describe the criminal to a police artist who then constructs a picture, I shall say that it is a picture *of* the criminal, even when after such a genesis the resulting picture has quite ceased to resemble the criminal. Similarly, had a photograph of Julius Caesar been xeroxed, and the xerox copy televised to a monastery, where it was copied by a monk, and so was reproduced down through the ages, I would call the resulting copy, no matter how distorted, no matter who, if anyone, it resembled, a picture *of* Julius Caesar.[24]

A police artist's reconstruction of Santa Claus, based on a careful reading of the poem *The Night Before Christmas*, is not a picture *of* anyone no matter how many people make themselves up so that it exactly resembles them, and no matter whether the artist regards the poem as fact or fiction. Even if in combining facial features of known statistical frequencies the artist correctly judges that the resulting picture will resemble someone or other, that person has no special causal efficacy in the production of the picture and so it still will not be a picture *of* anyone. And if the story of Medusa originated in imagination or hallucination (as opposed to misperception or misapprehension), then a rendering based on that legend is *of* no one, notwithstanding the existence of any past, present, or future snake-haired women.

In addition to the link with reality provided by the relation of resemblance the descriptive content of a picture determines its *vividness*. A faded picture showing the back of a man wearing a cloak and lurking in shadow will lack vividness. A clear picture, head on, full length, life size, showing fingerprints, etc. would be counted highly vivid. What is counted as vivid may to some extent depend on special interests. To the clothier, nude portraits may be lacking in detail, while to the foot fetishist a picture showing only the left big toe may leap from the canvas. Though special interests may thus weight detail, I would expect that increase in detail always increases vividness. It should be clear that there are no necessary connections between how vivid a picture is and whether it is *of* anyone or whether it resembles anyone.

Returning now to names, it is their descriptive content that determines what if anything they denote. Thus, denotation is the analogue for names to resemblance for pictures. The genetic character of a name in a given person's usage will account for how he *acquired* the name, that is how he heard of such a thing and, if he believes that such a thing exists, how he came to believe it. It is the genetic character of the name that determines what if anything it is a name *of*. (I here use the same nomenclature, '*of*', for names as for pictures.) The user-dependence of this notion is required by the fact that Ralph and Fred may each have acquired the name "John Smith," but in such a way that for Ralph it is a name *of* one John Smith while for Fred it is a name *of* another John Smith.

I would suppose that students of rhetoric realize that most of the lines of argument traditionally classified as 'informal fallacies' (*ad hominem, ad vericundiam*, etc.) are commonly considered relevant or even determinative by reasonable men.[25] Cases such as that of the two John Smiths, which emphasize the importance of genetic features in language use, indicate limitations that must be placed on the traditional dichotomy between *what* we believe (assert, desire, etc.) and *how* we came to believe it.

Let us attempt to apply these considerations to the case of proper names. Proper names denote each of the usually many persons so dubbed. Ralph may acquire a proper name in a number of different ways. He may have attended a dubbing with the subject present. I reconstruct such dubbings as consisting of a stipulative association of the name with a perception *of* the subject. Thus, the name becomes a name *of* the subject, and as it passes from Ralph to others retains this feature in the manner of the picture *of* Julius Caesar. We may of course dub on the basis of a hallucination, in which case the name is a name *of* nothing, though it will still denote each actual person, if any, that may be so dubbed. Dubbings sometimes take place with the subject absent, in which case some other name (usually a description) stands in for the perception, and the stipulatively introduced proper name takes its genetic character from the stand-in name. If the latter only denotes the subject (and is not a name *of* the subject for the user in question), the proper name can do no better. This having a name *of x*, I shall later take to be essential to having a belief about *x*, and I am unwilling to adopt any theory of proper names which permits me to perform a dubbing in absentia, as by solemnly declaring "I hereby dub the first child to be born in the twenty-second century 'Newman 1'," and thus grant myself standing to have beliefs about that as yet unborn child. Another presumably more common way to acquire a proper name is in casual conversation or reading, e.g. from the headline, "Mayor Indicted; B. J. Ortcutt sought by F.B.I.". In such cases we retrace the causal sequence from Ralph back through his immediate source to its immediate source and so on. An especially difficult case of this sort arises when someone other than Ortcutt, say Wyman, is introduced to Ralph as Ortcutt. Suppose that the introduction took place with intent to deceive and that Fred, who made the introduction, acquired the name "Ortcutt" as a name *of* Ortcutt. Clearly we should count "Ortcutt" as a name *of* Wyman for Ralph, but also, through Fred, as a name *of* Ortcutt. The situation is analogous to the composite photograph made by the split mirror technique. But here the much greater vividness of the perceptual half of the equation may outweigh the dim reflection of Ortcutt.

I leave to the reader the useful exercise of constructing cases of names (not necessarily proper) which are analogues to each of the cited cases of pictures.

The notion of a vivid name is intended to go to the purely internal aspects of individuation. Consider typical cases in which we would be likely to say that Ralph knows x or is acquainted with x. Then look only at the conglomeration of images, names, and partial descriptions which Ralph employs to bring x before his mind. Such a conglomeration, when suitably arranged and regimented, is what I call a vivid name. As with pictures, there are degrees of vividness and the whole notion is to some degree relative to special interests. The crucial feature of this notion is that it depends only on Ralph's current mental state, and ignores all links whether by resemblance or genesis with the actual world. If the name is such, that on the assumption that there exists some individual x whom it both denotes and resembles we should say that Ralph knows x or is acquainted with x, then the name is vivid.

The vivid names "represent" those persons who fill major roles in that *inner story* which consists of all those sentences which Ralph believes. I have placed 'represent' here in scarequotes to warn that there may not actually exist anything which is so "represented." Ralph may enjoy an inner story totally out of contact with reality, but this is not to deny it a cast of robust and clearly delineated characters. Life is often less plausible than art. Of course a vivid name should make an existence *claim*. If Ralph does not believe that there is a Santa Claus, I would not call any Santa Claus name vivid, no matter how lively it is in other respects.

There are certain features which may contribute strongly to vividness but which I feel we should not accept as absolute requirements. It is certainly too much to require that a vivid name must provide Ralph with a means of recognizing its purported object under all circumstances, for we do not follow the careers of even those we know best that closely. There are always gaps. We sometimes even fail to recognize ourselves in early photographs or recent descriptions, simply because of gaps in our self-concept.[26] It also seems to me too much to require that Ralph believes himself to have at some time perceived the purported object of a vivid name since a scholar may be better acquainted with Julius Caesar than with his own neighbor. Some have also suggested that the appropriate kind of name must provide Ralph with the means of locating its purported object. But parents and police are frequently unable to locate persons well known to them. Also, a vivid biography of a peasant somewhere in Asia, may involve none but the vaguest spatio-temporal references.

One might understand the assertion, "Ralph has an opinion as to who Ortcutt is" as a claim that Ralph can place Ortcutt among the leading characters of his inner story, thus that Ralph believes some sentence of the form $\ulcorner \alpha = \text{Ortcutt} \urcorner$ with α vivid. This, I believe, is the view of Hintikka. Hintikka institutionalizes the sense of 'represents' with usual quotes by allowing existential generalization on the leading character or inner individual "represented" by a vivid name. Although his symbolism allows him to distinguish between those inner individuals which are actual and those which are not, a central role is assigned to something close to what I call a vivid name.[27] In emphasizing this conceptual separation of vividness, which makes a name a *candidate* for exportation, from those features depending on genesis and resemblence, which determine what actual person, if anyone, the name really represents (without quotes), Hintikka (if I have him right) and I are in agreement.

It is a familiar fact of philosophy that no idea, description, or image can insure itself against non-natural causes. The most vivid of names may have had its origin in imagination or hallucination. Thus, to freely allow exportation a name must not only be vivid but must also be a name *of* someone, and indeed a name *of* the person it denotes. This last is an accuracy requirement which no doubt is rarely satisfied by the most vivid names we use. Our most vivid names can be roughly characterized as those elaborate descriptions containing all we believe about a single person. Such names will almost certainly contain inaccuracies which will prevent them from actually denoting anyone. Also such names are often not *of* a single person but result from conflation of information about several persons (as in Fred's prevaricating introduction of Wyman to Ralph).

One proposal for handling such difficulties would be to apply the method of best fit to our most vivid names, i.e. to seek the individual who comes closest to satisfying the two conditions: that the name denotes him and is *of* him. But it seems that this technique would distort the account of conflations, never allowing us to say that there are two persons whom Ralph believes to be one. There is an alternate method which I favor. Starting with one of our most vivid names, form the largest core, all of which is *of* the same person and which denotes that person. A vivid name resulting from conflation may contain more than one such core name. The question is whether such a core, remaining after excision of inaccuracy, is yet vivid. If so, I will say that

the core name *represents* the person whom it both denotes and is *of* to Ralph.

Our task was to characterize a relation between Ralph, a name, and a person, which could replace Δ in a variant analysis of **Bel.** For this I will use the above notion of representation. To repeat, I will say α *represents* x *to* Ralph (symbolized: "**R**(α, x, Ralph)") if and only if (i) α denotes x, (ii) α is a name *of* x for Ralph, and (iii) α is (sufficiently) vivid. Our final version of (33) is the following variant of (36):

(44)   ∃α[**R**(α, Ortcutt, Ralph) & Ralph **B** ⌜α is a spy⌝].

X

Part of our aim was to restrict the range of persons with whom Ralph is *en rapport* (in the sense of **Bel**). This was done by means of clauses (ii) and (iii). Clause (ii) excludes all future persons such as Newman 1[28] and indeed any person past, present, or future who has not left his mark on Ralph. The addition of clause (iii) excludes any person who has not left a vivid mark on Ralph.

The crucial exportation step for the case of the shortest spy is now blocked, because in spite of Ralph's correct belief that such a person exists, "the shortest spy" is not, for Ralph, a name *of* him.[29]

Clause (iii) takes account of the desire to allow Ralph beliefs *about* (again in the sense of **Bel**) only those persons he 'has in mind', where the mere acquisition of, say, a proper name *of* x would not suffice to put x in mind. Furthermore, if we were to drop clause (iii), and allow any name which both denotes x and is a name *of* x to represent x to Holmes, then after Holmes observed the victim, "the murderer" would represent the murderer to him. And thus we would have:

∃y∃α[**R**(α, y, Holmes)&Holmes **B**⌜α = the murderer⌝].

which is our present analysis of:

∃y Holmes **Bel** ("x = the murderer," y).

which is, roughly, Quine's translation of:

There is someone whom Holmes believes to be the murderer.

But this last should presage an arrest and not the mere certification of homicide. Clause (iii) is intended to block such cases. At some point in his investigation, the slow accretion of evidence, all "pointing in a certain direction" may just push Holmes' description over the appropriate vividness threshold so that we *would* say that there is now someone whom Holmes believes to be the murderer.

Clause (iii) could also be used to block exportation of "the shortest spy." But that would not eliminate the need for clause (ii) which is still needed to insure that we export to the right individual.

Although I believe that all three clauses are required to block all the anomalies of exportation, I am less interested in a definitive analysis of that particular inference than I am in separating and elucidating certain notions which may be useful in epistemological discussions. According to my analysis, Ralph must have quite a solid conception of x before we can say that Ralph believes x to be a spy. By weakening the accuracy requirements on the notion of representation we obtain in general new relational senses of belief.[30] Any such notion, based on a clearly specified variant of (36), may be worthy of investigation.

XI

A vivid name is a little bit like a standard name, but not much. It can't guarantee existence to its purported object, and although it has a kind of inner reliability by way of Ralph's use of such names to order his inner world, a crucial condition of reliability—the determinateness of standard identities—fails. A standard identity is an identity sentence in which both terms are standard names. It is corollary to the reliability of standard names, that standard identities are either true under all circumstances or false under all circumstances. But not so for identities involving vivid names. We can easily form two vivid names, one describing Bertrand Russell as logician, and another describing Russell as so-

cial critic, which are such that the identity sentence simply can not be decided on internal evidence. In the case of the morning star and the evening star, we can even form names which allow us to locate the purported objects (if we are willing to wait for the propitious moment) without the identity sentence being determinate. Of course Ralph may believe the negation of the identity sentence for all distinct pairs of vivid names, but such beliefs may simply be wrong. And the names can remain vivid even after such inaccurate nonidentities are excised. It may happen that Ralph comes to change his beliefs so that where he once believed a nonidentity between vivid names, he now believes an identity. And at some intermediate stage of wonder he believes neither the identity nor the nonidentity. Such Monte Cristo cases may be rare in reality (though rife in fiction),[31] but they are nevertheless clearly possible. They could be ruled out only by demanding an unreasonably high standard of vividness, to wit: no gaps, or else by adding an artificial and ad hoc requirement that all vivid names contain certain format items, e.g. exact place and date of birth. Either course would put us out of *rapport* with most of our closest friends. Thus, two vivid names can represent the same person to Ralph although Ralph does not believe the identity sentence. He may simply wonder, or he may disbelieve the identity sentence and so believe of one person that he is two. Similarly two vivid names can represent different persons to Ralph although Ralph does not believe the non-identity sentence. Again, Ralph may either suspend judgment or disbelieve the non-identity and so believe of two persons that they are one. Since this last situation is perhaps more plausible than the others, it is important to see that theoretically the cases are on a par. In fact, a case where Ralph has so conflated two persons and is then disabused by his friend Fred, becomes a case of believing one person to be two simply by assuming that Ralph was right in the first place and that Fred lied.

Quine acknowledges that Ralph can believe of one person that he is two on Quine's own understanding of **Bel,** when he remarks, as mentioned in VI above, that

(32)   Ralph **Bel** ("**x** is not a spy," Ortcutt),

and

(33)   Ralph **Bel** ("**x** is a spy," Ortcutt),

do not express an inconsistency on Ralph's part and do not imply (34). The background story justifying (32) and (33) involves Ralph twice spotting Ortcutt but under circumstances so different that Ralph was unaware that he was seeing the same man again. Indeed he believed he was not seeing the same man again, since on the one occasion he thought, "There goes a spy," and on the other, "Here is no spy." My point is that though one may quibble about whether each or either of the names of Ortcutt were vivid in the particular cases as described by Quine,[32] and so question whether in those cases exportation should have been permitted, no plausible characterization of appropriate conditions for vividness can prevent analogous cases from arising.

Cases of the foregoing kind, which agree with Quine's intuitions, argue an inadequacy in his regimentation of language. For in the same sense in which (32) and (33) do not express an inconsistency on Ralph's part, neither should (33) and

(45)   ~Ralph **Bel** ("**x** is a spy," Ortcutt)

express an inconsistency on ours. Indeed it seems natural to claim that (45) is a consequence of (32). But the temptation to look upon (33) and (45) as contradictory is extremely difficult to resist. The problem is that since Quine's **Bel** suppresses mention of the specific name being exported, he can not distinguish between

(46) $\exists\alpha[\mathbf{R}(\alpha,$ Ortcutt, Ralph) & ~ Ralph **B** $\ulcorner\alpha$ is a spy$\urcorner]$

and

(47)   ~$\exists\alpha[\mathbf{R}(\alpha,$ Ortcutt, Ralph) & Ralph **B** $\ulcorner\alpha$ is a spy$\urcorner]$

If (45) is read as (46), there is no inconsistency with (32); in fact, on this interpretation (45) is a consequence of (32) (at least on the assump-

tion that Ralph does not have contradictory beliefs). But if (45) is read as (47) (Quine's intention, I suppose), it is inconsistent with (33) and independent of (32).

So long as Ralph can believe of one person that he is two, as in Quine's story, we should be loath to make either (46) or (47) inexpressible.[33] If (33) is read as (44), we certainly must retain some way of expressing (47) since it expresses the negation of (33). Is it important to retain expression of (46)? In Quine's story, something stronger than (46) holds, namely (32), which we now read as:

(48) $\exists\alpha[\mathbf{R}(\alpha,$ Ortcutt, Ralph)&Ralph **B** $\ulcorner\alpha$ is not a spy$\urcorner]$

But we can continue the story to a later time at which Ralph's suspicions regarding even the man at the beach have begun to grow. Not that Ralph now proclaims that respected citizen to be a spy, but Ralph now suspends judgment as to the man's spyhood. At this time (48) is false, and (46) is true. If we are to have the means to express such suspensions of judgment, something like (46) is required.

I have gone to some trouble here to indicate the source of the notational inadequacy in the possibility of a single person bearing distinct exportable names not believed to name the same thing, and also to argue in favor of maintaining the possibility of such names. I have done this because logicians working in this field have for the most part been in accord with Quine in adopting the simpler language form. In my view the consequence of adopting such a form is either to exclude natural interpretations by setting an impossibly high standard for vividness, and thus for exportation, or else to make such partial expressions of suspended judgment as (46) inexpressible.

XII

When earlier I argued for Frege's method— seek the intermediate entity—it was on the grounds that a clarified view of the problem was worth at least a momentary ontological risk. But now it appears that to give adequate expression to the epistemological situation requires explicit quantificational certification of the status of such entities. I am undismayed and even would urge that the conservative course so far followed of taking expressions as the intermediate entities is clearly inadequate to the task. Many of our beliefs have the form: "The color of her hair is _____," or "The song he was singing went _____," where the blanks are filled with images, sensory impressions, or what have you, but certainly not words. If we cannot even *say* it with words but have to paint it or sing it, we certainly cannot believe it with words.

My picture theory of meaning played heavily on the analogy between names and pictures. I believe that the whole theory of sense and denotation can be extended to apply to pictures as well as words. (How can an identity "sentence" with the components filled by pictures be both true and informative?) If we explicitly include such visual images among names, we gain a new perspective on the claim that we can definitively settle the question of whether Bernard J. Ortcutt is such that Ralph believes him to be a spy by confronting Ralph with Ortcutt and asking "Is *he* a spy?" Ralph's response will depend on recognition, a comparison of current images with stored ones. And stored images are simply one more form of description, worth perhaps a thousand words, but thoroughly comparable to words. Thus Ralph's answer in such a situation is simply one more piece in the whole jigsaw of his cognitive structure. He might answer "yes" for some confrontations (compare—"yes" for some names), "no" for others, and withhold judgment for still others.

The suggested extension of the intermediate entities poses an interesting problem for the ontologist. Must we posit a realm of special mental entities as values for the variables used in analyzing the relational sense of belief, or will a variant on the trick of taking sentences as the objects of belief also account for beliefs involving visual images, odors, sounds, etc.?[34]

XIII

There are, I believe, two rather different problem areas connected with the analysis of intermediate contexts. The first problem area, which lies squarely within what is usually called the philosophy of language, involves chiefly the more fundamental nonrelational interpretation of intermediate contexts. It calls for an explanation of the seemingly logically deviant behavior of expressions in such contexts and perhaps also for a more exact statement of just what inferences, if any, are valid for such contexts. Here I feel that Frege's method outlines a generally acceptable solution. I especially appreciate the fact that for Frege intermediate contexts are not seen as exceptions to a powerful and heretofore general logical theory but rather are seen as fully accessible to that theory with the noted anomalies explained as due to a misreading of "initial conditions" leading to an inappropriate application of the laws. This accounting for seemingly aberrant phenomena in terms of the correct application of a familiar theory is explanation at its most satisfying. By contrast, the view I have associated with Quine—that intermediate contexts are referentially inarticulate—contents itself with a huge and unobvious class of "exceptions to the rules." This is shabby explanation, if explanation at all.

The second problem area specifically concerns the relational interpretation of intermediate contexts. Here I have tried to show how Frege's method, though it may provide a basis for unifying the relational and nonrelational interpretation of a given intermediate context and though it immediately provides for some form of quantification in, does not by itself necessarily provide the most interesting (and perhaps indispensable) relational interpretation. Further analysis, often specific to the context in question, may be required in order to produce an appropriately discriminating form of Δ which will yield results in conformity with our intuitive demands. Indeed, such an investigation may well lead far beyond the philosophy of language proper into metaphysics and epistemology. I know of no earlier source than "Quantifiers and Propositional Attitudes" in which relational uses of intermediate contexts are so clearly identified throughout an area of concern more urgent than modal logic. In that article Quine early expressed his remarkable insights into the pervasiveness of the relational forms and the need for a special analysis of their structure. And in fact following Quine's outlook and attempting to refine the conditions for valid applications of exportation, one might well arrive at the same metaphysical and epistemological insights as those obtained in attempting to refine Δ. What is important is that we should achieve some form of analysis of these contexts without recourse to the very idioms we are attempting to analyze.

The problem of interpreting the most interesting form of quantification in, appears in various guises: as the problem of making trans-world identifications, as the problem of finding favored names, and as the problem of distinguishing 'essential' from 'accidental' properties. The present paper suggests two polar techniques for finding favored names. It is curious and somehow satisfying that they so neatly divide the objects between them, the one applying only to objects capable of being perceived (or at least of initiating causal chains), the other applying only to purely abstract objects. I am well aware of obscurities and difficulties in my formulations of the two central notions—that of a standard name and that of a name being *of* an object for a particular user. Yet both seem to me promising and worthy of further investigation.

ACKNOWLEDGMENTS

The first half of my reflections was read to the Harvard Philosophy Colloquium in January 1966. Its writing was aided by conversations with Montgomery Furth. The present ending has been influenced by a number of different persons, most significantly by Saul Kripke and Charles Chastain. But they should not be held to blame for it. Furth, who also read the penultimate version, is responsible for any remaining deficiencies aside from section IX about which he is skeptical. My research has been partially supported by N.S.F. Grant GP-7706.

NOTES

1. This paper is intended as a commentary on Quine's "Quantifiers and Propositional Atti-

tudes." Quine's article was first published in 1956 and I have been thinking about it ever since. Quine has not been idle while I have been thinking, but his subsequent writings do not seem to have repudiated any part of "Quantifiers and Propositional Attitudes" [reprinted in this volume] which remains, to my mind, the best brief introduction to the field.

2. The quotation is from *Word and Object*, p. 144, wherein the inspiration for 'opaque' is explicitly given. The assimilation of intermediate occurrences to accidental ones might fairly be said to represent a *tendency* on Quine's part. The further evidence of *Word and Object* belies any simplistic characterization of Quine's attitudes toward intermediate occurrences.

3. In "Three Grades of Modal Involvement," p. 172 and other places. An intriguing suggestion for notational efficiency at no loss (or gain) to Quine's theory is to take advantage of the fact that occurrences of variables within opaque contexts which are bindable from without are prohibited, and use the vacated forms as "a way of indicating, selectively and changeably, just what positions in the contained sentence are to shine through as referential on any particular occasion" (*Word and Object*, p. 199). We interpret, "Hegel believed that x is greater than five" with bindable "x," as "x is such that Hegel believed it to be greater than five" which is modeled on (8). Similarly, "Hegel believed that x is greater than y" is now read as, "x and y are such that Hegel believed the former to be greater than the latter." (8) itself could be rendered as, "$\exists x[x = $ nine & Hegel believed that x is greater than five]," and still not be a logical consequence of (5).

4. The reader will recognize that I have incorporated, without reference, many themes upon which Quine has harped, and that I have not attempted to make my agreement with him explicit at each point at which it occurs. Suffice it to say that the agreements far outweigh the disagreements, and that in both the areas of agreement and of disagreement I have benefited greatly from his writings.

5. See especially the end of "Three Grades of Modal Involvement." I am informed by scholarly sources that Aristotelian essentialism has its origin in "Two Dogmas of Empiricism." It reappears significantly in "Reply to Professor Marcus," where essential properties of numbers are discussed, and in *Word and Object*, p. 199, where essential properties of persons are discussed. I will later argue that the two cases are unlike.

6. In "A Formulation of the Logic of Sense and Denotation."

7. See *Meaning and Necessity*, section 9, for the discovery of the explicandum, and section 40 for the discovery of the explicans.

8. See "On Sense and Nominatum," pp. 58, 59 [see p. 201, this volume] in *Translations from the Philosophical Writings of Gottlob Frege.*

9. The acute reader will have discerned a certain similarity in function, though not in foundation, between the Frege quotes and another familiar quotation device.

10. These parallels are exhibited at some length in my dissertation, *Foundations of Intensional Logic.*

11. A drawback to this position is that the resulting *correct* applications of Leibniz' Law are rather unexciting. More interesting intermediate entities can be obtained by taking what Carnap, in *Meaning and Necessity* calls 'intensions'. Two expressions have the same intension, in this sense, if they are logically equivalent. Other interesting senses of 'intension' might be obtained by weakening the notion of logical equivalence to logical equivalence within sentential logic, intuitionistic logic, etc. Church suggests alternatives which might be understood along these lines.

12. I have approximately followed the notational devices used by Quine in "Quantifiers and Propositional Attitudes." Neither of us recommend the notation for practical purposes, even with the theory as is. An alternative notation is suggested in note 3 above.

13. Also, see *Word and Object*, p. 211, for an implicit use of exportation.

14. The "nearly" of "nearly analytic" is accounted for by a small scruple regarding the logic of singular terms. If a language L containing the name '$\iota y F y$' is extended to a metalanguage L' containing the predicate "Δ" for denotation-in-L and also containing the logical particles, including quotes, in their usual meaning, then I regard

$$[\exists x \ x = \iota y F y \rightarrow \Delta('\iota y F y', \iota y F y)]$$

as fully analytic in L'. My reasons for thinking so depend, in part, on my treatment of quotation names as standard names, for which see section VIII. I am being careful, because Quine suggests disagreement in an impatient footnote to "Notes on the Theory of Reference" (I am grateful to Furth, who recalled the footnote.) I do not know whether our disagreement, if a fact, is over quotation or elsewhere. The whole question of analyticity is less than crucial to my line of argument.

15. For a recent expression see *Word and Object*, section 41.

16. The same difficulty was noticed, independently, by John Wallace and reported in a private communication.

17. Quoted from the end of Quine's "Reply to Professor Marcus." I fully agree with Quine's characterization of the case, though not with the misinterpretation of Church's review of "Notes on Existence and Necessity" from which Quine's characterization springs.

18. See the discussion of what Carnap calls *L-determinate individual expressions* in *Meaning and Necessity,* section 18, and also Tarski's discussion of what he calls *structural descriptive names* in "The Concept of Truth in Formalized Languages," section 1.

19. The latter wonder is not to be confused with an ontological anxiety concerning the nature of nine, which is more appropriately expressed by dropping the word "number" in the wonder description.

20. Benacerraf so concludes in "What Numbers Could Not Be."

21. The present discussion of standard names is based on that in the more technical environment of my dissertation, pp. 55–57.

22. Given this understanding of **Nec**, it is interesting to note that on certain natural assumptions '$\Delta_N(\alpha, y)$' is itself expressed by '**Nec**($\ulcorner \alpha = \mathbf{x} \urcorner, y$)'.

23. Note that an attempt to identify the object perceived in terms of resemblance with the perception rather than in terms of the causal chain leading to the perception would seriously distort an account of misperception.

24. The corresponding principle for determining who it is that a given proper name, as it is used by some speaker, names, was first brought to my attention by Saul Kripke. Kripke's examples incorporated both the indirect path from person named to person naming and also the possible distortions of associated descriptions.

The existence of a relatively large number of persons with the same proper name gives urgency to this problem even in mundane settings. In theoretical discussions it is usually claimed that such difficulties are settled by "context." I have recently found at least vague recognition of the use of genetic factors to account for the connection between name and named in such diverse sources as Henry Leonard: "Probably for most of us there is little more than a vaguely felt willingness to mean . . . whatever the first assigners of the name intended by it." (*An Introduction to Principles of Right Reason*, section 30.2), and P. F. Strawson: "[T]he identifying description . . . may include a reference to another's reference to that particular . . . So one reference may borrow the credentials . . . from another; and that from another." (*Individuals*, footnote 1, p. 182). Though in neither case are genetic and descriptive features clearly distinguished.

Kripke's insights and those of Charles Chastain, who has especially emphasized the role of *knowledge* in order to establish the desired connection between name and named, are in large part responsible for the heavy emphasis I place on genetic factors.

25. Although it is useful for scholarly purposes to have a catalogue of such "fallacies" (such as that provided in Carney and Scheer, *Fundamentals of Logic*), the value of such discussions in improving the practical reasoning of rational beings seems to me somewhat dubious. A sensitive discussion of a related form of argument occurs in Angell, *Reasoning and Logic*, especially pp. 422–423.

26. Such failures may also be due to self-deception, an inaccurate self-concept, but then the purported object does not exist at all.

27. Insofar as I understand Hintikka's "Individuals, Possible Worlds, and Epistemic Logic," the domain of values of the bound variables fluctuates with the placement of the bound occurrences of the variables. If, in a quantifier's matrix, the occurrences of the variable bound to the quantifier fall only within uniterated epistemological contexts, then the variables range over possible(?) individuals "represented" by vivid names. If, on the other hand, no occurrences of the variable fall within epistemological (or other opaque) contexts, then the variables range over the usual actual individuals. And if the variable occurs both within and without an epistemological context, then the values of the variables are inner individuals which are also actual. Thus if Ralph believes in Santa Claus, and σ is Ralph's vivid Santa Claus description, Hintikka would treat "$\ulcorner$Ralph believes that σ = Santa Claus$\urcorner$," as true and as implying "∃x Ralph believes that x = Santa Claus," but would treat "∃x[x = Santa Claus & Ralph believes that x = Santa Claus]" and presumably "∃x[∃y y = x& Ralph believes that x = Santa Claus]" as false, and not as consequences of "$\ulcorner$σ = Santa Claus & Ralph believes that σ = Santa Claus$\urcorner$."

28. I disregard precognition explained by a reverse causal chain.

29. We might say in such cases that the name *specifies* its denotation, in the sense in which a set of specifications, though not generated by the object specified, is written with the intention that there is or will be an object so described.

30. One such weakened notion of representation is that expressed by "Ralph **Bel** ($\ulcorner α = x \urcorner$,*y*)," analyzed as in (44) using our current **R**, which here, in contrast to the situation for Δ_N (see reference 22 above), is not equivalent to "**R**(α,*y*, Ralph)." Still this new notion of representation, when used in place of our current **R** in an analysis of the form of (44), leads to the same relational sense of belief.

31. Note especially the "secret identity" genre of children's literature containing Superman, Batman, etc.

32. At least one author, Hintikka, has seemed unwilling to allow Ralph a belief *about* Ortcutt merely on the basis of Ralph's few glimpses *of*

Ortcutt skulking around the missile base. See his "Individuals, Possible Worlds, and Epistemic Logic," footnote 13.

33. Another way out is to accept the fact that two names may represent the same person to Ralph though Ralph believes the nonidentity, but to put an ad hoc restriction on exportation. For example to analyze (33) as: "∃α[**R**(α, Ortcutt, Ralph) & Ralph **B**$\ulcorner$α is a spy$\urcorner$]& ~∃α[**R**(α, Ortcutt, Ralph) & ~Ralph **B**$\ulcorner$α is a spy$\urcorner$]." This prevents exportation where contradiction threatens. But again much that we would like to say is inexpressible in Quine's nomenclature.

34. It should be noted that in Church's "On Carnap's Analysis of Statements of Assertion and Belief" serious objections are raised to even the first step.

BIBLIOGRAPHY

R. B. Angell, *Reasoning and Logic* (New York: 1963).

P. Benacerraf, "What Numbers Could Not Be," *Philosophical Review*, 74 (1965) 47–73.

R. Carnap, *Meaning and Necessity* (Chicago: 1947) 2d ed., 1956.

D. Carney and K. Scheer, *Fundamentals of Logic* (New York: 1964).

A. Church, "A Formulation of the Logic of Sense and Denotation," in *Structure, Method, and Meaning*, ed. by P. Henle, M. Kallen, and S. K. Langer (New York: 1951).

A. Church, "On Carnap's Analysis of Statements of Assertion and Belief," *Analysis* 10 (1949–50) 97–99.

A. Church, Review of Quine's "Notes on Existence and Necessity," *Journal of Symbolic Logic*, 8 (1943) 45–47.

G. Frege, "On Sense and Reference," originally published in *Zeitschrift für Philosophie und philosophische Kritik*, 100 (1892) 25–50; translated in *Translations from the Philosophical Writings of Gottlob Frege*, ed. by P. Geach and M. Black (Oxford:1960)

K. J. Hintikka, "Individuals, Possible Worlds, and Epistemic Logic", *Noûs*, 1 (1967) 33–62.

D. Kaplan, *Foundations of Intensional Logic* (Dissertation), University Microfilms, (Ann Arbor: 1964).

H. S. Leonard, *An Introduction to Principles of Right Reason* (New York: 1957).

W. V. Quine, "Notes on Existence and Necessity," *The Journal of Philosophy*, 40 (1943) 113–127.

W. V. Quine, "Two Dogmas of Empiricism," *Philosophical Review*, 60 (1951) 20–43; reprinted in [15].

W. V. Quine, "Notes on the Theory of Reference", in [15].

W. V. Quine, *From a Logical Point of View* (Cambridge, Mass: 1953), 2nd ed., 1961.

W. V. Quine, "Three Grades of Modal Involvement," in *Proceedings of the XIth International
Congress of Philosophy, Brussels, 1953*, vol.
14, pp. 65–81, Amsterdam; reprinted in [20].

W. V. Quine, "Quantifiers and Propositional Attitudes," *The Journal of Philosophy*, 53 (1956)
177–187; reprinted (minus 15 lines) in [20],
[and in this volume].

W. V. Quine, *Word and Object* (New York: 1960).

W. V. Quine, "Reply to Professor Marcus,"
Synthese, 13 (1961) 323–330; reprinted in [20].

W. V. Quine, *The Ways of Paradox and Other
Essays* (New York: 1966).

P. F. Strawson, *Individuals* (London: 1959).

A. Tarski, "The Concept of Truth in Formalized
Languages," originally published in Polish in
*Prace Towarzystwa Naukowego
Warszawskiego*, Wydzial III, no. 34 (1933);
translated in A. Tarski, *Logic, Semantics,
Metamathematics* (Oxford: 1956) pp. 152–278.

Semantic Innocence and Uncompromising Situations   30

JON BARWISE AND JOHN PERRY

Since Frege, philosophers have become hardened to the idea that content sentences in talk about propositional attitudes may strangely refer to such entities as intensions, propositions, sentences, utterances and inscriptions . . . *If we could but recover our pre-Fregean semantic innocence,* I think it would be plainly incredible that the words "the earth moves," uttered after the words "Galileo said that," mean anything different, or refer to anything else, than is their wont when they come in other environments.

Donald Davidson, "On Saying That"[1]

I. SITUATIONS COMPROMISED

The present authors have managed to recover their pre-Fregean semantic innocence by rediscovering an old idea, that statements stand for situations, complexes of objects and properties in the world. The idea is found in various forms in Russell, Wittgenstein, and Austin, and more recently in Gustav Bergmann and other midwestern realists, but it has had little appeal for those whose philosophy of language is guided by the traditional model of formal semantics.

Situations were compromised by Frege's supposition that the reference of a sentence must be a truth-value. This approach left no room for situations, and major figures such as Church, Quine, and Davidson have followed

Frege in this regard. Carnap tried to take propositions as the designata of sentences in his early *Introduction to Semantics,* and his propositions were something like states of affairs or situations. But Church, in his review of this book, gave a formal proof that this could not work.[2] This argument used ideas from Frege to show that the reference of a sentence must be a truth-value, granted principles to which Carnap was committed.

We have developed a model-theoretic conception of semantics which takes situations seriously. We were forced to do this to give an innocent account of the semantics of perception and belief, respectively. Having developed situation semantics, we remembered the old proof that it was impossible. Reexamining Church's argument from this new perspective shows that it conflates two quite different ways of looking at the relation between statements and situations.

In this paper we sketch (quite briefly) enough of our conception of situations and their types to allow us to share our reexamination. A fuller development of situation semantics will appear in due course.

II. TYPES OF SITUATIONS

The basic picture we wish to promote goes like this. The world, at least the common-

From *Midwest Studies in Philosophy, Volume VI: The Foundations of Analytic Philosophy,* Peter French, Theodore Uehling, Jr., and Howard K. Wettstein, eds. (Minneapolis: University of Minnesota Press, 1981), pp. 387–403.

sense world that human language reflects, consists not just of objects and sets of objects, nor of objects, properties, and relations, but of objects having properties and standing in relations to one another. There are parts of the world, clearly recognized (although not precisely individuated) in common sense and human language, that we call situations.

We are certain that situations are part of the world because we see them (as when we see Hoover Tower casting a shadow on Stanford), because we find ourselves in situations (our being late with this paper puts us in an embarrassing one), and because we find we have always believed them (as we have frequently believed that Columbus discovered America). States of affairs are situations, events and episodes are situations in time, scenes are visually perceived situations, changes are sequences of situations, and facts are situations enriched (or polluted) by language.

Situations have properties of two sorts, internal and external. The cat's walking on the piano distressed Henry. Its doing so is what we call an external property of the event. The event consists of a certain cat performing a certain activity on a certain piano; these are its internal properties.

Simple indicative statements classify situations according to their internal properties, by stating that the actual situation is a certain *type* of situation. To represent the internal properties or type of a situation we use partial functions that take sequences of relations and objects as arguments and 1 or 0 as values. The type of situation that distressed Henry is one in which

$$s(\text{on, the cat, the piano}) = 1$$

The type of situation s' in which the cat is not walking on the piano but is where he belongs, on the mat, satisfies

$$s'(\text{on, the cat, the piano}) = 0$$
$$s'(\text{on, the cat, the mat}) = 1.$$

Belief in the world is belief in a largest situation; its type we call the world type.

We take properties and relations seriously; they are neither meanings nor sets of individuals nor sets of sequences of individuals. The domain A of individuals and the domain R of relations are parallel products of conceptual activity, that of individuation. They are equally abstract but equally the most concrete items we deal with in perception and in language. Individuation provides the articulation of the world necessary for language to get a hold on it.

Actual situations are part of the actual world. The conceptual activity that individuates the world lets us classify the situations according to their types. However, once we have some of the facts, we realize that they might have been otherwise, that there are situation types that are not realized by actual situations. These unrealized situation types are involved in many of our hopes, fears, intentions, and beliefs. Much of our mental life and hence the language we use to describe that mental life involves such unrealized situation types.

III. INTERPRETATION AND EVALUATION

How does language get a hold on the world? It does so at the most rudimentary level by having simple indicative statements describe types of situations, and a sentence's meaning is what suits it for this task. But meaning is a notoriously slippery and complex notion, conflating many distinct aspects of the use of language. Just as the number 100 is the sum of many different columns of smaller numbers, so are there many ways one might try to break down meaning into smaller components. Certain ways of doing this are rather well entrenched in philosophy: Frege's reference versus sense, Carnap's extension versus intension. More recently David Kaplan has advocated a three-level system of character, intension (or content), and extension.[3] Our own attempt also has three levels: *linguistic meaning*, *interpretation*, and *evaluation*.

About linguistic meaning we shall have little to say here, except by way of examples indicating how it gives rise to interpretation, but must be kept distinct from it. This we have learned from Kaplan's work on indexicality. (It is also an important insight of Austin's, and

Austin's work in general is valuable for the situation-oriented philosopher.)[4] Kaplan superimposes his top layer, character, on a possible-worlds semantics. Character and intension or content he sees as aspects of Frege's notion of sense. We believe the bottom two layers of this structure are in need of drastic reorganization, and that the top can benefit from awareness of the situations below. Our middle layer is *not* Frege's sense, for our interpretations are complexes of objects and properties, not denizens of a Fregean third realm, and not procedures or functions from possible worlds to extensions that have been used by recent philosophers of language to interpret Frege's senses. Objects and properties are found at Frege's level of reference. But Frege's notion of reference reflects his view that a realm of sense is available to provide needed specificity for embedded statements. We think this is quite misguided; hence our middle level is at best a drastic reworking of reference.

There is much that can be explored at the levels of interpretation and evaluation that seems to be largely insulated from other complexities of linguistic meaning. We do this by following two methodological principles. Our first principle is that, at the level of interpretation, indicative statements stand for, describe, or *designate* (as we will officially say) types of situations.

Our second principle is a version of compositionality, the claim that the meaning of a statement is a function of the meanings of its parts. Stated so vaguely, it could hardly be false.

Frege used this principle in his theory at both levels: the reference of a complex expression is a function of the references of its parts and similarly for sense. Our second methodological principle is the principle of modest and flexible compositionality: be compositional at the level of interpretation, but be modest in our goals, and not overly rigid. Modestly, bite off as little as possible from "meaning" so as to make the interpretations of a whole functions of the interpretation of its parts. Flexibly, realize that there may be more than one way to make a whole out of parts.

There are deliberate ambiguities in these principles. When we said that statements are to designate situation types, we used the plural to mask a complication. Namely, a single statement does not designate a single situation type, but a set of situation types. For example, "Someone is asleep" does not describe a single situation type, that of some particular individual being asleep; rather, it describes the type of situation in which *someone* is asleep. That is, it will designate the set of types of situations in which someone is asleep.

Similarly "Jackie or Molly has fleas" designates the set of types of situations in which either Jackie or Molly or both have fleas. We shall call a set of situation types a *proposition* so that statements designate propositions.

Another ambiguity in the first principle is that between statement and sentence, and here our first principle begins to interact with our second. The sentence "I am a Nebraskan" has a linguistic meaning that is independent of which English speaker uses it, or when (within bounds of time where the individual words do not take on different meanings or the whole becomes idiomatic). However, it expresses different propositions (types of situations) depending on who says it. Said by the first author, the resulting statement designates a set of unrealized types of situations. As said by the second, the resulting statement is different and contains the actual world type among those it designates.

In our emphasis on statements and types of situations we follow J. L. Austin in his famous paper "Truth." However, Austin tried to have his "descriptive conventions" take one straight from sentences to situation types, a move which conflates two steps that need to be kept separate. (Here Austin failed to implement the insight mentioned above; Kaplan's system does.) The way that utterances of "I am a Nebraskan" give rise to different statements is an important part of linguistic meaning, but one that gets in the way of having sentences designate situation types. Hence our emphasis on statements.[5]

A sentence is a sentence of some language, and part of what the language provides is the linguistic meaning of the sentence. In a particular use, the linguistic meaning provides interpretations of the parts and the whole. The interpretation of the whole is to be the set of situation types designated by the statement. (This is an oversimplification; as we shall see. The interpretation of the parts underdetermines the interpretation of the whole.) In general, the statement will have one interpretation that is independent of the way things really are in the world: that is, an interpretation determined by the statement, the set A of objects, and the set R of relations, but independent of the structure of the world as it happens to be. This must be the case since we can interpret statements that turn out to be false or that have to do with situations that are inaccessible to us.

Let us now turn to our second methodological principle—modest and flexible compositionality. First, let us look at a trivial application. The interpretation of "Jackie barks" is to be a proposition, the set of situation types s in which Jackie barks, i.e.,

$$\{s \mid s(\text{is barking, Jackie}) = 1\}.$$

It is also to be a function of the interpretation of the parts of the statement, so "Jackie" must supply the object Jackie and "barks" the property of barking. That is, the simplest choice of interpretations compatible with our principles is to interpret "Jackie" as Jackie and "barks" as the property of barking. At the level of interpretation, then, we find objects as the interpretations of names, variables, and other noncomplex terms, properties and relations as the interpretation of simple predicates, and propositions (i.e., sets of situation types) as the interpretation of statements.

There is a tendency in twentieth-century philosophy of language to conflate properties with meanings; this must be avoided. When the first author says "Mollie is this color," pointing to a rug of a certain color, and the second author says "Jackie is this color," pointing to a book, they use exactly the same verb phrase with the same meaning. But if the colors of the rug and the book are different, the predicates stand for quite different properties in the two statements.

To carry the analysis of interpretation one step further, let us find out what the interpretation of a complex predicate, or verb phrase, like "loves Mary" is. At first there is a problem. We interpret "loves" by a two-place relation l and "Mary" by Mary, and need to get out of the two some property—the property of loving Mary. Do we need to assume that this is a primitive or can we construct it out of what we have on hand?

To show how to construct it, we start from our first principle. For any a in A, we want the statement that a loves Mary to be interpreted as the set of situation types s in which a loves Mary, $s(l, a, \text{Mary}) = 1$. Call this proposition, this set of situation types, p(a). The function from any a in A to p(a) has two important properties: (1) it can be defined solely in terms of the interpretations l of "loves" and Mary of "Mary," and (2) from this function and any $a \in A$ we can construct the proposition that a loves Mary, namely, p(a). These are just the properties we require of an interpretation of "loves Mary."

Thus, we define P to be the set of all propositions obtainable from A and R, and we call any function from A into P a *complex property*. They are our analogue of Russell's propositional functions. Any primitive property p can be identified with a complex property p*—the property of having p—by defining p*(x) to be the proposition that x has p,

$$p^*(x) = \{s \in S \mid s(p,x) = 1\}.$$

So, in general, the interpretation of a verb phrase is a complex property.

A moment's thought will convince the reader that the conjunction of two statements ϕ and ψ should be interpreted by intersection of their respective interpretations. If we use $[\![\phi]\!]$ to denote the interpretation of ϕ, then $[\![\phi$ and $\psi]\!] = [\![\phi]\!] \cap [\![\psi]\!]$. Similarly, $[\![\phi$ or $\psi]\!] = [\![\rho]\!] \cup [\![\psi]\!]$. What about negation?

Austin, in "Truth," laments the confusion between falsity and negation, and with this we must agree. In the situation we are aware of here in our study, it is not true that Jackie is barking. Jackie is not present to our senses; she is just not part of this situation. Thus, while the proposition that Jackie is barking does not contain the type of the situation we are aware of, neither does the proposition that Jackie *is not* barking. Knowing Jackie, she probably is barking at home. Thus, the statement that Jackie is not barking is interpreted as the set of types s such that s (is barking, Jackie) = 0, whereas the statement "It is false that Jackie is barking" can be interpreted as {s | s(is barking, Jackie) ≠ 1}. Only this last proposition contains the situation we are aware of. Since situation types are partial world types, they never take on more than one value 0 or 1, but being partial, they may take on neither. This does not mean that we have a "three-valued logic." A statement is either true or it is not.

Situation semantics is much more flexible than more traditional approaches in ways that should please the linguist or philosopher of language who has not let traditional logic get too firm a hold on his thought processes. The proposal we are making leads to a rethinking of much of traditional logic. Certain classically simple concepts like negation and material implication are seen as conflations of several notions, brought about by working with only a single situation—the world.

In speaking of flexible compositionality, however, we had in mind another and absolutely central aspect of our theory. Recall that our system has three levels: meaning, interpretation, and evaluation. The idea behind the third category is this. Often by taking a look at the world or at some part of the world (or even at some pertinent situation type that does not fit the world) an expression can be fitted with a "value-laden interpretation"—an interpretation that depends on how the situation type arranges things. This value-laden interpretation is an alternative contribution that the expression can make to the interpretation of the statement of which it forms a part.

Some obvious sorts of evaluation consist in (1) determining whether a given type of situation is in a given proposition; (2) determining the extension of a property in a given situation; (3) determining the properties an individual has in a given situation. We think

that certain traditional semantical categories, such as Frege's *bedeutung* or the more modern notion of extension, are sort of a jumble between interpretation and evaluation, provoked by the central role of evaluation in understanding language. Thus propositions have been taken to be truth-values, properties conflated with extensions, and in Montague's work individuals have almost been identified with sets of properties.

Sensitivity to the differences between value-free and value-laden interpretations of statements is dulled by the logical tradition that ignored situations. For unembedded sentences in simple situations, value-laden and value-free interpretations will not be so different, and in particular their truth-values will agree, so long as the salient situation type belongs to a part of the world.

But the distinction is hard to ignore when sentences are embedded in perception and belief contexts. Thus everyone can feel the two readings of

Sally saw a dog with fleas jump in the pool.

or

Sally thinks the dean's secretary is a dean.

One who fails to see the alternative interpretations when the statements are unembedded is forced to find an alternative source for the ambiguity of the embedding statements. The appeal is naturally to scope, and this way of looking at things is so engrained as to be confused with the phenomena itself. We see the ambiguity as simply a matter of the interpretation of the embedded sentence, not a matter of scope.

Applied to definite descriptions, the value-free, value-laden distinction is simply Donnellan's distinction between attributive and referential uses.[6] Russell's theory of definite descriptions focused on their value-free or attributive use, Frege's and Strawson's on their value-laden use. Donnellan saw that these should not be alternative theories, but alternative uses accounted for by a single theory. Donnellan was unsure what sort of ambiguity he was drawing attention to; some philosophers have thought he was simply calling attention to the potential ambiguity, due to scope, when sentences containing definite descriptions were embedded. We think that Donnellan put his finger on a straightforward semantic ambiguity, and that the attributive–referential distinction is one manifestation of a ubiquitous and important phenomenon of value loading.

IV. INNOCENT SEMANTICS

One can find two reasons in Frege for giving up innocence. The first is that substitution of co-referential expressions within statements embedded in certain linguistic contexts does not preserve truth of the whole embedding statement. Such contexts are now often called, following Quine, "referentially opaque." Propositional attitudes are widely believed to be referentially opaque. We believe that by and large they are not. In any case, there should be general agreement that *some* are not. One such context is nonepistemic perception:

(1) Sally sees Mollie run.

Another is ordinary belief:

Sally believes that my dog is running.

Some arguments for referential opacity seem to be based on ignoring the difference between value-laden and value-free interpretation. One might argue, for example, that non-epistemic perception is opaque, citing the falsity of

(1)′ Sally sees the dog with the red collar run.

But (1)′ is only false if the description is used attributively; that is, if the type of scene Sally is said to see has the property of having a red collar as a constituent. But so used, the substitution of "the dog with the red collar" for "Mollie" does not preserve interpretation. On the other hand, if the description is value-loaded (using a type of a larger portion of the world than Sally sees to do the loading), (1)′ is true if (1) is, given that Mollie is the dog in question.

Some arguments for referential opacity seem based on a confusion between conversa-

tional implicatures and semantic entailments. Thus we think that "Smith believes Cicero was an orator" does not imply, but at most suggests, that Smith would check "Cicero was an orator" true. The suggestion is clearly cancelable: "Smith believes that Cicero was an orator, but only knows to call him 'Tully'."[7]

In any case, it seems clear to us that there are transparent sentence-embedding propositional attitudes. But Frege's second reason for giving up innocence was a set of considerations that convinced him that any such contexts would be equivalent to "It is true that . . ."

In "Sense and Reference" he asks what the reference of an entire declarative sentence should be, when it is "concerned with the reference of its words." He concludes that it is the truth-value. A key point in favor of this is that the truth-value of an expression remains unchanged when a part of the sentence is replaced by an expression having the same reference. "What else but the truth-value could be found," asks Frege, "that belongs quite generally to every sentence if the reference of its components is relevant, and remains unchanged by substitutions of the kind in question?"[8]

An innocent semantics takes the reference of the statement—that aspect of signification that depends on the reference of its parts—to be just that which contributes to the reference of the wholes in which it is embedded. If we take the reference of the sentence to be its truth value, an innocent semantics is hopeless, as Frege sees:

If now the truth value of a sentence is its reference, then on the one hand all true sentences have the same reference and so, on the other hand, do all false sentences. From this we can see that in the reference of a sentence all that is specific is obliterated.[9]

Given that Mollie is running and Richard lying, this would leave an innocent semantics committed to the equivalence of

(1) Sally sees Mollie run
(2) Sally sees Richard lie

or

(3) Sally believes that Mollie is running

(4) Sally believes that Richard is lying.

A semantics that could not grant these pairs different truth values would be quite hopeless.

The tradition has come to grips with Frege's loss of innocence in two ways: (i) for plausibly opaque propositional attitudes, treat the sentences as embedded and the semantics as guilty; (ii) for undeniably transparent propositional attitudes, treat the embedding of the sentence as illusory, adopting an analysis that removed the seemingly transparent position out of its spot in the embedded sentence. The semantics for that portion of the sentence left embedded will again be noninnocent.

Our approach is to treat the sentence as embedded and the semantics as innocent, and to deny that the problems that Frege and others have seen with this approach amount to much of anything.

For example, we take a statement of the form *X sees S* to embed a statement S, and to be true just in case X sees a scene (a specific kind of situation) that belongs to some type in the interpretation of S. We take *X believes that S,* in its most central and ordinary uses, to say that X has a certain complex relational property built of the objects and properties that are constituents of the proposition that S. In both cases, the parts of the embedded statement have their usual interpretations in the whole. What can be wrong with this innocent approach?

V. THE FREGE–CHURCH SLINGSHOT

Frege's own arguments against innocence do not seem very impressive. To his question, "What else but the truth value could be found, that belongs quite generally to every sentence if the reference of its components is relevant, and remains unchanged by substitutions . . . ?" we answer, "The situations designated." In the situation, all that is specific is not lost.

Again, Frege says that "the reference of a sentence may always be sought, whenever the reference of its components is involved, and this is the case when and only when we are inquiring after the truth-value." This seems to imply that we are only interested in the reference of the components of a sentence when we are inquiring about its truth value; but this is not so. If I am told "Smith believes his neighbor is a fool," I might be quite interested in the reference of "his neighbor," without caring at all about the truth of the embedded sentence.

There is, however, a very influential argument, virtually a priori, suggested no doubt by Frege's remarks, laid down explicitly by Church in his review of Carnap, and deployed in various forms with formal rigor and ruthless vigor by Quine, Davidson, and others, which seems to rule out the very possibility of a nontrivial situation semantics. The argument is so small, seldom encompassing more than half a page, and employs such a minimum of ammunition—a theory of descriptions and a popular notion of logical equivalence—that we dub it *the slingshot.* As developed by Church, the conclusion is that all sentences with the same truth-value must designate the same thing. As developed by Quine, we are put in the dilemma of either accepting "extensionality," which means seeing no distinction between (1) and (2) or (3) and (4), or losing our innocence and accepting opacity. Davidson used the slingshot to rule out straighforward innocent semantics, and then applied incredible resources of ingenuity to recover lost innocence in roundabout ways.

Church gives a form of the slingshot in the opening sections of his *Introduction to Mathematical Logic,* to motivate taking truth values as the key notion in developing logic. This version of the argument is especially interesting because, being for a reader who does not already know logic, Church cannot fall back on an appeal to any accepted notion of logical equivalence. This makes it eminently suited for reexamination, to see just where it goes wrong. Church considers these sentences:

(5) Sir Walter Scott is the author of *Waverley.*

(6) Sir Walter Scott is the man who wrote the twenty-nine *Waverley* novels altogether.

(7) The number, such that Sir Walter Scott is the man that wrote that many *Waverley* novels altogether, is twenty-nine.

(8) The number of counties in Utah is twenty-nine.

Church argues that as we go from each sentence to the next, what the sentences denote is the same. But the first and last seem to have nothing of importance in common except their truth value; he says, "Elaboration of examples of this kind leads us quickly to the conclusion, as at least plausible, that all true sentences have the same denotation."[10]

Sentence (6) results from (5) by replacement of one description by another, where both descriptions describe the same person, Scott. Sentence (8) results from (7) by a similar move, with the descriptions describing the same number, twenty-nine. The step from (6) to (7), however, is of a different sort. Church says that (6), though perhaps not synonymous with (7), "is at least so nearly so as to ensure having the same denotation."[11]

The argument is like an ambiguous figure or an Escher drawing. If you are aware of situations, you have to keep shifting perspective to let the argument trick you. From one perspective the first and last steps are fine but the middle step is all wrong. From a second perspective the middle step is reasonably good but the first and last steps are completely unfounded.

Intuitively, situations are complexes of objects and relations (under which we shall from now on subsume properties). Given this conception, the role of the parts of the sentence is to identify objects and relations out of which the complex is constructed. Let us hold this in mind, and go through the steps of the argument from both perspectives.

To get from (5) to (6), we need to suppose that the great difference between "the author of *Waverley*" and "the man who wrote the twenty-nine *Waverley* novels altogether" makes absolutely no difference to the situations described by the two sentences, that is, that the contribution these two descriptions make to the situation is just to identify Scott. Thus, the first perspective is the one where all four definite descriptions are interpreted by

the objects they happen to describe, Scott in two cases, the number twenty-nine in the other two.

But from this perspective, the step from (6) to (7) does not work at all. Recall we are attempting to show that all four sentences must designate the same situations. But from our current perspective, (6) designates a situation whose only constituent object is Scott, whereas, (7) designates one whose only constituent object is the number twenty-nine.

Now let us focus on the step from (6) to (7). If we attempt to see these sentences as designating the same situation, then it must be that of Scott's having written exactly twenty-nine *Waverley* novels altogether. To see them as designating this situation, however, we must pay close attention to the properties involved in the definite descriptions. This is not unreasonable. If you take situations seriously, it is quite natural to distinguish two ways in which descriptions might contribute to the sentence. The need is for the materials to build a situation, a complex of objects and properties, and why should the description not contribute the individual described or the properties involved in the description of the situation?

Thus, the second perspective, which is suggested anyway if we take situations seriously, is the one where "the author of *Waverley*" is not interpreted simply as Scott, but contributes the complex of objects and properties it mentions to the situations the sentence describes. But this perspective is absolutely fatal to the step from (5) to (6) or from (7) to (8). The descriptions of Scott, and those of twenty-nine even more so, contribute radically different objects and properties to the overall situation. Sentence (7) designates twenty-nine's being the number of *Waverley* novels Scott wrote, but sentence (8) designates twenty-nine's being the number of counties in Utah: distinct situations if ever there were distinct situations.

So we see that from the first perspective, the one Frege would have us take, where in the reference of the description all that is specific is obliterated, the first and last steps of the argument are fine but the middle is wrong. From the second perspective, more in line with Russell's theory of descriptions, the middle step comes off better but the first and the last steps are wrong. Under neither reading are we compelled to accept the argument.

The connection between the slingshot and Russell's theory of descriptions was, in effect, commented on by Gödel in his essay "Russell's Mathematical Logic," for he used a sort of reverse slingshot to motivate Russell's theory:

But different true sentences may indicate different true things. Therefore, this view about sentences makes it necessary either to drop the above mentioned principle (of compositionality) . . . or to deny that a descriptive phrase denotes the object described. Russell did the latter by taking the viewpoint that a descriptive phrase denotes nothing at all but only has meaning in context, . . .[12]

Gödel goes on to say that he cannot help feeling that the puzzling conclusion of the slingshot "has only been evaded by Russell's theory of descriptions and that there is something behind it which is not yet completely understood."[13]

We believe that "something" was gotten at by Donnellan, with the referential and attributive distinction, and that this version of the slingshot, and every version of it, simply turns on shifts from value-free to value-laden interpretations. We value load the definite descriptions for the first step, take them as value-free for the next, and then load them again to finish the argument.

Church speaks of the intimate relation between (6) and (7) but, as he is introducing logical ideas at this point, does not exploit the fact that they are logically equivalent in the traditional sense: true in just the same models. From one perspective they are both identity statements (*Scott is Scott, twenty-nine is twenty-nine*, respectively). From the other they are contingent, but nevertheless true in just the same models. For the philosopher who has learned the traditional notion of logical equivalence, it is easy to be impressed by this. It might seem that logically equivalent statements must stand for the same thing; they must, after all, be equivalent in their *logical* powers or they would not be called that. But

this line of thought would use the idea that all true sentences stand for the same thing as a premise for an argument where it is also the conclusion. If sentences designate truth values, then, of course, sentences that have the same truth value under all assignments to the nonlogical constants will be equivalent in what they designate. But if statements designate something else, they might be equivalent in truth value in virtue of logical structure, while being nonequivalent in what they designate. On our theory, "logical equivalence" is a misnomer for the relation between statements true in the same models; such statements need not have the same subject matter, in the sense of objects and properties designated by their parts, at all. As soon as such "logically equivalent" statements differing in subject matter are embedded in other statements, the differences in their logical powers become evident. The standard notion of logical equivalence plays an important role in the uses of the slingshot to which we now turn.

VI. QUINE AND THE SLINGSHOT

Quine uses various forms of the slingshot throughout his writings. One of the most explicit of these uses comes in his discussion of what he calls the extensionality principle: statements occur within other statements either truth functionally or opaquely, which forces one to give up semantic innocence.[14] When we suppose that (1) and (3) might be true, and (2) and (4) false, but still maintain that the parts of the embedded sentences make their usual contributions to the wholes, we are violating the extensionality principle.

Quine does not say that such violation is impossible, only that it is "not easy." Suppose S and S' are true and that F is a referentially transparent sentence-embedding context. Quine wants to argue that if F(S) is true, so is F(S'), and conversely. First note that

(A)
$\{x \mid S \ \& \ x = \varnothing\} = \{ x \mid S' \ \& \ x = \varnothing\} = \{\varnothing\}$
(B)
S is logically equivalent to $[\{\varnothing\} = \{ x \mid S \ \& \ x = \varnothing\}]$
S' is logically equivalent to $[\{\varnothing\} = \{x \mid S' \ \& \ x = \varnothing\}]$

From F(S) we obtain $F([\{\varnothing\} = \{x \mid S \& x = \varnothing\}])$ by substitution of logical equivalents, then we obtain $F([\{\varnothing\} = \{x \mid S' \& x = \varnothing\}])$ by (A) and the referential transparency of F, and then F(S') by another substitution of logical equivalents. If S and S' are both false, trade $\varnothing$ for $\{\phi\}$. Thus, if F is referentially transparent, it will treat sentences that just happen to have the same truth-values alike.

Quine finds in this argument "compelling" grounds for the principle of extentionality, a principle he was to come to advocate for the whole of science.[15] And yet he quite explicitly observes that for it to work we must suppose not only that the embedding context is transparent but that logical equivalents are interchangable in it. The argument simply takes us from the premise that transparent contexts do not discriminate among "logically equivalent" statements to the conclusion that they do not discriminate among statements that happen to be equivalent in truth value.

All the versions of the slingshot turn on the fact that logically equivalent statements can differ in subject matter, i.e., in what individuals and relations their parts designate.

Let us call a context that is transparent and in which logical equivalents are interchangeable *unconcerned* (about subject matter). Those that are transparent but in which logical equivalents are not interchangeable we shall call *concerned*. There seem to be a number of clearly concerned contexts. The most compelling is perception:

(9)   Fred sees Betty enter.
(10)   Fred sees Betty enter and (Sally smoke or Sally not smoke).

The statements embedded in (9) and (10) are logically equivalent. "Fred sees" seems clearly a transparent context. And yet we cannot go from (9) to (10). If we did, we should have to admit that Fred either saw Sally smoke or saw Sally not smoke, even though, as we may suppose, Fred has never laid eyes on Sally. The admission would be forced by the principles:

If Fred sees P and Q, then Fred sees Q

If Fred sees P or Q, then Fred sees P or Fred sees Q.

One could of course deny one of these principles to save the principle of extensionality, or one could deny that perception statements such as (9) and (10) are transparent. But we see no motive for either move. Quine seems to convey the attitude that unconcerned contexts are in the natural order of things, but, to be fair, does not say that there are no concerned contexts. His argument has to do with his statement operator "nec," and he carefully stipulates that logical equivalents are interchangeable within it without change of truth value. Other writers are not always so careful.

VII. DAVIDSON AND THE SLINGSHOT

The term "slingshot" was originally suggested to us by Donald Davidson's use of this compact piece of philosophical artillery in his wars against some of the giants of our industry. It is an essential part of his criticisms of Reichenbach on events and of Austin on truth, for example. The biggest giant Davidson takes on is Frege, however, for Davidson has consistently resisted the idea that statements embedded in propositional attitudes retain specificity by referring to Fregean senses. For this resistance, and for his recognition of situations, particularly in the analysis of action statements, he should be applauded. Unfortunately, Davidson was blocked from the most straightforward implementation of these insights by his devotion to the slingshot, a weapon constructed of Frege's own materials. To vary the pun, although Davidson resisted original *sinn,* he succumbed to original *bedeutung.*

To see how the slingshot corrupts Davidson, let us briefly look at his criticisms of Reichenbach. In *Elements of Symbolic Logic* Reichenbach developed a formal symbolic logic in which he quantified over situations, events, and facts. For Reichenbach the terms "fact" and "event" were synonymous, and events "have the physical existence of things, and not the fictitious existence of situations."[16] Thus his events and facts are analogous to our situations, his situations to our situation types.

Reichenbach sees a close relation between statements like (11) and (12):

(11)   Scott wrote *Waverley*
(12)   The event of Scott writing *Waverley* took place.

He refers to such statements as alternative ways of "splitting" a situation: "thing splitting" and "event splitting." The close relation is that a certain situation "corresponds" to (11) which is referred to by the description in (12). Reichenbach does not think that there is any singular term, manifest or hidden, in (11) that refers to the situation; only the statement as a whole has this relation to it; the transformation from (11) to (12) is "holistic."

Davidson finds much of value in Reichenbach's theory.[17] He acknowledges and emphasizes the importance of recognizing situations in resolving a number of problems about the logic of action statements. But he has to reject the leading component of Reichenbach's idea: he does not think (11) can correspond to the situation referred to by the description in (12) unless (11) also contains a (hidden) argument place for events. At this point, we think, Davidson purchases philosophical insight at the cost of syntactic plausibility.

The villain here is the slingshot. It convinces Davidson that Reichenbach's proposal is "radically defective," in leading inevitably to the conclusion that there is only one big event. The deployment of the slingshot depends on the principle,

> If S and S' are logically equivalent, then, for every event e, e consists in the fact that S if and only if e consists in the fact that S'.

This is just the assumption that "e consists in the fact that" provides an unconcerned context. Here Davidson is being less cautious than Quine was, perhaps more awed by the phrase "logical equivalence." There is no reason at all to suppose this operator would be unconcerned, as should now be pretty clear. The natural development of the idea of a statement corresponding to an event or class of events will have that event or class of events determined by the objects and properties the

parts of the statement designate. And logically equivalent statements can have parts that designate very different sets of objects and relations. Reichenbach would have no reason to accept the principle.

Logical equivalence as an unargued-for criterion for statement codesignation plays a key role in another important paper of Davidson's. In "Truth and Meaning" he considers the possibility of a semantical system something like ours.[18] Our level of interpretation is an aspect of meaning that is assigned to statements in a (modest and flexible) way as a function of the interpretations of the parts. Such a system, Davidson argues, must conclude that all true sentences have the same meaning, and so, too, all the false ones. This version of the slingshot takes up very little room:

> But now suppose that 'R' and 'S' abbreviate any two sentences alike in truth value. Then the following four sentences have the same reference:
>
> (1) R
> (2) $\hat{x}(x = x.R) = \hat{x}(x = x)$
> (3) $\hat{x}(x = x.S) = \hat{x}(x = x)$
> (4) S
>
> For (1) and (2) are logically equivalent, as are (3) and (4), whereas (3) differs from (2) only in containing the singular term '$\hat{x}(x = x.S)$' where (2) contains '$\hat{x}(x = x.R)$' and these refer to the same thing if S and R are alike in truth value.[19]

This difficulty for such a theory of meaning looms when we make two assumptions Davidson describes as reasonable:

> that logically equivalent singular terms have the same reference; and that a singular term does not change its reference if a contained singular term is replaced by another with the same reference.[20]

Davidson notes that the argument is essentially Frege's, cites Church, and says that "the argument does not depend on any particular identification of the entities to which sentences are supposed to refer."

Although we do not speak this way, in assigning interpretations to whole statements, we might be said to be treating them as singular terms. Let us look at Davidson's two principles, then, from the perspective of someone who treats statements as singular terms referring to situations. The first principle would be totally unacceptable, for it is really simply the rejection of this very idea. This is not surprising, since it was the rejection of the whole idea by Frege that led to the use of "logical equivalence" that the statement of the principle exploits. In spite of what Davidson says, it is hard to imagine any among those who have decided that statements designate at all who would accept this principle, except those who had decided they designate truth values. The second principle is ambiguous, depending on whether complex singular terms are given a value-free or value-laden interpretation. Taken the first way, and assuming the first principle, the first step in the argument works but not the second. Taken the second way, the first step fails.

VIII. FINAL REMARKS

In many contexts embedded statements seem to contribute something more specific than their truth-values to the embedding statement. Frege's choice of the truth-value as that which belongs to the statement in virtue of the references of its parts precluded taking this appearance at face value. His approach was to look to another aspect of meaning for the specificity provided by the embedded statement. Others who are skeptical of meaning beyond reference, like Quine, have been led to doubt the very intelligibility of such statement-embedding contexts. A third approach is to recognize that statements do contribute something to the larger wholes in which they are found, something that turns on the designations of their parts, but to deny that when this occurs they are truly embedded. Quine takes this attitude too at times, and Davidson's article from which our opening quotation was taken adopts a radical version of this approach. Perhaps a combination of the first and third attitudes is something like philosophical orthodoxy. Frege's approach is taken toward certain cases ("de dicto"): the statement is embedded, but what it provides does not turn on the reference of its parts. The

third attitude is taken toward other cases ("de re"): the parts of the contained statement do provide their designations to the whole, but the statements are not really embedded, they only seem to be at the level of superficial syntax.

An alternative is to question Frege's original decision. Here we think the slingshot has had a real and unfortunate influence. Perhaps its most important use was the first, Church's in his review of Carnap's *Introduction to Semantics*. Church used principles internal to Carnap's system to show that it must have truth-values as the designations of sentences, rather than the situation-like propositions Carnap had intended. Church's argument turned on the principle that "L-equivalent" sentences have the same designation and on the assumption that substitution of two quite different singular terms designating the null class preserved the designation of the sentence in which they occur ('Λ' and '$(\lambda x)(x = x \& \sim \ldots)$', where ' $\ldots$ ' is some true but not L-true sentence). His argument seems decisive against Carnap's system as it stands. One possible response would have been to rethink Carnap's principles about designation and his conception of propositions, to see if the slingshot could be avoided. But both Church and Carnap went in another direction and assumed that what is specific is not to be found in the reference of the sentence. Awesomely formal deployments of the slingshot seem to put this beyond question. One can see the whole development of possible-worlds semantics, and much else in the philosophy of language of the past thirty years, as an outgrowth of this response to Church's deployment of the slingshot against Carnap.

We like to view situation semantics and possible-worlds semantics as two lines meeting in a single point, that point being where there is only one world and one situation. We believe a more workable semantics for natural language can be developed along the line we are proposing and that many of the valuable insights of the possible worlds approach can be incorporated into it. It may turn out, however, that the semantic facts will not fit such a narrow-minded view, and that we will have to look at the complex plane determined by the two lines. If so, we leave it to the reader to decide which line is the real axis and which is the imaginary.

NOTES

1. Donald Davidson, "On Saying That," reprinted in *The Logic of Grammar,* ed. Donald Davidson and Gilbert Harman (Encino, Calif.: 1975), p. 152. Originally published in *Synthese* 19 (1968–69). Our italics. [Reprinted in this volume.]
2. Rudolf Carnap, *Introduction to Semantics* (Cambridge: 1942); Alonzo Church, "Carnap's *Introduction to Semantics,*" *Philosophical Review* 52 (1943):298–305.
3. David Kaplan, "Dthat" [reprinted in this volume] and "On the Logic of Demonstratives," in *Contemporary Perspectives in the Philosophy of Language,* ed. Peter A. French, Theodore E. Uehling, Jr., and Howard K. Wettstein (Minneapolis: 1979), pp. 383–412.
4. J. L. Austin, *Philosophical Papers* (Oxford: 1961). See particularly "Truth" and "Unfair to Facts."
5. We try to use "sentence" and "statement" properly, except when discussing the views of others where it seems inappropriate.
6. Keith Donnellan, "Reference and Definite Descriptions," *Philosophical Review* 75 (1966): 281–304 [reprinted in this volume]; "Putting Humpty Dumpty Together Again," *Philosophical Review* 77 (1968):203–15. Ruth Marcus remarks in passing in "Modalities and Intensional Languages," *Synthese* 14 (1962), that descriptions can function as proper names, i.e., "purely referentially"; she takes their normal use to be more like the attributive; see page 283.
7. See J. O. Urmson, "Criteria of Intentionality," in *Logic and Philosophy for Linguists* ed. J. M.

E. Moravcsik (The Hague: 1974), pp. 226–37. See also Jon Barwise, "Scenes and Other Situations," unpublished paper, Stanford University, and John Perry, "Belief and Acceptance," *Midwest Studies in Philosophy* 5 (1980):533–42 and "The Problem of the Essential Indexical," *Noûs* 13 (1979):3–21.
8. Gottlob Frege, "On Sense and Reference" [reprinted in this volume] in *Translations from the Philosophical Writings of Gottlob Frege,* ed. and trans. Peter Geach and Max Black (Oxford: 1960) p. 64.
9. *Ibid.,* 65.
10. Alonzo Church, *Introduction to Mathematical Logic* (Princeton: 1956), p. 25.
11. *Ibid.*
12. Kurt Gödel, "Russell's Mathematical Logic," reprinted in *Philosophy of Mathematics,* ed. Paul Benacerraf and Hilary Putnam (Englewood Cliffs, N.J.: 1966), pp. 214–15.
13. *Ibid.*
14. W. V. Quine, "Three Grades of Modal Involvement," in *Ways of Paradox,* revised and enlarged edition (Cambridge: 1976), pp. 163–64.
15. W. V. Quine, "The Scope and Language of Science," in *Ways of Paradox,* p. 242.
16. Hans Reichenbach, *Elements of Symbolic Logic* (New York: 1966), p. 272. Relevant sections are reprinted in *The Logic of Grammar,* ed. Davidson and Harman.
17. Donald Davidson, "The Logical Form of Action Sentences," in *The Logic of Grammar,* pp. 235–46. This essay was originally published in *The Logic of Decision and Action,* ed. Nicholas Rescher (Pittsburgh: 1967).
18. Donald Davidson, "Truth and Meaning" [reprinted in this volume] in *Philosophical Logic,* ed. J. W. Davis et al. (Dordrecht: 1969) pp. 1–20. This essay was originally published in *Synthese* 17 (1967).
19. *Ibid.,* p. 3 [p. 80, this volume].
20. *Ibid.,* pp. 2–3 [p. 82, this volume].

SUGGESTED FURTHER READING

Barwise, Jon, Scenes and Other Situations, *The Journal of Philosophy* 78 (1981), 369–397.

Barwise, Jon and John Perry, *Situations and Attitudes* (Cambridge: MIT Press, 1983).

Carnap, Rudolf, *Meaning and Necessity,* 2d ed. (Chicago: University of Chicago Press, 1956).

Church, Alonzo, On Carnap's Analysis of Statements of Assertion and Belief, *Analysis* 10 (1950), 97–99.

Hintikka, Jaakko, *Knowledge and Belief* (Ithaca, Cornell University Press, 1962).

Hintikka, Jaakko, Semantics for Propositional Attitudes, in *Philosophical Logic,* ed. J. W. Davis *et al.* (Dordrecht: D. Reidel, 1969), pp. 21–45.

Kripke, Saul, A Puzzle About Belief, in *Meaning and Use,* ed. Asa Margalit (Dordrecht: D. Reidel, 1979), pp. 239–283.

Loar, Brian, *Mind and Meaning* (Cambridge: Cambridge University Press, 1981).

Marcus, Ruth Barcan, A Proposed Solution to a Puzzle About Belief, in *Midwest Studies in Philosophy,* vol. 6, ed. Peter A. French, Theodore E. Uehling, Jr., and Howard K. Wettstein (Minneapolis: University of Minnesota Press, 1981), pp. 501–510.

Marcus, Ruth Barcan, Rationality and Believing the Impossible, *Journal of Philosophy* 80 (1983), 321–329.

Quine, W. V., Reference and Modality, in *From a Logical Point of View* 2d ed. (New York: Harper & Row, 1961), pp. 139–159.

Partee, Barbara, Belief-Sentences and the Limits of Semantics, in *Processes, Beliefs and Questions,* ed. Stanley Peters and Esa Saarinen (Dordrecht: D. Reidel, 1982), pp. 88–106.

Van Fraassen, Bas. Propositional Attitudes in Weak Pragmatics, *Studia Logica* (38) 365–374.

VI

METAPHOR

Any adequate theory of language or language use must be able to account for not just the wide variety of literal utterances but those used as figures of speech. Of these, metaphor is one of the most conspicuous. As explained earlier, there are two basic approaches to meaning: a semantic approach and a pragmatic approach. John Searle's "Metaphor" explains metaphor within Grice's pragmatic theory of conversation and his own theory of speech acts. Metaphors are similar to indirect speech acts in that both are conversationally implied due to the nonfulfillment of conversational maxims.

Donald Davidson's article, "What Metaphors Mean," is a semantic treatment of metaphor that is consistent with his general theory of meaning presented in "Truth and Meaning."

Significant differences notwithstanding, Searle and Davidson agree that there is no important sense in which sentences used metaphorically have a metaphorical meaning. Both emphasize that in the utterance of a metaphor the metaphorical sentence retains its literal meaning and that the literal meaning of the sentence must be understood in order for the metaphor to be understood. Davidson states something like this as his thesis: "metaphors mean what the words, in their most literal interpretation, mean, and nothing more."

JOHN R. SEARLE

FORMULATING THE PROBLEM

If you hear somebody say, "Sally is a block of ice," or "Sam is a pig," you are likely to assume that the speaker does not mean what he says literally but that he is speaking metaphorically. Furthermore, you are not likely to have very much trouble figuring out what he means. If he says, "Sally is a prime number between 17 and 23," or "Bill is a barn door," you might still assume he is speaking metaphorically, but it is much harder to figure out what he means. The existence of such utterances—utterances in which the speaker means metaphorically something different from what the sentence means literally—poses a series of questions for any theory of language and communication: What is metaphor, and how does it differ from both literal and other forms of figurative utterances? Why do we use expressions metaphorically instead of saying exactly and literally what we mean? How do metaphorical utterances work, that is, how is it possible for speakers to communicate to hearers when speaking metaphorically inasmuch as they do not say what they mean? And why do some metaphors work and others not?

In my discussion, I propose to tackle this latter set of questions—those centering around the problem of how metaphors work—both because of its intrinsic interest, and because it does not seem to me that we shall get an answer to the others until this fundamental question has been answered. Before we can begin to understand it, however, we need to formulate the question more precisely.

The problem of explaining how metaphors work is a special case of the general problem of explaining how speaker meaning and sentence or word meaning come apart. It is a special case, that is, of the problem of how it is possible to say one thing and mean something else, where one succeeds in communicating what one means even though both the speaker and the hearer know that the meanings of the words uttered by the speaker do not exactly and literally express what the speaker meant. Some other instances of the break between speaker's utterance meaning and literal sentence meaning are irony and indirect speech acts. In each of these cases, what the speaker means is not identical with what the sentence means, and yet what he means is in various ways dependent on what the sentence means.

It is essential to emphasize at the very beginning that the problem of metaphor concerns the relations between word and sentence meaning, on the one hand, and speaker's meaning or utterance meaning, on the other. Many writers on the subject try to

From *Metaphor and Thought*, Andrew Ortony, ed. (Cambridge: Cambridge University Press, 1979), pp. 92–123.

locate the metaphorical element of a meta-phorical utterance in the sentence or expressions uttered. They think there are two kinds of sentence meaning, literal and metaphorical. However, sentences and words have only the meanings that they have. Strictly speaking, whenever we talk about the metaphorical meaning of a word, expression, or sentence, we are talking about what a speaker might utter it to mean, in a way that departs from what the word, expression, or sentence actually means. We are, therefore, talking about possible speaker's intentions. Even when we discuss how a nonsense sentence, such as Chomsky's example, "Colorless green ideas sleep furiously," could be given a metaphorical interpretation, what we are talking about is how a speaker could utter the sentence and mean something by it metaphorically, even though it is literally nonsensical. To have a brief way of distinguishing what a speaker means by uttering words, sentences, and expressions, on the one hand, and what the words, sentences, and expressions mean, on the other, I shall call the former *speaker's utterance meaning,* and the latter, *word,* or *sentence meaning.* Metaphorical meaning is always speaker's utterance meaning.

In order that the speaker can communicate using metaphorical utterances, ironical utterances, and indirect speech acts, there must be some principles according to which he is able to mean more than, or something different from, what he says, whereby the hearer, using his knowledge of them, can understand what the speaker means. The relation between the sentence meaning and the metaphorical utterance meaning is systematic rather than random or ad hoc. Our task in constructing a theory of metaphor is to try to state the principles which relate literal sentence meaning to metaphorical utterance meaning. Because the knowledge that enables people to use and understand metaphorical utterances goes beyond their knowledge of the literal meanings of words and sentences, the principles we seek are not included, or at least not entirely included, within a theory of semantic competence as traditionally conceived. From the point of view of the hearer, the problem of

a theory of metaphor is to explain how he can understand the speaker's utterance meaning given that all he hears is a sentence with its word and sentence meaning. From the point of view of the speaker, the problem is to explain how he can mean something different from the word and sentence meaning of the sentence he utters. In light of these reflections, our original question, How do metaphors work? can be recast as follows: What are the principles that enable speakers to formulate, and hearers to understand, metaphorical utterances? and How can we state these principles in a way that makes it clear how metaphorical utterances differ from other sorts of utterances in which speaker meaning does not coincide with literal meaning?

Because part of our task is to explain how metaphorical utterances differ from literal utterances, to start with we must arrive at a characterization of literal utterances. Most—indeed all—of the authors I have read on the subject of metaphor assume that we know how literal utterances work; they do not think that the problem of literal utterances is worth discussing in their account of metaphor. The price they pay for this is that their accounts often describe metaphorical utterances in ways that fail to distinguish them from literal ones.

In fact, to give an accurate account of literal predication is an extremely difficult, complex, and subtle problem. I shall not attempt anything like a thorough summary of the principles of literal utterance but shall remark on only those features which are essential for a comparison of literal utterance with metaphorical utterance. Also, for the sake of simplicity, I shall confine most of my discussion of both literal and metaphorical utterance to very simple cases, and to sentences used for the speech act of assertion.

Imagine that a speaker makes a literal utterance of a sentence such as

(1) Sally is tall
(2) The cat is on the mat
(3) It's getting hot in here.

Now notice that in each of these cases, the literal meaning of the sentence determines, at least in part, a set of truth-conditions; and because the only illocutionary force indicating devices (see Searle, 1969) in the sentences are assertive, the literal and serious utterance of one of these sentences will commit the speaker to the existence of the set of truth conditions determined by the meaning of that sentence, together with the other determinants of truth conditions. Notice, furthermore, that in each case the sentence only determines a definite set of truth conditions relative to a particular context. That is because each of these examples has some indexical element, such as the present tense, or the demonstrative "here," or the occurrence of contextually dependent definite descriptions, such as "the cat" and "the mat."

In these examples, the contextually dependent elements of the sentence are explicitly realized in the semantic structure of the sentence: One can see and hear the indexical expressions. But these sentences, like most sentences, only determine a set of truth conditions against a background of assumptions that are not explicitly realized in the semantic structure of the sentence. This is most obvious for (1) and (3), because they contain the relative terms "tall" and "hot." These are what old-fashioned grammarians called "attributive" terms, and they only determine a definite set of truth conditions against a background of factual assumptions about the sort of things referred to by the speaker in the rest of the sentence. Moreover, these assumptions are not explicitly realized in the semantic structure of the sentence. Thus, a woman can be correctly described as "tall" even though she is shorter than a giraffe that could correctly be described as "short."

Though this dependence of the application of the literal meaning of the sentence on certain factual background assumptions that are not part of the literal meaning is most obvious for sentences containing attributive terms, the phenomenon is quite general. Sentence (2) only determines a definite set of truth conditions given certain assumptions about cats, mats, and the relation of being on. However, these assumptions are not part of the semantic content of the sentence. Sup-

pose, for example, that the cat and mat are in the usual cat-on-mat spatial configuration, only both cat and mat are in outer space, outside any gravitational field relative to which one could be said to be "above" or "over" the other. Is the cat still *on* the mat? Without some further assumptions, the sentence does not determine a definite set of truth conditions in this context. Or suppose all cats suddenly became lighter than air, and the cat went flying about with the mat stuck to its belly. Is the cat still on the mat?

We know without hesitation what are the truth-conditions of, "The fly is on the ceiling," but not of, "The cat is on the ceiling," and this difference is not a matter of meaning, but a matter of how our factual background information enables us to apply the meanings of sentences. In general, one can say that in most cases a sentence only determines a set of truth conditions relative to a set of assumptions that are not realized in the semantic content of the sentence. Thus, even in literal utterances, where speaker's meaning coincides with sentence meaning, the speaker must contribute more to the literal utterance than just the semantic content of the sentence, because that semantic content only determines a set of truth conditions relative to a set of assumptions made by the speaker, and if communication is to be successful, his assumptions must be shared by the hearer (for further discussion of this point, see Searle, 1978).

Notice finally that the notion of similarity plays a crucial role in any account of literal utterance. This is because the literal meaning of any general term, by determining a set of truth conditions, also determines a criterion of similarity between objects. To know that a general term is true of a set of objects is to know that they are similar with respect to the property specified by that term. All tall women are similar with respect to being tall, all hot rooms similar with respect to being hot, all square objects similar with respect to being square, and so on.

To summarize this brief discussion of some aspects of literal utterance, there are three features we shall need to keep in mind in our account of metaphorical utterance. First, in literal utterance the speaker means what he says; that is, literal sentence meaning and speaker's utterance meaning are the same; second, in general the literal meaning of a sentence only determines a set of truth conditions relative to a set of background assumptions which are not part of the semantic content of the sentence; and third, the notion of similarity plays an essential role in any account of literal predication.

When we turn to cases where utterance meaning and sentence meaning are different, we find them quite various. Thus, for example, (3) could be uttered not only to tell somebody that it is getting hot in the place of utterance (literal utterance), but it could also be used to request somebody to open a window (indirect speech act), to complain about how cold it is (ironical utterance), or to remark on the increasing vituperation of an argument that is in progress (metaphorical utterance). In our account of metaphorical utterance, we shall need to distinguish it not only from literal utterance, but also from these other forms in which literal utterance is departed from, or exceeded, in some way.

Because in metaphorical utterances what the speaker means differs from what he says (in one sense of "say"), in general we shall need two sentences for our examples of metaphor—first the sentence uttered metaphorically, and second a sentence that expresses literally what the speaker means when he utters the first sentence and means it metaphorically. Thus (3), the metaphor (MET):

(3) (MET) It's getting hot in here.

corresponds to (3), the paraphrase (PAR):

(3) (PAR) The argument that is going on is becoming more vituperative

and similarly with the pairs:

(4) (MET) Sally is a block of ice
(4) (PAR) Sally is an extremely unemotional and unresponsive person
(5) (MET) I have climbed to the top of the greasy pole (*Disraeli*)

(5) (PAR) I have after great difficulty become prime minister
(6) (MET) Richard is a gorilla
(6) (PAR) Richard is fierce, nasty, and prone to violence.

Notice that in each case we feel that the paraphrase is somehow inadequate, that something is lost. One of our tasks will be to explain this sense of dissatisfaction that we have with paraphrases of even feeble metaphors. Still, in some sense, the paraphrases must approximate what the speaker meant, because in each case the speaker's metaphorical assertion will be true if, and only if, the corresponding assertion using the PAR sentence is true. When we get to more elaborate examples, our sense of the inadequacy of the paraphrase becomes more acute. How would we paraphrase the following?

(7) (MET)
   My Life had stood—a Loaded Gun—
   In Corners—till a Day
   The Owner passes—identified
   And carried Me away—

   (*Emily Dickinson*)

Clearly a good deal is lost by

(7) (PAR) My life was one of unrealized but readily realizable potential (a loaded gun) in mediocre surroundings (corners) until such time (a day) when my destined lover (the owner) came (passed), recognized my potential (identified), and took (carried) me away.

Yet, even in this case, the paraphrase or something like it must express a large part of speaker's utterance meaning, because the truth-conditions are the same.

Sometimes we feel that we know exactly what the metaphor means and yet would not be able to formulate a literal PAR sentence because there are no literal expressions that convey what it means. Thus even for such a simple case as

(8) (MET) The ship ploughed the sea,

we may not be able to construct a simple paraphrase sentence even though there is no obscurity in the metaphorical utterance. And indeed metaphors often serve to plug such semantic gaps as this. In other cases, there may be an indefinite range of paraphrases. For example, when Romeo says:

(9) (MET) Juliet is the sun,

there may be a range of things he might mean. But while lamenting the inadequacy of paraphrases, let us also recall that paraphrase is a symmetrical relation. To say that the paraphrase is a poor paraphrase of the metaphor is also to say that the metaphor is a poor paraphrase of its paraphrase. Furthermore, we should not feel apologetic about the fact that some of our examples are trite or dead metaphors. Dead metaphors are especially interesting for our study, because, to speak oxymoronically, dead metaphors have lived on. They have become dead through continual use, but their continual use is a clue that they satisfy some semantic need.

Confining ourselves to the simplest subject-predicate cases, we can say that the general form of the metaphorical utterance is that a speaker utters a sentence of the form "S is P" and means metaphorically that S is R. In analyzing metaphorical predication, we need to distinguish, therefore, between three sets of elements. Firstly, there is the subject expression "S" and the object or objects it is used to refer to. Secondly, there is the predicate expression "P" that is uttered and the literal meaning of that expression with its corresponding truth conditions, plus the denotation if there is any. And thirdly, there is the speaker's utterance meaning "S is R" and the truth-conditions determined by that meaning. In its simplest form, the problem of metaphor is to try to get a characterization of the relations between the three sets, S, P, and R^1, together with a specification of other information and principles used by speakers and hearers, so as to explain how it is possible to utter "S is P" and mean "S is R," and how it is possible to communicate that meaning from speaker to hearer. Now, obviously, that is not all there is to understand about metaphorical utterances; the speaker does more than just assert that S is R, and the peculiar effectiveness of metaphor will have to be explained in terms of how he does more than just assert

that S is R and why he should choose this roundabout way of asserting that S is R in the first place. But at this stage we are starting at the beginning. At the very minimum, a theory of metaphor must explain how it is possible to utter "S is P" and both mean and communicate that S is R.

We can now state one of the differences between literal and metaphorical utterances as applied to these simple examples: In the case of literal utterance, speaker's meaning and sentence meaning are the same; therefore the assertion made about the object referred to will be true if and only if it satisfies the truth-conditions determined by the meaning of the general term as applied against a set of shared background assumptions. In order to understand the utterance, the hearer does not require any extra knowledge beyond his knowledge of the rules of language, his awareness of the conditions of utterance, and a set of shared background assumptions. But, in the case of the metaphorical utterance, the truth-conditions of the assertion are not determined by the truth-conditions of the sentence and its general term. In order to understand the metaphorical utterance, the hearer requires something more than his knowledge of the language, his awareness of the conditions of the utterance, and background assumptions that he shares with the speaker. He must have some other principles, or some other factual information, or some combination of principles and information that enables him to figure out that when the speaker says, "S is P," he means "S is R." What is this extra element?

I believe that at the most general level, the question has a fairly simple answer, but it will take me much of the rest of this discussion to work it out in any detail. The basic principle on which all metaphor works is that the utterance of an expression with its literal meaning and corresponding truth-conditions can, in various ways that are specific to metaphor, call to mind another meaning and corresponding set of truth-conditions. The hard problem of the theory of metaphor is to explain what exactly are the principles according to which the utterance of an expression can metaphorically call to mind a different set of truth-conditions from the one determined by its literal meaning, and to state those principles precisely and without using metaphorical expressions like "call to mind."

SOME COMMON MISTAKES ABOUT METAPHOR

Before attempting to sketch a theory of metaphor, I want in this section and the next to backtrack a bit and examine some existing theories. Roughly speaking, theories of metaphor from Aristotle to the present can be divided into two types.[2] Comparison theories assert that metaphorical utterances involve a *comparison* or *similarity* between two or more *objects* (e.g., Aristotle, 1952a, 1952b; Henle, 1965), and semantic interaction theories claim that metaphor involves a *verbal opposition* (Beardsley, 1962) or *interaction* (Black, 1962b) between two *semantic contents,* that of the expression used metaphorically, and that of the surrounding literal context. I think that both of these theories, if one tries to take them quite literally, are in various ways inadequate; nonetheless, they are both trying to say something true, and we ought to try to extract what is true in them. But first I want to show some of the common mistakes they contain and some further common mistakes made in discussions of metaphor. My aim here is not polemical; rather, I am trying to clear the ground for the development of a theory of metaphor. One might say the endemic vice of the comparison theories is that they fail to distinguish between the claim that the statement of the comparison is part of the *meaning,* and hence the *truth-conditions,* of the metaphorical statement, and the claim that the statement of the similarity is the *principle of inference,* or a step in the process of *comprehending,* on the basis of which speakers produce and hearers understand metaphor. (More about this distinction later.) The semantic interaction theories were developed in response to the weaknesses of the comparison theories, and they have little independent argument to recommend them other than the weakness of their rivals: Their endemic vice is the failure to appreciate the

distinction between sentence or word meaning, which is never metaphorical, and speaker or utterance meaning, which can be metaphorical. They usually try to locate metaphorical meaning in the sentence or some set of associations with the sentence. In any event, here are half a dozen mistakes, which I believe should be noted:

It is often said that in metaphorical utterances there is a change in meaning of at least one expression. I wish to say that on the contrary, strictly speaking, in metaphor there is never a change of meaning; diachronically speaking, metaphors do indeed initiate semantic changes, but to the extent that there has been a genuine change in meaning, so that a word or expression no longer means what it previously did, to precisely that extent the locution is no longer metaphorical. We are all familiar with the processes whereby an expression becomes a dead metaphor, and then finally becomes an idiom or acquires a new meaning different from the original meaning. But in a genuine metaphorical utterance, it is only because the expressions have not changed their meaning that there is a metaphorical utterance at all. The people who make this claim seem to be confusing *sentence* meaning with *speaker's* meaning. The metaphorical utterance does indeed mean something different from the meaning of the words and sentences, but that is not because there has been any change in the meanings of the lexical elements, but because the speaker means something different by them; speaker meaning does not coincide with sentence or word meaning. It is essential to see this point, because the main problem of metaphor is to explain how speaker meaning and sentence meaning are different and how they are, nevertheless, related. Such an explanation is impossible if we suppose that sentence or word meaning has changed in the metaphorical utterance.

The simplest way to show that the crude versions of the comparison view are false is to show that, in the production and understanding of metaphorical utterances, there need not be any two objects for comparison. When I say metaphorically

(4)   (MET) Sally is a block of ice,

I am not necessarily quantifying over blocks of ice at all. My utterance does not entail literally that

(10) $(\exists x)$ (x is a block of ice),

and such that I am comparing Sally to x. This point is even more obvious if we take expressions used as metaphors which have a null extension. If I say

(11)   Sally is a dragon

that does not entail literally

(12) $(\exists x)$ (x is a dragon).

Or, another way to see the same thing is to note that the negative sentence is just as metaphorical as the affirmative. If I say

(13)   Sally is not a block of ice,

that, I take it, does not invite the absurd question: Which block of ice is it that you are comparing Sally with, in order to say that she is not like it? At its *crudest,* the comparison theory is just muddled about the referential character of expressions used metaphorically.

Now, this might seem a somewhat minor objection to the comparison theorists, but it paves the way for a much more radical objection. Comparison theories which are explicit on the point at all, generally treat the statement of the comparison as part of the meaning and hence as part of the truth conditions of the metaphorical statement. For example, Miller is quite explicit in regarding metaphorical statements as statements of similarity, and indeed for such theorists the meaning of a *metaphorical* statement is always given by an explicit *statement* of similarity. Thus, in their view, I have not even formulated the problem correctly. According to me, the problem of explaining (simple subject-predicate) metaphors is to explain how the speaker and hearer go from the literal sentence meaning "S is P" to the metaphorical utterance meaning "S is R." But, according to them, that is not the utterance meaning; rather the utterance meaning must be expressible by an statement of similarity, such as "S

is like P with respect to R," or in Miller's case, the metaphorical statement "S is P" is to be analyzed as, "There is some property F and some property G such that S's being F is similar to P's being G." I will have more to say about this thesis and its exact formulation later, but at present I want to claim that though similarity often plays a role in the *comprehension* of metaphor, the metaphorical assertion is not necessarily an *assertion* of similarity. The simplest argument that metaphorical assertions are not always assertions of similarity is that there are true metaphorical assertions for which there are no objects to be designated by the P term, hence the true metaphorical statement cannot possibly presuppose the existence of an object of comparison. But even where there are objects of comparison, the metaphorical assertion is not necessarily an assertion of similarity. Similarity, I shall argue, has to do with the production and understanding of metaphor, not with its meaning.

A second simple argument to show that metaphorical assertions are not necessarily assertions of similarity is that often the metaphorical assertion can remain true even though it turns out that the statement of similarity on which the inference to the metaphorical meaning is based is false. Thus, suppose I say,

(6)   (MET) Richard is a gorilla

meaning

(6)   (PAR) Richard is fierce, nasty, prone to violence, and so forth.

And suppose the hearer's inference to (6 PAR) is based on the belief that

(14)   Gorillas are fierce, nasty, prone to violence, and so forth,

and hence (6 MET) and (14), on the comparison view, would justify the inference to

(15)   Richard and gorillas are similar in several respects; *viz,* they are fierce, nasty, prone to violence, and so forth,

and this in turn would be part of the inference pattern that enabled the hearer to conclude that when I uttered (6 MET) I meant (6 PAR). But suppose ethological investigation shows, as I am told it has, that gorillas are not at all fierce and nasty, but are in fact shy, sensitive creatures, given to bouts of sentimentality. This would definitely show that (15) is false, for (15) is as much an assertion about gorillas as about Richard. But would it show that when I uttered (6 MET), what I said was false? Clearly not, for what I meant was (6 PAR), and (6 PAR) is an assertion about Richard. It can remain true regardless of the actual facts about gorillas; though, of course, what expressions we use to convey metaphorically certain semantic contents will normally depend on what we take the facts to be.

To put it crudely, "Richard is a gorilla," is just about Richard; it is not literally about gorillas at all. The word "gorilla" here serves to convey a certain semantic content other than its own meaning by a set of principles I have yet to state. But (15) is literally about both Richard and gorillas, and it is true if and only if they both share the properties it claims they do. Now, it may well be true that the hearer employs something like (15) as a step in the procedures that get him from (6 MET) to (6 PAR), but it does not follow from this fact about his *procedures of comprehension* that this is part of the *speaker's utterance meaning* of (6 MET); and, indeed, that it is not part of the utterance meaning is shown by the fact that the metaphorical statement can be *true* even if it turns out that gorillas do not have the traits that the metaphorical occurrence of "gorilla" served to convey. I am not saying that a metaphorical assertion can *never* be equivalent in meaning to a statement of similarity—whether or not it is would depend on the intentions of the speaker; but I am saying that it is not a necessary feature of metaphor—and is certainly not the point of having metaphor—that metaphorical assertions are equivalent in meaning to statements of similarity. My argument is starkly simple: In many cases the metaphorical statement and the corresponding similarity statement cannot be equivalent in meaning because they have different truth conditions. The difference between the view I am attacking and the one I

shall espouse is this. According to the view I am attacking, (6 MET) *means* Richard and gorillas are similar in certain respects. According to the view I shall espouse, similarity functions as a comprehension strategy, not as a component of meaning: (6 MET) says that Richard has certain traits (and to figure out what they are, look for features associated with gorillas). On my account the *P* term need not figure literally in the statement of the truth conditions of the metaphorical statement at all.

Similar remarks apply incidentally to similes. If I say,

(16)   Sam acts like a gorilla

that need not commit me to the truth of

(17)   Gorillas are such that their behavior resembles Sam's.

For (16) need not be about gorillas at all, and we might say that "gorilla" in (16) has a metaphorical occurrence. Perhaps this is one way we might distinguish between figurative similes and literal statements of similarity. Figurative similes need not necessarily commit the speaker to a literal statement of similarity.

The semantic interaction view, it seems to me, is equally defective. One of the assumptions behind the view that metaphorical meaning is a result of an interaction between an expression used metaphorically and other expressions used literally, is that all metaphorical uses of expressions must occur in sentences containing literal uses of expressions, and that assumption seems to me plainly false. It is, incidentally, the assumption behind the terminology of many of the contemporary discussions of metaphor. We are told, for example, that every metaphorical sentence contains a "tenor" and a "vehicle" (Richards, 1936) or a "frame" and a "focus" (Black, 1962b). But it is not the case that every metaphorical use of an expression is surrounded by literal uses of other expressions. Consider again our example (4): In uttering, "Sally is a block of ice," we referred to Sally using her proper name literally, but we need not have. Suppose, to use a mixed metaphor, we refer to Sally as "the bad news." We would then say, using a mixed metaphor

(18)   The bad news is a block of ice.

If you insist that the "is" is still literal, it is easy enough to construct examples of a dramatic change on Sally's part where we would be inclined, in another mixed metaphor, to say

(19)   The bad news congealed into a block of ice.

Mixed metaphors may be stylistically objectionable, but I cannot see that they are necessarily logically incoherent. Of course, most metaphors do occur in contexts of expressions used literally. It would be very hard to understand them if they did not. But it is not a logical necessity that every metaphorical use of an expression occurs surrounded by literal occurrences of other expressions and, indeed, many famous examples of metaphor are not. Thus Russell's example of a completely nonsensical sentence, "Quadrilaterality drinks procrastination," is often given a metaphorical interpretation as a description of any postwar four-power disarmament conference, but none of the words, so interpreted, has a literal occurrence; that is, for every word the speaker's utterance meaning differs from the literal word meaning.

However, the most serious objection to the semantic interaction view is not that it falsely presupposes that all metaphorical occurrences of words must be surrounded by literal occurrence of other words, but rather, that even where the metaphorical occurrence is within the context of literal occurrences, it is not in general the case that the metaphorical speaker's meaning is a result of any interaction among the elements of the sentence in any literal sense of "interaction." Consider again our example (4). In its metaphorical utterances, there is no question of any interaction between the meaning of the "principal subject" ("Sally") and the "subsidiary subject" ("block of ice"). "Sally" is a proper name; it does not have a meaning in quite the way in which "block of ice" has a meaning. Indeed, other expressions could have been used to produce the same metaphorical predication. Thus,

(20)   Miss Jones is a block of ice

or

(21)   That girl over there in the corner is a block of ice

could have been uttered with the same metaphorical utterance meaning.

I conclude that, as general theories, both the object comparison view and the semantic interaction view are inadequate. If we were to diagnose their failure in Fregean terms, we might say that the comparison view tries to explain metaphor as a relation between references, and the interaction view tries to explain it as a relation between senses and beliefs associated with references. The proponents of the interaction view see correctly that the mental processes and the semantic processes involved in producing and understanding metaphorical utterances cannot involve references themselves, but must be at the level of intentionality, that is, they must involve relations at the level of beliefs, meanings, associations, and so on. However, they then say incorrectly that the relations in question must be some unexplained, but metaphorically described, relations of "interaction"[3] between a literal frame and a metaphorical focus.

Two final mistakes I wish to note are not cases of saying something false about metaphors but of saying something true which fails to distinguish metaphor from literal utterance. Thus it is sometimes said that the notion of similarity plays a crucial role in the analysis of metaphor, or that metaphorical utterances are dependent on the context for their interpretation. But, as we saw earlier, both of these features are true of literal utterances as well. An analysis of metaphor must show how similarity and context play a role in metaphor different from their role in literal utterance.

A FURTHER EXAMINATION OF THE COMPARISON THEORY

One way to work up to a theory of metaphor would be to examine the strengths and weaknesses of one of the existing theories. The obvious candidate for this role of stalking horse is a version of the comparison theory that goes back to Aristotle and can, indeed, probably be considered the common-sense view—the theory that says all metaphor is really literal simile with the "like" or "as" deleted and the respect of the similarity left unspecified. Thus, according to this view, the metaphorical utterance, "Man is a wolf," means "Man is like a wolf in certain unspecified ways"; the utterance, "You are my sunshine," means "You are like sunshine to me in certain respects," and "Sally is a block of ice," means "Sally is like a block of ice in certain but so far unspecified ways."

The principles on which metaphors function, then, according to this theory are the same as those for literal statements of similarity together with the principle of ellipsis. We understand the metaphor as a shortened version of the literal simile.[4] Since literal simile requires no special extralinguistic knowledge for its comprehension, most of the knowledge necessary for the comprehension of metaphor is already contained in the speaker's and hearer's semantic competence, together with the general background knowledge of the world that makes literal meaning comprehensible.

We have already seen certain defects of this view, most notably that metaphorical statements cannot be equivalent in meaning to literal statements of similarity because the truth conditions of the two sorts of statements are frequently different. Furthermore, we must emphasize that even as a theory of metaphorical comprehension—as opposed to a theory of metaphorical meaning—it is important for the simile theory that the alleged underlying similes be literal statements of similarity. If the simile statements which are supposed to explain metaphor are themselves metaphorical or otherwise figurative, our explanation will be circular.

Still, treated as theory of comprehension, there does seem to be a large number of cases where for the metaphorical utterance we can construct a simile sentence that does seem in some way to explain how its metaphorical meaning is comprehended. And, indeed, the fact that the specification of the values of R is left vague by the simile statement may, in fact, be an advantage of the theory, inasmuch as metaphorical utterances are often vague in precisely that way: it is not made *exactly* clear what the R is supposed to be when we say that S is P, meaning metaphorically that S is R. Thus, for example, in analyzing Romeo's metaphorical statement, "Juliet is the sun," Cavell (1976, pp. 78–9) gives as part of its explanation that Romeo means that his day begins with Juliet. Now, apart from the special context of the play, that reading would never occur to me. I would look for other properties of the sun to fill in the values of R in the formula. In saying this I am not objecting to either Shakespeare or Cavell, because the metaphor in question, like most metaphors, is open-ended in precisely that way.

Nonetheless, the simile theory, in spite of its attractiveness, has serious difficulties. First, the theory does more—or rather, less—than fail to tell us how to compute the value of R exactly: So far it fails to tell us how to compute it at all. That is, the theory still has almost no explanatory power, because the task of a theory of metaphor is to explain how the speaker and hearer are able to go from "S is P" to "S is R," and it does not explain that process to tell us that they go from "S is P" to "S is R" by first going through the stage "S is like P with respect to R" because we are not told how we are supposed to figure out which values to assign to R. Similarity is a vacuous predicate: any two things are similar in some respect or other. Saying that the metaphorical "S is P" implies the literal "S is like P" does not solve our problem. It only pushes it back a step. The problem of understanding literal similes with the respect of the similarity left unspecified is only a part of the problem of understanding metaphor. How are we supposed to know, for example, that the utterance, "Juliet is the sun," does not mean "Juliet is for the most part gaseous," or "Juliet is 90 million miles from the earth," both of which properties are salient and well-known features of the sun.

Yet another objection is this: It is crucial to the simile thesis that the simile be taken literally; yet there seem to be a great many metaphorical utterances where there is no relevant literal corresponding similarity between S and P. If we insist that there are always such similes, it looks as if we would have to interpret them metaphorically, and thus our account would be circular. Consider our example (4), "Sally is a block of ice." If we were to enumerate quite literally the various distinctive qualities of blocks of ice, none of them would be true of Sally. Even if we were to throw in the various beliefs that people have about blocks of ice, they still would not be literally true of Sally. There simply is no class of predicates, $R,$ such that Sally is literally like a block of ice with respect to R where R is what we intended to predicate metaphorically of Sally when we said she was a block of ice. Being unemotional is not a feature of blocks of ice because blocks of ice are not in that line of business at all, and if one wants to insist that blocks of ice are literally unresponsive, then we need only point out that that feature is still insufficient to explain the metaphorical utterance meaning of (4), because in that sense bonfires are "unresponsive" as well, but

(22)   Sally is a bonfire

has a quite different metaphorical utterance meaning from (4). Furthermore, there are many similes that are not intended literally. For example, an utterance of "My love is like a red, red rose" does not mean that there is a class of literal predicates that are true both of my love and red, red roses and that express what the speaker was driving at when he said his love was like a red, red rose.

The defender of the simile thesis, however, need not give up so easily. He might say that many metaphors are also examples of other figures as well. Thus, "Sally is a block of ice" is not only an example of metaphor, but of hyperbole as well.[5] The metaphorical utterance meaning is indeed derived from the simile, "Sally is like a block of ice," but then both the metaphor and the simile are cases of *hyperbole;* they are exaggerations, and in-

deed, many metaphors are exaggerations. According to this reply, if we interpret both the metaphor and the simile hyperbolically, they are equivalent.

Furthermore, the defender of the simile thesis might add that it is not an objection to the simile account to say that some of the respects in which Sally is like a block of ice will be specified metaphorically, because for each of these metaphorical similes we can specify another underlying simile until eventually we reach the rock bottom of literal similes on which the whole edifice rests. Thus "Sally is a block of ice" means "Sally is like a block of ice," which means "She shares certain traits with a block of ice, in particular she is very cold." But since "cold" in "Sally is very cold" is also metaphorical, there must be an underlying similarity in which Sally's emotional state is like coldness, and when we finally specify these respects, the metaphor will be completely analyzed.

There are really two stages to this reply: First, it points out that other figures such as hyperbole sometimes combine with metaphor, and, secondly, it concedes that some of the similes that we can offer as translations of the metaphor are still metaphorical, but insists that some recursive procedure of analyzing metaphorical similes will eventually lead us to literal similes.

Is this reply really adequate? I think not. The trouble is that there do not seem to be any literal similarities between objects which are cold and people who are unemotional that would justify the view that when we say metaphorically that someone is cold what we mean is that he or she is unemotional. In what respects exactly are unemotional people like cold objects? Well, there are some things that one can say in answer to this, but they all leave us feeling somewhat dissatisfied.

We can say, for example, that when someone is physically cold it places severe restrictions on their emotions. But even if that is true, it is not what we meant by the metaphorical utterance. I think the only answer to the question, "What is the relation between cold things and unemotional people?" that would justify the use of "cold" as a metaphor for lack of emotion is simply that as a matter of perceptions, sensibilities, and linguistic practices, people find the notion of coldness associated in their minds with lack of emotion. The notion of being cold just is associated with being unemotional.

There is some evidence, incidentally, that this metaphor works across several different cultures: It is not confined to English speakers (cf. Asch, 1958). Moreover, it is even becoming, or has become, a dead metaphor. Some dictionaries (for example, the *O.E.D.*) list lack of emotion as one of the meanings of "cold." Temperature metaphors for emotional and personal traits are in fact quite common and they are not derived from any literal underlying similarities. Thus we speak of a "heated argument," "a warm welcome," "a lukewarm friendship," and "sexual frigidity." Such metaphors are fatal for the simile thesis, unless the defenders can produce a literal R which S and P have in common, and which is sufficient to explain the precise metaphorical meaning which is conveyed.

Because this point is bound to be contested, it is well to emphasize exactly what is at stake. In claiming that there are no sufficient similarities to explain utterance meaning, I am making a negative existential claim, and thus not one which is demonstrable from an examination of a finite number of instances. The onus is rather on the similarity theorist to state the similarities and show how they exhaust utterance meaning. But it is not at all easy to see how he could do that in a way that would satisfy the constraints of his own theory.

Of course, one can think of lots of ways in which any S is like any P, e.g., ways in which Sally is like a block of ice, and one can think of lots of F's and G's such that Sally's being F is like a block of ice's being G. But that is not enough. Such similarities as one can name do not exhaust utterance meaning and if there are others that do, they are certainly not obvious.

But suppose with some ingenuity one could think up a similarity that would exhaust utterance meaning. The very fact that it takes so much ingenuity to think it up makes it unlikely that it is the underlying principle of the metaphorical interpretation, inasmuch as the metaphor is obvious: There is no difficulty for any native speaker to explain what it means. In "Sam is a pig," both utterance meaning and similarities are obvious, but in "Sally is a block of ice," only the utterance meaning is obvious. The simpler hypothesis, then, is that this metaphor, like several others I shall now discuss, functions on principles other than similarity.

Once we start looking for them, this class of metaphors turns out to be quite large. For example, the numerous spatial metaphors for temporal duration are not based on literal similarities. In "time flies," or "the hours crawled by," what is it that time does and the hours did which is literally like flying or crawling? We are tempted to say they went rapidly or slowly respectively, but of course "went rapidly" and "went slowly" are further spatial metaphors. Similarly, taste metaphors for personal traits are not based on properties in common. We speak of a "sweet disposition" or a "bitter person," without implying that the sweet disposition and the bitter person have literal traits in common with sweet and bitter tastes which exhaust the utterance meaning of the metaphorical utterance. Of course, sweet dispositions and sweet things are both pleasant, but much more is conveyed by the metaphor than mere pleasantness.

So deeply embedded in our whole mode of sensibility are certain metaphorical associations that we tend to think there *must* be a similarity, or even that the association itself is a form of similarity. Thus, we feel inclined to say that the passage of time *just is like* spatial movement, but when we say this we forget that "passage" is only yet another spatial metaphor for time and that the bald assertion of similarity, with no specification of the respect of similarity, is without content.

The most sophisticated version of the simile thesis I have seen is by George Miller, and I shall digress briefly to consider some of its special features. Miller, like other simile theorists, believes that the meanings of metaphorical statements can be expressed as statements of similarity, but he offers a special kind of similarity statement (rather like one of Aristotle's formulations, by the way) as the form of "reconstruction" of metaphorical statements. According to Miller, metaphors of the form "*S is P*", where both *S* and *P* are noun phrases, are equivalent to sentences of the form

(23) $(\exists F) (\exists G) \{\text{SIM } [F(S), G(P)]\}$.

Thus, for example, "Man is a wolf," according to Miller would be analyzed as

(24)   There is some property *F* and some property *G* such that man's being *F* is similar to a wolf's being *G*.

And when we have metaphors where a verb or predicate adjective *F* is used metaphorically in a sentence of the form "*x is F*" or "*xF's*", the analysis is of the form

(25) $(\exists G) (\exists y) \{\text{SIM } [G(x), F(y)]\}$.

Thus, for example, "The problem is thorny" would be analyzed as

(26)   There is some property *G* and some object *y* such that the problem's being *G* is similar to *y*'s being thorny.

I believe this account has all the difficulties of the other simile theories—namely, it mistakenly supposes that the use of a metaphorical predicate commits the speaker to the existence of objects of which that predicate is literally true; it confuses the truth conditions of the metaphorical statement with the principles under which it is comprehended; it fails to tell us how to compute the values of the variables (Miller is aware of this problem, he calls it the problem of "interpretation" and sees it as different from the problem of "reconstruction"); and it is refuted by the fact that not all metaphors have literal statements of similarity underlying them. But it has some additional problems of its own. In my view, the most serious weakness of Miller's account is that according to it the semantic contents of most metaphorical utterances have too many predicates, and, in fact, rather few metaphors really satisfy the formal structure he provides us with. Consider, for example, "Man is a

wolf." On what I believe is the most plausible version of the simile thesis, it means something of the form

(27)   Man is like a wolf in certain respects *R*.

We could represent this as

(28) SIM_R (man, wolf).

The hearer is required to compute only one set of predicates, the values for *R*. But according to Miller's account, the hearer is required to compute no less than three sets of predicates. Inasmuch as similarity is a vacuous predicate, we need to be told in which respect two things are similar for the statement that they are similar to have any informative content. His formalization of the above metaphorical utterance is

(29) $(\exists F) (\exists G) \{\text{SIM } [F(\text{man}), G(\text{wolf})]\}$.

In order to complete this formula in a way that would specify the respect of the similarity we would have to rewrite it as

(30) $(\exists F) (\exists G) (\exists H) \{\text{SIM}_H [F(\text{man}), G(\text{wolf})]\}$.

But both the reformulation (30), and Miller's original (29), contain too many predicate variables: When I say, "Man is a wolf," I am not saying that there are some *different* sets of properties that men have from those that wolves have, I am saying that they have the *same* set of properties (at least on a sympathetic construal of the simile thesis, that is what I am saying). But according to Miller's account, I am saying that man has one set of properties *F*, wolves have a different set of properties *G*, and man's having *F* is similar to wolves having *G* with respect to some other properties *H*. I argue that this "reconstruction" is (a) counterintuitive, (b) unmotivated, and (c) assigns an impossible computing task to the speaker and hearer. What are these *F*'s, *G*'s and *H*'s supposed to be? And how is the hearer supposed to figure them out? It is not surprising that his treatment of the interpretation problem is very sketchy. Similar objections apply to his accounts of other syntactical forms of metaphorical utterances.

There is a class of metaphors, that I shall call "relational metaphors," for which something like his analysis might be more appropriate. Thus, if I say

(8)   The ship ploughed the sea

or

(31)   Washington is the father of his country,

these might be interpreted using something like his forms. We might treat (8) as equivalent to

(32)   There is some relation R which the ship has to the sea and which is similar to the relation that ploughs have to fields when they plough fields;

and (31) as

(33)   There is some relation R which Washington has to his country and which is like the relation that fathers have to their offspring.

And (32) and (33) are fairly easily formalized à la Miller. However, even these analyses seem to me to concede too much to his approach: (8) makes no reference either implicitly or explicitly to fields and (31) makes no reference to offspring. On the simplest and most plausible version of the simile thesis (8) and (31) are equivalent to:

(34)   The ship does something to the sea which is like ploughing

and

(35)   Washington stands in a relation to his country which is like the relation of being a father.

And the hearer's task is simply to compute the intended relations in the two cases. By my account, which I shall develop in the next section, similarity does not, in general, function as part of the truth-conditions either in Miller's manner or in the simpler version; rather, when it functions, it functions as a strategy for interpretation. Thus, very crudely, the way that similarity figures in the interpretation of (8) and (31) is given by

(36)   The ship does something to the sea (to figure out what it is, find a relationship like ploughing)

and

(37)   Washington stands in a certain relationship to his country (to figure out what it is, find a relationship like that of being a father).

But the hearer does not have to compute any respects in which these relations are similar, inasmuch as that is not what is being asserted. Rather, what is being asserted is that the ship is doing something to the sea and that Washington stands in a certain set of relations to his country, and the hearer is to figure out what it is that the ship does and what the relations are that Washington stands in by looking for relations similar to ploughing and being a father of.

To conclude this section: The problem of metaphor is either very difficult or very easy. If the simile theory were true, it would be very easy, because there would be no separate semantic category of *metaphors*—only a category of *elliptical utterances* where "like" or "as" had been deleted from the uttered sentence. But alas, the simile theory is not right, and the problem of metaphor remains very difficult. I hope our rather lengthy discussion of the simile theory has been illuminating in at least these respects. First, there are many metaphors in which there is no underlying literal similarity adequate to explain the metaphorical utterance meaning. Second, even where there is a correlated literal statement of similarity, the truth conditions, and hence the meaning of the metaphorical statement and the similarity statement are not, in general, the same. Third, what we should salvage from the simile theory is a set of strategies for producing and understanding metaphorical utterances, using similarity. And fourth, even so construed, that is, construed as a theory of interpretation rather than of meaning, the simile theory does not tell us how to compute the respects of similarity or which similarities are metaphorically intended by the speaker.

THE PRINCIPLES OF METAPHORICAL INTERPRETATION

The time has now come to try to state the principles according to which metaphors are produced and understood. To reiterate, in its simplest form, the question we are trying to answer is, How is it possible for the speaker to say metaphorically "*S* is *P*" and mean "*S* is *R*," when *P* plainly does not mean *R*; furthermore, How is it possible for the hearer who hears the utterance "*S* is *P*" to know that the speaker means "*S* is *R*"? The short and uninformative answer is that the utterance of *P* calls to mind the meaning and, hence, truth conditions associated with *R,* in the special ways that metaphorical utterances have of calling other things to mind. But that answer remains uninformative until we know what are the principles according to which the utterance calls the metaphorical meaning to mind, and until we can state these principles in a way which does not rely on metaphorical expressions like "calls to mind." I believe that there is no single principle on which metaphor works.

The question, "How do metaphors work?" is a bit like the question, "How does one thing remind us of another thing?" There is no single answer to either question, though similarity obviously plays a major role in answering both. Two important differences between them are that metaphors are both restricted and systematic; restricted in the sense that not every way that one thing can remind us of something else will provide a basis for metaphor, and systematic in the sense that metaphors must be communicable from speaker to hearer in virtue of a shared system of principles.

Let us approach the problem from the hearer's point of view. If we can figure out the principles according to which hearers understand metaphorical utterances, we shall be a long way toward understanding how it is possible for speakers to make metaphorical utterances, because for communication to be possible, speaker and hearer must share a common set of principles. Suppose a hearer hears an utterance such as, "Sally is a block of ice," or "Richard is a gorilla," or "Bill is a barn door." What are the steps he must go through in order to comprehend the metaphorical meaning of such utterances? Obviously an answer to that question need not specify a set of steps that he goes through consciously; instead it must provide a rational

reconstruction of the inference patterns that underlie our ability to understand such metaphors. Furthermore, not all metaphors will be as simple as the cases we shall be discussing; nonetheless, a model designed to account for the simple cases should prove to be of more general application.

I believe that for the simple sorts of cases we have been discussing, the hearer must go through at least three sets of steps. First, he must have some strategy for determining whether or not he has to seek a metaphorical interpretation of the utterance in the first place. Secondly, when he has decided to look for a metaphorical interpretation, he must have some set of strategies, or principles, for computing possible values of *R,* and third, he must have a set of strategies, or principles, for restricting the range of *R*'s—for deciding which *R*'s are likely to be the ones the speaker is asserting of *S.*

Suppose he hears the utterance, "Sam is a pig." He knows that that cannot be literally true, that the utterance, if he tries to take it literally, is radically defective. And, indeed, such defectiveness is a feature of nearly all of the examples that we have considered so far. The defects which cue the hearer may be obvious falsehood, semantic nonsense, violations of the rules of speech acts, or violations of conversational principles of communication. This suggests a strategy that underlies the first step: *Where the utterance is defective if taken literally, look for an utterance meaning that differs from sentence meaning.*

This is not the only strategy on which a hearer can tell that an utterance probably has a metaphorical meaning, but it is by far the most common. (It is also common to the interpretation of poetry. If I hear a figure on a Grecian Urn being addressed as a "still unravish'd bride of quietness," I know I had better look for alternative meanings.) But it is certainly not a necessary condition of a metaphorical utterance that it be in any way defective if construed literally. Disraeli might have said metaphorically

(5) (MET) I have climbed to the top of the greasy pole,

though he had in fact climbed to the top of a greasy pole. There are various other cues that we employ to spot metaphorical utterances. For example, when reading Romantic poets, we are on the lookout for metaphors, and some people we know are simply more prone to metaphorical utterances than others.

Once our hearer has established that he is to look for an alternative meaning, he has a number of principles by which he can compute possible values of R. I will give a list of these shortly, but one of them is this: *When you hear "S is P," to find possible values of* R *look for ways in which* S *might be like* P, *and to fill in the respect in which* S *might be like* P, *look for salient, well-known, and distinctive features of* P *things*.

In this case, the hearer might invoke his factual knowledge to come up with such features as that pigs are fat, gluttonous, slovenly, filthy, and so on. This indefinite range of features provides possible values of R. However, lots of other features of pigs are equally distinctive and well known, for example, pigs have a distinctive shape and distinctive bristles. So, in order to understand the utterance, the hearer needs to go through the third step where he restricts the range of possible R's. Here again the hearer may employ various strategies for doing that but the one that is most commonly used is this: *Go back to the* S *term and see which of the many candidates for the values of* R *are likely or even possible properties of* S.

Thus, if the hearer is told, "Sam's car is a pig," he will interpret that metaphor differently from the utterance, "Sam is a pig." The former, he might take to mean that Sam's car consumes gas the way pigs consume food, or that Sam's car is shaped like a pig. Though, in one sense, the metaphor is the same in the two cases, in each case it is restricted by the S term in a different way. The hearer has to use his knowledge of S things and P things to know which of the possible values of R are plausible candidates for metaphorical predication.

Now, much of the dispute between the interaction theories and the object comparison theories derives from the fact that they can be construed as answers to different questions. The object comparison theories are best construed as attempts to answer the question of stage two: "How do we compute the possible values of R?" The interaction theories are best construed as answers to the question of stage three: "Given a range of possible values of R, how does the relationship between the S term and the P term restrict that range?" I think it is misleading to describe these relations as "interactions," but it seems correct to suppose that the S term must play a role in metaphors of the sort we have been considering. In order to show that the interaction theory was also an answer to the question of stage two, we would have to show that there are values of R that are specifiable, given S and P together, that are not specifiable given P alone; one would have to show that S does not *restrict* the range of R's but in fact creates new R's. I do not believe that can be shown, but I shall mention some possibilities later.

I said that there was a variety of principles for computing R, given P—that is, a variety of principles according to which the utterance of P can call to mind the meaning R in ways that are peculiar to metaphor. I am sure I do not know all of the principles that do this, but here are several (not necessarily independent) for a start.

Principle 1

Things which are P are by definition R. Usually, if the metaphor works, R will be one of the salient defining characteristics of P. Thus, for example,

(38)   (MET) Sam is a giant

will be taken to mean

(38)   (PAR) Sam is big,

because giants are by definition big. That is what is special about them.

Principle 2

Things which are P are contingently R. Again, if the metaphor works, the property R should be a salient or well known property of P things.

(39)   (MET) Sam is a pig

will be taken to mean

(39)   (PAR) Sam is filthy, gluttonous, sloppy, and so on.

Both principles 1 and 2 correlate metaphorical utterances with literal similes, "Sam is like a giant," "Sam is like a pig," etc. Notice in connection with this principle and the next that small variations in the P term can create big differences in the R terms. Consider the differences between "Sam is a pig," "Sam is a hog," and "Sam is a swine."

Principle 3

Things which are P are often said or believed to be R, even though both speaker and hearer may know that R is false of P. Thus,

(7)   (MET) Richard is a gorilla

can be uttered to mean

(7)   (PAR) Richard is mean, nasty, prone to violence, and so on,

even though both speaker and hearer know that in fact gorillas are shy, timid, and sensitive creatures, but generations of gorilla mythology have set up associations that will enable the metaphor to work even though both speaker and hearer know these beliefs to be false.

Principle 4

Things which are P are not R, nor are they like R things, nor are they believed to be R, nonetheless it is a fact about our sensibility, whether culturally or naturally determined, that we just do perceive a connection, so that utterance of P is associated in our minds with R properties.
Thus,

(4)   (MET) Sally is a block of ice
(40)   (MET) I am in a black mood
(41)   (MET) Mary is sweet
(42)   (MET) John is bitter

(43)   (MET) The hours $\left\{ \begin{array}{l} \text{crept} \\ \text{crawled} \\ \text{dragged} \\ \text{sped} \\ \text{whizzed} \end{array} \right\}$ by as we waited for the plane

are sentences that could be uttered to mean metaphorically that: Sally is unemotional; I am angry and depressed; Mary is gentle, kind, pleasant, and so on; John is resentful; and the hours seemed (of varying degrees of duration) as we waited for the plane; even though there are no literal similarities on which these metaphors are based. Notice that the associations tend to be scalar: degrees of temperature with ranges of emotion, degrees of speed with temporal duration, and so forth.

Principle 5

P things are not like R things, and are not believed to be like R things, nonetheless the condition of being P is like the condition of being R. Thus, I might say to someone who has just received a huge promotion

(44)   You have become an aristocrat,

meaning not that he has personally become *like* an aristocrat, but that his new status or condition is like that of being an aristocrat.

Principle 6

There are cases where P and R are the same or similar in meaning, but where one, usually P, is restricted in its application, and does not literally apply to S. Thus, "addled" is only said literally of eggs, but we can metaphorically say

(45)   This soufflé is addled
(46)   That parliament was addled

and

(47)   His brain is addled.

Principle 7

This is not a separate principle but a way of applying principles 1 through 6 to simple cases which are not of the form "S is P" but relational metaphors, and metaphors of other syntactical forms such as those involving verbs and predicate adjectives. Consider such relational metaphors as

(48)   Sam devours books

(8)   The ship ploughs the sea

(31)   Washington was the father of his country.

In each case, we have a literal utterance of two noun phrases surrounding a metaphorical utterance of a relational term (it can be a transitive verb, as in (48) and (8) but it need not be, as in (31)). The hearer's task is not to go from "*S* is *P*" to "*S* is *R*" but to go from "*SP*-relation *S'*" to "*S R*-relation *S'*" and the latter task is formally rather different from the former because, for example, our similarity principles in the former case will enable him to find a property that *S* and *P* things have in common, namely, *R*. But in the latter, he cannot find a relation in common, instead he has to find a relation *R* which is different from relation *P* but similar to it in some respect. So, as applied to these cases, principle 1, for example, would read

   P-relations are by definition *R*-relations.

For example, *ploughing* is by definition partly a matter of moving a substance to either side of a pointed object while the object moves forward; and though this definitional similarity between the *P*-relation and the *R*-relation would provide the principle that enables the hearer to infer the *R*-relation, the respect of similarity does not exhaust the context of the *R*-relation, as the similarity exhausts the content of the *R* term in the simplest of the "*S* is *P*" cases. In these cases, the hearer's job is to find a relation (or property) that is similar to, or otherwise associated with, the relation or property literally expressed by the metaphorical expression *P;* and the principles function to enable him to select that relation or property by giving him a respect in which the *P*-relation and the *R*-relation might be similar or otherwise associated.

Principle 8

According to my account of metaphor, it becomes a matter of terminology whether we

want to construe metonymy and synecdoche as special cases of metaphor or as independent tropes. When one says, "*S* is *P*," and means that "*S* is *R*," P and R may be associated by such relations as the part–whole relation, the container–contained relation, or even the clothing and wearer relation. In each case, as in metaphor proper, the semantic content of the *P* term conveys the semantic content of the *R* term by some principle of association. Since the principles of metaphor are rather various anyway, I am inclined to treat metonymy and synecdoche as special cases of metaphor and add their principles to my list of metaphorical principles. I can, for example, refer to the British monarch as "the Crown," and the executive branch of the U.S. government as "the White House" by exploiting systematic principles of association. However, as I said, the claim that these are special cases of metaphor seems to me purely a matter of terminology, and if purists insist that the principles of metaphor be kept separate from those of metonymy and synecdoche, I can have no nontaxonomical objections.

In addition to these eight principles, one might wonder if there is a ninth. Are there cases where an association between *P* and *R* that did not previously exist can be created by the juxtaposition of *S* and *P* in the original sentence? This, I take it, is the thesis of the interaction theorists. However, I have never seen any convincing examples, nor any even halfway clear account, of what "interaction" is supposed to mean. Let us try to construct some examples. Consider the differences between

(49)   Sam's voice is $\left\{ \begin{array}{l} \text{mud} \\ \text{gravel} \\ \text{sandpaper} \end{array} \right\}$

and

(50)   Kant's second argument for the transcendental deduction

   is so much $\left\{ \begin{array}{l} \text{mud} \\ \text{gravel} \\ \text{sandpaper} \end{array} \right\}$

The second set clearly gives us different metaphorical meanings—different values for

R—than the first trio, and one might argue that this is due not to the fact that the different *S* terms restrict the range of possible *R*'s generated by the *P* terms, but to the fact that the different combinations of *S* and *P* create new *R*'s. But that explanation seems implausible. The more plausible explanation is this. One has a set of associations with the *P* terms, "mud," "gravel," and "sandpaper." The principles of these associations are those of principles 1 through 7. The different *S* terms restrict the values of *R* differently, because different *R*'s can be true of voices than can be true of arguments for transcendental deductions. Where is the interaction?

Because this section contains my account of metaphorical predication, it may be well to summarize its main points. Given that a speaker and a hearer have shared linguistic and factual knowledge sufficient to enable them to communicate literal utterance, the following principles are individually necessary and collectively sufficient to enable speaker and hearer to form and comprehend utterances of the form "*S* is *P*," where the speaker means metaphorically that *S* is *R* (where $P \neq R$).

First, there must be some shared strategies on the basis of which the hearer can recognize that the utterance is not intended literally. The most common, but not the only strategy, is based on the fact that the utterance is obviously defective if taken literally.

Second, there must be some shared principles that associate the *P* term (whether the meaning, the truth conditions, or the denotation if there is any) with a set of possible values of *R*. The heart of the problem of metaphor is to state these principles. I have tried to state several of them, but I feel confident that there must be more.

Third, there must be some shared strategies that enable the speaker and the hearer, given their knowledge of the *S* term (whether the meaning of the expression, or the nature of the referent, or both), to restrict the range of possible values of *R* to the actual value of *R*. The basic principle of this step is that only those possible values of *R* which determine possible properties of *S* can be actual values of *R*.

METAPHOR, IRONY, AND INDIRECT SPEECH ACTS

To conclude, I wish to compare briefly the principles on which metaphor works with those on which irony and indirect speech acts work. Consider first a case of irony. Suppose you have just broken a priceless K'ang Hsi vase and I say ironically, "That was a brilliant thing to do." Here, as in metaphor, the speaker's meaning and sentence meaning are different. What are the principles by which the hearer is able to infer that the speaker meant, "That was a stupid thing to do," when what he heard was the sentence, "That was a brilliant thing to do"? Stated very crudely, the mechanism by which irony works is that the utterance, if taken literally, is obviously inappropriate to the situation. Since it is grossly inappropriate, the hearer is compelled to reinterpret it in such a way as to render it appropriate, and the most natural way to interpret it is as meaning the *opposite* of its literal form.

I am not suggesting that this is by any means the whole story about irony. Cultures and subcultures vary enormously in the extent and degree of the linguistic and extralinguistic cues provided for ironical utterances. In English, in fact, there are certain characteristic intonational contours that go with ironical utterances. However, it is important to see that irony, like metaphor, does not require any conventions, extralinguistic or otherwise. The principles of conversation and the general rules for performing speech acts are sufficient to provide the basic principles of irony.

Now consider a case of an indirect speech act. Suppose that in the usual dinner-table situation, I say to you, "Can you pass the salt?" In this situation you will normally take that as meaning, "Please pass the salt." That is, you will take the question about your ability as a request to perform an action. What are the principles on which this inference works? There is a radical difference between indirect speech acts, on the one hand, and irony and metaphor, on the other. In the indirect speech act, the speaker means what he says. However, in addition, he means

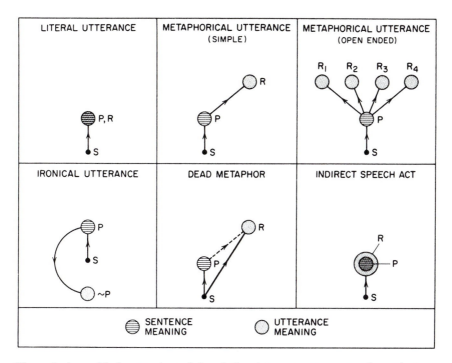

Figure 1. A graphical comparison of the relations between sentence meaning and utterance meaning where the sentence meaning is S is P and the utterance meaning is S is R, that is, where the speaker utters a sentence that means literally that the object S falls under the concept P, but where the speaker means by his utterance that the object S falls under the concept R.

a. *Literal Utterance.* A speaker says S is P and he means S is P. Thus the speaker places object S under the concept P, where P = R. Sentence meaning and utterance meaning coincide.

b. *Metaphorical Utterance (simple).* A speaker says S is P but means metaphorically that S is R. Utterance meaning is arrived at by going through literal sentence meaning.

c. *Metaphorical Utterance (open ended).* A speaker says S is P, but means metaphorically an indefinite range of meanings, S is R_1, S is R_2, etc. As in the simple case, utterance meaning is arrived at by going through literal meaning.

d. *Ironical Utterance.* A speaker means the opposite of what he says. Utterance meaning is arrived at by going through sentence meaning and then doubling back to the opposite of sentence meaning.

e. *Dead Metaphor.* The original sentence meaning is bypassed and the sentence acquires a new literal meaning identical with the former metaphorical utterance meaning. This is a shift from the metaphorical utterance (simple), *b* above, to the literal utterance, diagram *a*.

f. *Indirect Speech Act.* A speaker means what he says, but he means something more as well. Thus utterance meaning includes sentence meaning but extends beyond it.

something more. Sentence meaning is part of utterance meaning, but it does not exhaust utterance meaning. In a very simplified form (for a more detailed account, see Searle, 1975), the principles on which the inference works in this case are: First, the hearer must have some device for recognizing that the utterance might be an indirect speech act. This requirement is satisfied by the fact that in the context, a question about the hearer's ability lacks any conversational point. The hearer, therefore, is led to seek an alternative meaning. Second, since the hearer knows the rules of speech acts, he knows that the ability to pass the salt is a preparatory condition on the speech act of requesting him to do so. Therefore, he is able to infer that the question about his ability is likely to be a polite request to perform the act. The differences and similarities between literal utterances, metaphorical utterances, ironical utterances, and indirect speech acts are illustrated in Figure 1.

The question of whether all metaphorical utterances can be given a literal paraphrase is one that must have a trivial answer. Interpreted one way, the answer is trivially yes; interpreted another way, it is trivially no. If we interpret the question as, "Is it possible to find or to invent an expression that will exactly express the intended metaphorical meaning R, in the sense of the truth conditions of R, for any metaphorical utterance of 'S is P,' where what is meant is that S is R?" the answer to that question must surely be yes. It follows trivially from the Principle of Expressibility (see Searle, 1969) that any meaning whatever can be given an exact expression in the language.

If the question is interpreted as meaning, "Does every existing language provide us exact devices for expressing literally whatever we wish to express in any given metaphor?" then the answer is obviously no. It is often the case that we use metaphor precisely because there is no literal expression that expresses exactly what we mean. Furthermore, in metaphorical utterances, we do more than just state that S is R; as figure 4 shows, we state that S is R by way of going through the meaning of "S is P." It is in this sense that we

feel that metaphors somehow are intrinsically not paraphrasable. They are not paraphrasable, because without using the metaphorical expression, we will not reproduce the semantic content which occurred in the hearer's comprehension of the utterance.

The best we can do in the paraphrase is reproduce the truth-conditions of the metaphorical utterance, but the metaphorical utterance does more than just convey its truth conditions. It conveys its truth-conditions by way of another semantic content, whose truth-conditions are not part of the truth-conditions of the utterance. The expressive power that we feel is part of good metaphors is largely a matter of two features. The hearer has to figure out what the speaker means—he has to contribute more to the communication than just passive uptake—and he has to do that by going through another and related semantic content from the one which is communicated. And that, I take it, is what Dr. Johnson meant when he said metaphor gives us two ideas for one.

ACKNOWLEDGMENTS

I am indebted to several people for helpful comments on earlier drafts of this article, and I especially want to thank Jerry Morgan, Andrew Ortony, Paul Rauber, and Dagmar Searle.

NOTES

1. It is essential to avoid any use–mention confusions when talking about these sets. Sometimes we will be talking about the words, other times about meanings, other times about references and denotations, and still other times about truth conditions.
2. I follow Beardsley (1962) in this classification.
3. Even in Black's clarification of interaction in terms of "implication-complexes" there still does not seem to be any precise statement of the principles on which interaction works. And the actual example he gives, "Marriage is a zero-sum game," looks distressingly like a comparison metaphor: "Marriage is *like* a zero-sum game in that it is an adversary relationship between two parties in which one side can benefit only at the expense of the other." It is hard to see what the talk about interaction is supposed to add to this analysis.

4. By "literal simile," I mean literal statement of similarity. It is arguable that one should confine "simile" to nonliteral comparisons, but that is not the usage I follow here.

5. Furthermore, it is at least arguable that "block of ice" functions metonymously in this example.

BIBLIOGRAPHY

Aristotle. 1952a. [Rhetoric]. Translated by W. R. Roberts. In W. D. Ross, ed., *The Works of Aristotle,* vol. 11: *Rhetorica, De rhetorica ad Alexandrum, Poetica.* Oxford: Clarendon Press.

——1952b. [*Poetics*]. Translated by I. Bywater. In W. D. Ross, ed., *The Works of Aristotle* (vol. 11): *Rhetorica, De rhetorica ad Alexandrum, Poetica.* Oxford: Clarendon Press.

Asch, S. E. 1958. The metaphor: A psychological inquiry. In R. Tagiuri and L. Petrullo, eds., *Person Perception and Interpersonal Behavior.* Stanford, Calif.: Stanford University Press.

Beardsley, M. C. 1958. *Aesthetics: Problems in the philosophy of criticism.* New York: Harcourt Brace and Co.

——1962. The metaphorical twist. *Philosophy and Phenomenological Research,* 22, 293–307.

Black, M. 1962a. *Models and Metaphors.* Ithaca, N.Y.: Cornell University Press.

——1962b. Metaphor. In M. Black, *Models and Metaphors.* Ithaca, N.Y.: Cornell University Press.

Cavell, S. 1976. *Must We Mean What We Say?* Cambridge: Cambridge University Press.

Henle, P., ed. 1965. *Language, Thought, and Culture.* Ann Arbor: University of Michigan Press.

Miller, G. 1979. Images and Models, Similes and Metaphors. In Andrew Ortony, ed. *Metaphor and Thought.* Cambridge: Cambridge University Press.

Richards, I. A. 1936. *The Philosophy of Rhetoric.* London: Oxford University Press.

Searle, J. R. 1969. *Speech Acts.* Cambridge: Cambridge University Press.

——1975. Indirect speech acts. In P. Cole and J. L. Morgan, eds., *Syntax and Semantics,* vol. 3: *Speech Acts.* New York: Academic Press.

——1978. Literal meaning. *Erkenntnis,* 13. 207–24.

What Metaphors Mean   32

DONALD DAVIDSON

Metaphor is the dreamwork of language and, like all dreamwork, its interpretation reflects as much on the interpreter as on the originator. The interpretation of dreams requires collaboration between a dreamer and a waker, even if they be the same person; and the act of interpretation is itself a work of the imagination. So too understanding a metaphor is as much a creative endeavor as making a metaphor, and as little guided by rules.

These remarks do not, except in matters of degree, distinguish metaphor from more routine linguistic transactions: all communication by speech assumes the interplay of inventive construction and inventive construal. What metaphor adds to the ordinary is an achievement that uses no semantic resources beyond the resources on which the ordinary depends. There are no instructions for devising metaphors; there is no manual for determining what a metaphor "means" or "says"; there is no test for metaphor that does not call for taste.[1] A metaphor implies a kind and degree of artistic success; there are no unsuccessful metaphors, just as there are no unfunny jokes. There are tasteless metaphors, but these are turns that nevertheless have brought something off, even if it were not worth bringing off or could have been brought off better.

This paper is concerned with what meta-

phors mean, and its thesis is that metaphors mean what the words, in their most literal interpretation, mean, and nothing more. Since this thesis flies in the face of contemporary views with which I am familiar, much of what I have to say is critical. But I think the picture of metaphor that emerges when error and confusion are cleared away makes metaphor a more, not a less, interesting phenomenon.

The central mistake against which I shall be inveighing is the idea that a metaphor has, in addition to its literal sense or meaning, another sense or meaning. This idea is common to many who have written about metaphor: it is found in the works of literary critics like Richards, Empson, and Winters; philosophers from Aristotle to Max Black; psychologists from Freud and earlier, to Skinner and later; and linguists from Plato to Uriel Weinreich and George Lakoff. The idea takes many forms, from the relatively simple in Aristotle to the relatively complex in Black. The idea appears in writings which maintain that a literal paraphrase of a metaphor can be produced, but it is also shared by those who hold that typically no literal paraphrase can be found. Some stress the special insight metaphor can inspire and make much of the fact that ordinary language, in its usual functioning, yields no such insight. Yet this view too sees metaphor as a form of communication

From *On Metaphor,* Sheldon Sacks, ed. (Chicago: University of Chicago Press, 1978), pp. 29–46. © 1978 by Donald Davidson.

alongside ordinary communication; it conveys truths or falsehoods about the world much as plainer language does, though the message may be considered more exotic, profound, or cunningly garbed.

The concept of metaphor as primarily a vehicle for conveying ideas, even if unusual ones, seems to me as wrong as the parent idea that a metaphor has a special meaning. I agree with the view that metaphors cannot be paraphrased, but I think this is not because metaphors say something too novel for literal expression but because there is nothing there to paraphrase. Paraphrase, whether possible or not, is appropriate to what is *said:* we try, in paraphrase, to say it another way. But if I am right, a metaphor doesn't say anything beyond its literal meaning (nor does its maker say anything, in using the metaphor, beyond the literal). This is not, of course, to deny that a metaphor has a point, nor that that point can be brought out by using further words.

In the past those who have denied that metaphor has a cognitive content in addition to the literal have often been out to show that metaphor is confusing, merely emotive, unsuited to serious, scientific, or philosophic discourse. My views should not be associated with this tradition. Metaphor is a legitimate device not only in literature but in science, philosophy, and the law: it is effective in praise and abuse, prayer and promotion, description and prescription. For the most part I don't disagree with Max Black, Paul Henle, Nelson Goodman, Monroe Beardsley, and the rest in their accounts of what metaphor accomplishes, except that I think it accomplishes more and that what is additional is different in kind.

My disagreement is with the explanation of how metaphor works its wonders. To anticipate: I depend on the distinction between what words mean and what they are used to do. I think metaphor belongs exclusively to the domain of use. It is something brought off by the imaginative employment of words and sentences and depends entirely on the ordinary meanings of those words and hence on the ordinary meanings of the sentences they comprise.

It is no help in explaining how words work in metaphor to posit metaphorical or figurative meanings, or special kinds of poetic or metaphorical truth. These ideas don't explain metaphor, metaphor explains them. Once we understand a metaphor we can call what we grasp the "metaphorical truth" and (up to a point) say what the "metaphorical meaning" is. But simply to lodge this meaning in the metaphor is like explaining why a pill puts you to sleep by saying it has a dormative power. Literal meaning and literal truth-conditions can be assigned to words and sentences apart from particular contexts of use. This is why adverting to them has genuine explanatory power.

I shall try to establish my negative views about what metaphors mean and introduce my limited positive claims by examining some false theories of the nature of metaphor.

A metaphor makes us attend to some likeness, often a novel or surprising likeness, between two or more things. This trite and true observation leads, or seems to lead, to a conclusion concerning the meaning of metaphors. Consider ordinary likeness or similarity: two roses are similar because they share the property of being a rose; two infants are similar by virtue of their infanthood. Or, more simply, roses are similar because each is a rose, infants, because each is an infant.

Suppose someone says "Tolstoy was once an infant." How is the infant Tolstoy like other infants? The answer comes pat: by virtue of exhibiting the property of infanthood, that is, leaving out some of the wind, by virtue of being an infant. If we tire of the phrase "by virtue of," we can, it seems, be plainer still by saying the infant Tolstoy shares with other infants the fact that the predicate "is an infant" applies to him; given the word "infant," we have no trouble saying exactly how the infant Tolstoy resembles other infants. We could do it without the word "infant"; all we need is other words that mean the same. The end result is the same. Ordinary similarity depends on groupings established by the ordinary meanings of words. Such similarity is natural and unsurprising to the extent that familiar ways of grouping objects are tied to usual meanings of usual words.

A famous critic said that Tolstoy was "a great moralizing infant." The Tolstoy referred to here is obviously not the infant Tolstoy but Tolstoy the adult writer; this is metaphor. Now in what sense is Tolstoy the writer similar to an infant? What we are to do, perhaps, is think of the class of objects which includes all ordinary infants and, in addition, the adult Tolstoy and then ask ourselves what special, surprising property the members of this class have in common. The appealing thought is that given patience we could come as close as need be to specifying the appropriate property. In any case, we could do the job perfectly if we found words that meant exactly what the metaphorical "infant" means. The important point, from my perspective, is not whether we can find the perfect other words but the assumption that there is something to be attempted, a metaphorical meaning to be matched. So far I have been doing no more than crudely sketching how the concept of meaning may have crept into the analysis of metaphor, and the answer I have suggested is that since what we think of as garden variety similarity goes with what we think of as garden variety meanings, it is natural to posit unusual or metaphorical meanings to help explain the similarities metaphor promotes.

The idea, then, is that in metaphor certain words take on new, or what are often called "extended," meanings. When we read, for example, that "the Spirit of God moved upon the face of the waters," we are to regard the word "face" as having an extended meaning (I disregard further metaphor in the passage). The extension applies, as it happens, to what philosophers call the extension of the word, that is, the class of entities to which it refers. Here the word "face" applies to ordinary faces, and to waters in addition.

This account cannot, at any rate, be complete, for if in these contexts the words "face" and "infant" apply correctly to waters and to the adult Tolstoy, then waters really do have faces and Tolstoy literally was an infant, and all sense of metaphor evaporates. If we are to think of words in metaphors as directly going about their business of applying to what they properly do apply to, there is no difference between metaphor and the introduction of a new term into our vocabulary: to make a metaphor is to murder it.

What has been left out is any appeal to the original meaning of the word. Whether or not metaphor depends on new or extended meanings, it certainly depends in some way on the original meanings; an adequate account of metaphor must allow that the primary or original meanings of words remain active in their metaphorical setting.

Perhaps, then, we can explain metaphor as a kind of ambiguity: in the context of a metaphor, certain words have either a new or an original meaning, and the force of the metaphor depends on our uncertainty as we waver between the two meanings. Thus when Melville writes that "Christ was a chronometer," the effect of metaphor is produced by our taking "chronometer" first in its ordinary sense and then in some extraordinary or metaphorical sense.

It is hard to see how this theory can be correct. For the ambiguity in the word, if there is any, is due to the fact that in ordinary contexts it means one thing and in the metaphorical context it means something else; but in the metaphorical context we do not necessarily hesitate over its meaning. When we do hesitate, it is usually to decide which of a number of metaphorical interpretations we shall accept; we are seldom in doubt that what we have is a metaphor. At any rate, the effectiveness of the metaphor easily outlasts the end of uncertainty over the interpretation of the metaphorical passage. Metaphor cannot, therefore, owe its effect to ambiguity of this sort.[2]

Another brand of ambiguity may appear to offer a better suggestion. Sometimes a word will, in a single context, bear two meanings where we are meant to remember and to use both. Or, if we think of wordhood as implying sameness of meaning, then we may describe the situation as one in which what appears as a single word is in fact two. When Shakespeare's Cressida is welcomed bawdily into the Grecian camp, Nestor says, "Our general doth salute you with a kiss." Here we are to take "general" two ways: once as applying to Agamemnon, who is the general; and once, since she is kissing everyone, as applying to no one in particular, but everyone in general. We really have a conjunction of two sentences: our general, Agamemnon, salutes you with a kiss; and everyone in general is saluting you with a kiss.

This is a legitimate device, a pun, but it is not the same device as metaphor. For in metaphor there is no essential need of reiteration; whatever meanings we assign the words, they keep through every correct reading of the passage.

A plausible modification of the last suggestion would be to consider the key word (or words) in a metaphor as having two different kinds of meaning at once, a literal and a figurative meaning. Imagine the literal meaning as latent, something that we are aware of, that can work on us without working in the context, while the figurative meaning carries the direct load. And finally, there must be a rule which connects the two meanings, for otherwise the explanation lapses into a form of the ambiguity theory. The rule, at least for many typical cases of metaphor, says that in its metaphorical role the word applies to everything that it applies to in its literal role, and then some.[3]

This theory may seem complex, but it is strikingly similar to what Frege proposed to account for the behavior of referring terms in modal sentences and sentences about propositional attitudes like belief and desire. According to Frege, each referring term has two (or more) meanings, one which fixes its reference in ordinary contexts and another which fixes its reference in the special contexts created by modal operators or psychological verbs. The rule connecting the two meanings may be put like this: the meaning of the word in the special contexts makes the reference in those contexts to be identical with the meaning in ordinary contexts.

Here is the whole picture, putting Frege together with a Fregean view of metaphor: we are to think of a word as having, in addition to its mundane field of application or reference,

two special or supermundane fields of application, one for metaphor and the other for modal contexts and the like. In both cases the original meaning remains to do its work by virtue of a rule which relates the various meanings.

Having stressed the possible analogy between metaphorical meaning and the Fregean meanings for oblique contexts, I turn to an imposing difficulty in maintaining the analogy. You are entertaining a visitor from Saturn by trying to teach him how to use the word "floor." You go through the familiar dodges, leading him from floor to floor, pointing and stamping and repeating the word. You prompt him to make experiments, tapping objects tentatively with his tentacle while rewarding his right and wrong tries. You want him to come out knowing not only that these particular objects or surfaces are floors but also how to tell a floor when one is in sight or touch. The skit you are putting on doesn't *tell* him what he needs to know, but with luck it helps him to learn it.

Should we call this process learning something about the world or learning something about language? An odd question, since what is learned is that a bit of language refers to a bit of the world. Still, it is easy to distinguish between the business of learning the meaning of a word and using the word once the meaning is learned. Comparing these two activities, it is natural to say that the first concerns learning something about language, while the second is typically learning something about the world. If your Saturnian has learned how to use the word "floor," you may try telling him something new, that *here* is a floor. If he has mastered the word trick, you have told him something about the world.

Your friend from Saturn now transports you through space to his home sphere, and looking back remotely at earth you say to him, nodding at the earth, "floor." Perhaps he will think this is still part of the lesson and assume that the word "floor" applies properly to the earth, at least as seen from Saturn. But what if you thought he already knew the meaning of "floor," and you were remembering how Dante, from a similar place in the heavens, saw the inhabited earth as "the small round floor that makes us passionate"? Your purpose was metaphor, not drill in the use of language. What difference would it make to your friend which way he took it? With the theory of metaphor under consideration, very little difference, for according to that theory a word has a new meaning in a metaphorical context; the occasion of the metaphor would, therefore, be the occasion for learning the new meaning. We should agree that in some ways it makes relatively little difference whether, in a given context, we think a word is being used metaphorically or in a previously unknown, but literal way. Empson, in *Some Versions of Pastoral,* quotes these lines from Donne: "As our blood labours to beget / Spirits, as like souls as it can, . . . / So must pure lover's soules descend. . . ." The modern reader is almost certain, Empson points out, to take the word "spirits" in this passage metaphorically, as applying only by extension to something spiritual. But for Donne there was no metaphor. He writes in his *Sermons,* "The spirits . . . are the thin and active part of the blood, and are a kind of middle nature, between soul and body." Learning this does not matter much; Empson is right when he says, "It is curious how the change in the word [that is, in what we think it means] leaves the poetry unaffected."[4]

The change may be, in some cases at least, hard to appreciate, but unless there is a change, most of what is thought to be interesting about metaphor is lost. I have been making the point by contrasting learning a new use for an old word with using a word already understood; in one case, I said, our attention is directed to language, in the other, to what language is about. Metaphor, I suggested, belongs in the second category. This can also be seen by considering dead metaphors. Once upon a time, I suppose, rivers and bottles did not, as they do now, literally have mouths. Thinking of present usage, it doesn't matter whether we take the word "mouth" to be ambiguous because it applies to entrances to rivers and openings of bottles as well as to animal apertures, or we think there is a single wide field of application

that embraces both. What does matter is that when "mouth" applied only metaphorically to bottles, the application made the hearer *notice* a likeness between animal and bottle openings. (Consider Homer's reference to wounds as mouths.) Once one has the present use of the word, with literal application to bottles, there is nothing left to notice. There is no similarity to seek because it consists simply in being referred to by the same word.

Novelty is not the issue. In its context a word once taken for a metaphor remains a metaphor on the hundredth hearing, while a word may easily be appreciated in a new literal role on a first encounter. What we call the element of novelty or surprise in a metaphor is a built-in aesthetic feature we can experience again and again, like the surprise in Haydn's Symphony no. 94, or a familiar deceptive cadence.

If metaphor involved a second meaning, as ambiguity does, we might expect to be able to specify the special meaning of a word in a metaphorical setting by waiting until the metaphor dies. The figurative meaning of the living metaphor should be immortalized in the literal meaning of the dead. But although some philosophers have suggested this idea, it seems plainly wrong. "He was burned up" is genuinely ambiguous (since it may be true in one sense and false in another), but although the slangish idiom is no doubt the corpse of a metaphor, "He was burned up" now suggests no more than that he was very angry. When the metaphor was active, we would have pictured fire in the eyes or smoke coming out of the ears.

We can learn much about what metaphors mean by comparing them with similes, for a simile tells us, in part, what a metaphor merely nudges us into noting. Suppose Goneril had said, thinking of Lear, "Old fools are like babes again"; then she would have used the words to assert a similarity between old fools and babes. What she did say, of course, was "Old fools are babes again," thus using the words to intimate what the simile declared. Thinking along these lines may inspire another theory of the figurative or special meaning of metaphors: the figurative meaning of a metaphor is the literal meaning of the corresponding simile. Thus "Christ was a chronometer" in its figurative sense is synonymous with "Christ was like a chronometer," and the metaphorical meaning once locked up in "He was burned up" is released in "He was like someone who was burned up" (or perhaps "He was like burned up").

There is, to be sure, the difficulty of identifying the simile that corresponds to a given metaphor. Virginia Woolf said that a highbrow is "a man or woman of thoroughbred intelligence who rides his mind at a gallop across country in pursuit of an idea." What simile corresponds? Something like this, perhaps: "A highbrow is a man or woman whose intelligence is like a thoroughbred horse and who persists in thinking about an idea like a rider galloping across country in pursuit of . . . well, something."

The view that the special meaning of a metaphor is identical with the literal meaning of a corresponding simile (however "corresponding" is spelled out) should not be confused with the common theory that a metaphor is an elliptical simile.[5] This theory makes no distinction in meaning between a metaphor and some related simile and does not provide any ground for speaking of figurative, metaphorical, or special meanings. It is a theory that wins hands down so far as simplicity is concerned, but it also seems too simple to work. For if we make the literal meaning of the metaphor to be the literal meaning of a matching simile, we deny access to what we originally took to be the literal meaning of the metaphor, and we agreed almost from the start that *this* meaning was essential to the working of the metaphor, whatever else might have to be brought in in the way of a nonliteral meaning.

Both the elliptical simile theory of metaphor and its more sophisticated variant, which equates the figurative meaning of the metaphor with the literal meaning of a simile, share a fatal defect. They make the hidden meaning of the metaphor all too obvious and accessible. In each case the hidden meaning is to be found simply by looking to the literal meaning of what is usually a painfully trivial simile.

This is like that—Tolstoy like an infant, the earth like a floor. It is trivial because everything is like everything, and in endless ways. Metaphors are often very difficult to interpret and, so it is said, impossible to paraphrase. But with this theory, interpretation and paraphrase typically are ready to the hand of the most callow.

These simile theories have been found acceptable, I think, only because they have been confused with a quite different theory. Consider this remark by Max Black:

When Schopenhauer called a geometrical proof a mousetrap, he was, according to such a view, *saying* (though not explicitly): "A geometrical proof is *like* a mousetrap, since both offer a delusive reward, entice their victims by degrees, lead to disagreeable surprise, etc." This is a view of metaphor as a condensed or elliptical *simile*.[6]

Here I discern two confusions. First, if metaphors are elliptical similes, they say *explicitly* what similes say, for ellipsis is a form of abbreviation, not of paraphrase or indirection. But, and this is the more important matter, Black's statement of what the metaphor says goes far beyond anything given by the corresponding simile. The simile simply says a geometrical proof is like a mousetrap. It no more *tells* us what similarities we are to notice than the metaphor does. Black mentions three similarities, and of course we could go on adding to the list forever. But is this list, when revised and supplemented in the right way, supposed to give the *literal* meaning of the simile? Surely not, since the simile declared no more than the similarity. If the list is supposed to provide the figurative meaning of the simile, then we learn nothing about metaphor from the comparison with simile— only that both have the same figurative meaning. Nelson Goodman does indeed claim that "the difference between simile and metaphor is negligible," and he continues, "Whether the locution be 'is like' or 'is,' the figure *likens* picture to person by picking out a certain common feature. . . ."[7] Goodman is considering the difference between saying a picture is sad and saying it is like a sad person. It is clearly true that both sayings liken picture to person, but it seems to me a mistake to claim that either way of talking "picks out" a common feature. The simile says there is a likeness and leaves it to us to pick out some common feature or features; the metaphor does not explicitly assert a likeness, but if we accept it as a metaphor, we are again led to seek common features (not necessarily the same features the associated simile suggests; but that is another matter).

Just because a simile wears a declaration of similitude on its sleeve, it is, I think, far less plausible than in the case of metaphor to maintain that there is a hidden second meaning. In the case of simile, we note what it literally says, that two things resemble one another; we then regard the objects and consider what similarity would, in the context, be to the point. Having decided, we might then say the author of the simile intended us—that is, meant us—to notice that similarity. But having appreciated the difference between what the words meant and what the author accomplished by using those words, we should feel little temptation to explain what has happened by endowing the words themselves with a second, or figurative, meaning. The point of the concept of linguistic meaning is to explain what can be done with words. But the supposed figurative meaning of a simile explains nothing; it is not a feature of the word that the word has prior to and independent of the context of use, and it rests upon no linguistic customs except those that govern ordinary meaning.

What words do do with their literal meaning in simile must be possible for them to do in metaphor. A metaphor directs attention to the same sorts of similarity, if not the same similarities, as the corresponding simile. But then the unexpected or subtle parallels and analogies it is the business of metaphor to promote need not depend, for their promotion, on more than the literal meanings of words.

Metaphor and simile are merely two among endless devices that serve to alert us to aspects of the world by inviting us to make comparisons. I quote a few stanzas of T. S. Eliot's "The Hippopotamus":

The broad-backed hippopotamus
Rests on his belly in the mud;
Although he seems so firm to us
He is merely flesh and blood.

Flesh and blood is weak and frail,
Susceptible to nervous shock;
While the True Church can never fail
For it is based upon a rock.

The hippo's feeble steps may err
In compassing material ends,
While the True Church need never stir
To gather in its dividends.

The 'potamus can never reach
The mango on the mango-tree;
But fruits of pomegranate and peach
Refresh the Church from over sea.

Here we are neither told that the Church resembles a hippopotamus (as in simile) nor bullied into making this comparison (as in metaphor), but there can be no doubt the words are being used to direct our attention to similarities between the two. Nor should there be much inclination, in this case, to posit figurative meanings, for in what words or sentences would we lodge them? The hippopotamus really does rest on his belly in the mud; the True Church, the poem says literally, never can fail. The poem does, of course, intimate much that goes beyond the literal meanings of the words. But intimation is not meaning.

The argument so far has led to the conclusion that as much of metaphor as can be explained in terms of meaning may, and indeed must, be explained by appeal to the literal meanings of words. A consequence is that the sentences in which metaphors occur are true or false in a normal, literal way, for if the words in them don't have special meanings, sentences don't have special truth. This is not to deny that there is such a thing as metaphorical truth, only to deny it of sentences. Metaphor does lead us to notice what might not otherwise be noticed, and there is no reason, I suppose, not to say these visions, thoughts, and feelings inspired by the metaphor, are true or false.

If a sentence used metaphorically is true or false in the ordinary sense, then it is clear that it is usually false. The most obvious semantic difference between simile and metaphor is that all similes are true and most metaphors are false. The earth is like a floor, the Assyrian did come down like a wolf on the fold, because everything is like everything. But turn these sentences into metaphors, and you turn them false; the earth is like a floor, but it is not a floor; Tolstoy, grown up, was like an infant, but he wasn't one. We use a simile ordinarily only when we know the corresponding metaphor to be false. We say Mr. S. is like a pig because we know he isn't one. If we had used a metaphor and said he was a pig, this would not be because we changed our mind about the facts but because we chose to get the idea across a different way.

What matters is not actual falsehood but that the sentence be taken to be false. Notice what happens when a sentence we use as a metaphor, believing it false, comes to be thought true because of a change in what is believed about the world. When it was reported that Hemingway's plane had been sighted, wrecked, in Africa, the New York *Mirror* ran a headline saying, "Hemingway Lost in Africa," the word "lost" being used to suggest he was dead. When it turned out he was alive, the *Mirror* left the headline to be taken literally. Or consider this case: a woman sees herself in a beautiful dress and says, "What a dream of a dress!"—and then wakes up. The point of the metaphor is that the dress is like a dress one would dream of and therefore isn't a dream-dress. Henle provides a good example from *Anthony and Cleopatra* (2.2):

The barge she sat in, like a burnish'd throne
Burn'd on the water

Here simile and metaphor interact strangely, but the metaphor would vanish if a literal conflagration were imagined. In much the same way the usual effect of a simile can be sabotaged by taking the comparison too earnestly. Woody Allen writes, "The trial, which took place over the following weeks, was like a circus, although there was some difficulty getting the elephants into the courtroom."[8]

Generally it is only when a sentence is taken to be false that we accept it as a metaphor and start to hunt out the hidden implication. It is probably for this reason that most metaphorical sentences are *patently* false, just as all similes are trivially true. Absurdity or contradiction in a metaphorical sentence guarantees we won't believe it and invites us, under proper circumstances, to take the sentence metaphorically.

Patent falsity is the usual case with metaphor, but on occasion patent truth will do as well. "Business is business" is too obvious in its literal meaning to be taken as having been uttered to convey information, so we look for another use; Ted Cohen reminds us, in the same connection, that no man is an island.[9] The point is the same. The ordinary meaning in the context of use is odd enough to prompt us to disregard the question of literal truth.

Now let me raise a somewhat Platonic issue by comparing the making of a metaphor with telling a lie. The comparison is apt because lying, like making a metaphor, concerns not the meaning of words but their use. It is sometimes said that telling a lie entails saying what is false; but this is wrong. Telling a lie requires not that what you say be false but that you think it false. Since we usually believe true sentences and disbelieve false, most lies are falsehoods; but in any particular case this is an accident. The parallel between making a metaphor and telling a lie is emphasized by the fact that the same sentence can be used, with meaning unchanged, for either purpose. So a woman who believed in witches but did not think her neighbor a witch might say, "She's a witch," meaning it metaphorically; the same woman, still believing the same of witches and her neighbor but intending to deceive, might use the same words to very different effect. Since sentence and meaning are the same in both cases, it is sometimes hard to prove which intention lay behind the saying of it; thus a man who says "Lattimore's a Communist" and means to lie can always try to beg off by pleading a metaphor.

What makes the difference between a lie and a metaphor is not a difference in the words used or what they mean (in any strict sense of meaning) but in how the words are used. Using a sentence to tell a lie and using it to make a metaphor are, of course, totally different uses, so different that they do not interfere with one another, as say, acting and lying do. In lying, one must make an assertion so as to represent oneself as believing what one does not; in acting, assertion is excluded. Metaphor is careless to the difference. It can be an insult, and so be an assertion, to say to a man "You are a pig." But no metaphor was involved when (let us suppose) Odysseus addressed the same words to his companions in Circe's palace; a story, to be sure, and so no assertion—but the word, for once, was used literally of men.

No theory of metaphorical meaning or metaphorical truth can help explain how metaphor works. Metaphor runs on the same familiar linguistic tracks that the plainest sentences do; this we saw from considering simile. What distinguishes metaphor is not meaning but use—in this it is like assertion, hinting, lying, promising, or criticizing. And the special use to which we put language in metaphor is not—cannot be—to "say something" special, no matter how indirectly. For a metaphor *says* only what shows on its face—usually a patent falsehood or an absurd truth. And this plain truth or falsehood needs no paraphrase—it is given in the literal meaning of the words.

What are we to make, then, of the endless energy that has been, and is being, spent on methods and devices for drawing out the content of a metaphor? The psychologists Robert Verbrugge and Nancy McCarrell tell us that:

Many metaphors draw attention to common systems of relationships or common transformations, in which the identity of the participants is secondary. For example, consider the sentences: *A car is like an animal, Tree trunks are straws for thirsty leaves and branches.* The first sentence directs attention to systems of relationships among energy consumption, respiration, self-induced motion, sensory systems, and, possibly, a homunculus. In the second sentence, the resemblance is a more constrained type of transformation: suction of fluid

through a vertically oriented cylindrical space from a source of fluid to a destination.[10]

Verbrugge and McCarrell don't believe there is any sharp line between the literal and metaphorical uses of words; they think many words have a "fuzzy" meaning that gets fixed, if fixed at all, by a context. But surely this fuzziness, however it is illustrated and explained, cannot erase the line between what a sentence literally means (given its context) and what it "draws our attention to" (given its literal meaning as fixed by the context). The passage I have quoted is not employing such a distinction: what it says the sample sentences direct our attention to are facts expressed by paraphrases of the sentences. Verbrugge and McCarrell simply want to insist that a correct paraphrase may emphasize "systems of relationships" rather than resemblances between objects.

According to Black's interaction theory, a metaphor makes us apply a "system of commonplaces" associated with the metaphorical word to the subject of the metaphor: in "Man is a wolf" we apply commonplace attributes (stereotypes) of the wolf to man. The metaphor, Black says, thus "selects, emphasizes, suppresses, and organizes features of the principal subject by implying statements about it that normally apply to the subsidiary subject."[11] If paraphrase fails, according to Black, it is not because the metaphor does not have a special cognitive content, but because the paraphrase "will not have the same power to inform and enlighten as the original. . . . One of the points I most wish to stress is that the loss in such cases is a loss in cognitive content; the relevant weakness of the literal paraphrase is not that it may be tiresomely prolix or boringly explicit; it fails to be a translation because it fails to give the insight that the metaphor did."[12]

How can this be right? If a metaphor has a special cognitive content, why should it be so difficult or impossible to set it out? If, as Owen Barfield claims, a metaphor "says one thing and means another," why should it be that when we try to get explicit about what it means, the effect is so much weaker—"put it that way," Barfield says, "and nearly all the tarning, and with it half the poetry, is lost."[13] Why does Black think a literal paraphrase "inevitably says too much—and with the wrong emphasis"? Why inevitably? Can't we, if we are clever enough, come as close as we please?

For that matter, how is it that a simile gets along without a special intermediate meaning? In general, critics do not suggest that a simile says one thing and means another— they do not suppose it *means* anything but what lies on the surface of the words. It may make us think deep thoughts, just as a metaphor does; how come, then, no one appeals to the "special cognitive content" of the simile? And remember Eliot's hippopotamus; there there was neither simile nor metaphor, but what seemed to get done was just like what gets done by similes and metaphors. Does anyone suggest that the *words* in Eliot's poem have special meanings?

Finally, if words in metaphor bear a coded meaning, how can this meaning differ from the meaning those same words bear in the case where the metaphor *dies*—that is, when it comes to be part of the language? Why doesn't "He was burned up" as now used and meant mean *exactly* what the fresh metaphor once meant? Yet all that the dead metaphor means is that he was very angry—a notion not very difficult to make explicit.

There is, then, a tension in the usual view of metaphor. For on the one hand, the usual view wants to hold that a metaphor does something no plain prose can possibly do and, on the other hand, it wants to explain what a metaphor does by appealing to a cognitive content—just the sort of thing plain prose is designed to express. As long as we are in this frame of mind, we must harbor the suspicion that it *can* be done, at least up to a point.

There is a simple way out of the impasse. We must give up the idea that a metaphor carries a message, that it has a content or meaning (except, of course, its literal meaning). The various theories we have been considering mistake their goal. Where they think they provide a method for deciphering an encoded content, they actually tell us (or

try to tell us) something about the *effects* metaphors have on us. The common error is to fasten on the contents of the thoughts a metaphor provokes and to read these contents into the metaphor itself. No doubt metaphors often make us notice aspects of things we did not notice before; no doubt they bring surprising analogies and similarities to our attention; they do provide a kind of lens or lattice, as Black says, through which we view the relevant phenomena. The issue does not lie here but in the question of how the metaphor is related to what it makes us see.

It may be remarked with justice that the claim that a metaphor provokes or invites a certain view of its subject rather than saying it straight out is a commonplace; so it is. Thus Aristotle says metaphor leads to a "perception of resemblances." Black, following Richards, says a metaphor "evokes" a certain response: "a suitable hearer will be led by a metaphor to construct a . . . system."[14] This view is neatly summed up by what Heraclitus said of the Delphic oracle: "It does not say and it does not hide, it intimates."[15]

I have no quarrel with these descriptions of the effects of metaphor, only with the associated views as to *how* metaphor is supposed to produce them. What I deny is that metaphor does its work by having a special meaning, a specific cognitive content. I do not think, as Richards does, that metaphor produces its result by having a meaning which results from the interaction of two ideas; it is wrong, in my view, to say, with Owen Barfield, that a metaphor "says one thing and means another"; or with Black that a metaphor asserts or implies certain complex things by dint of a special meaning and *thus* accomplishes its job of yielding an "insight." A metaphor does its work through other intermediaries—to suppose it can be effective only by conveying a coded message is like thinking a joke or a dream makes some statement which a clever interpreter can restate in plain prose. Joke or dream or metaphor can, like a picture or a bump on the head, make us appreciate some fact—but not by standing for, or expressing, the fact.

If this is right, what we attempt in "paraphrasing" a metaphor cannot be to give its meaning, for that lies on the surface; rather we attempt to evoke what the metaphor brings to our attention. I can imagine someone granting this and shrugging it off as no more than an insistence on restraint in using the word "meaning." This would be wrong. The central error about metaphor is most easily attacked when it takes the form of a theory of metaphorical meaning, but behind that theory, and statable independently, is the thesis that associated with a metaphor is a cognitive content that its author wishes to convey and that the interpreter must grasp if he is to get the message. This theory is false, whether or not we call the purported cognitive content a meaning.

It should make us suspect the theory that it is so hard to decide, even in the case of the simplest metaphors, exactly what the content is supposed to be. The reason it is often so hard to decide is, I think, that we imagine there is a content to be captured when all the while we are in fact focusing on what the metaphor makes us notice. If what the metaphor makes us notice were finite in scope and propositional in nature, this would not in itself make trouble; we would simply project the content the metaphor brought to mind onto the metaphor. But in fact there is no limit to what a metaphor calls to our attention, and much of what we are caused to notice is not propositional in character. When we try to say what a metaphor "means," we soon realize there is no end to what we want to mention.[16] If someone draws his finger along a coastline on a map, or mentions the beauty and deftness of a line in a Picasso etching, how many things are drawn to your attention? You might list a great many, but you could not finish since the idea of finishing would have no clear application. How many facts or propositions are conveyed by a photograph? None, an infinity, or one great unstatable fact? Bad question. A picture is not worth a thousand words, or any other number. Words are the wrong currency to exchange for a picture.

It's not only that we can't provide an exhaustive catalogue of what has been attended to when we are led to see something in a new light; the difficulty is more fundamental. What we notice or see is not, in general, propositional in character. Of course it *may* be, and when it is, it usually may be stated in fairly plain words. But if I show you Wittgenstein's duck-rabbit, and I say, "It's a duck," then with luck you see it as a duck; if I say, "It's a rabbit," you see it as a rabbit. But no proposition expresses what I have led you to see. Perhaps you have come to realize that the drawing can be seen as a duck or as a rabbit. But one could come to know this without ever seeing the drawing as a duck or as a rabbit. Seeing as is not seeing that. Metaphor makes us see one thing as another by making some literal statement that inspires or prompts the insight. Since in most cases what the metaphor prompts or inspires is not entirely, or even at all, recognition of some truth or fact, the attempt to give literal expression to the content of the metaphor is simply misguided.

The theorist who tries to explain a metaphor by appealing to a hidden message, like the critic who attempts to state the message, is then fundamentally confused. No such explanation or statement can be forthcoming because no such message exists.

Not, of course, that interpretation and elucidation of a metaphor are not in order. Many of us need help if we are to see what the author of a metaphor wanted us to see and what a more sensitive or educated reader grasps. The legitimate function of so-called paraphrase is to make the lazy or ignorant reader have a vision like that of the skilled critic. The critic is, so to speak, in benign competition with the metaphor-maker. The critic tries to make his own art easier or more transparent in some respects than the original, but at the same time he tries to reproduce in others some of the effects the original had on him. In doing this the critic also, and perhaps by the best method at his command, calls attention to the beauty or aptness, the hidden power, of the metaphor itself.

NOTES

1. I think Max Black is wrong when he says, "The rules of our language determine that some

expressions must count as metaphors." He allows, however, that what a metaphor "means" depends on much more: the speaker's intention, tone of voice, verbal setting, etc. "Metaphor," in his *Models and Metaphors* (Ithaca, N.Y.: 1962), p. 29.

2. Nelson Goodman says metaphor and ambiguity differ chiefly "in that the several uses of a merely ambiguous term are coeval and independent" while in metaphor "a term with an extension established by habit is applied elsewhere under the influence of that habit"; he suggests that as our sense of the history of the "two uses" in metaphor fades, the metaphorical word becomes merely ambiguous (*Languages of Art* [Indianapolis, Ind.: 1968]. p. 71). In fact in many cases of ambiguity, one use springs from the other (as Goodman says) and so cannot be coeval. But the basic error, which Goodman shares with others, is the idea that two "uses" are involved in metaphor in anything like the way they are in ambiguity.

3. The theory described is essentially that of Paul Henle. Metaphor, in *Language, Thought and Culture*, ed. Henle (Ann Arbor, Mich: 1958).

4. William Empson, *Some Versions of Pastoral* (London: 1935), p. 133.

5. J. Middleton Murray says a metaphor is a "compressed simile," *Countries of the Mind*, 2d ser. (Oxford: 1931), p. 3. Max Black attributes a similar view to Alexander Bain, *English Composition and Rhetoric*, enl. ed. (London: 1887).

6. Black, p. 35.

7. Goodman, pp. 77–78.

8. Woody Allen, *New Yorker*, 21 November 1977, p. 59.

9. Ted Cohen, "Figurative Speech and Figurative Acts," *Journal of Philosophy* 72 (1975): 671. Since the negation of a metaphor seems always to be a potential metaphor, there may be as many platitudes among the potential metaphors as there are absurds.

10. Robert R. Verbrugge and Nancy S. McCarrell, "Metaphoric Comprehension: Studies in Reminding and Resembling," *Cognitive Psychology* 9 (1977): 499.

11. Black, pp. 44–45.

12. Ibid., p. 46.

13. Owen Barfield, "Poetic Diction and Legal Fiction," in *The Importance of Language*, ed. Max Black/Englewood Cliffs, N.J. 1962), p. 55.

15. I use Hannah Arendt's attractive translation of "σημαίνει": it clearly should not be rendered as "mean" in this context.

16. Stanley Cavell mentions the fact that most attempts at paraphrase end with "and so on" and refers to Empson's remark that metaphors are "pregnant" (*Must We Mean What We Say?* (New York: 1969), p. 79). But Cavell doesn't explain the endlessness of paraphrase as I do, as can be learned from the fact that he thinks it distinguishes metaphor from some ("but perhaps not all") literal discourse. I hold that the endless character of what we call the paraphrase of a metaphor springs from the fact that it attempts to spell out what the metaphor makes us notice, and to this there is no clear end. I would say the same for any use of language.

SUGGESTED FURTHER READING

Beardsley, Monroe, Metaphor, in *The Encyclopedia of Philosophy*, vol. 5, pp. 284–289.

Black, Max, Metaphor, in *Models and Metaphor* (Ithaca: Cornell University Press, 1954), pp. 41–60.

Fogelin, Robert, *Figuratively Speaking* (New Haven: Yale University Press, 1988).

Johnson, Mark, ed., *Philosophical Perspectives on Metaphor* (Minneapolis: University of Minneapolis Press, 1981).

Kittay, Eva, *Metaphor: Its Cognitive Force and Linguistic Structure* (Oxford: Clarendon Press, 1987).

Lakoff, George and Mark Johnson, *Metaphors We Live By* (Chicago: University of Chicago Press, 1980).

Martinich, A. P., A Theory for Metaphor, *Journal of Literary Semantics*, 13 (1984), 35–56.

Ortony, Andrew, ed., *Metaphor and Thought* (Cambridge: Cambridge University Press, 1980).

Sacks, Sheldon, ed., *On Metaphor* (Chicago: University of Chicago Press, 1981).

VII

THE NATURE OF LANGUAGE

The issue of what the nature of language is can be approached from many different perspectives and can be motivated by different worries. Three are represented in this section.

First, in the latter half of the twentieth century, the approach favored by most philosophers who have wondered about the issue has been to consider whether human languages are or can be private. The *locus classicus* for the view that private languages are possible has been some chapters in John Locke's *Essay Concerning Human Understanding,* first published in 1690. Further, not only does Locke hold that private languages are possible, but that private languages are necessary. That is, he holds that necessarily every language is private and that the meaning or signification of those words that have a meaning is necessarily an idea in the mind of the speaker: "A Man cannot make his Words the Signs either of Qualities in Things, or of Conceptions in the Mind of another, whereof he has none in his own" (*Essay Concerning Human Understanding,* III. ii. 2). The reason is that if a person were to try to have his words signify either something in another's mind or even in a physical object, then the speaker would mean by his words something of which he had no knowledge (since all that a person knows are his own ideas). And for a speaker to use a sign "of he knows not what . . . is in Truth to be the Signs of nothing" (*Essay,* III. ii. 2).

Locke clearly holds that the proper and immediate signification of meaningful words is the idea for which the word stands in the speaker and in the speaker alone. A word cannot signify both an idea of the speaker and an idea in someone else's mind, according to Locke; for then the word would both immediately signify the speaker's idea and not immediately signify the speaker's own idea (because it signifies an idea in another person's mind). Implicit in this argument is the premise that a word can immediately signify only one thing.

The purpose of language according to Locke is to make each person's private, invisible thoughts known to others. According to Locke, a speaker utters a word, say, "red," by which he signifies his own idea of redness with the intention of getting the audience to think of red also. Opponents of Locke's theory of language can exploit this statement of the purpose of language in order to demonstrate the impossibility of a private language. They can argue that by Locke's own account of meaning and his own reasoning about why a word must signify only the speaker's idea, no one one can ever know any one else's ideas. Recall that Locke had said that a word cannot signify an idea in another person's mind because no one can ever have this idea in his own mind. Jones's ideas belong only to Jones, and Smith can never have them. If this is true, then the purpose Locke states for language, that it is to make each person's private, invisible ideas known to others, cannot be achieved. Smith can never have Jones's ideas in his mind. That is one objection to the idea of a private language.

Another objection to Locke's explanation of the nature of language is that, if it were true, then no one could ever know that he had successfully communicated anything. The reason is this. Suppose the speaker immediately signifies by the word "red" some idea to which only he has access, and suppose that his utterance of the word "red" causes the audience to think of some idea. Since the speaker cannot see and does not have any other access to the audience's mind, there is never any way for the speaker to know whether he has succeeded in communicating. But since any reasonable person would concede that speakers are at least sometimes sure that their attempt to communicate has succeeded, Locke's view of the nature of language must be wrong.

These objections to the notion of a private language are simple and straightforward. Ludwig Wittgenstein's reasoning in his *Philosophical Investigations* (1954) was much more subtle, which in part explains why scholars do not agree about what he meant by a private language or how he argued for his view.

For the purposes of discussion, let us define a private language as one in which the meanings of the words refer to entities that only the speaker could have access to, and let us suppose that each person's pain is something to which only the person in pain can have cognitive access (a dubious assumption). The reason Wittgenstein thinks that the meaning of the word "pain" cannot be a sensation to which only the speaker has access is that a language is something that can be used for communication. But if the audience could never have access to the speaker's pain and the pain is the meaning of "pain," then the audience could never know the meaning of "pain," and communication would necessarily fail. In his article "Wittgenstein on Privacy," John Cook emphasizes that Wittgenstein's argument assumes that people do communicate about pains. This is important because many critics of Wittgenstein reason in this way: the meaning of "pain" is a speaker's pain; since Wittgenstein holds that if such is the case, talk about pain is impossible; but talk about pain is not impossible; therefore, Wittgenstein's view is mistaken. What these critics do not understand is that Wittgenstein is developing a kind of *reductio ad absurdum* argument against them. He agrees that talk about pain is not impossible and agrees that if the meaning of "pain" is a private sensation of pain, then such talk is impossible. He concludes that the meaning of "pain" is not a private sensation of pain. In other words, Wittgenstein assumes that "pain"—language is used to communicate and then tries to show that the meaning of "pain" cannot require a reference to a pain of which no other person can have knowledge. His view is consistent with the proposition that individuals have and feel pains, and consistent with the proposition that all individuals feel the same thing when they feel the same pain. But these matters are independent of the issue about the nature of language.

There are many confusions surrounding the ways in which sensations are and are not private and how the way in which they are private may affect the nature of language. John Cook has an elegant refutation of the view that since no one can feel another person's sensation, no one can know what sensation that person is experiencing. He points out that if such an argument were valid, then so is this one: since no one can have another person's shadow, no one can know anything about that person's shadow.

A defender of the private language view might respond that Wittgenstein nevertheless ignores the importance of the difference between the privacy of one's own pain and the publicness of a shadow. However, the alleged privacy of pain is ultimately irrelevant. The issue of whether language is private or not does not hang on whether pains or sensations are private or not. The nature of language can be misdescribed even if public objects are the objects of reference. Wittgenstein's argument would be similar even if someone held that the meaning of "red" is the experience of seeing red. It is a fact that many people can see the same red object, say, a candle, and it is the publicness of at least some red objects, their accessibility to speaker and audience, that is crucial to the meaning of "red."

If someone were to reply that "red" has a dual meaning, a public redness and the private redness (the sensation of red that is unique to each person), Wittgenstein would point out that the private redness is superfluous so far as the semantic issue is concerned. Suppose a person had a different qualitative sensation each time he saw a red object but that he used the word "red" in all observable ways as the other members of the linguistic community did. Then it would be true to say that he knew what the word "red" meant or knew the meaning of the word "red." This shows the superfluity or irrelevance of the private sensation so far as the meaning of the word "pain" is concerned. Again, this does not mean that sensations play no role in language.

So far, the discussion has focused on the nature of the object of meaning or reference, and nothing has been said about whether there is only one or many speakers of the language. The question about private languages has been in effect, "Can the meaning of a word be identified with a private entity?" The discussion can be focused in a very different way so that the relevant question is, "Can a human language be spoken by only one person?" For the purposes of answering this question, one can assume that the alleged objects of meaning are not private in the sense that only one person could have access to them. And the question also does not concern how a sole individual might learn a language. To make both of these points clear, let us ask whether a Robinson Crusoe, who was raised an English speaker, could continue to say such things as, "There's a coconut" and mean that there is a coconut; or whether, if all but one member of a linguistic community died, the sole surviving member would have a language.

Wittgenstein, I think, would answer these questions in the negative and would deny that there could be a language spoken only by one person. One reason has to do with the connection between language and rules. Linguistic communication is rule-governed behavior, and it does not make sense to say that someone is following a rule unless there is some way of judging whether the rule has been followed or broken. The speaker himself cannot be the final arbiter of this. The judge of whether a rule has been followed or not, like any standard of evaluation, must be separate from and independent of the matter to be decided. A speaker may think that he knows that he is following a rule, but there is a difference between thinking that one is doing something and doing it.

A. J. Ayer is not persuaded and explains why in "Can There Be a Private Language?" He thinks that there is nothing privileged about the publicness of the meaning-verification that Wittgenstein seems to require. All justification and verification of whatever sort must end somewhere. Further, all justification must end with some sense perception—for example, seeing or hearing the judgment of other people that one has or has not followed a rule of speaking correctly—so one may just as well end with one's own private sensation. (As part of an objection to Ayer's view, consider this line of reasoning: every judicial decision must end with some person's decision, so one may just as well end with the village idiot's decision.)

Saul Kripke in *On Rules and Private Language* in effect responds to Ayer by saying that Wittgenstein recognizes that all verification ends somewhere and that one might always doubt the veracity of one's perceptions. But Wittgenstein's point is that, skepticism notwithstanding, he has correctly described how human languages do work; that humans in fact do end their justification with certain rule-governed, publicly observable behavior and not with private sensations; and such a practice does not require any justification. According to Kripke, it is Wittgenstein's view that the ordinary practices of human beings do not need the kind of justification that the skeptic requires. Just as custom alone justifies the ordinary belief in causal relations, custom alone justifies the actual social practice and understanding of language: "the success of the practices . . . depends on the brute empirical fact that we agree with each other in our responses." And there is no further fact of the matter. Kripke calls this solution Humean, after the eighteenth-century philosopher David Hume, who responded to the challenge of skepticism by saying that human beings have a natural propensity for believing that they know things and it does not need to be justified.

While it is not clear how Ayer would respond to this line, it is clear that he disagrees with Wittgenstein on other matters. According to Ayer, it is a merely contingent matter whether one or many people speak a language, and he appeals to the possible existence of a real Robinson Crusoe to make the point. If Crusoe says, "That's a coconut" upon seeing a coconut, why isn't it true that he means that that's a coconut? Of if he says, "I have a pain," why isn't it true that he means that he has a pain? Ayer correctly recognizes that it is not significant whether material objects or sensations are the alleged meanings of terms. If a person is alone, then for all practical purposes one object is no more private than any other. Nonetheless, there is a reply to Ayer. He confuses Crusoe's vocalizations (that is, the sounds produced using human vocal cords), "That's a coconut," and "I have a pain," which are isomorphic or isophonic with English, with genuine instances of English. If a voice synthesizer randomly fit together sounds until it emitted the sound, "I have a pain," it would not follow that the voice synthesizer meant that it had a pain. It is tendentious or question-begging for Ayer to argue that since a scenario can be constructed that involves producing noises that sound like English that therefore English is being spoken. But Ayer has shown only that Crusoe's ability to vocalize remains the same, not that these vocalizations count as language. Crusoe would not be ordering or questioning or promising by means of any of his utterances, I would maintain, because there is no one to be ordered, questioned, or promised except, though it is dubious, himself. And if he could not be doing any of these things what sense does it make to say that he is stating or asserting that there's a coconut or that he is in pain? For the point and purpose of describing something is to inform someone of the described situation. Since Crusoe lacks such a purpose, he is going through the motions of language without speaking one. It is also useful to recall Austin's observation in "Performative Utterances" that one cannot just make a statement about anything at any time.

Another way to put the foregoing point is to say that if there is a private descriptive language, then there is a private performative language. One can easily describe a "private marriage" ceremony in which Crusoe says the words, "I take this woman to be my wife," and later to the extent possible, performs acts analogous to marital acts, such as making his own breakfast and worrying about mortgage payments. But he still wouldn't be married.

In addition to the acoustic identity between Crusoe's utterances and English, another possible source for Ayer's confusion on this point may be that he confuses himself and his readers with an audience for Crusoe. Ayer, who constructs the scenario, has the impression that he understands what Crusoe is saying, because he recognizes Crusoe's vocalizations as English and he knows what he wants Crusoe to mean by them. But it is illegitimate for Ayer to think of himself as part of Crusoe's audience. Crusoe is alone; his utterances cannot serve any function that language must have in order to deserve the name, and for all that Crusoe knows, his utterances do not have the purpose or regularity one must know they have in order to count as part of language.

A second approach to thinking about the nature of language is to think of language as a formal system that correlates sentences with meanings in a systematic way. These correlations can be represented as ordered pairs consisting of sentences as the first members, and meanings (sets of possible worlds) as the second. David Lewis, who is sympathetic to this goal, nonetheless thinks it can be coupled with a view something like Wittgenstein's. According to this latter view, language is a social phenomena, in which utterances initiate behavior and allow people to understand the beliefs and desires of others. Lewis suggests a synthesis of these two perspectives according to which humans use the formal system as a means of communication. This is possible because members of a community share two conventions: truth and trust. Speakers of indicative sentences try to tell the truth and their audiences trust that they will. Speakers of imperative sentences trust that their audiences will make the sentences true, while the audiences try to do so. Lewis's article is a powerful attempt to reconcile the Wittgensteinian and Austinian view of language with the formal view of logicians and many linguists.

The third approach to the nature of language developed from the work of Noam Chomsky, who rejects both Lewis's characterization of language and the attempt at synthesis, at least so far as linguistics is concerned. On Chomsky's view, language is a certain component of the human brain, and linguistics is a branch of brain science. For this reason, language is objectively real, and theories about it are true or false in the same sense that any scientific theory is. Since brain science is in its infancy, linguistic theory is still relatively naive, and the abstractness of its descriptions of the brain is relatively unsophisticated. Contemporary linguistics is to an adequate theory of the brain as eighteenth-century chemistry is to contemporary chemistry.

Another consequence of identifying language with a structure of the brain is that there is an objectively true description of it, at least in general. The apparently great differences between English, Finnish, and Japanese are probably not very great as they exist in the brains of English, Finnish, and Japanese speakers. Putting the point picturesquely, he says that, viewed by an angel, all human languages would look identical. What he means is that, viewed from afar, apparently large differences between, say, English and Japanese speakers, are in fact very small differences. He points out that biologists have discovered that very minor differences at the microscopic level of genetic components generate apparently large differences at the macroscopic level of biological form and behavior. Moreover, the ordinary idea that English, Spanish, and Japanese are different "languages" does not have any scientific validity. There are no sharp or principled borders between one so-called language and another. The German spoken near the Dutch border is more easily understood by Dutch speakers than by German speakers in certain remote areas. All of these considerations are connected with Chomsky's belief that there is, for all human languages, a universal grammar, which is a component of the brain of every normal human being.

Chomsky contrasts his view that language is a "subsystem of the mind/brain," which he dubs "I-language" (intensional language), with several other competing views. The most important of these is the view he attributes to David Lewis, according to which human language is "E-language" (extensional language), that is, an infinite set of strings of symbols for which there are an infinite number of possible grammars. On such a view, language is thought of as a mathematical entity. One objection to this way of construing human language is that its determinate set of symbols does not correspond to the utterances of human speakers, which include semi-grammatical and other sorts of borderline cases. Another problem is that its view of semantics as relating syntactic structures (strings of words or other symbols) with models, usually set theoretic models, is mistaken. Semantics is the study of the relation between language and the world, not some mental or otherwise artificial representation device.

Another consequence of Chomsky's view is that he has no sympathy with the Wittgensteinian view, as interpreted by Anthony Kenny, that to know a language is to be able or to have a disposition to speak, read, understand, and so on. Chomsky points out that a speaker can improve his ability to speak and write without changing his knowledge of the language, and that one's ability to use language can be lost, perhaps from an injury, and then regained by taking a drug without ever having lost that very language at all. Since language is a component of the brain, it is also not essentially tied to communication. Linguistic communication is merely one of several uses to which language can be put: it can also be used to remember things, make private computations, and write personal poetry.

Contradicting Quine's view in "Two Dogmas of Empiricism," Chomsky argues that it is obvious that there are determinate semantic relations and analytic sentences if one thinks about certain sentences that have a relational structure and involve intentional activities, for example, "If John persuaded Bill to go to college, then Bill went to college." Thus, there is a legitimate distinction to be made between truths of meaning and truths of fact.

Can There Be a Private Language?   33

A. J. AYER

In a quite ordinary sense, it is obvious that there can be private languages. There can be, because there are. A language may be said to be private when it is devised to enable a limited number of persons to communicate with one another in a way that is not intelligible to anyone outside the group. By this criterion, thieves' slang and family jargons are private languages. Such languages are not strictly private, in the sense that only one person uses and understands them, but there may very well be languages that are. Men have been known to keep diaries in codes which no one else is meant to understand. A private code is not, indeed, a private language, but rather a private method of transcribing some given language. It is, however, possible that a very secretive diarist may not be satisfied with putting familiar words into an unfamiliar notation, but may prefer to invent new words: the two processes are in any case not sharply distinct. If he carries his invention far enough he can properly be said to be employing a private language. For all I know, this has actually been done.

From this point of view, what makes a language private is simply the fact that it satisfies the purpose of being intelligible only to a single person, or to a restricted set of people. It is necessary here to bring in a reference to purpose, since a language may come to be intelligible only to a few people, or even only to a single person, merely by falling into general disuse: but such "dead" languages are not considered to be private, if the limitation of their use was not originally intended. One may characterize a private language by saying that it is not in this sense meant to be alive. There is, however, no reason, in principle, why it should not come alive. The fact that only one person, or only a few people, are able to understand it is purely contingent. Just as it is possible, in theory, that any code should be broken, so can a private language come to be more widely understood. Such private languages are in general derived from public languages, and even if there are any which are not so derived, they will still be translatable into public languages. Their ceasing to be private is then just a matter of enough people becoming able to translate them or, what is more difficult but still theoretically possible, not to translate but even so to understand them.

If I am right, then, there is a use for the expression "private language" which clearly allows it to have application. But this is not the use which philosophers have commonly given it. What philosophers usually seem to have in mind when they speak of a private language is one that is, in their view, necessarily private, in as much as it is used by some particular person to refer only to his own private experiences: for it is often held that for a language to be public it must refer to what is publicly observable: if a person could limit himself to describing his own sensations or feelings, then, strictly speaking, only he would understand what he was saying; his utterance might indirectly convey some information to others, but it could not mean to them exactly what it meant to him. Thus, Carnap who gives the name of "protocol language" to any set of sentences which are used to give "a direct record" of one's own experience argues, in his booklet on The Unity of Science,[1] that if an utterance like "Thirst now," belonging to the protocol language of a subject S_1 is construed as expressing "only what is immediately given" to S_1 it cannot be understood by anyone else. Another subject S_2 may claim to be able to recognize and so to refer to S_1's thirst, but "strictly speaking" all that he ever recognizes is some physical state of S_1's body. "If by 'the thirst of S_1' we understand not the physical state of his body, but his sensations of thirst, i.e., something nonmaterial, then S_1's thirst is fundamentally beyond the reach of S_2's recognition."[2] S_2 cannot possibly verify any statement which refers to S_1's thirst, in this sense, and consequently cannot understand it. "In general," Carnap continues, "every statement in any person's protocol language would have sense for that person alone. . . . Even when the same words and sentences occur in various protocol languages, their sense would be different, they could not even be compared. Every protocol language could therefore be applied only solipsistically: there would be no intersubjective protocol language. This is the consequence obtained by consistent adherence to the usual view and terminology (rejected by the author)."[3]

Since Carnap wishes to maintain that people can understand one another's protocol statements, if only on the ground that this is a necessary condition for statements made in what he calls the physical language to be intersubjectively verifiable, he draws the inference that "protocol language is a part of physical language." That is, he concludes that sentences which on the face of it refer to private experiences must be logically equivalent to sentences which describe some physical state of the subject. Other philosophers have followed him in giving a physicalist interpreta-

tion to the statements that one makes about the experiences of others, but have stopped short of extending it to all the statements that one may make about one's own. They prefer to hold that certain sentences do serve only to describe the speaker's private experiences, and that, this being so, they have a different meaning for him from any that they can possibly have for anybody else.

In his *Philosophical Investigations* Wittgenstein appears to go much further than this. He seems to take the view that someone who attempted to use language in this private way would not merely be unable to communicate his meaning to others, but would have no meaning to communicate even to himself; he would not succeed in saying anything at all. "Let us", says Wittgenstein,[4] "imagine the following case: 'I want to keep a diary about the recurrence of a certain sensation. To this end I associate it with the sign 'S' and write this sign in a calendar for every day on which I have the sensation.—I will remark first of all that a definition of the sign cannot be formulated.—But still I can give myself a kind of ostensive definition.—How? Can I point to the sensation? Not in the ordinary sense. But I speak, or write the sign down, and at the same time I concentrate my attention on the sensation—and so, as it were, point to it inwardly.—But what is this ceremony for? for that is all it seems to be! A definition surely serves to establish the meaning of a sign.— Well, that is done precisely by the concentration of my attention; for in this way I impress on myself the connexion between the sign and the sensation.—But 'I impress it on myself' can only mean: this process brings it about that I remember the connexion *right* in the future. But in the present case I have no criterion of correctness. One would like to say: whatever is going to seem right to me is right. And that only means that here one can't talk about 'right'."

Again, "What reason have we for calling 'S' the sign for a *sensation?* For 'sensation' is a word of our common language, not of one intelligible to me alone. So the use of the word stands in need of a justification which everybody understands."[5]

This point is then developed further: "Let us imagine a table (something like a dictionary) that exists only in our imagination. A dictionary can be used to justify the translation of a word X into a word Y. But are we also to call it a justification if such a table is to be looked up only in the imagination?—'Well, yes: then it is a subjective justification'.—But justification consists in appealing to something independent.—'But surely I can appeal from one memory to another. For example, I don't know if I have remembered the time of departure of a train right and to check it I call to mind how a page of the time-table looked. Isn't it the same here?' No; for this process has got to produce a memory which is actually *correct*. If the mental image of the time-table could not itself be *tested* for correctness, how could it confirm the correctness of the first memory? (As if someone were to buy several copies of the morning paper to assure himself that what it said was true.)

Looking up a table in the imagination is no more looking up a table than the image of the result of an imagined experiment is the result of an experiment."[6]

The case is quite different, Wittgenstein thinks, when the sensation can be coupled with some outward manifestation. Thus he maintains that the language which we ordinarily use to describe our "inner experiences" is not private because the words which one uses to refer to one's sensations are "tied up with [one's] natural expressions of sensation"[7] with the result that other people are in a position to understand them. Similarly he grants that the person who tries to describe his private sensation by writing down the sign "E" in his diary might find a use for this sign if he discovered that whenever he had the sensation in question it could be shown by means of some measuring instrument that his blood pressure rose. For this would give him a way of telling that his blood pressure was rising without bothering to consult the instrument. But then, argues Wittgenstein, it will make no difference whether his recognition of the sensation is right or not. Provided that whenever he thinks he recognizes it, there is independent evidence that his blood pressure

rises, it will not matter if he is invariably mistaken, if the sensation which he takes to be the same on each occasion is really not the same at all. "And that alone shows that the hypothesis that [he] makes a mistake is mere show."[8]

Let us examine this argument. A point to which Wittgenstein constantly recurs is that the ascription of meaning to a sign is something that needs to be justified: the justification consists in there being some independent test for determining that the sign is being used correctly; independent, that is, of the subject's recognition, or supposed recognition, of the object which he intends the sign to signify. His claim to recognize the object, his belief that it really is the same, is not to be accepted unless it can be backed by further evidence. Apparently, too, this evidence must be public: it must, at least in theory, be accessible to everyone. Merely to check one private sensation by another would not be enough. For if one cannot be trusted to recognize one of them, neither can one be trusted to recognize the other.

But unless there is something that one is allowed to recognize, no test can ever be completed: there will be no justification for the use of any sign at all. I check my memory of the time at which the train is due to leave by visualizing a page of the time-table; and I am required to check this in its turn by looking up the page. But unless I can trust my eyesight at this point, unless I can recognize the figures that I see written down, I am still no better off. It is true that if I distrust my eyesight I have the resource of consulting other people; but then I have to understand their testimony, I have correctly to identify the signs that they make. Let the object to which I am attempting to refer be as public as you please, let the word which I use for this purpose belong to some common language, my assurance that I am using the word correctly, that I am using it to refer to the "right" object, must in the end rest on the testimony of my senses. It is through hearing what other people say, or through seeing what they write, or observing their movements, that I am enabled to conclude that their use of the word agrees with mine. But if without further ado I can recognize such noises or shapes or movements why can I not also recognize a private sensation? It is all very well for Wittgenstein to say that writing down the sign "E," at the same time as I attend to the sensation, is an idle ceremony. How is it any more idle than writing down a sign, whether it be the conventionally correct sign or not, at the same time as I observe some "public" object? There is, indeed, a problem about what is involved in endowing any sign with meaning, but it is no less of a problem in the case where the object for which the sign is supposed to stand is public than in the case where it is private. Whatever it is about my behavior that transforms the making of a sound, or the inscription of a shape, into the employment of a sign can equally well occur in either case.

But, it may be said, in the one case I can point to the object I am trying to name, I can give an ostensive definition of it; in the other I cannot. For merely attending to an object is not pointing to it. But what difference does this make? I can indeed extend my finger in the direction of a physical object, while I pronounce what I intend to be the object's name; and I cannot extend my finger in the direction of a private sensation. But how is this extending of my finger itself anything more than an idle ceremony? If it is to play its part in the giving of an ostensive definition this gesture has to be endowed with meaning. But if I can endow such a gesture with meaning, I can endow a word with meaning, without the gesture.

I suppose that the reason why the gesture is thought to be important is that it enables me to make my meaning clear to others. Of course they have to interpret me correctly. If they are not intelligent, or I am not careful, they may think that I am pointing to one thing when I really intend to point to another. But successful communication by this method is at least possible. The object to which I mean to point is one that they can observe. On the other hand, no amount of gesturing on my part can direct their attention to a private sensation of mine, which *ex hypothesi* they cannot observe, assuming fur-

ther that this sensation has no "natural expression." So I cannot give an ostensive definition of the word which I wish to stand for the sensation. Nor can I define it in terms of other words, for how are they to be defined? Consequently I cannot succeed in giving it any meaning.

This argument is based on two assumptions, both of which I believe to be false. One is that in a case of this sort it is impossible, logically impossible, to understand a sign unless one can either observe the object which it signifies, or at least observe something with which this object is naturally associated. And the other is that for a person to be able to attach meaning to a sign it is necessary that other people should be capable of understanding it too. It will be convenient to begin by examining the second of these assumptions which leads on to the first.

Imagine a Robinson Crusoe left alone on his island while still an infant, having not yet learned to speak. Let him, like Romulus and Remus, be nurtured by a wolf, or some other animal, until he can fend for himself; and so let him grow to manhood. He will certainly be able to recognize many things upon the island, in the sense that he adapts his behavior to them. Is it inconceivable that he should also name them? There may be psychological grounds for doubting whether such a solitary being would in fact invent a language. The development of language, it may be argued, is a social phenomenon. But surely it is not self-contradictory to suppose that someone, uninstructed in the use of any existing language, makes up a language for himself. After all, some human being must have been the first to use a symbol. And even if he did so as a member of a group, in order to communicate with the other members, even if his choice of symbols was socially conditioned, it is at least conceivable that it should originally have been a purely private enterprise. The hypothesis of G. K. Chesterton's dancing professor about the origin of language, that it came "from the formulated secret language of some individual creature" is very probably false, but it is certainly not unintelligible.

But if we allow that our Robinson Crusoe

could invent words to describe the flora and fauna of his island, why not allow that he could also invent words to describe his sensations? In neither case will he be able to justify his use of words by drawing on the evidence provided by a fellow creature: but while this is a useful check, it is not indispensable. It would be difficult to argue that the power of communication, the ability even to keep a private diary, could come to him only with the arrival of Man Friday. His justification for describing his environment in the way that he does will be that he perceives it to have just those features which his words are intended to describe. His knowing how to use these words will be a matter of his remembering what objects they are meant to stand for, and so of his being able to recognize these objects. But why should he not succeed in recognizing them? And why then should he not equally succeed in recognizing his sensations? Undoubtedly, he may make mistakes. He may think that a bird which he sees flying past is a bird of the same type as one which he had previously named, when in fact it is of a different type, sufficiently different for him to have given it a different name if he had observed it more closely. Similarly, he may think that a sensation is the same as others which he has identified, when in fact, in the relevant aspects, it is not the same. In neither case may the mistake make any practical difference to him, but to say that nothing turns upon a mistake is not to say that it is not a mistake at all. In the case of the bird, there is a slightly greater chance of his detecting his mistake, since the identical bird may reappear: but even so he has to rely upon his memory for the assurance that it is the identical bird. In the case of the sensation, he has only his memory as a means of deciding whether his identification is correct or not. In this respect he is indeed like Wittgenstein's man who buys several copies of the morning paper to assure himself that what it says is true. But the reason why this seems to us so absurd is that we take it for granted that one copy of a morning paper will duplicate another; there is no absurdity in buying a second newspaper, of a different type, and using it to check the first. And in a place where there was only one morning newspaper, but it was so pro-

duced that misprints might occur in one copy without occuring in all, it would be perfectly sensible to buy several copies and check them against each other. Of course there remains the important difference that the facts which the newspaper reports are independently verifiable, in theory if not always in practice. But verification must stop somewhere. As I have already argued, unless something is recognized, without being referred to a further test, nothing can be tested. In the case of Crusoe's sensation, we are supposing that beyond his memory there is no further test. It does not follow that he has no means of identifying it, or that it does not make sense to say that he identifies it right or wrong.

So long as Crusoe remains alone on the island, so long, that is, as he communicates only with himself, the principal distinction which he is likely to draw between "external" objects and his "inner" experiences is that his experiences are transient in a way that external objects are not. He will not be bound to draw even this distinction; his criteria for identity may be different from our own; but it is reasonable to suppose that they will be the same. Assuming, then, that his language admits the distinction, he will find on the arrival of Man Friday that it acquires a new importance. For whereas he will be able to teach Man Friday the use of the words which he has devised to stand for external objects by showing him the objects for which they stand, he will not, in this way, be able to teach him the use of the words which he has devised to stand for his sensations. And in the cases where these sensations are entirely private, in the sense that they have no "natural expressions" which Man Friday can identify, it may well be that Crusoe fails to find any way of teaching him the use of the words which he employs to stand for them. But from the fact that he cannot teach this part of his language to Man Friday it by no means follows that he has no use for it himself. In a context of this sort, one can teach only what one already understands. The ability to teach, or rather the ability of someone else to learn, cannot therefore be a prerequisite for understanding.

Neither does it necessarily follow, in these circumstances, that Man Friday will be incapable of learning the meaning of the words which Crusoe uses to describe his private sensations. It is surely a contingent fact that we depend upon ostensive definitions, to the extent that we do, for learning what words mean. As it is, a child is not taught how to describe his feelings in the way he is taught to describe the objects in his nursery. His mother cannot point to his pain in the way that she can point to his cup and spoon. But she knows that he has a pain because he cries and because she sees that something has happened to him which is likely to cause him pain; and knowing that he is in pain she is able to teach him what to call it. If there were no external signs of his sensation she would have no means of detecting when he had them, and therefore could not teach him how to describe them. This is indeed the case, but it might easily be otherwise. We can imagine two persons being so attuned to one another that whenever either has a private sensation of a certain sort, the other has it too. In that case when one of them described what he was feeling the other might very well follow the description, even though he had no "external" evidence to guide him. But how could either of them ever know that he had identified the other's feeling correctly? Well, how can two people ever know that they mean the same by a word which they use to refer to some "public" object. Only because each finds the other's reactions appropriate. Similarly one may suppose that Man Friday sympathizes when Crusoe's private sensation is painful, and congratulates him when it is pleasant, that he is able to say when it begins and when it stops, that he correctly describes it as being rather like such and such another sensation, and very different from a third, thereby affording proof that he also understands the words that stand for these sensations. Admittedly, such tests are not conclusive. But the tests which we ordinarily take as showing that we mean the same by the words which we apply to public objects are not conclusive either: they leave it at least theoretically open that we do not after all mean quite the same. But from the fact that the tests are not conclusive it does not, in either case,

follow that they have no force at all. It is true also that such tests as the expressed agreement about the duration of the experience require that the two men already share a common language, which they have no doubt built up on the basis of common observations. It would indeed be difficult, though still, I think, not necessarily impossible, for them to establish communication if all their experience were private, in Wittgenstein's sense. But even if their understanding each other's use of words could come about only if some of the objects which these words described were public, it would not follow that they all must be so.

It is not even necessary to make the assumption that Man Friday comes to know what Crusoe's sensations are, and so to understand the words which signify them, through having similar sensations of his own. It is conceivable that he should satisfy all the tests which go to show that he has this knowledge, and indeed that he should actually have it, even though the experience which he rightly ascribes to Crusoe is unlike any that he has, or ever has had, himself. It would indeed be very strange if someone had this power of seeing, as it were, directly into another's soul. But it is strange only in the sense that it is something which, on causal grounds, we should not expect to happen. The idea of its happening breaks no logical rule. An analogous case would be that of someone's imagining, or seeming to remember, an experience which was unlike any that he had ever actually had. To allow that such things are possible is, indeed, to admit innate ideas, in the Lockean sense, but that is not a serious objection. The admission is not even inconsistent with the prevalent varieties of empiricism. It can still be made a rule that in order to understand a word which signifies a sensation one must know what it would be like to have the sensation in question: that is, one must be able to identify the sensation when one has it, and so to verify the statement which describes it. The peculiarity of the cases which we are envisaging is just that people are credited with the ability to identify experiences which they have not previously had. There may indeed be causal objections to the hypothesis that this can ever happen. The point which concerns us now is that these objections are no more than causal. The ways in which languages are actually learned do not logically circumscribe the possibilities of their being understood.

If the sort of insight which we have been attributing to Man Friday were commonly possessed, we might well be led to revise our concepts of publicity and privacy. The mistake which is made by philosophers like Carnap is that of supposing that being public or being private, in the senses which are relevant to this discussion, are properties which are somehow attached to different sorts of objects, independently of our linguistic usage. But the reason why one object is publicly and another only privately accessible is that in the one case it makes sense to say that the object is observed by more than one person and in the other it does not. Tables are public; it makes sense to say that several people are perceiving the same table. Headaches are private: it does not make sense to say that several people are feeling the same headache. But just as we can assimilate tables to headaches by introducing a notation in which two different persons' perceiving the same table becomes a matter of their each sensing their own private "tabular" sense-data, so we could assimilate headaches to tables by introducing a notation in which it was correct to speak of a common headache, which certain people only were in a condition to perceive. As things are, this notation would not be convenient. But if people were so constituted that they were communally exposed to headaches in the way that they are communally exposed to the weather, we might cease to think of headaches as being necessarily private. A London particular might come to be a local headache as well as, or instead of, a local fog. Certain persons might escape it, just as certain persons, for one reason or another, may fail to perceive the fog. But the fog exists for all that, and so, given this new way of speaking, would the public headache. The conditions which would make this way of speaking useful do not, indeed, obtain; but that they do not is, once again, a purely contingent fact.

The facts being what they are, we do not have a use for such expressions as "S_2's feeling S_1's thirst" or "S_2's observing the sensation of thirst which S_1 feels." On the other hand, we do attach a meaning to saying that the same physical object, or process, or event, for instance a state of S_1's body, is observed by S_2 as well as by S_1. Does it follow, as Carnap thinks, that for this reason S_2 cannot understand a statement which refers to S_1's feeling of thirst, whereas he can understand a statement which refers to the condition of S_1's body? Suppose that we modified our rules for identity, in a way that many philosophers have proposed, and allowed ourselves to say that what was ordinarily described as S_1 and S_2's observing the same physical event was "really" a case of each of them sensing his own sense-data which, while they might be qualitatively similar, could not be literally the same. Should we thereby be committed to denying that either could understand what the other said about this physical event? Surely not. And equally the fact that S_2 cannot feel, or inspect, S_1's feelings in no way entails that he cannot understand what S_1 says about them. The criteria for deciding whether two people understand each other are logically independent of the fact that we do, or do not, have a use for saying that literally the same objects are perceived by both.

I conclude, first, that for a person to use descriptive language meaningfully it is not necessary that any other person should understand him, and, secondly, that for anyone to understand a descriptive statement it is not necessary that he should himself be able to observe what it describes. It is not even necessary that he should be able to observe something which is naturally associated with what it describes, in the way that feelings are associated with their "natural expressions." If we insist on making it a necessary condition for our understanding a descriptive statement that we are able to observe what it describes, we shall find ourselves disclaiming the possibility of understanding not merely statements about other people's private sensations, but also statements about the past; either that, or reinterpreting them in such a way that they change their reference, as when philosophers substitute bodily states for feelings, and the future for the past. Both courses, I now think, are mistaken. No doubt it is a necessary condition for my understanding a descriptive statement that it should be, in some way, verifiable. But it need not be directly verifiable, and even if it is directly verifiable, it need not be directly verifiable by me.

NOTES

1. 76ff.
2. p. 79.
3. p. 80.
4. *Philosophical Investigations*, 1.258.
5. *Op. cit.*, 1.261.
6. *Op. cit.*, 1.265.
7. *Op. cit.*, 1.256.
8. *Op. cit.*, 1.270.

Wittgenstein on Privacy 34

Recent discussions of Wittgenstein's treatment of the idea of a private language have made it clear that the point of what Wittgenstein is doing has been widely misunderstood. I should here like to take one step toward remedying that situation. A chief complaint against Wittgenstein is that he does not make it sufficiently clear what the idea of a private language includes—what is meant by "a private language."[1] It is this complaint that I mean to examine, and I will argue that there can be no such genuine complaint even though it is true that Wittgenstein does not say clearly what is meant by "a private language." He does not try to make this clear because the idea under investigation turns out to be irremediably confused and hence can be only suggested, not clearly explained. Moreover, the philosophical idea of a private language is confused not merely in that it supposes a mistaken notion of language (or meaning) but in its very notion of the privacy of sensations. It is this last point which is generally missed and which I mean here to insist on.

I

The philosophical idea of a private language is a consequence of the following argument (hereafter called *A*):

No one can know that another person is in pain or is dizzy or has any other sensation, for sensations are private in the sense that no one can feel

(experience, be acquainted with) another person's sensations.

The conclusion of argument *A* leads, in turn, to the further conclusion that no one can be taught the names of sensations; each of us must give these words their meanings independently of other people and of other people's use of sensation words. (The missing premise here is that in order to teach another person the name of a sensation, it would be necessary to check his use of the word, and this would require knowing from time to time what sensation the learner is having.) The result is the idea that anyone who says anything about his sensations is saying something which he alone can understand. Names of sensations, the word "sensation" itself, and the expression "same sensation" will have no genuine public use, only a private use.

It is this consequence of *A* that Wittgenstein refers to in section 243 of the *Investigations*[2] when he asks whether we could imagine a language whose words "refer to what can only be known to the person speaking; to his immediate private sensations. So another person cannot understand the language." But having raised this question, he almost immediately (*Inv.* 246–254) launches attacks against both the premise and the conclusion of *A*. That is, he undertakes to show that the very notion of privacy on which the description of this language depends is a tangle of confusions. Hence, when he returns

From *Philosophical Review*, volume 74 (1965).

in section 256 to the consideration of "the language which describes my inner experiences and which only I myself can understand," he points out that (contrary to argument A) our ordinary use of sensation words is not such a language. Thus, the temptation behind the idea of a private language has already been disposed of. What Wittgenstein goes on to do, then, in the ensuing discussion of this "language which only I myself can understand" is to "assume the abrogation of the normal language-game," that is, to consider what the result would be "if we cut out human behavior, which is the expression of sensation" (*Inv.* 288). He introduces the discussion as follows: "But suppose I didn't have my natural expression of sensation, but only had the sensation? And now I simply *associate* names with sensations and use these names in descriptions" (*Inv.* 256). Here we have what might be an allusion to Descartes, who assumes that even if his philosophical doubts be justified, so that he has "no hands, no eyes, no flesh, no blood, nor any senses," still he can privately understand and inwardly speak a language. It is this picture of language as a phenomenon made possible by "some remarkable act of mind" (*Inv.* 38) that Wittgenstein means to investigate. In rejecting this idea of a private language, then, what he rejects is not our normal language game but a philosophically truncated version of it. Defenders of argument A, however, because they must regard sensations as only privately namable, must regard Wittgenstein's rejection of this either as a rejection of our normal language game or as committing him to an extremely odd account of our normal language game. Thus, on the one hand, Wittgenstein has been "refuted" on the grounds that since sensations are private, and since each of us does have names of sensations in his vocabulary, there could not be any real difficulty in the idea of a private language: "the ordinary language of pains is . . . a counter-example against Wittgenstein's thesis."[3] On the other hand, it has been argued that since sensations are private, and since Wittgenstein denies the possibility of naming private objects, he must be denying that

ordinary language contains any genuine names of sensations: on Wittgenstein's view "private sensations do not enter into pain language games."[4]

In order to expose the errors of these two views, it is necessary to bring out the force of Wittgenstein's attack on argument A. I have given the argument in a form commonly found, but as it stands certain of its premises are suppressed. The premise

(P_1)   No one can feel (experience, be acquainted with) another person's sensations

does not entail the conclusion

(C)   No one can know what sensations another person is having.

Argument A, as it stands, is really no better than (and I will show that it cannot be made to be better than) the following argument: "No one can have another person's shadow, and therefore no one can know anything about another person's shadow." This argument is unsatisfactory for the obvious reason that the premise has no bearing on how one gets to know something about another person's shadow. In the same way, the premise of A has no bearing on how one gets to know about another person's sensations. And yet it is just this bearing that (P_1) is thought to have by those who advance argument A. What, then, are their suppressed premises? One of them must be this:

(P_2)   The proper and necessary means of coming to know what sensation another person is having is to feel that person's sensation.

With this premise added, argument A purports to be denying that anyone can avail himself of the sole proper means of ascertaining what sensations another person is having. Hence, what the argument must also show, if it is to be at all plausible, is that the sole proper means of ascertaining whether another person is in pain, for example, is to feel his pain. This is usually thought to be shown as follows:

(P_3)   Anyone who has a sensation *knows* that he has it because he feels it, and whatever can be known to exist by being felt cannot be known (in the same sense of "known") to exist in any other way.

With these two premises added, is argument *A* complete? In recent defenses of the argument it has been common to add to (P_1) the qualification that the impossibility of experiencing another person's sensations is a *logical* impossibility. What bearing this qualification has on the form of the argument will depend on which of the several current interpretations is placed on "logical impossibility." I will examine these interpretations in sections II and III and will show that they fail to make sense of the claim that no one can feel another person's sensations. Therefore, I will give no further attention here to the qualification that (P_1) expresses a logical impossibility. In the remainder of this section I will try to bring out the force of Wittgenstein's attack on the premises (P_2) and (P_3) which purport to state a necessary condition for knowing what sensation another person is having.

What these premises say is that I can *know* that I am in pain because I *feel* my pain and that if anyone else is to know that I am in pain, he too will have to feel my pain. What the argument presupposes, then, is that there is a genuine use of the verb "to know" as an expression of certainty with first-person present-tense sensation statements. This is essential to the argument, for what the conclusion (*C*) states is that no one can know, in this sense of "to know" appropriate to first-person sensation statements, what sensations another person is having. Hence, if this presupposition of the argument should turn out to be indefensible, we must reject not only (P_2) and (P_3) but also the conclusion. For if the alleged use of "to know" is spurious, then all three are infected by the confusion.

Does it make sense, then, to say "I know that I am in pain"? Consider the following. A man has been complaining for several days that his stomach hurts dreadfully, though he has sought no relief for it. His wife has nagged him repeatedly, "You're in pain, so go to a doctor!" Might he not at last exclaim in exasperation, "I *know* I'm in pain, but we can't *afford* a doctor"? No one would want to

maintain that this expression of exasperation was unintelligible. What argument *A* presupposes, however, is not that "I know I am in pain" be intelligible as an expression of exasperation but that it be intelligible as an expression of certainty. What, then, would be necessary for it to be an expression of certainty? Consider the following case. Someone asks you whether it is raining; you tell him that it is, and then he asks, "Are you certain?" Here one might reply, "Yes, I know it's raining; I'm looking out the window." (This might be a telephone conversation, for example.) Now, what is the function of "I know" here? To put it roughly and briefly, the function of these words is to indicate that in answering the question one is not merely guessing or taking someone's word for it or judging from what one saw ten minutes before or something else of the sort. Their function is to indicate that one is in as good a position as one could want for answering the question "Is it raining?" What makes it possible to use "I know" here as an expression of certainty is that it would be intelligible for someone to suppose that the speaker is not, in the particular instance, in as good a position as one could want for correctly answering a certain question or making a certain statement. More generally, for "I know that . . ." to be an expression of certainty, it is at least necessary that the sense of the sentence filling the blank allow the speaker to be ignorant in some circumstances of the truth-value of statements made by means of the sentence (or equivalents thereof). But now, it is just this, as Wittgenstein points out (*Inv.* 246 and pp. 221–222), that does *not* hold for "I am in pain."

It should be noticed that Wittgenstein is not saying that the addition of the words "I know" to "I am in pain" would be *pointless* and therefore senseless. That might be said of the following case. The two of us are seated in such a way that you cannot see out the window, although I can. As you notice that it is time for you to leave, you ask me whether it is still raining. I peer out the window, straining to see in the failing light, and then go to the window, open it, and put my hand out. As

I close the window, wiping the drops from my hand, I say, "Yes, it is raining rather hard." Because you have watched me take the necessary pains to answer your question, you would have nothing to gain by asking, "Are you certain?" or "Do you *know* that it is?" For the same reason, I would not be telling you anything by adding to my answer the words "I know. . . . " If I were to add them, you might cast about for an explanation: did he think I didn't see him put his hand out? Or: is adding those words some eccentricity of his, like the character in one of Dostoevsky's novels who is always adding "No, sir, you won't lead me by the nose"? If no explanation is found (and it would not be an explanation to say that I added those words because they were *true*), my utterance of them would have to be judged senseless. But for all that, in the situation we began by describing, if someone in the street had seen me put my hand out, he might have said of me, "He knows it's raining." Or had my wife called from the next room to ask whether I knew it was raining, I could have answered that I do know.

Now the point that Wittgenstein is making about "I am in pain" can be made clear by the contrast with "It is raining." The sense of the latter sentence is such that, although in a given situation my *saying* to a particular person "I *know* it is raining" may be senseless, still in that same situation I could be said by some other person to know that it is raining. In that same situation I may be asked by someone whether I know it is raining and may sensibly answer the question. By contrast, the sense of "I am in pain" (or of any other first-person present-tense sensation statement) does not provide for *any* situation such that the addition of the words "I know" would be an expression of certainty. It would not be merely pointless to utter the sentence "I know I am in pain" (indeed, we have seen how its utterance might express exasperation); it is rather that no utterance of it could be sensibly taken to be an expression of certainty.[5]

Wittgenstein's point here is often missed because, instead of considering what function the words "I know" could have in "I know I'm

in pain," one wants to say something like this: "Surely a man who is in pain could not be like the man who has a stone in his shoe but does not know it because he does not feel the stone. A man who has a pain *feels* it, and if he feels it, he must *know* he's in pain." But this is making a wrong assimilation of "I feel a pain in my knee" to "I feel a stone in my shoe," which will be discussed below. At any rate, what we are inclined to contrast is the case of a man in pain with the case of a man with a (possibly unnoticed) stone in his shoe, and we want to mark the contrast by saying that, invariably, the man in pain *knows* that he is in pain. But this is a wrong way of marking the contrast. The right way is to say that whereas it makes sense to speak of ignorance and knowledge, doubt and certainty, in the case of the stone in the shoe, it does not make sense to speak this way in the case of the man in pain. Or as I would prefer to put it (see section III below): the moves that are part of the one language game are not part of the other.

I have not here argued for Wittgenstein's point; I have merely tried to clarify it. To argue for it, I should have to go some way toward showing the "incorrigibility" of first-person sensation statements. It is not clear to me, however, what "showing this" would involve. The most one could do, I should think, is to provide reminders as to how the names of sensations are taught, for example, that such teaching contains no counterpart of teaching a child to put a color sample under a better light or to move in closer for a better look. Also, one might show a person that where he thinks we can (or do) doubt or make mistakes about our sensations, he has merely oddly described something else. For instance, I have heard it objected against Wittgenstein that we sometimes exclaim "Ouch!" in anticipation of a pain which never comes, but it would be misleading, at best, to call this "a mistake about *being* in pain." There is also the fact that such words as "stomachache," "headache," and "dizziness" are partly diagnostic. Thus, a doctor might correct someone by saying, "It's not stomachache you have; it's appendicitis!" Or a man might correct himself by saying, "Never mind the aspirin; I didn't have a headache, after all. It was just this tight hat I've been wearing." These are corrections of mistaken diagnoses. Another objection that is raised is that victims of accidents sometimes hysterically scream that they are in dreadful pain, although they are scarcely injured. But it should be clear that the screamings of hysterical people are no more to be counted genuine uses of language than are the ravings of delirious people or the mumblings of sleepwalkers. It is not my intention here to answer all such objections; I have no idea how many an ingenious person might propose or how far he would go to defend them.

The preceding discussion has shown, in so far as showing this is possible, that the alleged use of "to know" presupposed by argument *A* is not a use at all but a confusion. Thus, an essential presupposition of argument *A* has been defeated, and the argument will have to be abandoned. The possible criticisms of *A*, however, are by no means exhausted. In the remainder of this section I will deal with several points related to those already made. Sections II and III will present Wittgenstein's criticisms of (P_1) and the claim that it states a logical impossibility.

There is a use of the verb "to feel" (as in "I feel a stone in my shoe") that is related to the verb "to know" in the following way. If I am asked how I know that there is a stone in my shoe or that the grass is wet or that a certain man has a pulse beat, there will be cases in which it will be correct to answer, "I know because I feel it." I will call this the *perceptual sense* of "to feel." Now it is clear that argument *A* presupposes that it makes sense to speak of feeling (in the perceptual sense) a pain or an itch or dizziness. (P_3) says that I can *know* that I am in pain because I *feel* my pain. It no doubt contributes to the plausibility of this that we commonly say such things as "I feel a slight pain in my knee when I bend it." That this is not the perceptual sense of "to feel" should be clear from the fact that in all such sentences the words "I feel" may be replaced by either "I have" or "there is" without altering the sense of the sentence (cf.

Inv. 246). Thus, "I feel a slight pain in my knee" comes to the same as "There is a slight pain in my knee." Such substitutions are not possible when "to feel" is used in the perceptual sense. "I feel a stone in my shoe" implies, but does not mean the same as, "There is a stone in my shoe." It will make sense to say, "There was a stone in my shoe, but I didn't feel it," whereas it will not make sense to say, as an admission of ignorance, "There was a pain in my knee, but I didn't feel it." Sensation words cannot be the objects of verbs of perception in first-person sentences. And once this is seen, the plausibility of argument *A* altogether disappears. For when it is recognized that it does not make sense to say "I know that I am in pain because I feel it," it will no longer be tempting to say, "Another person can know that I am in pain only if he feels it."

There remain difficulties with argument *A* which have gone generally unnoticed. (P_2) purports to state the proper and necessary means of ascertaining what sensations another person is having, and what it says is that one must feel his sensation. But even within the presuppositions of the argument this is inadequate: it ought to require not only that one feel the other person's sensation but also that one correctly identify it as being *his*. The plausibility of *A* depends on its seeming to be analogous to something like this: to ascertain whether my neighbor's crocuses are in bloom, as opposed to merely taking his word for it, I must see his crocuses. But I must also know which are his and which are mine, and I know this by knowing where the line runs between our gardens. I identify our respective crocuses by identifying our gardens, and this is presupposed in the sense of "I saw his crocuses" and "He saw my crocuses." But how am I supposed to distinguish between the case in which I am in pain (whether he is or not) and the case in which he is in pain and I feel it? How do I know whose pain I feel? I will postpone the discussion of this question until the next section, but it is worth noticing how far the analogy with seeing my neighbor's crocuses has been carried. Thus, Russell says that "we cannot *enter into the minds of others* to observe the thoughts and emotions which we infer from their behavior."[6] The italicized phrase seems to provide a criterion of identity of the same kind as in the case of the crocuses, but of course it does not. It merely raises the further question of how one is to identify whose mind one has "entered into." What that question should show is that one is being led on by an analogy that has no application. Why, in the first place, is one tempted to speak of "feeling another's sensations"? A part of the answer is that one thinks that just as such a sentence as "My neighbor's crocuses are in bloom" has a place in its grammar for both "I know because I *saw* them" and "I didn't see them but took his word for it," so the sentence "He is in pain" should have a place in its grammar for both "I know because I *felt* his pain" and "I didn't feel his pain but took his word for it." And now if we somehow exclude "I felt his pain," it will seem that we are left with "I only took his word for it." If, instead of seeing for myself, I ask my neighbor whether certain of his flowers are in bloom, this may be owing to a garden wall. It may seem that some comparable circumstance must account for the fact that we ask people what they feel. "Other people can tell us what they feel," says Russell, "but we cannot directly observe their feelings."[7] Thus is argument A born. It makes out the difference between first- and third-person sensation statements to rest on a matter of circumstance (like being unable to see my neighbor's crocuses), whereas Wittgenstein has made us realize that the difference resides in the language game itself. The difference does not rest on some circumstance, and therefore argument A, which purports to name such a circumstance with the words "being unable to feel another's sensations," is inherently confused.

There remains a difficulty with premise (P_3) related to the above. (P_3) states that I can know what sensations I am having because I feel them. Now if someone wants to defend argument A, he will have to show how it is supposed to account not only for what we have here called "sensation statements" but also for their negations: "I am not in pain" and "He is not in pain." This may not seem to pose a difficulty if one thinks he understands

Russell's phrase about entering into the minds of others to observe their thoughts and emotions. For if one enters a room to observe what is there, one may also observe that nothing is there or that certain things are not there. But if one does not pretend to understand Russell's phrase, how (on the presuppositions of argument A) is one supposed to understand either "I am not in pain" or "He is not in pain"? The same difficulty may be raised about negative statements containing "dream" or "image" instead of "pain" (see *Inv.* 448). But if we stick to the case of bodily sensations, one might be tempted to substitute for the word "mind" in Russell's phrase the word "body." One would then suppose that if someone says, "I didn't feel any pain in my knee that time," he is reporting an observation: I felt around in my knee for a pain and found none. But what is the feeling in this case? Is it the same feeling as when feeling pain? But if not that, then what? There *is* such a thing as making oneself receptive to pain—and even to pain in a particular place. (Perhaps a doctor wants to know whether your injured knee still hurts when it is bent in a certain way.) One relaxes, stops moving and talking, and then one feels pain—or one does not. But although there is no difficulty with the idea of being receptive to pain when there is no pain, it is not even prima facie plausible to speak of a feeling which might have disclosed a pain but did not. How, for instance, could one make out the difference between not feeling for pain and feeling for a pain but finding none? Here all talk about a kind of observation appropriate to sensations becomes obvious nonsense. On the presuppositions of argument A, then, no account of negative sensation statements can be even suggested. It was tempting to say: "I can know that I am in pain because I *feel* my pain, and that is what I cannot do in the case of another person." But the plausibility of this is lost if one says, "I can know that I am not in pain because I can *feel* the absence of pain in myself, and that is what I cannot feel in the case of another person." One would want to reply: perhaps you are feeling the absence of it right now!

II

The one premise of argument *A* which we have so far neglected is in some respects the most pertinacious: "No one can feel (have) another person's sensations." I remarked in section I that it is now commonplace to say that this premise expresses a "logical impossibility." This is intended, no doubt, as an improvement over older ways of talking. Russell once said of our sensations and images that they "cannot, even theoretically, be observed by anyone else."[8] But substituting "not even logically possible" for "not even theoretically possible" has proved to be an empty gesture, for the meaning of "logically impossible" has at best remained dubious. Two interpretations are current. (1) Some philosophers have held that to say that it is logically (or conceptually) impossible that *p* is to say no more and no less than that the sentence "*p*" is senseless. In the present case, this would amount to saying that such sentences as "I felt his pain" and "He feels my dizziness" are senseless.[9] (2) Others seem to hold that to say that it is logically (or conceptually) impossible that *p* is to say, not that "*p*" is senseless, but that the negation of "*p*" is a necessary truth. In the present case, this would amount to saying that a sentence such as "I did not feel his pain" (or perhaps "Any pain I feel is my own pain") expresses a necessary truth.[10] Both versions speak of sentences—one saying that certain sentences are senseless, the other saying that the negations of those sentences express necessary truths. This presents a difficulty.

Any sentence may, so far as logic can foresee, find its way into some nonphilosophical context. Thus, in the last section a context was imagined in which the sentence "I know I'm in pain" was uttered as an expression of exasperation. No one would want to say that in that context the person who exclaimed, "I know I'm in pain!" was uttering either nonsense or a necessary truth—any more than they would want to say this of "Business is business." Now there are, no doubt, a great many philosophical propositions for which it would be extremely difficult, if not impossi-

ble, to provide a nonphilosophical context. But it should be clear that to specify merely a sentence is not to specify what (according to which view you take) is said to be senseless or to express a necessary truth. At this point it is tempting to say that, in the context I imagined for it, the sentence "I know I'm in pain" was not meant literally. Similarly, someone might insist that if we were ever to say, "I feel your pain," this could not, at any rate, be *literally* true. Thus, Ayer says that "it is logically impossible that one person should *literally* feel another's pain."[11] What is said to be logically impossible, then, is what is expressed by "I feel his pain" in its literal sense. But can we now apply either of the aforementioned versions of logical impossibility? Those who adopt version (1) would find themselves in the odd position of saying that it is the literal *sense* of a sentence which is senseless. (This is what Wittgenstein warns against in saying that "it is not the sense as it were that is senseless" [*Inv.* 500].) Those who adopt either (1) or (2) will somehow have to specify, for the particular sentence, what its alleged literal sense is. One way of attempting this is by presenting the parts of the sentence (either words or expressions) in some familiar context in which *they* have the desired meaning and then specifying that it is when the sentence in question combines the words or expressions as used in *these* contexts that it has its literal sense. But what could it mean to speak of transferring a word or expression *and its meaning* from a context in which it has a particular use to a sentence in which it has no use at all (except as a part of speech)—and certainly not the use it had in the context from which it was allegedly transferred? The most that would seem to be possible here is that one might be under the *impression* that he had combined the original meanings into the sentence. This, I think, is exactly the case with philosophers who declare either that certain sentences are senseless or that their negations are necessary truths.

To illustrate this point, I want to consider a fictitious philosophical argument designed both for its transparency and for its similarity to the case of someone's saying that no one can have another person's sensations. Here, then, is the argument of an imaginary philosopher:

We commonly speak of a child as having his father's build, but this is really absurd when you come to think of it. How *could* someone have another person's build? I know what it is for someone to have his father's watch or for someone to have another man's coat, but no one could literally have another person's build. A build is not something which, like a coat, can be removed and passed around from person to person. That is not even conceivable. And this is why no one can have another person's build. So when, ordinarily, we say of someone that he has another person's build, or when we say that two people have the *same* build, we are using these words, not in their literal sense, but in a sense that is arbitrary and does not fit the meaning of the words at all. We are saying only that the one person has a build that is *like* the other person's, not that he has the other person's build itself. It is the same when we say that a child has her mother's eyes. We don't mean this literally—that her mother's eyes have been transplanted into her head. Of course, this could theoretically be done. But having another's build, in the literal sense, is not even theoretically possible. No amount of surgical skill will enable doctors to transfer a build from one person to another. They may graft skin and bone, but each person will still have a build all his own, not someone else's. Builds, one might say, are among the most inviolable forms of private property.

Now what has happened in this argument? Our imaginary philosopher purports to have identified the "literal sense" of such sentences as "He has your build" and "You have your father's build" and to have discovered that these sentences, in their literal sense, mean something impossible. But what is being referred to here as the literal sense of "He has your build"? What I should like to suggest is that though this is no sense at all, what may strike one as being the literal sense—the real meaning—of "He has your build" is this sentence construed on analogy with such a sentence as "He has your coat." The temptation so to construe it lies, of course, in the surface similarity of the two sentences. Moreover, quite apart from these sentences, there is our familiar use of possessives in "my build," "your build," and so forth, and one

may be tempted to construe this use of possessives on analogy with possessives of ownership. That this is a false analogy can be shown as follows. In order to use a possessive of ownership (as in "his coat") to make a true statement, we must correctly identify the owner of the article. It is this identification that makes the difference between saying, "*His* coat is too large for him," and saying merely, "*That* coat is too large for him." If I should say, "His coat is too large for him," without having made the correct identification, I can be corrected by being told, for example, "That's not *his* coat; it's his father's." Now contrast this case with one in which I notice a child's build and comment, "His build is rather angular." Here the step of identifying an owner plays no part: I need only observe the child. And so my statement could not be challenged by someone saying, "The build *is* rather angular, but are you sure that it's *his*?" This question would be senseless because, intended as a particular kind of challenge to my statement, it wrongly presupposes that in the language game played with "his build" there is a move of the same kind as in the language game played with "his coat," that is, the identification of an owner. But now it is just this question that would have to make sense if the so-called "literal sense" of "He has his father's build" were to *be* a sense. Hence, the "literal sense" was no sense at all.

To put the matter in another way, what would not make sense would be to ask, as though requesting an identification, "Whose build does he have: his own or his father's?" But in its so-called "literal sense" the sentence "He has his father's build" was supposed to be a sentence of the kind used in answering that supposedly genuine identification question. So again, the "literal sense" was no sense at all. Here it is important to notice that in thus rejecting the "literal sense" of "He has his father's build" we must also reject its correlatives, "I have my own build" and "Everyone has his own build." For these sentences, too, in the context of the above argument, are supposed to be of the kind used in answering that supposedly genuine identification question. But as we have seen, there is no such genuine question, and so there are no answers either. The question and the answers we were made to believe in by the analogy with "He has his father's coat" are not moves in the language game played with the word "build." Hence, what we were to understand as involving some kind of impossibility—namely, "literally having another's build"—and also what we were to take as being necessarily true—namely, "I have my own build"—turn out to be illusions. Therefore the statement "Builds are private" must be given up.

The points I have made here apply, *mutatis mutandis,* to the philosophical assertion "Sensations are private," where this is meant as "No one can have another person's sensations." I will not rehearse the arguments again. It is enough to say that in order to be in a position to use correctly the expression "his pain" (as in "His pain is worse, so you had better give him a hypo"), it is sufficient to know *who* is in pain. There is no further step required here comparable to that of identifying an owner as in the use of "his coat." (Hence in the first-person case, where there is no question of *who* is in pain [*Inv.* 404–408], there is no identification of any kind.) Or to put the point in still another way, when we say of someone, "His pain is quite severe," the word "his" is performing the same function (apart from surface grammar) as the word "he" in "He is in severe pain." It was this that Wittgenstein meant to bring out when, in reply to "Another person can't have my pains," he asked: "Which pains are my pains?" (*Inv.* 253). He did not intend that one should *answer* that question, saying something like "All the pains I have are mine." He intended, rather, that that "answer" and the "question" that prompts it should be recognized as spurious, as not belonging to the language game.[12] Hence, for the reasons adduced in the previous case, when it is said that no one can, literally, have another person's pain, the supposed literal sense is no sense at all.

Before leaving the topic of possessives, it will be well to notice a source of frequent confusion. It was briefly mentioned in section I that such words as "stomachache" and "headache" are partly diagnostic. Thus, a man might say, "Never mind the aspirin; I didn't have a headache after all. It was only this tight hat I've been wearing." Now it is easy to imagine a use of possessives related to this in the following way. Philosophers have imagined wireless connections of some sort being set up between people such that when one of them is in pain the other is, too. In such cases, it is suggested, the question "Whose headache do I have?" would come to have the following use. It will be correct to answer that I have my own headache when, on detaching the wireless device, the pain continues unaffected, but if instead the pain immediately stops, it will be correct to say that I did not have my own headache, that I had Smith's headache, and so forth. Now granting all this, it is still important to be clear about two points. First, the sentence "I did not have my own headache" will not mean the same as "I was not in pain." The man who asks, "Whose headache do I have?" will be one of whom it will be true to say, "He is in pain" or even "He is in severe pain." Secondly, when we say of a person, "He is in severe pain," we also say indifferently, "His pain is severe." (As noted above, the words "he" and "his" in these two sentences perform the same function.) So the statement "His pain was severe" will be true even though it is also true that he did not have his own headache. Because "his pain" in the former statement is not an answer to an identification question, it does not compete with the new idiom. Moreover, this would remain true even if we should lapse into using the word "pain" in the same kind of way we have here imagined the word "headache" to be used. That is, even if we should superimpose on our present use of "pain" the question "Whose pain do I have?" with the possible answer "I have Smith's pain," it will still be possible to say of me "His pain is severe" in case I am in severe pain. It is thus as a comment on this use of possessives that one can say: any pain I feel will be mine. The mistakes one is inclined to make here are, first, to suppose that this is a truth about the nature of pains or of human beings, and secondly, to suppose that the word "mine" here is a possessive of ownership. Those who have sought to avoid the first mistake by resorting to talk about "logical impossibility" have nevertheless persisted in the second mistake, and thus they have reinforced the fundamental confusion by serving it up in a terminology that commands great respect. We can see more clearly what this amounts to if we return to the argument of our imaginary philosopher. Having concluded that no one can have another person's build, he might go on to argue that therefore we need never worry that the build someone has will not last out his lifetime owing to its previous hard use by another person. Now if a more up-to-date philosopher were to offer further relief from this worry by maintaining that it is not even *logically* possible to have another's build, this would be merely a perpetuation of the original confusion. This is what happens when philosophers seek to strengthen argument *A* by adding that it is a *logical* impossibility to feel another's sensations.

If we can make any sense of the insistence that pains are private—that is, that any pain I feel is my own—this amounts to no more than a comment on the kind of possessive commonly used with the word "pain." Of course, this is not what philosophers have supposed they were saying with the premise "No one can feel another's pain," but since nothing but this can be intelligibly made of that premise, it can hardly do the job that philosophers have given it. There would not be even the semblance of plausibility in an argument running: no one can know what sensations another person has, because the possessives commonly used with names of sensations are not possessives of ownership.

III

The preceding section began with two criticisms of the view that "No one can have another's pain" expresses a logical impossibility. The criticisms were these: (a) when something is said to be logically impossible it is necessary to specify more than a sentence, but what must be specified cannot be the sense of a sentence, for it is absurd to speak of

the sense as being senseless; and (b) attempts at specifying such a sense must come to grief in requiring the parts of the sentence (either words or expressions) to retain their meaning though shorn of their use. Have my own arguments of the preceding section avoided these criticisms?

The chief difficulty with the views against which these criticisms were directed is that they propose to deal with sentences, and then in order to specify what is said to be logically impossible, they find themselves resorting to talk about the literal sense of a sentence. This is what Wittgenstein meant to oppose when he wrote: "When a sentence is called senseless, it is not as it were its sense that is senseless. But a combination of words is being excluded from the language, withdrawn from circulation" (*Inv.* 500). But what does it mean to speak of "a combination of words being excluded from the language"? *What* is being excluded from *what*? When Wittgenstein says, for example, that "it can't be said of me at all (except perhaps as a joke) that I *know* I am in pain" (*Inv.* 246), he does not mean to exclude the joke. In fact, one can think of a variety of contexts for the sentence "Now he *knows* he's in pain." (Think of how a torturer might say it.) So again I ask: what is being excluded from what? The answer to this can be seen from the following segment of argument from section II:

If I should say, "His coat is too large for him," without having made the correct identification, I can be corrected by being told, for example, "That's not *his* coat; it's his father's." Now contrast this case with one in which I notice a child's build and comment, "His build is rather angular." Here the step of identifying an owner plays no part: I need only observe the child. And so my statement could not be challenged by someone saying, "The build *is* rather angular, but are you sure it's *his*?" This question would be senseless because, *intended as a particular kind of challenge to my statement*, it wrongly presupposes that in the language game played with "his build" there is a move of the same kind as in the language game played with "his coat," that is, the identification of an owner.

What is appealed to here is the reader's familiarity with a pair of language games.

What is said to be senseless is not merely a combination of words but rather an attempt, by means of a combination of words, to make in one language game a move that belongs only to the other language game. In other words, by showing that the apparent analogy between the language games is in fact a false one, the argument shows that if one tried making the moves suggested by the analogy, one would not be *saying* anything but would be merely under the impression that he was. It is this mistaken *impression* of saying something that the argument condemns as senseless, and therefore (to answer our original question) the argument cannot be accused of saying that the *sense* of some sentence is senseless. It should be evident, however, that an argument of this kind, unless it is carefully formulated, is peculiarly open to misunderstanding. For in order to specify what it is that one is condemning as nonsense, one must repeat that nonsense in *some* form, and if a reader insists on taking one's words "straight" at this point and thus looks for or imagines a sense where none was intended, then one's argument will have the paradoxical air of trying to prove that the sense of something is senseless.

Since the point I have been making here is important to Wittgenstein's thought, it is worth noticing the following pair of passages. The first is from Moore's report of Wittgenstein's 1930–1933 lectures:

[Wittgenstein] then implied that where we say "This makes no sense" we always mean "This makes nonsense *in this particular game*"; and in answer to the question "Why do we call it 'nonsense'? what does it mean to call it so?" said that when we call a sentence "nonsense," it is "because of some similarity to sentences which have sense," and that "nonsense always arises from forming symbols analogous to certain uses, where they have no use."[13]

The second passage is from *The Blue Book:*

It is possible that, say in an accident, I should . . . see a broken arm at my side, and think it is mine when really it is my neighbor's. . . .On the other hand, there is no question of recognizing a person when I say I have a toothache. To ask "are you sure that it's *you* who have pains?" would be nonsensical. Now, when in this case no error is possible, it is because the move which we might be inclined to think of as an error, a "bad move," *is no move of the game at all.* (We distinguish in chess between good and bad moves, and we call it a mistake if we expose the queen to a bishop. But it is no mistake to promote a pawn to a king.)[14]

It is clear that Wittgenstein came to think that there is more than one kind of senselessness, but the description of the kind mentioned here is the description of "No one can feel another person's pain."[15]

Going back now, briefly, we can say one thing more about the so-called "literal sense" of "He has his father's build" or "I feel your pain." Seeming to see in such sentences a sense that is somehow impossible is a queer sort of illusion, produced by seeing one pattern of grammar on analogy with another and quite different pattern of grammar. This sort of illusion is not altogether peculiar to philosophy, however. Seeming to see in a sentence a meaning that is somehow impossible is the stuff of which grammatical jokes are made (cf. *Inv.* III). Consider, for example, a cartoon by S. J. Perelman. It shows a distraught gentleman rushing into a doctor's office clutching a friend by the wrist and whimpering: "I've got Bright's disease, and he has mine." This is more than a play on the name "Bright's disease." The surface grammar reminds one of such a sentence as "I've got his hat, and he has mine," as used to report a mix-up in the coatroom. So the caption gives the illusion of making sense—of reporting an extraordinary mix-up, which the doctor is supposed to set straight. And yet "getting the joke" consists in feeling its senselessness. So there seems to be a sense that is somehow senseless. But what we understand here is not a *sense* but rather the two language games that have been (humorously) assimilated. When this is intentional and fairly obvious, it produces a laugh; when it is unintentional and unrecognized, it may seem to provide an original and penetrating insight into the nature of things. Thus, in the case of my imaginary philosopher, once he is captivated by the grammatical analogy suggested by "He has his father's build," he is led to treat the word "build" at every turn on analogy with the word "coat." The whole complex grammar of words for physical objects opens out before him as a new field for the word "build" to run in. A new range of sentences is thus opened up, suggesting what appear to be new "speculative possibilities"— builds being removed like coats, being passed around from person to person, becoming more worn and shabby with the years, and so forth. When we are captivated by such an analogy, we may succumb to temptation and play in these new fields. But we may also feel considerable resistance here, for the grammatical analogy behind it is a false one, and the signs of this may be too clear to be missed altogether. My imaginary philosopher expresses this felt resistance by insisting that "no one can literally have another's build." This, of course, does not reject the analogy; it merely denies that the supposed "speculative possibilities" can ever be realized. Nor would it improve matters to say that the impossibility involved is a *logical* one. This would be merely a new jargon for calling a halt to the analogy in midcourse. One finds the same thing when David Pole, in his commentary on the *Investigations,* writes: "In some sense experience is clearly private; one person cannot be said literally to feel another's feeling," and this cannot be said, he thinks, because grammar "forbids us" to say it.[16] This talk of grammar "forbidding us" to say something is nothing but the most recent jargon for calling a halt to an analogy whose oddness has begun to dawn on one. Because Pole is still in the clutches of the analogy, he is under the impression that there is some "literal sense" of the phrase "feeling another's feelings" which grammar somehow forbids. Because in general he thinks that grammar forbids us at many points to express a sense that we fully understand, he vehemently opposes Wittgenstein's expressed intention to "bring words back from their metaphysical to their everyday use" (*Inv.* 116). Thus, he speaks of Wittgenstein's "characteristic anxiety to pin language down within the limits of its origins" and of Wittgenstein's

insistence that "existing usage is to be accepted as we find it and never tampered with."[17] The result of this, Pole warns, is that "the advance of speculation may well be halted; thought may well be 'contained' within its existing frontiers."[18] What Pole fails to recognize is that the "metaphysical use" from which Wittgenstein wants to "bring words back" is not a *use* but the illusion of a use. Wittgenstein himself says that to reform language "for particular practical purposes . . . is perfectly possible. But these are not the cases we have to do with" (*Inv.* 132).

IV

There is another expression for the idea that sensations are private. It is said that no two people can have (feel) the *same* sensation. This has an analogue in the case of our imaginary philosopher, who argues that when we say of someone that he has his father's build or that they have the same build, "we only mean that the one person has a build that is *like* the other's, not that he has the other person's build itself." He means to say that, however alike they may be, there are two builds here, not one. This, of course, is a mistake as to how builds are counted, but it goes with his prior mistake of taking possessives as used with "build" to be possessives of ownership. He reasoned that if we say, "His build is rather angular, and so is mine," there must be two builds: his and mine. But this is wrong. If one wanted to count builds, one would proceed differently—as one would proceed to count diseases or habits or the gaits of horses. One counts in such cases in accordance with more or less detailed descriptions. A five-gaited horse is one that can ambulate in accordance with five descriptions of foot movements, and two horses are performing the same gait if their foot movements fit the same relevant description. What would not make sense (if one meant to be using "gait" in its present sense) would be to say, "They are performing different gaits which are exactly alike." To say that this makes no sense is to say that the identity of a gait is just given by a description of it. To count two gaits among those being performed, one must make out some difference in foot movement that would be relevant in describing (identifying) gaits. In the same way, a person has the same build he had before if he still fits the same (relevant) description; and if ten people fit that description, then all ten have the same build. Our imaginary philosopher's error lay in this: having confused the use of "his build" with that of "his coat," he inevitably repeated the mistake with "same build" and "same coat." Of course it does make sense to speak of two coats being exactly alike, for one may identify coats independently of descriptions of them. Now, no doubt we do say things as "His build is exactly like mine," but this is not used in opposition to "He and I have the same build." It is rather that "same" and "exactly like" are used interchangeably here, as in the case of color we might say indifferently either "The color here is exactly like the color over there" or "This is the same color here as over there." Whichever we say, there is but one color— red, for example—and it would be a mistake to say: there cannot be only *one* color, for there is *this* color *here* and also *that* color *there*.

The point is that there is no such thing as being just *the same*—no such thing as identity pure and simple. It would be a mistake to think that the same is the same whether we are speaking of builds or coats or gaits or sensations. "Same" must always be understood together with some general term, such as "build" or "coat," and the criterion of identity in any particular case is determined by the general term involved. Or when we use the phrase "the same one," it is determined by the general term that is understood in the context to have been replaced by "one." Similarly, there is no such thing as being an individual pure and simple. It is always a matter of being one build or one coat, and the criterion for counting will vary with the general term. Now one consequence of failing to be clear on this point is that we may unwittingly take the criterion of identity determined by one kind of general term as showing us the meaning of "same" by itself, with the result that we construe the use of "same" with all general terms on this one model. Thus, my imaginary

philosopher supposed that if someone were to have the *same* build as his father, he would be getting an already well-worn article. He was clearly taking as his paradigm the use of "same" with words for physical objects and supposing that *that* is what "same build" must mean. The same mistake is made by Ayer when he writes:

> The question whether an object is public or private is fundamentally a question of . . . the conventions which we follow in making judgements of identity. Thus physical objects are public because it makes sense to say of different people that they are perceiving the same physical object; mental images are private because it does not make sense to say of different people that they are having the same mental image; they can be imagining the same thing, but it is impossible that their respective mental images should be literally the same.[19]

When Ayer speaks of "judgements of identity" and "being literally the same," he is taking the use of "same" with words for physical objects as his paradigm for all uses of "same." So he thinks that if two people were to see the same mental image, they would be in a position to add to, correct, and corroborate one another's descriptions in the same kind of way as we do when two of us have seen the same house.

But we do, of course, constantly speak of two people having the same image or the same sensation. The identity of an image is given by the description of that of which it is an image (cf. *Inv.* 367), and thus we say, "There is one image that keeps coming back to me: that little boy standing there . . .," and someone else may remark, "I have that same image." Again, someone descending in an elevator for the first time may complain of the funny feeling in his stomach, and someone else tells him, "I get the same sensation; it will go away when the elevator stops." Nor would it be odd for someone to say, "We always get the same pain whenever it rains: an intense aching in the joints." Now we may also say, "He gets a pain exactly like mine," but nothing turns on the choice of idiom. We say indifferently either "Now I have the same pain in both knees" or "Now there is a pain in my left knee exactly like the one in my right knee." As Wittgenstein remarks: "In so far as it makes sense to say that my pain is the same as his, it is also possible for us both to have the same pain" (*Inv.* 253). His point is that where it is correct to say, "His pain is the same as mine," it is also correct to say, "We have the same pain." It would be a mistake to think that "same pain" here really means "two pains exactly alike." Ayer, for example, has said that though we speak of two people having the same pain or the same thought, "same" here does not have the meaning of "numerical identity."[20] Apparently he thinks that in all such cases we are comparing two pains or thoughts or images. But Ayer gives no defense of this, except by invoking the very doctrine he is trying to defend: that sensations and thoughts are private. But since Ayer wants to treat this doctrine as a thesis about language, it is begging the question to appeal to the doctrine to decide what *must* be the meaning of "same pain," "same image," and so on. If he were not captivated by the doctrine, he would see that if someone says, "He and I get the same pain in damp weather: an intense aching in the joints," then intense aching is counted as one pain. Another pain would be, for example, the searing sting of a pulled muscle.

The confusion about identity can show up in still another way, which Wittgenstein deals with as follows:

I have seen a person in a discussion on this subject strike himself on the breast and say: "But surely another person can't have THIS pain!"—The answer to this is that one does not define a criterion of identity by emphatic stressing of the word "this" [*Inv.* 253].

What Wittgenstein describes here would be exactly analogous to our imaginary philosopher gesturing toward his body and saying: "But surely another person can't have *this* build!" Although the mistake is more obvious here, it is the same: the word "this" can be used to refer to a particular pain or build only in accordance with the criterion of identity provided by the use of the general term. The word "this" does not itself carry a criterion of

identity. As we have already seen, to speak of a particular pain would be, for example, to speak of intense aching in the joints, and *that* is something that many people have. How, then, could someone think that by stressing the word "this" he could refer to a pain that he alone can have? Wittgenstein remarks that "what the emphasis does is to suggest the case in which we are conversant with such a criterion of identity, but have to be reminded of it" (*Inv.* 253). That is, we might use the emphatic "*this*" to clear up a misunderstanding that has occurred because the general term involved is used at different times with different criteria of identity. To take the stock example, we might clear up in this way a misunderstanding resulting from the type-token ambiguity of the word "letter." ("No, I meant that you should count *this* letter, too.") This will succeed, of course, only if the alternative use of the general term is already well known to us, so that the emphatic "*this*" has only to remind us of it, for as Wittgenstein says, the emphasis "does not define" the kind of identity that is meant. Is there, then, a familiar use of sensation words with a criterion of identity that is reflected in "But surely another person can't have *this* pain!"?

There is a class of episode words that must be considered here. Such expressions as "dizzy spell," "toothache," and sometimes "pain" are used with a criterion of identity quite different from any described above. Although it makes sense to speak of having had the same sensation or image or dream on several occasions, it does not make sense to speak of having had the same dizzy spell on several occasions, unless this means that one was *still* having the dizzy spell. Similarly, there is a use of the word "toothache" such that if someone with a toothache should remark that he had one just like it two years ago, it could only be a joke or a confusion to suggest, "Perhaps it is the same one again." Toothaches are episodes of pain, just as dizzy spells are episodes of dizziness, so that answering the question, "How many toothaches have you had?" requires a reference to particular occasions. Moreover, the episodes are counted by reference to particular persons, so that if I were to count the number of toothaches my children had had, and on some date two of them had suffered from toothache, I should have to count two toothaches for that date. This would be like having to keep count of the number of tantrums they have or the number of somersaults they turn in a day. To refer to a particular tantrum or a particular somersault is to refer to what *one* person did at some time. Thus, if a mother has described one of her children's tantrums, someone else might remark that her child had had a tantrum "exactly like that"; he, too, threw himself on the floor and held his breath until he turned blue. "Exactly like" is used here in contrast, not with "same," but with "rather like," "rather different," and so forth. That is, it would not be asked: "Do you suppose they may have had the same one and not just two exactly alike?" This kind of identification question has no place in the grammar of "tantrum," and so neither do its two answers: "Yes, they did have the same one" and "No, they did not have the same one, only two exactly alike." Now this same point holds for the grammar of "toothache": the identification question "Did they have the same one?" has no place and so neither do its answers. That is, it would not make sense to say, as if in answer to that question, *either* "They had the same toothache" or "They did not have the same toothache." Now the relevance of this point can be seen if we bear in mind the inclination to think of sensations as being objects of perception. If we think of first-person sensation statements on analogy with eyewitness reports, the question will arise whether our reports of sensations could be corroborated or denied by other "eyewitnesses." So the question becomes "Can two people feel the same toothache?" But as between answering that two people *can* feel the same toothache and answering that they *cannot*, we seem to be faced with a Hobson's choice. For the former alternative will seem to be excluded a priori—that is, we will want to say (without knowing quite why, perhaps): "It can't be the *same* toothache if there are *two* people in pain." This, of course, is the influence of the criterion of identity (de-

scribed above) in the use of the word "toothache." But with one of the pairs of "answers" thus excluded a priori, it will seem that the other one *must* be true, and thus "No two people can feel the same toothache" comes to be called "a necessary truth." From this one easily concludes that we cannot know anything about another person's toothaches.

This, then, is the complicated story behind the idea that in "Sensations are private" we have a "necessary truth" or that "No one can feel another's pain" expresses a "logical impossibility." The notion of "logical impossibility" was meant to be contrasted with "physical impossibility," but borrowing a remark of Wittgenstein's from another context, we might say: it made the difference "look *too slight*. . . . An unsuitable type of expression is a sure means of remaining in a state of confusion. It as it were bars the way out" (*Inv.* 339). The "state of confusion" in the present case is that of argument *A*—that of thinking that (as Wittgenstein once imagined it being expressed) "a man's thinking [or dream or toothache] goes on within his consciousness in a seclusion in comparison with which any physical seclusion is an exhibition to public view" (*Inv.* p. 222). It is worth remarking, perhaps, that there is an altogether unproblematic sense in which our sensations may be private: we can sometimes keep them to ourselves. In this sense we often speak of a man's thoughts on some subject being private. No doubt most of our sensations are private in this sense once we pass beyond childhood.

V

In section I it was mentioned that if argument *A* is taken to be sound, it will be seen to have the following consequence: no one can be taught the names of sensations; each of us must give these words their meanings independently of other people and their use of sensation words, and therefore no one can know what other people mean by them. With argument *A* now disposed of, we can also reject this consequence of it. We were taught the names of sensations by others—by others who knew what our sensations were. So we speak a common language. If one fails to see that Wittgenstein has already established this point before he takes up the question "Can there be a private language?" (*Inv.* 256ff.), then one may suppose that what is in question is our actual use of sensation words. As was mentioned in section I, it has been argued against Wittgenstein that since sensations are private, and since we do have names of sensations in our vocabularies, Wittgenstein could not have exposed any real difficulties in the idea of a private language. This argument has now been sufficiently disposed of in the preceding sections: the requisite notion of "privacy" is defective. There has recently been published, however, another version of this misunderstanding, which is likely to gain currency, and which I will therefore briefly discuss.

In his recent book on Wittgenstein, George Pitcher has taken the following view of the matter: (a) "Everyone acknowledges that sensations are private, that no one can experience another person's sensations, so that the special felt quality of each person's sensations is known to him alone,"[21] so (b) it must be acknowledged also that if there were to be genuine names of sensations, they would have to get their meanings by private ostensive definitions, but (c) since Wittgenstein rejects the possibility of any word acquiring meaning in this way, he must be taken to be denying that in ordinary language there are any genuine names of sensations.[22] Therefore, (d) on Wittgenstein's view, in the language game we play with the word "pain," for example, a person's "private sensations do not enter in."[23] This means that if we have just seen a man struck down by a car and find that "he is moaning, bleeding, crying out for help, and says he is in great pain," and if we "rush to help him, see that doctors are called, do everything we can to make him comfortable," still that wretched man's sensations "are completely unknown to us; we have no idea what he might be feeling—what the beetle in his box might be like. But this is no . . . stumbling block to the playing of the language-game, for they are not in the least

needed. We proceed in exactly the same way no matter what his sensations may be like."[24]

If this reads like an attempted *reductio ad absurdum* of Wittgenstein, it was not intended as such. But one is not surprised to find Pitcher concluding that Wittgenstein's "ideas are obviously highly controversial" and open to "powerful objections."[25] In fact, Pitcher's "exposition" is altogether inaccurate. Wittgenstein, as we have seen, rejects the first step (a) in the argument. As for step (b), Wittgenstein not only rejects private ostensive definitions, as Pitcher sees, but also explicitly presents an alternative account of how names of sensations are possible (*Inv.* 244, 256). But since (b) is essential to reaching the conclusion (d), how does Pitcher manage to attribute this conclusion to Wittgenstein? The answer is that Pitcher has misunderstood certain passages in which Wittgenstein opposes the idea of "the private object." As can be seen from the above quotation, one of these is the passage in which Wittgenstein creates the analogy of the beetle in the box (*Inv.* 293). There are several other passages similarly misunderstood (for example, *Inv.* 297), but I will deal with only this one.

Pitcher quotes only the following lines from the beetle-in-the-box passage:

Suppose everyone had a box with something in it: we call it a "beetle." No one can look into anyone else's box, and everyone says he knows what a beetle is only by looking at *his* beetle.—Here it would be quite possible for everyone to have something different in his box. One might even imagine such a thing constantly changing.—But suppose the word "beetle" had a use in these people's language?—If so it would not be used as the name of a thing. The thing in the box has no place in the language-game at all; not even as a *something:* for the box might even be empty.—No, one can "divide through" by the thing in the box; it cancels out, whatever it is [*Inv.* 293].

Without quoting the final, crucial sentence, Pitcher remarks: "The analogy with pain is perfectly clear."[26] By this he seems to mean at least that pains are, as it were, in a box and cut off from public view, so that they have (as Wittgenstein says of the thing in the box) "no place in the language-game at all." But so far from this being Wittgenstein's actual view, it is what he calls a "paradox" (*Inv.* 304). What the beetle-in-the-box passage is meant to bear an analogy to is not our use of sensation words but the philosophical picture of that use. Pitcher has reversed the sense of the passage, and he has done so because he takes Wittgenstein to agree that sensations are private objects. But the intention of the passage is clearly shown in the final sentence, which Pitcher does not quote: "That is to say: if we construe the grammar of the expression of sensation on the model of 'object and name' the object drops out of consideration as irrelevant." The word "if" here is crucial, for it is not Wittgenstein's view but the one he opposes that construes the grammar of the expression of sensation on the model of "object and name," and therefore it is not Wittgenstein, as Pitcher thinks, who is committed to the paradoxical consequence that in the use of the word "pain," for example, the sensation drops out as irrelevant. The point of the passage, then, is quite the opposite of what Pitcher supposes. Rather than showing that sensations cannot have names, it shows that since the view that sensations are private allows sensations to have "no place in the language-game" and thereby makes it impossible to give any account of the actual (that is, the "public") use of sensation words, we must, if we are to give an account of that language game, reject the view that sensations are private. In Wittgenstein's words, we must reject "the grammar which tries to force itself on us here" (*Inv.* 304). We have seen that the idea that sensations are private results from construing the grammar of sensation words on analogy with the grammar of words for physical objects. One consequence of this false grammatical analogy is that we are led to think that the names of sensations must get their meanings by private ostensive definitions. Wittgenstein, on the other hand, gives this account of learning the name of a sensation: "words are connected with the primitive, the natural, expressions of the sensation and used in their place. A child has hurt himself and he cries; and then adults talk to him and teach him exclamations and, later, sentences"

(*Inv.* 244). It is in this way that sensations get their place in the language game.

It is clear that Pitcher cannot have grasped this last point, for although he quotes he does not understand Wittgenstein's remark (*Inv.* 246) that it is either false or nonsensical to suppose that no one can know whether another person is in pain. He takes Wittgenstein to agree with him that I cannot "determine that another person feels the same sensation I do: to do that, I would have to be able to feel his . . . , and that is impossible."[27] It is not surprising, then, that Pitcher should fail to understand Wittgenstein's reminder of how names of sensations are taught. It is surprising, however, that he should think that the view of sensation words rejected by Wittgenstein is our "common-sensical attitude."[28] Whatever Pitcher may have meant by this phrase, it at least indicates that he has failed to see how very queer is the idea that sensations are essentially private. Could it be that the child who comes crying with a bumped head and who screams when it is touched is giving his peculiar expression to an itching scalp? Or that the giggling child who comes wriggling back for more tickling is really a grotesque creature coming back for more pain? Or that the person who staggers, gropes for support, blinks, and complains that the room is whirling is exhibiting, not dizziness, but a feeling of bodily exhilaration? No, the idea of the private object is not one that turns up in our common thought and practice; it turns up only in those odd moments when we are under the influence of a false grammatical analogy.

NOTES

1. See, e.g., the papers by H.-N. Castañeda and J. F. Thomson in *Knowledge and Experience* (Pittsburgh: 1964), ed. C. D. Rollins. Thomson (pp. 121–123) asks, "What kind of language is here being envisaged?" and concludes that Wittgenstein's account is "obscure." The controversy over whether there can be a private language rages, he thinks, over "some unexplained sense of 'private language,'" and so "the claim that Wittgenstein answered it [must be] obscure." Castañeda (p. 129) says that "the idea of a private language is so obscure that

there are many senses of 'privacy,' " and he implies that "Wittgenstein's definition of a private language" is not "an honest effort at giving the idea of a private language a full run" (p. 90).

2. *Philosophical Investigations* (New York: 1953), hereafter abbreviated as *Inv.* Unless otherwise indicated, numbered references will refer to sections of part I.

3. Castañeda, *op. cit.*, p. 94.

4. George Pitcher, *The Philosophy of Wittgenstein* (Englewood Cliffs, N.J.: 1964), p. 299.

5. This point has been widely missed. Castañeda, for example, argues "it is odd, because pointless, to inform another person that one believes or thinks that one is in pain, or to insist that one knows that one is in pain. But this fact about ordinary *reporting* in no way shows that there are no facts that would be reported if one were to make pointless assertions. The pointlessness of the assertions is not only compatible with their intelligibility, but even presupposes it" (*op. cit.*, p. 94). I do not know what could be meant here by "pointless assertions," i.e., what would make them *assertions*. But it should be clear that Wittgenstein's point about "I know I'm in pain" is quite different from the point I have made about the sometimes senseless addition of "I know" to "It is raining," and this is the difference Castañeda has missed. The same mistake is made (in almost the same words) in Ayer's criticism of Wittgenstein in "Privacy," *Proceedings of the British Academy* (1959), p. 48.

6. *Human Knowledge* (New York: 1948), p. 193 (my italics).

7. *The Analysis of Mind* (London: 1951), p. 118.

8. *Ibid.*, p. 117.

9. "The barriers that prevent us from enjoying one another's experiences are not natural but logical. . . . It is not conceivable that there should be people who were capable of having one another's pains, or feeling one another's emotions. And the reason why this is inconceivable is *simply that we attach no meaning to such expressions* as 'I am experiencing your headache,' 'She is feeling his remorse,' 'Your state of anger is numerically the same as mine.' " A. J. Ayer, *The Foundations of Empirical Knowledge* (London: 1953), pp. 138–139 (my italics).

10. For example, Castañeda, who regards it as a logical impossibility to experience another's sensations (*op. cit.*, p. 90), seems to take this view of "logical impossibilities." In his discussion of the sentence "I believed falsely at time *t* that I was in pain at *t*" (which he says would be regarded as meaningless by Wittgensteinians), he gives his own position as follows: "But obviously 'I believed falsely at *t* that I was in pain at *t*' is meaningful; it expresses a conceptual contradiction; its negation is a necessary truth" (*ibid.*, p. 93).

11. *The Problem of Knowledge* (Edinburgh: 1956), p. 202 (my italics).

12. In another passage (*Inv.* 411) Wittgenstein asks us to consider a "practical (nonphilosophical)" application for the question "Is this sensation *my* sensation?" Perhaps he was thinking that this form of words might be used in place of "Am I the *only* one having this sensation?" which would be like asking, "Am I the *only* one who is dizzy?"

13. G. E. Moore, *Philosophical Papers* (London: 1959), pp. 273–274.

14. Wittgenstein, *The Blue and Brown Books* (Oxford: 1958), p. 67 (the last italics are mine).

15. Another kind of senselessness is that illustrated in section I by the sometimes senseless addition of the words "I know" to "It is raining." Other examples are noticed in *Inv.* 117, 349, 514, 670, p. 221, and elsewhere.

16. *The Later Philosophy of Wittgenstein* (London: 1958), pp. 68–69.

17. *Ibid.*, pp. 91 and 94.

18. *Ibid.*, p. 95.

19. *The Problem of Knowledge*, p. 200.

20. *The Foundations of Empirical Knowledge*, p. 139; and *The Problem of Knowledge*, p. 199.

21. *Op. cit.*, p. 297.

22. *Ibid.*, pp. 281–300.

23. *Ibid.*, p. 299.

24. *Ibid.*

25. *Ibid.*, p. 313.

26. *Ibid.*, p. 298.

27. *Ibid.*, p. 288.

28. *Ibid.*, p. 283.

On Rules and Private Language   35

SAUL KRIPKE

... A common view of the 'private language argument' in *Philosophical Investigations* assumes that it begins with section 243, and that it continues in the sections immediately following.[1] This view takes the argument to deal primarily with a problem about 'sensation language'. Further discussion of the argument in this tradition, both in support and in criticism, emphasizes such questions as whether the argument invokes a form of the verification principle, whether the form in question is justified, whether it is applied correctly to sensation language, whether the argument rests on an exaggerated scepticism about memory, and so on. Some crucial passages in the discussion following §243—for example, such celebrated sections as §258 and §265—have been notoriously obscure to commentators, and it has been thought that their proper interpretation would provide the key to the 'private language argument'.

In my view, the real 'private language argument' is to be found in the sections *preceding* §243. Indeed, in §202 *the conclusion is already stated explicitly:* "Hence it is not possible to obey a rule 'privately': otherwise thinking one was obeying a rule would be the same thing as obeying it." I do not think that Wittgenstein here thought of himself as *anticipating* an argument he was to give in greater detail later. On the contrary, the crucial considerations are all contained in the discussion leading up to the conclusion stated in §202. The sections following §243 are meant

to be read in the light of the preceding discussion; difficult as they are in any case, they are much less likely to be understood if they are read in isolation. The 'private language argument' as applied to *sensations* is only a special case of much more general considerations about language previously argued; sensations have a crucial role as an (apparently) convincing *counterexample* to the general considerations previously stated. Wittgenstein therefore goes over the ground again in this special case, marshalling new specific considerations appropriate to it. It should be borne in mind that *Philosophical Investigations* is not a systematic philosophical work where conclusions, once definitely established, need not be reargued. Rather the *Investigations* is written as a perpetual dialectic, where persisting worries, expressed by the voice of the imaginary interlocutor, are never definitively silenced. Since the work is not presented in the form of a deductive argument with definitive theses as conclusions, the same ground is covered repeatedly, from the point of view of various special cases and from different angles, with the hope that the entire process will help the reader see the problems rightly.

The basic structure of Wittgenstein's approach can be presented briefly as follows: A certain problem, or in Humean terminology, a 'sceptical paradox', is presented concerning the notion of a rule. Following this, what Hume would have called a 'sceptical solution'

From *On Rules and Private Language* (Cambridge: Harvard University Press, 1982).

475

to the problem is presented. There are two areas in which the force, both of the paradox and of its solution, are most likely to be ignored, and with respect to which Wittgenstein's basic approach is most likely to seem incredible. One such area is the notion of a mathematical rule, such as the rule for addition. The other is our talk of our own inner experience, of sensations and other inner states. In treating both these cases, we should bear in mind the basic considerations about rules and language. Although Wittgenstein has already discussed these basic considerations in considerable generality, the structure of Wittgenstein's work is such that the special cases of mathematics and psychology are not simply discussed by citing a general 'result' already established, but by going over these special cases in detail, in the light of the previous treatment of the general case. By such a discussion, it is hoped that both mathematics and the mind can be seen rightly: since the temptations to see them wrongly arise from the neglect of the same basic considerations about rules and language, the problems which arise can be expected to be analogous in the two cases. In my opinion, Wittgenstein did not view his dual interests in the philosophy of mind and the philosophy of mathematics as interests in two separate, at best loosely related, subjects, as someone might be interested both in music and in economics. Wittgenstein thinks of the two subjects as involving the same basic considerations. For this reason, he calls his investigation of the foundations of mathematics "analogous to our investigation of psychology" (p. 232). It is no accident that essentially the same basic material on rules is included in both *Philosophical Investigations* and in *Remarks on the Foundations of Mathematics*,[2] both times as the basis of the discussions of the philosophies of mind and of mathematics, respectively, which follow.

In the following, I am largely trying to present Wittgenstein's argument, or, more accurately, that set of problems and arguments which I personally have gotten out of reading Wittgenstein. With few exceptions, I am *not* trying to present views of my own;

neither am I trying to endorse or to criticize Wittgenstein's approach. In some cases, I have found a precise statement of the problems and conclusions to be elusive. Although one has a strong sense that there is a problem, a rigorous statement of it is difficult. I am inclined to think that Wittgenstein's later philosophical style, and the difficulty he found (see his preface) in welding his thought into a conventional work presented with organized arguments and conclusions, is not simply a stylistic and literary preference, coupled with a *penchant* for a certain degree of obscurity,[3] but stems in part from the nature of his subject.

I suspect—for reasons that will become clearer later—that to attempt to present Wittgenstein's argument precisely is to some extent to falsify it. Probably many of my formulations and recastings of the argument are done in a way Wittgenstein would not himself approve. So the present paper should be thought of as expounding neither 'Wittgenstein's' argument nor 'Kripke's': rather Wittgenstein's argument as it struck Kripke, as it presented a problem for him.

As I have said, I think the basic 'private language argument' *precedes* section 243, though the sections following 243 are no doubt of fundamental importance as well. I propose to discuss the problem of 'private language' initially without mentioning these latter sections *at all*. Since these sections are often thought to *be* the 'private language argument', to some such a procedure may seem to be a presentation of Hamlet without the prince. Even if this is so, there are many other interesting characters in the play.

. . . In §201 Wittgenstein says, "this was our paradox: no course of action could be determined by a rule, because every course of action can be made to accord with the rule." In this section of the present essay, in my own way I will attempt to develop the "paradox" in question. The "paradox" is perhaps the central problem of *Philosophical Investigations*. Even someone who disputes the conclusions regarding 'private language', and the philosophies of mind, mathematics, and logic, that Wittgenstein draws from his problem, might well regard the problem itself as an important contribution to philosophy. It may be regarded as a new form of philosophical scepticism.

Following Wittgenstein, I will develop the problem initially with respect to a mathematical example, though the relevant sceptical problem applies to all meaningful uses of language. I, like almost all English speakers, use the word "plus" and the symbol '+' to denote a well-known mathematical function, addition. The function is defined for all pairs of positive integers. By means of my external symbolic representation and my internal mental representation, I 'grasp' the rule for addition. One point is crucial to my 'grasp' of this rule. Although I myself have computed only finitely many sums in the past, the rule determines my answer for indefinitely many new sums that I have never previously considered. This is the whole point of the notion that in learning to add I grasp a rule: my past intentions regarding addition determine a unique answer for indefinitely many new cases in the future.

Let me suppose, for example, that '68 + 57' is a computation that I have never performed before. Since I have performed—even silently to myself, let alone in my publicly observable behavior—only finitely many computations in the past, such an example surely exists. In fact, the same finitude guarantees that there is an example exceeding, in both its arguments, all previous computations. I shall assume in what follows that '68 + 57' serves for this purpose as well.

I perform the computation, obtaining, of course, the answer '125'. I am confident, perhaps after checking my work, that '125' is the correct answer. It is correct both in the arithmetical sense that 125 is the sum of 68 and 57, and in the metalinguistic sense that "plus," as I intended to use that word in the past, denoted a function which, when applied to the numbers I called "68" and "57," yields the value 125.

Now suppose I encounter a bizarre sceptic. This sceptic questions my certainty about my answer, in what I just called the 'metal-inguistic' sense. Perhaps, he suggests, as I used the term "plus" in the past, the answer I intended for '68 + 57' should have been '5'! Of course the sceptic's suggestion is obviously insane. My initial response to such a suggestion might be that the challenger should go back to school and learn to add. Let the challenger, however, continue. After all, he says, if I am now so confident that, as I used the symbol '+', my intention was that '68 + 57' should turn out to denote 125, this cannot be because I explicitly gave myself instructions that 125 is the result of performing the addition in this particular instance. By hypothesis, I did no such thing. But of course the idea is that, in this new instance, I should apply the very same function or rule that I applied so many times in the past. But who is to say what function this was? In the past I gave myself only a finite number of examples instantiating this function. All, we have supposed, involved numbers smaller than 57. So perhaps in the past I used "plus" and '+' to denote a function which I will call 'quus' and symbolize by '⊕'. It is defined by:

$$x \oplus y = x + y \text{ if } x, y < 57$$
$$= 5 \text{ otherwise.}$$

Who is to say that this is not the function I previously meant by '+'?

The sceptic claims (or feigns to claim) that I am now misinterpreting my own previous usage. By "plus," he says, I *always meant* quus;[4] now, under the influence of some insane frenzy, or a bout of LSD, I have come to misinterpret my own previous usage.

Ridiculous and fantastic though it is, the sceptic's hypothesis is not logically impossible. To see this, assume the common sense hypothesis that by '+' I *did* mean addition. Then it would be *possible,* though surprising, that under the influence of a momentary 'high', I should misinterpret all my past uses of the plus sign as symbolizing the quus function, and proceed, in conflict with my previous linguistic intentions, to compute 68 plus 57 as 5. (I would have made a mistake, not in mathematics, but in the supposition that I had accorded with my previous linguistic intentions.) The sceptic is proposing that I have made a mistake precisely of this kind, but with a plus and quus reversed.

Now if the sceptic proposes his hypothesis sincerely, he is crazy; such a bizarre hypothesis as the proposal that I always meant quus is absolutely wild. Wild it indubitably is, no doubt it is false; but if it is false, there must be some fact about my past usage that can be cited to refute it. For although the hypothesis is wild, it does not seem to be a priori impossible.

Of course this bizarre hypothesis, and the references to LSD, or to an insane frenzy, are in a sense merely a dramatic device. The basic point is this. Ordinarily, I suppose that, in computing '68 + 57' as I do, I do not simply make an unjustified leap in the dark. I follow directions I previously gave myself that uniquely determine that in this new instance I should say '125'. What are these directions? By hypothesis, I never explicitly told myself that I should say '125' in this very instance. Nor can I say that I should simply 'do the same thing I always did,' if this means 'compute according to the rule exhibited by my previous examples.' That rule could just as well have been the rule for quaddition (the quus function) as for addition. The idea that in fact quaddition *is* what I meant, that in a sudden frenzy I have changed my previous usage, dramatizes the problem.

In the discussion below the challenge posed by the sceptic takes two forms. First, he questions whether there is any *fact* that I meant plus, not quus, that will answer his sceptical challenge. Second, he questions whether I have any reason to be so confident that now I should answer '125' rather than '5'. The two forms of the challenge are related. I am confident that I should answer '125' because I am confident that this answer also accords with what I *meant*. Neither the accuracy of my computation nor of my memory is under dispute. So it ought to be agreed that *if* I meant plus, then unless I wish to change my usage, I am justified in answering (indeed compelled to answer) '125', not '5'. An answer to the sceptic must satisfy two conditions. First, it must give an account of what fact it is (about my mental state) that consti-

tutes my meaning plus, not quus. But further, there is a condition that any putative candidate for such a fact must satisfy. It must, in some sense, show how I am justified in giving the answer '125' to '68 + 57'. The 'directions' mentioned in the previous paragraph, that determine what I should do in each instance, must somehow be 'contained' in any candidate for the fact as to what I meant. Otherwise, the sceptic has not been answered when he holds that my present response is arbitrary. Exactly how this condition operates will become much clearer below, after we discuss Wittgenstein's paradox on an intuitive level, when we consider various philosophical theories as to what the fact that I meant plus might consist in. There will be many specific objections to these theories. But all fail to give a candidate for a fact as to what I meant that would show that only '125', not '5', is the answer I 'ought' to give.

The ground rules of our formulation of the problem should be made clear. For the sceptic to converse with me at all, we must have a common language. So I am supposing that the sceptic, provisionally, is not questioning my *present* use of the word "plus"; he agrees that, according to my *present* usage, '68 plus 57' denotes 125. Not only does he agree with me on this, he conducts the entire debate with me in my language as I *presently* use it. He merely questions whether my present usage agrees with my past usage, whether I am *presently* conforming to my *previous* linguistic intentions. The problem is not "How do I know that 68 plus 57 is 125?", which should be answered by giving an arithmetical computation, but rather "How do I know that '68 plus 57', as I *meant* 'plus' in the *past*, should denote 125?" If the word "plus" as I used it in the past, denoted the quus function, not the plus function ('quaddition' rather than addition), then my *past* intention was such that, asked for the value of '68 plus 57', I should have replied '5'.

I put the problem in this way so as to avoid confusing questions about whether the discussion is taking place 'both inside and outside language' in some illegitimate sense.[5] If we are querying the meaning of the word "plus," how can we use it (and variants, like 'quus') at the same time? So I suppose that the sceptic assumes that he and I agree in our *present* uses of the word "plus": we both use it to denote addition. He does *not*—at least initially—deny or doubt that addition is a genuine function, defined on all pairs of integers, nor does he deny that we can speak of it. Rather he asks why I now believe that by "plus" in the *past*, I meant addition rather than quaddition. If I meant the former, then to accord with my previous usage I should say '125' when asked to give the result of calculating '68 plus 57'. If I meant the latter, I should say '5'.

The present exposition tends to differ from Wittgenstein's original formulations in taking somewhat greater care to make explicit a distinction between use and mention, and between questions about present and past usage. About the present example Wittgenstein might simply ask, "How do I know that I should respond '125' to the query '68 + 57'?" or "How do I know that '68 + 57' comes out 125?" I have found that when the problem is formulated this way, some listeners hear it as a sceptical problem about *arithmetic:* "How do I know that 68 + 57 is 125?" (Why not answer this question with a mathematical proof?) At least at this stage, scepticism about arithmetic should not be taken to be in question: we may assume, if we wish, that 68 + 57 *is* 125. Even if the question is reformulated 'metalinguistically' as "How do I know that 'plus', as I use it, denotes a function that, when applied to 68 and 57, yields 125?", one may answer, "Surely I know that 'plus' denotes the plus function and accordingly that '68 plus 57' denotes 68 plus 57. But if I know arithmetic, I know that 68 plus 57 is 125. So I know that '68 plus 57' denotes 125!" And surely, if I use language at all, I cannot doubt coherently that "plus," as I now use it, denotes plus! Perhaps I cannot (at least at this stage) doubt this about my *present* usage. But I can doubt that my *past* usage of "plus" denoted plus. The previous remarks—about a frenzy and LSD—should make this quite clear.

Let me repeat the problem. The sceptic doubts whether any instructions I gave myself in the past compel (or justify) the answer '125' rather than '5'. He puts the challenge in terms of a sceptical hypothesis about a change in my usage. Perhaps when I used the term "plus" in the *past,* I always meant quus: by hypothesis I never gave myself any explicit directions that were incompatible with such a supposition.

Of course, ultimately, if the sceptic is right, the concepts of meaning and of intending one function rather than another will make no sense. For the sceptic holds that no fact about my past history—nothing that was ever in my mind, or in my external behavior—establishes that I meant plus rather than quus. (Nor, of course, does any fact establish that I meant quus!) But if this is correct, there can of course be no fact about which function I meant, and if there can be no fact about which particular function I meant in the *past,* there can be none in the *present* either. But before we pull the rug out from under our own feet, we begin by speaking as if the notion that at present we mean a certain function by "plus" is unquestioned and unquestionable. Only *past* usages are to be questioned. Otherwise, we will be unable to *formulate* our problem.

Another important rule of the game is that there are no limitations, in particular, no *behaviorist* limitations, on the facts that may be cited to answer the sceptic. The evidence is not to be confined to that available to an external observer, who can observe my overt behavior but not my internal mental state. It would be interesting if nothing in my external behavior could show whether I meant plus or quus, but something about my inner state could. But the problem here is more radical. Wittgenstein's philosophy of mind has often been viewed as behavioristic, but to the extent that Wittgenstein may (or may not) be hostile to the 'inner', no such hostility is to be assumed as a premise; it is to be argued as a conclusion. So whatever 'looking into my mind' may be, the sceptic asserts that even if God were to do it, he still could not determine that I meant addition by "plus."

This feature of Wittgenstein contrasts, for example, with Quine's discussion of the 'indeterminacy of translation'.[6] There are many points of contact between Quine's discussion and Wittgenstein's. Quine, however, is more than content to assume that only behavioral evidence is to be admitted into his discussion. Wittgenstein, by contrast, undertakes an extensive introspective[7] investigation, and the results of the investigation, as we shall see, form a key feature of his argument. Further, the way the sceptical doubt is presented is not behavioristic. It is presented from the 'inside'. Whereas Quine presents the problem about meaning in terms of a linguist, trying to guess what someone *else* means by his words on the basis of his behavior, Wittgenstein's challenge can be presented to me as a question about *myself:* was there some past fact about me— what I 'meant' by plus—that mandates what I should do now?

To return to the sceptic. The sceptic argues that when I answered '125' to the problem '68 + 57', my answer was an unjustified leap in the dark; my past mental history is equally compatible with the hypothesis that I meant quus, and therefore should have said '5'. We can put the problem this way: When asked for the answer to '68 + 57', I unhesitatingly and automatically produced '125', but it would seem that if previously I never performed this computation explicitly I might just as well have answered '5'. Nothing justifies a brute inclination to answer one way rather than another. . . . Wittgenstein has invented a new form of scepticism. Personally I am inclined to regard it as the most radical and original sceptical problem that philosophy has seen to date, one that only a highly unusual cast of mind could have produced. Of course he does not wish to leave us with his problem, but to solve it: the sceptical conclusion is insane and intolerable. It is his solution, I will argue, that contains the argument against 'private language'; for allegedly, the solution will not admit such a language. But it is important to see that his achievement in posing this problem stands on its own, independently of the value of his own solution of it and the resultant argument against private language. For, if we see Wittgenstein's problem as a real one, it is clear that he has often been read from the wrong perspective. Readers, my previous self certainly included, have often

been inclined to wonder: "How can he prove private language impossible? How can I possibly have any difficulty identifying my own sensations? And if there were a difficulty, how could 'public' criteria help me? I must be in pretty bad shape if I needed external *help* to identify my own sensations!" But if I am right, a proper orientation would be the opposite. The main problem is *not,* "How can we show private language—or some other special form of language—to be *impossible?*"; rather it is, "How can we show *any language* at all (public, private, or what-have-you) to be *possible?*"[8] It is not that calling a sensation 'pain' is easy, and Wittgenstein must invent a difficulty.[9] On the contrary, Wittgenstein's main problem is that it appears that he has shown *all* language, *all* concept formation, to be impossible, indeed unintelligible.

It is important and illuminating to compare Wittgenstein's new form of scepticism with the classical scepticism of Hume; there are important analogies between the two. Both develop a sceptical paradox, based on questioning a certain *nexus* from past to future. Wittgenstein questions the nexus between past 'intention' or 'meanings' and present practice: for example, between my past 'intentions' with regard to 'plus' and my present computation '68 + 57 = 125'. Hume questions two other nexuses, related to each other: the causal nexus whereby a past event necessitates a future one, and the inductive inferential nexus from the past to the future.

The analogy is obvious. It has been obscured for several reasons. First, the Humean and the Wittgensteinian problems are of course distinct and independent, though analogous. Second, Wittgenstein shows little interest in or sympathy with Hume: he has been quoted as saying that he could not read Hume because he found it "a torture".[10] Furthermore, Hume is the prime source of some ideas on the nature of mental states that Wittgenstein is most concerned to attack.[11] Finally (and probably most important), Wittgenstein never avows, and almost surely would not avow, the label 'sceptic', as Hume explicitly did. Indeed, he has often appeared to be a 'common-sense' philosopher, anxious to defend our ordinary conceptions and dissolve traditional philosophical doubts. Is it not Wittgenstein who held that philosophy only states what everyone admits?

Yet even here the difference between Wittgenstein and Hume should not be exaggerated. Even Hume has an important strain, dominant in some of his moods, that the philosopher never questions ordinary beliefs. Asked whether he "be really one of those sceptics, who hold that all is uncertain," Hume replies "that this question is entirely superfluous, and that neither I, nor any other person, was ever sincerely and constantly of that opinion."[12] Even more forcefully, discussing the problem of the external world: "We may well ask, *What causes induce us to believe in the existence of body?* but 'tis in vain to ask, *Whether there be body or not?* That is a point, which we must take for granted in all our reasonings."[13] Yet this oath of fealty to common sense begins a section that otherwise looks like an argument that the common conception of material objects is irreparably incoherent!

When Hume is in a mood to respect his professed determination never to deny or doubt our common beliefs, in what does his 'scepticism' consist? First, in a sceptical *account* of the causes of these beliefs; and second, in sceptical analyses of our common notions. In some ways Berkeley, who did not regard his own views as sceptical, may offer an even better analogy to Wittgenstein. At first blush, Berkeley, with his denial of matter, and of any objects 'outside the mind' seems to be *denying* our common beliefs; and for many of us the impression persists through later blushes. But not for Berkeley. For him, the impression that the common man is committed to matter and to objects outside the mind derives from an erroneous metaphysical interpretation of common talk. When the common man speaks of an 'external material object' he does not really mean (as we might say *sotto voce*) an *external material object* but rather he means something like 'an idea produced in me independently of my will'.[14]

Berkeley's stance is not uncommon in philosophy. The philosopher advocates a view apparently in patent contradiction to common sense. Rather than repudiating common sense, he asserts that the conflict comes from a philosophical misinterpretation of common language—sometimes he adds that the misinterpretation is encouraged by the 'superficial form' of ordinary speech. He offers his own analysis of the relevant common assertions, one that shows that they do not really say what they seem to say. For Berkeley this philosophical strategy is central to his work. To the extent that Hume claims that he merely analyses common sense and does not oppose it, he invokes the same strategy as well. The practice can hardly be said to have ceased today.[15]

Personally I think such philosophical claims are almost invariably suspect. What the claimant calls a 'misleading philosophical misconstrual' of the ordinary statement is probably the natural and correct understanding. The real misconstrual comes when the claimant continues, "All the ordinary man really means is . . ." and gives a sophisticated analysis compatible with his own philosophy. Be this as it may, the important point for present purposes is that Wittgenstein makes a Berkeleyan claim of this kind. For—as we shall see—his solution to his own sceptical problem begins by agreeing with the sceptics that there is no 'superlative fact' (§192) about my mind that constitutes my meaning addition by "plus" and determines in advance what I should do to accord with this meaning. But, he claims (in §§183–93), the appearance that our ordinary concept of meaning demands such a fact is based on a philosophical misconstrual—albeit a natural one—of such ordinary expressions as "he meant such-and-such," "the steps are determined by the formula," and the like. How Wittgenstein construes these expressions we shall see presently. For the moment let us only remark that Wittgenstein thinks that any construal that looks for something in my present mental state to differentiate between my meaning addition or quaddition, or that will consequently show that in the future I should say '125' when asked about '68 + 57', *is* a misconstrual and attributes to the ordinary man a notion of meaning that *is* refuted by the man a notion of meaning that *is* refuted by the sceptical argument. "We are," he says in §194—note that Berkeley could have said just the same thing!—"like savages, primitive people, who hear the expressions of civilized men, put a false interpretation on them, and then draw the queerest conclusions from it." Maybe so. Personally I can only report that, in spite of Wittgenstein's assurances, the 'primitive' interpretation often sounds rather good to me . . .

In his *Enquiry,* after he has developed his "Sceptical Doubts Concerning the Operations of the Understanding," Hume gives his "Sceptical Solution of These Doubts." What is a 'sceptical' solution? Call a proposed solution to a sceptical philosophical problem a *straight* solution if it shows that on closer examination the scepticism proves to be unwarranted; an elusive or complex argument proves the thesis the sceptic doubted. Descartes gave a 'straight' solution in this sense to his own philosophical doubts. An a priori justification of inductive reasoning, and an analysis of the causal relation as a genuine necessary connection or nexus between pairs of events, would be straight solutions of Hume's problems of induction and causation, respectively. A *sceptical* solution of a sceptical philosophical problem begins on the contrary by conceding that the sceptic's negative assertions are unanswerable. Nevertheless our ordinary practice or belief is justified because—contrary appearances notwithstanding—it need not require the justification the sceptic has shown to be untenable. And much of the value of the sceptical argument consists precisely in the fact that he has shown that an ordinary practice, if it is to be defended at all, cannot be defended in a certain way. A sceptical solution may also involve—in the manner suggested above—a sceptical analysis or account of ordinary beliefs to rebut their *prima facie* reference to a metaphysical absurdity.

The rough outlines of Hume's sceptical solution to his problem are well known.[16] Not an a priori argument, but custom, is the source of our inductive inferences. If *A* and *B* are two types of events which we have seen constantly conjoined, then we are conditioned—Hume is a grandfather of this modern psychological notion—to expect an event of type *B* on being presented with one of type *A.* To say of a particular event *a* that it caused another event *b* is to place these two events under two types, *A* and *B*, which we expect to be constantly conjoined in the future as they were in the past. The idea of necessary connection comes from the 'feeling of customary transition' between our ideas of these event types.

The philosophical merits of the Humean solution are not our present concern. Our purpose is to use the analogy with the Humean solution to illuminate Wittgenstein's solution to his own problem. For comparative purposes one further consequence of Hume's sceptical solution should be noted. Naively, one might suppose that whether a particular event *a* causes another particular event *b*, is an issue solely involving the events *a* and *b* alone (and their relations), and involves no other events. If Hume is right, this is not so. Even if God were to look at the events, he would discern nothing relating them other than that one succeeds the other. Only when the particular events *a* and *b* are thought of as subsumed under two respective event types, *A* and *B*, which are related by a generalization that *all* events of type *A* are followed by events of type *B*, can *a* be said to 'cause' *b*. When the events *a* and *b* are considered by themselves alone, no causal notions are applicable. This Humean conclusion might be called: the impossibility of private causation.

Can one reasonably protest: surely there is nothing the event *a* can do with the *help* of other events of the same type that it cannot do by itself! Indeed, to say that *a*, by itself, is a sufficient cause of *b* is to say that, had the rest of the universe been removed, *a* still would have produced *b!* Intuitively this may well be so, but the intuitive objection ignores Hume's sceptical argument. The whole point of the sceptical argument is that the common notion of one event 'producing' another, on which the objection relies, is in jeopardy. It appears that there is no such relation as 'production' at all, that the causal relation is fictive. After the sceptical argument has been seen to be unanswerable on its own terms, a sceptical solution is offered, containing all we can salvage of the notion of causation. It just is a feature of this analysis that causation makes no sense when applied to two isolated events, with the rest of the universe removed. Only inasmuch as these events are thought of as instances of event types related by a regularity can they be thought of as causally connected. If two particular events were somehow so *sui generis* that it was logically excluded that they be placed under any (plausibly natural) event types, causal notions would not be applicable to them.

Of course I am suggesting that Wittgenstein's argument against private language has a structure similar to Hume's argument against private causation. Wittgenstein also states a sceptical paradox. Like Hume, he accepts his own sceptical argument and offers a 'sceptical solution' to overcome the appearance of paradox. His solution involves a sceptical interpretation of what is involved in such ordinary assertions as "Jones means addition by '+'." The impossibility of private language emerges as a corollary of his sceptical solution of his own paradox, as does the impossibility of 'private causation' in Hume. It turns out that the sceptical solution does not allow us to speak of a single individual, considered by himself and in isolation, as ever meaning anything. Once again an objection based on an intuitive feeling that no one else can affect what I mean by a given symbol ignores the sceptical argument that undermines any such naive intuition about meaning.

I have said that Wittgenstein's solution to his problem is a sceptical one. He does not give a 'straight' solution, pointing out to the silly sceptic a hidden fact he overlooked, a condition in the world which constitutes my meaning addition by "plus." In fact, he agrees with his own hypothetical sceptic that there is no such fact, no such condition in either the 'internal' or the 'external' world. Admittedly, I am expressing Wittgenstein's view more straightforwardly than he would ordinarily allow himself to do. For in denying that there is any such fact, might we not be expressing a philosophical thesis that doubts or denies something everyone admits? We do not wish to doubt or deny that when people speak of themselves and others as meaning something by their words, as following rules, they do so with perfect right. We do not even wish to deny the propriety of an ordinary use of the phrase "the fact that Jones meant addition by such-and-such a symbol," and indeed such expressions do have perfectly ordinary uses. We merely wish to deny the existence of the 'superlative fact' that philosophers misleadingly attach to such ordinary forms of words, not the propriety of the forms of words themselves.

It is for this reason that I conjectured above that Wittgenstein's professed inability to write a work with conventionally organized arguments and conclusions stems at least in part, not from personal and stylistic proclivities, but from the nature of his work. Had Wittgenstein—contrary to his notorious and cryptic maxim in §128—stated the outcomes of his conclusions in the form of definite theses, it would have been very difficult to avoid formulating his doctrines in a form that consists in apparent sceptical denials of our ordinary assertions. Berkeley runs into similar difficulties. Partly he avoids them by stating his thesis as the denial of the existence of 'matter', and claiming that 'matter' is a bit of philosophical jargon, not expressive of our common-sense view. Nevertheless he is forced at one point to say—apparently contrary to his usual official doctrine—that he denies a doctrine "strangely prevailing amongst men."[17] If, on the other hand, we do not state our conclusions in the form of broad philosophical theses, it is easier to avoid the danger of a denial of any ordinary belief, even if our imaginary interlocuter (e.g. §189; see also §195)[18] accuses us of doing so. Whenever our opponent insists on the perfect propriety of an ordinary form of expression (e.g. that "the steps are determined by the formula," "the future application is already present"), we can insist that if these expressions are properly understood, we agree. The danger comes when we try to give a precise formulation of exactly what it is that we *are* denying—*what* 'erroneous interpretation' our opponent is placing on ordinary means of expression. It may be hard to do this without producing yet another statement that, we must admit, is *still* 'perfectly all right, properly understood'.

So Wittgenstein, perhaps cagily, might well disapprove of the straightforward formulation given here. Nevertheless I choose to be so bold as to say: Wittgenstein holds, with the sceptic, that there is no fact as to whether I mean plus or quus. . . . Let me, then, summarize the 'private language argument' as it is presented in this essay. (1) We all suppose that our language expresses concepts— "pain," "plus," "red"—in such a way that, once I 'grasp' the concept, all future applications of it are determined (in the sense of being uniquely *justified* by the concept grasped). In fact, it seems that no matter what is in my mind at a given time, I am free in the future to interpret it in different ways—for example, I could follow the sceptic and interpret "plus" as "quus." In particular, this point applies if I direct my attention to a sensation and name it; nothing I have done determines future applications (in the justificatory sense above). Wittgenstein's scepticism about the determination of future usage by the past contents of my mind is analogous to Hume's scepticism about the determination of the future by the past (causally and inferentially). (2) The paradox can be resolved only by a 'sceptical solution of these doubts', in Hume's classic sense. This means that we must give up the attempt to find any fact about me in virtue of which I mean "plus" rather than "quus," and must then go on in a certain way. Instead we must consider how we actually use: (i) the categorical assertion that an individual is following a given rule (that he means addition by 'plus'); (ii) the conditional assertion that "if an individual follows such-and-such a rule, he must do so-and-so on a given occasion" (e.g., "if he means addition by '+', his answer to '68 + 57' should be '125' "). That is to say, we must look at the circumstances under which these assertions are introduced into discourse, and their role and utility in our lives. (3) As long as we consider a single individual in isolation, all we

can say is this: An individual often does have the experience of being confident that he has 'got' a certain rule (sometimes that he has grasped it "in a flash"). It is an empirical fact that, after that experience, individuals often are disposed to give responses in concrete cases with complete confidence that proceeding this way is 'what was intended'. We cannot, however, get any further in explaining on this basis the use of the conditionals in (ii) above. Of course, dispositionally speaking, the subject is indeed determined to respond in a certain way, say, to a given addition problem. Such a disposition, together with the appropriate 'feeling of confidence', could be present, however, even if he were not really following a rule at all, or even if he were doing the 'wrong' thing. The justificatory element of our use of conditionals such as (ii) is unexplained. (4) If we take into account the fact that the individual is in a community, the picture changes and the role of (i) and (ii) above becomes apparent. When the community accepts a particular conditional (ii), it accepts its *contraposed* form: the failure of an individual to come up with the particular responses the community regards as right leads the community to suppose that he is not following the rule. On the other hand, if an individual passes enough tests, the community (endorsing assertions of the form (i)) accepts him as a rule follower, thus enabling him to engage in certain types of interactions with them that depend on their reliance on his responses. Note that this solution explains how the assertions in (i) and (ii) are introduced into language; it does *not* give conditions for these statements to be true. (5) The success of the practices in (3) depends on the brute empirical fact that we agree with each other in our responses. Given the sceptical argument in (1), this success cannot be explained by 'the fact that we all grasp the same concepts'. (6) Just as Hume thought he had demonstrated that the causal relation between two events is unintelligible unless they are subsumed under a regularity, so Wittgenstein thought that the considerations in (2) and (3) above showed that all talk of an individual following rules has reference to him as a member of a community, as in (3). In particular, for the conditionals of type (ii) to make sense, the community must be able to judge whether an individual is indeed following a given rule in particular applications, i.e. whether his responses agree with their own. In the case of avowals of sensations, the way the community makes this judgement is by observing the individual's behavior and surrounding circumstances.

A few concluding points regarding the argument ought to be noted. First, following §243, a 'private language' is usually defined as a language that is logically impossible for anyone else to understand. The private language argument is taken to argue against the possibility of a private language in this sense. This conception is not in error, but it seems to me that the emphasis is somewhat misplaced. What is really denied is what might be called the 'private model' of rule following, that the notion of a person following a given rule is to be analyzed simply in terms of facts about the rule follower and the rule follower alone, without reference to his membership in a wider community. (In the same way, what Hume denies is the private model of causation: that whether one event causes another is a matter of the relation between these two events alone, without reference to their subsumption under larger event types.) The impossibility of a private language in the sense just defined does indeed follow from the incorrectness of the private model for language and rules, since the rule following in a 'private language' could only be analyzed by a private model, but the incorrectness of the private model is more basic, since it applies to all rules. I take all this to be the point of §202.

Does this mean that Robinson Crusoe, isolated on an island, cannot be said to follow any rules, no matter what he does?[19] I do not see that this follows. What does follow is that *if* we think of Crusoe as following rules, we are taking him into our community and applying our criteria for rule following to him.[20] The falsity of the private model need not mean that a *physically isolated* individual cannot be said to follow rules; rather that an individual, *considered in isolation* (whether or

not he is physically isolated), cannot be said to do so. Remember that Wittgenstein's theory is one of assertability conditions. Our community can assert of any individual that he follows a rule if he passes the tests for rule following applied to any member of the community.

Finally, the point just made in the last paragraph, that Wittgenstein's theory is one of assertability conditions, deserves emphasis. Wittgenstein's theory should not be confused with a theory that, for any *m* and *n,* the value of the function we mean by "plus," *is* (by definition) the value that (nearly) all the linguistic community would give as the answer. Such a theory would be a theory of the *truth* conditions of such assertions as "By 'plus' we mean such-and-such a function," or "By 'plus' we mean a function, which, when applied to 68 and 57 as arguments, yields 125 as value." (An infinite, exhaustive totality of specific conditions of the second form would determine which function was meant, and hence would determine a condition of the first form.) The theory would assert that 125 is the value of the function meant for given arguments, if and only if '125' is the response nearly everyone would give, given these arguments. Thus the theory would be a social, or community-wide, version of the dispositional theory, and would be open to at least some of the same criticisms as the original form. I take Wittgenstein to deny that he holds such a view, for example, in *Remarks on the Foundations of Mathematics,* v, §33 [vii, §40]: "Does this mean, e.g., that the definition of the same would be this: same is what all or most human beings take for the same?—Of course not."[21] (See also *Philosophical Investigations,* p. 226, "Certainly the propositions, 'Human beings believe that twice two is four' and 'Twice two is four' do not mean the same"; and see also §§240–1.) One must bear firmly in mind that Wittgenstein has no theory of truth-conditions—necessary and sufficient conditions—for the correctness of one response rather than another to a new addition problem. Rather he simply points out that each of us *automatically* calculates new addition problems (without feeling the need to check with the community whether our procedure is proper); that the community feels entitled to correct a deviant calculation; that in practice such deviation is rare, and so on. Wittgenstein thinks that these observations about sufficient conditions for justified assertion are enough to illuminate the role and utility in our lives of assertion about meaning and determination of new answers. What follows from these assertability conditions is *not* that the answer everyone gives to an addition problem is, by definition, the correct one, but rather the platitude that, if everyone agrees upon a certain answer, then no one will feel justified in calling the answer wrong.

Obviously there are countless relevant aspects of Wittgenstein's philosophy of mind that I have not discussed.[22] About some aspects I am not clear, and others have been left untouched because of the limits of this essay.[23] In particular, I have not discussed numerous issues arising out of the paragraphs *following* §243 that are usually called the 'private language argument', nor have I really discussed Wittgenstein's attendant positive account of the nature of sensation language and of the attribution of psychological states. Nevertheless, I do think that the basic 'private language argument' precedes these passages, and that only with an understanding of this argument can we begin to comprehend or consider what follows. That was the task undertaken in this essay.

NOTES

1. Unless otherwise specified (explicitly or contextually), references are to *Philosophical Investigations*. The small numbered units of the *Investigations* are termed 'sections' (or 'paragraphs'). Page references are used only if a section reference is not possible, as in the second part of the *Investigations*. Throughout I quote the standard printed English translation (by G. E. M. Anscombe) and make no attempt to question it except in a very few instances. *Philosophical Investigations* has undergone several editions since its first publication in 1953 but the paragraphing and pagination remain the same. The publishers are Basil Blackwell, Oxford and Macmillan, New York.

    This essay does not proceed by giving detailed exegesis of Wittgenstein's text but rather develops the arguments in its own way. I recommend that the reader reread the *Investigations* in the light of the present exegesis and see whether it illuminates the text.

2. Basil Blackwell, Oxford: 1956. In the first edition of *Remarks on the Foundation of Mathematics* the editors assert (p. vi) that Wittgenstein appears originally to have intended to include some of the material on mathematics in *Philosophical Investigations*. The third edition (1978) includes more material than earlier editions and rearranges some of the sections and divisions of earlier editions. When I wrote the present work, I used the first edition. Where the references differ, the equivalent third edition reference is given in square brackets.

3. Personally I feel, however, that the role of stylistic considerations here cannot be denied. It is clear that purely stylistic and literary considerations meant a great deal to Wittgenstein. His own stylistic preference obviously contributes to the difficulty of his work as well as to its beauty.

4. Perhaps I should make a remark about such expressions as "By 'plus' I meant quus (or plus)," "By 'green' I meant green," etc. I am not familiar with an accepted felicitous convention to indicate the object of the verb 'to mean'. There are two problems. First, if one says, "By 'the woman who discovered radium' I meant the woman who discovered radium," the object can be interpreted in two ways. It may stand for a woman (Marie Curie), in which case the assertion is true only if 'meant' is used to mean referred to (as it can be used); or it may be used to denote the *meaning* of the quoted expression, not a woman, in which case the assertion is true with 'meant' used in the ordinary sense. Second, as is illustrated by 'referred to', 'green', 'quus', etc. above, as objects of 'meant', one must use various expressions as objects in an awkward manner contrary to normal grammar. (Frege's difficulties concerning unsaturatedness are related.) Both problems tempt one to put the object in quotation marks, like the subject; but such a usage conflicts with the convention of philosophical logic that a quotation denotes the expression quoted. Some special 'meaning marks', as proposed for example by David Kaplan, could be useful here. If one is content to ignore the first difficulty and always use 'mean' to mean denote (for most purposes of the present paper, such a reading would suit at least as well as an intensional one; often I speak as if it is a *numerical function* that is meant by plus), the second problem might lead one to nominalize the objects—'plus' denotes the plus function, 'green' denotes greeness, etc. I contemplated using italics (" 'plus' means *plus*"; " 'mean' may mean *denote*"), but I decided that

normally (except when italics are otherwise appropriate, especially when a neologism like 'quus' is introduced for the first time), I will write the object of 'to mean' as an ordinary roman object. The convention I have adopted reads awkwardly in the written language but sounds rather reasonable in the spoken language.

Since use–mention distinctions are significant for the argument as I give it, I try to remember to use quotation marks when an expression is mentioned. However, quotation marks are also used for other purposes where they might be invoked in normal non-philosophical English writing (for example, in the case of " 'meaning marks' " in the previous paragraph, or " 'quasi-quotation' " in the next sentence). Readers familiar with Quine's 'quasi-quotation' will be aware that in some cases I use ordinary quotation where logical purity would require that I use quasi-quotation or some similar device. I have not tried to be careful about this matter, since I am confident that in practice readers will not be confused.

5. I believe I got the phrase "both inside and outside language" from a conversation with Rogers Albritton.

6. See W. V. Quine, *Word and Object* (MIT, The Technology Press, Cambridge, Massachusetts: 1960) especially chapter 2, "Translation and Meaning" (pp. 26–79). See also *Ontological Relativity and Other Essays* (Columbia University Press, New York and London: 1969), especially the first three chapters (pp. 1–90); and see also "On the Reasons for the Indeterminacy of Translation," *The Journal of Philosophy*, vol. 67 (1970), pp. 178–83.

7. I do not mean the term 'introspective' to be laden with philosophical doctrine. Of course much of the baggage that has accompanied this term would be objectionable to Wittgenstein in particular. I simply mean that he makes use, in his discussion, of our own memories and knowledge of our 'inner' experiences.

8. So put, the problem has an obvious Kantian flavor.

9. See especially the discussions of 'green' and 'grue' above, [not reprinted in this volume] which plainly could carry over to pain (let 'pickle' apply to pains before *t*, and tickles thereafter!); but it is clear enough by now that the problem is completely general.

10. Karl Britton, "Portrait of a Philosopher," *The Listener*, LIII, no. 1372 (June 16, 1955), p. 1072, quoted by George Pitcher, *The Philosophy of Wittgenstein* (Prentice Hall, Englewood Cliffs, N.J.: 1964), p. 325.

11. Much of Wittgenstein's argument can be regarded as an attack on characteristically Humean (or classical empiricist) ideas. Hume posits an introspectible qualitative state for each of our

psychological states (an 'impression'). Further, he thinks that an appropriate 'impression' or 'image' can constitute an 'idea', without realizing that an image in no way tells us how it is to be applied. Of course the Wittgensteinian paradox is, among other things, a strong protest against such suppositions.

12. David Hume, *A Treatise of Human Nature,* ed. L. A. Selby-Bigge, Clarendon Press, Oxford: 1888), Book I, part IV, section I (p. 183 in the Selby-Bigge edition).

13. Hume, *ibid.,* Book I, part IV, Section II (p. 187 in the Selby-Bigge edition). Hume's occasional affinities to 'ordinary language' philosophy should not be overlooked. Consider the following: "Those philosophers, who have divided human reason into *knowledge and probability,* and have defined the first to be *that evidence, which arises from the comparison of ideas,* are obliged to comprehend all our arguments from causes or effects under the general term of probability. But tho' everyone be free to use his terms in what sense he pleases . . . 'tis however certain, that in common discourse we readily affirm, that many arguments from causation exceed probability, and may be received as a superior kind of evidence. One would appear ridiculous, who would say, that 'tis only probable the sun will rise tomorrow, or that all men must dye . . ." (*ibid.,* Book I, part III, section XI, p. 124 in the Selby-Bigge edition).

14. George Berkeley, *The Principles of Human Knowledge,* §§29–34. Of course the characterization may be oversimplified, but it suffices for present purposes.

15. It is almost 'analytic' that I cannot produce a common contemporary example that would not meet with vigorous opposition. Those who hold the cited view would argue that, in this case, their analyses of ordinary usage are really correct. I have no desire to enter into an irrelevant controversy here, but I myself find that many of the 'topic-neutral' analyses of discourse about the mind proposed by contemporary materialists are just the other side of the Berkeleyan coin.

16. Writing this sentence, I find myself prey to an appropriate fear that (some) experts in Hume and Berkeley will not approve of some particular thing that I say about these philosophers here. I have made no careful study of them for the purpose of this paper. Rather a crude and fairly conventional account of the 'rough outlines' of their views is used for purposes of comparison with Wittgenstein.

17. Berkeley, *The Principles of Human Knowledge,* §4. Of course Berkeley might mean that the prevalence of the doctrine stems from the influence of philosophical theory rather than common sense, as indeed he asserts in the next section.

18. §189: "But *are* the steps then *not* determined by the algebraic formula?" In spite of Wittgenstein's interpretation within his own philosophy of the ordinary phrase "the steps are determined by the formula", the impression persists that the interlocutor's characterization of his view is really correct. See §195: "But I don't mean that what I do now (in grasping a sense) determines the future use *causally* and as a matter of experience, but that in a *queer* way, the use itself is in some sense present," which are the words of the interlocutor, and the bland reply. "But of course it is, 'in *some* sense'! Really the only thing wrong with what you say is the expression "in a queer way". The rest is all right; and the sentence only seems queer when one imagines a different language-game for it from the one in which we actually use it."

19. See . . . A. J. Ayer, "Can there be a Private Language?" [reprinted in this volume]. Ayer assumes that the 'private language argument' excludes Crusoe from language [and] takes this alleged fact to be fatal to Wittgenstein's argument. . . . Others, pointing out that a 'private language' is one that others *cannot* understand (see the preceding paragraph in the text), see no reason to think that the 'private language argument' has anything to do with Crusoe (as long as we could understand his language). My own view of the matter, as explained very briefly in the text, differs somewhat from all these opinions.

20. If Wittgenstein would have any problem with Crusoe, perhaps the problem would be whether we have any 'right' to take him into our community in this way, and attribute our rules to him. See Wittgenstein's discussion of a somewhat similar question in §§199–200, and his conclusion, "Should we still be inclined to say they were playing a game? What right would one have to say so?"

21. Although, in the passage in question, Wittgenstein is speaking of a particular language-game of bringing something else and bringing the same, it is clear in context that it is meant to illustrate his general problem about rules. The entire passage is worth reading for the present issue.

22. [. . .] As members of the community correct each other, might a given individual correct himself? Some question such as this was prominent in earlier discussions of verificationist versions of the private language argument. Indeed, in the absence of Wittgenstein's sceptical paradox, it would appear that an individual remembers his own 'intentions' and can use one memory of these intentions to correct another mistaken memory. In the presence of the paradox, any such 'naive' ideas are meaningless. Ultimately, an individual may simply have conflicting brute inclinations, while the upshot of the matter depends on his will alone. The situation is not analogous to the case of the community, where distinct individuals have distinct and independent wills, and where, when an individual is accepted into the community, others judge that they can rely on his response (as was described in the text above). No corresponding relation between an individual and himself has the same utility. Wittgenstein may be indicating something like this in §268.

23. I might mention that, in addition to the Humean analogy emphasized in this essay, it has struck me that there is perhaps a certain analogy between Wittgenstein's private language argument and Ludwig von Mises's celebrated argument concerning economic calculation under socialism. (See e.g., his *Human Action*, 2d ed., Yale University Press, New Haven: 1963, chapter 26, pp. 698–715, for one statement.) According to Mises, a rational economic calculator (say, the manager of an industrial plant) who wishes to choose the most efficient means to achieve given ends must compare alternative courses of action for cost effectiveness. To do this, he needs an array of prices (e.g. of raw materials, or machinery) set by *others*. If *one* agency set *all* prices, it could have no rational basis to choose between alternative courses of action. (Whatever seemed to it to be right would be right, so one cannot talk about right.) I do not know whether the fact bodes at all ill for the private language argument, but my impression is that although it is usually acknowledged that Mises's argument points to a real difficulty for centrally planned economies, it is now almost universally rejected as a theoretical proposition.

Languages and Language　　36

DAVID LEWIS

I. THESIS

What is a language? Something which assigns meanings to certain strings of types of sounds or of marks. It could therefore be a function, a set of ordered pairs of strings and meanings. The entities in the domain of the function are certain finite sequences of types of vocal sounds, or of types of inscribable marks; if σ is in the domain of a language £, let us call σ a *sentence of* £. The entities in the range of the function are meanings; if σ is a sentence of £, let us call £(σ) the *meaning of σ in* £. What could a meaning of a sentence be? Something which, when combined with factual information about the world—or factual information about *any* possible world—yields a truth-value. It could therefore be a function from worlds to truth-values—or more simply, a set of worlds. We can say that a sentence σ is true in a language £ at a world w if and only if w belongs to the set of worlds £(σ). We can say that σ is true in £ (without mentioning a world) if and only if our actual world belongs to £(σ). We can say that σ is *analytic* in £ if and only if every possible world belongs to £(σ). And so on, in the obvious way.

II. ANTITHESIS

What is language? A social phenomenon which is part of the natural history of human beings; a sphere of human action, wherein people utter strings of vocal sounds, or inscribe strings of marks, and wherein people respond by thought or action to the sounds or marks which they observe to have been so produced.

This verbal activity is, for the most part, rational. He who produces certain sounds or marks does so for a reason. He knows that someone else, upon hearing his sounds or seeing his marks, is apt to form a certain belief or act in a certain way. He wants, for some reason, to bring about that belief or action. Thus his beliefs and desires give him a reason to produce the sounds or marks, and he does. He who responds to the sounds or marks in a certain way also does so for a reason. He knows how the production of sounds or marks depends upon the producer's state of mind. When he observes the sounds or marks, he is therefore in a position to infer something about the producer's state of mind. He can probably also infer something about the conditions which caused that state of mind. He

From *Language, Mind and Knowledge*, Keith Gunderson, ed. (Minneapolis: University of Minnesota Press, 1975), pp. 3–35. AUTHOR'S NOTE: This paper was originally prepared in 1968 and was revised in 1972. The 1968 draft appears in Italian translation as "Lingue e ligua," *Versus*, 4 (1973): 2–21.

may merely come to believe these conclusions, or he may act upon them in accordance with his other beliefs and his desires.

Not only do both have reasons for thinking and acting as they do; they know something about each other, so each is in a position to replicate the other's reasons. Each one's replication of the other's reasons forms part of his own reason for thinking and acting as he does; and each is in a position to replicate the other's replication of his own reasons. Therefore the Gricean mechanism[1] operates: X intends to bring about a response on the part of Y by getting Y to recognize that X intends to bring about that response; Y does recognize X's intention, and is thereby given some sort of reason to respond just as X intended him to.

Within any suitable population, various regularities can be found in this rational verbal activity. There are regularities whereby the production of sounds or marks depends upon various aspects of the state of mind of the producer. There are regularities whereby various aspects of responses to sounds or marks depend upon the sounds or marks to which one is responding. Some of these regularities are accidental. Others can be explained, and different ones can be explained in very different ways.

Some of them can be explained as conventions of the population in which they prevail. Conventions are regularities in action, or in action and belief, which are arbitrary but perpetuate themselves because they serve some sort of common interest. Past conformity breeds future conformity because it gives one a reason to go on conforming; but there is some alternative regularity which could have served instead, and would have perpetuated itself in the same way if only it had got started.

More precisely: a regularity R, in action or in action and belief, is a *convention* in a population P if and only if, within P, the following six conditions hold. (Or at least they almost hold. A few exceptions to the "everyone"s can be tolerated.)

(1) Everyone conforms to R.

(2) Everyone believes that the others conform to R.

(3) This belief that the others conform to R gives everyone a good and decisive reason to conform to R himself. His reason may be that, in particular, those of the others he is now dealing with conform to R; or his reason may be that there is general or widespread conformity, or that there has been, or that there will be. His reason may be a practical reason, if conforming to R is a matter of acting in a certain way; or it may be an epistemic reason, if conforming to R is a matter of believing in a certain way. First case: according to his beliefs, some desired end may be reached by means of some sort of action in conformity to R, provided that the others (all or some of them) also conform to R; therefore he wants to conform to R if they do. Second case: his beliefs, together with the premise that others conform to R, deductively imply or inductively support some conclusion; and in believing this conclusion, he would thereby conform to R. Thus reasons for conforming to a convention by believing something—like reasons for belief in general—are believed premises tending to confirm the truth of the belief in question. Note that I am *not* speaking here of practical reasons for acting so as to somehow produce in oneself a certain desired belief.

(4) There is a general preference for general conformity to R rather than slightly-less-than-general conformity—in particular, rather than conformity by all but any one. (This is not to deny that some state of *widespread* nonconformity to R might be even more preferred.) Thus everyone who believes that at least almost everyone conforms to R will want the others, as well as himself, to conform. This condition serves to distinguish cases of convention, in which there is a predominant coincidence of interest, from cases of deadlocked conflict. In the latter cases, it may be that each is doing the best he can by conforming to R, given that the others do so; but each wishes the others did not conform to R, since he could then gain at their expense.

(5) R is not the only possible regularity meeting the last two conditions. There is at least one alternative R' such that the belief that the others conformed to R' would give

everyone a good and decisive practical or epistemic reason to conform to R' likewise; such that there is a general preference for general conformity to R' rather than slightly-less-than-general conformity to R'; and such that there is normally no way of conforming to R and R' both. Thus the alternative R' could have perpetuated itself as a convention instead of R; this condition provides for the characteristic arbitrariness of conventions.

(6) Finally, the various facts listed in conditions (1) to (5) are matters of *common* (or *mutual*) knowledge: they are known to everyone, it is known to everyone that they are known to everyone, and so on. The knowledge mentioned here may be merely potential: knowledge that would be available if one bothered to think hard enough. Everyone must potentially know that (1) to (5) hold; potentially know that the others potentially know it; and so on. This condition ensures stability. If anyone tries to replicate another's reasoning, perhaps including the other's replication of his own reasoning, . . . , the result will reinforce rather than subvert his expectation of conformity to R. Perhaps a negative version of (6) would do the job: no one disbelieves that (1) to (5) hold, no one believes that others disbelieve this, and so on.

This definition can be tried out on all manner of regularities which we would be inclined to call conventions. It is a convention to drive on the right. It is a convention to mark poisons with skull and crossbones. It is a convention to dress as we do. It is a convention to train beasts to turn right on "gee" and left on "haw." It is a convention to give goods and services in return for certain pieces of paper or metal. And so on.

The common interests which sustain conventions are as varied as the conventions themselves. Our convention to drive on the right is sustained by our interest in not colliding. Our convention for marking poisons is sustained by our interest in making it easy for everyone to recognize poisons. Our conventions of dress might be sustained by a common aesthetic preference for somewhat uniform dress, or by the low cost of mass-produced clothes, or by a fear on everyone's part

that peculiar dress might be thought to manifest a peculiar character, or by a desire on everyone's part not to be too conspicuous, or—most likely—by a mixture of these and many other interests.

It is a platitude—something only a philosopher would dream of denying—that there are conventions of language, although we do not find it easy to say what those conventions are. If we look for the fundamental difference in verbal behavior between members of two linguistic communities, we can be sure of finding something which is arbitrary but perpetuates itself because of a common interest in coordination. In the case of conventions of language, that common interest derives from our common interest in taking advantage of, and in preserving, our ability to control others' beliefs and actions to some extent by means of sounds and marks. That interest in turn derives from many miscellaneous desires we have; to list them, list the ways you would be worse off in Babel.

III. SYNTHESIS

What have languages to do with language? What is the connection between what I have called *languages*, functions from strings of sounds or of marks to sets of possible worlds, semantic systems discussed in complete abstraction from human affairs, and what I have called *language*, a form of rational, convention-governed human social activity? We know what to *call* this connection we are after: we can say that a given language $\pounds$ is *used by*, or is a (or the) language *of*, a given population P. We know also that this connection holds by virtue of the conventions of language prevailing in P. Under suitably different conventions, a different language would be used by P. There is some sort of convention whereby P uses $\pounds$—but what is it? It is worthless to call it a convention to use $\pounds$, even if it can correctly be so described, for we want to know what it is to use $\pounds$.

My proposal[2] is that the convention whereby a population P uses a language $\pounds$ is a convention of *truthfulness* and *trust* in $\pounds$. To be truthful in $\pounds$ is to act in a certain way: to try never to utter any sentence of £ that are not true in £. Thus it is to avoid uttering any sentence of £ unless one believes it to be true in £. To be trusting in £ is to form beliefs in a certain way: to impute truthfulness in £ to others, and thus to tend to respond to another's utterance of any sentence of £ by coming to believe that the uttered sentence is true in £.

Suppose that a certain language £ is used by a certain population P. Let this be a perfect case of normal language use. Imagine what would go on; and review the definition of a convention to verify that there does prevail in P a convention of truthfulness and trust in £.

(1) There prevails in P at least a regularity of truthfulness and trust in £. The members of P frequently speak (or write) sentences of £ to one another. When they do, ordinarily the speaker (or writer) utters one of the sentences he believes to be true in £; and the hearer (or reader) responds by coming to share that belief of the speaker's (unless he already had it), and adjusting his other beliefs accordingly.

(2) The members of P believe that this regularity of truthfulness and trust in £ prevails among them. Each believes this because of his experience of others' past truthfulness and trust in £.

(3) The expectation of conformity ordinarily gives everyone a good reason why he himself should conform. If he is a speaker, he expects his hearer to be trusting in £; wherefore he has reason to expect that by uttering certain sentences that are true in £ according to his beliefs—by being truthful in £ in a certain way—he can impart certain beliefs that he takes to be correct. Commonly, a speaker has some reason or other for wanting to impart some or other correct beliefs. Therefore his beliefs and desires constitute a practical reason for acting in the way he does: for uttering some sentence truthfully in £.

As for the hearer: he expects the speaker to be truthful in £, wherefore he has good reason to infer that the speaker's sentence is true in £ according to the speaker's beliefs. Commonly, a hearer also has some or other reason to believe that the speaker's beliefs are correct (by and large, and perhaps with exceptions for certain topics); so it is reasonable for him to infer that the sentence he has heard is probably true in £. Thus his beliefs about the speaker give him an epistemic reason to respond trustingly in £.

We have coordination between truthful speaker and trusting hearer. Each conforms as he does to the prevailing regularity of truthfulness and trust in £ because he expects complementary conformity on the part of the other.

But there is also a more diffuse and indirect sort of coordination. In coordinating with his present partner, a speaker or hearer also is coordinating with all those whose past truthfulness and trust in £ have contributed to his partner's present expectations. This indirect coordination is a four-way affair: between present speakers and past speakers, present speakers and past hearers, present hearers and past speakers, and present hearers and past hearers. And whereas the direct coordination between a speaker and his hearer is a coordination of truthfulness with trust for a single sentence of £, the indirect coordination with one's partner's previous partners (and with *their* previous partners, etc.) may involve various sentences of £. It may happen that a hearer, say, has never before encountered the sentence now addressed to him; but he forms the appropriate belief on hearing it—one such that he has responded trustingly in £—because his past experience with truthfulness in £ has involved many sentences grammatically related to this one.

(4) There is in P a general preference for general conformity to the regularity of truthfulness and trust in £. Given that most conform, the members of P want all to conform. They desire truthfulness and trust in £ from each other, as well as from themselves. This general preference is sustained by a common interest in communication. Everyone wants occasionally to impart correct beliefs and bring about appropriate actions in others by means of sounds and marks. Everyone wants to preserve his ability to do so at will. Everyone wants to be able to learn about the parts of the world that he cannot observe for himself by observing instead the sounds and marks of his fellows who have been there.

(5) The regularity of truthfulness and trust in £ has alternatives. Let £' be any language that does not overlap £ in such a way that it is possible to be truthful and trusting simultaneously in £ and in £', and that is rich and convenient enough to meet the needs of *P* for communication. Then the regularity of truthfulness and trust in £' is an alternative to the prevailing regularity of truthfulness and trust in £. For the alternative regularity, as for the actual one, general conformity by the others would give one a reason to conform; and general conformity would be generally preferred over slightly-less-than-general conformity.

(6) Finally, all these facts are common knowledge in *P*. Everyone knows them, everyone knows that everyone knows them, and so on. Or at any rate none believes that another doubts them, none believes that another believes that another doubts them, and so on.

In any case in which a language £ clearly is used by a population *P,* then, it seems that there prevails in *P* a convention of truthfulness and trust in £, sustained by an interest in communication. The converse is supported by an unsuccessful search for counterexamples: I have not been able to think of any case in which there is such a convention and yet the language £ is clearly not used in the population *P.* Therefore I adopt this definition, claiming that it agrees with ordinary usage in the cases in which ordinary usage is fully determinate:

a language £ is *used by* a population *P* if and only if there prevails in *P* a convention of truthfulness and trust in £, sustained by an interest in communication.

Such conventions, I claim, provide the desired connection between languages and language-using populations.

Once we understand how languages are connected to populations, whether by conventions of truthfulness and trust for the sake of communication or in some other way, we can proceed to redefine relative to a population all those semantic concepts that we previously defined relative to a language. A string of sounds or of marks is a sentence of *P* if and only if it is a sentence of some language £ which is used in *P*. It has a certain meaning in *P* if and only if it has that meaning in some language £ which is used in *P*. It is true in *P* at a world *w* if and only if it is true at *w* in some language £ which is used in *P*. It is true in *P* if and only if it is true in some language £ which is used in *P*.

The account just given of conventions in general, and of conventions of language in particular, differs in one important respect from the account given in my book *Convention.*[3]

Formerly, the crucial clause in the definition of convention was stated in terms of a conditional preference for conformity: each prefers to conform if the others do, and it would be the same for the alternatives to the actual convention. (In some versions of the definition, this condition was subsumed under a broader requirement of general preference for general conformity.) The point of this was to explain why the belief that others conform would give everyone a reason for conforming likewise, and so to explain the rational self-perpetuation of conventions. But a reason involving preference in this way must be a practical reason for acting, not an epistemic reason for believing. Therefore I said that conventions were regularities in action alone. It made no sense to speak of believing something in conformity to convention. (Except in the peculiar case that others' conformity to the convention gives one a practical reason to conform by acting to somehow produce a belief in oneself; but I knew that this case was irrelevant to ordinary language use.) Thus I was cut off from what I now take to be the primary sort of conventional coordination in language use: that between the action of the truthful speaker and the responsive believing of his trusting hearer. I resorted to two different substitutes.

Sometimes it is common knowledge how the hearer will want to act if he forms various beliefs, and we can think of the speaker not only as trying to impart beliefs but also as trying thereby to get the hearer to act in a way that speaker and hearer alike deem appropriate under the circumstances that the speaker believes to obtain. Then we have speaker-hearer coordination of action. Both conform to a convention of truthfulness for the speaker plus appropriate responsive action by the hearer. The hearer's trustful believing need not be part of the content of the convention, though it must be mentioned to explain why the hearer acts in conformity. In this way we reach the account of "signaling" in *Convention*, chapter IV.

But signaling was all too obviously a special case. There may be no appropriate responsive action for the hearer to perform when the speaker imparts a belief to him. Or the speaker and hearer may disagree about how the hearer ought to act under the supposed circumstances. Or the speaker may not know how the hearer will decide to act; or the hearer may not know that he knows; and so on. The proper hearer's response to consider is *believing*, but that is not ordinarily an action. So in considering language use in general, in *Convention*, chapter V, I was forced to give up on speaker-hearer coordination. I took instead the diffuse coordination between the present speaker and the past speakers who trained the present hearer. Accordingly, I proposed that the convention whereby a population *P* used a language £ was simply a convention of truthfulness in £. Speakers conform; hearers do not, until they become speakers in their turn, if they ever do.

I think now that I went wrong when I went beyond the special case of signaling. I should have kept my original emphasis on speaker-hearer coordination, broadening the definition of convention to fit. It was Jonathan Bennett[4] who showed me how that could be done: by restating the crucial defining clause not in terms of preference for conformity but rather in terms of reasons for conformity—practical or *epistemic* reasons. The original conditional preference requirement gives way now to clause (3): the belief that others conform gives everyone a reason to conform likewise, and it would be the same for the alternatives to the actual convention. Once this change is made, there is no longer any obstacle to including the hearer's trust as part of the content of a convention.

(The old conditional preference requirement is retained, however, in consequence of the less important clause (4). Clause (3) as applied to practical reasons, but not as applied to epistemic reasons, may be subsumed under (4).)

Bennett pointed out one advantage of the change: suppose there is only one speaker of an idiolect, but several hearers who can understand him. Shouldn't he and his hearers comprise a population that uses his idiolect? More generally, what is the difference between (a) someone who does not utter sentences of a language because he does not belong to any population that uses it, and (b) someone who does not utter sentences of the language although he does belong to such a population because at present—or always, perhaps—he has nothing to say? Both are alike, so far as action in conformity to a convention of truthfulness goes. Both are vacuously truthful. In *Convention*, I made it a condition of truthfulness in £ that one sometimes does utter sentences of £, though not that one speaks up on any particular occasion. But that is unsatisfactory: what degree of truthful talkativeness does it take to keep up one's active membership in a language-using population? What if someone just never thought of anything worth saying?

(There is a less important difference between my former account and the present one. Then and now, I wanted to insist that cases of convention are cases of predominant coincidence of interest. I formerly provided for this by a defining clause that seems now unduly restrictive: in any instance of the situation to which the convention applies, everyone has approximately the same preferences regarding all possible combinations of actions. Why *all?* It may be enough that they agree in preferences to the extent specified in my present clause (4). Thus I have left out the further agreement-in-preferences clause.)

IV. OBJECTIONS AND REPLIES

Objection: Many things which meet the definition of a language given in the thesis—many functions from strings of sounds or of marks to sets of possible worlds—are not really possible languages. They could not possibly be adopted by any human population. There may be too few sentences, or too few meanings, to make as many discriminations as language-users need to communicate. The meanings may not be anything language-users would wish to communicate about. The sentences may be very long, impossible to pronounce, or otherwise clumsy. The language may be humanly unlearnable because it has no grammar, or a grammar of the wrong kind.

Reply: Granted. The so-called languages of the thesis are merely an easily specified superset of the languages we are really interested in. A language in a narrower and more natural sense is any one of these entities that could possibly—possibly in some appropriately strict sense—be used by a human population.

Objection: The so-called languages discussed in the thesis are excessively simplified. There is no provision for indexical sentences, dependent on features of the context of their utterance: for instance, tensed sentences, sentences with personal pronouns or demonstratives, or anaphoric sentences. There is no provision for ambiguous sentences. There is no provision for nonindicative sentences: imperatives, questions, promises and threats, permissions, and so on.

Reply: Granted. I have this excuse: the phenomenon of language would be not too different if these complications did not exist, so we cannot go too far wrong by ignoring them. Nevertheless, let us sketch what could be done to provide for indexicality, ambiguity, or nonindicatives. In order not to pile complication on complication we shall take only one at a time.

We may define an *indexical language* £ as a function that assigns sets of possible worlds not to its sentences themselves, but rather to sentences paired with possible occasions of their utterance. We can say that σ is true in £ at a world w on a possible occasion o of the utterance of σ if and only if w belongs to £(σ,o). We can say that σ is true in £ on o (without mentioning a world) if and only if the world in which o is located—our actual world

if o is an actual occasion of utterance of σ, or some other world if not—belongs to £(σ,o). We can say that a speaker is truthful in £ if he tries not to utter any sentence σ of £ unless σ would be true in £ on the occasion of his utterance of σ. We can say that a hearer is trusting in £ if he believes an uttered sentence of £ to be true in £ on its occasion of utterance.

We may define an *ambiguous language* £ as a function that assigns to its sentences not single meanings, but finite sets of alternative meanings. (We might or might not want to stipulate that these sets are nonempty.) We can say that a sentence σ is true in £ at w under some meaning if and only if w belongs to some member of £(σ). We can say that σ is true in £ under some meaning if and only if our actual world belongs to some member of £(σ). We can say that someone is (minimally) truthful in £ if he tries not to utter any sentence σ of £ unless σ is true in £ under some meaning. He is trusting if he believes an uttered sentence of £ to be true in £ under some meaning.

We may define a *polymodal language* £ as a function which assigns to its sentences meanings containing two components: a set of worlds, as before; and something we can call a *mood:* indicative, imperative, etc. (It makes no difference what things these are—they might, for instance, be taken as code numbers.) We can say that a sentence σ is indicative, imperative, etc., in £ according as the mood-component of the meaning £(σ) is indicative, imperative, etc. We can say that a sentence σ is true in £, regardless of its mood in £, if and only if our actual world belongs to the set-of-worlds-component of the meaning £(σ). We can say that someone is truthful in £ with respect to indicatives if he tries not to utter any indicative sentence of £ which is not true in £; truthful in £ with respect to imperatives if he tries to act in such a way as to make true in £ any imperative sentence of £ that is addressed to him by someone in a relation of authority to him; and so on for other moods. He is trusting in £ with respect to indicatives if he believes uttered indicative sentences of £ to be true in £; trusting in £ with respect to imperatives if he expects his utterance of an imperative sentence of £ to result in the addressee's acting in such a way as to make that sentence true in £, provided he is in a relation of authority to the addressee; and so on. We can say simply that he is truthful and trusting in £ if he is so with respect to all moods that occur in £. It is by virtue of the various ways in which the various moods enter into the definition of truthfulness and of trust that they deserve the familiar names we have given them. (I am deliberating stretching the ordinary usage of "true," "truthfulness," and "trust" in extending them to nonindicatives. For instance, truthfulness with respect to imperatives is roughly what we might call *obedience* in £.)

Any natural language is simultaneously indexical, ambiguous, and polymodal; I leave the combination of complications as an exercise. Henceforth, for the most part, I shall lapse into ignoring indexicality, ambiguity, and nonindicatives.

Objection: We cannot always discover the meaning of a sentence in a population just by looking into the minds of the members of the population, no matter what we look for there. We may also need some information about the causal origin of what we find in their minds. So, in particular, we cannot always discover the meaning of a sentence in a population just by looking at the conventions prevailing therein. Consider an example: What is the meaning of the sentence "Mik Karthee was wise" in the language of our 137th-century descendants, if all we can find in any of their minds is the inadequate dictionary entry: "Mik Karthee: controversial American politician of the early atomic age"? It depends, we might think, partly on which man stands at the beginning of the long causal chain ending in that inadequate dictionary entry.

Reply: If this doctrine is correct, I can treat it as a subtle sort of indexicality. The set of worlds in which a sentence σ is true in a language £ may depend on features of possible occasions of utterance of σ. One feature of a possible occasion of utterance—admittedly a more recondite feature than the time, place,

or speaker—is the causal history of a dictionary entry in a speaker's mind.

As with other kinds of indexicality, we face a problem of nomenclature. Let a *meaning*₁ be that which an indexical language £ assigns to a sentence σ on a possible occasion *o* of its utterance: £(σ, *o*), a set of worlds on our account. Let a *meaning*₂ be that fixed function whereby the meaning₁ in £ of a sentence σ varies with its occasions of utterance. Which one is a meaning? That is unclear—and it is no clearer which one is a sense, intension, interpretation, truth-condition, or proposition.

The objection says that we sometimes cannot find the meaning₁ of σ on *o* in *P* by looking into the minds of members of *P*. Granted. But what prevents it is that the minds do not contain enough information about *o:* in particular, not enough information about its causal history. We have been given no reason to doubt that we can find the meaning₂ of σ in *P* by looking into minds; and that is all we need do to identify the indexical language used by *P*.

An exactly similar situation arises with more familiar kinds of indexicality. We may be unable to discover the time of an utterance of a tensed sentence by looking into minds, so we may know the meaning₂ of the sentence uttered in the speaker's indexical language without knowing its meaning₁ on the occasion in question.

Objection: It makes no sense to say that a mere string of sounds or of marks can bear a meaning or a truth-value. The proper bearers of meanings and truth-values are particular speech acts.

Reply: I do not say that a string of types of sounds or of marks, by itself, can bear a meaning or truth-value. I say it bears a meaning and truth-value relative to a language, or relative to a population. A particular speech act by itself, on the other hand, can bear a meaning and truth-value, since in most cases it uniquely determines the language that was in use on the occasion of its performance. So can a particular uttered string of vocal sounds, or a particular inscribed string of marks, since in most cases that uniquely determines the particular speech act in which it was produced, which in turn uniquely determines the language.

Objection: It is circular to give an account of meanings in terms of possible worlds. The notion of a possible world must itself be explained in semantic terms. Possible worlds are models of the analytic sentences of some language, or they are the diagrams or theories of such models.[5]

Reply: I do not agree that the notion of a possible world ought to be explained in semantic terms, or that possible worlds ought to be eliminated from our ontology and replaced by their linguistic representatives—models or whatever.

For one thing, the replacement does not work properly. Two worlds indistinguishable in the representing language will receive one and the same representative.

But more important, the replacement is gratuitous. The notion of a possible world is familiar in its own right, philosophically fruitful, and tolerably clear. Possible worlds are deemed mysterious and objectionable because they raise questions we may never know how to answer: are any possible worlds five-dimensional? We seem to think that we do not understand possible worlds at all unless we are capable of omniscience about them—but why should we think that? Sets also raise unanswerable questions, yet most of us do not repudiate sets.

But if you insist on repudiating possible worlds, much of my theory can be adapted to meet your needs. We must suppose that you have already defined truth and analyticity in some base language—that is the price you pay for repudiating possible worlds—and you want to define them in general, for the language of an arbitrary population P. Pick your favorite base language, with any convenient special properties you like: Latin, Esperanto, Begriffsschrift, Semantic Markerese, or what have you. Let's say you pick Latin. Then you may redefine a language as any function from certain strings of sound or of marks to sentences of Latin. A sentence σ of a language £ (in your sense) is true, analytic, etc., if and only if £(σ) is true, analytic, etc., in Latin.

You cannot believe in languages in my sense, since they involve possible worlds. But I can believe in languages in your sense. And I can map your languages onto mine by means of a fixed function from sentences of Latin to sets of worlds. This function is just the language Latin, in my sense. My language £ is the composition of two functions: your language £, and my language Latin. Thus I can accept your approach as part of mine.

Objection: Why all this needless and outmoded hypostasis of meanings? Our ordinary talk about meaning does not commit us to believing in any such entities as meanings, any more than our ordinary talk about actions for the sake of ends commits us to believing in any such entities as sakes.

Reply: Perhaps there are some who hypostatize meanings compulsively, imagining that they could not possibly make sense of our ordinary talk about meaning if they did not. Not I. I hypostatize meanings because I find it convenient to do so, and I have no good reason not to. There is no point in being a part-time nominalist. I am persuaded on independent grounds that I ought to believe in possible worlds and possible beings therein, and that I ought to believe in sets of things I believe in. Once I have these, I have all the entities I could ever want.

Objection: A language consists not only of sentences with their meanings, but also of constituents of sentences—things sentences are made of—with their meanings. And if any language is to be learnable without being finite, it must somehow be determined by finitely many of its constituents and finitely many operations on constituents.

Reply: We may define a class of objects called *grammars*. A grammar Γ is a triple comprising (1) a large finite *lexicon* of *elementary constituents* paired with meanings; (2) a finite set of *combining operations* which build larger constituents by combining smaller constituents, and derive a meaning for the new constituent out of the meanings of the old ones; and (3) a *representing operation* which effectively maps certain constituents onto strings of sounds or of marks. A grammar Γ generates a function which assigns meanings to certain constituents, called *constituents in* Γ. It generates another function which assigns meanings to certain strings of sounds or of marks. Part of this latter function is what we have hitherto called a language. A grammar uniquely determines the language it generates. But a language does not uniquely determine the grammar that generates it, not even when we disregard superficial differences between grammars.

I have spoken of meanings for constituents in a grammar, but what sort of things are these? Referential semantics tried to answer that question. It was a near miss, failing because contingent facts got mixed up with the meanings. The cure, discovered by Carnap,[6] is to do referential semantics not just in our actual world but in every possible world. A meaning for a name can be a function from worlds to possible individuals; for a common noun, a function from worlds to sets; for a sentence, a function from worlds to truth-values (or more simply, the set of worlds where that function takes the value truth). Other derived categories may be defined by their characteristic modes of combination. For instance, an adjective combines with a common noun to make a compound common noun; so its meaning may be a function from common-noun meanings to common-noun meanings, such that the meaning of an adjective-plus-common-noun compound is the value of this function when given as argument the meaning of the common noun being modified. Likewise a verb phrase takes a name to make a sentence; so its meaning may be a function that takes the meaning of the name as argument to give the meaning of the sentence as value. An adverb (of one sort) takes a verb phrase to make a verb phrase, so its meaning may be a function from verb-phrase meanings to verb-phrase meanings. And so on, as far as need be, to more and more complicated derived categories.[7]

If you repudiate possible worlds, an alternative course is open to you: let the meanings for constituents in a grammar be phrases of Latin, or whatever your favorite base language may be.

A grammar, for us, is a semantically interpreted grammar—just as a language is a semantically interpreted language. We shall not be concerned with what are called grammars or languages in a purely syntactic sense. My definition of a grammar is meant to be general enough to encompass transformational or phrase-structure grammars for natural language[8] (when provided with semantic interpretations) as well as systems of formation and valuation rules for formalized languages. Like my previous definition of a language, my definition of a grammar is too general: it gives a large superset of the interesting grammars.

A grammar, like a language, is a set-theoretical entity which can be discussed in complete abstraction from human affairs. Since a grammar generates a unique language, all the semantic concepts we earlier defined relative to a language £—sentencehood, truth, analyticity, etc.—could just as well have been defined relative to a grammar Γ. We can also handle other semantic concepts pertaining to constituents, or to the constituent structure of sentences.

We can define the meaning in Γ, denotation in Γ, etc., of a subsentential constituent in Γ. We can define the meaning in Γ, denotation in Γ, etc., of a *phrase:* a string of sounds or of marks representing a subsentential constituent in Γ via the representing operation of Γ. We can define something we may call the *fine structure of meaning* in Γ of a sentence or phrase: the manner in which the meaning of the sentence or phrase is derived from the meanings of its constituents and the way it is built out of them. Thus we can take account of the sense in which, for instance, different analytic sentences are said to differ in meaning.

Now the objection can be restated: what ought to be called a language is what I have hitherto called a grammar, not what I have hitherto called a language. Different grammar, different language—at least if we ignore superficial differences between grammars. Verbal disagreement aside, the place I gave to my so-called languages ought to have been given instead to my so-called grammars. Why not begin by saying what it is for a grammar Γ to be used by a population *P?* Then we could go on to define sentencehood, truth, analyticity, etc., in *P* as sentencehood, truth, analyticity, etc., in whatever grammar is used by *P*. This approach would have the advantage that we could handle the semantics of constituents in a population in an exactly similar way. We could say that a constituent or phrase has a certain meaning, denotation, etc., in *P* if it has that meaning, denotation, etc., in whatever grammar is used by *P*. We could say that a sentence or phrase has a certain fine structure of meaning in *P* if it has it in whatever grammar is used by *P*.

Unfortunately, I know of no promising way to make objective sense of the assertion that a grammar Γ is used by a population *P* whereas another grammar Γ′, which generates the same language as Γ, is not. I have tried to say how there are facts about *P* which objectively select the languages used by *P*. I am not sure there are facts about *P* which objectively select privileged grammars for those languages. It is easy enough to define truthfulness and trust in a grammar, but that will not help: a convention of truthfulness and trust in Γ will also be a convention of truthfulness and trust in Γ′ whenever Γ and Γ′ generate the same language.

I do not propose to discard the notion of the meaning in *P* of a constituent or phrase, or the fine structure of meaning in *P* of a sentence. To propose that would be absurd. But I hold that these notions depend on our methods of evaluating grammars, and therefore are no clearer and no more objective than our notion of a *best* grammar for a given language. For I would say that a grammar Γ is used by *P* if and only if Γ is a best grammar for a language £ that is used by *P* in virtue of a convention in *P* of truthfulness and trust in £; and I would define the meaning in *P* of a constituent or phrase, and the fine structure of meaning in *P* of a sentence, accordingly.

The notions of a language used by *P,* of a meaning of a sentence in *P,* and so on, are independent of our evaluation of grammars. Therefore I take these as primary. The point is not to refrain from ever saying anything that depends on the evaluation of grammars. The point is to do so only when we must, and that is why I have concentrated on languages rather than grammars.

We may meet little practical difficulty with the semantics of constituents in populations, even if its foundations are as infirm as I fear. It may often happen that all the grammars anyone might call best for a given language will agree on the meaning of a given constituent. Yet there is trouble to be found: Quine's examples of indeterminacy of reference[9] seem to be disagreements in constituent semantics between alternative good grammars for one language. We should regard with suspicion any method that purports to settle objectively whether, in some tribe, "gavagai" is true of temporally continuant rabbits or timeslices thereof. You can give their language a good grammar of either kind—and that's that.

It is useful to divide the claimed indeterminacy of constituent semantics into three separate indeterminacies. We begin with undoubted objective fact: the dependence of the subject's behavioral output on his input of sensory stimulation (both as it actually is and as it might have been) together with all the physical laws and anatomical facts that explain it. (a) This information either determines or underdetermines the subject's system of propositional attitudes: in particular, his beliefs and desires. (b) These propositional attitudes either determine or underdetermine the truth conditions of full sentences—what I have here called his language. (c) The truth-conditions of full sentences either determine or underdetermine the meanings of subsentential constituents—what I have here called his grammar.

My present discussion has been directed at the middle step, from beliefs and desires to truth conditions for full sentences. I have said that the former determine the latter—provided (what need not be the case) that the beliefs and desires of the subject and his fellows are such as to comprise a fully determinate convention of truthfulness and trust in some definite language. I have said nothing here about the determinacy of the first step; and I am inclined to share in Quine's doubts about the determinacy of the third step.

Objection: Suppose that whenever anyone

is party to a convention of truthfulness and trust in any language £, his competence to be party to that convention—to conform, to expect conformity, etc.—is due to his possession of some sort of unconscious internal representation of a grammar for £. That is a likely hypothesis, since it best explains what we know about linguistic competence. In particular, it explains why experience with some sentences leads spontaneously to expectations involving others. But on that hypothesis, we might as well bypass the conventions of language and say that £ is used by P if and only if everyone in P possesses an internal representation of a grammar for £.

Reply: In the first place, the hypothesis of internally represented grammars is not an explanation—best or otherwise—of anything. Perhaps it is *part* of some theory that best explains what we know about linguistic competence; we can't judge until we hear something about what the rest of the theory is like.

Nonetheless, I am ready enough to believe in internally represented grammars. But I am much less certain that there are internally represented grammars than I am that languages are used by populations; and I think it makes sense to say that languages might be used by populations even if there were no internally represented by grammars. I can tentatively agree that £ is used by P if and only if everyone in P possesses an internal representation of a grammar for £, if that is offered as a scientific hypothesis. But I cannot accept it as any sort of analysis of "£ is used by P," since the analysandum clearly could be true although the analysans was false.

Objection: The notion of a convention of truthfulness and trust in £ is a needless complication. Why not say, straightforwardly, that £ is used by P if and only if there prevails in P a convention to bestow upon each sentence of £ the meaning that £ assigns to it? Or, indeed, that a grammar Γ of £ is used by P if and only if there prevails in P a convention to bestow upon each constituent in Γ the meaning that Γ assigns to it?

Reply: A convention, as I have defined it, is a regularity in action, or in action and belief. If that feature of the definition were given up,

I do not see how to salvage any part of my theory of conventions. It is essential that a convention is a regularity such that conformity by others gives one a reason to conform; and such a reason must either be a practical reason for acting or an epistemic reason for believing. What other kind of reason is there?

Yet there is no such thing as an action of bestowing a meaning (except for an irrelevant sort of action that is performed not by language-users but by creators of language) so we cannot suppose that language-using populations have conventions to perform such actions. Neither does bestowal of meaning consist in forming some belief. Granted, bestowal of meaning is conventional in the sense that it depends on convention: the meanings would have been different if the conventions of truthfulness and trust had been different. But bestowal of meaning is not an action done in conformity to a convention, since it is not an action, and it is not a belief-formation in conformity to a convention, since it is not a belief-formation.

Objection: The beliefs and desires that constitute a convention are inaccessible mental entities, just as much as hypothetical internal representations of grammars are. It would be best if we could say in purely behavioristic terms what it is for a language £ to be used by a population P. We might be able to do this by referring to the way in which members of P would answer counterfactual questionnaires; or by referring to the way in which they would or would not assent to sentences under deceptive sensory stimulation; or by referring to the way in which they would intuitively group sentences into similarity-classes; or in some other way.

Reply: Suppose we succeeded in giving a behavioristic operational definition of the relation "£ is used by P." This would not help us to understand what it is for £ to be used by P; for we would have to understand that already, and also know a good deal of common-sense psychology, in order to check that the operational definition was a definition of what it is supposed to be a definition of. If we did not know what it meant for £ to be used by P, we would not know what sort of behavior on the part of members of P would indicate that £ was used by P.

Objection: The conventions of language are nothing more nor less than our famously obscure old friends, the rules of language, renamed.

Reply: A convention of truthfulness and trust in £ might well be called a rule, though it lacks many features that have sometimes been thought to belong to the essence of rules. It is not promulgated by any authority. It is not enforced by means of sanctions except to the extent that, because one has some sort of reason to conform, something bad may happen if one does not. It is nowhere codified and therefore is not "laid down in the course of teaching the language" or "appealed to in the course of criticizing a person's linguistic performance."[10] Yet it is more than a mere regularity holding "as a rule"; it is a regularity accompanied and sustained by a special kind of system of beliefs and desires.

A convention of truthfulness and trust in £ might have as consequences other regularities which were conventions of language in their own right: specializations of the convention to certain special situations. (For instance, a convention of truthfulness in £ on weekdays.) Such derivative conventions of language might also be called rules; some of them might stand a better chance of being codified than the overall convention which subsumes them.

However, there are other so-called rules of language which are not conventions of language and are not in the least like conventions of language: for instance, "rules" of syntax and semantics. They are not even regularities and cannot be formulated as imperatives. They might better be described not as rules, but as clauses in the definitions of entities which are to be mentioned in rules: clauses in the definition of a language £, of the act of being truthful in £, of the act of stating that the moon is blue, etc.

Thus the conventions of language might properly be called rules, but it is more informative and less confusing to call them conventions.

Objection: Language is not conventional. We have found that human capacities for language acquisition are highly specific and dictate the form of any language that humans can learn and use.

Reply: It may be that there is less conventionality than we used to think: fewer features of language which depend on convention, more which are determined by our innate capacities and therefore are common to all languages which are genuine alternatives to our actual language. But there are still conventions of language; and there are still convention-dependent features of language, differing from one alternative possible convention of language to another. That is established by the diversity of actual languages. There are conventions of language so long as the regularity of truthfulness in a given language has even a single alternative.

Objection: Unless a language-user is also a set-theorist, he cannot expect his fellows to conform to a regularity of truthfulness and trust in a certain language £. For to conform to this regularity is to bear a relation to a certain esoteric entity: a set of ordered pairs of sequences of sound-types or of mark-types and sets of possible worlds (or something more complicated still, if £ is a natural language with indexicality, ambiguity, and nonindicatives). The common man has no concept of any such entity. Hence he can have no expectations regarding such an entity.

Reply: The common man need not have any concept of £ in order to expect his fellows to be truthful and trusting in £. He need only have suitable particular expectations about how they might act, and how they might form beliefs, in various situations. He can tell whether any actual or hypothetical particular action or belief-formation on their part is compatible with his expectations. He expects them to conform to a regularity of truthfulness and trust in £ if any particular activity or belief-formation that would fit his expectations would fall under what we—but not *he*—could describe as conformity to that regularity.

It may well be that his elaborate, infinite system of potential particular expectations can only be explained on the hypothesis that he has some unconscious mental entity somehow analogous to a general concept of £—say, an internally represented grammar. But it does not matter whether this is so or not. We are concerned only to say what system of expectations a normal member of a language-using population must have. We need not engage in psychological speculation about how those expectations are generated.

Objection: If there are conventions of language, those who are party to them should know what they are. Yet no one can fully describe the conventions of language to which he is supposedly a party.

Reply: He may nevertheless know what they are. It is enough to be able to recognize conformity and nonconformity to his convention, and to be able to try to conform to it. We know ever so many things we cannot put into words.

Objection: Use of language is almost never a rational activity. We produce and respond to utterances by habit, not as the result of any sort of reasoning or deliberation.

Reply: An action may be rational, and may be explained by the agent's beliefs and desires, even though that action was done by habit, and the agent gave no thought to the beliefs or desires which were his reason for acting. A habit may be under the agent's rational control in this sense: if that habit ever ceased to serve the agent's desires according to his beliefs, it would at once be overridden and corrected by conscious reasoning. Action done by a habit of this sort is both habitual and rational. Likewise for habits of believing. Our normal use of language is rational, since it is under rational control.

Perhaps use of language by young children is not a rational activity. Perhaps it results from habits which would not be overridden if they ceased to serve the agent's desires according to his beliefs. If that is so, I would deny that these children have yet become party to conventions of language, and I would deny that they have yet become normal members of a language-using population. Perhaps language is first acquired and afterward becomes conventional. That would not conflict with anything I have said. I am not concerned with the way in which language is acquired, only with the condition of a normal member of a language-using population when he is done acquiring language.

Objection: Language could not have originated by convention. There could not have been an agreement to begin being truthful and trusting in a certain chosen language, unless some previous language had already been available for use in making the agreement.

Reply: The first language could not have originated by an agreement, for the reason given. But that is not to say that language cannot be conventional. A convention is so-called because of the way it persists, not because of the way it originated. A convention need not originate by convention—that is, by agreement—though many conventions do originate by agreement, and others could originate by agreement even if they actually do not. In saying that language is convention-governed, I say nothing whatever about the origins of language.

Objection: A man isolated all his life from others might begin—through genius or a miracle—to use language, say to keep a diary. (This would be an accidentally private language, not the necessarily private language Wittgenstein is said to have proved to be impossible.) In this case, at least, there would be no convention involved.

Reply: Taking the definition literally, there would be no convention. But there would be something very similar. The isolated man conforms to a certain regularity at many different times. He knows at each of these times that he has conformed to that regularity in the past, and he has an interest in uniformity over time, so he continues to conform to that regularity instead of to any of various alternative regularities that would have done about as well if he had started out using them. He knows at all times that this is so, knows that he knows at all times that this is so, and so on. We might think of the situation as one in which a convention prevails in the population of different time-slices of the same man.

Objection: It is circular to define the meaning in P of sentences in terms of the beliefs held by members of P. For presumably the members of P think in their language. For instance, they hold beliefs by accepting suitable sentences of their language. If we do not already know the meaning in *P* of a sentence, we do not know what belief a member of *P* would hold by accepting that sentence.

Reply: It may be true that men think in language, and that to hold a belief is to accept a sentence of one's language. But it does not follow that belief should be analyzed as acceptance of sentences. It should not be. Even if men do in fact think in language, they might not. It is at least possible that men—like beasts—might hold beliefs otherwise than by accepting sentences. (I shall not say here how I think belief should be analyzed.) No circle arises from the contingent truth that a member of *P* holds beliefs by accepting sentences, so long as we can specify his beliefs without mentioning the sentences he accepts. We can do this for men, as we can for beasts.

Objection: Suppose a language £ is used by a population of inveterate liars, who are untruthful in £ more often than not. There would not be even a regularity—still less a convention, which implies a regularity—of truthfulness and trust in £.

Reply: I deny that £ is used by the population of liars. I have undertaken to follow ordinary usage only where it is determinate; and, once it is appreciated just how extraordinary the situation would have to be, I do not believe that ordinary usage is determinate in this case. There are many similarities to clear cases in which a language is used by a population, and it is understandable that we should feel some inclination to classify this case along with them. But there are many important differences as well.

Although I deny that the population of liars *collectively* uses £, I am willing to say that each liar *individually* may use £, provided that he falsely believes that he is a member—albeit an exceptional, untruthful member—of a population wherein there prevails a convention of truthfulness and trust in £. He is in a position like that of a madman who thinks he belongs to a population which uses £, and behaves accordingly, and so can be said to use £, although in reality all the other members of this £-using population are figments of his imagination.

Objection: Suppose the members of a population are untruthful in their language £ more often than not, not because they lie, but because they go in heavily for irony, metaphor, hyperbole, and such. It is hard to deny that the language £ is used by such a population.

Reply: I claim that these people *are* truthful in their language £, though they are not *literally truthful* in £. To be literally truthful in £ is to be truthful in another language related to £, a language we can call literal-£. The relation between £ and literal-£ is as follows: a good way to describe £ is to start by specifying literal-£ and then to describe £ as obtained by certain systematic departures from literal-£. This two-stage specification of £ by way of literal-£ may turn out to be much simpler than any direct specification of £.

Objection: Suppose they are often untruthful in £ because they are not communicating at all. They are joking, or telling tall tales, or telling white lies as a matter of social ritual. In these situations, there is neither truthfulness nor trust in £. Indeed, it is common knowledge that there is not.

Reply: Perhaps I can say the same sort of thing about this non-serious language use as I did about nonliteral language use. That is: their seeming untruthfulness in nonserious situations is untruthfulness not in the language £ that they actually use, but only in a simplified approximation to £. We may specify £ by first specifying the approximation language, then listing the signs and features of context by which nonserious language use can be recognized, then specifying that when these signs or features are present, what would count as untruths in the approximation language do not count as such in £ itself. Perhaps they are automatically true in £, regardless of the facts; perhaps they cease to count as indicative.

Example: what would otherwise be an untruth may not be one if said by a child with crossed fingers. Unfortunately, the signs and features of context by which we recognize nonserious language use are seldom as simple, standardized, and conventional as that. While they must find a place somewhere in a full account of the phenomenon of language, it may be inexpedient to burden the specification of £ with them.

Perhaps it may be enough to note that these situations of non-serious language use must be at least somewhat exceptional if we are to have anything like a clear case of use of £; and to recall that the definition of a convention was loose enough to tolerate some exceptions. We could take the nonserious cases simply as violations—explicable and harmless ones—of the conventions of language.

There is a third alternative, requiring a modification in my theory. We may say that a *serious communication situation* exists with respect to a sentence σ of £ whenever it is true, and common knowledge between a speaker and a hearer, that (a) the speaker does, and the hearer does not, know whether σ is true in £; (b) the hearer wants to know; (c) the speaker wants the hearer to know; and (d) neither the speaker nor the hearer has other (comparably strong) desires as to whether or not the speaker utters σ. (Note that when there is a serious communication situation with respect to σ, there is one also with respect to synonyms or contradictories in £ of σ, and probably also with respect to other logical relatives in £ of σ.) Then we may say that the convention whereby P uses £ is a convention of truthfulness and trust in £ in serious communication situations. That is: when a serious communication situation exists with respect to σ, then the speaker tries not to utter σ unless it is true in £, and the hearer responds, if σ is uttered, by coming to believe that σ is true in £. If that much is a convention in P, it does not matter what goes on in other situations: they use £.

The definition here given of a serious communication resembles that of a signaling problem in *Convention*, chapter IV, the difference being that the hearer may respond by belief-formation only, rather than by what speaker and hearer alike take to be appropriate action. If this modification were adopted, it would bring my general account of language even closer to my account in *Convention* of the special case of signaling.

Objection: Truthfulness and trust cannot be a convention. What could be the alternative to uniform truthfulness—uniform untruthfulness, perhaps? But it seems that if such untruthfulness were not intended to deceive, and did not deceive, then it too would be truthfulness.

Reply: The convention is not the regularity of truthfulness and trust *simpliciter*. It is the regularity of truthfulness and trust in some particular language £. Its alternatives are possible regularities of truthfulness and trust in other languages. A regularity of uniform untruthfulness and non-trust in a language £ can be redescribed as a regularity of truthfulness and trust in a different language anti-£ complementary to £. Anti-£ has exactly the same sentences as £, but with opposite truth conditions. Hence the true sentences of anti-£ are all and only the untrue sentences of £.

There is a different regularity that we may call a regularity of truthfulness and trust *simpliciter*. That is the regularity of being truthful and trusting in whichever language is used by one's fellows. This regularity neither is a convention nor depends on convention. If any language whatever is used by a population *P*, then a regularity (perhaps with exceptions) of truthfulness and trust *simpliciter* prevails in *P*.

Objection: Even truthfulness and trust in £ cannot be a convention. One conforms to a convention, on my account, because doing so answers to some sort of interest. But a decent man is truthful in £ if his fellows are, whether or not it is in his interest. For he recognizes that he is under a moral obligation to be truthful in £: an obligation to reciprocate the benefits he has derived from others' truthfulness in £, or something of that sort. Truthfulness in £ may bind the decent man against his own interest. It is more like a social contract than a convention.

Reply: The objection plays on a narrow sense of "interest" in which only selfish interests count. We commonly adopt a wider sense. We count also altruistic interests and interests springing from one's recognition of obligations. It is this wider sense that should be understood in the definition of convention. In this wider sense, it is nonsense to think of an obligation as outweighing one's interests. Rather, the obligation provides one interest which may outweigh the other interests.

A convention of truthfulness and trust in £ is sustained by a mixture of selfish interests, altruistic interests, and interests derived from obligation. Usually all are present in strength; perhaps any one would be enough to sustain the convention. But occasionally truthfulness in £ answers only to interests derived from obligation and goes against one's selfish or even altruistic interests. In such a case, only a decent man will have an interest in remaining truthful in £. But I dare say such cases are not as common as moralists might imagine. A convention of truthfulness and trust among scoundrels might well be sustained—with occasional lapses—by selfish interests alone.

A convention persists because everyone has reason to conform if others do. If the convention is a regularity in action, this is to say that it persists because everyone prefers general conformity rather than almost-general conformity with himself as the exception. A (demythologized) social contract may also be described as a regularity sustained by a general preference for general conformity, but the second term of the preference is different. Everyone prefers general conformity over a certain state of general nonconformity called the state of nature. This general preference sets up an obligation to reciprocate the benefits derived from others' conformity, and that obligation creates an interest in conforming which sustains the social contract. The objection suggests that, among decent men, truthfulness in £ is a social contract. I agree; but there is no reason why it cannot be a social contract and a convention as well, and I think it is.

Objection: Communication cannot be explained by conventions of truthfulness alone. If I utter a sentence σ of our language £, you—expecting me to be truthful in £—will conclude that I take σ to be true in £. If you think I am well informed, you will also conclude that probably σ is true in £. But you will draw other conclusions as well, based on your legitimate assumption that it is for some good reason that I chose to utter σ rather than

remain silent, and rather than utter any of the other sentences of £ that I also take to be true in £. I can communicate all sorts of misinformation by exploiting your beliefs about my conversational purposes, without ever being untruthful in £. Communication depends on principles of helpfulness and relevance as well as truthfulness.

Reply: All this does not conflict with anything I have said. We do conform to conversational regularities of helpfulness and relevance. But these regularities are not independent conventions of language; they result from our convention of truthfulness and trust in £ together with certain general facts—not dependent on any convention—about our conversational purposes and our beliefs about one another. Since they are byproducts of a convention of truthfulness and trust, it is unnecessary to mention them separately in specifying the conditions under which a language is used by a population.

Objection: Let £ be the language used in P, and let £− be some fairly rich fragment of £. That is, the sentences of £− are many but not all of the sentences of £ (in an appropriate special sense if £ is infinite); and any sentence of both has the same meaning in both. Then £− also turns out to be a language used by P; for by my definition there prevails in P a convention of truthfulness and trust in £−, sustained by an interest in communication. Not one but many—perhaps infinitely many—languages are used by P.

Reply: That is so, but it is no problem. Why not say that any rich fragment of a language used by P is itself a used language?

Indeed, we will need to say such things when P is linguistically inhomogeneous. Suppose, for instance, that P divides into two classes: the learned and the vulgar. Among the learned there prevails a convention of truthfulness and trust in a language £; among P as a whole there does not, but there does prevail a convention of truthfulness and trust in a rich fragment £− of £. We wish to say that the learned have a common language with the vulgar, but that is so only if £−, as well as £, counts as a language used by the learned.

Another case: the learned use $£_1$, the vulgar

use £$_2$, neither is included in the other, but there is extensive overlap. Here £$_1$ and £$_2$ are to be the most inclusive languages used by the respective classes. Again we wish to say that the learned and the vulgar have a common language: in particular, the largest fragment common to £$_1$ and £$_2$. That can be so only if this largest common fragment counts as a language used by the vulgar, by the learned, and by the whole population.

I agree that we often do not count the fragments; we can speak of *the* language of *P*, meaning by this not the one and only thing that is a language used by *P*, but rather the most inclusive language used by *P*. O⁻ we could mean something else: the union of all the languages used by substantial subpopulations of *P*, provided that some quite large fragment of this union is used by (more or less) all of *P*. Note that the union as a whole need not be used at all, in my primary sense, either by *P* or by any subpopulation of *P*. Thus in my example of the last paragraph, *the* language of *P* might be taken either as the largest common fragment of £$_1$ and £$_2$ or as the union of £$_1$ and £$_2$.

Further complications arise. Suppose that half of the population of a certain town uses English, and also uses basic Welsh; while the other half uses Welsh, and also uses basic English. The most inclusive language used by the entire population is the union of basic Welsh and basic English. The union of languages used by substantial subpopulations is the union of English and Welsh, and the proviso is satisfied that some quite large fragment of this union is used by the whole population. Yet we would be reluctant to say that either of these unions is the language of the population of the town. We might say that Welsh and English are the two languages of the town, or that basic English and basic Welsh are. It is odd to call either of the two language-unions a language; though once they are called that, it is no further oddity to say that one or the other of them is the language of the town. There are two considerations. First: English, or Welsh, or basic English, or basic Welsh, can be given a satisfactory unified grammar; whereas the language-unions cannot. Second: English, or Welsh, or basic Welsh, or basic English, is (in either of the senses I have explained) the language of a large population outside the town; whereas the language-unions are not. I am not sure which of the two considerations should be emphasized in saying when a language is the language of a population.

Objection: Let £ be the language of *P;* that is, the language that ought to count as the most inclusive language used by *P*. (Assume that *P* is linguistically homogenous.) Let £+ be obtained by adding garbage to £: some extra sentences, very long and difficult to pronounce, and hence never uttered in *P*, with arbitrary chosen meanings in £+. Then it seems that £+ is a language used by *P*, which is absurd.

A sentence never uttered at all is *a fortiori* never uttered untruthfully. So truthfulness-as-usual in £ plus truthfulness-by-silence on the garbage sentences constitutes a kind of truthfulness in £+; and the expectation thereof constitutes trust in £+. Therefore we have a prevailing regularity of truthfulness and trust in £+. This regularity qualifies as a convention in *P* sustained by an interest in communication.

Reply: Truthfulness-by-silence is truthfulness, and expectation thereof is expectation of truthfulness; but expectation of truthfulness-by-silence is not yet trust. Expectation of (successful) truthfulness—expectation that a given sentence will not be uttered falsely—is a necessary but not sufficient condition for trust. There is no regularity of trust in £+, so far as the garbage sentences are concerned. Hence there is no convention of truthfulness and trust in £+, and £+ is not used by *P*.

For trust, one must be able to take an utterance of a sentence as evidence that the sentence is true. That is so only if one's degree of belief that the sentence will be uttered falsely is low, not only absolutely, but as a fraction of one's degree of belief—perhaps already very low—that the sentence will be uttered at all. Further, this must be so not merely because one believes in advance that the sentence is probably true: one's degree of belief that the sentence will be uttered falsely must be substantially lower than the product of one's degree of belief that the sentence will be uttered times one's prior degree of belief that it is false. A garbage sentence of £+ will not meet this last requirement, not even if one believes to high degrees both that it is true in £+ and that it never will be uttered.

This objection was originally made, by Stephen Schiffer, against my former view that conventions of language are conventions of truthfulness. I am inclined to think that it succeeds as a counterexample to that view. I agree that £+ is not used by *P,* in any reasonable sense, but I have not seen any way to avoid conceding that £+ is a possible language—it might *really* be used—and that there does prevail in *P* a convention of truthfulness in £+, sustained by an interest in communication. Here we have another advantage of the present account over my original one.

Objection: A sentence either is or isn't analytic in a given language, and a language either is or isn't conventionally adopted by a given population. Hence there is no way for the analytic–synthetic distinction to be unsharp. But not only can it be unsharp; it usually is, at least in cases of interest to philosophers. A sharp analytic–synthetic distinction is available only relative to particular rational reconstructions of ordinary language.

Reply: One might try to explain unsharp analyticity by a theory of degrees of convention. Conventions do admit of degree in a great many ways: by the strengths of the beliefs and desires involved, and by the fraction of exceptions to the many almost-universal quantifications in the definition of convention. But this will not help much. It is easy to imagine unsharp analyticity even in a population whose conventions of language are conventions to the highest degree in every way.

One might try to explain unsharp analyticity by recalling that we may not know whether some worlds are really possible. If a sentence is true in our language in all worlds except some worlds of doubtful possibility, then that sentence will be of doubtful analyticity. But this will not help much either.

Unsharp analyticity usually seems to arise because we cannot decide whether a sentence would be true in some bizarre but clearly possible world.

A better explanation would be that our convention of language is not exactly a convention of truthfulness and trust in a single language, as I have said so far. Rather it is a convention of truthfulness and trust in whichever we please of some cluster of similar languages: languages with more or less the same sentences, and more or less the same truth-values for the sentences in worlds close to our actual world, but with increasing divergence in truth-values as we go to increasingly remote, bizarre worlds. The convention confines us to the cluster, but leaves us with indeterminacies whenever the languages of the cluster disagree. We are free to settle these indeterminacies however we like. Thus an ordinary, open-textured, imprecise language is a sort of blur of precise languages—a region, not a point, in the space of languages. Analyticity is sharp in each language of our cluster. But when different languages of our cluster disagree on the analyticity of a sentence, then that sentence is unsharply analytic among us.

Rational reconstructions have been said to be irrelevant to philosophical problems arising in ordinary, unreconstructed language. My hypothesis of conventions of truthfulness and trust in language-clusters provides a defense against this accusation. Reconstruction is not—or not always—departure from ordinary language. Rather it is selection from ordinary language: isolation of one precise language, or of a subcluster, out of the language-cluster wherein we have a convention of truthfulness and trust.

Objection: The thesis and the antithesis pertain to different subjects. The thesis, in which languages are regarded as semantic systems, belongs to the philosophy of artificial languages. The antithesis, in which language is regarded as part of human natural history, belongs to the philosophy of natural language.

Reply: Not so. *Both* accounts—just like almost any account of almost anything—can most easily be applied to simple, artificial, imaginary examples. Language-games are just as artificial as formalized calculi.

According to the theory I have presented, philosophy of language is a single subject. The thesis and antithesis have been the property of rival schools; but in fact they are complementary essential ingredients in any adequate account either of languages or of language.

NOTES

1. H. P. Grice, "Meaning," *Philosophical Review*, 66(1957):377–388.
2. This proposal is adapted from the theory given in Erik Stenius, "Mood and Language-Game," *Synthese*, 17(1967):254–274.
3. (Harvard University Press, Cambridge, Mass.: 1969). A similar account was given in the original version of this paper, written in 1968.
4. Personal communication, 1971. Bennett himself uses the broadened concept of convention differently, wishing to exhibit conventional meaning as a special case of Gricean meaning. See his "The Meaning-Nominalist Strategy," *Foundations of Language*, 10(1973):141–168.
5. Possible worlds are taken as models in S. Kripke, "A Completeness Theorem in Modal Logic," *Journal of Symbolic Logic*, 24(1959):1–15; in Carnap's recent work on semantics and inductive logic, discussed briefly in sections 9, 10, and 25 of "Replies and Systematic Expositions," *The Philosophy of Rudolf Carnap*, ed. P. Schilpp; and elsewhere. Worlds are taken as state-descriptions—diagrams of models—in Carnap's earlier work: for instance, section 18 of *Introduction to Semantics*. Worlds are taken as complete, consistent novels—theories of models—in R. Jeffrey, *The Logic of Decision*, section 12.8.
6. "Replies and Systematic Expositions," section 9.v. A better-known presentation of essentially the same idea is in S. Kripke, "Semantical Considerations on Modal Logic," *Acta Philosophica Fennica*, 16(1963):83–94.
7. See my "General Semantics," *Synthese*, 22 (1970):18–67.
8. For a description of the sort of grammars I have in mind (minus the semantic interpretation) see N. Chomsky, *Aspects of the Theory of Syntax*, and G. Harman, "Generative Grammars without Transformation Rules," *Language*, 37 (1963):597–616. My "constituents" correspond to semantically interpreted deep phrase-markers, or sub-trees thereof, in a transformational grammar. My "representing operation" may work in several steps and thus subsumes both the transformational and the phonological components of a transformational grammar.
9. W. V. Quine, "Ontological Relativity," *Journal of Philosophy*, 65(1968):185–212; *Word and Object*, pp. 68–79.
10. P. Ziff, *Semantic Analysis*, pp. 34–35.

NOAM CHOMSKY

Before entering into the question of language and problems of knowledge, it may be useful to clarify some terminological and conceptual issues concerning the concepts "language" and "knowledge" which, I think, have tended to obscure understanding and to engender point-less controversy.

To begin with, what do we mean by "language"? There is an intuitive common-sense concept that serves well enough for ordinary life, but it is a familiar observation that every serious approach to the study of language departs from it quite sharply. It is doubtful that the common-sense concept is even coherent, nor would it matter for ordinary purposes if it were not. It is, in the first place, an obscure sociopolitical concept, having to do with colors on maps and the like, and a concept with equally obscure normative and teleological elements, a fact that becomes clear when we ask what lan-guage a child of five, or a foreigner learning English, is speaking—surely not my lan-guage, nor any other language, in ordinary usage. Rather we say that the child and foreigner are "on their way" to learning English, and the child will "get there," though the foreigner probably will not, ex-cept partially. But if all adults were to die from some sudden disease, and children of five or under were to survive, whatever it is

that they were speaking would become a typical human language, though one that we say does not now exist. Ordinary usage breaks down at this point, not surprisingly: its concepts are not designed for inquiry into the nature of language.

Or consider the question of what are called "errors." Many, perhaps most speakers of what we call "English" believe that the word "livid," which they have learned form the phrase "livid with rage," means "red" or "flushed." The dictionary tells us that it means "pale." In ordinary usage, we say that the speakers are wrong about the meaning of this word of their language, and we would say this even if 95%, or perhaps 100% of them made this "error." On the other hand, if dictionaries and other normative documents were de-stroyed with all memory of them, "livid" would then mean "flushed" in the new lan-guage. Whatever all this might mean, it plainly has nothing to do with an eventual science of language, but involves other no-tions having to do with authority, class struc-ture, and the like. Unless the concept of "community norms" or "conventions" is clari-fied in some manner yet to be addressed—if this is possible at all in a coherent way—one should be cautious about accepting arguments concerning meaning that make free use of such ideas, taking them to be clear enough;

This is a slightly revised version of a paper delivered at a conference in Madrid, April 28, 1986.

they are not. We understand this easily enough in connection with pronunciation; thus to say that the pronunciation of one dialect is "right" while that of another is "wrong" makes as much sense as saying that it is "right" to talk Spanish and "wrong" to talk English. Such judgments, whatever their status, plainly have nothing to do with the study of language and mind, or human biology; or more accurately, they have to do with some vastly broader inquiry into the interaction of cognitive systems, some complex that is well beyond our current grasp and that we are unlikely ever to comprehend unless the elements that enter into it are identified and understood. The question of "error of interpretation" or "misuse" has much the same status.

Note that a person can be mistaken about his or her own language. Thus if "livid" in fact means "flushed" in my current language, and I tell you that it means "pale" in my language, then I am wrong, just as I would be wrong if I told you, perhaps in honest error, that in my language "whom" is always used for a direct object, not "who," or if I were to deny some feature of the urban dialect that I speak natively. Judgments about oneself are as fallible as any others, but that is not what is at issue here.

All of this is, or should be, commonplace. Correspondingly, every serious approach to the study of language departs from the common-sense usage, replacing it by some technical concept. The choices have generally been questionable ones. The general practice has been to define "language" as what I have called elsewhere "E-language," where "E" is intended to suggest "extensional" and "externalized." The definition is "extensional" in that it takes language to be a set of objects of some kind, and it is "externalized" in the sense that language, so defined, is external to the mind/brain. Thus a set, however chosen, is plainly external to the mind/brain.

As a side comment, let me say that I will use mentalistic terminology freely, but without any dubious metaphysical burden; as I will use the terms, talk about mind is simply talk about the brain at some level of abstraction that we believe to be appropriate for under-

standing crucial and essential properties of neural systems, on a par with discussion in nineteenth-century chemistry of valence, benzene rings, elements, and the like, abstract entities of some sort that one hoped would be related, ultimately, to the then-unknown physical entities. To say that the world includes elements with valence of two which therefore behave in a certain way, or benzene rings, etc., is to say that whatever the elementary constituents of the world may be, their properties are such that they are correctly described in these terms at this level of abstraction. To say that the world includes such abstract entities as neural nets (it is the abstract structure that we take to be roughly invariant through time or among individuals, not the molecules, specific orientations, etc.) or mental representations is to say something similar about the brain. Mentalistic inquiry, so understood, is justified insofar as it yields insight and theoretical understanding of phenomena that concern us, and from another point of view, insofar as it facilitates inquiry into brain mechanisms. Just as nineteenth-century chemistry provided a guide to subsequent investigations of more "fundamental" physical entities, so one can expect the same to be true of the brain sciences, which have little idea what to seek without some awareness of the properties of the yet-to-be-discovered mechanisms. Mentalism, in short, is just normal scientific practice, and an essential step towards integrating the study of the phenomena that concern us into the more "fundamental" natural sciences. I might add that it is generally pointless to demand too much clarity in these matters. As the history of physics and even mathematics shows, clarity about foundational issues (e.g., in mathematics, the notions of limit or even proof) develops as a result of inquiry and is not a necessary preliminary to it; foundational questions and questions of conceptual clarity are often premature, and can often be approached and settled only as research progresses without too much concern about exactly what one is talking about.

A typical formulation of a notion of E-language is the definition of "language" by the distinguished American linguist Leonard Bloomfield as "the totality of utterances that can be made in a speech community," the latter another abstract entity, assumed to be homogeneous.[1] Another approach, based ultimately on Aristotle's conception of language as a relation of sound and meaning, is to define "language" as a set of pairs (*s, m*), where *s* is a sentence or utterance, and *m* is a meaning, perhaps represented as some kind of set-theoretical object in a system of possible worlds, a proposal developed by David Lewis among others. There are other similar proposals.

Under any of these proposals, a grammar will be a formal system of some kind that enumerates or "generates" the set chosen to be "the language," clearly an infinite set for which we seek a finite representation.

The concept "E-language" and its variants raise numerous questions. In the first place, the set is ill defined, not simply in the sense that it may be vague, with indeterminate boundaries, but in a deeper sense. Consider what are sometimes called "semi-grammatical sentences," such as "the child seems sleeping." Is this in the language or outside it? Either answer is unacceptable. The sentence clearly has a definite meaning. An English speaker interprets it in a definite way, quite differently from the interpretation that would be given by a speaker of Japanese. Hence it cannot simply be excluded from the set "E-English," though it is plainly not well formed. But speakers of English and Japanese will also differ in how they interpret some sentence of Hindi—or for that matter how they will interpret a wide variety of noises—so then all languages and a vast range of other sounds also fall within English, a conclusion that makes no sense. It is doubtful that there is any coherent solution to this range of problems. The fact is that a speaker of English, Japanese, or whatever, has developed a system of knowledge that assigns a certain status to a vast range of physical events, and no concept of E-language, nor any construct developed from it, is likely to be able to do justice to this essential fact.

A second problem has to do with choice of grammar. Evidently, for any set there are many grammars that will enumerate it. Hence it has commonly been argued, most notably by

W. V. Quine, that choice of grammar is a matter of convenience, not truth, like the choice of "a grammar" for the well-formed sentences of arithmetic in some notation. But now we face real questions about the subject matter of the study of language. Clearly, there is some fact about the mind/brain that differentiates speakers of English from speakers of Japanese, and there is a truth about this matter, which is ultimately a question of biology. But sets are not in the mind/brain, and grammars can be chosen freely as long as they enumerate the E-language, so the study of E-language, however constructed, does not seem to bear on the truth about speakers of English and Japanese; it is not, even in principle, part of the natural sciences, and one might argue that it is a pointless pursuit, a kind of chasing after shadows. Many philosophers—W. V. Quine, David Lewis, and others—have concluded that linguists must be in error when they hold that they are concerned with truths about the mind/brain, though clearly there are such truths about language for someone to be concerned with; they also hold that puzzling philosophical problems are raised by the claim that grammars are "internally represented" in some manner. Others (Jerrold Katz, Scott Soames, and others) have held that linguistics is concerned with some Platonic object that we may call "P-language," and that P-English is what it is independently of what may be true about the psychological states or brains of speakers of English. One can see how these conclusions might be reached by someone who begins by construing language to be a variety of E-language.

There is little point arguing about how to define the term "linguistics," but it is plain that there is an area of investigation, let us call it "C-linguistics" (cognitive linguistics) which is concerned with the truth about the mind/brains of the people who speak C-English and C-Japanese, suitably idealized. This subject belongs strictly within the natural sciences in principle, and its links to the main body of the natural sciences will become more explicit as the neural mechanisms responsible for the structures and principles discovered in the study of mind come to be understood. As I noted earlier, the status of this study of language and mind is similar to that of nineteenth-century chemistry or pre-DNA genetics; one might argue that it is similar to the natural sciences at every stage of their development. In any event, C-linguistics raises no philosophical problems that do not arise for scientific inquiry quite generally. It raises numerous problems of fact and interpretation, but of a kind familiar in empirical inquiry.

The status of P-linguistics, or of the study of E-language generally, is quite different. Thus the advocates of P-linguistics have to demonstrate that in addition to the real entities C-English, C-Japanese, etc., and the real mind/brains of their speakers, there are other Platonic objects that they choose to delineate somehow and study. Whatever the merits of this claim, we may simply put the matter aside, noting that people may study whatever abstract object they construct. This still leaves the apparent problem noted by Quine, Lewis, and others who argue that it is "folly" to claim that one of a set of "extensionally equivalent systems of grammar" that enumerate the same E-language is correctly attributed to the speaker-hearer as a property physically encoded in some manner, whereas another one merely happens to enumerate the E-language but is not a correct account of the speaker's mind/brain and system of knowledge. Plainly this conclusion cannot be correct, given that, as they agree, there is surely some truth about the mind/brain and the system of knowledge represented in it, so some error must have crept in along the way.

Note that the question is not one of metaphysical realism, or of choice of theory in science. Take whatever view one wants on these matters, and it is still alleged that some further philosophical problem, or "folly," arises in the case of attribution of one grammar but not another extensionally equivalent one to a speaker-hearer, a conclusion that is transparently in error, but seems to be as well founded as the correct conclusion that there is no "true" grammar of arithmetic. So we seem to be left with a puzzle.

A third class of problems that arise from the study of E-language has to do with the properties of these sets. Sets have formal properties, so it seems to be meaningful to ask

whether human E-languages have certain formal properties: are they context-free, or recursive, or denumerable? All of these choices have been affirmed, and denied, but the point is that the questions are taken seriously, though it is far from clear that the questions are even meaningful. The answers are also thought to have some crucial bearing on questions of parsing and learnability, but quite wrongly, for reasons discussed years ago.[2]

All of this is, in my view, quite confused and pointless, because the notion of E-language is an artifact, with no status in an eventual science of language. E-languages can be selected one way or another, or perhaps better, not at all, since there appears to be no coherent choice and the concept appears to be useless for any empirical inquiry. In particular, it is quite mistaken to hold, as many do, that an E-language is somehow "given," and that there is no particular problem in making sense of the idea that a person uses a particular E-language, but that in contrast there are serious problems if not pure folly in the contention that a particular "grammar" for that E-language, but not some other one, is in fact used by the speaker. Clearly infinite sets are not "given." What is given to the child is some finite array of data, on the basis of which the child's mind develops some system of knowledge X, where X determines the status of arbitrary physical objects, assigning to some of them a phonetic form and meaning. With a different finite array of data—from Japanese rather than English, for example— the system of knowledge attained will differ, and the question of what the systems in the mind/brain really are is as meaningful as any other question of science. As for the E-language, it does raise innumerable problems, probably unanswerable ones, since whatever it is, if anything, it is more remote from mechanisms and at a higher level of abstraction than the internally represented system of knowledge, the "correct grammar" that is alleged to raise such difficulties.

The source of all of these problems resides in an inappropriate choice of the basic concept of the study of language, namely "language." The only relevant notion that has a real status is what is usually called "grammar." Here again we find an unfortunate terminological decision, which has undoubtedly been misleading. Guided by the misleading and inappropriate analogy to formal languages, I and others have used the term "language" to refer to some kind of E-language, and have used the term "grammar" with systematic ambiguity—a fact that has always been spelled out clearly, but has nevertheless caused confusion: the term "grammar" has been used to refer to the linguist's theory, or to the subject matter of that theory. A better usage would be to restrict the term "grammar" to the theory of the language, and to understand the language as what we may call "I-language," where "I" is to suggest "intensional" and "internalized." The I-language is what the grammar purports to describe: a system represented in the mind/brain, ultimately in physical mechanisms that are now largely unknown, and is in this sense *internalized;* a system that is *intensional* in that it may be regarded as a specific function considered in intension—that is, a specific characterization of a function—which assigns a status to a vast range of physical events, including the utterance "John seems to be sleeping," the utterance "John seems sleeping," a sentence of Hindi, and probably the squeaking of a door, if we could do careful enough experiments to show how speakers of English and Japanese might differ in the way they "hear" this noise.

As contrasted with E-language, however construed, I-languages are real entities, as real as chemical compounds. They are in the mind, ultimately the brain, in the same sense as chemical elements, organic molecules, neural nets, and other entities that we construct and discuss at some appropriate abstract level of discussion are in the brain. They are what they are, and it is a problem of science to discover the true account of what they are, the grammar for the speaker in question. The story presented by many philosophers is entirely backwards. It is the E-language, not the I-language (the "grammar," in one of the two senses in which this systematically ambiguous phrase has been used), that poses philosophical problems, which are probably not worth trying to solve, since the concept is of no interest and has no status. It may, indeed, be pure "folly" to construct and discuss it, to ask what formal properties E-languages have, and so on. I suspect it is. In particular, the analogy to formal systems of arithmetic and so on is largely worthless, and should be discarded, though other analogies to arithmetic and logic, as systems of mentally represented knowledge, are quite definitely worth pursuing, and raise quite interesting questions, yet to be seriously explored. The debates of the past generation about these matters seem to me a classic example of the philosophical errors that arise from misinterpreting concepts of ordinary language—in this case, developing a useless, perhaps quite senseless concept, and assuming erroneously that it is the relevant scientific notion that corresponds to, or should replace, some concept of ordinary language—a source of philosophical error that was clearly exposed in the eighteenth-century critique of the theory of ideas, if not earlier, and has more recently been brought to general attention by Wittgenstein.

Let us now use the term "language" to refer to I-language, and the term "grammar" to refer to the theory of an I-language. What about the term "universal grammar," recently resurrected and given a sense that is similar to the traditional one, but not identical, since the entire framework of thinking has been radically modified? The term "universal grammar" has also been used with systematic ambiguity, to refer to the linguist's theory and to its subject matter. In keeping with our effort to select terms so as to avoid pointless confusion, let us use the term "universal grammar" to refer to the linguist's theory only. The topic of universal grammar is, then, the system of principles that specify what it is to be a human language. This system of principles is a component of the mind/brain prior to the acquisition of a particular language. It is plausible to suppose that this system constitutes the initial state of the language faculty, considered to be a subsystem of the mind/brain.

This initial state, call it S_0, is apparently a common human possession to a very close approximation, and also appears to be unique to humans, hence a true species property. It is what it is, and theories concerning it are true or false. Our goal is to discover the true theory of universal grammar, which will deal with the factors that make it possible to acquire a particular I-language and that determine the class of human I-languages and their properties. Looked at from a certain point of view, universal grammar describes a "language acquisition device," a system that maps data into language (I-language). A theory of universal grammar, like a particular proposed grammar, is true or false in whatever sense any scientific theory can be true or false. For our purposes, we may accept the normal reaalist assumptions of the practicing scientist, in this connection. Whatever problems may arise are not specific to this enterprise, and are surely far better studied in connection with the more developed natural sciences.

Crucially, (I-)languages and S_0 are real entities, the basic objects of study for the science of language, though it may be possible to study more complex abstractions, such as speech or language communities; any further such inquiry will surely have to presuppose grammars of (I-)language and universal grammar, and always has in practice, at least tacitly, even when this is explicitly denied, another confusion that I will not pursue here. An I-language—henceforth, simply "a language"— is the state attained by the language faculty under certain external conditions. I doubt very much that it makes any sense to speak of a person as *learning* a language. Rather, a language grows in the mind/brain. Acquiring language is less something that a child does than something that happens to the child, like growing arms rather than wings, or undergoing puberty at a certain stage of maturation. These processes take place in different ways depending on external events, but the basic lines of development are internally determined. The evidence seems to me overwhelming that this is true of language growth.

Let us now consider the question of knowledge. The language a person has acquired underlies a vast range of knowledge, both "knowledge-how" and "knowledge-that." A person whose mind incorporates the language English (meaning, a particular I-language that falls within what is informally called "English")

knows how to speak and understand a variety of sentences, knows that certain sounds have certain meanings, and so on. These are typical cases of knowing-how and knowing-what, ordinary propositional knowledge in the latter case, and this of course does not exhaust the range of such knowledge. It seems entirely reasonable to think of the language as a system that is internalized in the mind/brain, yielding specific cases of propositional knowledge or knowledge how to do so and so. We now have to consider at least three aspects of knowledge: (1) the internalized system of knowledge of the language, (2) knowing how to speak and understand, and (3) knowledge that sentences mean what they do (etc.).

It is common among philosophers, particularly those influenced by Wittgenstein, to hold that "knowledge of language is an ability," which can be exercised by speaking, understanding, reading, talking to oneself: "to know a language just is to have the ability to do these and similar things,"[3] and indeed more generally knowledge is a kind of ability. Some go further and hold that an ability is expressible in dispositional terms, so that language becomes, as Quine described it, "a complex of present dispositions to verbal behavior." If we accept this further view, then two people who are disposed to say different things under given circumstances speak different languages, even if they are identical twins with exactly the same history, who speak the same language by any sensible criteria we might establish. There are so many well-known problems with this conception that I will simply drop it, and consider the vaguer proposal that knowledge of language is a practical ability to speak and understand (Michael Dummet, Anthony Kenny, and others, in one or another form).

This radical departure from ordinary usage is, in my view, entirely unwarranted. To see how radical is the departure from ordinary usage, consider the consequences of accepting it, now using "ability" in the sense of ordinary usage. In the first place, ability can improve with no change in knowledge. Thus suppose Jones takes a course in public speaking or in composition, improving his ability to speak and understand, but learning nothing new about his language. The language that Jones speaks and understands is exactly what it was before, and his knowledge of language has not changed, but his abilities have improved. Hence knowledge of language is not to be equated with the ability to speak, understand, etc.

Similarly, ability to use langauge can be impaired, and can even disappear, with no loss of knowledge of language at all. Suppose that Smith, a speaker of English, suffers Parkinson's disease, losing entirely the ability to speak, understand, etc. Smith then does not have "the ability to do these and similar things," and therefore does not have knowledge of English, as the term is defined by Kenny, Dummett, and others. Suppose that use of the chemical L-Dopa can restore Smith's ability completely, as has been claimed (it does not matter whether the facts just noted are accurate; since we are dealing with a conceptual question, it is enough that they could be, as is certainly the case). Now what has happened during the recovery of the ability? On the assumption in question, Smith has recovered knowledge of English from scratch with a drug, after having totally lost that knowledge. Curiously, Smith recovered knowledge of *English,* not of *Japanese,* though no evidence was available to choose between these outcomes; he regained knowledge of his original English with no experience at all. Had Smith been a speaker of Japanese, he would have recovered Japanese with the same drug. Evidently, something remained fully intact while the ability was totally lost. In normal usage, as in our technical counterpart to it, we would say that what remained fully intact was "possession of the language," knowledge of English, showing again that knowledge cannot be reduced to ability.[4]

Note that there are cases where we would say that a person retains an ability but is incapable of exercising it, say a swimmer who cannot swim because his legs and arms are tied. But that is surely an entirely different kind of case than the one we are now considering, where the ability is lost but the knowledge is retained.

To sustain the thesis that knowledge is ability, we would have to invent some new concept of ability, call it "K-ability," which we

understand in the sense of knowledge. Then we could say that Jones, who improved his ability to speak with no change in his knowledge of English, retained his K-ability to speak (etc.) without change; and Smith fully retained his K-ability while entirely losing his ability to use English, in the normal sense of "ability." Plainly this is pointless. The invented concept K-ability is invested with all the properties of knowledge, and diverges radically from the quite useful ordinary concept of ability. It is true that knowledge is K-ability, since we have defined the novel invented term "K-ability" to have the properties of knowledge, but that is hardly an interesting conclusion.

Exactly this tack is taken by Anthony Kenny, in the face of conceptual arguments such as those just reviewed. Thus in the case of the patient with Parkinson's disease, Kenny says that he did indeed have the ability to use the language when he had no ability to use the language, thus shifting to "K-ability," plainly, since the ability was totally lost.[5] Crucially, K-ability diverges radically from ability, and is like knowledge, as we can see from the fact that a person may have entirely lost the ability to speak and understand while entirely retaining the K-ability, can improve the ability with the K-ability unmodified, etc.

Kenny also assumes that there is a contradiction between my conclusion concerning the person who has lost the ability while retaining the knowledge and my statement elsewhere (which he accepts) that there might in principle be a "Spanish pill" that would confer knowledge of Spanish on a person who took it. There is no inconsistency. The issue in connection with aphasia or Parkinson's disease has nothing to do with a pill for acquiring a certain language; rather, the point is that the person in the *Gedankenexperiment* reacquires ability to use *exactly the same language that he had* (knowledge of which he never lost); the same dose of L-dopa restores ability to speak English to the English speaker and ability to speak Japanese to the Japanese speaker; it is not an "English pill." The same holds true of the person whose ability changes while his knowledge—or K-ability, if one prefers—remains constant.

It is curious that this attempt to maintain a clearly untenable thesis by inventing a new term "ability" that is used in the sense of "knowledge" and is radically different from "ability" in its normal sense is presented in the spirit of Wittgenstein, who constantly inveighed against such procedures and argued that they are at the root of much philosophical error, as in the present case.

Note that essentially the same arguments show that knowing-how cannot be explained in terms of ability, unless we adopt the same pointless procedure just discussed. Suppose a person knows how to ride a bicycle, loses this ability under some kind of brain injury, and then recovers it through administration of a drug, or when the effects of the injury recede. The person has made a transition from full ability, to no ability, to recovery of the original ability—not some other one. The argument is the same as before. Knowing-how is not simply a matter of ability, nor, surely, is knowing-that, contrary to much widely accepted doctrine. In fact, it is quite clear from closer investigation of the concept "knowing how." Rather, knowing-how involves a crucial cognitive element, some internal representation of a system of knowledge.[6] Since this matter is not germane here, I will not pursue it.

Could we say, then, that knowing how to speak and understand a language is in no formal way different from knowing how to ride a bicycle, as is commonly alleged, so that we need not be driven to assume a mentally-represented system of knowledge in the case of language? There are at least two fundamental problems with this line of argument. First, knowing-how in general involves a cognitive element, as just noted. Secondly, the "just like" argument is quite empty. We might as well say that there is no real problem in accounting for the ability that some people have to write brilliant poetry or wonderful quartets, or to discover deep theorems or scientific principles; it is just like knowing how to ride a bicycle. What possible point can there be to such proposals?

In any particular case, we have to discover what kind of cognitive structure underlies knowing how to do so-and-so or knowing that

such-and-such.[7] In pursuing such inquiry, we rely entirely on "best theory" arguments, and we discover, not surprisingly, that very different kinds of systems, cognitive or other, are involved. To say that it is all just "knowing how," hence unproblematic, is merely a form of anti-intellectualism, little more than an expression of lack of curiosity about features of the world, in this case, central features of human nature and human life.

In summary, to try to sustain the principle that knowing how to speak and understand a language reduces to a network of abilities, one has to use the term "ability" in some novel technical sense—in fact, a sense invested with all the properties of knowlege. Plainly this is pointless.

A rather striking feature of the widespread conception of language as a system of abilities, or a habit system of some kind, or a complex of dispositions, is that it has been completely unproductive. It led precisely nowhere. One cannot point to a single result or discovery about language, even of the most trivial kind, that derives from this conception. Here one must be a bit more precise. There was, in fact, a discipline that did obtain empirical results and that professed this doctrine, namely, American structural linguistics for many years. But the actual work carried out, and even the technical theories developed, departed from the doctrine at every crucial point. Thus, there is no relation between, say, the procedures of phonemic analysis devised and the concept of language as a habit system.[8] This latter belief did influence applied disciplines such as language teaching, very much to their detriment. But linguistics itself was essentially unaffected, except insofar as it was impoverished in vision and concerns by the doctrine it professed.

One might draw an analogy to operationalism in the sciences. This doctrine, widely professed at one time, undoubtedly had an influence in psychology. Namely, to the extent that it was followed in practice, it seriously impoverished the discipline. The principles were also professed in physics for a time, but I suspect that they had little impact there, since the scientists who professed the principles generally continued to do their work in utter contradiction to them, quite wisely. (We omit examples that are discussed in the standard literature; see, e.g., the reference in note 2.)

The central problem of the theory of language is to explain how people can speak and understand new sentences, new in their experience or perhaps in the history of the language. The phenomenon is not an exotic one, but is the norm in the ordinary use of language, as Descartes and his followers stressed in their discussion of what we may call "the creative aspect of language use," that is, the commonplace but often neglected fact that the normal use of language is unbounded in scope, free from identifiable stimulus control, coherent and appropriate to situations that evoke but do not cause it (a crucial distinction), arousing in listeners thoughts that they too might express in the same or similar ways. It is surprising how rarely the phenomenon was seriously addressed in the linguistics of the past century, until the mid-1950s at least, in part, perhaps, because of the conception of language as a system of habits, dispositions or abilities, Otto Jesperson being a rare and notable exception. When the question was addressed, the conventional answer was that new forms are produced and understood "by analogy" with familiar ones. (But this explanation in empty until an account is given of analogy, and none exists.)

In the past few years it has been shown that a wide range of phenomena from typologically quite different languages can be explained on the assumption that the language faculty of the mind/brain carries out digital computations following very general principles, making use of representations of a precisely determined sort, including empty categories of several kinds. This work then provides evidence, quite strong evidence I believe, for some rather striking and surprising conclusions: that the language faculty, part of the mind/brain, is in crucial part a system of digital computation of a highly restricted character, with simple principles that interact to yield very intricate and complex results. This is a rather unexpected property of a biological system. One must be alert to the possibility that the conclusion is an artifact, resulting from our mode of analysis, but the evidence suggests quite strongly that the conclusion reflects reality.

As far as I am aware, there is only one other known biological phenomenon that shares the properties of discrete infinity exhibited by language, and that involves similar principles of digital computation: namely, the human number faculty, also apparently a species property, essentially common to the species and unique to it, and, like human language, unteachable to other organisms, which lack the requisite faculties. There are, for example, numerous animal communication systems, but they are invariably finite (the calls of apes) or continuous (the "language" of bees, continuous in whatever sense we can say this of a physical system; the human gestural system; etc.). Note that the difference between human languages and these communication systems is not one of "more" or "less," but one of difference in quality; indeed, it is doubtful that any sense can be given to the idea that human language is a communication system, though it can be used for communication along with much else. These observations suggest that at some remote period of evolutionary history, the brain developed a certain capacity for digital computation, for employing recursive rules and associated mental representations, thus acquiring the basis for thought and language in the human sense, with the arithmetical capacity perhaps latent as a kind of abstraction from the language faculty, to be evoked when cultural conditions allowed, much later, in fact never in the case of some societies, so it appears. Notice that there is surely no reason to suppose that every trait is specifically selected.

The phenomena of the languages of the world appear to be highly diverse, but, increasingly, it has been shown that over a large and impressive range they can be accounted for by the same principles, which yield highly varied results as the properties of lexical items vary from language to language. Thus in Spanish, there are clitic pronouns, including the reflexive, while in English there are not, so that the forms of English and Spanish, say in causative constructions, look quite different. But the principles that govern them appear to be essentially the same, their consequences differing by virtue of a lexical property of the pronominal system: in Spanish, but not in English, there is a system of pronouns that are lexically marked as affixes, and therefore must attach to other elements. The manner in which these affixes attach, and the targets to which they adjoin, are determined by the very same principles that determine the formation of complex syntactic constructions such as operator-variable constructions and others, so it now appears.

In other languages, many more items are identified in the lexicon as affixes, and the same syntactic principles determine complex morphological forms that reflect in another way the same underlying and near universal underlying structures.[9] Thus in Japanese, the causative element is not a verb, like Spanish *hacer* or English *make,* but rather an affix, so a verb must move from the embedded clause to attach to it, yielding what appears to be a monoclausal causative as distinct from the English-Spanish biclausal causative; in Spanish too there is a reflection of the same process when *se* raises to the main verb in the sentence "Juan se hizo afeitar," as if *hizo-afeitar* were a single word. The point is that as lexical items vary, the very same principles determine a wide range of superficially different complex phenomena in typologically quite different languages.

The principles of universal grammar are fixed as constituent elements of the language faculty, but languages plainly differ. How do they differ? One way has already been noted: they differ in properties of lexical items, though here too the options are narrowly constrained by general principles. Beyond that, it seems that the principles allow for a limited range of variation. That variation is limited has often been explicitly denied. The leading American linguist Edward Sapir held that languages can vary "without assignable limit," and Martin Joos put forth what he called the "Boasian" view, referring to Franz Boas, one of the founders of modern linguistics: namely, that "languages could differ from each other without limit and in unpredictable ways." Such views echo William Dwight Whitney, who greatly influenced Ferdinand de Saussure, and who emphasized "the infinite diversity of human speech."

Such views perhaps appeared tenable in some form if one regarded language as a habit system, a network of practical abilities, a complex of dispositions, and the like. In that case, language would be constrained only by whatever general conditions constrain the development of abilities and habits in general, by what are sometimes called "generalized learning mechanisms," if these exist. But this conception does not allow one even to approach the essential features of normal language use, as has been demonstrated beyond reasonable doubt in my view; and as already noted, the conception has been entirely unproductive.

Assuming without further discussion that this conception must be abandoned, the question of language variation will take on a new form in the context of a general revision of the framework of inquiry into problems of natural language. A conceptual change of this nature was proposed about thirty years ago, reviving in a new form some long-forgotten approaches to the study of natural language. This rather sharp conceptual change underlies the research program that has been given the name "generative grammar," referring to the fact that the grammar—or as we are now more properly calling it "the language"—generates an unbounded range of specific consequences, assigning a status to every expression and thus providing the mechanisms for the creative aspect of language use. The central questions of the study of language, conceived along the lines of the earlier discussion, now become the following:

1.
    (i) What is the system of knowledge attained by a person who speaks and understands a language?
    (ii) How is that knowledge acquired?
    (iii) How is that knowledge put to use?

The last question has two aspects, the production problem and the perception problem. The second question, how language is acquired, is a variant of what we might call "Plato's problem," raised for example when Socrates demonstrated that a slave boy with no training in geometry in fact knew geometry, perhaps the first psychological (thought-)-experiment. The problem is not a trivial one: people know a great deal more than can possibly be accounted for in terms of the standard paradigms of epistemology (or perhaps more accurately, what they know is different from what one might expect in these terms), language being a striking example. The production problem might be called "Descartes's problem," referring to one of the central Cartesian criteria for the existence of other minds: namely, when experiment demonstrates that another creature that resembles us exhibits the creative aspect of language use, then it would only be reasonable to attribute to the creature a mind like ours. In more recent years, a similar idea has been called "the Turing Test." This problem, one aspect of more general problems concerning will and choice, remains beyond the scope of serious human inquiry in fact, and may be so in principle, rather as Descartes suggested. In any event, having nothing to say about it, I will put it aside, keeping just to the perception problem, or what is sometimes called "the parsing problem" (restricting attention to certain computational aspects).

These questions were posed as constituting the research program of generative grammar about thirty years ago, along with an argument to the effect that prevailing answers to them in terms of habit systems and the like were completely unacceptable for reasons already briefly discussed. What alternative, then, can we propose? I will keep to the terminology suggested above, departing from earlier usage.

The first proposal was that a language is a rule system, where the kinds of rules and their interrelations are specified by universal grammar. In one familiar conception, the rules included context-free rules, lexical rules, transformational rules, phonological rules (in a broad sense), and what were misleadingly called "rules of semantic interpretation" relating syntactic structures to representations in a system sometimes called "LF," suggesting "logical form" but with certain qualifications. This term "rules of semantic interpretation" is misleading, as David Lewis among others has pointed out,

because these rules relate syntactic objects, mental representations. They relate syntactic structures and LF-representations, which are syntactic objects. The term "semantics" should properly be restricted to the relation between language and the world, or to use of language, some might argue. The criticism is accurate, but it applies far more broadly. In fact, it applies in exactly the same form to what Lewis and others call "semantics," where "meanings" are set-theoretic objects of some sort: models, "pictures," situations and events, or whatever. These are mental representations,[10] not elements of the world, and the problem arises of how they are related to the world. It is often assumed that the relation is trivial, something like incorporation, so that it is unnecessary to provide a justification for these particular systems of mental representation, but it is easy to show that this cannot be true unless we trivialize our conception of what the world is by restricting attention to something like what Nelson Goodman calls "versions," all mental representations, abandoning (perhaps as meaningless) the question of why one collection of "versions" is jointly acceptable or "right" and others not, that is, not pursuing the common-sense answer: that certain versions are jointly "right" because of their accord with reality. But if we take this tack, which I do not suggest, semantics disappears and we are only studying various systems of mental representation. In fact, much of what is called "semantics" is really the study of the syntax of mental representations. It is a curious fact that those who correctly call their work in this area "syntax" are said to be avoiding semantics, while others who incorrectly describe their studies of syntax as "semantics" are said to be contributing to semantics.[11]

Adopting this conception of language, a language is a complex of rules of the permitted format, interconnected in a way permitted by universal grammar. In contrast to the conception of language in terms of habit systems or abilities, this was an extremely productive idea, which led quickly to a vast increase in the range of phenomena brought under investigation, with many discoveries about facts of language, even quite simple ones, that had never been noted or explored. Furthermore, the array of phenomena discovered and investigated were made intelligible at some level, by providing partial rule systems that accounted for their properties. The depth of explanation, however, could never really be very great. Even if appropriate rule systems could be constructed, and even if these systems were found to be restricted in type, we would always want to know why we have these kinds of rules and not others. Thus, languages typically have rules that allow the direct object of a verb to function as its subject, though it is still being interpreted as the object; but the converse property does not exist. Or consider again causative constructions, say, the form that we can give in abstract representation as (2), where the element CAUSE may be a word as in Spanish-English or an affix as in Japanese:

(2)   problems CAUSE [that Y lies]

The principles of universal grammar permit a realization of this abstract form as something like (3), where CAUSE is an affix, or with CAUSE-*lie* associated in a closely linked verb sequence as in Spanish:

(3)   problems CAUSE-lie Y

But the form (4) does not underlie a possible realization as (5):

(4)   [that Y lies] CAUSE problems
(5)   Y CAUSE-lie problems

Subject-object asymmetries of this sort are found very widely in language. They reflect in part the fact that subject-verb-object sentences are not treated in natural language as two-term relations as is familiar in logical analysis, but rather in the more traditional terms of Aristotelian logic and the universal grammar of the pre-modern period, as subject-predicate structures with a possibly complex predicate. In part, the asymmetries appear to follow from a newly discovered principle governing empty categories of the sort illustrated earlier. But whatever the explanation, problems of this nature abound, and an approach in terms of rule systems leaves them unsolved, except in a rather

superficial way. From another point of view, there are simply too many possible rule systems, even when we constrain their form, and we thus do not achieve a convincing answer to our variant of Plato's problem.

Recognition of these facts has been at the core of the research program of the past twenty-five years. The natural approach has been to abandon the rules in favor of general principles, so that the question of why we have one choice of rules rather than another simply does not arise. Thus if there are no rules for the formation of passive constructions, or interrogatives, or relative clauses, or phrase structure, and no rules that change grammatical functions such as causative and others, then the question why we have certain rules, not others, does not arise. Increasingly, it has become clear that rules are simply epiphenomena, on a par with sentences in the sense that they are simply "projected" from the (I-) language, viewed in a certain way. But as distinct from sentences, which exist in mental representation and are realized in behavior, there is no reason to believe that rules of the familiar form exist at all, they have no status in linguistic theory and do not constitute part of mental representation or enter into mental computations, and we may safely abandon them, so it appears. We are left with general principles of universal grammar.

If there were only one possible human language, apart from lexical variety, we would then have a simple answer to our variant of Plato's problem: universal grammar permits only one realization apart from lexicon, and this is the language that people come to know when they acquire appropriate lexical items through experience in some manner. But clearly the variety of languages is greater than this, so this cannot be the complete story—though it is probably closer to true than has been thought in the past. Thus in languages such as English or Spanish, verbs and prepositions precede their objects, and the same is true of adjectives and nouns, as in such expressions as "proud of Mary" (where "Mary" is the object of "proud" with a semantically empty preposition *of* introduced automatically as a kind of case-marker for reasons determined by universal grammar) and "translation of the book" with a similar analysis. The categories noun, verb, adjective, and preposition (more generally, adposition) are the *lexical categories*. The general principles of universal grammar determine the kinds of phrases in which they appear as *heads*. The lexical entry itself determines the number and category of the *complements* of these heads and their semantic roles, and the general principles of phrase structure determine a limited range of other possibilities.

There is, however, an option left underdetermined by the principles of universal grammar. English and Spanish settle this option by placing the head invariably *before* its complements. We may say that they choose the "head-initial" value of the "head parameter." In Japanese, in contrast, verbs, adpositions, adjectives, and nouns *follow* their complements. The range of phrase structures in the two languages is very similar, and accords with quite general principles of universal grammar, but the languages differ in one crucial choice of the head parameter: the language may choose either the "head-initial" or the "head-final" value of this parameter. In fact, this is only the simplest case, and there is a very limited range of further options depending on directionality of assignment of abstract case and semantic roles, a matter that has been explored by Hilda Koopman, Lisa Travis, and others, but we may put these further complexities aside.

A crucial fact about the head parameter is that its value can be determined from very simple data. There is good reason to believe that this is true of all parameters; we must deal with the crucial and easily demonstrated fact that what a person knows is vastly underdetermined by available evidence, and that much of this knowledge is based on no direct evidence at all. Empty categories and their properties provide a dramatic example of this pervasive phenomenon, almost entirely ignored in earlier work. Thus a person is provided with no direct evidence about the position and various properties of elements that have no physical realization. There is little doubt that this problem of "poverty of stimulus" is in fact the norm rather than the exception. It must be, then, that the values of parameters are set by the kinds of simple data

that are available to the child, and that the rich, complex, and highly articulated system of knowledge that arises, and is shared with others of somewhat different but equally impoverished experience, is determined in its basic features by the principles of the initial state S_0 of the language faculty. Languages may appear to differ, but they are cast in the same mold. One might draw an analogy to the biology of living organisms. Apparently, the biochemistry of life is quite similar from yeasts to humans, but small changes in timing of regulatory mechanisms of the cells and the like can yield what to us seem to be vast phenomenal differences, the difference between a whale and a butterfly, a human and a microbe, and so on. Viewed from an angel's point of view, with numerous other possible though not actual physical worlds under consideration, all life might appear identical apart from trivialities. Similarly, from an angel's point of view, all languages would appear identical, apart from trivialities, their fundamental features determined by facts about human biology.

The language itself (again, as always, in the sense of I-language) may be regarded as nothing more than an array of choices for the various parameters, selected in accord with whatever options universal grammar permits. Since there are a finite number of parameters, each finite-valued (probably two-valued), it follows that there are a finite number of possible languages. One can see at once why questions concerning the formal properties of natural languages are largely irrelevant; there are few questions of mathematical interest to raise concerning finite sets.

Here a qualification is necessary. We are separating out the lexicon (to which I will briefly return), a system that in principle can extend without bound though with sharp constraints in many languages (thus in English, we may always add another monomorphemic name of arbitrary length), and we are considering only what we might call "core language," to be distinguished from a "periphery" of marked and specifically learned exceptions; irregular verbs, idioms, and the like. These may presumably vary without bound apart from time and memory limitations, though surely in a manner that is sharply constrained in type. It is the core language that is nothing other than an array of values for parameters. I assume, of course, that the distinction between core and periphery is a real-world distinction, not a matter of convenience or pragmatic choice, except insofar as this is true of theories in chemistry and other branches of natural science, a consideration irrelevant here. For obvious reasons, the periphery is of much less interest for the basic psychological-biological questions to which linguistics is directed, if conceived along the lines of the previous discussion, and I will ignore it here.

Keeping to the core, then, there are finitely many possible languages. What a person knows, when that person speaks and understands a language, is a vocabulary and a particular array of values of parameters: an I-language. Once the parameters are set and lexical items acquired, the entire system functions, assigning a status to a vast range of expressions in a precise and explicit manner, even those that have never been heard or produced in the history of language (and well beyond, as noted earlier). Others understand what we say, because they have the same biological nature and sufficiently similar experience with simple utterances.

Turning to Plato's problem, a language is acquired by determining the values of the parameters of the initial state on the basis of simple data, and then the system of knowledge is represented in the mind/brain and is ready to function—though it might not function if the person lacks the ability to use it, perhaps because of some brain injury or the like. As for the parsing problem, it presumably should be solved along such lines as these: the hearer identifies words, and on the basis of their lexical properties, projects a syntactic structure as determined by principles of universal grammar and the values of the parameters. Connections and associations among these elements, including the empty categories that are forced to appear, are determined by other principles of universal grammar, perhaps parametrized. Thus given the sentence "a quién se hizo Juan afeitar," the mind of the speaker of Spanish automatically assigns a structure with two

empty categories, one the subject of "afeitar," another its object. Principles of universal grammar then produce a contradiction, in the manner informally described earlier, and the sentence receives no coherent interpretation, though of course it has a status; thus the Spanish speaker assigns to it a lexical and syntactic structure, and might even be able to "force" a certain meaning, if the sentence were produced by a foreigner, by me for example. A monolingual speaker of English will also assign a certain status to this expression, at least in some kind of phonetic representation, very likely considerably more.

The abandonment of rule systems in favor of a principles-and-parameters approach, which has been gradually developing over the past twenty-five years and has been achieved to a substantial extent only in the past half-dozen years, has been extremely productive. It has, once again, led to a vast leap in empirical coverage, with entirely new empirical materials discovered in well-studied languages, and with languages of great typological variety incorporated within essentially the same framework. The depth of explanation has also advanced considerably, as it has become possible to explain why there are processes described by certain rules but not others. The principles now being developed yield very sharp and surprising predictions about languages of varied types, predictions which sometimes prove accurate, and sometimes fail in highly instructive ways. My guess is that we are at the beginning of a radically new and highly productive phase in the study of language.

The shift of perspective from rule systems to a principles-and-parameters approach might be regarded as a second major conceptual change in the development of generative grammar, the first being the conceptual change noted earlier as part of the so-called "cognitive revolution," from a conception of language as a system of habits or abilities to a mentalistic approach that regards language as a computational system of the mind/brain—a step towards integrating the study of language to the natural sciences, for the reasons discussed earlier. The second shift of perspective is more theory-internal than the first, but is in a sense a much sharper break from the tradition, for two reasons. One is that the "cognitive revolution" of the 1950s was in many respects a rediscovery in different terms of ideas and insights that had been developed long before, both in psychology and the study of language, during the seventeenth century "cognitive revolution." A second is that the rule system developed in early generative grammar were in certain respects a formalization, in a different framework, of traditional notions about the way sentences are constructed and interpreted. The shift to a principles-and-parameters approach introduces ideas that have only a remote resemblance to those of the traditional or modern study of language, and the basic notion of the discipline and the ways in which problems are formulated and addressed take on a considerably different form as well.

The principles-and-parameters approach yields a rather new way of thinking about questions of typology and comparative-historical linguistics. Consider again the analogy of speciation in biology. Apparently, small changes in the way fixed mechanisms function can produce large-scale phenomenal differences, yielding different species of organisms. In general, a slight change in the functioning of a rigidly structured and intricate system can yield very complex and surprising clusters of changes as its effects filter through the system. In the case of language, change of a single parameter may yield a cluster of differences which, on the surface, appear disconnected, as its effects filter through the invariant system of universal grammar. There is reason to believe that something of the sort is correct. Thus, among the Romance languages, French has a curious status. It differs from the other Romance languages in a cluster of properties, and it appears that these differences emerged fairly recently, and at about the same time. It may be that one parameter was changed—the null subject parameter that permits subject to be suppressed, some have speculated—yielding a cluster of other modifications through the mechanical working of the principles of universal grammar, and giving French something of the look of a Germanic language. At the same time, French and Spanish share certain features distinguishing them from Italian, and there are numerous other complexities as we look at the actual languages, or "dialects" as they are called. Similarly, we find most remarkable similarities among languages that have no known historical connection, suggesting that they have simply set crucial parameters the same way. These are essentially new questions, which can now be seriously formulated for the first time and perhaps addressed.

As conceptions of language have changed over the years, so has the notion of what counts as a "real result." Suppose we have some array of phenomena in some language. In the era of structural-descriptive linguistics, a result consisted in a useful arrangement of the data. As Zellig Harris put it in the major theoretical work of structural linguistics, a grammar provides a compact one-one representation of the phenomena in a corpus of data. Some, for example Roman Jakobson, went further in insisting on conformity to certain general laws, particularly in phonology, but in very limited ways.

Under the conception of language as a rule system, this would no longer count as a significant result; such a description poses rather than solves the problem at hand. Rather, it would be necessary to produce a rule system of the permitted format that predicts the data in question and in nontrivial cases, infinitely more. This is a much harder task, but not a hopeless one; there are many possible rule systems, and, with effort, it is often possible to find one that satisfies the permitted format, if this is not too restricted.

Under the more recent principles-and-parameters approach, the task becomes harder still. A rule system is simply a description: it poses rather than solves the problem, and a "real result" consists of a demonstration that the phenomena under investigation, and countless others, can be explained by selecting properly the values of parameters in a fixed and invariant system of principles. This is a far harder problem, made still more difficult by the great expansion of empirical materials in widely differing languages that have come to be partially understood, and to which any general theory must be responsible. Where the problem can be solved, we have results of some depth, well beyond anything imaginable earlier. It is an important fact that the problem is now intelligibly formulable, and that solutions are being produced over an interesting range, while efforts to pursue this inquiry are unearthing a large mass of new and unexplored phenomena in a wide variety of languages that pose new challenges, previously unknown.

This discussion has been based on the assumption that lexical items are somehow learned and available, suggesting that apart from parameter-setting, language acquisition as well as parsing and presumably the creative use of language (in the unlikely event that we can come to understand anything about this matter) are to a large extent determined by properties of the lexicon. But acquisition of lexical items poses Plato's problem in a very sharp form. As anyone who has tried to construct a dictionary or to work in descriptive semantics is aware, it is a very difficult matter to describe the meaning of a word, and such meanings have great intricacy and involve the most remarkable assumptions, even in the case of very simple concepts, such as what counts as a possible "thing." At peak periods of language acquisition, children are "learning" many words a day, meaning that they are in effect learning words on a single exposure. This can only mean that the concepts are already available, with all or much of their intricacy and structure predetermined, and the child's task is to assign labels to concepts, as might be done with very simple evidence.

Many have found this conclusion completely unacceptable, even absurd; it certainly departs radically from traditional views. Some, for example Hilary Putnam, have argued that it is entirely implausible to suppose that we have "an innate stock of notions" including *carburetor, bureaucrat,* etc.[12] If he were correct about this, it would not be particularly to the point, since the problem arises in a most serious way in connection with simple words such as "table," "person," "chase," "persuade," etc. But his argument for the examples he mentions is not compelling. It is that to have given us this innate stock of notions, "evolution would have had to be able to anticipate all the contingencies of future physical and cultural environments. Obviously it didn't and couldn't do this." A very similar argument had long been accepted in immunology; namely, the number of antigens is so immense, including even artificially synthesized substances that had never existed in the world, that it was considered absurd to suppose that evolution had provided "an innate stock of antibodies"; rather, formation of antibodies must be a kind of "learning process" in which the antigens played an "instructive role." But this assumption has been challenged, and is now widely assumed to be false. Niels Kaj Jerne won the Nobel Prize for his work challenging this idea, and upholding his own conception that an animal "cannot be stimulated to make specific antibodies, unless it has already made antibodies of this specificity before the antigen arrives," so that antibody formation is a selective process in which the antigen plays a selective and amplifying role.[13] Whether or not Jerne is correct, he certainly could be, and the same could be true in the case of word meanings, the argument being quite analogous.

Furthermore, there is good reason to suppose that the argument is at least in substantial measure correct, even for such words as *carburetor* and *bureaucrat,* which, in fact, pose the familiar problem of poverty of stimulus if we attend carefully to the enormous gap between what we know and the evidence on the basis of which we know it. The same is true of technical terms of science and mathematics, and it is quite surely the case for the terms of ordinary discourse. However surprising the conclusion may be that nature has provided us with an innate stock of concepts, and that the child's task is to discover their labels, the empirical facts appear to leave open few other possibilities. Other possibilities (say, in terms of "generalized learning mechanisms") have not, to my knowledge, been coherently formulated, and if they are some day formulated, it may well be that the apparent issue will dissolve.

To the extent that anything is understood about lexical items and their nature, it seems that they are based on conceptual structures of a very specific and closely integrated type. It has been argued plausibly that concepts of a locational nature, including goal and source of action, object moved, place, etc., enter widely into lexical structure, often in quite abstract ways. In addition, notions like actor, recipient of action, event, intention, and others are pervasive elements of lexical structure, with their specific properties and permitted interrelations. Consider, say, the words *chase* or *persuade*. Like their Spanish equivalents, they clearly involve a reference to human intention. To chase Jones is not only to follow him, but to follow him with the intent of staying on his path, perhaps to catch him. To persuade Smith to do something is to cause him to decide or intend to do it; if he never decides or intends to do it, we have not succeeded in persuading him. Furthermore, he must decide or intend by his own volition, not under duress; if we say that the police persuaded Smith to confess by torture, we are using the term ironically. Since these facts are known essentially without evidence, it must be that the child approaches language with an intuitive understanding of concepts involving intending, causation, goal of action, event, and so on, and places the words that are heard in a nexus that is permitted by the principles of universal grammar, which provide the framework for thought and language, and are common to human languages as conceptual systems that enter into various aspects of human life.

Notice further that we appear to have connections of meaning, analytic connections, in such cases as these; we have a rather clear distinction between truths of meaning and truths of fact. Thus, if John persuaded Bill to go to college, then Bill at some point decided or intended to go to college; otherwise, John did not persuade Bill to do so. This is a truth of meaning, not of fact. The *a priori* framework of human thought, within which language is acquired, provides necessary connections among concepts, reflected in connections of meaning among words, and more broadly, among expressions involving these words. Syntactic relations provide a rich array of further examples. It appears, then, that one of the central conclusions of modern philoso-phy is rather dubious: namely, the contention, often held to have been established by work of Quine and others, that one can make no principled distinction between questions of fact and questions of meaning, that it is a matter of more or less deeply held belief. Philosophers have, I think, been led to this dubious conclusion, which is held by some (e.g., Richard Rorty) to have undermined centuries of thought, by concentrating on an artificially narrow class of examples, in particular, on concepts that have little or no relational structure: such sentences as "cats are animals." Here, indeed, it is not easy to find evidence to decide whether the sentence is true as a matter of meaning or fact, and there has been much inconclusive debate about the matter. When we turn to more complex categories with an inherent relational structure such as *persuade* or *chase*, or to more complex syntactic constructions, there seems little doubt that analytic connections are readily discerned.

Furthermore, the status of a statement as a truth of meaning or of empirical fact can and must be established by empirical inquiry, and considerations of many sorts may well be relevant; for example, inquiry into language acquisition and variation among languages. The question of the existence of analytic truths and connections, therefore, is an empirical one, to be settled by empirical inquiry that goes well beyond the range of evidence ordinarily brought to bear. Suppose that two people differ in their intuitive judgments as to whether I can persuade John to go to college without his deciding or intending to do so. We are by no means at an impasse. Rather, we can construct conflicting theories and proceed to test them. One who holds that the connection between *persuade* and *decide* or *intend* is conceptual will proceed to elaborate the structure of the concepts, their primitive elements, and so on, and will seek to show that other aspects of the acquisition and use of language can be explained in terms of the very same assumptions about the innate structure of the language faculty, in the same language and others, and that the same concepts play a role in other aspects of thought and understanding. One who holds that the connection is one of deeply held belief, not connection of meaning, has the task of developing a general theory of belief fixation that will yield the right conclusions in these and numerous other cases. One who holds that the connection is based on the "semantic importance" of sentences relating *persuade* and *decide* or *intend* (i.e., that these sentences play a prominent role in inference, or serve to introduce the term *persuade* to the child's vocabulary, and thus are more important than others for communication[14]) faces the task of showing that these empirical claims, which appear to lack any plausibility, are in fact true. The first task seems far more promising to me, but it is a matter of empirical inquiry, not pronouncements on the basis of virtually no evidence. The whole matter requires extensive rethinking, and much of what has been generally assumed for the past several decades about these questions appears to be dubious at best. There is, it seems clear, a rich conceptual structure determined by the initial state of the language faculty (perhaps drawing from the resources of other genetically determined faculties of mind), waiting to be awakened by experience, much in accord with traditional rationalistic conceptions and even, in some respects, the so-called "empiricist" thought of James Harris, David Hume, and others.

I think we are forced to abandon many commonly accepted doctrines about language and knowledge. There is an innate structure that determines the framework within which thought and language develop, down to quite precise and intricate details. Language and thought are awakened in the mind, and follow a largely predetermined course, much like other biological properties. They develop in a way that provides a rich structure of truths of meaning. Our knowledge in these areas, and I believe elsewhere—even in science and mathematics—is not derived by induction, by applying reliable procedures, and so on; it is not grounded or based on "good reasons" in any useful sense of these notions. Rather, it grows in the mind, on the basis of our biological nature, triggered by appropriate experience, and in a limited way shaped by experience that settles options left open by the innate structure of mind. The result is an elaborate structure of cognitive systems, systems of knowledge and belief, that reflects the very nature of the human mind, a biological organ like others, with its scope and limits. This conclusion, which seems to me well-supported by the study of language and I suspect holds far more broadly, perhaps universally in domains of human thought, compels us to rethink fundamental assumptions of modern philosophy and of our general intellectual culture, including assumptions about scientific knowledge, mathematics, ethics, aesthetics, social theory and practice, and much else, questions too broad and far-reaching for me to try to address here, but questions that should, I think, be subjected to serious scrutiny from a point of view rather different from those that have conventionally been assumed.

NOTES

1. For references, here and below, see my *Knowledge of Language: Its Nature, Origin and Use* (New York: Praeger, 1986).
2. For discussion, see my *Aspects of the Theory of Syntax* (Cambridge: MIT Press, 1965). Here the concept of E-language is put to the side, and the object of inquiry is taken to be (1) the set of potential utterances $s_1, s_2, \ldots$ made available by universal phonetics (a part of universal grammar, UG); (2) the set of potential structural descriptions $SD_1, SD_2, \ldots$ made available by UG; (3) the set of potential grammars $G_1, G_2, \ldots$ made available by UG; a function f provided by UG that associates a set of SD's with each pair (s_i, G_j), and an "evaluation metric" provided by UG that orders grammars and thus determines their accessibility, given data. UG is understood to be the initial stage of the language faculty, a genetically determined species property, and a particular G_i is understood to be the steady state attained by the language faculty, given linguistic data, what I will call below a particular I-language. As discussed there, however, one chooses to define E-language, if at all, the formal properties of such sets (i.e., the "generative capacity" of grammars) is a matter of no clear relevance to questions of learnability, or surely parsability, given that as was well-known, languages do not meet this condition.
3. Anthony Kenny, *The Legacy of Wittgenstein* (Oxford: Basil Blackwell, 1984), p. 138. Elsewhere Kenny speaks of "the futility of [my] attempt to separate knowledge of English from the ability to use—the mastery of—the lan-

guage." But to deny his identification of knowledge with ability is not to hold that knowledge can be "separated" from ability, whatever that means exactly.

4. Suppose that someone prefers to say that the knowledge of English was indeed lost, but that something else was retained. Then that "something else" is the only matter of interest for the new theory that will replace the old theory of knowledge, and the same conclusions follow: the only concept of significance, which plays the role of the now abandoned notion "knowledge," is this "possession of language" that cannot be identified with ability to speak and understand. Clearly there is no point in these moves.

5. He also invests the invented concept of K-ability with curious properties, holding that had the patient not recovered, he would not have had the K-ability when he lost the ability; but since the concept is invented, he may give it whatever properties he likes. To be precise, Kenny is not discussing the example given here but one that is identical in all relevant respects: an aphasic who loses all ability to use language and then recovers the ability in full when the effects of the injury recede. He also shifts from "ability" to "capacity," saying that when the person lacked the ability he had the capacity, thus using "capacity" in the sense of "knowledge" or "K-ability." In my *Rules and Representations* (New York: Columbia University Press, 1980), to which he refers in this connection, I pointed out that "capacity" is often used in a much looser sense than "ability," so that a shift to "capacity" may disguise the inaccuracy of a characterization of knowledge in terms of ability. Kenny's discussion is also marred in other respects. Thus he notes that my usage of mentalistic terminology is quite different from his, but then criticizes my usage because it would be nonsensical on his assumptions, which is correct but hardly relevant, since I was precisely challenging these assumptions, for the reasons reviewed here.

6. See my "Knowledge of Language," in K. Gunderson, ed., *Language, Mind and Knowledge* (Minneapolis: University of Minnesota Press, 1975).

7. If there is one. Note that I have not tried to establish that this must always be the case but rather that it is in the case of language; or that knowledge can never be reduced to ability, but rather that it cannot be in general, and in particular cannot be in the case of knowledge of language.

8. One cannot speak of strict inconsistency, since the concept of language as a habit system was regarded as a matter of fact, while the procedures of linguistic analysis devised by many of the more sophisticated theorists were regarded as simply a device, one among many, with no truth claim.

9. For very important recent discussion of this matter, see Mark Baker, *A Theory of Grammatical Function* (Chicago: University of Chicago Press, 1988).

10. At least, if we are doing C-linguistics, with empirical content. If not, then further clarification is required. The inquiry is in any event not semantics in the sense of empirical semantics, a study of relations between the language and something extralinguistic.

11. On a personal note, my own work, from the beginning, has been largely concerned with the problem of developing linguistic theory so that the representations provided in particular languages will be appropriate for explaining how sentences are used and understood, but I have always called this "syntax," as it is, even though the motivation is ultimately semantic; see, e.g., my *Logical Structure of Linguistic Theory* (1955–56; published in part in 1975, New York: Plenum), *Syntactic Structures* (The Hague: Mouton, 1957). This work is correctly described as syntax, but it deals with questions that others incorrectly term "semantic," and it is, I suspect, one crucial way to study semantics.

12. See Putnam, "Meaning and Our Mental Life," manuscript, 1985.

13. For discussion in a linguistic-cognitive context, see my *Rules and Representations* (New York: Columbia University Press, 1980), 136f.; and Jerne's Nobel Prize lecture, "The Generative Grammar of the Immune System," *Science* 229.1057–9, September 13, 1985.

14. The proposal of Paul M. Churchland, *Scientific Realism and the Plasticity of Mind* (Cambridge University Press, 1979; 1986, 51f.).

SUGGESTED FURTHER READING

Baker, G. P. and P. M. S. *Hacker, Skepticism, Rules and Language* (New York: Basil Blackwell, 1984).

Kenny, Anthony, Cartesian Privacy, in *Wittgenstein: The Philosophical Investigations,* ed. George Pitcher (Garden City, N.Y.: Anchor Books, 1966), pp. 352–370.

Lewis, David. *Convention* (Cambridge: Harvard University Press, 1969).

Lewis, David. *Counterfactuals* (Cambridge: Harvard University Press, 1973).

Locke, John. *An Essay Concerning Human Understanding,* Book III, chapters I–IV.

Rhees, Rush. Can There Be a Private Language? *Proceedings of the Aristotelian Society Supplementary Volume* 28 (1954), 77–94.

Strawson, P. F., Review of *Philosophical Investigations, Mind* 63 (1954), 70–99.

Winch, Peter, Facts and Superfacts, *The Philosophical Quarterly* 33 (1983), 398–404.